D1866775

Heinrich von Kleist

Günter Blamberger

Heinrich von Kleist

The Biography

Translated from German by
Sebastian Goth and Kelly Kawar

BRILL | WILHELM FINK

Title of the original German edition: Günter Blamberger, *Heinrich von Kleist. Biographie*
© S. Fischer, Frankfurt a. M. 2011

Cover illustration: Heinrich von Kleist (1777–1811), reproduction of a miniature painted by Peter Friedel, made for Kleist's fiancée Wilhelmine von Zenge, mentioned in Kleist's letter to her of April 9, 1801.

The translation of this work was funded by Geisteswissenschaften International – Translation Funding for Work in the Humanities and Social Sciences from Germany, a joint initiative of the Fritz Thyssen Foundation, the German Federal Foreign Office, the collecting society VG WORT, and the Börsenverein des Deutschen Buchhandels (German Publishers & Booksellers Association).

Sponsored by the

Federal Ministry
of Education
and Research

This publication was realized through the kind support of the Morphomata Center for Advanced Studies at the University of Cologne, sponsored by the Federal Ministry of Education and Research under the project number 01UK1505. Responsibility for the contents of the publication lies with the authors.

Bibliographic information published by the Deutsche Nationalbibliothek
The Deutsche Nationalbibliothek lists this publication in the Deutsche Nationalbibliografie;
detailed bibliographic data available online http://dnb.d-nb.de

All rights reserved. No part of this publication may be reproduced, translated, stored in a retrieval system, or transmitted in any form or by any means, electronic, mechanical, photocopying, recording or otherwise, without prior written permission from the publisher.

© 2021 Wilhelm Fink Verlag, an imprint of the Brill-Group
(Koninklijke Brill NV, Leiden, The Netherlands; Brill USA Inc., Boston MA, USA;
Brill Asia Pte Ltd, Singapore; Brill Deutschland GmbH, Paderborn, Germany)

www.fink.de

Copy editing: Karena Weduwen
Cover design: Evelyn Ziegler, Munich
Production: Brill Deutschland GmbH, Paderborn

ISBN 978-3-7705-6574-0 (hardback)
ISBN 978-3-8467-6574-6 (e-book)

Contents

CHAPTER I

Dead or Alive?

Or, How to Capture Kleist

Imaginary travel. This parlor game was well loved at the turn of the 19th century. Women especially loved it, for in real life, if they traveled at all, they were only allowed to do so in the company of a man or disguised as one, which was what Heinrich von Kleist's sister Ulrike did. Sitting at a table blindfolded, a player moves her hand slowly over a map until she comes to a stop, with pointed finger, at a random location and proceeds to imagine her journey to that place. She moves without difficulty, unlike real life, where the art of traveling can become an art of calculation—at least according to Enlightenment philosopher Denis Diderot. In his "Elements of Physiology" ("Eléments de physiologie"; 1774–80), Diderot warns against following one's natural instincts if while sitting in a carriage the horses suddenly bolt toward a precipice or a river. Anyone in this situation would want to jump out of the carriage immediately, but in which direction? Toward the front wheel which moves away from the jumper, or toward the rear wheel which threatens to move toward him? Instinctively, Diderot writes, one would jump toward the front wheel. A fatal error. If one wants to avoid being crushed by one of the two massive wheels, one must jump toward the rear wheel while the moving carriage simultaneously pulls him forward. Only in this way can one get on the diagonal that traverses the safe space between the two wheels. Being saved, then, depends on the interplay of force vectors, the forces of jumping backward and being moved forward.[1]

In the summer of 1801, Kleist was on his way from Strasbourg to Paris with his sister Ulrike. The journey took them 8 days—120 hours on the road—and they were fortunate, as Kleist acknowledges in a letter to his friend Karoline von Schlieben on July 18, 1801. In Butzbach, near Frankfurt am Main, they take a short break in front of an inn. While seated in the carriage, suddenly, a donkey, with a horrid cry, frightens their horses into a full-speed bolt. What does Kleist do?

> I reached for the reins, but they were hanging loose beneath the horses' chests, and before I had a chance to realize the magnitude of the danger, the carriage had already turned over with us, and we were thrown—And, so, a human life depended on the mere braying of a donkey? And what if my life had ended at this moment, had I lived *for that*? For that? *This* would have been all that Heaven

© WILHELM FINK VERLAG, 2021 | DOI:10.30965/9783846765746_002

> had intended for this dark, inscrutable, earthly life, and nothing more—? But, for now, it was not over—*why* Heaven had spared our lives, who can know? In short, we raised ourselves from the pavement, alive and unscathed, and held each other close. The carriage lay overturned, wheels in the air, one of them completely smashed, the shaft broken, the harnesses torn. All of this cost us three Louis d'or and twenty-four hours. We continued our journey the next morning—when will be the last?[2]

Clearly, Kleist does not have Diderot's advice in mind. He does not jump out of the carriage and, in an attempt to rescue himself, does not count on a parallelogram of forces in a movement-image of carriage-horse-human, as Diderot describes, but relies on forces of his own. He wants to grab the reins and take control of the sudden and hardly stoppable event by his own volition, but fails. His survival is a matter of luck. *Fortuna* rules, but Kleist thinks instantly of *Fatum*, of the persistence of a life that could have ended by the whim of a donkey's bray. Kleist's record, at this point in his life, was less than remarkable: In the summer of 1801, he was a twenty-three-year-old, largely aimless traveler—without a sense of home, without a profession, without any savings, always scheming new projects—on his way to Paris to resume his study of the natural sciences he had recently given up in his hometown, Frankfurt an der Oder. This was one of the many projects in his life that had not gone according to plan. A letter from Kleist to his fiancée Wilhelmine von Zenge of June 1801, written on his way to Paris, reveals that he does not really know how to carry on. "Everything seems confused inside me, all tangled like the fibers on the distaff," he writes. "[E]ven my desires change, and first one and then the other is overshadowed, like things in a landscape when clouds lengthen over it."[3] This lack of direction was hard to cope with for Kleist, who, since adolescence, had been fascinated by figures of control, and who wanted to take hold of life like he did the reins of the carriage horses. Two years prior to his journey to Paris, in May 1799, Kleist writes to his sister:

> A traveler who knows his destination, and the route to that destination, has a travel plan. What a travel plan is for the traveler, a life plan is for the person in general. To undertake a journey without an itinerary would mean leaving to Chance whether we should reach a goal, which we ourselves would not foreknow. To live without an itinerary for our life would mean leaving to Chance whether we should arrive at happiness of which we ourselves have no prior conception.
>
> It is really incomprehensible to me how a person can live without a plan for his life, and in the secure way I make use of the present, I feel with such inwardness the calm with which I look to the future, the priceless happiness that my life plan affords me; while the condition of being without a life plan, without a firm vocation, forever hesitant between uncertain desires, ever in contradiction to my sense of duty, a plaything of Chance, a puppet on the string of fate—such

> an ignoble condition would seem to me so contemptible, would render me so unhappy, that I would by far prefer death.[4]

Apart from the chance event of a donkey's bray, from which no one is safe, for Kleist, one should be in control of one's life in the same way that one is of one's travels. But what if life consists of experiments whose outcomes can no longer be predicted? How would somebody like Kleist manage? How did he cope with the fact that his life had not turned out as planned, did not add up to a coherent project with a clear goal, but remained a tangled patchwork without predetermined pattern—a patchwork identity, as sociologists today would call it? Such questions might seem pertinent only to contemporary life, but they are historically relevant too. Kleist might have been, as Thomas Mann once wrote, "a man unique in every respect, whose achievement and career seemed to violate all known codes and patterns."[5] His difficulties in conceiving of and following a life plan, however, were not unique to him. Rather, they were representative of a generational problem faced by those born after 1770. This generation, raised on Enlightenment values of autonomy and self-determination, was caught up in the turmoil of the Napoleonic Wars, which gave rise to political instability, the need for comprehensive social reform, and the destabilization of the estate system in the German states. The lives of aristocrats, in particular, became dangerously indeterminate, as their sense of stability derived from the social hierarchy of the estate system weakened and the possibility for social mobility increased. Such a gain in freedom could be experienced as a loss of orientation.[6] In contrast to the time of the old estate-based society, at the turn of the 19th century, it was not uncommon for somebody like Kleist to spend his life searching for its meaning.

It was a time of change and thus crisis, full of tensions that ought not be resolved and harmonized retrospectively in a biography. This is to avoid boredom and an overly simplistic biographical account—to protect the reader as much as the individual being portrayed. In Kleist's case this is not an easy task, as with all people who die early and in an extraordinary manner. As the great essayist Walter Benjamin once remarked about the correlation between a person's age at death and the way he is remembered: "A man […] who died at thirty-five will appear to *remembrance* at every point in his life as a man who dies at the age of thirty-five."[7] This holds true for Kleist, who died at the age of thirty-four. Almost every biographer writes Kleist's story by starting from its monstrous end, trying to discern in the wounds of his body those of his soul. Kleist's suicide at Lake Wannsee in 1811 is regarded as the final catastrophe in a life presented as a story of permanent crisis—the last consequence of a nonconformist who, coming from a prominent Prussian military family, resigned his commission in the army, left his studies, broke off his engagement with the daughter of a general, quit his attempt at a career in the civil service, received no recognition as a writer from his contemporaries, and failed at his ambitious journalistic project, the *Berlin Evening Paper* (*Berliner Abendblätter*). A single string of disappointments and failures to account for Kleist's self-sacrifice. And yet it is the other way around: As a result of his puzzling death, Kleist biographers have read his life retrospectively under the sign of melancholia and have thus regarded his works as documents of suffering.

It seems more reasonable to try to understand a life not from the perspective of its end, but from its beginnings, from the formative years of childhood. Yet even this biographical convention has its pitfalls, as a memorable story by German writer Wolfgang Hildesheimer teaches us. The story is entitled "Insurance Agent's Guest Performance," from *Loveless Legends* (*Lieblose Legenden*), a collection of short stories first published in 1952. Its protagonist's name is Frantisek Hdrla, a famous pianist whose career choice the narrator presents as the logical conclusion of the education he received from his musically gifted parents. The career 'mommy' and 'daddy' chose for this child prodigy becomes disrupted by a chance encounter with an insurance agent. At just ten years old, the boy is already excited about a side job. His pursuit of this double talent is unstoppable. At the end of this story that makes a mockery of the principle of causality, it will come as no surprise that the pianist sells insurance policies to the audience during intermission. What *is* surprising is that biographers so willingly believe in the temporal succession of events as the necessary result of cause and effect—putting the writer on Freud's couch, or behaving, in the good old German tradition, like the omniscient narrator of a *Bildungsroman*, who arranges the events of a life into a continuum and rounds them out into an organic whole.

One thing is for certain: Kleist never mastered the reassuring pattern of Johann Wolfgang Goethe's *Wilhelm Meister's Apprenticeship*, neither in his work nor his life. It makes little sense, then, to spin him a biography that retrospectively fills in gaps and draws in warp threads from the end—or the beginning—of his life. Instead of such a narrative technique, which reduces the complexity of real life, oversimplifying, arresting, and finalizing its events in terms of cause and effect—ultimately taking the perspective of death—I opt for the open, indeterminate perspective of life and, thus, for a narrative technique committed to the present. One has to remain at eye-level with the present and, alongside Kleist and from the perspective of his experience, think through the various options he was confronted with—be in the moment with him—suspending one's knowledge of what the future holds. This perspective still allows me to narrate linearly and chronologically, as any biographer would—but not teleologically. I abandon the narrative suspense created by the anticipation of a plot's ending and refrain from fixating on a particular outcome—on an imminent climax or a spectacular ending. Instead, I seek to capture the unsettling or astonishing in each phase of Kleist's life, the explosive nature of each of his experiments in living and writing.

The source material for such an endeavor is scarce, consisting of correspondences—letters written and received by Kleist—and accounts from his contemporaries. In a biography one typically extrapolates from a writer's life to make sense of his or her work; with Kleist one is tempted to do the exact opposite. But one should not thoughtlessly fall prey to this temptation. This does not mean one ought to ignore a writer's work when drawing his portrait. A biography on Kleist without a reading of his tragedy *Penthesilea* would be as absurd as a biography on Napoleon without a description of the French invasion of Russia.[8] With Kleist, though, there is no simple one-to-one correspondence between his life and work. 'Melancholy, the muse. Poetry, the remedy.' The sentiment expressed in this dictum, familiar to Kleist's contemporaries from Goethe's *The Sorrows of Young Werther*, did not pertain to Kleist. For him writing neither expressed nor alleviated his sorrows, and it did not provide his life with a sense of stability. This is not to say that Kleist's work did not engage with the conflicts of his life and his time. One is still allowed to ask: How did the author produce his work? And what kind of author did the work produce? A preliminary answer is: The relationship between life and writing resembles a 'parallel campaign.' In both life and writing, Kleist placed himself in a pre-Modernist laboratory, so to speak; he experimented recklessly with explosive material which, a century later, demolished the edifice of tradition. How, then, does one become—against the conventions of the philosophical and literary establishment of one's time—a "model for posterity,"[9] as Adam Müller once called his friend Kleist? Unlike Goethe, Kleist was in no sense moderate. The author of the cannibalistic Penthesilea and cruel political realist Herrmann treated "his topics like a sex offender treats a woman," as German playwright Heiner Müller once said of Kleist.[10] Kleist's ideas have a future in Modernism and Postmodernism, from Friedrich Nietzsche to Franz Kafka to Heiner Müller, but they had no currency for his contemporaries in the 19th century, where, following Goethe's verdict on Kleist, his ideas were stigmatized as pathological. But what kind of past did they have? Kleist scholarship tends to ignore this question. Kleist's experiments in life and writing were not created *ex nihilo*. He was no god creating out of nothing. One has to locate the grounds for his rejection of bourgeois idealism, the relations to, for instance, the aristocratic theories of 'cool conduct'[11] by Niccolò Machiavelli and Baltasar Gracián. But why did Kleist turn his back on idealism at all, and thus on philosophical and aesthetic measures that prevent and minimize social and individual risk? Why was he, in his writing as well as his life, fascinated by crises, catastrophes, and the loss of control? How did a one-time soldier with an unremarkable literary education become one of the greatest innovators of German literature? Unlike his contemporaries Goethe, Friedrich Hölderlin, Novalis, or E.T.A. Hoffmann, Kleist did not portray intellectual protagonists in his works. There are no musicians, painters, or poets, nor was he a theoretical mind proffering insight into his writing and life, as Goethe does in his *Poetry and Truth*. Kleist denies us a glimpse into his workshop. Where, then, might we discover the generative cores from which his creativity developed? These are enough questions for now, knowing that this biography will raise more questions than it will answer, as answers are so quickly forgotten. Questions, however—to rework an aphorism from Nietzsche's *On the Genealogy of Morality*—burn themselves in the memory, as they never cease "*to hurt*."[12]

CHAPTER II

Noblesse Oblige

Kleist's Lineage and Station

Il Gattopardo. The Leopard. One can easily surmise the character of a noble family by the animal featured in its coat of arms. Giuseppe Tomasi di Lampedusa's Prince of Salina, however, has lost his instinct to bite. In the face of the jackals and hyenas who outnumber him, his new strength has become melancholia. Maybe two are better than one—at least that is how it appears in the Kleist family coat of arms:[1] a white-silver shield with a red crossbar and, both above and underneath it, some sort of 'red dog,' or a fox, which is what it appears to be at first sight—and sometimes even Kleist scholars say so,[2] without, however, capitalizing on what it might mean for Kleist's works. After all, in his essay "On the Gradual Fabrication of Thoughts While Speaking" ("Über die allmählige Verfertigung der Gedanken beim Reden"), Kleist recounts a fable by Jean de La Fontaine in which a fox is condemned to death by the king of animals, the lion, who needs to sacrifice a sinner in order to appease the heavens as the plague rages among the animals. The fox escapes his fate by talking his way out, proving himself to be an expert in the art of invention. Could this great master of imagination be the same heraldic animal of the Kleists, corresponding to the family's motto: "All Kleists poets"?[3] Corresponding, too, to Baltasar Gracián's prudence rule for aristocrats in distress: "If you cannot clothe Yourself in Lionskin use Foxpelt"?[4] A rule of prudence that Herrmann, Prince of Cherusci, in Kleist's play *The Battle of Herrmann* (*Die Herrmannsschlacht*) knows how to exploit, when the Romans, with their superior military strength, become the victim of his art of deception. Kleist thus envisions Herrmann as a model for contemporary rulers in their struggle against the seemingly all-powerful Napoleon.

What can be seen twice on the Kleist family shield is, unfortunately, not a fox, but a wolf—in spite of the red color—which, in its doubling, is typical of Pomeranian coats of arms. Heraldic tinctures are not naturalistic colors adhering to the laws of optics. They follow their own logic, which can be seen, for example, in the principle of modifying fore- and backgrounds according to the obligatory variation of colors and metals. Heraldic tinctures cover the pictorial and geometrical elements of a coat of arms regardless of the 'nature' of what they represent. Thus, a position in a coat of arms can be colored red if the background is white-silver, and vice versa. The animals on the Kleist coat of arms are,

© WILHELM FINK VERLAG, 2021 | DOI:10.30965/9783846765746_003

Fig. 1
The Kleist family coat of arms

therefore, no red foxes, but color-coded wolves, which, in the reverse case—if the background were red instead of silver—could be, and indeed would have to be, silver or gold.[5] In Kleist's coat of arms, a helmet sits enthroned on top of the shield of wolves and is adorned with three inverted hunting spears, each aiming at a rose, symbolizing not the power of imagination but that of combat. Hence, "The Martial Wolf" of Gotthold Ephraim Lessing's fable[6] fits the Kleist family better than the fox, notwithstanding the family motto. By no means were all of the Kleists poets. There were only three: Ewald Christian von Kleist, the Rococo poet; Franz Alexander von Kleist, a cousin and contemporary of Heinrich, who remains a marginal figure in literary history, his works all but forgotten;[7] and Heinrich von Kleist. Soldiers dominate the Kleist family. Between 1640 and 1892, the Kleists produced twenty-three Prussian generals alone. In 1806, at the time of Prussia's defeat by Napoleon in the twin battles of Jena and Auerstedt, the army list registered fifty officers by the name of Kleist. No other Prussian noble family had produced more.[8]

The Kleists were an old Pomeranian noble family with Wendish origins, which can be traced back to the 13th century. A document from 1289 identifies someone by the name of 'Clest' as witness for a land grant to the Bukow monastery near Belgard,[9] located between Stettin and Danzig, which is where the Clest (or Klest) estate was located. At that time peace had finally prevailed in the region that had been so long-contested during the German eastward expansion. The early Kleist family records attest to a mix of Christianized Wends and German settlers. The political situation, however, remained unstable for a long time and, at the beginning of the 15th century, the Kleists took advantage of their Pomeranian feudal lord Bogislaw VIII's absence, fighting the Teutonic Order, to start a feud. They raided their neighbors' estates, setting their houses on fire, ravaging their fields, and stealing their livestock.[10] It was not until Bogislaw X that control over the Pomeranian nobility—which had become too independent, as the example of the Kleists illustrates—was regained. This was achieved by issuing letters of enfeoffment verifying (or disputing) a family's lineage and land ownership. The Kleists received their first such letter on April 13, 1477,[11] and its renewal was continued with each succeeding feudal lord. It is from this point onward that the Kleist family tree can be traced, without a break, in all of its branches.

'Pomerania is burnt down': So goes a German children's song about the aftermath of the Thirty Years' War, in the course of which—with the extinction of the old House of Greifen—Eastern Pomerania was ceded to the Elector of Brandenburg. As a privy councilor, one Ewald von Kleist helped Friedrich Wilhelm, the Great Elector, in his peace negotiations with Sweden. He then went on to establish the new Prussian rule over Eastern Pomerania in Kolberg on Friedrich's behalf.[12] So the Kleists were able to maintain their privileged position within the state. And just as it was under Pomeranian rule, members of the Kleist family under Prussian rule had a choice between "writing, warfare, or agriculture,"[13] which is to say: civil service, military office, or estate ownership. By the 18th century, however, this aristocratic free choice was encroached upon by the great increase in population ushered in by the age of Enlightenment. If an inheritance was limited, later-born sons were often left without their own estate, forcing them into a lifelong struggle with poverty. And with nothing to bequeath to a future progeny, they often chose a celibate existence.[14]

One such member of the Prussian nobility who found himself without rule over land and people was the Anacreontic poet Ewald Christian von Kleist. A friend of Lessing and the inspiration for his character Major von Tellheim in the comedy *Minna von Barnhelm or the Soldiers' Happiness*, Ewald Christian was one of the most prominent poets of the Frederician era. He was born in 1715 and died a legendary death in the Battle of Kunersdorf in 1759—one of the bloodiest battles of the Seven Years' War. His unsettled life foreshadows the life choices Heinrich von Kleist would be burdened with. Ewald Christian was the second son of Ewald Joachim von Kleist, who, in 1735, due to financial problems, had to mortgage the family estate of Zeblin to Paul von Humboldt—the grandfather of the brothers Wilhelm and Alexander von Humboldt—for thirty years.

Fig. 2
Ewald Christian von Kleist (1715–1759)

Hence, there was no money on his father's side. Ewald Christian studied law in Königsberg, where he also attended lectures in philosophy and mathematics. He became an "army officer in Denmark" in 1736, "as he could not immediately secure a position as a civil servant."[15] During his furlough he fell in love with a woman named Wilhelmine—just like Heinrich von Kleist would—whose last name, however, was not von Zenge, but von der Goltz. But, in 1747, Wilhelmine married somebody else because, over the course of almost ten years, Ewald Christian had not managed to find the lucrative profession that would have allowed him to start a family. By contrast, through a combination of guile and magnanimity, Lessing's Minna von Barnhelm manages to save her marriage to her impoverished lover, whose honor had been offended, by posing as a disinherited mismatch for Tellheim. The difference between Minna and Wilhelmine is, of course, one of theater and reality—the comedy turned to tragedy: Joining Friedrich the Great's army in 1741, Major Ewald Christian von Kleist saved himself from lost honor, a broken heart, and the monotony of garrison life, first by escaping into poetry and then into death—seeking recognition as a poet and in his glorious death on the battlefield. Likewise, Heinrich von Kleist would scheme ideas for burning himself in the memory of his contemporaries and posterity. His predecessor had succeeded in cultivating the demeanor of a melancholic nobleman, poet, and soldier, the vanishing point of which was death. Thus his "Funeral Song" ("Grab-Lied") reads: "Woe unto thee! for thou art dead. / Thou wilt no longer see the dawn. / [...] And yet thou wilt no longer see, / The struggle of the virtuous man, / Who wants, ashamed of being bare, / And cries his mortal life away." And even his "Birth Song" ("Geburtslied") opens, "Woe unto thee, for thou art born! / The world, a mighty house of fools, / Awaits thee for thy misery," closing with the following line: "Beset by woe, for he's alive!" Finally, we have the closing lines of his "Ode to the Prussian Army" ("Ode an die preußische Armee"): "I hope I will one day—may Heaven grant it to me!— / Ahead a handful heroes march. / I see thee, prideful enemy! the rabble doest thou flee, / And I, in raging turmoil, find honor or my death."[16]

The crucial term in the closing line of the ode is honor, which has nothing to do with patriotism. Rather, aristocratic honor is characterized by its reference to the individual and his family lineage. In defending one's family name, one thereby defends one's own. Heinrich von Kleist's father, Joachim Friedrich von Kleist, born in 1728, knew this all too well. A veteran of the Seven Years' War, he served as a battalion commander in Frankfurt an der Oder. Despite years of service in the Prussian army, however, he never ascended past the rank of major, due to Friedrich the Great's disappointment with the infantry regiments stationed in Ruppin and Frankfurt an der Oder upon his review of the Prussian troops in 1783. In consequence, Majors von Pirch and von Kleist were denied promotion by Friedrich the Great for not "fully applying themselves to their service."[17] Von Pirch immediately requested resignation from service, as did Kleist's father, who wrote the following letter to the King: "Your Majesty is the master of my life but not of my honor. The former has not been forfeited, the latter has been offended. I therefore implore Your Majesty most obediently for my resignation from service, commend myself and my family to destiny, and shall die, Your Royal Majesty's [most humble Joachim Friedrich von Kleist]."[18] Von Pirch was granted resignation; Kleist was not. He died without ever again being promoted by Friedrich the Great or by his successor Friedrich Wilhelm II.

One can only speculate as to what, exactly, might have displeased Friedrich the Great at the time, and whether his reproach of Battalion Commander Kleist was actually intended for the regimental commander, Prince Leopold von Braunschweig, who treated his soldiers too humanely for the King's liking.[19] And one can only speculate as to why Kleist's father chose to remain in the Frankfurt regiment. Financial reasons may have played a role. When Franz Heinrich von Kleist, Kleist's father's elder brother, inherited the family estate

Fig. 3
Joachim Friedrich von Kleist (1728–1788), Heinrich von Kleist's father

of Schmenzin, in the county of Belgard, the siblings were merely compensated with money. Without an estate, Joachim Friedrich could not become a country nobleman. So he studied for a short time at the University of Frankfurt an der Oder,[20] and it was not until 1749, when his service as a military officer began, that he was able to secure a livelihood. His earnings were enough to buy the small estate of Guhrow near Cottbus in the Spreewald in 1783, which he leased out. And in 1788 he managed to buy a townhouse in Frankfurt near St. Mary's Church at 26 Große Oderstraße, which the family had already been renting for several years. There, Heinrich von Kleist was born in 1777. His birthplace, however, can no longer be seen in today's Frankfurt, as the house burnt down at the end of World War II.[21]

The house was big, as it had to provide enough space for a large family. Joachim Friedrich married twice. His first marriage in 1767, at the age of forty-one, was to Caroline Luise von Wulffen, who was fourteen years old at the time and who gave birth to two daughters, Wilhelmine (1772) and Ulrike (1774). One week after Ulrike's birth, Caroline Luise died from complications related to childbirth at the age of nineteen. Soon thereafter, Kleist's father married a second time, to Juliane Ulrike von Pannwitz, a twenty-eight-year-old, fortuneless daughter from a family of military officers, which resided in Lower Lusatia and Silesia. With Juliane, Kleist's father had more children: Friederike (1775), Auguste (1776), Heinrich (1777), Leopold (1780), and Juliane (1784). In keeping

Fig. 4
Heinrich von Kleist's birthplace

Fig. 5
Juliane Ulrike von Kleist, née von Pannwitz (1746–1793), with her son Heinrich von Kleist

with tradition Heinrich von Kleist, his father's fifth child and first son following four daughters, was to be heir.

Bernd Heinrich Wilhelm von Kleist, as his name goes in full, was born on October 18, 1777, at one o'clock in the morning, at least according to the entry in the church registry recorded by the pastor who baptized him in the garrison town

Frankfurt an der Oder, in the Protestant consistory of Berlin-Charlottenburg.[22] Kleist, himself, had no doubt that his birthday was October 10, as confirmed in a letter he wrote to his fiancée Wilhelmine von Zenge on October 10, 1800, wherein he partakes in the birthday ritual par excellence: well-wishing for the future.[23] What is thus repeated year after year is what persists in the memory; in any case, the pastor may have easily misheard the date or written it down incorrectly. So, if one wants to celebrate Kleist's birthday, it should be done on October 10; any credibility ascribed to his birth record is merely the result of scant documentation of Kleist's childhood. Surviving documents written by friends and relatives fill only a few pages,[24] and Kleist, himself, did not reveal anything about his childhood. With Johann Wolfgang Goethe it is the opposite case; we are well informed by his relatives and friends, and Goethe carefully archived or transcribed the memories of his childhood, both fictionally, in *Wilhelm Meister's Apprenticeship*, and autobiographically, in *Poetry and Truth*. This difference in attentiveness to Kleist's and Goethe's childhoods has little to do with their respective standings or the different ways their contemporaries remembered them. Rather, it concerns the ethics of their respective social station—namely, the difference between aristocratic and bourgeois notions of family and childhood. It was not until the 18th century that the emphasis on intimacy and affection in bourgeois child-rearing engendered the paradigm of 'childhood' still familiar to us today. And, at the same time, this concern laid the foundation for the psychology of 'coming-of-age,' best expressed in the *Bildungsroman* and the autobiographical works so representative of the period. In *Poetry and Truth*, for example, Goethe describes, in detail, his father's personal commitment to his education and expounds on the significance of the puppet theater he inherited from his grandmother in the development of his imaginative, inventive, and expressive powers. By contrast, we know almost nothing about the emotional life of Kleist's family, nor do we have any sense of the degree to which Kleist's talents were fostered, particularly his poetic imagination. The sparse source material we do have stems from memories recorded decades after Kleist's death, rendering it largely unreliable—at times, peculiar or contradictory—and therefore incomparable to Goethe's careful and subtle character studies.

One such recorded memory describes the eleven-year-old Heinrich in competition with his brother Leopold, who was three years younger than him. The boys were asked to write poems singing the praises of their uncle's new cow barn. Only Leopold's poem survived (and perhaps this is not entirely unfortunate): "Stand, oh stand, thou solid building / Century on century, / Let no storm or fire ravage / Thy so stately symmetry. [...] And when someday thou collapsest / All at once, tremendously, / Then let legend tell forever / What a barn thou

Fig. 6 Auguste von Kleist (1776–1818), Kleist's sister

Fig. 7 Leopold von Kleist (1780–1837), Kleist's brother

used to be."[25] Heinrich seems not to have been able to write something similarly apocalyptic at this early age, losing, as he did, against his brother, along with the promised sum of money. Nevertheless, his early years in Frankfurt in the company of his siblings are said to have been "cheerful and good," according to another source. And yet another suggests the opposite—that Kleist's "childhood had been made bitter because his private tutors did not think it worth their while to consider the boy's unique constitution, disciplining him for mistakes he made, though their way of treating him was mostly to blame. The consequence of this was that, on the one hand, the boy retreated, sheepishly, into himself. On the other hand, he displayed unruly, defiant behavior. Both went *against his nature*, because by nature Kleist was open, gentle, dreamy, generous." A third account quotes Kleist's private tutor Christian Ernst Martini, who is said to have experienced Kleist's temperament in the following ambivalent terms: "an untamable fiery spirit, thrown into a state of exaltation by the merest trifles; of erratic temper, but of admirable intelligence when it came to the enhancement of his knowledge; inspired by love and a genuine eagerness for learning; in short, the most open and diligent mind in the world but, at the same time, unambitious."[26]

We are thus left with artist legends and childhood stories rather than reliable accounts: Kleist's childhood is not documented in writing. No one seemed to have had any interest in it, which was not uncommon for an aristocratic military family of that time. That Kleist wrote a yet-to-be-discovered autobiographical work entitled *Story of My Soul* (*Geschichte meiner Seele*),[27] one can choose to believe or not. The fact is, he never wrote a coming-of-age novel, and in his literary work, childhood experiences, as such, are of no concern. If he does portray family life, he presents it in a state of upheaval, thus turning otherwise noble houses bourgeois. Kleist takes pleasure in exposing the deep divide between the ideal and the reality of the bourgeois nuclear family—the illusion of a paternal authority justified by natural law, which is to say, the incompatibility of sovereign power and tenderness in child rearing, as well as the incompatibility of sensuality and friendship in married life. The dark novella "The Foundling" ("Der Findling") is a particularly extreme example of this.[28]

Yet Kleist's upbringing was certainly not bourgeois. It followed the aristocratic model, which meant growing up in an extended, patriarchally organized family, being educated by a private tutor and at boarding school, and spending adolescence in the military. His parents' marriage, then, which was entered into shortly after the death of Joachim Friedrich's first wife, was more likely a pact for securing care of the two existing infants, Wilhelmine and Ulrike, than a love match following the bourgeois ideal—despite, of course, the constant supply of children, which brings to mind Immanuel Kant's austere notion of marriage as a pact for the mutual use of each other's sexual organs. From an economic perspective the idea of a Prussian nobleman without a substantial estate giving in to his reproductive drive was anything but wise, as the death of Kleist's father in 1788 went on to prove. There are painted portraits of Kleist's parents,[29] but no written account of their characters, no details of them from Kleist's memory. His father, who died in June 1788 when Kleist was ten, is completely absent from his letters. His mother died in February 1793. Soon thereafter, Kleist writes a letter to his aunt Auguste Helene von Massow, in which he only briefly remembers the deceased as a caring, benevolent mother, before going on to recount, in detail, his experiences on his journeys and in the garrison.[30] The terse reference to his mother's death reveals his etiquette, but it may also point to the distance between parents and their children in the extended aristocratic family.

As for his education, Kleist did not receive a public one. Instead, as befitted his station, he was raised by the Huguenot nanny Jeanne-Elisabeth Nogier, who took care of the children in the Kleist household for twelve years, beginning in 1782.[31] He was taught by a private tutor, the theologian and, later, principal of the town school in Frankfurt an der Oder, Christian Ernst Martini. Kleist studied under Martini together with his cousin Carl von Pannwitz, who, Martini tells us, suffered from melancholia, became an officer at the age of fifteen (as Kleist did), and ended his life by shooting himself with a pistol on October 10, 1795, Kleist's presumed birthday.[32] In January 1788 Kleist was sent to Berlin to continue his education. He stayed *in Mitte*—as one would say today, referring to the city center—at 54 Kronenstraße, at the corner of Charlottenstraße, in a private boarding house run by the Huguenot preacher Samuel Henri Catel, together with his cousins Ernst von Schönfeldt and Wilhelm von Pannwitz, Carl's elder brother, who would go on to marry Kleist's sister Auguste in 1802. Presumably, Kleist received lessons at a private school run by Catel's brother-in-law Frédéric Guillaume Hauchecorne on Mohrenstraße as well as at the Collège Royal François, the Berlin Huguenots' secondary school at the Werderscher Markt, where the curriculum consisted of Latin and French, French literature and philosophy, as well as fencing, horseback riding, and dancing, among other things.[33] But Kleist's school days in Berlin did not even last six months before he had to return to Frankfurt an der Oder upon his father's death in June 1788. There is no source material on the four years of his life that followed, leading up to his enlistment in the military in 1792. This means we know practically nothing about Kleist's education due to the poor culture of writing in this family of military officers. But it would be false to conclude that Kleist was therefore poorly educated. In fact, his literary works prove the opposite, taking up literary, mythological, and historical topics: *The Schroffenstein Family* (*Die Familie Schroffenstein*), William Shakespeare's *Romeo and Juliet*; *Penthesilea*, the Greek myth of the Amazons; *The Battle of Herrmann*, the liberation war of the Germans against the Romans. Kleist's use of the canon, however, entails a challenging of convention so persistent and radical that his contemporaries found reason to question his education, particularly his understanding of Classical Antiquity. It is remarkable that Kleist made no attempt to justify, on a theoretical level, his creative use of the Western literary and cultural canon in his letters and his aesthetical and poetological reflections. Put differently: Kleist's education had no system or agenda but followed the shifting interests of an autodidact.

The lack of source material means that we cannot reliably determine the scope of experiences that defined Kleist's childhood. Thus, what follows is a miscellany of events taken from the 'cultural timetable' of the years 1777 to 1792, in an attempt to approximate the context in which he grew up: In 1777 *Hamlet* is staged in Hamburg and the enthusiasm for Shakespeare within the Sturm und Drang movement conquers the German stages; Germany's most famous mathematician, Carl Friedrich Gauß, is born; French painter Jean-Baptiste Greuze paints a broken jug. In 1778 Voltaire and Jean-Jacques Rousseau die; German men imitate Werther's style of dress, wearing their hair

Fig. 8 Frankfurt an der Oder, etching of 1826

unpowdered, donning a blue tailcoat, yellow vest and pants, and brown boots; Georg Christoph Lichtenberg writes his essay *On Physiognomy; against the Physiognomists* (*Ueber Physiognomik; wider die Physiognomen*) in opposition to Johann Kaspar Lavater. In 1779 Lessing's *Nathan the Wise* is published; Pastor Oberlin founds a nursery school; Lichtenberg introduces the terms 'positive' and 'negative' electricity. In 1780 Friedrich Nicolai erects the first Christmas tree in Germany; the fountain pen is invented. In 1781 Austria abolishes serfdom, torture, and the censorship of journals and books, and allows for the immigration of non-Catholics; Kant's *Critique of Pure Reason* is published; Lessing dies; first attempts are made at constructing a parachute. In 1782 James Watt invents the steam engine; Friedrich Schiller's *The Robbers* moves the audience in Mannheim; the last witch is executed, by sword, in Switzerland; Goethe is ennobled. In 1783 the Montgolfier brothers perform the first hot air balloon flight; Karl Philipp Moritz founds the *Magazine for Empirical Psychology* (*Magazin für Erfahrungsseelenkunde*). In 1784 Kant asks "What is Enlightenment?"; Goethe experiments with hot air balloons; Austria issues a ban on emigration. In 1785 the first of Karl Philipp Moritz's *Anton Reiser* is published; two explorers cross the English Channel in a gas balloon; Jakob Grimm is born and, with that, today's German Studies; the seismometer is invented; the *Times* is founded in London. In 1786 Gottfried August Bürger's *Adventures of Baron Munchhausen* (*Abenteuer des Freiherrn von Münchhausen*) causes a sensation; Wolfgang Amadeus Mozart composes *The Marriage of Figaro*; Friedrich the Great dies. In 1787 the first ascent of Mont Blanc is made; Mozart composes *Don Giovanni*. In 1788 Goethe ends his relationship with Charlotte von Stein and meets Schiller; Adolph Baron Knigge's *On Human Relations* (*Über den Umgang mit Menschen*) is published; Prussian secondary schools introduce university qualification exams; a British penal colony is founded in Sydney. In 1789 the French Revolution begins; George Washington becomes the first president of the United States of America; at his inaugural lecture in Jena, Schiller asks "What is, and to What End Does One Study Universal History?" ("Was heißt und zu welchem Ende studiert man Universalgeschichte"); at the Philanthropinum in Dessau physical education enters into the curriculum. In 1790 the short Titus cut replaces the hedgehog hairstyle with a tail; Mozart composes *Così fan tutte*; in Haiti a revolution breaks out; Kant's *Critique of the Power of Judgment* is published; Adam Smith dies in England and Benjamin Franklin in the United States. In 1791 hoop skirts and top hats become popular in Europe; the Brandenburg Gate is finished after three years of construction; Mozart dies and is buried in a common grave; Luigi Galvani's frog leg experiments cause a sensation; Goethe is appointed director of the Weimar Court Theater. In 1792 Mary Wollstonecraft writes *A Vindication of the Rights of Woman*; France introduces civil marriages; the United States dollar becomes the country's standard unit of money; France declares war on Austria; in June Kleist begins his military service in Potsdam.

Let us now return from this panorama of Kleist's time to his life. But, since we do not even know the young Kleist's hiding places and the secret page-turners of his nursery and classroom, there is little reason to conjecture about the influence of the streets, squares, and people of the city in which Kleist spent most of the first fourteen years of his life. A trade, university, and garrison town, Frankfurt an der Oder had a population of around 12,500 at the turn of the 19th century, and was at the cultural periphery of the German states.[34] It is all too understandable that Kleist would go on to praise Dresden as a cultural and artistic center, for it was soldiers who determined life in Frankfurt, not students and professors. Biographers searching for the impact of Frankfurt on Kleist's works may speculate as to whether the "hurly-burly of the fair" in the trade city "exalted Kleist's imagination" and initiated "the story writer's later affinity for foreign and adventurous themes."[35] In his letter of March 1793, the fifteen-year-old writes to his aunt that, after the death of his mother, Frankfurt "had ceased to be a happy place."[36] After that, nothing could tie him to Frankfurt—neither his studies, which he began in 1799 and quit after a mere three semesters, nor his engagement to Wilhelmine, daughter of the regimental commander, whose family lived next door to the Kleist family home. Kleist was always traveling, and he soon fled from Frankfurt, not so much to escape its provincialism but its aristocracy. His disappearance from the city had to do with the uncertainty of his financial and professional situations, which were under close scrutiny in Frankfurt, where people knew him. Dreams of rebirth could only be realized out of the sight of his relatives and friends.

Kleist's struggles did not begin with his mother's sudden death from fever in 1793; they began with his father's death, from edema, in June 1788. Kleist was then pulled out of his boarding school in Berlin; his family evidently had financial problems and was still not well liked by the crown. His father had been denied promotion since 1783 and, after his death, Kleist's mother's appeal for a pension was likewise declined. Fruitless, too, was her pleading letter to Friedrich Wilhelm II requesting his assistance in certifying the validity of her husband's will. Joachim Friedrich had appointed his wife, Juliane, sole heir, but due to formal errors, the will was annulled. The assets were to then be divided among his children, but Juliane contested the decision. In September 1790 an inheritance settlement was reached, which separated the children, proprietarily, from their mother and put them under the legal guardianship of Judicial Commissioner Georg Friedrich Dames until they reached their full legal age, which was, at the time, twenty-four. This meant that Kleist did not have access to his inheritance until October 1801. The settlement agreement itemized Joachim Friedrich's assets: the leased estate of Guhrow, which had to be divested for 30,000 Reichsthaler in 1797; the family house in Frankfurt, which had appreciated at 6,000 Reichsthaler; and cash in the amount of 3,738 Reichsthaler in gold and 4,431 Thaler Courant.[37] With these holdings an extended family like the Kleists was able to continue living in a manner befitting its station for a few more years, but the family had to be frugal, as one of Kleist's letters to his sister Ulrike of February 1795 suggests. He thanks his sister for the vest she had gifted him, commenting that, for the time it took her to knit it, she must have passed up on sleigh rides, masquerades, balls, comedies, and other "pleasures of the city, which are otherwise so delightful"—a backhanded thanks Ulrike must have found "rather distasteful," as Kleist anticipates.[38]

Ultimately, Joachim Friedrich's estate was not enough to secure the family's livelihood. So the Kleist sons had to seek employment, though they were prohibited from pursuing bourgeois professions due to the division of labor among the estates instituted by Friedrich the Great and codified in the Prussian General State Laws in 1794. And because there were so few positions in higher governmental offices, it was only natural that Heinrich and, later, Leopold, at just fourteen years of age, were sent to serve in the military. Their mother requested that the King admit her eldest son to the Prussian Military Academy in Berlin, where the sons of Prussian nobility, with the financial support of the crown, were reared into well-educated officers, but her requests were denied. The time of the old swashbuckler had been over in Prussia since Friedrich the Great, and the various Prussian cadet schools were meant to cultivate an elite of sophisticated leaders. The Military Academy in Berlin, for instance, offered Latin, French, German, math, geography, history, and philosophy, as well as lessons in fencing, horseback riding, and dancing, as befitting the students' station. The 'learned' officer—in the likes of Gerhard von Scharnhorst, Carl von Clausewitz, Neidhardt von Gneisenau, or even Kleist's fellow officers Johann Jakob August Otto Rühle von Lilienstern and Adolf Heinrich Ernst von Pfuel—was in high demand. It was the 'learned' officer that prompted military reform at the turn of the 19th century.[39] Rühle went on to become chief of the Prussian General Staff and inspector general of military education, while Pfuel became minister of war and prime minister of Prussia. Kleist, however, having been denied the chance to receive a comprehensive education, was thus also denied access to the elites. After what he considered "seven irretrievably lost years,"[40] Kleist left his military career to begin studying the sciences. One cannot help but wonder how things might have turned out had the King accepted him into the military academy. Speculation is futile, but there is no doubt that this missed career opportunity determined the course of Kleist's life as much as the expropriation of his family and the untimely loss of his parents did.

Rather than an elite academy, then, Kleist entered an elite military unit. On June 1, 1792, the boy became a corporal,[41] joining the Potsdam Guard Regiment No. 15 as an officer cadet. At the turn of the year, the regiment left the garrison to take up winter quarters in Frankfurt am Main, joining the War of the First Coalition, in which Prussia and Austria fought against the forces of revolutionary France. Only a single letter of this period survived—the earliest surviving Kleist letter, composed in March 1793. Eight pages long, it shows that the now fifteen-year-old is more suited for the life of a writer than a child soldier.[42] The letter is addressed to his "most gracious Aunt" Auguste Helene von Massow, an elder sister of his mother. As his mother had just died in the previous month, Kleist appeals to his aunt as a surrogate. In this sense the letter is one of flattery and supplication, with strategic remarks such as: "The thought of you, best Aunt of mine, brings tears to my eyes, for at the time I think of my late loving mother, and the thought of her goodness comforts me, and I at least may think of myself as a not entirely *forsaken* orphan." Kleist repeatedly draws upon the motif of the "*forsaken* orphan" and crafts the self-portrait of an impoverished, yet, honest young nobleman who keeps in order his knapsack and sleeping quarters and endures his meager meals. At the same time he pleads the authenticity of his poverty, which, he argues, distinguishes him from other "sons," who "often lie to their parents about their misfortunes." The letter is also a war report with boastful outbursts such as: "The French, or rather that gang of robbers, are now everywhere getting pummeled." First and foremost, however, it is a travel narrative with atmospheric descriptions of landscapes, with geographic-topographic notes and historico-cultural reminiscences. It is a travel narrative with an adventure story woven into it, telling of a fight with a highway robber who tried to hold up Kleist's carriage somewhere between Gotha and Eisenach, sending the horses into a bolt. And the letter, itself, is framed by reflections on how to write a letter. It begins: "Dear Aunt, I hardly know what to describe or tell you first! Shall I describe the views of the beautiful countryside or those of beautiful cities, magnificent palaces, elegant gardens, the terrible cannon or legions of soldiers? I would forget one thing and write down another if I did not tell you everything from the beginning. I will therefore proceed with the description of my journey." Kleist decidedly understands letter writing as a problem of narration, and he quickly abandons his aspiration of a linear account in favor of a complex narrative pattern that skillfully links heterogeneous motifs. At the letter's conclusion he expresses regret that all his "powers of eloquence are exhausted"—that he does not know how to continue—and he begs his aunt "not to be too critical about this mishmash of a letter, and to read it carefully." But the "mishmash of a letter" is more than just a rhetorical expression; it indicates Kleist's awareness of the hybrid nature of the letter genre—its suitability for the mixing of genres, forms, and styles, as well as fiction and reality. It also expresses Kleist's intuition that every letter is an artifact, an artwork of montage and collage. We are thus invited to see Kleist's letters, beginning with his first, as a poetic field of experimentation and practice, which is how he, himself, understood letter writing, long before deciding to become a writer. This is best demonstrated in the mental exercises he assigns to Wilhelmine in a letter from November 1800—not, however, without first trying these exercises in creative writing himself, supplying his fiancée with a model for her responses. To questions such as: What is delightful? Elevating? Terrifying? Moving? Admirable? Consoling? Deceptive? etc., he provides answers such as: delightful, e.g. the depiction of a day in May, a peach blossom, a joyful bride; moving, e.g. eulogies over the deceased, a sunset, etc.[43]

Kleist's letters are exercises in composition—a 'magazine of ideas' and a testing ground for his later storytelling—though they do not serve as immediate source material for his works in the way that Rainer Maria Rilke's letters from Paris do for his novel *The Notebooks of Malte Laurids Brigge*. So if one treats them as biographical source material, one has to be prepared for the blurring of the line between poetry and truth that define them at the outset—and that is what makes them exceptional. Crafting a particular image

Fig. 9 Uniforms of the Guard Regiment

of oneself, as such, is nothing unusual in letters. But letters written in one's early years are typically thought of as sincere and unaffected. Kleist's letter to his aunt, whom he hopes will take on the 'forsaken orphan,' emotionally and financially, appeals to her benevolence. His detailed description of his living conditions at the Frankfurt winter quarters serves this end: Having only vegetables and sometimes a side of soup for lunch; having to pay for his own food; having to share with his servant lad a single dark room in which there is only one bed, available only at a fee of one Reichsthaler per week, an exorbitant price, as Kleist suggests, giving us a sense of the cost of wartime living and his meager finances. Kleist's inheritance amounted only to about five to six thousand Reichsthaler, but he did not have access to it before turning twenty-four, anyhow, which is why he relied upon his aunt, and later turned to other relatives, particularly his sister Ulrike. Being financially dependent on his family forced him to write many a begging letter.

Kleist wrote the letter to his "most gracious Aunt" in 1793. Shortly thereafter, from Frankfurt am Main, the guard regiment dispatched for the Rhine campaign against the French revolutionary armies. The regiment was involved in the bombing and siege of Mainz in the spring and summer of 1793, and they succeeded in suppressing the Jacobin Republic of Mainz when the French forces surrendered on July 22, 1793. The next operation was the Palatinate; in the course of its recapture in 1793/94, the regiment engaged in bloody combats, among them, the Battles of Pirmasens, Kaiserslautern, Frankenthal, Hochspeyer, and Trippstadt.[44] But it would be wrong to think of this war as a constant battle. Primarily, it consisted of marches and camp life, problems with the food supply, miserable sanitary conditions, and enduring severe weather conditions.[45] Battles only made for a few days of a campaign once the opposing armies found each other and arranged their troops, which was particularly hard in the Palatinate Forest, whose topography prevented the standing army from implementing its linear tactics, consisting of mile-long frontlines. The Palatinate required a more mobile style of warfare geared toward smaller units and individual soldiers.[46] This also meant that officers could no longer seek shelter behind the common soldiers fighting in the rank-and-file formation typical of Frederician warfare. In the traditional linear tactics, an officer's job was not to kill or get killed, but to stay beside or behind the ranks—usually positioned behind each other in lines of three or four—in order to keep them in line and, despite their fear of dying, drive them into battle and shoot deserters when necessary.[47] It is unlikely, however, that Kleist was able to hide behind the backs of common soldiers during the battles in the Palatinate; he was likely engaged in man-to-man combat.

Military theorist Carl von Clausewitz describes how such a novice to the battlefield must have felt when "[t]he air is filled with hissing bullets that sound like a sharp crack if they pass close to one's head. For a final shock, the sight of men being killed and mutilated moves our pounding hearts to awe and pity."[48]

Kleist must have drawn on similar experiences when he expressed his longing for peace in a letter to his sister Ulrike on February 25, 1795: "May Heaven only grant us peace, so that with more humane endeavors we might atone the time that we are now murdering so immorally."[49] Compare this to Kleist's earliest surviving poem, entitled "The Higher Peace" ("Der höhere Frieden"). According to Kleist, it was written at the beginning of his military service. In 1808 it was published in the journal *Phöbus*, which Kleist edited together with Adam Müller. It is a youthful poem, which, in all its naïveté, was likely composed before the beginning of the war. In it religion, nature, and, most of all, poetry still serve as a refuge from the atrocities of war. But Kleist's real war experiences must have shattered his hope that "the thunder-chariot of war" would not "disturb the song of nightingales, / Which pervades my peaceful breast with glee."[50] Kleist's longing for peace, which he was certainly not alone in,[51] was fulfilled in April 1795, when Prussia withdrew from the First Coalition and entered into the Peace of Basel treaty with the French Republic. After this betrayal Prussia's reputation was ruined in the eyes of the members of the First Coalition and the Holy Roman Empire of the German Nation. The establishment of a neutral zone in northern Germany merely served Prussia's own power interests. The French militia, in which military talents could prove themselves as leaders independent of any noble title due to the policy of mass conscription, had shown the Prussian army of professionals and mercenaries, still organized according to social station, its limits. Moreover, Prussia had overexerted itself fighting two wars at the same time: to the west, the devastating and ultimately failing Rhine campaign against the French, which Heinrich took part in; to the east, campaigns against Poland, together with Russia and Austria, which Heinrich's brother Leopold was part of. Poland was defeated in 1795, and the Polish territories were subsequently divided among the victorious powers. Prussia gained large territories in the east, whose administration became difficult; it had been in financial trouble for a long time, which was the impetus for signing the Peace of Basel, making it possible for the guard regiment to return home. Among the officers, however, Prussia's withdrawal from the Rhine campaign was perceived as inglorious, as it demoralized the troops. Be that as it may, in June 1795 Kleist was back in Potsdam, now seventeen years old and promoted to ensign, as his younger brother Leopold was before him. His childhood—ended by the war—belonged to the past.

Yet there are certain similarities between children and soldiers. Both regularly find themselves in new, unknown, or dangerous situations. During the years of childhood and war, one lives most intensively. This is why memory holds on to these years most tightly, and why they often recur in letters and autobiographical accounts. But not so with Kleist. His childhood and adolescent years, up until his resignation from the military in 1799, are nearly unwritten. Put numerically: We have 2 letters from the period before 1799 and 254 letters from the years 1799 to 1811.[52] What is remarkable about the letters after 1799 is that the past does not serve as a reference point; Kleist's thoughts are focused on the present and the future, with few exceptions, such as his sentimental recounting of a war-time journey on the Rhine in a letter to Adolphine von Werdeck of July 1801, and his suicide letters, of course. It is as if Kleist wanted to start anew, without any obligations to his lineage and station. Yet, during his time at the Potsdam garrison, he still had to will himself to perform his duties as a noble officer, as he knew from his father. Despite Kleist's relative silence in letters, however, we are rather well informed about his military years up to 1799, thanks to the recorded memories of his regimental comrades and acquaintances from Potsdam.

The Prussian military of the 18th century served as a proxy for the patriarch and the sovereign, a correctional facility for common soldiers, and an educational institution that befitted the noble officers' station. Not courage, but discipline was the highest principle, because a regiment that falls into disorder becomes uncontrollable and stands no chance in war. The officers had to discipline the common soldiers during their military training in the garrison. Corporal punishment in cases of suspected insubordination was routine business, due to the fact that soldiers did not consider arrest a punishment, given how much they disliked the service, and their pay was too low to impose fines. The noble officers' relationship to common soldiers, who were recruited from Prussian peasantry or foreign countries, was generally marked by contempt and disregard, with no sensibility for the dignity of subordinates. Corporal punishment was not only a deliberate humiliation to the common soldiers, who were—with an average age of thirty years—often considerably older than their noble officers; it also led to serious physical injuries and even death. As noted in a polemical work of the era, an officer "can flog, he can rampage, he can push teeth in, he can send you to hell, he can—like an Oriental despot—whip a poor servant to death for his amusement without having to fear punishment for all these brutalities."[53] The guard regiment—in which Kleist served as an officer for seven years—did not only distinguish itself from all other regiments through impeccable discipline, but also through exacting rigor; in the 1770s it attracted attention due to the fact that several soldiers committed suicide.[54]

From the beginning of his time in the Potsdam garrison, Kleist likely sided with the military reformers, who regarded as senseless the "miserable puppet theater" that turns "soldiers into marionettes,"[55] not least for reasons of military tactics. After all, Prussia had fought so badly against France in the Rhine campaign precisely because the French soldiers were not driven by fear of their superior officer but by patriotism and personal responsibility. In a letter to his former tutor, Martini, on March 19, 1799, Kleist criticizes the disciplinary tactics of the Prussian army in an attempt to justify his resignation. His criticism is anything but original, encapsulating established views on the Prussian army's need to reform:

> The greatest wonders of military discipline, while objects of awe to all experts, became objects of my own most heartfelt contempt; the officers I regarded as so many drillmasters, the soldiers as so many slaves, and when the whole regiment was performing its tricks, it seemed to me a living monument to tyranny. What is more, I began to feel keenly the evil effect that my position was making on my character. I was often compelled to punish when I would gladly have pardoned, or I pardoned when I should really have punished; and, in either case, saw *myself* as the punishable one. At such moments, the wish to leave such a profession began to grow within me as a matter of course, constantly martyred as I was between two completely incompatible principles, and always in doubt whether to act as an officer or as a human being, for I consider it an impossibility to combine the obligations of both under present conditions in the military.[56]

For these officers the world was divided into duties and privileges. The field days in spring and fall and the drills were part of the duties; the generous leaves were part of the privileges. Kleist took advantage of his time off to gain a 'general education,' so to speak, in the social and intellectual life of Potsdam—the arts and sciences—as befitted his station. This is likely what made bearable his seven years in the guard regiment. Life in Potsdam—the summer residence of the Prussian kings—was more exciting than in Frankfurt an der Oder. Kleist lived in the new part of town, in the Dutch Quarter, near Nauener Straße, and he made friends inside and outside of his regiment—friends who supported him emotionally and, sometimes, financially throughout his life. Among those were three noble families, regarded as liberal for their value of philosophical, literary, and moral education over courtly etiquette: Staff Captain Friedrich Wilhelm Christian von Kleist, a distant cousin of Heinrich, and his wife Marie, daughter of the Huguenot preacher Albert Samuel Gualtieri;

Marie's sister, Amélie Henriette von Massenbach and her husband Christian Karl August Ludwig von Massenbach, who wrote mathematical and military theory treatises and was later blamed for Prussia's defeat in the 1806 Battle of Jena; and, lastly, Adolphine von Werdeck and her husband Christoph Wilhelm von Werdeck, state councilor in Potsdam. Whether the soirées at their private homes were more familial or frequented by philosophers, poets, and artists as prominent as those at the Berlin salon of Rahel Varnhagen (with whom Kleist met frequently in the spring of 1810), we do not know. It is quite possible, however, that the conversations among the officers at times resembled duels, using words instead of weapons. In his short essay "On the Gradual Fabrication of Thoughts While Speaking," written for Rühle von Lilienstern in 1805/06, Kleist reflects on the act of speaking at such public events. We know from its military imagery that the essay concerns a rather agonistic culture of conversing, as opposed to small talk. It is embarrassing, says Kleist, to want to participate in an "animated conversation"—feeling inflamed and excited—but without a sense of control over language, because "where we may assume equal clarity of thought, he who can talk faster than his opponent will enjoy a distinct advantage, for, in a manner of speaking, he leads more troops into the field."[57]

Most likely, the ladies of the house were at the center of these battles of words in Potsdam (just as they were, later, in Berlin). Kleist felt close to Adolphine von Werdeck and Marie von Kleist, the latter in particular. Marie, who did not have a happy marriage, getting divorced in 1812, was sixteen years older than Kleist. She was not a maternal figure, though, as their active correspondence shows. She served as lady-in-waiting to the legendary Queen Luise of Prussia and repeatedly advocated for Kleist's case to Friedrich Wilhelm III. From 1805 to 1810 she secured her protégé a pension allegedly coming from Queen Luise but actually paid for by Marie herself. In the end she felt deeply resentful that Kleist decided to die with such a "fame-seeking, vain fool"[58] as Henriette Vogel. Feeling betrayed, she unfortunately destroyed most of the letters Kleist had written to her. Allegedly, Kleist also had a "true affair of the heart" with a general's daughter named Luise von Linckersdorf during his time in Potsdam. Their breakup had a tremendous impact on him, who "henceforth neglected his appearance, withdrew from society and took up serious study of the philosophical sciences," incurring "the indignation of his superior, General von Rüchel."[59]

Cherchez la femme? That the broken-hearted should take refuge in the sciences is unusual enough, probably even more so for a noble officer. It is more likely that Kleist's interest in the sciences, literature, and music were nurtured by his comrades from the regiment, particularly the graduates of the Military Academy in Berlin: Ernst von Pfuel and Rühle von Lilienstern, Kleist's closest friends during and after his time in Potsdam. With Rühle, who joined the guard regiment in 1795, Kleist played music in a quartet of officers. They traveled to the Harz Mountains together in the summer of 1798, which they were able to fund through concert performances. The two other members of the quartet were Carl Heinrich von Gleißenberg and Hartmann von Schlotheim. According to Romantic writer Clemens Brentano, Kleist was in fact "one of the greatest virtuosi on the flute and clarinet."[60] Kleist also shared his interest in mathematics, philosophy, and the study of Greek and Latin with Rühle. They were supported by Heinrich Ludwig Bauer, vice-principal of the Great Town School in Potsdam, who gave lectures and private lessons in the garrison on behalf of Friedrich Wilhelm III. To his former tutor Martini, Kleist later played down Bauer's importance, writing that he did "not" receive "a significant amount of help" from him.[61]

Rühle, with whom Kleist was able to study well, seems to have been the more theoretical mind of the two friends. He went on to become inspector general of military education. Pfuel, by contrast, who had served the guard regiment since 1797, was a keen sportsman. He suggested exercises in climbing and swimming for the soldiers and later established the first military swimming facility in the Berlin district of Kreuzberg. Pfuel also served as a diplomat for various sovereigns, and, in 1848, was Prussia's prime minister and minister of war for two months.[62] Kleist regarded Pfuel enthusiastically. In a letter from January 1805, Kleist swoons over Pfuel who made "a marvelous impression" on his "heart" with his "eloquence." Moreover, his body "could have served an artist as a model for study"—his "small head, with its curly hair, [his] sturdy neck, broad shoulders, lean body, altogether the very picture of vigor, as though modeled after the most beautiful young steer ever bred in honor of Zeus." He continues: "You restored the age of the Greeks in my heart; I could have slept with you, my dear boy; [...]. I had often, as I watched you step into the lake at Thun, contemplated your handsome body with almost *maidenly* feelings. [...] I shall never marry, you will be wife to me, children and grandchildren!"[63] This letter, discovered in the Pfuel family archive in 1902, is the foundation of all speculation about Kleist's sexual identity, which persists to the present day. On the one hand, scholars have pointed to the rhetoric associated with the cult of friendship in this sentimental era, of which there are ample examples.[64] Kleist's famous predecessor, the poet Ewald von Kleist, for instance, assures Johann Wilhelm Ludwig Gleim, the leading figure of the Anacreontic poets, that: "Truly I love you more than all the maidens in the world."[65] On the other hand, scholars have taken the letter as evidence of Kleist's sexual orientation and then gone on to divine its possible genealogy, looking for its origins in his time at boarding school or with the military or on a trip to the island of

Rügen in 1796, accompanied by his siblings and his friend Ludwig von Brockes, who also accompanied Kleist on his mysterious journey to Würzburg in 1800, and who, like Kleist, never married.[66] Moreover, there is speculation about whether Kleist himself, due to the "absence of women in the military," "experienced the traditionally-female first hand," was "subjected to a man's will," whether he was "seduced," "possibly not without force"—that is, whether he fell victim to an overpowering officer not unlike the poor Marquise of O— in Kleist's eponymous novella.[67] Certainly, homosexual relationships were not unheard of in the Prussian military at the turn of the 19th century and were a part of Kleist's circle. Indeed, the father of Kleist's cousin and childhood friend Carl von Pannwitz warned his son about such temptations in a nine-page letter. The son, who, at the beginning of the Polish campaign, shared a room with his superior, should not sacrifice his honor and health "to lust" and become "a miserable creature for the rest of his life." These words of warning fuel speculation about the motive for Carl's suicide in 1795 on the homeward march from battle in Poland.[68]

Was Kleist, then, a homosexual, or an abused child soldier as some scholars have suggested? Or, perhaps he was bisexual? After all, in Thun, 1802, Kleist did not only look at Pfuel with pleasure, but also at a Swiss girl who shared a house with him on the Aar island, which Kleist confessed to his sister, but not his fiancée Wilhelmine.[69] And one could keep going. Was he androgynous? One only has to look at the miniature painted by Peter Friedel in April 1801—the only authentic portrait of Kleist, a present for Wilhelmine[70]—to get that impression, or think of the children's cross-dressing in Kleist's first work *The Schroffenstein Family*, or the Amazon queen Penthesilea, uncertain of her gender. Ultimately, the question of the nature of Kleist's desire cannot be answered. Any thesis on Kleist's homosexuality is viable only if one is less interested in truth than in the "art of intellectual midwifery"[71]—that is, in promoting new readings of Kleist's work. It has been claimed, for instance, that the need Kleist and Thomas Mann as well as other homosexual writers felt to write periphrastically, to camouflage their forbidden desire, may have nurtured their literary creativity.[72] The French term *camouflage* originally refers to the disguise of military fortifications and thus carries a double meaning: to brace oneself and to disguise. In the case of Kleist, then, his camouflage would fortify his work, both safeguarding and walling-in his sexuality. But more interesting than the defensive is the offensive, productive nature of camouflage: The silence imposed on taboos may have produced profound displacements. One is left to wonder, for example, if sexual relations turn into racial relations—if it is not the 'man-woman' Kleist manifest as the mestiza Toni in "The Betrothal in Santo Domingo" ("Die Verlobung in St. Domingo"), whose love of Swiss officer Gustav, from "the banks of the Aar,"[73] re-enacts Kleist's 'betrothal' to Ernst von Pfuel in Thun. This subtext would at least explain why the price for this transgression is Toni's and Gustav's deaths. The pleasure the reader can take in such readings is that of a detective exposing techniques of camouflage and making connections between text and subtext, not so much for the redemptive recognition, let alone stigmatization, of Kleist as a 'homosexual,' but to gain an always-hypothetical insight into his creative process. This approach can also lead to readings that do not take 'sacred' texts such as Kleist's famous essay "On the Puppet Theater" ("Über das Marionettentheater") quite so seriously. Is it not remarkable that two men should stand in a dark park one winter evening to discuss such delicate questions as the grace of a naked sixteen-year-old boy in a bathhouse?[74]

It remains difficult to examine Kleist's life and discern what is in fact a secret and what is merely a smokescreen. One is thus glad to have recourse to an essay he wrote during his time at the Potsdam garrison, which delineates the principles of his character formation. Kleist presumably wrote the essay at the end of 1798 or beginning of 1799, and dedicated it to his military comrade Rühle. He also reiterated its central passages in a letter to his former tutor Martini in March 1799. The essay's ambitious, convoluted title "Essay: How to find the certain Path to Happiness and—even amid Life's greatest Tribulations—enjoy the Journey undeterred!" ("Aufsatz, den sichern Weg des Glücks zu finden und ungestört—auch unter den größten Drangsalen des Lebens, ihn zu genießen!") indicates its significance to Kleist. It is a manifesto that marks the end of Kleist's adolescence—he was twenty-one years old at the time—and lays the foundation for a new beginning. Soon after finishing it, Kleist quits the army and begins his studies in Frankfurt an der Oder. The essay reveals his understanding of this transitional period in his life in terms of a classic philosophical gesture: the linking of happiness and virtue. In his *Nicomachean Ethics* Aristotle states: "For the truly good and wise person, we believe, bears all the fortunes of life with dignity and always does the noblest thing in the circumstances."[75] Kleist, on his part, defines "happiness as encouragement for virtue, virtue as the path to happiness" and then concludes that "*the best individual is the happiest individual.*"[76] The circular logic of this premise indicates that Kleist is not yet confident about his argument. He has a hard time bringing happiness and virtue into relation with one another without running into problems, for two reasons: On the one hand, he has to distinguish between internal and external happiness—those true pleasures that lie "in the gratifying observation of the moral beauty of our own beings"—and *Fortuna*, the goddess of chance, as that which "fools" call happiness. On the other hand, virtue has to prove itself as the master of *Fortuna*. For this to work, Kleist would have to have a clear conception of what virtue is, or what means are necessary for happiness to become independent of ever-changing "external circumstances."

And yet what is peculiar about Kleist's essay is that the notion of virtue itself is never defined. Instead, Kleist repeatedly emphasizes the unrepresentability of virtue, writing that he "associate[s] with this concept only a vague understanding; [...]. It appears to me like a lofty, sublime, unnameable phenomenon, for which I seek in vain a word to express it in language, and in vain a form through which to express it with a picture." Kleist hopes that his "inarticulate representation" of virtue will gradually become coherent as he enumerates some of its characteristics—"noble-mindedness, love of humankind, constancy, modesty, contentment, etc." They do not, however, succeed in bringing about a "resolution" to the "riddle." Kleist thus compensates for the unrepresentability of virtue by generating entirely heterogenous images of happiness. Happiness lies, he writes, "in the gratifying observation of the moral beauty of our own beings," echoing Schiller's congruence of grace and dignity or Shaftesbury's notion of moral grace. "[E]ven in chains and in irons," there are "exalted delightful feelings for the virtuous sage," Kleist continues, drawing on the tradition of Baroque stoicism. And yet Kleist will go on to free himself from the chains and irons of his military commission. Moreover, drawing on the tradition of *Ecce homo*, Kleist reminds us of the example of "that one best and most noble of all human beings, who suffered death on the cross for humankind," before returning to Aristotelian ethics, specifically the concept of *mesotés*. He writes that in life we should "always travel straight on the middle road" and "never aim in our desires for the dizzying heights," which he uses his journey to the Harz Mountains to exemplify. "[T]he view from great extraordinary heights," such as the Blocksberg Mountain, he writes, "promises so little happiness," while "the view from the intermediate and less lofty elevation of the *Regenstein Mountain*" holds much greater pleasures. Finally, Greek mythology is made to serve as proof: Homer's story about the front court of Mount Olympus, where there stood "two large vessels, one filled with pleasure, the other with deprivation." Kleist argues that "the individual to whom the gods mete out equal portions from both vessels is the happiest," "the most unhappy of all is the one who receives from only one of the vessels." All of these esteemed examples are, however, of little use. The essay never makes good on what Kleist promises Rühle at its outset: "I am happy in advance that I will persuade you that this [the congruence of happiness and virtue] is so." Instead, Kleist directs Rühle—as much as himself—from theory to practical life, to future life experiences:

> We do not know the words of the incantation; time alone conducts them in and of itself, in order to calm and pacify the remarkably disharmonious forms that agitate deep inside and drive us to distraction. And all the young men, whom we see alongside and around us, naturally share this fate with us. All their moves

> and motions appear to be nothing but the effect of an imperceptible but powerful jolt, which irresistibly drags them along. They appear to me like comets that roam the universe in random ovals until they finally find a law of motion and an orbit.

Accordingly, the "law of motion" must first be found, it does not precede motion. Advanced, elaborate calculations, such as developing a life plan or determining a path to happiness, hold no sway over the power of chance. Instead, order and disorder are bound to each other. At the heart of Kleist's essay lies a contradiction that would later serve as the generative core of his life and writing. He discovers crises, risks, chance events as sources of innovation. However, as a young man, Kleist is not yet able to tolerate such contingencies. Hence, in May 1799, he writes to his sister Ulrike that a life without a plan and goal is "contemptible," "a game of chance." He refuses to be "a puppet on the string of fate" and, thus, "forever dependent."[77] This resistance to chance undermines the practical insight of Kleist's essay on happiness. Virtue must not be left indeterminate; order must prevail, though not the discipline of the military, but rather the systematics of science. Self-cultivation toward autonomy is his new life motto rather than assuming the ready-made career path of his family. For Kleist this means leaving the military to study in Frankfurt an der Oder—a return to his hometown, possibly due to financial reasons, for no more than one year, after which he plans to study in Göttingen.[78] On April 4, 1799, by cabinet order, he is granted the resignation he had asked for. In addition, Friedrich Wilhelm III assures him that he has "nothing to object to" regarding Kleist's intention to study, and he would remain gracious if Kleist were to strive to "become a particularly useful civil servant." Kleist responds that he does not intend to join the army again, whether to fight for a foreign country or for his "Fatherland," which he instead aims to serve "in a civilian capacity."[79]

The Potsdam guard regiment seemed to have lost its sheen for Kleist's friends too. Pfuel and Rühle also desired resignation from their commissions as Prussian officers, but they did not successfully assert themselves against their families and military superiors.[80] Kleist appears to have been more assertive. He describes to his former tutor Martini, not without self-satisfaction, the resistance he had to overcome when he presented his new life plan to his family in Frankfurt:

> They said I was too old to study. At this I smiled to myself, because I have long foreseen that my fate is to live and die a student, even if I were to go to my grave a hoary old man. They broached my limited means; they pointed out the doubtful prospect for bread on my new-chosen path, the promised security of my old one. The destiny that faced me, years of studying some dry discipline, years of torment

> with the dry drudgery of an unpaid teaching assistantship, in order eventually to earn some meager bread: these they painted for me in such Baroque colors that if it had occurred to me even in a dream to exchange my present position, in many respects so advantageous, for such a future, I should have had to chide myself for being the most ridiculous simpleton ever to come along.[81]

Kleist had probably long harbored reasons for leaving the military life. The question is why he chose to do so in the spring of 1799. His claim to Martini that his "attraction to the realm of knowledge" could not be satisfied in the "military" contradicts his admission that in Potsdam he had been "more of a student than a soldier."[82] His superiors apparently did not keep him from pursuing his independent studies. On the contrary, Kleist's regimental commander, Major General Ernst Friedrich Wilhelm von Rüchel—commissioned to reorganize the Prussian military education system—must surely have been sympathetic to Kleist's cause. We know from Kleist's friend, Romantic writer Johann Ludwig Tieck, that the King had even been willing to grant Kleist an "unlimited leave" "so he could study."[83] We are thus left to wonder if Kleist's decision to quit his commission was motivated by his frustration over the Prussian military's resistance to reform, a sentiment common among the officers at the time. After all, he was committed to reforming the soldierly profession and, in 1798, even expressed his beliefs in a letter to the King. Due to what he believed to be a flawed, unrefined presentation of his position, however, he never ended up sending it to the King, and instead forwarded it to Martini.[84] Why, then, did Kleist resign from his commission in the spring of 1799? Did the King's *Instruction for the Entire Prussian Infantry* (*Instruktion für die gesamte preußische Infanterie*), which upheld the rigid Frederician discipline, play a role? Or was the decision to leave a profession that secured his livelihood indeed the expression of the idealist desire for freedom of somebody eager to educate himself, as Kleist suggests in his letters? Could not his decision also have had to do with his general political disappointment that Friedrich Wilhelm III did not join the Second Coalition against the French? The new King, who ascended to the throne in November 1797, disappointed any hopes for a policy shift in the spring of 1799 by settling for neutrality, which was popular among the Prussian people but highly controversial among the nobility. Delegations from Great Britain, Russia, and Austria had tried to convince Friedrich Wilhelm III to join a campaign to liberate Holland; after all, in 1794 the Netherlands had fallen into French hands because of Prussia's reservation. Even some ministers of the Prussian cabinet strongly and repeatedly advocated for joining the campaign. The King however—as a dispatch from the Russian ambassador to Berlin, Count Nikita Panin, of 1799 attests—appeared weak, hesitant, and incapable of leading the state.[85]

Perhaps the King's passivity irritated Kleist, who belonged to the same generation as the King and whom Kleist knew well. Perhaps Kleist realized that Prussia could not be successfully governed with a melancholic sitting on the throne and that the Prussian military's honor and reputation in Europe had not improved since 1794/95, when the King's father had abandoned the powers of the First Coalition. In any event, Kleist left his regiment at a time when the King's indecisive politics were being publicly debated, given that the new ruler's 'grace period' had come to an end. No clear statement from Kleist on this matter has survived, so whether or not he voted with his feet, so to speak, remains up for speculation. A year later, in November 1800, he complained to his sister Ulrike that the King had not been very friendly toward him, and commented, impudently, that: "[I]f he has no use for me, then I have even less for him. For it might not be at all hard for me to find a new King, but hard indeed for him to search out new subjects."[86] Whether Kleist renounced his lineage and station by resigning from the military—that is, whether he deliberately gave up noble conventions in favor of a bourgeois existence—is another question.[87] The fact that Kleist refrains from using his noble title in his confessional letter to Martini, in which he justifies his decision to alter his life plans, and continues to sign most of his letters with 'Heinrich Kleist' until 1803, suggests so. But the more one tries to dissociate oneself from traditions, the more one stays bound to them, it would seem. Kleist's alternatives in 1799 do not consist of 'bourgeois' or 'aristocrat,' but 'human being' or 'officer.' There is no sign that Kleist underwent a complete embourgeoisement in the years that followed. Rather, the question is whether Kleist alienates and withdraws himself from his hereditary noble milieu or if there are remnants of 'being noble' beyond the biographical threshold of 1799.

If 'being noble' is understood as a cultural system comprising an aristocratic mentality, typical ways of life, and ritualized manners of behavior and speech, how is it experienced?[88] First and foremost: as a constant struggle to stay at the top, to maintain the honor of one's house and one's social privileges, to remain a part of the social power elite, and retain cultural hegemony. Not equality, as in the bourgeoisie, but inequality is the natural foundation of the aristocratic notion of law and freedom. Kleist will never shake this trusted pillar of aristocratic self-understanding. Even after 1799 his life continued to be determined by an agonistic sentiment. He continually looked for the means and strategies, across various professional fields, to get back to—and remain—at the top. Traveling modestly on the "middle road," as avowed in his Happiness essay of 1798, never satisfied him. He was committed to distinguishing himself through fame and honor in the manner of an aristocrat. For example, in a letter to Wilhelmine from Switzerland in 1802 regarding the conditions for his return home, he writes: "In short, either I return to my Fatherland a famous man, or not at all."[89] And in the following year, 1803, while working on his tragedy *Robert Guiscard, Duke of the Normans* (*Robert Guiskard, Herzog der Normänner*), Kleist admits to his sister Ulrike that his sole goal was "to weave the wreath of immortality," "to wrestle down yet one more wreath of fame to place beside the many already achieved by our family." But he is unsuccessful. He burns his tragedy before it is complete, writing to his sister: "Heaven denies me fame, the highest earthly possession. I throw back in its face, like a willful child, everything else I have. [...] I go now to my death," the honorable, "beautiful death of the battlefield."[90] He signs the letter 'Heinrich *von* Kleist.' Throughout his life Kleist perceived himself as "a man of honor," and if offended demanded "satisfaction," when necessary, as he does on February 22, 1811, from Prussian state councilor Friedrich von Raumer, whom Kleist holds responsible for the failure of his newspaper project, the *Berlin Evening Paper*. Raumer is prepared to face Kleist in a duel, but Prussian chancellor Karl August von Hardenberg intercedes.[91]

The honor of a nobleman—and its defense—is a theme that permeates Kleist's life and work, as do other aristocratic patterns of behavior, as we will see in the following chapters. Kleist's biography cannot be split into an aristocratic pre-existence up to 1799 and a self-determined existence shaped by a bourgeois-idealist ethic after 1799. Rather, his biography proceeds in cycles of leaving and returning to a life befitting his station, converging the traditional with the modern, and characterized by an instability typical of other biographies in the time of crisis in the late 18th century.[92] Kleist's decision to pursue his studies or, later, to become a writer should not be seen as decisions made in favor of a bourgeois professional career that supplants the entitlement of noble birth with merit. In his letter to Martini of March 1799, Kleist emphasized his desire to study "not for lack of bread, not for improving my outlook for bread" but for the sake of his "attraction to the realm of knowledge."[93] This is an idealist thought, familiar to us from Schiller's 1798 inaugural lecture in Jena, in which he sought to develop curricula for "philosophical minds" rather than "bread-and-butter scholars." At the same time, however, attempting to avoid the stigma of breadwinning corresponds to the aristocratic way; and, at the turn of the 19th century, it is also a common impetus for those pursuing the life of an artist. Hence, the bourgeois notion of genius and the aristocratic claim of exclusivity converge.[94] Leisure and inspiration have belonged together since the ancient times; drudgery has never been for aristocrats. Aristotle knew this when he introduced the concept of *scholé*. The University of Frankfurt, where Kleist began his studies in the spring of 1799, promised this freedom.

CHAPTER III

Science or Fiction?

Kleist's Studies in Frankfurt an der Oder and the Kant Crisis

Nowadays, the yellow signs at Frankfurt's city limits proudly state: "University Town Frankfurt/Oder." In 1996 the Heinrich von Kleist Department for Literature and Politics was established at the *Alma mater Viadrina*,[1] and in 2005 a graduate school was founded. Understanding the humanities as a complement to the life sciences, the school poses interdisciplinary questions about literature's function as a medium for reflecting on knowledge, thereby facilitating the study of 'forms of life and the know-how of living.'[2] As a student Kleist would have no doubt appreciated such intellectual experiments, for reasons that will be illustrated in this chapter.

In the spring of 1799, when Kleist enrolled with high hopes at the Viadrina, the State University of Brandenburg was anything but a center of academic innovation. Rather, it was the place where the King's subjects trained to become Prussian civil servants. A university of only local significance, it would have registered third—at best—among the city's most distinctive features, trailing behind the garrison and the trade fair. Frankfurt was not a 'university town.' It had only one bookstore, and the university consisted of just a few buildings around the Lebus Gate and on Oderstraße. Nineteen full professors, adjunct professors, and private lecturers taught approximately 220 students—about one-tenth the population of the Frankfurt military personnel.[3] There were few aristocrats among the students, and descendants of old, established noble families were almost entirely absent, as the university primarily served educated members of the lower estate, providing opportunities for social advancement. Only one in eight students possessed a title of nobility. Most of the entries in the 'father's profession' section of the enrollment lists consisted of peasants, craftsmen, and civil servants, with professions such as: butcher, tailor, councilor of justice, pedagogue, shoemaker, castle gardener, etc.[4] It is no wonder, then, that the professors conducting Kleist's admission interview were skeptical of his decision to study, reminding him of his far better prospects in the military.[5] At home, too, his aunt Helene von Massow must have had little understanding of his choice. And, so, it is not surprising that in his letters Kleist relayed practically nothing about his student life in Frankfurt, where he seems to have made no friends.

© WILHELM FINK VERLAG, 2021 | DOI:10.30965/9783846765746_004

Fig. 10 University of Frankfurt an der Oder, main building

A letter to his sister Ulrike of November 12, 1799, attests to Kleist's social isolation. He is in his second semester and appears to be studying with 'ardent effort' and a Faustian thirst for knowledge. But he admits that he has to force himself to be social, conversing once a day with the family next door, the von Zenges, whose "crisscrossing chatter," he writes, hardly constitutes conversation. He mentions feelings of "anxiousness" and "uneasiness" taking hold of him "more and more often" in social situations and "abortive attempts" to explain to people his "higher interest." "I am afraid," he continues, "that, as a result, I may end up like most professional scholars: rude in their manner, or *rêche* as the French say, and inept at social life." What are we to make of this anxiety? Kleist admits that "*self-cultivation in the social sense*" reached by "much company, much babble, much aggressiveness and superficiality" is not his "goal." His "higher interest" requires "loneliness, cogitation, concentration and thoroughness"; right now his "behavior cannot please," and his goal must be "taken for foolish." In sum, he writes: "[T]hey laugh at me as I walk these streets just as they once laughed at Columbus, who hoped to find the East Indies in the West."[6]

Kleist, the *homo academicus*, fully committed to his "higher interest"—to his scientific quest for truth—feels out of place in Frankfurt, the garrison and trade fair town, and would have preferred to be studying in Göttingen, the city of scholars? As a Prussian subject Kleist was not permitted to study outside of his home state—though, for his advanced studies, he had planned to transfer to the prestigious university in Göttingen, where he would devote himself "to the higher theology, to mathematics, philosophy, and physics."[7] He should have avoided the comparison with Columbus though. Older sisters easily see through such narcissistic delusions of grandeur, no matter how elaborately concealed in dialectical feats: It is a "misconception," writes Kleist to Ulrike, that a scholar is quiet in social situations "out of pride." He is quiet, rather, out of "humility." The enthusiasm someone else has for "a book, for example, or a poem, or a novel," he continues, can be conveyed to others to great effect, but who would understand him if he had "plumbed to the foundations of a basic mathematical truth, the sublimity and grandeur of which likewise fill [his] mind and soul"?[8] It is rather troubling that Kleist claims for himself the habits of a scholar, and even an explorer, for the purpose of masking his self-doubt. His mania guises his melancholia, as it were. Kleist—the "military-academic hybrid"[9]—is, after all, little more than a new student with limited educational experience, lagging behind his peers at a small-town university without "giants" and "distinguished scholars."[10]

The Viadrina was founded as early as 1506, but it never gained great acclaim in the academic world. In 1811 it was closed in favor of the newly founded Friedrich Wilhelm University in Berlin, and its collections were relocated to the University of Wrocław. The closure had nothing to do with Wilhelm von Humboldt, the great Prussian university reformist, who had studied at the Viadrina for some time himself. In fact, Humboldt, who championed for a decentralized education policy, fought against the university's closing in spite of having ridiculed the school—during his student days there—to a Berlin friend: "If you know anybody who wants to earn a doctorate but does not know much, just send him over. Here, all he needs to do is stand around for an hour and pretend he wants to defend his thesis. As the professor does not only host the defense for him, he also defends the thesis."[11] Humboldt's comment attests to the fact that the Viadrina was better suited for vocational training than for earning an academic qualification. Ultimately, the school's practice of accommodating students by graduating them after cursory professional training, an implicit criticism of Humboldt's, is a far cry from Kleist's university ideal. Kleist, the zealous truth-seeker and would-be scholar, was out of place at the Viadrina. His scholarly project was destined to fail from the beginning. While Kleist was willing to prepare "for some official position," what he soon needed to admit to himself and others was how unimaginable he found the prospect of studying diplomacy, law, or economics. Though he could see himself in another profession, an "honorable one," even if it would not provide him "with much glory": an "*academic position*."[12] This is what Kleist assures his fiancée Wilhelmine von Zenge of in the spring of 1800, when—after three semesters of general studies in scientific methodology—the time had come for him to decide on an area of specialization, such as jurisprudence or cameralism, preparing him for a practical career. Kleist, however, evaded this decision, abandoning his studies in the summer of 1800.

Yet his experiment at the Viadrina was not entirely useless; it made a lasting impact on his life and work. It provided him with material for the "little magazine of ideas" he began compiling in preparation for "the literary profession," as he reveals in a letter to Wilhelmine on November 18, 1800.[13] The future Kleist's experiments in thought and writing would oscillate between science and fiction—between scientific and literary thought experiments.

But what, exactly, would he have been able to study at the Viadrina, and who were his professors? The best source for answering these questions is a historical account of the institution, written by the Frankfurt historian and university librarian, Carl Renatus Hausen, published in 1800.[14] According to Hausen, the Viadrina had four distinct schools. An interview was conducted in order to determine whether an entering student's educational background sufficed to qualify him for one of the 'higher' schools—theology, law, or medicine—which offered professional degrees, or whether he required general coursework in the School of Philosophy. The latter was the case with Kleist, for whom the university register indicates no previous educational experience, stating tersely: "[He declares:] Coming from the guard regiment in Potsdam."[15] Kleist was likely unfazed by this qualification, as unspecialized general education courses must have suited his wide-ranging intellectual interests. Indeed, prior to his enrollment he had announced in his letter to his tutor Christian Ernst Martini on March 1799 that he intended to complete his "studies in pure mathematics and pure logic," strengthen his "Latin skills," and attend "a lecture on literary encyclopedia."[16] Strong language skills in Latin were especially necessary because the lectures in Frankfurt were held in Latin. A year later, in the discussion of potential professions in his letter to Wilhelmine, Kleist does not even mention theology or medicine. His awareness of the programs at Frankfurt is limited exclusively to the Schools of Philosophy and Law. Accordingly, one can deduce the names of professors whose teaching and research may have influenced Kleist.

There were six full professors at the School of Philosophy: historian Carl Renatus Hausen; theologian and philosopher Gotthilf Samuel Steinbart; Professor of Philosophy and Rhetoric Johann Gottlob Schneider; economist and cameralist Georg Heinrich Borowsky; physicist and mathematician Johann

Gottfried Huth; and Christian Ernst Wünsch, who taught philosophy, pharmacy, mathematics, and physics. In his letters Kleist mentions Huth[17] and Wünsch[18] by name. Aside from that, associate professor Karl Dietrich Hüllmann, a historian, who advised Kleist on his class schedule, is the only professor Kleist names from the School of Philosophy.[19] There were three full professors at the School of Law: Ludwig Gottfried Madihn, Johann Friedrich Reitemeier, and Johann Christian Friedrich Meister. We have evidence that Kleist attended a lecture taught by Madihn,[20] and as the list of his university fees reveals, Kleist perfected his Latin skills with the help of the classicist Georg Christian Immanuel Kalau, who had been vice-principal at the Lyceum, a secondary school for girls in Frankfurt an der Oder, since 1798.[21]

Given the small size of the faculty, it was easy for the student Kleist to evaluate and rank his professors. Out of all of them, he seems to have most identified with Wünsch, who serves as Kleist's second example of the unsuitability scholars are destined for in social life—second only to Columbus, of course: "Our brilliant Professor Wünsch, who certainly occupies the front rank and towers above all others here in Frankfurt," writes Kleist to Ulrike in November 1799, "would nevertheless, I am certain, be reduced to the greatest perplexity by the insipid banter of the silliest little girl."[22] It seems that Kleist put his claim to the test when he, in all his enthusiasm for his professor, prompted "Zengen's family and [his own] along with other ladies from Frankfurt" to attend Wünsch's "lecture on experimental physics." Hoping to spark Ulrike's interest, he promoted it as a "mineral water treatment for their benefit and pleasure."[23] Even after he had quit his studies, Kleist spoke passionately about Wünsch and, in November 1800, advised his fiancée to use Wünsch's *Cosmological Conversations for Young Friends of the Knowledge of Nature* (*Kosmologische Unterhaltungen für junge Freunde der Naturerkenntniß*) as a guide to "practice independent thinking."[24] Some renowned contemporaries, however, did not share Kleist's appreciation of Wünsch. Alexander von Humboldt, who in 1787/88 attended Wünsch's lectures on economics (which, at the time, meant agriculture), thought he was a "half-crazy scholar," whose ignorance and teaching style were "far from whetting [his] interest in botany." And in his polemic on Wünsch's theory of spectral colors, Johann Wolfgang Goethe refers to him, derogatorily, as the "strange" or "whimsical Wünsch," who provides young men with "a cautionary tale of how actually talented men can go astray." The history of science confirms Humboldt's and Goethe's verdicts on Wünsch, whose work did not stand the test of time.[25] The cosmos of the provincial university seems to have been a closed one, with the local 'greats' unrivaled. Unlike today, it was not possible for students of Kleist's

Frankfurt to inform themselves about international research standards by way of academic journals and the internet. Still, the question remains as to what, exactly, attracted Kleist to Wünsch.

Christian Ernst Wünsch was a colorful, picaresque figure with a venturesome career. Born in 1744 as the son of a weaver in the Ore Mountains, he started out as a master weaver himself. It was a fellow weaver who introduced him to the basic principles of mathematics. Initially no more than a coincidence, his interest in mathematics soon turned into a hobby. When a business deal fell through, Wünsch decided to emigrate to India but only made it as far as Leipzig, where he earned money and a scholarship building wooden planetariums for a public fascinated with the 1769 comet lighting up the night sky. In 1776 Wünsch habilitated from the School of Philosophy at Leipzig University with a defense of his thesis on sound conduction and aerostatics. He gave his first lectures and, a year later—to ensure financial stability—became a doctor of medicine with a dissertation on the sensory physiology of the ear. Wünsch, however, ruined his chance for advancement in the School of Medicine by falling in love with the twelve-year-old daughter of the Professor of Practical Medicine. He thus changed his profession once more, becoming a translator of scientific studies for several publishing houses in Leipzig. In 1783 he published a five-hundred-page-long study, entitled *Horus*, in which he argues, among other things, that religious ideas are nothing more than the hypostatization and mythologization of the figurative language originally used to describe empirical observations of the heavens and earth. It made no difference that Wünsch published his *Horus* anonymously and tenaciously denied authorship; his reputation as a godless heretic stuck with him for the rest of his life. But, from 1778 to 1780, Wünsch reaped the fruits of his labors in scientific translation, transforming the knowledge he gleaned there into a three-volume work of popular science that was met with great success and frequent reprints—*Cosmological Conversations for Young Friends of the Knowledge of Nature*, a book that Kleist read extensively and even recommended to his fiancée. And in 1783, benefiting from the Enlightened Prussian monarch, the free-spirited Wünsch was offered the chair of Mathematics and Physics at the Viadrina. At first Wünsch was not particularly happy about his new position, believing Frankfurt an der Oder to be too "provincial," with "houses far too small and miserable."[26] But, having had no other offers for a professorship, he accepted his fate, and even rose to the position of university rector, receiving a student-led torchlight procession in front of his home upon the university's closure in 1811. Wünsch did not move to Wrocław but stayed in Frankfurt until his death in 1828. Apart from some minor scientific studies, he finished out his career as a writer publishing primarily autobiographical works.

D. Christian Ernst Wünsch
Professor zu Frankfurth an der Oder
Kosmologische
Unterhaltungen
für
junge Freunde der Naturerkenntniß.
Erster Band
von den Himmelskörpern.
Zweite Auflage.
Mit neunzehn Kupfertafeln.
Leipzig
bei Joh. Gottlob Immanuel Breitkopf
1791.

Fig. 11
Cosmological Conversations for Young Friends of the Knowledge of Nature by Christian Ernst Wünsch (1744–1828)

By the time of Kleist's adolescence, Wünsch had already become a local celebrity in 'provincial' Frankfurt. And long before beginning his studies there—during his time as a soldier—it is likely that Kleist had already read the long-selling *Cosmological Conversations*.[27] But what was it, exactly, that so fascinated Kleist about Wünsch? After all, Wünsch was not a distinguished scholar with groundbreaking ideas; he was no original genius. His biography was a patchwork, concluding with the modest fortune of a position as a civil servant in a small town, but preceded by multiple career changes—some more successful than others—showing him to be the type of person for whom the 17th to 19th centuries had the somewhat derogatory term *Projektmacher* ('project-maker'). A 'project-maker' does not pursue a single project, but many. He is in the business of 'making projects.'[28] A 'project-maker' changes his life plans when opportunity knocks; he deals in the public good but as an agent of his own agenda. A 'project-maker' does not follow the bourgeois model of individuation as a steady path of self-cultivation; he relies on chance rather than providence, on a bricolage of ideas rather than a systematic approach. He seeks adventures and, at the same time, society's approval of them; and he is often a hero, but only in imagination, whose character—rightly or wrongly—is seen as undependable, given his flights of fancy. In other words, he is somebody who deceives himself as much as he does others. And yet the opposite may also be true. A 'project-maker' may be considered a true "model for posterity,"[29] as he often develops a "feeling for projects—which one might call fragments of the future,"[30] as Romantic writer Friedrich Schlegel concedes in his *Athenaeum Fragment* 22. The viability of these projects, however, is often questioned.

Kleist relied on strength of character to stave off chance—on education, autonomy, and individuality—at least that is what he claims in his Happiness essay. Yet, in spite of his intentions, he, too, ended up a 'project-maker.' Kleist's post-military life was marked by constant shifts, including numerous reinventions as a scholar, farmer and family man, civil servant, industrial spy, bookseller, and editor. Only his posthumous fame could have assured him that writing was his true vocation. And while he had no plans of emigrating to India to become a tradesman only to then end up a builder of wooden planetariums in Leipzig, he did make it to France and Switzerland, and dreamed of emigrating to Australia with his friends Rühle von Lilienstern and Ernst von Pfuel.[31] And it was with Pfuel, in 1805, that Kleist conceived a plan for a hydrostatic submersible, which would have undoubtedly sunk had the two put their plan to action, given their faulty calculations of the underwater pressure.[32] Kleist's other technological projects were similarly bold and ahead of their time, such as his invention of an artillery "*projectile* or *cannonball* express" for the rapid transmission of messages.[33] An article published in the *Berlin Evening Paper* in 1811, entitled "Know, Create, Destroy, Preserve" ("Wissen, Schaffen, Zerstören, Erhalten")—whose author remains unknown—envisions the "artificial creation of an organic, or even living body," the possibility of "creating animals, or even humans, in a mechanical or chemical way." It also imagines the use of "machines to dig a hole through the earth to the Antipodeans" in order to listen in on "nature's most secret creative workshop." In doing so, one would eventually "come across water," which would, in turn, necessitate the production of a functional "diving bell."[34] Such dreams are 'science fiction,' as it were—no longer the subject of ridicule, as it had been in Christian Felix Weiße's 1766 comedy *The Project-Maker* (*Der Projektmacher*), composed in the spirit of the Enlightenment, whose protagonist schemes of digging tunnels through the center of the earth in hopes of reaching the Antipodeans.

But while Kleist's professor Wünsch was able to make the leap from adventurer to civil servant, Kleist was not. For him occasionalist leanings did not combine well with plain opportunism and reliance on chance events, so the principle of contingency, alone, became his rule for life. And while Wünsch was eccentric, he was no model for such radicalism. Rather, it was his teachings that reinforced Kleist's belief that the ambition of the 'project-maker' was more timely than hopes for the stable life called for in his Happiness essay.[35] Especially compelling was a basic law of nature which, at the time, was understood to govern physical and moral phenomena alike: the Law of Charges. At the turn of the 19th century, this law can be found in every experimental physics textbook, including Johann Christian Polykarp Erxleben's *Elements of Natural Philosophy* (*Anfangsgründe der Naturlehre*). Published in 1794 in its sixth edition, annotated by Georg Christoph Lichtenberg, Erxleben's text served as a basis for Wünsch's lectures, which Kleist attended enthusiastically. According to Erxleben,

> [t]he force an electrified body exerts over an electrically neutral body when placed in the atmosphere of the former is that it produces in the latter—due to the force of electric matter to repel like charges, or attract matter of unlike charge—a charge opposite of its own.[36]

The law of electric polarization caused by electrostatic influence can also be found in Wünsch's work of popular science *Cosmological Conversations*, which summarizes the contemporary state of research in the field of electricity.[37] During Kleist's time the latest discoveries in electricity dominated discussion in the same way innovations in computer technology do today; they were part of everyday conversation—thanks, in part, to a distant relative of Kleist's: Ewald von Kleist, who, in 1745, invented a device for storing static electricity. A glass jar, the so-called Kleistian jar, which was more widely known as the Leyden jar because, in 1746, the Dutch scientist Pieter van Musschenbroek of Leyden also invented a capacitor marketed more successfully to the masses. In his essay "On the Gradual Fabrication of Thoughts While Speaking" of 1805/06, Kleist describes the onset of the French Revolution as an electrophysical phenomenon. Kleist reads Mirabeau's 'electrifying' speech of June 1789—in which he opposes Louis XVI's command to dismiss the assembly of the estates—as a sudden strengthening of Mirabeau's "charge by a process of reaction" and, thereby, as a 'counter-charge' to the King's Master of Ceremonies, who relays the royal command. Kleist then goes on to explain Mirabeau's subsequent caution by the fact that, "having in the manner of a Kleistean Bottle discharged himself, he had once again become neutral." For Kleist the physical explanation of political events is not merely rhetorical or figurative, but literal. "This is," he continues, "a remarkable example of the correspondence between the phenomena of the physical and moral worlds."[38] Kleist holds on to this belief for the remainder of his life. His essay "The Very Last Word in Modern Educational Theory" ("Allerneuester Erziehungsplan"), published over several

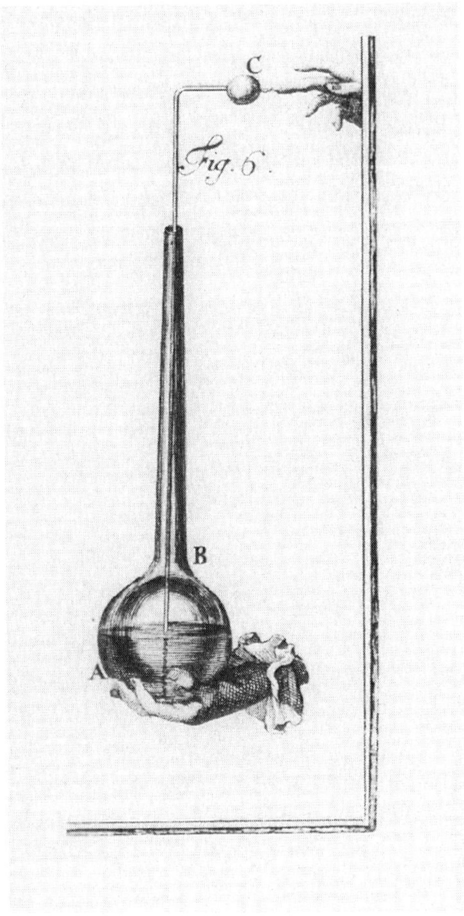

Fig. 12
Kleistian jar, invented by Ewald Jürgen von Kleist in 1745

issues of the *Berlin Evening Paper* in October and November of 1810, is one of many instances of Kleist's generalization of the law of static electricity. He writes:

> Physical science, in one of its newest chapters on the nature of electrical bodies, teaches us that when we bring an electrically neutral body in proximity with, or, to put it more technically, into the 'atmosphere' of, an electrically active body, the neutral one is suddenly activated too, and in fact assumes the opposite charge. [...] This remarkable law can be observed to operate in the moral as well as the physical realm, although, as far as we know, it has hardly received attention until now. A man in a condition of total indifference, for example, as to some issue or other, does not only instantly cease to be so upon contact with someone firmly opinioned in the matter, but his entire being (if we may so express it) modulates into polar opposition: he assumes the term + when the other is –, and – when the other is +.

Kleist calls this the "universal law of contradiction," which prevails "not only in matters of opinion and predilection, but in a much more general way in regard to feelings and passions, character and disposition."[39] Kleist may have also been influenced by a study written by his friend Adam Müller, entitled *The Doctrine of Opposites* (*Lehre vom Gegensatze*), of 1804, in which he posits the principle of contrariness as a general rule for life. Kleist had nevertheless been fascinated by the law of electric polarization since his student days in Frankfurt. With the principle of attraction and repulsion, he takes up a dualistic notion central to the theory of electricity, which—via Immanuel Kant and Johann Gottfried Herder—becomes a "universal law"[40] in the natural philosophy of the Romantics (particularly in F. W. J. Schelling), where it serves as a guiding principle for understanding the structural analogy of matter and mind, nature and morals, physics and psychology. Kleist, however, goes beyond the Romantics insofar as he does not attempt to sublate the polarity through a dialectical reconciliation of opposites or to counterbalance it through some other kind of synthesis.[41] In this refusal, among other things, lies the specifically Modern quality of Kleist. The law of polarity—to which Kleist was first introduced in Wünsch's lecture on experimental physics—gradually undermines his idealist vision of education, as it failed to align with his sense of a continuous, autonomous, and stable identity formation. By contrast, the law is a perfect fit for the 'project-maker,' whose calculations are always reckoning with variation and contingency. If all of socialization were subject to the principle of contrariness, then life would look like a wrestling match with ever-changing partners, as Kleist later illustrates in his essay "On Thinking Things Over: A Paradox," published in the *Berlin Evening Paper* on December 7, 1810:

> Life itself is a contest with fate, and the same is true for ordinary action as for wrestling. The athlete, at that moment when he is holding his opponent in his grip, simply has no recourse but to act spontaneously, on inspiration; and if he begins to calculate which muscles to contract and which limbs to move in order to throw him, he will always draw the short straw and be thrown himself. But afterwards, when he has either won or found himself flat on the floor, *that* would be the proper time and place to think it over, and decide which pressure threw his opponent, or with which foot he ought to have tripped him in order to remain standing himself. Whoever does not hold tightly to life like that wrestler, and, at every turn of contest, in the face of whatever oppositions, pressures, retreats and responses, does not feel and act with every fiber of his being, such a man, try as he might, will never make his mark in a conversation, still less on a field of battle.[42]

The 'principle of contrariness' can be expressed in an algebraic formula, in the opposition of positive and negative charges—an opposition whose terms are inextricably linked in their difference. It can also be rendered as a metaphor, namely in the image of a wrestling match, which is also determined by a polar relation in that the weakness of one wrestler becomes the strength of the other. A struggle simultaneously opposes and unites them; their unity is temporary and relative—a dynamic equilibrium. Sooner or later the struggle ends in victory or defeat and, with that, in a resolved opposition and potential for a new antagonism. As a formula for socialization, the principle of contrariness might look like this: One confronts person A and differentiates oneself from that person; one confronts person B and differentiates oneself from that person, and so on. It is this principle of individuation that determines Kleist's biography in its haphazard movement from one opponent to the next. This formula is far from a goal-oriented or even teleological notion of development, which is to say, a predictable life plan with predictable educational goals. The appeal of individuality runs dry when identity formation is understood as being dependent on situations of opposition; such a strategy establishes only relationships of difference, in which one's self is linked to an other in a struggle defined by mutual dependence. The (potential) arbitrariness of the other corresponds to the arbitrariness of one's self. There can be no talk of the ideal human's organic development as hoped for by Neohumanist pedagogy at the turn of the 19th century[43] because nothing whole could result from ever-changing constellations of influence; there is only the potentiality encountered in the dispositions of one's opponents. It is evident that the principle of contrariness also determines Kleist's poetics: Michael Kohlhaas, for instance, is "one of the most honourable as well as one of the most terrible men of his age"[44]—depending on whom he is opposing. There are many such ambiguous figures in Kleist's work, and rarely is there a balance of power that could put an end to the interplay of forces.

But let us return to the 'project-maker,' who, like Kleist's wrestler, often discovers that "[r]eflection, or thinking something over, finds its proper moment *after* rather than *before* an act."[45] The logic of behaving according to the demands of a given situation is grounded in the idea that knowledge is produced in the act itself—not the other way around, with knowledge and plans being simply transformed into action. The 'project-maker' engages in the behavior of someone taking part in an experiment, not knowing the outcome. The projects in Kleist's life and those of his literary works are largely set up so open-endedly—as explorative practices in novelty in the sense of a testing ground or an art of experimentation, in which necessity begets ingenuity. On February 5, 1801, Kleist writes to his sister:

> Dear Ulrike, it is a well-known commonplace that life is a game; and why is it difficult? Because one is forever expected to throw out a new card, but without knowing what is trump; by which I mean, one is forever expected to act but without knowing what is right. *Knowledge* cannot possibly be man's highest: to *do* is better than to *know*.[46]

Sometimes, however, the 'project-maker' Kleist becomes discouraged and suffers from his abundance of talents—especially when yet another project has failed, such as his tragedy *Guiscard*. On October 5, 1803, Kleist thus writes to Ulrike:

> But is it not really ignoble of Fate thus to stoop and lead around by the nose such a niddering thing as a human being? And does she not deserve to be thus spoken of, when she bequeaths us shares in gold mines, as it were, which after all our digging prove to be void of genuine metal? It was hell that gave me this half-talent of mine: heaven grants a whole one or none at all.[47]

In addition to explorative experiments, productive of new knowledge, there are those experiments that confirm the already-known. Kleist also participates in this latter form of the experimental culture of his time, which, in illustrating the findings of the natural sciences for educational purposes, hopes to charm the public with the joys of science.[48] This is what Wünsch was able to model for Kleist in Frankfurt. No longer a scientist, but a science communicator, Wünsch conducted spectacular experiments in his lectures, as he did for the ladies Wilhelmine von Zenge and Ulrike von Kleist. Kleist, in turn, according to his fiancée, saw himself as an "assistant teacher," who, she writes, "took great interest" in "entertaining" her and the other ladies with what he learned from Wünsch or "repeated" the knowledge they acquired in Wünsch's lecture.[49] Perhaps, as a student in Frankfurt, he even had access to a "superb collection of scientific instruments" to conduct his experiments, as he was able to do later in Berlin.[50] Be that as it may, Kleist's self-conception as a scholar had changed within a year. At the beginning of his studies, as we saw in his letter to his sister Ulrike from the fall of 1799, he still sees himself as a "professional scholar[]," "inept at social life." But by the spring of 1800, he seems convinced of both his pedagogical and communicative skills—an "*academic position*" would no doubt remain "open," he points out to Wilhelmine. Half a year after quitting his studies, in the fall of 1800, he assures his fiancée that "no field of knowledge seems too difficult to me," and therefore "the entire field of writing would stand open to me." He "could go to Paris to transplant the newest philosophy in that knowledge-hungry land," thus envisioning himself as a science communicator.[51]

His preferred training partner for this task—for reasons that will later be discussed—was Wilhelmine, whom he frequently pestered with didactic anecdotes on general principles and discoveries in the natural sciences, believing examples "may have the best effect, especially on women."[52] On November 16 and 18, 1800, he thus writes to her from Berlin that Newton discovered gravity because "an apple fell from a branch and landed at his feet"; that Galileo discovered the "law of the pendulum" by observing a swaying chandelier in a church; that Pilâtre became the "inventor of the art of ballooning" at the sight of smoke "ascending whirlingly from a chimney"; that Columbus, noticing a piece of driftwood on the shores of Portugal, arrived at the conclusion that beyond the sea must be more land, and thus went on to discover America.[53] Kleist lists these examples for Wilhelmine, one after the other, in order to prove to the "dear girl" that "*nothing* in nature is insignificant and indifferent and that *every* phenomenon is worthy of the attention of a *thinking* human being." "[B]ooks," he writes, "offer very bad moral instruction," and there is but "one splendid teacher, and that is *nature*." Following the examples comes the famous parable of the arched gate, which "remains standing" "*because all the stones tend to collapse at the same time*." "[F]rom this thought," Kleist continues, "I derived an indescribably heartening consolation [...]: I too would not collapse, even if everything were dragging me down."[54]

As one can see, Kleist is not interested in delivering systematic proof of scientific findings in this brief letter. His name-dropping of famous scientists allows him to tell entertaining biographical legends, while the science—made more obscure than transparent—is intended to evidence morally edifying truths. Moreover, his analogy of the arched gate, offered as proof of the reassuring equilibrium of forces, is poorly conceived, from both a physical and moral point of view. Firstly, Kleist neglects that there are not only vertical but also horizontal forces at work, which must be countered by abutments to keep the arch from collapsing. And secondly, he seems to overlook the fact that it is not a force within himself that would cause his collapse, but an external one, with "everything" dragging him down. Here, we thus see that Kleist does not actually learn from nature, but through his storytelling construes nature in terms of his needs. And he does it so convincingly that the image of 'stability in falling' becomes central to his appeals to Wilhelmine—until, that is, he no longer requires her support. Nor should we forget the formative power this image has over the posthumous recognition that Kleist, the suicide victim, would receive, or the influence it has on the reception of his work, in which the paradoxical trope recurs—in Prothoe's call to Penthesilea, for instance: "Stand steady, steady as the arch stands / just because each block composing it / wants to fall!"[55]

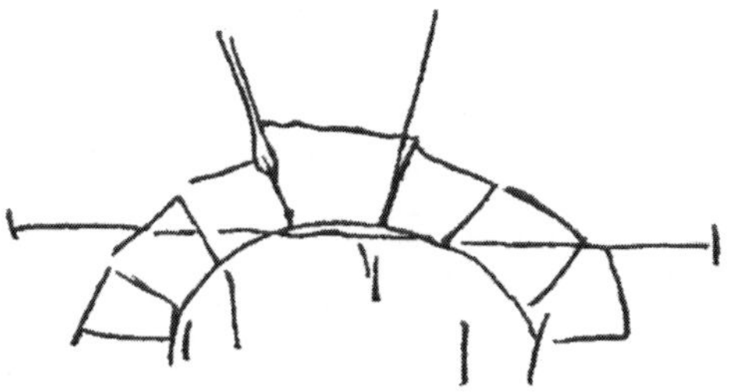

Fig. 13
Kleist's sketch of the arched gate in Würzburg

It is obvious that his studies in Frankfurt do not make Kleist a scientist, but only someone 'in the line of sciences,' which is not meant to sound belittling. Kleist's fascination with the sciences persists for the rest of his life, as the alliance of science and journalism in his *Berlin Evening Paper* attests, with its wide variety of articles on technological and scientific experiments.[56] The sciences supply Kleist with his stock, with his "magazine of ideas" for the entirety of his "literary profession"—for his letters, his essays, and especially his prose and plays.[57] But Kleist seems to have benefited from all of his studies in Frankfurt, not only experimental physics. In the chapters that follow, we will see, for example, the degree to which legal discourse shaped his literary thinking, beyond the novella *Michael Kohlhaas* or the comedy *The Broken Jug* (*Der zerbrochne Krug*). Unfortunately, one can only speculate as to what, exactly, Kleist may have learned from Ludwig Gottfried Madihn's and Johann Friedrich Reitemeier's lectures on law, or if his familiarity with Classical drama was facilitated by the classicist Johann Gottlieb Schneider and his historical-critical editions of Classical writers.[58] Moreover, the question of whether or not Kleist applies academic knowledge correctly in his literature seems misguided.[59] It would be better to inquire as to how scientific experiments are transformed into literary experiments, or to what degree the fragments from Kleist's 'magazine of ideas' serve as building blocks for his literary structures—what function they perform within a 'poetology of knowledge.'[60]

A good starting place takes us back to Kleist's knowledge of experimental physics and a peculiar scene from his first play, *The Schroffenstein Family* of 1802. Johann and Ottokar—the sons of the gruesome Count Rupert von Schroffenstein of the House of Rossitz—argue over Agnes, daughter of the mild-mannered Count Sylvester von Schroffenstein of the House of Warwand, with whom they are both in love:

OTTOKAR. Thou wouldst provoke me. 'Tis no use.
I know too well, to-morrow thou wilt take
My part.

JOHANN. Nay, nay, not so, for I will see
To that. For in my breast I'll make a wound
With needles tear it open every morn,
In order that my injury be made
Concrete.[61]

The annotations accompanying this scene in the German DKV-edition of Kleist's work regard Johann's words as a "metaphor for the 'suicide by an act of will'" later committed in *Penthesilea*.[62] However, Johann's words in this scene simply refer to a "galvanic stimulation experiment" familiar to Kleist's contemporaries, such as the ones Alexander von Humboldt or Johann Wilhelm Ritter conducted on themselves to then publish the findings in widely read works.[63] To demonstrate the principle of polarity, both Humboldt and Ritter connected themselves to electric circuits so that they could observe the reaction and counter-reaction of their various body parts when exposed to the positive and negative poles. To connect the galvanic circuit, Humboldt stuck needles into self-inflicted wounds on his shoulders, and physicist Johann Wilhelm Ritter even galvanized his own eyeballs, raising the power until he believed himself to have experienced, in the intensification of his sensation, the reversal into the opposite sensation. This would have provided evidence for the hope of all natural philosophy in the Romantic era: the unity concealed by opposites. For Ritter these self-experiments were ultimately experiments with death, as he slowly destroyed his body, dying in 1810 at the age of thirty-three.

Kleist's Johann is not a scientist but a lover, marked with all the signs of insanity, infatuated, primarily, with the purported unity of Eros and Thanatos. Following the dialogue with his brother Ottokar quoted above, he terrifies poor Agnes upon their next meeting with a strange confession. Waving a dagger, he announces: "Naught more, for thou art dead to me and like / A corpse./ 'Tis with shudder that I clasp / Thee to my heart." Agnes—apparently not so familiar with the polar reversal of sensations—must consider him murderous. Nor does she know how to respond to his tender plea: "I tell thee, take / This knife. Hast thou not stabbed me to the heart / Already?"[64] She cries for help. But, having fainted, she does not hear that Johann asks her to kill him out of love. Her call for help results in Johann being struck down by Jeronimo, who, in his fruitless attempt to reconcile the two families, falls victim to the family feud himself, just as Ottokar and Agnes do, swapping their clothes to disguise their true identity in an attempt to protect each other. Ultimately, Johann is the Counts Schroffenstein's only surviving child. The play of opposites in Kleist's tragedy kills off all hope, with the fathers Rupert and Sylvester von Schroffenstein becoming the murderers of their children. At the play's end

Sylvester offers Rupert his hand in reconciliation, "[*w*]*ith face turned away*," and Johann responds with the following words: "Bring wine! Be merry! Wine! Let's laugh / Ourselves to Death! It is a merry jest!"[65] According to one of Kleist's friends, Kleist seems to have felt the same way: "When, one day, [he] read his tragedy *The Schroffenstein Family* to us, the audience's laughter, along with the writer's, became so fierce and boundless during the last act that it was impossible for him to reach the final murder scene."[66]

There can thus be no talk of a "suicide by an act of will" with regard to Johann, unlike Penthesilea. Admittedly, if Agnes had allowed him, Johann, too, would have confused the contrary sensations of kissing and biting. In *Penthesilea* the reversal of opposites comprises its tragic core, whereas in *The Schroffenstein Family* it is merely an absurd "jest," a play-within-a-play. In Kleist's poetological toolbox, the principle of polarity can thus serve contradictory functions, confirming that it yields aesthetic rather than scientific evidence. The only galvanic experiments that Johann conducts are in his mind; hence, his psychological distress would have found no relief in electrostatic influence. In the same way his author Kleist experiments with scientific 'findings' from his 'magazine of ideas'—that is, not for science's sake but for the sake of his tragedy's architecture. It would thus be rash to read *The Schroffenstein Family* as a critique of science simply because Kleist has a fool cite galvanic experiments—or, more precisely, because his debut play, due to its temporal proximity to what scholars have labeled his Kant crisis, has always been read as the birth of literature from a critique of science. So far the opposite has been suggested: that Kleist's literature is born from his fascination with science. But perhaps this is yet another example of the universality of the polarity principle at work—an opposition whose terms are at once distinct and unified.

We do not know why Kleist ended his studies after three semesters. Was it because he was forced to pursue a 'bread-and-butter job'—an unbearable thought for Kleist, who considered himself a philosophical mind? Did Kleist, the autodidact, give up because "he lagged behind most of his [peers] in requisite background knowledge," as Romantic writer Ludwig Tieck suspects?[67] Or is the historian Friedrich Christoph Dahlmann right, who claims to have discerned in Kleist's "lecture notes" evidence of his conducting "military campaigns and serious, not just dilettantish studies at the university"?[68] Be that as it may, Kleist's letters show that he was unhappy with his situation as a student. As early as November 1799, Kleist complains that "[w]hen one has occupied oneself for so long with serious and abstract matters, things that nourish the mind," "the poor heart must go begging." "Happiness," Kleist continues, "cannot be explained as one explains a mathematical theorem, it must be experienced if it is to have any existence at all. Therefore, it is good to enliven the heart afresh from time to time with the enjoyment of the senses; and one should read at least *one* good poem daily, see *one* beautiful painting, hear *one* sweet melody, or exchange heart to heart words with a friend, and thus educate the more beautiful, I might say the more human, side of our nature as well."[69]

The mind-heart dichotomy has remained a commonplace since the middle of the 18th century. And the advice to devote oneself to a daily poem, painting, or melody Kleist took from Goethe. The wisdom thus comes less from his own experience than from his reading of *Wilhelm Meister's Apprenticeship*; Serlo pronounces it at the beginning of the fifth book. For Kleist, then, it seems a good education is no more than a pronouncement or quotation. To live in quotations, second-hand, detached from the world of experience, leads to a solitary life, makes a person "rude in their manner" and "inept at social life."[70] The teaching methods of the Frankfurt professors were apparently not geared toward the fostering of dialogue—that is, with perhaps the exception of Kleist's favorite professor Wünsch, who structured his *Cosmological Conversations* as a discussion between a private tutor and his students, as the title suggests. That said, *Cosmological Conversations* was written for a larger audience and not intended as a university textbook, and here, too, the monologues of the tutor Philalethes actually dominate the conversations. Kleist once remarked to his tutor Martini that, "what I do not understand when I read it, I understand even less when I hear it."[71] He processes his evidently disappointing experience at university in his essay "On the Gradual Fabrication of Thoughts While Speaking" of 1805/06, which closes with a critique of university exams, in which professors want to hear their ideas simply echoed back at them by a student instead of playing on his mind to sound its "proper tone." It thus seems that these professors are not very skilled in the "art of intellectual midwifery."[72] With this critique Kleist may be alluding to Kant's *Metaphysics of Morals* of 1797, which differentiates between an acroamatic teaching style, in which the students are merely listeners, and an erotematic or dialogical teaching style, in which teacher and students question and answer each other.[73] As Kleist argues most clearly in his "On the Gradual Fabrication of Thoughts While Speaking," a "certain agitation of the mind" is conducive to the process of thinking, for "it is not *we* who 'know'; it is rather a certain condition, in which we happen to be, that 'knows.'"[74] The one-time soldier Kleist links creativity with the agonistic: Novelty is born from a battle of words, not weapons.[75]

But it seems such a contentious student mindset was not quite welcome in Frankfurt. The soldier in Kleist, who was trained to take action, must have been disappointed by the intellectual culture of the Viadrina—or so it appears in the testimonies of his contemporaries, which portray him as a misfit and melancholic: "Kleist's extraordinary absentmindedness was the subject of ridicule among his friends," remembers Edward von Bülow, instantly relaying an anecdote: "One day after his lecture he went home to change his coat; but, absorbed in thought, he undressed completely, up to his shirt and was about to go to bed when his brother came in and, with boisterous laughter, woke him from his dreams."[76] Another source claims that, when among company, Kleist often stopped talking "all of a sudden, in the middle of a flood of words" and then descended into "gloomy rumination," "where he could not be made to speak again." There was something "dark and unsettling" in his personality, which was supposedly "most attractive to women."[77] And "by overstraining his powers," Kleist also "caused concern that he was confusing his thoughts rather than setting them straight."[78] During his student days, then, he may have already felt the way he did on October 10, 1800, in Würzburg, when he wrote his 'birthday letter' to Wilhelmine: "My soul resembles the desk of a philosopher who, in an attempt to conceive a new system, wrote down individual key concepts on scattered [*zerstreute*] papers."[79] This confession paints a picture of both mania and melancholia; while the appeal of the "philosopher" with his "key concepts" is a rather unconvincing portrait of Kleist, the scattered thoughts and experience of arbitrariness—which lead to wanderlust and fantasies of escape—certainly ring true. In his letter to Wilhelmine, his awareness of *Zerstreuung*, which connotes both dispersal and distraction, is charged with negative undertones; only later does it become a constructive means for evading a future marked by the trappings of stability—a means for fostering the distraction and the dispersal of knowledge he would embrace, above all, in literature.[80]

The Berlin doctors Sternemann and Greif performed two autopsies on the body of the suicide victim Kleist to finally establish the presence of "an abundance of thickened black bile," which they linked to an "eccentric mental condition" and an "excess of religious enthusiasm."[81] If we understand "religious enthusiasm" in the sense common at the turn of the 19th century—as the effect of a pietistic culture of repentance—then it certainly did not apply to Kleist. There is, nevertheless, some truth to it. Kleist's passion for "higher theology," which he understands as an umbrella term for the trinity of "mathematics, philosophy, and physics,"[82] does reveal a kind of Faustian drive for the absolute. Like Goethe's melancholic scholar, averse to academic specialization, Kleist is compelled to understand what binds the world together at its innermost core. But this urge cannot be satisfied. And the resulting disillusionment Kleist experiences manifests at times in melancholia and, eventually, in his literature, which grapples with the elusiveness of such knowledge. This elusiveness, of course, is what continues to constitute the unsettling power of Kleist's literature.

For a 'reciprocal illumination of the arts,' we can compare Kleist's self-portrait as a melancholic scholar with "scattered papers" on his desk to Albrecht Dürer's 1514 engraving *Melencolia I*, which is as much a thought-image as it is an image of a gloomy thinker. The center of the image portrays an angel with a somber countenance, embodying the melancholic genius in its Modern form: the figure of a scholar. It is significant that he is holding a compass in his hand, which, in medieval portrayals, pertains to God as the world's original architect. The Modern genius, however, surveys the world autonomously, and the leading science of the Renaissance is mathematics. For this reason, in addition to the tools of applied mathematics—such as the hand plane, saw, and straight edge—scattered around the angel are tools intended for the architect of a new, Modern world, along with figures from descriptive geometry, such as a sphere and a polyhedron. The newly constructed building depicted at the upper edge of the image, however, appears unfinished, with the ladder still leaning against its wall. And the scholarly architect sits idle, resting his head in his hand, appearing as if—in the midst of his work—he had been seized by doubt and despair. In this lies Dürer's subtle allusion to medieval theology, according to which a mathematician inevitably becomes melancholic when confronted with the limits of the mind and its inability to transcend the boundaries of mathematical systems to think the unthinkable in terms of space and time: the metaphysical. Melancholia is thus rendered as the insufficiency of the human intellect in the face of the absolute—a 'transcendental homelessness' and a despair over the fact that no form of scientific thinking could organize an array of scattered concepts into a closed system. In Dürer, this notion of melancholia is represented by the dispersal of the mathematical instruments around the dark angel.[83] In Kleist, we have the "scattered papers" on the desk of the dejected thinker.

There could also be something pathological in the melancholia Kleist experienced after quitting his studies, in the sense of the phenomenon of 'remanence'—in the self-reproach one feels in falling short of his potential.[84] And perhaps his family and fiancée, too, felt he had failed in some way. But Kleist preempts blame from both others and himself with passionate accounts of the skepticism he feels toward science after ending his studies, suggesting his melancholia should be understood as a frame of mind rather than an illness. He styles himself as a melancholic intellectual whose world fell apart when science could not help him arrive at eternal truths. In the first testimony of his so-called Kant crisis, he has already developed an entire arsenal of arguments for his self-defense. In his letter to Wilhelmine of March 1801, he explains:

Fig. 14 Albrecht Dürer, *Melencolia I*, 1514 (copper engraving)

I had already as a lad (I think by the Rhine, while reading Wieland) adopted the idea that Perfection is the goal of creation. I believed that after death we should progress from the level of perfection achieved on this planet to a higher one beyond, and that we should be able there to make use of that trove of truths collected here. From this notion I little by little developed a kind of personal religion, and the striving never to remain idle here on earth but to advance without cease to an ever higher stage of Education, became my sole principle of action. Education seemed to me the only goal worth the striving, and Truth the only wealth worth the having. [...]

I recently became familiar with the more recent so-called Kantean philosophy, and I may impart one of his leading ideas to you without fear of its shattering you as deeply, as painfully as it has me. Then too, you are not versed enough in the whole matter to grasp its import completely. I shall therefore speak as clearly as possible.

If everyone saw the world through green glasses, they would be forced to judge that everything they saw *was* green, and could never be sure whether their eyes saw things as they really are, or did not add something of their own to what they saw. And so it is with our intellect. We can never be certain that what we call Truth is really Truth, or whether it does not merely appear so to us. If the latter, then the Truth that we acquire here is *not* Truth after our death, and it is all a vain striving for a possession that may never follow us into the grave.

Ah, Wilhelmine, if the point of this thought does not strike you to your heart, do not smile at one who feels himself wounded by it to his most sacred inner being. My one, my highest goal has sunk from sight, and I have no other.

Since coming to the realization in my soul that Truth is nowhere to be known here on earth, I have not touched another book. I have paced idly in my room, I have sat by the open window, I have run from the house, an inner unrest at last drove me to the taverns and coffee houses, I have gone to plays and concerts for distraction [...]; and still my one thought, which my soul, with this tumult all around it, kept belaboring with burning anxiety, was this: your *only*, your *highest* goal has sunk from sight.

One morning I tried forcing myself to work, but an inward nausea overwhelmed my will. I felt an indescribable longing to weep on your neck, or at least to press some friend to my breast. I walked in very bad weather to Potsdam, arrived there drenched to the skin, embraced Leopold, Gleissenberg and Rühle, and felt better. [...]

Dear Wilhelmine, grant me time to travel. Studying is out of the question, it is impossible, it would serve no purpose. I would be condemned, if I stayed at home, to sit with my hands folded and think. I would rather walk and think. Movement on a journey would seem more bearable than this brooding in one place.[85]

The next day, on March 23, Kleist repeats the most important sentences, with minor variations, in a letter to his sister Ulrike. The purport is the same: "[E]verything that goes by the name of knowledge disgusts me."[86] To his fiancée, who seems to have tried to refute his 'green glasses' analogy, he answers that he "only used the eyes as an *explanatory example*," "since [he] might not allow [himself] the abstract language of philosophy."[87] His state of despair persists into his travels several months later. On June 3, 1801, Kleist writes to Wilhelmine from Göttingen "to impart something of [his] *inner* condition" to her:

> Everything seems confused inside me, all tangled like the fibers on the distaff, and I am hard put, when the spinning wheel of experience should be drawing out the thread of Truth, to wind it in an orderly way on the spindle of my mind. Indeed, even my desires change, and first one and then the other is overshadowed, like things in a landscape when clouds lengthen over it.

Perhaps, Kleist continues, "man's purpose is something more than *to think*—*work*, I feel, is the only thing that might bring me peace. What robs me of peace is really the impossibility of setting a goal for myself and the concern lest I in choosing too rashly choose falsely, and so miss my true calling and make a botch of my entire life."[88]

At this time Kleist no longer knows what he wants and no longer wants what he knows. The time of the Kant crisis is experienced, according to his words, as a lost sense of totality. He thus enters into a state of utter uncertainty, his melancholia the result of lost orientation in thought and action. In his letter he presents an exitless maze of thoughts. He is shaken to the core by Kant's philosophy, though this turbulence is ultimately the result of misunderstanding. In his *Critique of Pure Reason,* Kant denies the possibility of perceiving the objects of the empirical world as they are, *in themselves*. Rather, he argues, we perceive as the *a priori* of objects only that which we bring to them. In the act of cognition, we assign objects meaning; we do not reconstruct but, rather, *construct* an object's proper meaning. And we know that, long since Kant's time, his epistemology has been empirically validated by neurobiological research. According to the findings of Humberto Maturana and Francisco Varela, the human sense organs can only differentiate stimuli from their environment quantitatively, not qualitatively. The ears and eyes, for instance, measure the frequency of sound and light waves but do not distinguish their physical properties. What they communicate to the brain's nerve cells are, therefore, uncoded messages. The brain, thus, receives unspecified information—from its environment—to which it is left to assign meaning. The generation of meaning occurs in the brain's neural system, which is shut off from its environment, working self-referentially. The interpretation of information is thus independent of the structure of the environment, though it is dependent on the structure of the neural system, which may vary from individual to individual.[89]

From both a Kantian and neurobiological perspective, there is no such thing as an objective representation of reality—no model of reality capable of rendering absolute truth. Rationalists come to terms with this fact, but Kleist the scholar—a metaphysician striving to "acquire" a "Truth" that would remain valid even "after our death"—cannot. Kant, on the other hand, thrives at this

Fig. 15
Immanuel Kant (1724–1804)

impasse, and goes on to discern the instruments of our cognitive faculty for the making and classifying of perception: the networks of the mind or patterns of logical connections; the sensuous forms of our intuition of space and time; or the aesthetic forms of intuition, the underlying principles of our judgments of taste, etc. What Kant then discerns are schemes of inter-individual communication that convey subjective constructions of reality. Conventionalized, these schemes enable us to communicate with each other, and through them our thinking can achieve not an absolute, but a practical, workable truth. So, where thinking properly begins for Kant, it necessarily ends for Kleist. He has no interest in contemplating the structure of the human sense organs or, as it were, the structure of the "green glasses." Instead, he holds fast to his desire for the absolute, and grows desperate over the fact that reason cannot satisfy it. Kleist's crisis is of his own making. It is his folly and not Kant's—though Kleist does not see it this way. In his letter to Ulrike of March 23, 1801, he writes: "It seems I am to become another one of those victims of folly of which the Kantean philosophy already had so many on its conscience. [...] The thought that we here on earth may know nothing, nothing at all of Truth [...]: this thought has shattered me in the innermost sanctum of my soul.—My *single*, my *highest* goal is sunk from sight and I have no other."[90]

One can speculate about whom, aside from himself, Kleist categorized as a 'victim of folly,' or if Kleist ever read Kant in the original or merely studied lecture notes. And considering his ignorance of Kant, one might wonder if Kleist's crisis should instead be ascribed to Johann Gottlieb Fichte, which would further attest to Kleist's only partial understanding of the Romantic philosophy of the subject. One might also wonder if Kleist took the example of the "green glasses" from Friedrich Maximilian Klinger's novel *The Chain-bearer* (*Der Kettenträger*) or from another source, and so on—it is noteworthy, however, that in his letter to Wilhelmine of March 22, 1801, Kleist claims that his friend Rühle von Lilienstern gave him the novel in what would ultimately be the vain hope of consoling him *after* the onset of his Kant crisis.[91]

But whether Kleist's understanding of Kant was superficial or flawed is beside the point. What matters is, firstly, that he used his Kant crisis to excuse quitting his studies after the fact; secondly, that he used it to justify his escape from Frankfurt, which was to fulfill his desire to travel and his need to design a new life plan. Thirdly, we cannot forget the significance the crisis had for his literature and the creativity that resulted from his productive misreading: Kleist turns his melancholic reading of Kant's philosophy—in other words, his disinterest in analyzing the conditions of human cognition—into a grandiose semiotic crisis that becomes the generative core of his literary works. For the driving force of his work is the uncertainty in knowledge, language, and action expressed by his protagonists. Kleist owes it to his Kant crisis that his literary world is out of joint: The protagonists of his plays and prose tend to act from states of deep isolation and existential uncertainty; they conceive of themselves and their worlds according to their own rules, without knowing if their perception of the world aligns with that of other protagonists, and without knowing whether their version of reality provides a stable foundation for their actions. Hence, the blind and disoriented behavior we find in Kleist's first play, *The Schroffenstein Family*, where the fathers end up killing their own children by "mistake."[92] Whereas Kant seeks to analyze the human organs of cognition—of pure and practical reason—Kleist's tragedies of language, perception, and action are the result of an entirely different aim. He wants absolute knowledge, and he wants it immediately; reflecting on the mediation of the subject and object of cognition affords him no certainty. In a letter to his sister Ulrike of March 13/14, 1803, after, again, expressing doubt over language's capacity for communication, he writes: "I wish I could tear my heart from my body, pack it into this letter, and send it to you.—Silly thought."[93] To tear one's heart or brain out in order to avoid deception and disappointment is, indeed, a silly idea, but it appears to be, for Kleist, the only way to really get to know his own thoughts and those of others. Penthesilea understands Achilles only after she devours him, literally consuming his heart and brain; she fails "to stand / guard over [her] rash mouth" due to "a slip […] of the tongue," thus mistaking 'kissing' for 'biting.'[94] The act of cognition, here, is—in a double sense—a matter of taste.

What is often overlooked is the fact that the Kant crisis comprises only one reason for Kleist's skepticism toward science. The other comes into view in a letter to his friend Adolphine von Werdeck of July 29, 1801, written from Paris:

> I would so love to proceed with a *purely humane* kind of education, but knowledge makes us neither better nor happier. O very well, if we could perceive the entire aggregate of things! But is not the beginning and end of all knowledge wrapped in darkness? Or shall I apply every capacity, and all my powers, and my entire life to learn all there is to know about a single species of insect, or to assign one plant a place in the classification of things? Ah, how this one-sidedness revolts me! I believe that when Newton looked at a woman he calculated the curve of her breasts, and that what interested him about her heart was its liquid capacity in cubic measure. While kissing his young lady, the true chemist can think of nothing except that her breath consists of nitrogen and carbonaceous gases. Should the sun glowingly mount the heavens, nothing occurs to him except that it has not yet reached its zenith. He sees only the insect, not the earth that bears it, and when the pied woodpecker knocks at the pine, or the wood dove coos sweetly in the oak tree, it occurs to him how attractive they would look stuffed. The entire earth is merely the botanist's herbarium, and as for the weeping birch or the violet that blooms in its shadow, what interests him is its Linnaean name. For the mineralogist a landscape is beautiful only for its rocks, and if the Alpine granite soars to the clouds, he regrets not being able to put it in his pocket, and place it in his cabinet along with the other fossils—O, how depressing is this Cyclopean one-sidedness![95]

This satirical portrait of science provides yet another example of the literature sparked by Kleist's skepticism. It parodies the bias and limitations of any individual science, highlighting the tunnel vision of any given scholar or specialization and corresponding detachment from the interconnectivity of things. It makes clear, above all, that Kleist does not want to do things halfway. He wants the whole truth—the "entire aggregate of things." A hubristic goal to be sure, but one he could have reached, with great effort, had it not been for Kant, some might claim. Would it not have been possible for Kleist to study each of the sciences well enough to synthesize the fragmentation into a new whole? Was he simply uninterested in hard work? Could that have been the reason for giving up on his studies? This scenario seems unlikely. In fact, the critical diagnosis of scientific culture we find in his letter is typical of his time. Kleist's complaint about the scientist's isolation, the compartmentalization of his existence, is merely one site of the universal fragmentation of the human condition declaimed in Friedrich Schiller's *On the Aesthetic Education of Man in a Series of Letters*, published six years prior to Kleist's letter. In his sixth letter, Schiller notes:

> Once the increase of empirical knowledge, and more exact modes of thought, made sharper divisions between the sciences inevitable, and once the increasingly complex machinery of State necessitated a more rigorous separation of ranks and occupations, then the inner unity of human nature was severed too, and a disastrous conflict set its harmonious powers at variance. The intuitive and the speculative understanding now withdrew the hostility to take up positions in their respective fields [...]. While in the one a riotous imagination ravages the hard-won fruits of the intellect, in another the spirit of abstraction stifles the fire at which the heart should have warmed itself and the imagination been kindled. [...] That polypoid character of the Greek States, in which every individual enjoyed an independent existence but could, when need arose, grow into the whole organism, now made way for an ingenious clock-work, in which, out of the piecing together of innumerable but lifeless parts, a mechanical kind of collective life ensued. State and Church, laws and customs, were now torn asunder; enjoyment was divorced from labour, the means from the end, the effort from the reward. Everlastingly chained to a single little fragment of the Whole, man himself develops into nothing but a fragment; everlastingly in his ear the monotonous sound of the wheel that he turns, he never develops the harmony of his being, and instead of putting the stamp of humanity upon his own nature, he becomes nothing more than the imprint of his occupation or of his specialized knowledge.[96]

We have melancholia here too, but Schiller has a cure: A literature that harmoniously integrates what has been fragmented into a utopian 'anticipatory illumination.' While Kleist agrees with Schiller's diagnosis of the time, he rejects his prescribed treatment of the ideal of reconciliation. Kleist is not a mind of consensus, but conflict. The contemporary crisis of culture becomes his muse, but for him literature can provide no such 'remedy.' For, unlike the idealist aesthetics of autonomy, Kleist does not grant his literature exceptional status by having it governed by rules other than those of the real world. The fact that literature can provide no such remedy is also evident in the Frankfurt escape fantasies he entertained at the time of his Kant crisis; through travel he might "find the word that answers the riddle" and, thereby, resolve his "confusion."[97] Yet, unbeknownst to him, he already has it—*Zerstreuung*—though he had not yet found the right context. As he admits in his Kant letters, it did not help him in his skepticism toward science to run to "coffee houses and smoking dens," or "plays and concerts for distraction," nor did it help him to look for "love" to "distract" himself.[98] Kleist seeks refuge, but not within some kind of self-contained aesthetic realm. Traveling is essential to his quest, serving as a typically Romantic, anti-philistine means of evading the trappings of stability; so, too, is writing, so long as it does not—as idealist literature does—try to reconcile what has been disintegrated in the sciences through a 'utopian' practice of synthesis into a new organic whole. This rather paradoxical demand for a whole without synthesis is the realistic—rather than idealist—result of Kleist's Kant crisis.

Any idealist philosopher who "conceive[s] a new system," or at least wants to, may fall into despair over the array of "key concepts on scattered papers" lying on his desk.[99] But there is a more satisfying means of reaping the benefits of one's skepticism toward science. If totality cannot be found in the confines of a single concept, one can simply disperse all scientific ideas onto a different logical plane, such as literature—the ideal site for both dispersal and distraction—whose poetology involves the "intentional de-disciplinization and de-specialization of knowledge."[100] Kleist eventually takes this insight to heart, and it is what accounts for both the skepticism and fascination he would have for the sciences throughout his life and work. It is what makes Kleist's literature Modern. In its daring and arbitrary appropriation of scientific theorems, it poses a "Dadaism of science *avant la lettre*."[101] At every turn it surprises the reader with fragmented thoughts, detached, displaced from their original academic contexts. In his letter to his sister Ulrike of February 5, 1801, Kleist admits: "No subject is more important to me than any other, and if I have a preference, I am like a father whose favorite son is ever the one who happens to be nearest. But then again, must I go from one field of study to another, always swimming on the surface, and never touching to the depths? And so the pillar totters."[102]

'Yes,' as the answer is later revealed; to float freely from one field of study to another is permitted, so long as it happens within the institution of literature, and not the university. Swimming on the surface of the sciences is a good aesthetic trick for exciting the reader's desire for a story that can support myriad interpretations. Kleist's essay "On the Puppet Theater" deals with questions concerning aesthetics and the history of philosophy without in-depth reflection on or reference to philosophical or historical systems, and it is for this reason that it remains so widely read and interpreted. It is a melting pot for the sciences. Accordingly, the essay renders the "*path of the dancer's soul*" in a mathematical parable, as the relation of "numbers to their logarithms or asymptotes to their hyperbola," and it illustrates the idea of the return to paradise through a tool from optics—the image of a "concave mirror."[103] It is thus easy to see how Kleist managed to find stability while clutching a tottering pillar: in the 'gay science' of literature, which fulfills its proper function in the artistic ordering and disordering of the un-differentiated. This potential is what allows literature, unlike any specialized scientific discipline, to create multi-faceted reflections of life, which is, itself, a union of disparate elements.

In his letter to Ernst von Pfuel of January 7, 1805, Kleist writes self-confidently: "I can solve differential equations and I can write verses; are these not the extreme limits of human potential?"[104] He later echoes this thought in a fragment in the *Berlin Evening Paper*: "There are two categories of people: those who think in terms of metaphors and those who think in terms of formulas. Those who think in terms of both are very few; they comprise no separate category."[105] Kleist's studies in Frankfurt an der Oder were anything but vain. He could proudly announce that he knew both verses and differential equations, metaphors and formulas. Such double talents are, however, in no way rare at the turn of the 19th century, if one thinks of Goethe, Schiller, Novalis, Achim von Arnim, Adelbert von Chamisso, among others. Characteristic of the epochal threshold of 1800 is a diversity of interests. It is a period of transition, between the empiricism and rationalism of the 18th century and the positivism of the 19th century, in which literature and the sciences are brought together in tension; in which "imagination and fantasy complement the systematic faculty of reason and rationality as equal powers for creating knowledge of the world and human nature"; in which the destabilization of Enlightenment knowledge, experienced as a crisis, manifests as a "conflict between epistemes and aesthetics."[106] It is Romantic literature, in particular, that mediates between the speculative philosophical approach to the study of nature and the exact, scientific one. And more often than not, the art that originates here has, as E.T.A. Hoffmann puts it in *The Serapion Brethren*, "something of a Kaleidoscope character," and "its matters, though most adventitiously shaken together, do ultimately form more or less interesting combinations."[107]

The memory of this "period—so rich in words and ideas, so poor in true knowledge and genuine studies"—later "terrifies" and "appalls" 'genuine' natural scientists, who abandoned speculation in favor of strict empiricism, such as German chemist Justus Liebig, when he "recovers his senses from this frenzy."[108] Writers, by contrast, are inspired by such "frenzy." In this time of disciplinary formation within the sciences—in the "heroic heyday" of Alexander von Humboldt, Carl Friedrich Gauß, Alessandro Volta, Antoine Lavoisier, Joseph von Fraunhofer, Georg Ohm, Hermann von Helmholtz—Romanticism arises as a "counter-discourse, perhaps the result of having one's expectations disappointed when 'science' fails to provide a sense of the totality of things," and often articulates experiences that fall through the perceptual grid of the individual disciplines or are not quite "compatible with the sciences," such as experiences of the unconscious, dream, fantasy, madness, love, violence, etc.[109] Kleist can be compared to E.T.A. Hoffmann insofar as they are both 'project-makers' dealing in the sciences. They are tinkerers and bricoleurs, mixing the sciences up 'kaleidoscopically' in their works, undisciplining and carnivalizing their knowledge.

Such an undoing of the order of knowledge and representation should not be mistaken for the Postmodern play with arbitrariness—the sense that 'anything goes.' In 1801, when Kleist mockingly writes that "when Newton looked at a woman he calculated the curve of her breasts, and that what interested him about her heart was its liquid capacity in cubic measure"—or when he laments that the truth we acquire on earth through reason is no longer applicable "after our death"[110]—he offers a twofold reflection on the limits of scientific knowledge. The drive toward reason and the urge for the absolute remain unsatisfied because, alongside the world of scientific reason, there is a world of irrationality—of sexuality, eroticism, and metaphysics. Kleist will go on to address this antagonism between a potent, yet not omnipotent, reason and a constantly evolving irrationality in his literature—a conflict Albert Camus later called "absurd," which, in Latin, originally meant dissonant, disharmonious.[111]

But there is a second, more serious consequence of the Kant crisis. The melancholia Kleist suffers over the fact that we "can never be certain that what we call Truth is really Truth, or whether it does not merely appear so to us,"[112] leads him to a crossroads faced by many in the history of Western philosophy, from Plato to Friedrich Nietzsche: There, one must decide between piercing through the appearance of things toward their true being or exploring the possibilities of a thought that recognizes both the appearance of things and the unattainability of true being. Kleist chooses the latter, without losing sight of the first, and it is from this threshold position that the productive paradoxes of his writing originate. Following his Kant crisis of 1801, Kleist moves from the idealist 'otherworld' to the surface spectacle of empiricism. He turns from an optimistic moral philosopher to a skeptical moralist, reckoning with simulation and deception instead of truth. The starting point for Kleist's various experiments in the logical, moral, political, and aesthetic dimensions of appearances is the observation of human action in everyday life, most of which he makes while traveling.[113] But there is yet another cause for Kleist's 'gradual' disillusionment: his experience as a disappointed lover. During his studies in Frankfurt, the unsociable student who has made no new friends falls in love with the neighbor's daughter, Wilhelmine von Zenge. The following two chapters deal with Kleist's travels and his love.

Kleist did not end up becoming a scholar. He was thus spared a cell in the madhouse—one of the possible pathological consequences of intellectual narrow-mindedness. According to a letter to Wilhelmine of September 1800, during a tour of the "insane" unit at the Julius-Hospice in Würzburg, he was approached by "a professor, who had perhaps studied too hard," questioning him in Latin in such a manner that Kleist was "in all seriousness at a loss to answer, as though face to face with the most brilliant person in the world."[114] We are, thus, presented with another one of Kleist's satirical remarks on science, though less lighthearted than his mockery of Newton. And German writer Erich Kästner offers a fitting epilogue in his novel *Fabian*, wherein the eponymous hero Jakob Fabian earns his PhD in German studies with a dissertation entitled “Did Heinrich von Kleist Stutter?” Fabian subsequently abandons academia to work as an advertising copywriter and explore the Berlin nightlife. By contrast, his friend Labude continues his academic career, encaged by the university, which leads to his undoing: He submits his habilitation thesis on Lessing but, while waiting for his advisor’s protracted assessment, falsely fears his work has been rejected and shoots himself dead. Fabian, meanwhile, meets his end trying to rescue a boy who falls into a river. Fabian cannot swim.[115]

CHAPTER IV

The Misused Love Letters

Defending Kleist from His Fiancée and Critics

Literary critics, writes Walter Benjamin, approach "a book as lovingly as a cannibal spices a baby."[1] From biographers, by contrast, the reader expects 'kissing'—not 'biting.' And yet with Kleist it is the opposite: It is easy to be enthusiastic about his work, but more difficult to deal with his person. Especially after reading the letter he sent to his fiancée while traveling, in which he writes that, were he rich and were it not for her, he would look for pretty girls "at every house" and educate them in his own way, provided they had the "merest spark of soul" in them: "For this is what I must always do, and if a girl were quite perfect, but already wore her final polish, she would not be the one for me. I myself must form and educate her, and if not, it would be as with the mouthpiece of my clarinet." Bought by the dozens in the marketplace, Kleist explains that he once tried one of these mouthpieces and "got nothing out of it but sour, squeaky notes. So I cut a piece for myself from a fresh reed, formed it to my own lips, shaved and scraped away with my knife until it fit my embouchure exactly—and it works superbly. I played to my heart's content."[2]

A remark such as this upsets more than just outspoken feminists. In 1992, when German writer Monika Maron received the Kleist Prize from literary critic Marcel Reich-Ranicki in Regensburg, she admitted in her acceptance speech to having difficulties with the 'macho' Kleist. While she was able to get "close" to his works, she could not "reconcile" with "Kleist, the man."[3] To this remark Kleist would have perhaps responded in the same way he did to Adolphine von Werdeck in the fall of 1801: "You seem to be less pleased with Goethe's person than his works. But for Heaven's sake, gracious lady, if we were to expect of our poets that they be as exalted as their heroes, would there be any poets at all? And if people had to behave as they teach in their books, would anyone ever again write books for us?"[4]

Poets may not have to be heroes, but what is one to make of the man who needs "a spouse that shares [his] ideas" in order to become a poet, and who decides to "educate" his beloved "up to [his] level" with the help of an "educational plan"? The beloved is instructed to "read and learn" a series of books "without fail" and to prove her "lofty femininity" through letters to her itinerant lover in which she is to reflect on the "idea of separation," for example, and its "anguish or utility," because their "future peace and happiness depend

© WILHELM FINK VERLAG, 2021 | DOI:10.30965/9783846765746_005

upon this final test." In her despair the young woman, tested in this manner, copies the questions her lover poses to her and sends them to a young teacher whose enthusiastic answers she then passes off as her own. One can imagine how the story ends. But, despite the parallels, this is not the story of Heinrich von Kleist, Wilhelmine von Zenge, and her future husband Wilhelm Traugott Krug—author of a *Philosophy of Marriage* (*Philosophie der Ehe*) and successor to Immanuel Kant at the University of Königsberg. It is, instead, the story of three people from Seldwyla: Viktor, Gritli, and Wilhelm—characters from Gottfried Keller's *The Misused Love Letters* of 1865,[5] a story that parodies the 'civil improvement of women'[6] by their Enlightened husbands.

But what seemed ridiculous to Gottfried Keller from a historical distance was a genuine concern at the end of the 18th century, and considering Kleist within this context shows his behavior toward his fiancée as neither foolish nor macho. It is not Kleist who 'misuses' his love letters but Kleist's critics, in declaring them "unbearable" and scandalous for their profuse paternalism and narcissistic torture of the beloved.[7] Kleist's love letters are not a testimony to his personal failure but to the historical problem encountered in the transition from an aristocratic notion of marriage to a bourgeois union of love. In other words, as long as Kleist was still in love with Wilhelmine, he was acting according to the conventions of his time. Only in breaking his engagement to her did his actions gain a unique and Modern character. Kleist and Wilhelmine's affair reveals, from the very beginning, how difficult it was, at the turn of the 19th century, to simply declare one's love to another, even when that person was the neighbor's daughter. Feelings are not anthropological constants; every era loves differently. But when one's era has only a "mishmash"[8] of possibilities to offer in terms of a lover's role, an engagement becomes a search for orientation in an experiment with an uncertain outcome.

In the spring of 1799, the house next-door to Kleist's became lively. The von Zenge family moved in at Große Oderstraße with nine children, among them two attractive daughters, born in 1780 and 1782. At the perfect marital age, Wilhelmine and Louise did not leave the Kleist brothers cold. Leopold had an advantage as a lieutenant in the Frankfurt infantry regiment, whose new commander was Wilhelmine and Louise's father, Hartmann von Zenge—major general and "warrior of the school of Friedrich the Great."[9] Heinrich could not count on such capital. Having just resigned from his military commission, he was at first reticent, while Leopold, with his cheerful disposition, attempted to ease the Zenge daughters—who were mourning the loss of their hometown, Berlin—into their new life in the province. But when Leopold was transferred to the guard regiment in Potsdam, Heinrich's chance arose—though it was not easy to live down his brother. "We thought," writes Wilhelmine, "that he could not replace his brother, since he was very melancholic and dark, and talked very little. Soon, however, he accompanied us on all our walks, visited us with his sisters, played music and sang with me, and seemed to enjoy our company."[10] Wilhelmine's shift from "us" to "me" is telling, though she expressed herself cautiously to her new contender for marriage in this account of her first love. Her letter of June 16, 1803, to the philosophy professor Wilhelm Traugott Krug, whom she would marry in 1804, reveals the precarious balancing act she had to perform, knowing that—at the end of the 18th century—virginity was not only expected from a woman's body but also from her mind. Thus admonishes the widely read *Attempt at a Characterization of the Female Sex*: "[T]he girl that succeeds in possessing your heart must be innocent, the way she came forth from the arms of nature. She must not have exchanged love letters with any other man; she must be able to sincerely and without falsehood tell you: You are the *first* man I have ever loved and whom I will therefore love forever."[11] Kleist and Wilhelmine exchanged many love letters, but only one of her letters survived. Fortunately, there exists the account she gave to Krug, which was written with candor and fairness regarding her not-always-easy engagement to Kleist.

Unlike his brother, Kleist had neither the talent for nor an interest in jokes; he disliked the Zenge's "crisscrossing chatter."[12] The change in his life plan—giving up his military career—corresponded with a change in his manner. Among company Kleist no longer played the part of a chivalrous officer, like his brother did, but the part of a student in search of truth and virtue. He eschewed aristocratic conversational culture; depth, not surface, became his motto. This attitude did not make it any easier to approach Wilhelmine, though it might have aroused her curiosity, since the noblewoman also possessed a bourgeois heart. As she admits to Krug, even though she marveled at "courtly life" during her adolescence in Berlin, attending "operas, masquerades, and balls" "with great interest for a while, [her] heart felt very empty during all this, and [she] gladly returned home to [their] quiet domestic life."[13] This confession helps to explain why she—in provincial Frankfurt, far away from life at court—"listens [...] at times with interest"[14] to the dark and melancholic student Kleist, who is not at all amusing, charming, or quick witted, as is required for aristocratic amusement,[15] and why he, in turn, suspects in her a "sense for the finer things, something of a discernment for the nicer points," "even if she has not much to say in return."[16] Wilhelmine was wanting in education, as many noblewomen of her time were, lacking even the basis for a genuine understanding of German literature and philosophy, given the everyday language of Prussian aristocrats at the turn of the 19th century was French. Kleist

Fig. 16
Wilhelmine von Zenge (1780–1852), Kleist's fiancée

wanted to remedy this shortcoming by giving German lessons to Wilhelmine and her sisters, as well as his own sisters, through private lectures on experimental physics with Professor Wünsch, along with lectures he, himself, would give, elucidating Wünsch's teachings. According to Wilhelmine, Wünsch found the ladies to be "a very attentive audience," who repeat what they learn with their "assistant teacher, Mr. von Kleist," and write essays about Wünsch's lectures, which Kleist then corrects.[17] The problem of course remains as to how the "assistant teacher" should explain to his student that he was motivated by more than a love for teaching, without reverting to the old aristocratic art of complimenting. According to Wilhelmine in her letter to Krug, Kleist solved the problem in the following way:

> He asked for my permission to teach me the main rules of the German language, little by little, in short essays, which I gladly granted, and I studied diligently to reward him for his efforts.
>
> One night, when I was at Kleist's, he gave me what resembled an essay, enveloped in white paper, as usual, but how astounded I was when I opened it at home and found a letter from him in which he told me he had long been in love with me, and that I could make him very happy if I were to give him my hand. Until then, it had not crossed my mind that a man could ever fall in love with me because I always thought of myself as rather unsightly and unpleasant, and was never pleased with myself. I had always been fairly unbiased toward him, and was good to him as to a brother, but I did not love him, and I was taken aback by his confession because I had not the slightest idea—on the contrary, I always thought he preferred my sister Lotte to me.[18]

Wilhelmine was in truth anything but "unsightly," as a miniature by an unknown artist from the turn of the 19th century confirms.[19] She was taken aback by Kleist's declaration and, after confiding in her sister, writes to Kleist the next day that she "neither loves him" nor "wish[es] to become his wife" but "would always hold him dear as a friend."[20] Kleist's experiment in love thus seems to fail, but it should not be understood simply as a "surprise coup" that "only the most clever or most clumsy would carry out" (with Kleist belonging to the latter).[21] The only thing known for certain is that Kleist proposed in writing rather than in person, thus creating distance between Wilhelmine and himself. This distance corresponded to the fact that there had, until then, been no signs of love exchanged between the two, while also reflecting Kleist's hope that love might yet develop. Their correspondence takes the place of a heart-to-heart talk, thus granting Wilhelmine the freedom to reflect calmly on Kleist's declaration. Moreover, it spared him the need for dramatic overtures, which, in his time, would have manifested as either an aristocratic melodrama of refined gallantry or a bourgeois melodrama of diffidence and naïveté—the demonstration of insecurity serving as proof of authentic love and an inability for simulation.[22] Kleist was, therefore, neither coy nor clumsy when he secretly delivered his love letter to Wilhelmine. His letter should instead be seen as a means for opening up "interstices"[23] for the 'gradual fabrication' of feelings and for negotiating the right approach to marriage. But what would his options have been? According to the aristocratic tradition, love is not the cause but, at best, the effect of marriage; economic or political motives drove aristocratic marriages of convenience. It was the bourgeois, Enlightenment philosophy of marriage that propagated the ideal of a relationship based on love, in which love and virtue could conjoin on the basis of an individual's selection of a partner. Yet the bourgeois marriage did not require a sudden epiphanic moment of mutual passion. That would be the Romantic exception. The rule was, as German writer Sophie von La Roche writes in her novel *The History of Lady Sophia Sternheim*, first published in 1771: "A young woman; you know, is not to make the first advances."[24] This convention persisted even into the Modernist period. It appears in Thomas Mann's novel *The Magic Mountain* of 1924, in which Mynheer Peeperkorn and Hans Castorp—being faced with Madame Chauchat's dislike of Ludovico Settembrini—reassure themselves that women are "creatures not of action but of reaction; they do not initiate," but expect "to be intoxicated" by men's "desire."[25] It was the common expectation, then, that a woman's feelings develop only after a man's proposal of marriage; that this would take time was Kleist's only hope. He had to win Wilhelmine's love before he had any chance of success in asking Major General Hartmann von Zenge for his daughter's hand. Having left the military, with no money, no official position, and no estate, Kleist had no grounds for a relationship with Wilhelmine according to aristocratic convention.

After the failure of the first letter, Kleist tried to persuade Wilhelmine with a second one, but she refused to accept it. Eight days later he handed her the letter "once again with tearful eyes,"[26] in hopes of authenticating his feelings. While this emotional display was certainly an unusual scene for a former officer, it was a common trope in the bourgeois literature of the 18th century, with the eyes being regarded as the windows to the soul: "[T]o look into a crying eye is to see a soul in its pure nakedness."[27] Wilhelmine was thus moved to read Kleist's letter, the contents of which she detailed in her letter to Krug: "In this letter he asked what I found fault with in him, and he promised that I could make him into anything I wanted, I should just tell him how he could win my love. I wrote back to him and described the man that could make me happy. He made every effort to live up to this image so I finally gave him permission to write to my parents, and I promised him my hand as soon as they gave their consent."[28]

From the very beginning, then, Kleist and Wilhelmine's engagement had been based on a guarantee of mutual improvement. This fact often goes unnoticed, as the only surviving letters are Kleist's. Their relationship sought to balance diverging interests. Wilhelmine insisted on a marriage of social equals as well as a love match, while Kleist, who regarded aristocratic interests as restraints on his freedom, did his utmost to cultivate a bourgeois culture of feeling between them. Wilhelmine's parents supported their daughter and, in the spring of 1800, consented to the engagement on the condition that Kleist first prove himself. As Wilhelmine relays to Krug: "He had some assets but not enough for us to live on, but the King had promised to provide him with a government position as soon as he had completed his studies. My parents gave their consent but on the condition that we waited until he took a position, which pleased me."[29]

Though they were not officially engaged, having only received the consent of Wilhelmine's parents, Kleist's relationship with Wilhelmine did not remain a secret to the public. He thus felt the pressure to find an official position while still insecure about Wilhelmine's feelings. Shortly after his engagement agreement with the Zenges, he writes to her:

> After careful consideration, what more can I ultimately believe than that which I already knew half a year ago—I ask, what more can I know beyond the fact that you *value* me and that you love me like *a friend*?
>
> And yet I wish *more*, and yet I would like to *know* what your heart feels for me. Wilhelmine! Let me peer into your heart. Open it to me once with faith and candor. So much trust, so much unbounded trust from me surely merits *some*

> response from you. I do not wish to say you must love me simply because I love you; but you must confide in me as I have confided wholeheartedly in you. [...] Tell me if you love me—because why would you be ashamed of it? *Am I not noble*, Wilhelmine? [...] I believe I would be enraptured [...] if your hand could resolve itself to the writing down of these three words: *I love you*.
>
> Yes, Wilhelmine, say these three glorious words to me; they shall hold true for the rest of my life. Say them *once* and then let us soon get to the point where we do not need to repeat them to each other anymore. As *true faithfulness* and *true love* do not manifest themselves in words but in actions. Let us completely unbosom ourselves to each other so that we may at least know each other completely. [...] Trust and respect are the two inseparable cornerstones of love [...].
>
> Let us, therefore, be mindful of our conduct toward each other, with compassion and gentle rigor. At least I would, for my own part, wish that you would tell me openly anything that might displease you about me. I may dare to fulfill all your demands because I do not fear you will make excessive ones. At least continue to behave in such a way that I may place my highest happiness in your love and your respect; [...]. So, I shall also work for your own education, Wilhelmine, and to ever more refine and heighten the merits of the girl I love.
>
> And now another matter of importance, Wilhelmine. You know that I have already decided to prepare myself for some official position; but I am as yet undecided *which*. [...]
>
> Also, I would like to learn from you what you actually expect from a future by my side. I do not promise to fulfill the expectations you have set out for me; but I promise that I will—given the prospects are equally advantageous—choose the life path that comes closest to your wishes.[30]

Should he practice law? Become a diplomat? Work for the ministry of finance? Become a professor or an economist? Whatever it was Wilhelmine wrote in response, Kleist evaded making a decision on a bread-and-butter job, despite all promises. What is more remarkable about this letter is the fact that, in spite of their engagement, Kleist had yet to make Wilhelmine confess her love—that after a probationary period of a few months, she had not plainly expressed the nature and degree of her feelings for him. It thus appears that it was not she who was dependent on Kleist, but Kleist who was dependent on her, as anyone in such an unequal love match would be. Kleist scholarship generally assumes that Kleist's engagement was a questionable experiment in love from the outset, given the speculation surrounding his 'gender trouble,' his 'amphibian nature,' and his latent—or manifest—homosexuality, all of which result in the conjecture that his pursuit of marriage was driven by his need for "containment," the same way it would later do for Thomas Mann.[31] Accordingly, Kleist scholars read his instructions to Wilhelmine in his private, but not secret, letters—accessible, at least, to her family—as either simulations of masculinity congruent with the expectations of his time,[32] or, from the perspective of his individual struggle, as the desperate attempt to fashion himself as the fiancée's preceptor and domineering husband-to-be, given his loss of control over his life, which left him "utterly insecure with regard to the prospects of his life and career, tormented by the experience of continual failure." This reading reduces Kleist's 'love' to a compensatory function: "The letters, rife with repulsive impertinences, are real love letters, seeking affection, comfort, and support from the beloved partner." It also means to explain why "heartfelt, intimate, and tender words toward the fiancée" are first heard in the precarious final stage of their relationship and not at its beginning—the reverse order of a typical romance."[33] Regarding the beginning of the engagement, it has been succinctly noted that "[i]f Wilhelmine had expected that, after giving in to his advances, Kleist would turn out to be a tender lover and stop playing the schoolmaster, she must have found herself bitterly disappointed."[34]

The letter of spring 1800, which has been extensively quoted here, was written the day after Wilhelmine's parents gave their consent to hers and Kleist's engagement. Firstly, it shows that, from the very beginning, there was nothing Kleist would have liked more—unless one were to find grounds for fraudulent intent or self-delusion—than to be a "tender lover," that is, if the conventions of his time, not to mention his fiancée, had allowed for it. Secondly, it proves that Wilhelmine's reservations had a rather destabilizing effect on Kleist's psyche. She yields to Krug's demand for exclusivity and likely the entire truth about her affair with Kleist, writing to Krug that, "[e]ven if you were not the only one to have stirred my heart, I can still assure you that I have never loved so wholeheartedly as I love you."[35] Too bad for Kleist. His sense of awareness that Wilhelmine would never be fully his may explain why there are—alongside the 'intimate and tender words' in the opening passages of his letters to his "dearest, heart-treasured Minna,"[36] which must not be overlooked—frequent complaints about Wilhelmine's lack of love for him. And then there are the subtly and openly aggressive passages, such as the one quoted at the beginning of this chapter, in which Kleist lets on that he could easily 'form and educate' women other than Wilhelmine. Wilhelmine was probably fine with the fact that Kleist had to keep playing the schoolmaster even after their engagement. In any case, unlike Kleist's critics, she did not complain about it:

> He assigned me interesting questions, which I was to answer in writing, and he would revise them. He gave me useful books to read, about which I would give my judgments or take excerpts. He recited poems to me, and I was to repeat them or translate them into French. He also sharpened my wit and acumen through exercises in comparisons which I had to give to him in writing. He thus lived exclusively for me, I grew quite fond of him and made it my duty to live exclusively for

> him too. If, at times, I admitted to myself that he did not yet resemble the ideal man I had imagined, then I thought maybe there was no better one, as I did not know anybody whom I better liked. I carried out my plan in all sincerity.[37]

Kleist and Wilhelmine's love appears to have followed a give-and-take economy rather than an aneconomy of profusion, devotion, and passion. Kleist himself suggested this mode of exchange in the letter he wrote immediately following the engagement talk with Wilhelmine's parents, in which they granted their consent. But it is doubtful that this mode of exchange was consistent with his character. It is remarkable how within a single letter Kleist first begs for a confession of love, then struggles for faithfulness and respect—thus emphasizing reasons to marry that do not require the feeling of love[38]—and finally promises education in return. In the long run Kleist would not allow his expectations to be lowered so easily. Later, when Ludwig Tieck asks Wilhelmine for her letters from Kleist, she admits that she was "foolish to burn many of [them] [...], as they were all written with the utmost fervor."[39] While we do not know these letters of passion, it is important to at least know that, by Wilhelmine's account, they existed, and that of the thirty-five surviving letters he wrote to her, only four can be fully classified as schoolmasterly mental exercises.[40] It is therefore peculiar that Kleist scholars continue to assert that, "strangely enough," the "early Enlightenment model of the letter as essay," or *chreia*, dominates Kleist's love letters rather than the "so-called *natural letter*, geared more toward the personal, private exchange of thoughts and heartfelt revelations."[41] In fact, the opposite is true: Kleist follows Christian Fürchtegott Gellert's influential guide to letter-writing, first published in 1751, according to which "the language of the heart cannot be constrained to a *chreia*."[42]

Ultimately, Kleist's occasionally schoolmasterly attitude should be seen as an accessory to his love letters, and unoriginally so, as it was purely a matter of convention. Moreover, he was only ever acting in the position of Wünsch's "assistant teacher," relaying second-hand scientific findings to Wilhelmine. Kleist's intention to "work" on Wilhelmine's "education" to "ever more refine and heighten" her "merits"[43] is not scandalous but rather typical of the time, and the same is true of his thoughts on the nature and social function of men and women. Wilhelmine took no offense, unlike Kleist's critics, who speak of an "education dictatorship" or the "sublime sadism of Kleist's educational program," established to confirm male superiority or authority through "(pseudo-)logical maneuvers." "Self-opinionated hypocrisy! A die-hard bachelor would hardly be able to argue more deviously,"[44] reads the harsh verdict on the mental exercise Kleist shares with Wilhelmine in his letter of May 30, 1800, in which he asks "in the case of a married couple who have fulfilled every duty

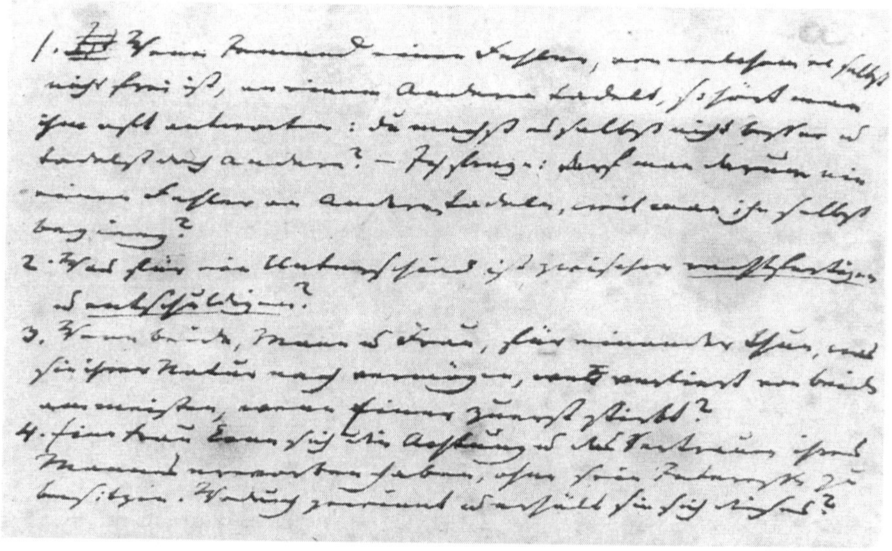

Fig. 17 Mental exercises for Wilhelmine von Zenge, Frankfurt an der Oder, spring to summer 1800

1. When someone reprimands someone else for a fault of which he himself is not free, one often hears the reply: "You do not do any better yourself; and yet you reprimand others?"—I ask: "Should one, therefore, never reprimand others for a mistake because one has made that mistake oneself?"
2. What is the difference between *justifying* and *excusing*?
3. If both man and woman do for each other what they are capable of doing according to their nature, which of them loses the most if one dies first?
4. A woman may have earned her husband's respect and trust without having earned his interest. How does she gain and maintain his interest? (DKV IV, 61)

toward one another, whose is the greater loss when the other dies?" Kleist uses this as an example to then develop the answer, step by step, with future mental exercises in mind. The most important sentences are:

> The man is not only husband to his wife, he is also a citizen of the state, while the woman is only a wife; the man has obligations not only to his wife but to his country, while the wife has no obligations to anyone but her husband; a wife's happiness, though indeed an irremissible concern for the man, is not his *only* one, he is also concerned for the happiness of his fellow countrymen, while the husband's happiness, contrariwise, is the *sole* concern of his wife [...]. The husband thus receives infinitely more from his wife than, conversely, she from him.
>
> It follows that the husband loses infinitely more when his wife dies than she does when he dies. The wife only loses protection from assaults on her honor and security, and sustenance for life's basic needs; the former she can regain in the law [...]; the latter she could inherit from her husband. But how does the wife intend to bequeath to her husband what he loses when she dies? He loses the

> very quintessence of his earthly happiness: with the death of his wife, the very wellsprings of his happiness are shut, he who lacks a wife lacks everything, and all she can bequeath to him is the sad memory of an erstwhile happiness, which can only make his condition the more melancholy.[45]

From today's point of view, it is hard to agree with Kleist's argument. Readers at the turn of the 19th century, however, would have, at most, noticed that Kleist adopts familiar distinctions between the sexes *sub specie mortis*—under the sign of death. To think of happiness only in relation to its loss may be typical of Kleist. But the generative core of the mental exercise consists of variations on the central tenets of the *Prussian Civil Code* (*Allgemeines Landrecht*) and Kant's theory of marriage law—two works born out of the spirit of reform at the end of the 18th century proving that the Enlightenment does not embrace women's emancipation. The role of the steersman—"fix[ing] the direction of the voyage wisely" and "steer[ing] the course with a strong arm"[46]—which Kleist frequently claims for himself with regard to Wilhelmine, is a role which, according to Kant, naturally befits the man: "*Woman* regardless of age is declared to be immature in civil matters; her husband is her natural curator." Thus states Kant's *Anthropology from a Pragmatic Point of View* of 1798, which also argues against a woman's effort to educate herself: "As concerns scholarly women: they use their *books* somewhat like their *watch*, that is, they carry one so that it will be seen that they have one; though it is usually not running or not set by the sun." Compared with Kant, Kleist's mental exercises for Wilhelmine seem almost emancipatory. Kleist does, after all, discuss the works of Friedrich Schiller or Jean-Jacques Rousseau with Wilhelmine, while Kant primarily defines women as natural beings or, literally, as a "domestic animal."[47] Kant's concept of marriage parallels the Prussian civil code, which went into effect in 1794. §184 states: "The husband is the head of the marital union"; in §188: "The husband is responsible for and authorized to defend the person, honor, and assets of his wife in and outside the court"; in §194 on the duties of women: "She is responsible for presiding over her husband's household affairs as befits his station and rank," etc.[48] The definition of the woman as a domestic being who devotes herself wholly to the husband's happiness can also be found in Rousseau's *Emile*, first published in 1762—a programmatic work that epitomizes Enlightenment pedagogy: "Thus the whole education of women ought to relate to men. To please men, to be useful to them, to make herself loved and honored by them [...]—these are the duties of women at all times, and they ought to be taught from childhood."[49] Unlike women, men have additional duties, as the Romantic writer Jean Paul knew: "So long as a woman loves, she loves right on, steadily. A man has to do something between whiles."[50] The man is both lover and citizen of the state, the woman is only lover; the man is split in his purpose, the woman is one. So goes the bourgeois ideal of harmony from the turn of the 19th century, which can also be found in Johann Gottlieb Fichte's philosophy of law.[51] The man finds wholeness in the woman. When she dies, he loses it. Kleist's melancholic conclusion to his mental exercise for Wilhelmine is founded in this belief.

Today's readers may be shocked by the ways that women were excluded from public life in order to ensure an ideal world—at least at home—for men. Yet, at the turn of the 19th century, the increasing prioritization of gender differences over social standing was regarded as a progressive step toward restabilizing a society whose feudal structures were dissolving. Kleist's instruction of Wilhelmine was neither outlandish nor particularly harsh; it was merely a reflection of the new bourgeois model of the woman as wife, homemaker, and mother, which a noblewoman like Wilhelmine, with her memories of social life at court in the royal capital, had to adapt to. Wilhelmine also had to learn to tolerate Kleist's tendency toward long-windedness in his mental exercises or, upon dreaming of his future family, his tendency to lose himself in passion and abstractions in sentences such as: "O lay this thought to your breast like a shield of adamant: *I was born to motherhood!* Let every other thought, every other wish be deflected from this impenetrable armor. What other purpose offered by the world could not deserve your contempt?"[52] The explanation for such enthusiasm is easy. Kleist loosely quotes from Christoph Martin Wieland's *Sympathies*.[53] When it came to matters of love, he had more reading than life experience to pull from, though this seems to change slightly in the summer of 1800 when Wilhelmine and Kleist lived next door to each other: Going for walks, intimate conversations in the arbor, reading together—according to Wilhelmine, the two lived together "very happily for half a year."[54]

The pressure on Kleist, however, was building. Having quit his studies, it was all the more urgent to his family as well as Wilhelmine's that he finally find a post. At the beginning of July 1800, he took time off for what would become the first of many travels, this time with his sister Ulrike to Sagard on the island of Rügen. There, he became acquainted with Ludwig von Brockes, a northern German nobleman of little means, who was a former law student and had served in the Danish military, currently employed as a private tutor in Göttingen. Born in 1767, Brockes was ten years older than Kleist and became his "intimate friend."[55] One can only speculate if it was during their time together on Rügen, that the two had—against Kleist's own declaration[56]—planned to leave on their mysterious Würzburg journey, which they took a few weeks later. Whatever the case, after his return Kleist could no longer stand to remain in Frankfurt: On August 14 he flees from his hometown. "[I]n the morning, in the semidarkness" his carriage rolls past Wilhelmine's house, to which his tearful eyes cling with a "burning desire." But after fifty miles of traveling his eyes have dried up. He arrives in Berlin that evening "well and in good spirits."[57] Kleist remains silent on the actual purpose of his journey. Even his sister Ulrike and Wilhelmine do not know, though he counts on their "unbreachable discretion," on their willingness to keep "the seemingly adventurous aspects of [his] journey" a secret, and lead all relatives and friends to believe that he went to stay in Berlin in order to inquire about an official position at court that had been promised to him upon his resignation from the military.[58] Wilhelmine, at least, is led to believe that the journey is meant to remove an impediment to their marriage, the nature of which remains a mystery down to the present day.

What chance was left for their relationship? When the two first met in 1799, Kleist was twenty-one years old, and Wilhelmine was nineteen; he was a student without concrete job prospects, and she had reached the marriageable age. In the spring of 1800, they became engaged on the condition that he find a position, and he subsequently quit his studies. In the fall of 1800, he traveled to Würzburg, and there became elated over the favorable solution he discovered for his undisclosed problems. In the winter of 1800/01, he went to Berlin to see if he was capable of taking up a government position. Ultimately reluctant to assume a post and disenchanted by Kantian philosophy, he fled Berlin in the spring of 1801 and traveled to Paris via Dresden. From July through November 1801, he stayed in the French capital under the pretense of devoting himself to the study of the sciences, and at the end of November he left again, this time to Switzerland via Frankfurt am Main. He stayed in Basel, followed by time in Bern, and in the spring of 1802, finally settled in a small house he rented on an island in the Aar, at the outflow of Lake Thun. But Kleist would be on the move for years, as we will see in the chapters to come. After leaving Frankfurt an der Oder in August of 1800, Wilhelmine only saw him again, briefly, two more times—Kleist visited her in his hometown at the beginning of November and at Christmas in 1800. It is, thus, no wonder their love failed, at least from today's perspective. Who, at the age of nineteen, would be willing to sustain a relationship for more than two years with a prospect-less, nomadic university dropout? At the end of the 18th century, however, an engagement was a contract not easily broken. The German philosopher Johann Gottfried Herder was engaged to Caroline Flachsland for eight years. "[I]t is a pleasure, to love from a distance!" he assures Caroline, at once admitting: "I do not blame you that the tiresome letter-writing languishes under your hand: as writing letters is nothing—but deception, presence, hope?"[59] What hope did Wilhelmine cling to when imagining her future with Kleist? The one left behind surely feels less loved; did the physical distance become an emotional one? What are the advantages and disadvantages of a love sustained through letters?

Fig. 18 Kleist's gift to Wilhelmine ("Trust in us, unity among us.")

As a farewell gift before his travels, Kleist did not only give Wilhelmine a tea cup and saucer engraved with the words "trust," "us," and "unity," forming—in German—the rebus: "Vertrauen auf uns, Einigkeit unter uns." ("Trust in us, unity among us.")[60] He also gave her a copy of Schiller's *Wallenstein*, urging her: "Read it, dear girl, I will read it too. Thus, our souls will coincide in a third object. [...] So dream away the time of our separation with the help of pleasant images. Everything *Max Piccolomini* says shall—if there is any similarity—relate to me;

everything that *Thekla* says shall—if there is any similarity—relate to you."[61] As is well known, in times of greatest hardship, Schiller's lovers stick together in spite of all fatherly constraints, sacrificing their lives for their love. Love is fate or nothing at all: This becomes Kleist's motto. "Imagine yourself aboard the ship of my happiness," he writes to Wilhelmine four days after leaving. "We shall sink beneath the waves *together*, or arrive joyfully in port *together*."[62] With each letter Kleist became more audacious, and the intensification of their correspondence increased the intensity of his confessions and demands. In Frankfurt, by contrast, under his family's watch, he had to, above all, play the role of dutiful schoolmaster. The proximity of his fiancée, not entirely taken by him, may have rather inhibited his dreams and desires. It was only from a distance, in the medium of the letter, in the freedom of his imagination, that they found complete expression. The depression that set in after parting in Frankfurt was followed by the euphoria of setting up in Berlin, and Kleist's mental exercises for Wilhelmine became rhetorical questions, no longer presented in dialectical treatises but in bourgeois daydreams. What would Wilhelmine prefer to be in the future: "Will she only need to part the thin curtains in this dimly lit room" of her house "in order to smile her morning greeting to me, or will she send a servant from the furthest wing of that palace to inquire as to whether her esteemed consort had enjoyed his repose?—O, dear Minna, no, surely, surely you do not want the latter."[63] But Kleist's fantasies are easy to see through. Through physical distance he creates intimacy. At the end of August, on his journey from Berlin to Leipzig, Kleist looks up at the night sky and sees Wilhelmine in the clouds' form: "[I]t lacked of nothing in regard to your person; your dress, the little gold cross, the way it lay"—at her bosom, one might add—"that hard hoop of your skirt that so often exasperated me, even the brown mole midway along your soft right arm. A thousand times I kissed it, and you. Then I drew you close to my breast and fell asleep in your arms."[64]

Could these be the words of someone planning to camouflage his homosexuality through a marriage? Kleist only dared such permissive remarks because he considered his letters a *cri de coeur*, and not a performance: "But it all turned into the sort of letter that can only be delivered by myself and in person, for, confidentially, it is my very heart. But you wish to see black on white, and so I shall paint my heart as well as I can on this paper."[65] Indeed, it is the medialization of his love that allowed for such heartfelt immediacy. In his letters he transforms distance into intimacy, quoting examples from contemporary literature in the process—a common practice in the culture of sentimentalism, and nothing exceptional at the end of the 18th century, let alone unique to Kleist. The best-known model is Rousseau's novel *Julie, or the New Heloise* of 1761. The story of the teacher Saint-Preux and his aristocratic student Julie d'Etange could not have a happy ending, but, as an experiment in transforming the aristocratic culture of feeling into a bourgeois one through the medium of the letter, the novel was epoch-making: "I have received your letter with the same transports your presence would have evoked, and in the exaltation of my joy a mere piece of paper stood me in stead of you. […] Do not then be surprised if your letters which depict you so well sometimes have the same effect on your worshipful lover as your presence. Rereading them I lose my reason, […] my blood takes fire and sizzles, I am seized with frenzy. I imagine I see you, touch you, hold you to my breast…. object of worship, bewitching maid, source of delight and ecstasy."[66] Thus writes Rousseau's Saint-Preux. Inversely, Kleist is preoccupied with the potential his letter to Wilhelmine contains for her arousal: "To think that this very paper I write on and hold and see before me, *you* will one day hold, and *you* will one day see—I kiss it […] and kiss it again, the precious paper that you will also kiss perhaps—and pretend to myself that my lips are already touching yours—for when I close my eyes I can imagine anything I wish."[67]

In the "seclusion" of writing "one has other ways of seeing and feeling than in involvement with the world," writes Rousseau in the preface to his epistolary novel.[68] To love in and through a medium has one advantage: It intensifies longing and desire and allows one to elevate one's own image as well as that of the beloved with unfettered caprice. The drawback is that any real encounter between the lovers can only disappoint, and so they must remain apart in order to maintain their illusions. Julie, ultimately, does not marry the passionate letter writer Saint-Preux, but Monsieur de Wolmar. Wilhelmine writes to her future husband Krug, clear-sightedly, that Kleist wanted to "shape her into an ideal," which "often troubled" her,[69] while Kleist's final letters to her repeatedly emphasize that he would return home only when he could "fulfill the expectations" that he "so foolishly aroused in people by so many boastful actions."[70] Letters, it seems, can lead to narcissistic delusions of grandeur that quickly shatter in the face of reality back home. In his final letter to Wilhelmine, Kleist alludes to his future career, but there is more to it than that. In continually prolonging his travels, he evaded both reproach from his family and, perhaps, erotic frustrations.

Love letters demand a response; any disruption in correspondence raises doubts. 'You are no longer loved' is the message of the letter that never arrives. That is another disadvantage of loving through letters. In a letter to his beloved Milena Jesenská, Franz Kafka attributes the phenomenon of letters that pass each other by or never arrive at their destination to the parasitic nature of the medium itself: "The easy possibility of writing letters […] must have brought wrack and ruin to the souls of the world. […] How did people ever get the idea they could communicate with one another by letter! [...] Writing letters [...] means exposing oneself to the ghosts, who are greedily waiting precisely for that. Written kisses never arrive at their destination; the ghosts drink them up along the way."[71] But Kleist took great care to avoid precisely that: "How easy it is for letters to be left behind at the post office or get lost elsewhere; but who would be so quick to worry?" Thus, Kleist tried to calm Wilhelmine and himself by suggesting they keep track of letters "sent" and "received" in a table appended to each of their letters.[72] He reassured Wilhelmine that the certainty of his love would be guaranteed by daily letters—an "almost continuous conversation"[73]—and urged her to do the same. In his letters he thought constantly about postal routes and destinations, but it did not help: "And still no news from you, my *dear* friend? Is there no messenger who could deliver a line from you to me? Is there no longer a connection between the two of us, no roads, no bridges. Did a chasm open up between us so that the countries can no longer hold out their arms—the country roads? [...] Or did some fiend of mistrust come between us after all to tear me away from your heart? [...] Wilhelmine! Am I worth nothing to you anymore?"[74]

Another ghostly element of written correspondence is the sender and receiver's transformation of one another into phantasmal figures. In person, speakers have the advantage of facial expressions and gestures; they may ask for clarification in the case of misunderstanding and react to shifts in mood. Written love, by contrast, is incorporeal; the "written word" appears "unalterable"—to adapt another phrase from Kafka—and the "opinions" of the receiver "are often only an expression of despair."[75] Equally discouraging is the temporal 'phase delay' to which letters are subject. Sender and receiver are never the same as they were when they last corresponded: "Dear, cherished Wilhelmine, when you write to me from one heart to another as you have done, why, I simply must answer you instantly, even if I were ten times busier than I am. O how it pains me to have sent off that melancholy letter in my bad mood the day before yesterday, which you must have received this very day when I received yours, which has so marvelously renewed love and spirit within me. Please forgive me this last outburst of my self-discontentment, do not even answer that letter, rather burn it entirely and, in its stead, read often this letter which I am writing joyfully and cheerfully for you with all my heart."[76] Love can founder on such confusions inherent to the letter, which, in the end, are blamed on the writer and never on the postal service. The longer the correspondence lasts, the less likely it is to fulfill its purpose, to bridge the "chasm" of misunderstanding until the lovers meet again. Wilhelmine must have sensed this too, when she responds to Kleist's untimely moodiness in January 1801 with the "suggestion to stop writing letters for a week or two to be able to write

[him] all the more. This correspondence must never be a cause of worry and trouble for you [Wilhelmine], it is solely meant to supplement a pleasure, namely that of talking to you in person."[77] Kleist abided with fewer letters to Wilhelmine. But the agitation continued, as evidenced by the anecdote of the unyielding French postmaster, which tells of Kleist being forced to run back and forth for hours across Paris in August 1801 because a postmaster refused to hand him one of Wilhelmine's letters without first seeing his passport.[78] The intimate, tender tone also continued, though descriptions of his travels began to take up more and more room. To think of Wilhelmine in the year and a half that followed meant "forgetting [her] (without forgetting, life itself is not possible) and frequently waking out of that forgetfulness."[79]

The same might be true for Wilhelmine. After having been apart for months on end, their correspondence must have felt like more of an obligation than a "pleasure" for both of them. The difficult task was to remain memorable across the distance. Especially when Wilhelmine began to doubt her future happiness, Kleist tried to understand the particular nature of their love within the more general context of a bourgeois love match and its inherently arduous trials. While Kleist's justification of his Würzburg journey in the fall of 1800 was still somewhat plausible—the removal of some mysterious obstacle to their marriage—fleeing from all potential posts in Berlin and the despair of the Kant crisis seem less convincing reasons for his journey to Paris in the spring of 1801. Hence, Kleist not only gives Wilhelmine a miniature portrait of himself when he leaves again;[80] he also promises her, as a "second gift," "the complete works of Rousseau," adding that, "I shall also indicate the order in which he is to be read. For the moment, let nothing deter you from finishing *Emile*."[81] Upon finishing Rousseau's *Emile*, Wilhelmine would have come across its fifth and final book, which deals with the education of women, the reciprocal relationship between the sexes, and the duties and hardships of engagement through the example of the engaged couple Emile and Sophie. Emile's mentor urges him to set out on an educational journey for at least two years, leaving his fiancée behind, in order to then "return worthy of her. Do not be vain as to believe that you already merit her. [...] Come and learn to bear her absence. Come and win the prize of fidelity, so that on your return you can lay claim to some honor from her and ask for her hand not as an act of grace but as a recompense." To Sophie's dismay the hesitant Emile allows himself to be persuaded and follows his mentor's advice. As they bid each other farewell, the couple exchanges edifying reading material in preparation for their respective roles of 'virtuous traveler' and 'honorable wife.' Emile receives a copy of François Fénelon's *Telemachus*, and Sophie receives Joseph Addison's *The Spectator*. Emile's mentor gives him detailed instructions for proper traveling, which he

Fig. 19
Jean-Jacques Rousseau (1712–1778)

considers necessary for acquiring practical knowledge: "The abuse of books kills science. Believing that we know what we have read, we believe that we can dispense with learning it. Too much reading only serves to produce presumptuous ignoramuses." Emile's educational journey is not only meant to equip him with knowledge about foreign countries and peoples but, most importantly, with knowledge about himself—his choice of career, where to settle with his family, etc.:

> But, before marrying, you must know what kind of man you want to be, what you want to spend your life doing, and what measures you want to take to assure yourself and your family of bread. Although one ought not to make such a care his principal business, one must nonetheless think about it once. Do you want to commit yourself to dependence on men whom you despise? Do you want to establish your fortune and determine your status by means of civil relations which will put you constantly at the discretion of others and force you to become a rascal yourself in order to escape from the clutches of other rascals? […] In what corner of the earth will you be able to say, 'Here I am master of myself and of the land which belongs to me?' […] Do you believe that it is so easy to find the country where one is always permitted to be a decent man? I agree that if there is any legitimate and sure means of subsisting without intrigue, without involvements, and without dependence, it is to live by cultivating one's own land with the labor of one's own hands. But where is the State where a man can say

> to himself, 'The land I tread is mine'? Before choosing this happy land, be well assured that you will find there the peace you seek. [...] I have a proposition to make to you. Let us consecrate the two years until your return to choosing an abode in Europe where you can live happily with your family [...].[82]

If one reads Kleist's life as a parallel to Rousseau's *Emile*, one can no longer claim with any certainty that it was stability Kleist so desperately sought in Wilhelmine's love. Instead, from the very beginning of their engagement, Kleist's love for her sought to manifest the experiences he had read about earlier in Rousseau, the mentor Kleist would follow in all of the major changes he made to his life plan in the years around 1800. *Julie, or, The New Heloise* showed him how, as a lover, to turn absence into presence through letters. *Emile* was even more to him, serving as a guide for all of life's major questions, whose teachings he took literally, as instructions. In it he found the 'curriculum' for—and legitimization of—his education of Wilhelmine, as well as the inspiration for his search for a "*wise, older* friend,"[83] a mentor and companion for his Würzburg journey. Rousseau also provided him with arguments in support of his refusal "to accept an official post" and be forged "with the hammer of tyranny" at court; to take a position whose "interest [...] I am not allowed to question"; to pursue a career in which people are "instructed" in the "art of deception"—such as the Prussian Technical Commission sessions that Kleist attended in Berlin in the winter of 1800, which was to prepare him to spy on foreign factories.[84] It was Rousseau who taught Kleist that nature—not books—is "the master teacher,"[85] and that a journey facilitates the acquisition of practical knowledge. From Rousseau Kleist learned to long for the countryside and to disdain the illusory life of the city, as we shall see later in his depictions of Berlin and Paris. At the beginning of September 1800, en route to Würzburg, Kleist shared with Wilhelmine, for the first time, his dreams of a small house in the country.[86] In November 1800 he made plans to settle down as a German teacher in French-speaking Switzerland and responded sympathetically when Wilhelmine deemed his plans "unfeasible," a position he was ultimately unable to maintain.[87] Almost a year later, on his birthday, on October 10, 1801, writing to Wilhelmine from Paris, he tries to convince her of his plan to "buy a farm of some sort in Switzerland, which could sustain [him]." He wishes, "in the most literal sense, *to become a peasant*, or to use a somewhat better sounding word, a farmer."[88] On October 27, 1801, he concedes that Wilhelmine's "agreement to this is of first importance."[89] On December 2, 1801, from Frankfurt am Main, already on his way to Switzerland, he begs her to reevaluate her hesitation and tells her in no uncertain terms that her answer to his letter "will be the moment that will decide [his] future happiness."[90]

Rousseau rewards Emile's years of travel with a happy ending: He sends him back home to his fiancée, where he is ultimately able to find happiness and freedom. This was not the case for the Prussian aristocrat Kleist, who preferred to forsake "the whole splendid lot of nobility and station and honor and wealth" for the sake of his "love" for Wilhelmine.[91] He had to go to 'free' Switzerland, following Rousseau's understanding that there are exceptions to a man's duty of "attachment" to the place of his birth, "circumstances in which a man can be more useful to his fellow citizens outside of his fatherland than if he were living in its bosom."[92] Kleist's suggestion to become a peasant and make Wilhelmine a farmer's wife was by no means as outlandish as it first sounds. It would be erroneous to imagine the two in rugged clothes and head scarf performing manual labor on the field or sitting at a warm hearth in an alpine cabin. Kleist was on the lookout for "manors"[93] in Switzerland, and Wilhelmine was meant to imagine a manorial economy, familiar from Prussia, with "at least two or three servant girls at [her] side." Having likely finished her reading of *Emile,* Wilhelmine knew that factual arguments were no match for Rousseau and thus opted for an emotional appeal: her attachment to her family home, the weakness of her constitution, or the headaches she suffered from when exposed to the sun. "Some of the reasons you give for your hesitation are rather odd," writes Kleist, and he was right.[94] Her reasons were fabricated. Wilhelmine was not overly attached to her family home. After all, she was considering a position as domina of the Lindow cloister.[95] Nor was she too proud: Two years later she would marry a commoner and move to Königsberg. The truth is that Wilhelmine had emotionally distanced herself from Kleist and admitted to herself that she "will never be his," and "stopped wishing to be so a long time ago." "My hope, and my expectation of a happy future, had long faded," she wrote to Krug in 1803.[96]

Whose love would be able to withstand a series of love letters such as the ones Kleist wrote to Wilhelmine after his departure from Berlin in 1801? If he had only been able to give himself the appearance of a stable partner and prospective husband. Instead, he insists on writing to her about his depressions: "Why am I condemned, like Tancred, to hurt the one I love by my every act?— But let me fall silent once and for all. The realization that my letters make you sad rather than happy, makes me loathe them so much I almost tore up this letter while writing these last lines."[97] It is characteristic of Kleist's paradoxical relationship with Wilhelmine that he was unable to "fall silent once and for all," and instead drew attention to the fundamental peril they found themselves in by comparing himself to Tancred, the Christian hero from Torquato Tasso's epic *Jerusalem Delivered*. Tancred does not only "hurt" but mistakenly kills the heathen warrior Clorinda, whom he loves, in battle. And so writes

Kleist: "At times on this journey I have felt as though I were heading straight for my abyss—and only the thought of dragging you down with me, you, my good true innocent girl, you who have surrendered yourself to me so completely, expecting to find your happiness through me—Ah, Wilhelmine, [...] I have often struggled with myself over whether it is not my *duty* to separate you from one who is surely rushing toward the abyss!" He then adds, consolingly: "I do not deserve to be unhappy, and shall not remain so forever. [...] What are your feelings? Ask your heart. Do not deceive me, just as I have firmly resolved never to deceive you."[98] *These* are the two letters Kleist sent in May and July 1801 in order to prevent Wilhelmine from leaving him.

And just as Kleist's travels reflect his fear of emotional intimacy, his letters reflect his fear of loneliness. They speak of his desperation and, at the same time, attempt to dispel his self-doubt as well as the doubts of those he wished to bind to himself. In this double effort the letters exhaust themselves. Whoever reads them becomes all the more doubtful of Kleist, and Kleist was aware of this fact. He thus played with the images he imagined people had of him from afar, especially with that of a sick person, further increasing their doubts:

> I am so in love with the idea of planting a field that it simply must happen. Think of mine as a sick man's heart, and grant my wish as a small covetousness that, being after all quite harmless, might be permitted. But to be serious, when I think over the past year, when I consider my curious bitterness toward myself and everything else around me, I must almost believe I am really ill. You, for example, my dear, my best Ullrique, how could I so intensely love you and, often in the same moment, injure your most delicate feelings? O, forgive me! I have not behaved any the better toward myself. You once advised me in Paris that to give up drinking beer might make me more cheerful, and I was very sensitive to so purely physical an explanation of my sorrow—now I can laugh about it, and I think I am on the road to recovery.[99]

Thus writes Kleist to his sister. And in imagining Wilhelmine—Ulrike's neighbor in Frankfurt an der Oder—reading along with her, one can understand why she refused to follow Kleist to Switzerland and lost all hope for their future.

So it was not the beer that made Kleist unhappy. He rejected materialist explanations, common in anthropology at the turn of the 19th century. Today, psychoanalysts would diagnose him with borderline syndrome or narcissistic personality disorder: considering his suicide and the many threats of suicide leading up to it; the traumatic experience of loss during his childhood and adolescence; his chronic sense of emptiness; his disorganized manner of attachment; his oscillations between the idealization and debasement of himself and the people closest to him, which keep all of the projects in his life from maturing and prevent his success from stabilizing; the continual longing for grandiosity, compensating the lack of love and recognition during his adolescence; his own humiliation as well as the humiliation of his father, who fell out of favor with the King.[100] Warranted or unwarranted, one can only speculate about these things. Kleist's suffering, if one assumes his perspective, is born from an affliction typical of his time—a suffering rooted in the instability of the lives of aristocrats at the turn of the 19th century. Time and again he emphasizes his resistance to a return to Prussia—in the letter to his sister quoted above, for instance, where he writes, "it would be impossible for me to show myself to people who had nurtured such hopes for me, impossible to answer when they asked me how I had fulfilled them. I am not what people think I am, their expectations oppress me."[101] Kleist's 'pre-melancholic situation' was the consequence of the confinement he suffered within his, as well as Wilhelmine's, family, so firmly set in the aristocratic tradition he believed obsolete—a tradition he was only able to transcend internally, through the development of a bourgeois ethics. His longing had a "quiet, obscure, unseen existence."[102] His retreat to Switzerland as prescribed by Rousseau presented a way out for a man who rejected the goals of aristocratic society and the means it provided him for action, though he had not yet established his own.

Wilhelmine cannot be blamed for being unwilling—unlike Kleist—to live in a state of uncertainty. Such a willingness would have required a different attitude from her—a readiness to self-sacrifice that might have afforded Kleist some happiness. Later Wilhelmine writes to Krug that she refused to go to Switzerland with Kleist but still wanted "to keep her word and fully devote herself to him."[103] While there can be no talk of complete devotion, sacrificial gestures clearly played a significant role in their correspondence, most prominently in Kleist's depiction of a ship accident on the Rhine: "Each person, forgetting the others, clung to one of the beams, and I did so too, to save *myself*. Ah, there is nothing more disgusting than this fear of death. Life is the one possession that only has value when it is held lightly. [...] Whoever loves life excessively, he is already morally dead; for his highest vital power, namely his ability to sacrifice it, molders even as he cultivates it."[104] Kleist's letters to his cousin Marie in November 1811 echo this sentiment. In them he distinguishes Henriette Vogel from his sister Ulrike with regard to the "art of self-sacrifice, of giving oneself entirely for what one loves." And he "would never have exchanged" Marie for Henriette "if she had wanted nothing more than to live with me."[105] Kleist's suicide was merely the final expression of his lifelong suppression of the instinctual drive toward self-preservation—the final expression of the fact that he, in principle, conceived freedom as an act that necessarily violated that same self-preservation. Without the sacrifice of every sense of security, innovation is possible neither in life nor in art. Kleist developed this sense of radicalism—which came to guide his literary productions—'gradually,' as he endured the sorrows that came with his loss of orientation in 1802. Since Wilhelmine lacked this radicality, Kleist only became free when he left her. At Christmas 1801 he responded harshly to her hesitation toward his proposal to move to Switzerland. After waiting a year before putting his plan into action, he reacted cruelly when she finally refused to go with him. He waited months to write to her, and took his time before responding to her letter relaying news, in poignant words, about the death of her brother Carl, her severe illness, and her need for help. Answering coldly from Thun on May 20, he writes that, after having "not stinted on entreaties and clarifications" as to why she should join him in Switzerland "in a great many letters," and after her refusal, "little was to be expected in the way of success from still another letter." He then ends melodramatically: "Dear girl, write me no more, I have no other wish than very soon to die."[106]

"He loved back what had been in him before," goes Rilke's poem "Narcissus."[107] Might this line explain Kleist's cruel silence—a power trip of *fort-da*? Could he no longer perceive his faraway Wilhelmine—whom he only invoked phantasmally in letters—as a person but only as a doll to be loved or rejected according to whim?[108] A better explanation for Kleist's harshness might be his "destructive character": After having waited so long and struggled so painfully, in vain, to find common ground with Wilhelmine, he smashed everything to pieces—opening up new pathways by ridding of that which stood in his way of a free life. At no point in his life is Kleist an "etui-man" looking to make things comfortable.[109] It was better to make a painful break, though this break does not invalidate his attempt at love at the beginning of their affair. Kleist did deliver on his promise to never marry anyone else.[110] Today, a therapist would diagnose him with a fear of commitment. From where did it originate? Kleist's 'gender trouble'—his unsettled 'masculinity' indicated in his subsequent letters—may be founded in a latent homosexuality but must be equally considered in relation to the failure of his marriage project. What might have happened had Wilhelmine been less hesitant at the beginning of their relationship? If Kleist had found in her somebody passionately in love with him? In his stories and plays, Kleist frequently conceives female protagonists who—actively or passively—come to embody a radical aneconomy of sacrifice by either giving themselves up completely, like Katie, or devouring everything out of love, like Penthesilea, or remaining unwavering, like Alcmene. It is also significant that even unconditional, passionate love is doubted and put to the test by Kleist's male heroes.

Kleist's love for Wilhelmine did not lead to a mutual recognition between lovers but to further self-awareness. Wilhelmine accepted the post at the Lindow cloister near Ruppin and later found herself a husband who, though he was beneath her in social standing, was able to secure her a living befitting her station. Kleist, on the other hand, liberated himself from a situation he felt constrained him, a situation of melancholic 'includence' or 'remanence' that kept him from fully realizing himself; and in this liberation he found himself as someone who, if necessary, could part with the wrong in a clear cut. He quit his military career as well as his studies in order to fulfill his potential, and he went on to abandon his plan—modeled on Rousseau's *Emile*—to get married. The foundation of the bourgeois ideal of education—so firmly cast in his Happiness essay—began to show cracks. Kleist no longer desired to travel—humbly, virtuously, and modestly—on the "middle road." At least in his break-up letter to Wilhelmine—which evokes his "writing" as the possibility of an existence proper to him—Kleist once again thinks in aristocratic terms. He talks of "fame" and "ambition": "It is quite probable that I shall never return to my Fatherland. There is one word in the German language which you women as a rule fail to understand, and that is ambition. There is only one condition under which I would return, and that is when I can fulfill the expectations that I so foolishly aroused in people by so many boastful actions. This is possible, but not very likely. In short, either I return to my Fatherland a famous man, or not at all. This remains as decided once and for all as the very nature of my being."[111] The "nature" of his "being" is experimental, casuistic. From this point on there was, for Kleist, no lasting obligation to the aristocratic or bourgeois way of life. He was no longer interested in establishing a stable identity. Instead, he dedicated himself to the new project of literary writing—a project that dissolved everything stable into fluidity and allowed for experimentation with identities, including gendered ones. Throughout his engagement Kleist was caught in a kind of pre-existence, fashioning his life according to the literary models of the Enlightenment—even the plan to settle in Switzerland was modeled on Rousseau. It was only after this that Kleist's free, autonomous authorship developed.

From the perspective of the outsider, someone firmly rooted in a bourgeois or aristocratic existence, such a way of life may have seemed dubious, foolish, suspect, or desperate. Wilhelmine's husband epitomized the solid, bourgeois judgment of Kleist. In 1805/06 he invited Kleist to social events at his house in Königsberg in order to observe what he called the "unpredictable and erratic being" of someone with "an unfortunate constitution."[112] Thirty years after Kleist's death, Krug imagines meeting his wife's ex-fiancé again in Heaven, where Kleist no longer understands "why he had been such a fool on earth

Fig. 20 Wilhelm Traugott Krug, Louise von Zenge, and Wilhelmine Krug, née von Zenge

and had always tortured himself with such gloomy thoughts." Krug goes on to imagine countering Kleist's self-reproach—more smugly than consolingly—with the remark that not every poet had to "always be discontent with the world," he, himself, having had "known many a happy poet" on earth.[113] The judgment of Kleist by his aristocratic relatives is similarly direct. Primarily, one has to secure a living. If someone like Kleist feels "the urge to become a poet," writes his cousin and financial advisor Wilhelm von Pannwitz, he could always "satisfy" it "on the side"[114] of his military career or official position—just as the famous example in his family, Ewald von Kleist, did, one should add.

After their separation, and as soon as June 1802, Wilhelmine returned to Kleist the miniature he gave her. Kleist would later leave it behind, carelessly, in a dresser at his house in Thun, when he left Switzerland for good. Several decades later Wilhelmine's sister Louise discovered the miniature.[115] "There is a touch of mockery in it that I do not like, I wish he [the painter Peter Friedel] had portrayed me more *truthfully*," Kleist writes, expressing his discontent to Wilhelmine, on April 9, 1801, in his letter accompanying the miniature.[116] Unjustly so. Friedel captured the melancholic 'includence' of Kleist's engagement period while also rendering the mockery at such a constraint, which was what helped Kleist to call off his engagement. As any good portrait, one can see in it, retrospectively, what in the past determined the future of a person.

Fig. 21 Kleist portrait, commissioned for Wilhelmine before his departure to Paris (the only authentic Kleist image, miniature by Peter Friedel, 1801)

There is a second surviving portrait of Kleist, which was painted in 1807 during his confinement in Fort de Joux, presumably by a fellow inmate. It is deemed authentic but of inferior artistic quality. As in Friedel's portrait Kleist comes across more boyish than manly, and it is difficult to tell if his expression is mischievous or insecure.[117] But the most accurate account of Kleist's appearance seems to be the record kept by the commander at Fort de Joux: "Henry-Bernd-Guillaume Kleist, Natif de Francfort (Oder) Agé de 28 Ans, Taille

Fig. 22
Kleist portrait during his confinement, Fort de Joux, March 1807

de 5 pieds trois pouces, Cheveux et Sourcils Chatains, Yeux Bleux, Nez petit, Bouche moyenne, Menton Rond, Visage Ovale."[118] Five Paris feet, three Paris inches—or five feet and seven inches. Brown hair and eyebrows, blue eyes, small nose, average-sized mouth, round chin, and oval face.

CHAPTER V

"I Felt as Though I Were Entering on a New Life"

Kleist's Travels, 1800–1802: Würzburg—Paris—Thun

"In a love affair, most people seek an eternal homeland. Others, but very few, eternal voyaging. The latter are melancholics, who believe that contact with Mother Earth is to be shunned. They seek the person who will keep the homeland's sadness far away from them. To that person they remain faithful. The medieval complexion-books understood the yearning of this human type for long journeys."[1] In Walter Benjamin's "Old Map," he writes about himself, not Kleist; though, as melancholics, the two are kindred spirits. There is thus a constellation written into Benjamin's thought-image which, in Kleist's case, both separates and unites loving and traveling. In both his love and his travels, Kleist sought a homeland he had never been to. He remained faithful to Wilhelmine as long as she, in her letters, kept the sadness of his former homeland far away from him. And when she tried to bring him back to his past—instead of setting off with him into the unknown—he left her. Kleist did not want his fatherland—"our melancholy Mark of Brandenburg"—anymore.[2] His travels did not, however, help him to escape his melancholia, that combination of longing and sorrow. While the homesick person knows the object of his desire, Kleist, in his yearning to travel, wanted to leave Frankfurt an der Oder in the late summer of 1800 without knowing where to go. His urge to travel was a longing for indeterminateness, moving him from one place to the next, as no place could satisfy him.

Let us take another look at his travels, but this time independent of his relationship with Wilhelmine. Did Kleist not merely share the restlessness of his contemporaries in a time of unrest? The Romantics—Wilhelm Wackenroder, Ludwig Tieck, Novalis, Adelbert von Chamisso, etc.—were always traveling, and so are the protagonists of Romantic literature—Lovell, Sternbald, Ofterdingen, Godwi, Fortunat, Schlemihl, and 'Good-for-Nothing.' Kleist, I argue, traveled as a Romantic; he embarked on a never-ending journey—at least in principle—on a quest for an indeterminate and unlocatable cure. This reading helps explain the aimlessness of his first long journey, whose destination, Würzburg, seems rather arbitrary, and whose success seems more than questionable. Kleist's actual destination was Vienna; Würzburg was only an alternative destination to Strasbourg. Thus, the designation given to Kleist's supposedly mysterious and legendary 'Würzburg journey' is problematic. Nevertheless, for decades Kleist

© WILHELM FINK VERLAG, 2021 | DOI:10.30965/9783846765746_006

Fig. 23 Robert Gernhardt, *Wanderlust*

scholars have—as tirelessly as unsuccessfully—sought to give Kleist's wanderlust direction and to ground his motivations not in the mentality typical of the Romantic era, but in a variety of more socially commensurable rationales. Yet for Kleist, himself, traveling was about the unspeakable—an indeterminate longing.[3] His scholars thus fall into his trap; as a Romantic nomad writing home from foreign places, Kleist reckoned with such philistines eager to turn a secret into a solvable riddle. His travel letters therefore posit a paradoxical mix of truth and disguise—of *dissimulatio* and *simulatio*. On the one hand, they hide the fact that his longing to travel was a *mysterium* even to himself—a secret beyond the limit of what can be said. On the other hand, they mislead the reader into believing that his motives are a mere *secretum*—a secret that has to be concealed for now but can later be told.[4]

The true secret of the Würzburg journey may be that there is no secret at all. It has no substance, is "no longer a content held within a form of interiority."[5] Kleist handled the secret as a form of pure exteriority—a play on the forms of secret-keeping and degrees of divulgence. "[A] journey without an explained purpose" could "cause concern to sympathetic friends," writes Kleist to his sister Ulrike on August 14, 1800. As Kleist reminds her, "if I hold back the truth, I have told no lies; and when I explain that the happiness, the honor, and perhaps the life of a human being might be saved by this journey, there is every reason to believe it." "[T]he life of a human being"—surely Kleist is referring to himself here, but how was his journey to save him? The answer is precisely what is kept secret, and it can only be so if his sister is willing to help him:

> In all this I count not only on your unbreachable discretion (for the seemingly adventurous aspects of my journey must remain concealed, and the world must learn no more than that I am in Berlin, on business with Struensee, which is in part true), but I count as well on your unshakable trust in my integrity, so that your faith in me will not waver even in the face of the most striking contradictions.[6]

Without Ulrike, Kleist's game of mystification would not have succeeded. What Kleist asks of his sister is less noble discretion than complicity in his simulation—that he left Frankfurt an der Oder to apply for an official position in Berlin and meet the demands of his, as well as Wilhelmine von Zenge's, family. Simulation in the face of the family is what Kleist demands of his fiancée too, but he gives her a privilege over Ulrike: The latter will only "know where I *am*, but you, my beloved girl, will always know where I *am going to be*."[7] Kleist creates two confidants of varying degrees who are in on a game with forms of secrecy whose substance remains opaque in spite of its clear social function: It binds Ulrike and Wilhelmine to Kleist, creating a sense of solidarity and intimacy, exciting their curiosity for withheld information and obliging them to read Kleist's letters with great care. Kleist instructs his sister Ulrike to engage in this play of exteriority without looking for interiority: "Leave off all questions, deductions and conjectures. They *must* come to nought, since you cannot *completely* understand me. Rely on what I tell you directly. It is true to the letter."[8]

"[T]rue to the letter"—not just "seemingly" "true"—is that Kleist's journey has something of the "adventurous," as he writes to his sister. This may point to the realm of the imaginary—to Kleist's tendency to fictionalize his life, as we shall later see. More importantly, according to a dictionary of Kleist's time, 'the adventurous' is linked to the notion of chance. According to Johann Christoph

Adelung's 1774 dictionary, an adventure is "a kind of coincidence, in which chance plays a greater role than forethought." It is etymologically derived from "Lat. *Adventus* or from *Eventus*."[9] Thus, the adventure stands in stark contrast to the idea of a life plan; it refers to sudden, chance events. But the adventure is not merely an "exemplary manifestation of chance"; for the adventurer it also signifies a "particular form of behavior when confronted with chance events" that takes into account the "unpredictability and contingency of any event."[10] According to German sociologist Georg Simmel, for the adventurer there is no regard for "continuity with life," or even any need to disregard it, because we know from the beginning that we have to do with something alien, untouchable, out of the ordinary."[11] Applied to Kleist's biography, this definition shows his departure from Frankfurt in the summer of 1800 as the beginning of his life as adventure. While pretending for his family that he was still 'in the ordinary,' he had already been experimenting in life '*out of* the ordinary.' During and through his journeys to Würzburg, Paris, and Thun, he acquired an awareness of contingency that would affect his thinking, his actions, and his writing. Kleist let himself be carried away; he made decisions in the spur of the moment, understanding chance as an opportunity. And when he gave an account of his life in his letters, he joined the episodic and the particular in loose association. All the while his mood swung as his awareness of the principle of contingency led to both moments of resignation and moments of hope—the hope that even the unexpected may not be impossible: a life as a science communicator in Paris, an estate owner in Switzerland, a writer surpassing even William Shakespeare and Johann Wolfgang Goethe, etc.

Kleist's 'road movie' probably followed no script. Or, better, it followed ever-changing plans and purposes, various immediate goals, instead of the one great distant goal. Even Kleist's accomplices Ulrike and Wilhelmine would not have approved of such capriciousness, which is why he made them believe that he was merely keeping his masterplan secret. To do so, he employed an old familiar technique of camouflage, obscuring his situation by heightening its complexity. He gave heterogeneous, incommensurable, and often contradictory suggestions about the possible objectives of his travels. It is for this reason that none of the numerous speculations on the motives for Kleist's Würzburg journey are entirely convincing. They can be classified into two categories: those who believe Kleist was seeking a medical procedure and those who believe he was trying to figure out his career path. The only thing Kleist scholars seem to be able to agree on is the *tertium comparationis* of all speculations: that the Würzburg journey served to remove an obstacle to Kleist and Wilhelmine's marriage. This is what Kleist's letter to Wilhelmine of August 21, 1800, suggests: The purpose of his journey is "worthy" and "*Our happiness* lies at the heart of it and, what is a main thing, *nothing can be lost* but *everything won*."[12] Yet why is it, then, that Brockes, his traveling companion, allegedly had "the same objective" as Kleist?[13] The 'obstacle' to Brockes' marriage was that Cäcilie von Ziegesar, the lady he loved, had just lost her husband and was prevented from remarrying by a provision of his will. Brockes had good reasons to distract himself from his gloomy thoughts on a journey. With regard to Cäcilie, however, he had nothing to gain from this journey. Brockes' assurance that there was a great "likelihood of a happy outcome" to his journey with Kleist and that "there is no danger in it, in any respect," can thus only refer to Kleist, who only passed on his friend's assertion to comfort Wilhelmine.[14] Less reassuring is a letter from Würzburg a few weeks later in which Kleist tells Wilhelmine she owes him "*eternal, heartfelt, tender thankfulness*" as a prize for the fact that he had left her only "to purchase [her] happiness at incredible cost to himself," indeed had "*risked his life*."[15] Who or what could have threatened Kleist's life? A medical procedure in Würzburg? The French soldiers occupying Würzburg? Nothing but dazzling ambiguity, rhetoric of hyperbole without substance? Whatever the answer is, Kleist played one grand game of cat-and-mouse, full of contradictions, and after his return from Würzburg there was but one thing for certain: The marriage with Wilhelmine still seemed impossible, and the secret of the Würzburg journey was never mentioned again in Kleist's letters. The mystery thus remains unsolved, depriving Kleist scholars of any peace. Let us for now review their major theses about Kleist's career plans.

Kleist left Frankfurt an der Oder hastily on August 14, 1800, this much is for certain, and he stayed in Berlin to pay a visit the following day to Carl August von Struensee, the Prussian minister of state since 1792, in charge of excise, customs, commerce, and manufacturing. Struensee, however, was out of town and would not return to Berlin until August 26. In the meantime Kleist visited Wilhelmine's brother Carl, consulted with the lawyer Johann Christian Friedrich Benecke about his sister Wilhelmine's divorce, went to a bookstore to buy Friedrich Schiller's *Wallenstein* for his fiancée, visited an exhibition of Johann Adam Breysig's *Panorama of Rome* (*Panorama der Stadt Rom*), and then traveled to Pasewalk to seek out a companion for his travel: Ludwig von Brockes, a friend he knew from his journey to the island of Rügen with Ulrike in the early summer of 1800. "I have confided completely in him, and he respected my intentions as soon as he heard them," Kleist writes to his fiancée on August 21. He continues: "I have brooded a long, long time on the matter [...], and so I am heading toward my goal almost with confidence. But before that I will certainly meet with *Struensee* to secure an alternative to fall back on."[16] These remarks suggest that the purpose of Kleist's journey was not defined by Struensee but had already been decided on before their meeting, which was scheduled for the morning of Kleist's departure from Berlin, August 28, and therefore could have only been brief, if it took place at all.[17] If it did take place, we can assume Kleist asked Struensee about the prospects of a position in the Prussian civil service and the deadline by which he had to make a decision. This would at least explain why Kleist so desperately wanted to return from Würzburg to Berlin before November 1, exactly on the date that he asked Struensee "most humbly for permission to attend the sessions of the Prussian Technical Commission" to see if he "may dare to devote [himself] to the study of commerce and manufacturing."[18] With this letter Kleist secured for himself, as he had announced earlier, "an alternative to fall back on." From this we can conclude, on the one hand, that Kleist's travel plan, which he had spent a "long, long time" conceiving, was probably not successful; on the other hand, however, it means that Kleist could have only exchanged his preferred plan with the alternative one if the former equally allowed him to figure out what career to pursue. Kleist's medical treatment in Würzburg—successful or not—would not have been equal to a career in the Prussian civil service, and thus speaks against this explanation of the Würzburg journey. Kleist's talk of an "alternative to fall back on" also puts into question speculations that he was acting on behalf of the government.

In recent years a thesis supported most notably by Eberhard Siebert has become particularly prominent. It suggests that Kleist spied on foreign industries for the Prussian government in order to promote himself for a position in the Technical Commission in Struensee's department, which was in charge of industrial espionage.[19] After Kleist's death his sister Ulrike allegedly claimed the Würzburg journey was "political in nature."[20] Kleist an agent on His Majesty's secret service? What speaks in favor of this thesis is the fact that Prussia was running behind the leading national economies of England and France and was, thus, reliant on spying on their technological advances. What also speaks in favor of this argument is that Kleist's alternative destinations—Vienna, Strasbourg, and Würzburg—were all equipped with factories that had developed new processes for chemical dyeing and bleaching. In the factory of Georg Pickel in Würzburg, Kleist could have spied on the production of a color called *Pickelgrün* to benefit the Prussian textile industry. Pickel was a professor at the University of Würzburg, and the practice sessions for his lectures were held at the laboratory of the Julius-Hospice, which Kleist visited. Did Kleist, then, "*risk*[] *his life*"—as he wrote to Wilhelmine—as a spy? Is this the reason Kleist and Brockes used the pseudonyms Klingstedt and Bernhoff during their journey? Does Struensee's assurance of an "alternative to fall back on" therefore not mean an alternative career, but rather the promise to protect and rescue the secret agent were he to be discovered? That seems hardly likely.

That the Prussian secret service should impart a spy mission to a former soldier and university drop-out—who knew nothing about the production of paint, let alone about being a secret agent—merely on the basis of his noble name, and allow him to freely choose his companion Brockes, who was equally inexperienced, seems as unlikely today as it must have been at the turn of the 19th century. Besides, not many secret agents would repeatedly reference their journey's secret objective in their letters. If it was not for a passage in Kleist's letter to his sister Ulrike of November 25, 1800, nobody would have ever conceived of the idea of him serving as a spy:

> The journey was the one part I could have enjoyed, while I was still not too precisely informed about it. But it is mainly a matter of wile and guile, and for these I have little expertise. The foreign factory owners do not invite knowledgeable people into the privacy of their workshops. The only way, then, is by wheedling, hypocrisy; in short, deceit—Yes, they have already instructed me in this art of deception—no, my darling Ulrike, it is not for me.[21]

"The journey"? Which one? Is Kleist referring to his Würzburg journey? If so, he would have already been trained in the art of espionage before his meeting with Struensee on August 28, 1800. By whom, though, we do not know. It is worth noting that, in his letter to Ulrike, Kleist could not have referred to what he had learned in the Technical Commission sessions. To his embarrassment, after his return from Würzburg, he had missed the first session on November 12, though he did make it to the second session on December 3, 1800. But would a candidate like Kleist need to sit in on a session to know that a position at the Technical Commission would involve, on the one hand, going on delightful journeys and, on the other hand, working as a spy? Would the young Kleist, given his high moral standards, have been capable of allowing himself involvement with the "art of deception," only to later change his mind due to his real-life experience as a spy in Würzburg? Kleist did, after all, assert to Wilhelmine regarding the intentions of his Würzburg journey that "any principled person *must*" respect them, "once he comprehends them."[22] We can assume, then, that Kleist—notoriously unwilling to take up an official position—came up with the argument about espionage being unethical the very moment a post in Struensee's department was about to become a reality and his family would have expected him to accept it.

What, then—if not industrial espionage—could have been the professional purpose of Kleist's journey? Given that all of Kleist's changing destinations—Vienna, Strasbourg, and Würzburg—were university towns, and given that he asked Ulrike in his letter of August 14, 1800, to send him his "paper on the Kantean philosophy" as well as "the cultural history,"[23] Ulrich Gall suggests that Kleist—far from his education at the Viadrina that was meant to prepare him for a practical career—was intending to write his doctoral or habilitation thesis at a different university.[24] After all, Kleist gives an obscure hint to Wilhelmine in his 'birthday letter' of October 10 from Würzburg, saying that their "time of trial" will go on. "In five years," however, writes Kleist, "I hope, the work will be done."[25] Did Kleist find a dissertation or habilitation committee in Würzburg and arrange to hand in his thesis at a deadline remarkably late for the university system of that time? Why would he have chosen the faraway Würzburg—undistinguished, threatened by the French, and on top of that Catholic—and not Göttingen if he wanted to continue his studies outside of Prussia? In March 1799, after his general studies at the Viadrina, Kleist had announced a transfer to the prestigious university in Göttingen.[26] Why would he have kept his plans for further academic qualifications secret from his and his fiancée's family? After all, following his return from Würzburg, he admits to Wilhelmine in his letter of November 13, 1800, that he is "not fitted for an official post," that if he were holding a position, he "would rush, rush to have" his duties "out of the way" so he could "turn once more to [his] beloved studies." In the same letter he continues that for his "future the entire field of writing would stand open" to him, that he could go to Paris "to transplant the newest philosophy in that knowledge-hungry land."[27] A week earlier Gottlob Johann Christian Kunth, director of the Technical Commission, writes to his minister Struensee that, when Kleist applied for a position with him in the civil service, he gave him the advice to "enroll at any university and qualify as a professor." He also thinks nothing of Kleist's desire to sit in on sessions of the "Technical Commission" in order to "assess his suitability for manufacturing and commerce affairs himself," because it would hardly benefit, in particular, somebody like Kleist "who, given his age, has no time to lose," and would provide him with "little opportunity for a general preparation for the civil service and definitely with no prospect of a promotion."[28] If at that time Kleist had an offer in his pocket to write a habilitation thesis at Würzburg University, he would have simply had to inform his family of Kunth's advice to evade a ministerial post in the Prussian government. Instead, he struggled for months sitting in on the sessions of the Technical Commission—a privilege he owed to a special permission from Struensee—only to end up fleeing from any prospect of an official position. He headed to Paris in the spring of 1801 calling on Kunth's advice of November 1800, despite the fact that his Kant crisis had put an end to his desire for an academic career.[29]

Even more spectacular, yet equally questionable, is a third hypothesis on Kleist's professional motives for the Würzburg journey. According to Dirk Grathoff, Kleist was looking to contact a Masonic lodge outside of Prussia in order to secure a scholarship for his philosophical education, possibly under the promise of a *quid pro quo*—an academic paper in defense of the Freemasons. Accordingly, Kleist was to refute the conspiracy theory which alleged that the German Illuminati in Paris provoked the French Revolution.[30] It is more likely, however, that he simply wanted to give his sponsors his paper on Immanuel Kant and the cultural history as references for his qualifications. Had Kleist been seeking membership with the Freemasons, he would have had to leave Prussia, since—thanks to the edict of October 20, 1798—becoming a Freemason was prohibited for all men under the age of twenty-five. Grathoff's thesis would thus work to account for the strict secrecy of the Würzburg journey, and for why Kleist and Brockes enrolled under false names at the University of Leipzig, were it not based on vague assumptions and conjectures. Given how popular Freemasonry was in Germany at the time, the fact that there were many Freemasons among Kleist's friends and acquaintances—the Frankfurt professors Madihn and Wünsch, his brother-in-law Pannwitz, his financial guardian Dames, and Minister Struensee—is of little significance. Kleist's travel companion Brockes appears to be on record as a member of a lodge in Göttingen in 1802. He was ten years older than Kleist and, thus, did not have to leave Prussia in 1800 to join the Freemasons, if he had not already been one at the time of the Würzburg journey. If Brockes' journey had "the same objective" as Kleist's, was he planning to vouch for Kleist in becoming a member of a lodge?[31] Grathoff further suggests that Lord Hugh Elliot, the British ambassador, whom Kleist and Brockes met in Leipzig, was a Freemason and convinced them not to go to Vienna, apparently based on information from his brother Sir Gilbert Earl of Minto, who served as envoy extraordinary in Vienna and knew about the difficult situation of the Freemasons in Austria. In Catholic Austria all Masonic lodges were shut down in 1794. Though it is hard to believe that Kleist and Brockes would have first learned this fact from Elliot. And why would Elliot have sent Kleist and Brockes to Würzburg (instead of Vienna), a city without a Masonic lodge? Grathoff refers to records of newcomers in two special issues of the *Würzburg Intelligence Paper* (*Extrablatt des Würzburger Intelligenzblattes*), according to which the famous physician and Freemason Christoph Wilhelm Hufeland stayed in Würzburg some time at the end of September or beginning of October, as did Gustav Count von Schlabrendorf from Paris in mid-October. Schlabrendorf was a member of the Leipzig lodge, Grathoff argues, and Elliot probably established a connection for Kleist and Brockes with him. Are we then to believe that Hufeland and Schlabrendorf—two prominent Freemasons—traveled to the French-occupied Würzburg expressly to commission a young and inexperienced student to write a politically charged paper in defense of the Freemasons? This scenario is far from plausible.[32] Moreover, no evidence exists in support of a meeting between Kleist and Hufeland or Schlabrendorf, nor is there any suggesting that Kleist ever became a member of the Freemasons after his Würzburg journey.

Meanwhile, the speculations on the medical motives of Kleist's Würzburg journey demonstrate how imaginative German Studies can be—and how imprudent it was of Kleist to ask his sister Ulrike to pay his debt to Brockes after the Würzburg journey. Because, despite promising that he would repay her in "one year"—when he would be "of age" and his financial guardianship would be over—he concludes his letter of request urging her that her support "will do him good after suffering for twenty-four years."[33] The economic context—Kleist's reference to his financial dependence—is hard to miss; and yet his biographers, from the 19th century to the present day, would rather suspect Kleist was impotent than insolvent: that in his Würzburg journey he sought remedy in a medical procedure for a congenital physical ailment in order to be fit for matrimony. After all, Kleist and Brockes boarded with the city surgeon Joseph Wirth, who, when accused of missing billeting orders for his two guests, professed to the Würzburg town council that one of the two students from Leipzig "was seriously ill."[34] This ill student is taken to refer to Kleist, as he himself relates that Brockes would always leave their quarters discreetly to go for a walk "[w]hile the doctor was visiting."[35] An unlicensed surgeon, such as Wirth, could be consulted to perform minor surgeries that established university doctors would decline, such as the simple treatment of phimosis, which is what Hans-Jürgen Schrader and Hans Dieter Zimmermann argue Wirth treated Kleist for.[36] Accordingly, this would explain the cheerfulness in Kleist's 'birthday letter' of October 10, 1800, in which he assures Wilhelmine—who had, in Frankfurt, laid out for him her idea of a happy marriage—that it "pained" him to think that he "could not fulfill [her] most sacred desires, but now, now—yet it need not be said." Thereafter Kleist invokes the image of Wilhelmine as the mother of three children, and he concludes by saying: "Good night, Wilhelmine, my betrothed, some day my wife, some day the *mother* of my children!"[37] Such a tonal upswing may allure us into thinking Kleist is now willing and able to procreate. However, one small link is still missing to complete the phimosis hypothesis: Can impotence be caused by phimosis? Now things get complicated: Schrader assumes Kleist's birthday was not on October 10 but—in accordance with the entry in the church register—on October 18. Kleist's Würzburg letter of October 10, in which he explicitly writes, "Yes, today is my birthday,"[38] supposedly refers—figuratively, as is common in the Pietist tradition—to the date of his "new birth," on which his 'twenty-four years of suffering' came to an end, and to "the beginning of the life that actually counted," the "overcoming of the old Adam through the new birth," which, in turn, "is often symbolized as a 'circumcision' or 'taking away of the foreskin' in the Pietist imagery (apparently based on biblical passages, such as Jer. 4:4 or Rom. 2:25–29)."[39] Kleist's sympathetic depiction of a young man at the Julius-Hospice who became addicted to masturbating further fueled the phimosis hypothesis because—as Max Morris argued as early as 1899—it served Kleist as a mirror image of the final stage of his own suffering.[40] According to the medical understanding of the time, phimosis led to itching, itching to masturbation, and masturbation to imagined or real impotence. However, it should be said that the doctors among Kleist scholars argue that the minor obstacle to his marriage was probably not cured by the surgeon Wirth, and indeed his marriage to Wilhelmine was never consummated. Kleist's works supposedly reflect this. On the one hand, many of his father characters are not the biological begetters of their children: Jupiter foists Heracles to Amphitryon, Piachi adopts the foundling, and Theobald Friedeborn has an illegitimate daughter, Katie. On the other hand, so the argument goes, Kleist's works contain depictions of radical sensuality. One is reminded of Penthesilea's and the Amazons' uninhibited sexuality, the rape of the Marquise of O—, the night Alcmene unknowingly spends with Jupiter, or Elvire's sensual yet painful encounters with Colino and Nicolo. It comes as no surprise, then, that Günter Blöcker concludes, in his analysis of Kleist's motif of the "literary cuckold," that Kleist employs it to "poetically compensate for the impotence of his own body."[41] It would be surprising, though, if Kleist had indeed traveled across half of Germany for such a quick and minor surgery, waiting weeks for the procedure to be performed in Würzburg. It would, of course, be understandable that he did not want to have a phimosis surgery performed in Frankfurt an der Oder or Berlin for reasons of discretion, but discretion does not warrant such a long journey to Würzburg. It would have been easy for Kleist to find an unlicensed surgeon like Wirth at his stopovers in Leipzig or Dresden. But perhaps Kleist's condition was not physical. And perhaps it required a lengthy, intensive treatment. So some speculate.

Maybe the treatment was mesmeric in nature, as Uffe Hansen suggests. Hansen establishes that Hugh Elliot met Franz Anton Mesmer as early as in the 1770s, during his time as minister plenipotentiary in Munich, and thereafter became a follower of the theory of animal magnetism. Elliot may have advised Kleist not to travel to Vienna, as the general appeal of the theory of animal magnetism was waning after Mesmer's practice had been shut in 1793, and to instead consult mesmerists in Strasbourg or Würzburg. Moreover, Hansen presumes that the doctors Kleist mentioned at the Julius-Hospice, Karl Kasper Seibold and Hermann Joseph Brünninghausen, had non-local mesmerists perform treatments in Würzburg to test the method. Perhaps they were tested even on Kleist, not at the Julius-Hospice, but at his quarters by prominent Frankfurt doctor and mesmerist Matthias Wilhelm de Neufville, who may have stayed in Würzburg in the early summer of 1800. What ailment Kleist supposedly suffered from, Hansen does not address, which makes his outspoken claim to have found "the key to the mystery of the Würzburg journey"—based on a few questionable clues—all the more disconcerting.[42] He derives his mesmerism hypothesis primarily from Kleist's allegedly anagrammatic wordplay with the name Wilhelm de Neufville in his story "The Betrothal in Santo Domingo." Guillaume de Villeneuve is the name of the benevolent plantation owner in Port-au-Prince, who, shamefully, gets killed by the ferocious Congo Hoango at the beginning of the story. It is in Villeneuve's house, too, that the sudden transformation of the mestiza Toni takes place—from an ally of Congo Hoango to the lover of the white refugee Gustav—the cause of which Hansen reads as the influence of unconscious, somnambulistic processes. Katharine Weder's recent, detailed study on Kleist's familiarity with the phenomenon of somnambulism and its poetization—apparent especially in his plays *Katie of Heilbronn* (*Das Käthchen von Heilbronn*) and *Prince Frederick of Homburg* (*Prinz Friedrich von Homburg*)—rejects Hansen's assumption of Kleist's long-term mesmeric treatment in Würzburg and instead reasserts some verifiable facts, namely that it was not until the fall and winter of 1807/08 that Kleist became acquainted with the theory of mesmerism through the lectures of Gotthilf Heinrich Schubert in Dresden.[43] It is thus hardly plausible that Kleist, as Hansen claims, "not only underwent a successful treatment, but also learned a new anthropology" from theory and practical experience: the demonstration of a "*different* state of mind" qua somnambulism, the unfolding of the latent potential of one's higher possibilities, unconscious to one's normal self.[44] Apart from the mesmerism hypothesis, I do agree—and will later show—that, in his travels after 1800, Kleist hoped for such epiphanic moments to transgress the Enlightenment imperative for an arduous progression through self-cultivation.

The different readings of the Würzburg journey are entertaining, but none is academically sound. And it does not help to suppose a combination of motives rather than the main one Kleist repeatedly alludes to in his letters of August 1800.[45] As stated at the beginning of this chapter, Kleist merely intends to create confusion through his letters so that he might render his situation obscure, and hide the fact that after his departure from Frankfurt an der Oder he actually embarked on a journey into the indeterminate, the indefinite. His is a journey that blends experience and hope with adventurous events and their fictional idealization. It is a journey in which the particular and episodic, which will become sources for his later literary work, is more important than the futile quest for 'the main purpose.' Let us therefore follow Kleist's description of his travel experiences and focus on the seemingly small details along the way rather than the alleged designation and purpose of the whole.

To begin, let us bring to mind the main stops of Kleist's itinerary from the summer of 1800 to the spring of 1802: In August 1800 Kleist leaves Frankfurt an der Oder, stays in Berlin at first, picks up his travel companion Ludwig von Brockes in Coblentz near Pasewalk, returns to Berlin again, presumably to talk to Minister Struensee, then sets out to Vienna with Brockes at the end of August. The two enroll at the University of Leipzig under false names as Klingstedt and Bernhoff and, at the beginning of September, stay in Dresden for a short time, where they meet Lord Elliot, the British ambassador, who causes them to change their itinerary. They then travel via Wittenberg, Freiberg, Zwickau, Bayreuth, and Ebrach to Würzburg, where they stay for two months. At the end of October, they return to Berlin via Meiningen, Naumburg, Halle, and Potsdam. In Berlin Kleist struggles, preparing for a civil service position in the Technical Commission until the spring of 1801, only to vanish to Paris with his sister Ulrike in mid-April, allegedly to continue his studies of the natural sciences. Their first major stopover is Dresden, where the two stay until mid-May, taking excursions through the Saxon and Bohemian countryside, to Moritzburg, Pillnitz, Tharandt, and Freiberg, to Teplitz, Lobositz, and Aussig. They then continue to Strasbourg via Leipzig, Halle, Halberstadt, Wernigerode, Ilsenburg, Goslar, Göttingen, Kassel, Butzbach, Rödelheim, Frankfurt am Main, Mainz, Mannheim, Heidelberg, and Durlach. At the end of June, the two siblings arrive in Paris, accompanied by their coachman. The initial plan was to stay for a year, but at the end of November, they both leave Paris in the direction of Frankfurt am Main, where they part ways. Ulrike returns home to Prussia, while Kleist's path leads him via Darmstadt, Heidelberg, and Karlsruhe to Basel. He is accompanied by the painter Friedrich Lose and stays in Basel for two weeks in December 1801. Lose and Kleist get into an argument, Kleist continues his journey to Bern, where he meets Heinrich Zschokke, Christoph Martin Wieland's son Ludwig, and the latter's brother-in-law Heinrich Geßner. He looks around for a manor and, at the beginning of February, arrives in Thun, where he stays until the summer of 1802. On May 20 he writes his harsh break-up letter to Wilhelmine from Thun.

This overview marks the stops and turns of the prominent travel routes intellectuals took at the turn of the 19th century: Romantic hikes through the Central German Uplands, the journey to post-revolutionary Paris or to the Helvetic Republic. Other destinations are missing: the educational journey to Italy, a trip to London, the metropolis of progress. Original genre pictures or descriptions of the landscape are hard to obtain from Kleist's travel letters, as many of his experiences are predetermined by the literature he reads. Kleist is on an expedition, though the unknown that he seeks to discover and explore in his movement does not lie in the external territory but the internal—the realm of possibilities hidden inside himself. Thus, his travel letters constitute a private archive: They are a fragmentary copy, so to speak, of his "magazine of ideas," the original of which Kleist scholars are still eagerly waiting to discover. With it Kleist prepares himself "for the field of writing," as he notes to Wilhelmine from Würzburg on November 18, 1800.[46] In this, perhaps only imaginary, magazine—and again in his travel letters—he gathers what he sees, experiences, and reads, not for sentimental reasons but for a practical potential. He is only interested in those of his experiences which can be used productively. Thus, Kleist 'reads' landscapes like Goethe does books, whose credo is: "As for the rest, I hate everything that merely instructs me without increasing or directly rousing my activity."[47] Kleist would likely agree with Goethe on this. He only describes what affects him and what is supposed to affect the letters' recipients. But his landscapes, cities, and people are not rendered with any kind of systematic approach. Kleist is not a scholarly observer who conducts regional studies following well-organized schemes—such as the sequence of topography, physical geography, and cultural geography—distinguishing them neatly from private experiences and reflections, as did the great travel writers of the first half of the 19th century, Alexander von Humboldt and Adelbert von Chamisso. Kleist's travel letters bring together landscape and city sketches, character portraits and philosophical speculations, political analyses and private confessions. As both a writer and traveler, Kleist seems to abandon himself to the principle of contingency. Kleist prefers to collect moments in which his preconceived notions and actual experiences are made indistinguishable.[48]

An example of this practice can be found at the outset of his journey, in Coblentz near Pasewalk, when Kleist joins his travel companion Brockes at the manor of Count von Eickstedt in August 1800. The Count is not at home, but Kleist still comes "to know him in his own house, even before setting eyes on him. Shaded rooms, beautifully furnished, much silver, still more crosses of St. John, portraits of the great: field marshals, counts, ministers, dukes, and he in the middle—life-size, in scarlet cape, on either breast the star of rank, the ribbon across his entire chest, in each corner of the frame a cross of the Knights of St. John." Just like the interior, Kleist renders the garden and estate in a mottled list: "many dairy houses, horses, people, cows, well-built and efficient barns, but never a one without that cross of St. John." Kleist follows this with four dashes: "– – – – We can know a snail by its shell, I cried, and just as surely I know the man who inhabits this place. [...] I found frugality and generosity, vainglory and abstemiousness, wisdom and folly all combined in a single person, for such was the Count von Eickstedt."[49] Barely out of the confines of Frankfurt an der Oder, Kleist develops a mordant sarcasm, proving how uncomfortable the comforts of Prussia have become to him. The crux of his account lies in what he leaves out: that the inward points of the cross of St. John originally referred to the Christian virtues of the Knights of St. John—prudence, justice, fortitude, and temperance. Count von Eickstedt's crosses, however, are little more than hollow ornaments, vain emblems of order and prosperity. Signifier and signified no longer correspond; the tradition has been emptied out. Yet Kleist's experience of the profaned cross of St. John gives way to a new symbol that is able to restore a sense of coherence, not only with regard to Count von Eickstedt's estate but to Prussia: the image of the snail shell. Mollusks move slowly and, when in danger, retreat inside their shells. For Kleist the snail is a symbol of Prussia's overly cautious maneuvers against the all-powerful Napoleon, which Kleist will continue to denounce even ten years later in the *Berlin Evening Paper*.

Kleist may have been tired of studying and disinterested in obtaining an official post, though his travels—his flights from Prussia in the summer of 1800 and in the spring of 1801—were not motivated by merely private reasons, but by his lack of social attachments and trust in the state. In his "scanty travel accounts," he had to camouflage this detachment with polite compliments to the Count von Eickstedt, which served to veil his sarcasm, or with geomorphological conjectures about and excuses for the national character of the Brandenburg people: "There is grain growing in sand, pines growing in sand, miserable villages, towns as though swept into a heap with a broom. All around the walls everything is so clean and tidy, you would often look in vain for so much as a ball of dust! It seems this entire northern stretch of Germany had been intended by nature to remain forever and always at the bottom of the sea, and that the sea itself had withdrawn so far only by a kind of mistake, as it were, thus forming a stretch of ground originally intended rather for whales and herrings than for people."[50] The situation is different when Kleist writes about Saxony. There, the people are "warm and friendly, most of them handsomely made, especially the girls. The *enclosure* of mountain life seems generally to affect the *emotions*, and there one finds many philosophers of sentiment, and of philanthropic attitude, and devotees of the arts, especially of music. The *spaciousness* of flat country rather stimulates the intellect, and there one finds the thinkers and polymaths. I would like to have been born where the valleys were not too steep, and the lands not too low-lying."[51] While such a conjunction of geomorphology and psychology may not stand the test of an empirical survey, and while Kleist's praise of the people of Saxony may be a cliché, what is significant about these marginal comments is that Kleist defines a homeland in terms of social attachment and emotional connection. Hence, one understands why Kleist did not want to travel on his own and—in his search for a homeland to which he had never been—relied on the company of a "*wise, older* friend,"[52] that is, a travel companion who shared with him the ideal of social attachment and knew how to put it into practice. Unlike Count von Eickstedt, Ludwig von Brockes would have truly deserved to wear the cross of St. John due to his knightliness, judging from Kleist's portrait of him in his letter to Wilhelmine of January 31, 1801:

> Of his virtues I, too, can only tell you little of general nature, or else this sheet of paper would not suffice. He was always honorable, not only in outward things, but in his innermost motivations. A deep sense of justice always held sway over him, and when he asserted it, he proved himself to always be so strong and yet so gentle at the same time. Gentleness was indeed the basis of his whole being. [...] Only on occasion was he hard, with the highly educated; not in action but in word, calling most of them pedants. His first principle was: *to do is better than to know*. [...] He always spoke of the intellect as cold, and of the heart as alone productive and creative. [...] I would like to concentrate on what was most characteristic of his nature, then—and that was his *unselfishness* [...]. Always guided by his loving soul, in every argument, he chose *never his own but always* the interest *of somebody else*; and he did so not only in important situations, in situations where people were watching him [...], even in the most unremarkable, most unnoticed cases (and that counts far more), his soul always showed itself with the same immaculate unselfishness.[53]

Brockes was not a longtime friend when Kleist, in Pasewalk in August 1800, asked him to accompany him on his Würzburg journey. The two had just met a few weeks earlier on the island of Rügen,[54] where Kleist had traveled with Ulrike for a short summer holiday. Brockes had studied law in Kiel and Göttingen, served in the Danish military, and worked as a private tutor in Göttingen. As mentioned earlier, he fell into unrequited love with a woman by the name of Cäcilie von Ziegesar, who had entered an aristocratic marriage of convenience with a baron thirty-five years her senior. Her husband died at the beginning of August 1800. Brockes hoped to renew his love but was unable to marry Cäcilie due to a testamentary provision of her late husband. Brockes died in 1815, when their love finally seemed to fulfill itself, in the arms of his fiancée.[55] Brockes' unhappy life was not the image of a successful *vita activa*. It is thus easy to understand that, in August 1800, Kleist and Brockes—two melancholics—had found each other, and together sought to escape from all the adversities of their existence. Kleist thinks of Brockes as his alter ego, writing to Wilhelmine on September 18, 1800, that Brockes "is constantly in conflict with nature because he, as he says, is unable to figure out his eternal destiny, and therefore does nothing for his worldly destiny."[56] Undoubtedly, it is from

Fig. 24
Ludwig von Brockes (1767–1815)

within this state of discord, and in his critique of 'cold' intellectualism, that Brockes guides Kleist through his Kant crisis.

But let us return to Kleist's portrait of Brockes from January 1801, in which he obliterates all contradictions in Brockes' character, idealizing him as a selfless hero as he laments Brockes' departure, for the latter had just left Berlin to accept a post in Mecklenburg. Kleist was eager to prove Brockes' altruism: About the beginning of their Würzburg journey, he says Brockes put all his own interests last, passed up the offer of an official position, and even led his family to believe their journey was taken on behalf of him, not Kleist. Brockes sacrificed six hundred Reichsthaler of his savings for the Würzburg journey, and also, when it came to trifles, he denied himself for his companion's sake: He would always choose the lesser bed for himself when they took up quarters along the way, or, at night, hold his weary friend if he happened to fall asleep on his chest, without sleeping himself. In Kleist's portrait the gentle melancholic becomes a man of action, embodying the utopian spirit of solidarity in the sense of Jean-Jacques Rousseau, who asserts selflessness over self-interest, rejection of ownership over *amour propre*, and "rapture of self-sacrifice" over a regard for one's "own advantage." Promoting such principles, Kleist tries enthusiastically to introduce Wilhelmine to a "*new era*": "Imagine how happy the world would be if everyone were to disregard their own advantage for another person's advantage."[57] Brockes, with his active love, served as the role model for this utopia, the companionship with him—construed as homoerotic by some Kleist scholars[58]—anticipated this happy existence. In his play *The Schroffenstein Family*, written in Switzerland in 1802, Kleist would evoke this utopia once more, in the unselfish trust and deliberate sacrifice of the lovers Agnes and Ottokar amidst a fatal world of self-interest and mistrust.

One does not have to be an idealist to know there is a right life in the wrong one. Since he identified with Brockes, Kleist knew only too well that Brockes' noble conduct was the result of a proud despair and the exception to the rule in a world of selfishness. It cannot be understood otherwise that Kleist, in the very same letter, confesses to Wilhelmine to "this sad clarity which reveals to me the thought behind every look, the meaning behind every word, the motive behind every action. It shows me everything that surrounds me, even my own nature in all its wretched nakedness, and the colorful mist vanishes, and all the veils thrown to please are lowered, and finally the heart is repulsed by the sight of such nakedness."[59] It seems Kleist learned to distinguish between the ideal and reality, appearance and being, on his journeys—between the "nimbus"[60] of Brockes' true virtues, hidden beneath his melancholia, and the merely decorative St. John's cross of Count von Eickstedt. Kleist's travels thus describe a journey of disillusionment, a journey from pre-existence to existence. The Enlightenment ideals of his adolescence collided with his experience.

Kleist's journey to Würzburg with Brockes is anything but convenient. He travels by ordinary stagecoaches, often day and night without much rest, not befitting his station—unlike a year later on his journey to Paris with Ulrike when he travels in stages with his own coach, horses, and a servant, and frequently stops to visit scholars, writers, and aristocratic peers. His journey to Würzburg is not an aristocratic grand tour.[61] Brockes and Kleist enroll at the University of Leipzig under false names. They call themselves Bernhoff, a student of economy, and Klingstedt, a student of mathematics, thus disguising their noble origins and obtaining the freedom to move and observe, as Goethe had done on his journey to Italy in 1786, when he hid behind the pseudonym Möller. From his journeys through the Saxon and Franconian uplands, Kleist mainly conveys Romantic moods, poetic "reveries," commonplace idylls inhabited by happiness, love, and beautiful, warm people, as in "the delightful valley of *Tharandt* [...]. Such valleys, narrow and secret, are the true birthplace of love."[62] Kleist's landscapes are conceived in opposition to the cold intellect and barrenness of Brandenburg—*en passant*, as it were, sketched in passing while sitting on the "open wagon," "constantly changing sights to left and right as in a raree-show [...]. We are flying like birds above the countryside. But then again we do not learn much this way."[63] There can thus be no talk of any reality reflected in Kleist's early writing. It is not until his urban portrayals that his empiricism gains the upper hand—that astonished contemplations on the never-before-seen begin to replace the critical clichés of the time.

Brockes and Kleist arrive in Würzburg on September 9 or 10, 1800, and they stay in the Franconian episcopal city for six weeks. They first take up quarters at the Hotel Zum Fränkischen Hof, an inn near the Julius-Hospice, as the local press reports. A few days later they find a new, cheaper yet rather pleasant accommodation with a city surgeon, Wirth, in a bourgeois house at Schmalzmarkt, built by German architect Balthasar Neumann. In his letters to Wilhelmine, Kleist initially takes pleasure in mocking the "true Catholic appearance" of the city occupied by the French, the tolling of the bells from thirty-nine steeples that continues "without respite": "Masses and *horae canonicae* alternate continually, and the beads of the rosaries are in constant motion. For thus is the deliverance of the city assured, and since the French are praying for its fall, the outcome depends on who prays the harder." He denounces the "murmuring of the priests" in Latin, and is "certain that all this busy zeal awakens not a single meaningful thought," that such "ceremony stifles the emotions"; he quips about the announcement of a procession to pray for "the extermination of all heretics" and so for the extermination of Wilhelmine and him as well, etc.[64] All of this criticism of Catholicism is commonplace for an Enlightened protestant, hardly original, and can be found two decades earlier, in a similar style, in the southern Germany travel accounts of Berlin publisher and critic Friedrich Nicolai.[65]

Yet Würzburg also has some surprises in store for Kleist, putting conventional perceptions to the test and challenging Kleist's point of view. Thus, Kleist is puzzled by a cabinet of natural specimens—birds, mosses, butterfly wings, and other materials—collected by a University of Würzburg professor not in order to classify them, but to do "something more lighthearted": "Without any other coloring he has used all these materials to *paint landscapes*, bouquets of flowers, people, etc., often strikingly true to life, with down for water, moss for leafage, pollen for earth, spider webs for sky."[66] The natural objects thus, themselves, become signs for other natural objects. The illusion seems deceptively real even as it announces its artificiality. "I am going to tell you later what this means,"[67] writes Kleist to Wilhelmine, and he delivers on his promise by way of his reflections on painting during his second visit to Dresden. On May 21, 1801, he explains to Wilhelmine that he envies the painters "with their palettes on their knees, their brushes in their hands, occupied with copying the beauty of nature, [...] these happy people untroubled by doubts about Truth, which nowhere exists."[68] Kleist will never attain the happy naïveté of these copyists. The Kant crisis of spring 1801 confirms his semiotic skepticism, already apparent in the fall of 1800 in the ambiguous quality of the natural signs in the Würzburg cabinet of specimens.[69]

But more than the gallery of plant and animal specimens, the gallery of the insane at the Julius-Hospice in Würzburg puts Kleist's capacity to perceive and represent to the test. Let us therefore quote the passage in its entirety:

> Among the insane we saw many things (some disgusting, some laughable) often informative and pitiable. Two people lay across each other like logs, totally withdrawn, and one might almost doubt whether they were human. On the other hand, a professor, who had perhaps studied too hard, approached us in a cheerful and pleasant manner, and began to harangue us in Latin, questioning us with such quickness and alacrity, and in such correct and syntactical Latin, that we were in all seriousness at a loss to answer, as though face to face with the most brilliant person in the world. In one cell, dressed all in black, sat a monk with a deeply thoughtful and serious expression. Slowly his eyes came to rest upon us, and it seemed he could weigh our innermost souls. Then he began, in a weak yet sonorous and heart-wrenching way, to admonish us against earthly joys, to remind us of life eternal and the holiness of prayer. We made no answer. He spoke with long pauses. At times he looked at us sorrowfully, as though giving us up nevertheless for lost. A slip of the tongue in the pulpit, and he was convinced, from that moment, that he had desecrated the word of God. Then we met a merchant who had gone mad out of pride and vexation, because his father had been ennobled, but without hereditary title upon his son. But most horrifying of all was the sight of a creature driven mad by an unnatural vice. An eighteen-year-old youth, only a short time ago of blooming handsomeness and still bearing certain traces of it about him, now lay wallowing in his own filth; with naked, dead-white and shriveled limbs, head slumped listlessly on a sunken breast, a dull, vein-streaked flush, as though of a consumptive, aglow on an otherwise bloodlessly white face, eyelids drooping, eyes dim and lusterless, his thin hair dry and already hoary as though with age, tongue parched and dry and lolling between pale, shriveled lips, his hands bound and sewn behind him—he failed of the strength to move his tongue in speech, he could barely draw each gasping breath—the nerves of his brain were not deranged so much as enfeebled, utterly exhausted, incapable of responding to his will, his entire life nothing but one prolonged, crippling swoon—O better to die a thousand deaths than live out one's only life like this! How terrible is nature's vengeance upon the transgressors of her will! O enough of this fearful image—[70]

Are these medical case studies or invented miniatures from Kleist's imagination? His visit to the Würzburg Hospice with Brockes is established as a fact. Kleist scholarship even believes to have found a real-life model for the eighteen-year-old youth that succumbed to the vice of masturbation.[71] Kleist purportedly describes the incomprehensibility, the aloofness of insanity. When faced with the monk and the figure of the "professor, who had perhaps studied too hard," Brockes and Kleist are "at a loss" for answers, and they escape the horrifying sight of the merchant and youth. At the same time Kleist draws attention to the literary quality of his portrayal. He and Brockes walk past the cells as if they were *tableaux vivants*, scenes from a play, whose particular selection and succession can arouse the suspicion that they are simulations rather than 'copies' of reality. Does the poor professor not confirm Brockes' and Kleist's skepticism toward scholarliness? Is the melancholic monk in the cell not a personification of Kleist's crisis of language, of his skepticism toward the correlation between sign and referent? An anticipation of his authorship insofar as the tragic events in Kleist's *The Schroffenstein Family* unfold from the awareness that language is nothing more than misspeaking, a distortion of truth?[72] Is the merchant's son Kleist's doppelganger—no longer bearing his noble title, dispossessed, and suffering from the humiliation of his father's aristocratic pride? How are we to understand the youth's "unnatural vice"? Is it a matter of self-reproach, a projection of Kleist's own lacking masculinity?[73] The answer to these questions is this: Kleist's portraits of the insane are all ambiguous figures that make it hard to tell whether he distorts himself or others to the point of recognition. The language Kleist uses to refer to reality is not symbolic, but symbolist. He does not browse the book of nature and copy from it, but rather pieces his very own world together in his "magazine of ideas," transforming experiences into lemmata, as it were.[74] He generates a dictionary with its own index and correspondences, whose most well-known entry is the arched gate of Würzburg, the paradoxical trope of 'stability in falling.'[75]

Kleist's travel writing is no great literature; it serves as a mere rehearsal for his future literary virtuosity. It proves that Kleist is a master of pathos—for instance, in his description of a sunset in Würzburg, whose basin forms a large "amphitheater," the terraces of the surrounding mountains serving as loges, "and in the highest place above stands God. And from the dome of the great theater the chandelier of the sun sinks down." Or, as a counterpoint to this, there is his depiction of the "superb spectacle" of a morning storm: "To the West stood the nocturnal storm, raging, like a tyrant, and in the East the sun rose, calm and quiet, like a hero. And the tempest flung its hissing bolts and assailed him with his thundering, but he, the divine star, remained silent, and rose higher, and gazed regally down on the restless fog cloud at his feet."[76] But Kleist also dials down the pathos. His travel letters prove that he is skilled at capturing the sublime but also familiar with the popular fiction of his time. His gallery of the insane at the Julius-Hospice playfully draws on set pieces of the Gothic novel. That Kleist is well versed in the gloomy does not come as a surprise. As a jokester, however, he has yet to be discovered. In any case, Kleist proves in Würzburg that he is also able to write satirical dialogues whose humor is not as inscrutable as it is in his supposed comedies *The Broken Jug*

Fig. 25 Würzburg, full view 1811

and *Amphitryon*. One need only look to Kleist and Brockes' purported conversation with a librarian in a Würzburg library, which Kleist writes down for Wilhelmine on September 14, 1800:

> "We would like to have a couple of good things to read."—"The collection is at your disposal."—"Something of Wieland?"—"I rather doubt it."—"Or Schiller, or Goethe?"—"They would be hard to find."—"What! Are all of their books loaned out? Are the people here such readers?"—"Hardly that."—"Who are the most avid readers here?"—"Lawyers, merchants, married ladies."—"And the unmarried ones?"—"They may not borrow books."—"And the students?"—"We have been instructed not to give them any."—"Well, then, please tell us, if so little reading is done here, where in the world are the works of Wieland or Goethe or Schiller?"—"By your leave, such things are never read here."—"You mean, you do not have them here in your library?"—"They are not allowed."—"What sort of books are all these on the shelves, then?"—"Chivalric romances. Nothing but chivalric romances. On the right, chivalric romances *with* ghosts; on the left, chivalric romances *without* ghosts, as you prefer."—"Ah! I see."[77]

But let us move from the Bavarian cabaret to the Prussian cabinet: Over a hurried five-day-journey, Kleist rushes back to Berlin at the end of October 1800 not to miss his chance at a ministerial post. Struensee seems to have given Kleist a November 1 deadline by which to make a decision. In his letters from the winter of 1800/01, Kleist hardly mentions the outside world in Berlin. He is too busy justifying to his fiancée, his sister, and himself why he is unable to accept the government position everyone has been expecting him to take. Being caught up in his justifications makes him lonely and, understandably, apprehensive about being in company: "The need to play a role, and an inner repugnance for it, make social gatherings burdensome for me, and I can only be happy in my own company, because there I can be what I really am." He even locks himself in his room for eight days in hopes of deciding on a new life plan, but "in the end [he] had to leave [his] room after all, and as undecided as ever."[78] The only thing that will help is to escape Berlin, to overcome his paralysis and regain some freedom to think and take action. To his sister and his fiancée, Kleist justifies his departure with his Kant crisis and his "inner disgust for all scholarly work,"[79] while to Minister Struensee he claims the opposite: the need to resume his scientific studies in Paris. This time, too, Kleist travels with a companion. Ulrike accompanies him. Though she is not his first choice, he relies on his sister's financial support. For a "third travel companion," "Brockes and Rühle would be the only ones, and both are bound by their positions."[80]

On their Würzburg journey Brockes was an ideal doppelganger for Kleist, reflecting him without showing his imperfections. By contrast, Ulrike reflects Kleist's bad conscience, especially since she had always had to bail him out. With her he took the family police, so to speak, on his journey to Paris. Thus, he had "partly" hoped that she "would not accept" his offer to accompany him "due to the great rashness and the extraordinary costs."[81] Ulrike, however, joined in immediately; she was—unlike Brockes—assertive and decisive, "the soul of a hero in a female body [...], a soul who has nothing of womankind about her except her hips, [...] a blunder on nature's part to have constructed a being neither male nor female, but wavering between the two like an amphibian," who "encounters every danger with coolness and presence of mind, but if a dog or a bull should appear unexpectedly, she trembles from head to foot." Thus goes the—not very kind—portrait of Ulrike Kleist creates to his Potsdam friend Adolphine von Werdeck in July 1801. He finally apologizes and excuses Ulrike by clarifying that her "only fault is to exceed the capacities of her sex."[82] In actuality, a miniature portrait of Ulrike, whose authenticity has not been verified, depicts anything but an Amazon.[83] But, after all, Kleist was not concerned with her physique, but her psyche. His critique of Ulrike—that a male soul lives in a female body—may in fact have been a veiled self-critique insofar as Kleist was aware that a female soul lived in his male body. He did not so much resent her but rather himself for the fact that she, unlike him, was able to perform the male role so naturally. Compared with her often rather passive and hesitant brother, Ulrike invariably proved to be the true head of the family, financing and protecting Kleist time and again. For instance, the

Fig. 26
Ulrike von Kleist (1774–1849),
Kleist's half-sister

time she fearlessly traveled in men's clothes to war-torn Switzerland to convey her brother from Bern to the safety of Oßmannstedt. In a Freudian slip of sorts, Kleist reveals his discontent with Ulrike's gender-bending in a letter of January 12, 1802, in which he once again begs his sister for money and confuses the grammatical gender: "My dear Ullrique, with you I must always keep quiet about certain things because I am embarrassed to speak up against someone who [*der*!] acts."[84] At the same time this relationship between the siblings—so strangely complementary in their 'gender trouble'—is the premise of their life-long bond. When Kleist continues on his journey from Paris to Switzerland without Ulrike, he writes in December 1801: "I wish you had stayed with me.—Are we not like body and soul, which often contradict each other and yet only part reluctantly."[85] It would be undue and clichéd to assume Kleist only feigned his attachment to his sister for the sake of money.

Just like her brother, and unlike her sisters, Ulrike never married. She lived with Kleist twice for a considerable time—in Paris in 1801 and in Berlin and Königsberg in 1805/06. For many years she did not have a place of her own, which she would have been able to afford had it not been for her continual financial support of Kleist. Instead, she lived with her relatives, namely her brothers-in-law in Pomerania or Cottbus. After Kleist's death and the long disputes about his debts, she succeeded in buying the family home in Frankfurt an der Oder in 1819, where she had established a girls' boarding school two years earlier which she continued to run until she sold the house in 1839. She became a very highly regarded citizen of Frankfurt, achieving affluence and becoming popular among the members of the Kleist family as a very lively, prosperous aunt. Even at the age of sixty, she took a big journey with her nieces Friederike and Auguste von Pannwitz through Germany, France, Switzerland, and Italy for nine months. Ulrike kept her brother's letters not only for the purpose of an eventual publication; she also organized and edited them, according to her own interests, as Kleist scholars argue: "Traces of a phantasmal dialogue between the sister and her dead brother become apparent during the years in which Ulrike, increasingly lonely, still lived in Frankfurt," notes Hans Joachim Kreutzer.[86] Never bound as a mother or wife—even though her brother constantly reminded her of her gender role—she seemed to feel the need to rebel one last time against him at the end of her life. In dying and through her death, she might have forcefully rid herself of the burden of guilt Kleist's suicide imposed upon his family and his sister in particular.[87] According to the account of Ulrike's niece Friederike, who took care of her, she became latently hostile and obstinate toward the end of her life. She began rejecting her medication and food, lamenting sleeplessly throughout the night for months on end, searching for mistakes she might have made in the past, until she finally died on February 5, 1849. Sigrid Weigel, who wrote a short biography on Ulrike, reads this as an at once self-destructive and self-liberating behavior, as a "*talking* illness": "[T]he repressed expressed itself, the once self-sacrificing became selfish. To come to find herself, after having put herself last her entire life, she had to distance herself from the image of the seventy-four-year-old spinster Miss von Kleist."[88]

But let us come back to the Paris journey of the two siblings. In mid-April 1801 Heinrich and Ulrike set forth from Berlin with their own carriage and a servant named Johann, whom they borrowed from Carl von Zenge. Their first stopover is Dresden, and this time—unlike during his first, short visit there during his Würzburg journey—Kleist is enraptured by the city. In May 1801 he writes enthusiastically to Wilhelmine that he doubts he will ever "find a city where the distractions [*Zerstreuung*] from life are so easy and pleasant as in Dresden. Nothing could have led me with such total forgetfulness from the melancholy fields of learned abstractions as has the art collected in this city. […] [S]uch things have no need of the intellect to be enjoyed, and work only on the heart and the senses. I felt so well at my first entry into this world of beauty, hitherto unknown to me."[89] *Zerstreuung*, connoting both dispersal and distraction, is the key word for Kleist after the Kant crisis, and its primary site is art.[90] Dresden with its picture gallery, displaying works of the Italian Renaissance and reproductions of Classical sculptures, illustrates how sorrow can be captured in the form of beauty, and how knowledge—which, in spite of all intellectual efforts,

Fig. 27
Raphael, *Sistine Madonna*, 1512–14

cannot be contained within a closed system—can be happily rounded out into an aesthetic totality. At least that is how it appears, with Kleist's diligent citation of the idealist platitudes to which Johann Joachim Winckelmann's reflections on Classical art tend to be reduced, even to the present day. But Kleist's reflections are a far cry from the complex, aesthetic and historical "Thoughts on the Imitation of Greek Works in Painting and the Art of Sculpture," which is the title of Winckelmann's Dresden essay of 1755, when he—like all travelers to Dresden—visits the main tourist attraction, Raphael's *Sistine Madonna*: "Every day I visited those ideal figures of the Greeks, and the masterpieces of the Italians, and each time I entered the gallery I stood for hours before the one Raphael of the collection, that Madonna and Child with its high seriousness, with its quiet greatness, and Ah! Wilhelmine! those two images that reminded me of two beings that I love."[91]

Kleist flirts a little and wraps his compliments for Wilhelmine in Winckelmann's words. Whoever thinks that this is more than Kleist being charming, that it can be read as true enthusiasm and support for the idealist notion of art, overlooks the fact that Kleist, in the very next sentence of his letter to Wilhelmine, expresses his envy for the young artists of Dresden, "occupied with copying the beauty of nature," "these happy people untroubled by doubts about Truth, which nowhere exists, and who instead live only for Beauty, which does indeed reveal itself to them at moments, at least to their imaginations."[92]

Kleist was envious because he was no longer satisfied with being an epigone of Classical art and its renaissance. He envied anyone not tortured "by doubts," anyone still able to join in harmony the beautiful, the true, and the good—aesthetics, epistemology, and ethics—be it in contemplating Classical art and its legacy or when enjoying "the greatest, the most uplifting music," still able to experience his faith in the "celebration" of the Catholic mass, "praying with conviction" like a pious man on the steps of the altar: "I felt an indescribable longing to throw myself down beside him and weep. Ah, a single drop of forgetfulness, and I would embrace Catholicism with a passion.—But that is exactly what I did not want to mention."[93] Kleist did express his doubts, however, and there was no going back. He may have allowed himself a little, temporary escape into forgetting through the contemplation of artistic—or natural—beauty. Dresden's picturesque surroundings provided him with ample charms for this. But, ultimately, Kleist's enthusiasm remained second-hand—something foreign, not his own. There is no way to hide the fact that, for the melancholic Kleist, the idyllic atmosphere of Dresden merely served as a façade to conceal the real terrors. In his literary works he later repeatedly invokes paintings from the Dresden picture gallery: For instance, in his story "The Earthquake in Chile" ("Das Erdbeben in Chili"), written in 1806, he quotes Ferdinand Bol's painting *Rest on the Flight into Egypt*.[94] The idyll, however, is brutally destroyed in Kleist's story. The same is true for the idealist notion of art in Kleist. Even in his earliest works—in *The Schroffenstein Family*, written one year after his stay in Dresden—Kleist presents it as a vision of utopia in which he may want to believe for a while but which he will eventually cross out or even ridicule, as he does in his debut play.

The two Kleists continue on their journey from Dresden to Leipzig, where they attend a lecture by the anthropologist Ernst Platner, who advised Ulrike beforehand to wear men's clothes to avoid a disturbance.[95] They carry on to Halle to see the mathematician Georg Simon Klügel and from there to Halberstadt to visit an eighty-three-year-old sage, Anacreontic poet Johann Wilhelm Ludwig Gleim, who, using the example of the Kleists' famous forefather Ewald von Kleist, reveals to the siblings why and how one goes from being a soldier to a poet. Gleim brings them into his study, bedecked with portraits of his well-known friends, among which Ewald von Kleist's stood "in the most prominent place," for having achieved "both": He had "performed a great deed" and "written a thing of beauty." Gleim then goes on to tell them an anecdote of how it was he "who had shown" the Prussian officer Ewald von Kleist "the road to Parnassus," which Kleist must have found deeply interesting, as suggested by his detailed retelling of the story in a letter to Wilhelmine:

Fig. 28
Johann Wilhelm Ludwig Gleim
(1719–1803)

> For Kleist, it seems, had been wounded in a duel, and lay in Potsdam. Gleim was regimental quartermaster and visited the sick man, without knowing much more about it. "Ah," said Kleist, "I am so very bored, unable even to read." "I'll tell you what," replied Gleim, "I'll come here from time to time and read something to you." Gleim was just at that time trying his hand at writing poems in the style of Anacreon, for the sport of it, and read to him, among others, an ode to death, that went something as follows: "Death, why do you seduce away my girl? Can you too fall in love?" And so it continues. Finally it ends: "What do you intend doing with her? With those lipless teeth of yours you might indeed bite girls, but surely not kiss them." At the thought of such a thing, of death with his bare, revolting teeth pressing against the red rosebud lips in a vain attempt to kiss, Kleist began to shake so with laughter that the bandage slipped from his wound. An army surgeon was called. "It is a lucky thing," he said, "for we have the beginnings here of a gangrene and tomorrow would have been too late." Out of thankfulness Kleist consecrated his life to the muse of poesy, for it was she who had saved him.[96]

Thus ends the tale of the primal scene of Ewald von Kleist's poetry, which one may believe or not. It is, in any case, edifying—both the poem and the events related—insofar as it suggests that one can beat death with wit and art. Ewald's biography tells rather of the opposite, of the realization that writing poetry does not help against melancholia, and that a grandiose self-sacrifice such as Ewald von Kleist's—which Lessing read as a suicide—burns itself into the memory of one's contemporaries. Looking back on the lives of the two Kleists, it is easy to see parallels.[97] But if we want to stay true to Kleist's present in 1801, we must refrain from seeing phantoms. That Gleim could have planted the idea in Kleist's head to become a writer for the sake of fame and honor, one cannot seriously maintain. What is particularly remarkable about the anecdote is that the end of Gleim's poem "To Death" indicates that the Grim Reaper "[c]annot mean to give" the girl "kisses" with his "lipless teeth,"[98] while Kleist, in his retelling of the anecdote, warns Death not to confuse kissing with biting. While typically Kleist-sounding, the passage does not suffice as an anticipation of his *Penthesilea.* It better serves to evidence that the early Kleist, as a letter writer, is more original when telling anecdotes than when portraying landscapes. His stories about the insane at the Julius-Hospice in Würzburg attest to this, and the anecdote about Ewald von Kleist, with its laconic pointedness, falls right in line with Kleist's splendid anecdotes in the *Berlin Evening Paper.*

From Halberstadt the siblings continue their journey through Germany—via Göttingen, Kassel, Frankfurt am Main, Mainz, and Koblenz—with many stopovers and visits that Kleist merely lists in the awareness of the transience of all experience, as he writes to Karoline von Schlieben, his new friend from Dresden, in July 1801: "[B]ut life's events follow swiftly and the heart is too confined to encompass them all, and those of the past are ever vanishing to make place for the new—Finally the heart is weary of the new, and surrenders itself exhausted to impressions whose transience it already feels beforehand. Ah, it must be desolate, empty and sad to outlive one's own heart."[99] Here, Kleist's new sense of time announces itself, which counters his future-oriented Enlightened adolescence and, at the same time, the eschatological awareness of Christians, who can always find comfort in the thought that this world is temporary and ephemeral and that eternity can only be gained in the next. Kleist seems to be condemned to passivity insofar as he, as a melancholic, is given to "sense" transience and loss "before the fact," that is, insofar as he considers loss—the potential consequence of his actions—not as imminent but as having always already taken place.[100] And yet he sees the danger resulting from such a reversal of time's arrow, and he knows how to handle it as well. The goal is to completely relinquish a linear, teleological understanding of the world and live entirely in the present, in the spur of the moment, as he writes to Adolphine von Werdeck, his friend from Potsdam, in July 1801: "Ah, this inborn vice of mine never to be able to seize the moment, and always to live in a place where I am not, and in a time that is either past or not yet come. In my homeland I was often in Paris, and now in Paris I am almost always back in my homeland."[101]

Kleist thinks in the subjunctive, like someone with a borderline personality disorder who knows the way out of a crisis and is unable to take it. The realization that it comes down to seizing "the moment" instead of hoping for the future, is not just a passing remark referring to the opposition of homeland and foreign land and to the enjoyment of the here and now. It is a crucial figure of thought for Kleist, which results from his always thinking ahead toward death and finding affirmation in extreme situations—such as the ones Kleist experiences on his journey to Paris. During a boat trip on the Rhine from Koblenz to Cologne, the boat he is on threatens to capsize during a storm; and in Butzbach near Frankfurt am Main, the carriage horses go into a full-speed bolt frightened by the braying of a donkey, flipping over the coach. The Kleist siblings survive despite the serious fall. The corresponding passage from Kleist's letter, familiar from the introductory chapter, is again quoted here:

> I reached for the reins, but they were hanging loose beneath the horses' chests, and before I had a chance to realize the magnitude of the danger, the carriage had already turned over with us, and we were thrown—And, so, a human life depended on the mere braying of a donkey? And what if my life had ended at this moment, had I lived *for that*? For that? *This* would have been all that Heaven had intended for this dark, inscrutable, earthly life, and nothing more—? But, for now, it was not over—*why* Heaven had spared our lives, who can know? In short, we raised ourselves from the pavement, alive and unscathed, and held each other close. The carriage lay overturned, wheels in the air, one of them completely smashed, the shaft broken, the harnesses torn. All of this cost us three Louis d'or and twenty-four hours. We continued our journey the next morning—when will be the last?[102]

Kleist's philosophizing in the face of his potential random death brings Michel de Montaigne's essay to mind—translated into German by Johann Daniel Tietz in 1753/54—bearing the descriptive title "That to Philosophize Is to Learn to Die" as borrowed from Cicero. Montaigne almost seems to take pleasure in reciting accidental deaths from the history of Western culture: Aeschylus was struck to death by a tortoise falling from the claws of an eagle above him in the sky; a Breton duke was accidentally crushed to death by the crowd attending the entry of Pope Clemens into Lyon in 1305; a brother of Montaigne was fatally struck above his right ear by a ball during a game, etc. Montaigne's conclusion is that death is unpredictable, yet omnipresent: "It is uncertain where death awaits us; let us await it everywhere. Premeditation of death is premeditation of freedom. He who has learned how to die has unlearned how to be a slave." Accordingly, to learn to die means to expect that "death is equally near us." Consequently, we should always live in such a way that we "can move out [...] without regret for anything at all." One must not "plan anything that takes so long, or at least not with the idea of flying into a passion if we cannot see it accomplished. [...] One day is equal to all days." Thus, for Montaigne "the advantage of living is not measured by length, but by us."[103]

Hence, to learn to die means to learn to live, which, according to Montaigne, primarily requires a different sense of time. If one can die anytime by accident, it only makes sense to live every day as if it were the first and last. What matters, then, is not the quantity but the quality of life. Death is no longer regarded *sub specie aeternitatis*, under the sign of eternity; instead life is viewed *sub specie mortis*, from the perspective of its finitude. This, then, has nothing to do with the Christian fear of the hereafter and comfort in the idea of eternal life; it is instead about grasping, through the awareness of one's mortality, the value of each day and refusing to waste even one. After his stormy boat trip on the Rhine, Kleist remarks that "only he who can throw [life] away lightly and joyfully can use it to great ends." One might lose the "fear of death"[104] by following the motto: Act in such a way that your actions are meaningful in and of themselves and are not reliant on a before or after. This moralist-prosaic, anti-idealist principle shapes Kleist's thought after his Kant crisis. For Kleist life becomes a permanent experiment in which a person gains knowledge only by way of experience, a "contest" in which the athlete—as Kleist puts it much later, in 1810, in the *Berlin Evening Paper*—"simply has no recourse but to act spontaneously, on inspiration."[105]

The Kant crisis and the experience of almost dying under rather absurd circumstances in Butzbach were critical for Kleist's future life and writing insofar as, through them, he came to understand both the possibilities and limits of knowledge. The ambition of reason to understand that which lies beyond reason—be it the irrational, continually emerging, or the absolute which transcends reason—cannot be satisfied. But reason does have its own realm where it is effective—the realm of human experience. From 1801 on Kleist moved, albeit reluctantly, from the idealist 'otherworld' to the surface spectacle of empiricism. Instead of dealing in the absolute and eternal, Kleist concentrated on the ephemeral and the often only seeming, on the observation of human behavior in everyday life. In doing so, he focused less on how people *should* behave and more on how they *actually* behaved.[106] The best place for studying such 'real' human behavior was Paris, the metropolis of the 19th century. At the beginning of July 1801, about three months after his distraught Kant letters, Kleist arrives—right on time for the celebration of the anniversary of the storming of the Bastille—in the French capital, which has, at the time, a population of seven hundred thousand and is the world's second largest city after London. Coming from the provincial Mark of Brandenburg, Kleist is confronted with the masses and their indifference, and he reacts with disgust—a stock critique of the Modern city. But remarkable is the particular position that Kleist goes on to adopt: Unlike Charles Baudelaire, Rainer Maria Rilke, or Walter Benjamin, he does not depict the shock of the flaneur, who loses himself in the crowd. "So this is where people come to live; I would have thought it is a city to die in," writes Rilke about Paris at the beginning of *The Notebooks of Malte Laurids Brigge*.[107] Kleist protects himself and keeps his distance from the crowd. The masses may be amorphous and caught up in ever-changing deceptions, but Kleist keeps his integrity as an individual by hardly ever leaving the house during his time in Paris, preferring to look out of his window at the 'street theater' below. On July 18, 1801, he writes to his Dresden friend Karoline von Schlieben:

> Of course here in Paris it [my heart] is as good as dead. I open my window and see nothing but this colorless, flat, stale city, with its high, gray slate roofs and formless chimneys, something of the top of the Tuileries, and mobs of people whom one has forgotten by the time they have turned the corner. So far I know only a few people, love nobody, and do not know if I ever will. For in capitals people are too shrewd to be open, too elegant to be true. Actors are what they are, taking turns at deceiving each other, while pretending not to notice. One passes another coldly; one wriggles through the crowds of people in the streets, who could not care less about their own kind; before one has caught an impression, it is already replaced by ten others; doing so, one does not get attached to anyone, and no one gets attached to us; one greets another politely, but one's heart is as useless here as one's lungs are under an airless campana, and if an emotion does escape once, it goes unheard like the sound of a flute during a hurricane.[108]

A sense of disgust professes itself in this passage, as does a fascination for the performative arts and theatrical passions of the French, for their propensity for "fireworks and light shows and spectacles and clownings."[109] The Parisians did not even shy away from simulating a life in close touch with nature in the suburbs of Paris. Kleist gives the example of the Hameau de Chantilly, a precursor, so to speak, of today's Disneyland Resort in Paris from the turn of the 19th century—a place of public amusement with artificial fishermen cottages, hunters, and shepherds, wherein the "most *raffiné* foods and finest wines are served up, but in wooden bowls and earthenware dishes; and so that nothing be lacking in this deception, one eats with forks of tin," only to then rush from the phony "Nature back to [the] Unnature" of Paris as the day comes to an end.[110] Kleist weighs the everyday behavior of the French against the ideals of their Enlightenment philosophy and must realize that they do not take seriously Rousseau, Claude Adrien Helvétius, and Denis Diderot—the heroes of the bourgeois Enlightenment for whom the Germans admire the French so much. To the French it does not really matter if "a person exhibits a great, deep, sublime soul." Above all, they want a person to "behave gracefully," to know how to dance, and to know the "fifteen formulae considered courtesies here,"[111] as in the feudal times before 1789. Behind these courtesies lies selfishness; the abolition of the estate system does not seem to have changed this fact. Kleist's letters from Paris indicate how his thinking in terms of substance, his call for a congruence of inner and outer beauty—encountered in his Happiness essay—becomes increasingly problematic. It did him no good that he locked himself in his Paris apartment in the Latin Quarter near the Sorbonne; at heart he had already been fully taken by the amalgamation of filth and radiance in the big city, as he suggests to Louise von Zenge in a superbly hubristic comparison of his fate with the river Seine: "[I]magine, finally, a river, which, like many a foreign youth, passes pure and clean through the city, but, saturated with manifold refuse, departs again, and indeed cuts through it in an almost straight line, as though wanting to hurry as fast as possible and on the shortest possible route through the nauseating place into which it has somehow blundered."[112]

However, it was not such smooth sailing for Kleist: He stayed in Paris for five months, until November 1801. After his Kant crisis he entered into another time of disillusionment. Following Paris Kleist's thoughts were dominated by complementary relations, or a 'simultaneity of the non-simultaneous,' with his mind torn between longing and experience: Enlightenment optimism, the bourgeois moral philosophy of his adolescence, and the skeptical moralism of the aristocratic, old European tradition coexisted. Considering Kleist's observations about French customs, the moralist tradition, in particular, seems relevant even in post-revolutionary times. In his letters Kleist may have frequently modified certain commonplaces like the opposition between reality and appearance, stability and labyrinthian, volatile movement, depth and superficiality, inside and outside, love and deception, authentic warm-heartedness and the coldness of self-fashioning.[113] But, ultimately, he had to realize that he had long lost the confidence to make such distinctions, and that perhaps it would be more truthful to refer back to the aristocratic theory of prudence of French moralist François de La Rochefoucauld, who, in his *Maxims* of 1664, points out the difficulty of differentiating between virtues and vices and thus the connectedness of what is thought to be separate—to such an extent, it seems that even Christian charity is a mere covering for self-love. On August 15, 1801, Kleist writes to his fiancée from Paris, devoid of any illusions:

> There is no use saying that a voice deep within confides secretly and clearly what is just. The same voice that calls on the Christian to forgive his enemies calls on the savage to roast him, and he eats him up with piety. If an inner conviction justifies such deeds, can it be trusted? What does it mean, in terms of results, to

> do evil? What is *evil*? *Absolute evil*? Myriad, connected and intertwined are the things of this world, every act is the mother of millions of others, and often the worst begets the best.[114]

In Paris Kleist began to think beyond good and evil—a way of thinking guided by empirically observable forms of behavior, focused, above all, on the motives and impacts of actions. What one finds in Kleist, then, is empiricism rather than idealism, combined with the attempt to analyze, genealogically, the difference between reality and appearance, and to figure out the workings of the human mind—an endeavor often doomed to fail. From this interest in the deceivability of human beings, Kleist later garners his ideas for writing, as the analysis of his debut play *The Schroffenstein Family* will illustrate.

He wrote his play in Switzerland, which he had set out to from Paris. The main purpose of his journey was to pursue a Rousseauian life in the countryside, in a free, democratic country. Kleist fled from the "abyss"[115] of the Paris metropolis to the other world of Swiss nature, followed by the other world of art, which had already given him comfort in Paris when he retreated from the hectic, uncaring, cold bustle on the streets to the Louvre, to warm himself "by the marbles, the Apollo Belvedere" or the "Medici Venus."[116] It was not science that gave him a sense of stability in Paris, even though he did attend lectures on the natural sciences there—as he had assured Struensee—facilitated by Wilhelm von Humboldt and Prussian ambassador Marquis Girolamo Lucchesini. It appears that Kleist had given up on his plan to make money with works of popular science.[117] In October 1801 he turned twenty-four, and, from there on, he was able to dispose of his inheritance without his financial guardian. This financial independence served as the basis for his project in Switzerland, which was nothing but a fantasy of self-creation through which he intended to break free, once and for all, from the restrictive terms of the career of a Prussian aristocrat. And so a month later, Kleist vanishes from Paris, aiming for 'rebirth' as a Swiss estate owner and writer.

Kleist does not seem to be reliant on Ulrike's money anymore. She accompanies him to Frankfurt am Main and then returns to Prussia. Kleist continues his journey with the painter Friedrich Lose—fiancé of his Dresden friend Karoline von Schlieben—via Heidelberg, Karlsruhe, and Strasbourg to the south. On December 16, 1801, he writes effusively to his sister from Basel: "It was a dark night when I entered my new homeland. [...] I felt as though I were entering on a new life."[118] What shines forth here is the epiphany of—as they say in the age of Goethe—a rebirth or new birth. In contrast to the Classical concept of palingenesis, personal re-creation is understood not as cyclical but meliorative. The concept of rebirth or new birth originates in Pietist doctrine. In its profanation as a purely metaphorical speech act, it was used almost excessively at the turn of the 19th century—mostly by sophisticated travelers who set out to foreign countries in hopes of defining themselves anew, like Goethe did in his *Italian Journey*, which popularized the concept of rebirth or new birth.[119] Identity formation was not conceived as linear and processual—following the model of a life plan—but as erratic. And it was not said to take place in public institutions, but was primarily conceived as a fantasy of self-creation—a self-projection independent of all realities, which remained fictional as long as it had not proved itself in social experience. There were lucky people who successfully acted out their dreams in real life, such as Goethe or Adelbert von Chamisso, who, in his *Peter Schlemihl's Wondrous Story* of 1814, gives his shadowless hero a stable identity as a botanizing globetrotter—thereby anticipating his own career path from a Romantic poet to a globetrotting natural scientist and curator of the Royal Herbarium in Berlin.[120] Kleist was not one of them. His dream of settling down as an estate owner in free, democratic Switzerland fell through within a few months. He did, nevertheless, start writing literature in Switzerland—yet he notoriously did not have any measurable success with his contemporaries.

His new start in Switzerland began, right away, with a personal disappointment. Kleist had a falling out with his travel companion, whom he had only just described to his sister in a letter from Basel as a "good person, who one can be rather fond of. His way of speaking is somewhat rough, but his deeds are gentle."[121] A week later Kleist writes a fierce letter to Lose from Liestal near Basel—a combination of anger and despair, accusation and regret, as though he were a narcissistically wounded lover raging against his beloved for failing to meet the image he projected of him. We know little of Lose. We do know that he married Karoline von Schlieben and that, in 1833, he died in madness in Mailand. In his relationship with Kleist, he seems to have had his hands full trying to avoid any 'gender trouble.' Kleist apparently expected more than friendship from Lose: "What was it we were seeking on our beautiful journey? Was it not peace from passion?" Thus goes Kleist's rhetorical question in his break-up letter, in which he returned to Lose the key to their shared apartment in Basel. Lose had probably already answered in no uncertain terms, but it was not the response Kleist had hoped for. Lose consoled him with hopes, telling him he may find "a female lover" in Switzerland.[122] Contrary to expectation, Kleist may have even succeeded doing so. After several failed attempts at purchasing a manor in Switzerland, he rented a small house on the Delosea Island in the Aar river at the outflow of Lake Thun for six months. A local fisherman's daughter kept house for him, "Mädeli [...] a sweet, amiable girl, the image of the Magdalene her namesake. We rise with the sun, she plants flowers for me

Fig. 29
Thun, Kleist house on an island in the Aar River (photograph, circa 1940)

in the garden, and prepares my food while I work for my eventual return to you; then we eat together; on Sundays she dresses in her beautiful Swiss costume, a present from me, and we row ashore; she goes to church in Thun, I climb the Schreckhorn, and after respective devotions we return together."[123] Kleist would have been better off going to church with Mädeli to confess that the idyll he paints for his sister Ulrike in his letter of May 1, 1802, is an outright lie, as the climb up the Schreckhorn alone—which is 13,379 feet high and over 40 miles away from Thun and still considered one of the most challenging of all the Bernese four-thousanders—would have quite exceeded the duration of a mass. There are many rumors surrounding Mädeli. After all, she takes up the position initially intended for Wilhelmine in Kleist's household in Thun, and, three weeks after the sentimental image of his idyllic life, Kleist writes his break-up letter to Wilhelmine. Nothing more can be said without speculation. To this day we do not know anything for certain about the identity of the young woman.[124]

There is also no direct evidence for what Kleist worked on during his time in Thun, whether he was still finishing *The Schroffenstein Family* or already beginning *Robert Guiscard*. One may assume though that the writer gave free reign to his imagination in Thun so as to be able to return to Prussia—"to you"—on account of his literary fame. Switzerland, as he soon had to realize, could not become his new homeland. The political situation in 1802 was too unstable. His departure to Switzerland may have been a belated reflex triggered by the 18th century's enthusiasm for Switzerland when the Old Swiss Confederacy—despite its absolutist structure—was the center of attraction for Enlightenment thinkers and the home to thinkers celebrated across Europe, such as Albrecht von Haller, Jean-Jacques Rousseau, Johann Jakob Bodmer, Salomon Geßner, Johann Heinrich Pestalozzi, and Johann Kaspar Lavater. The restructuring of Switzerland into a Helvetic Republic in 1798, following the French model, promised democratic conditions. In point of fact, however, the new centralized unitary state, originating from national uprisings, was a vassal state of France, disunited due to the conflict between the proponents of a unitary state and the federalists—supported by the majority of people—who wanted to restore the old canton system. The withdrawal of French forces in 1802 led to several skirmishes between these two parties, which were ended in 1803 once more by Napoleon's intervention and by restructuring the unitary state into a confederation while strengthening the independence of the individual cantons. It makes sense that even the 'project-maker' Kleist did not dare to buy a manor in Switzerland during such troubled times, even though he had studied a number of agricultural works for months and looked at several estates. On March 2, 1802, he writes to Heinrich Zschokke from Thun: "I am terrified by the mere possibility that I could become a Frenchman, rather than a Swiss citizen, by some sleight of hand."[125]

Zschokke, born in Magdeburg in 1771, studied in Frankfurt an der Oder, and became a lecturer at the Viadrina in 1792. In 1793 he gained success as a writer with his robber novel *Abällino, the Great Bandit*. In 1795/96, having grown tired of scholarship, he traveled through Switzerland and France, settled down in Switzerland in 1796 and, from 1798 on, as a vivid proponent of the unitary state, supported the new Republic as director of the Office for National Culture and governor of the cantons of Waldstätten, Ticino, and Basel. When the federalists started to gain the upper hand at the end of 1801, he resigned from his political positions and settled in Aarau. Zschokke's Prussian-Swiss biography, which exhibits several parallels to Kleist's, may have attracted Kleist; be that as it may, Kleist could not have had a better adviser in so troubled a political time in Switzerland. Zschokke knew—as Kleist writes to him "with astonishment"—how to "steer" his "life's ship with a steady hand away from the shores of the political world into the haven of philosophical tranquility."[126] Kleist promises to follow suit and "wait" in Thun to see "how the discord of things will resolve itself,"[127] but he does not have Zschokke's patience. The latter stayed in Switzerland and—from 1804 to his death—played a significant role as a chief forest commissioner and mining counselor as well as a politician in the canton of Aargau. Kleist, by contrast, left the country on October 17, 1802, the day of the collapse of the Helvetic Republic, when the federalists came into power.

Zschokke was one of three new friends Kleist had made in Switzerland. The second was the Bernese bookseller, publisher, and writer Heinrich Geßner—son of Salomon Geßner, the great Swiss poet of idylls—who published Kleist's *The Schroffenstein Family* in 1803. Heinrich Geßner married Christoph Martin Wieland's daughter Charlotte in 1795, whose brother Ludwig Wieland moved to Bern in 1800 and worked in the publishing house of his brother-in-law. Ludwig was the third in the group of friends: one Swiss national and three voluntary 'exiles' who dreamed of literary careers and lives of freedom in the Helvetic Republic in the center of Europe, even though the reality around them had long since signaled the end of this freedom. This diminishing freedom was the reason for Kleist's mood swings. On the one hand, he was cheerful as he "hovered about" and "embarked on adventures" with his three friends—whose "good humor" he shared—"wherever the path led them."[128] And, on the other hand, he felt depressive, sometimes longing for death, again and again reduced to a "quiet, obscure, unseen existence."[129] He writes to Zschokke that, if Zschokke were to visit him with Geßner, he should muse on a saying in Thun: "'I come, I know not whence. I am, I know not what. I am going, I know not whither. I am surprised to be so cheerful.'—I like this saying very much," Kleist continues, "and I cannot think of it without pleasure when I am going for a walk."[130] This pleasure is, according to Martin Luther's exegesis of the saying, highly questionable: "Hence, the saying is not true for Christians, which goes: 'I live and do not know how long; I die and do not know when; I am going and do not know whither; I am surprised to be so cheerful.' Such things are said by unbelievers, for whom all this is true. But a Christian knows full well where he is going, namely to the bosom of the Father."[131]

Luther's commentary on the saying shows how radical Kleist's "pleasure" in a movement that evades the trappings of stability[132] actually was. For Kleist Switzerland represented two contrasting things: melancholia and utopia. The latter, meaning 'no place,' suggests a place where he can lose himself and, at the same time, get to the bottom of his existence and reinvent himself in and through literature. The motto 'Melancholy, the muse. Poetry, the remedy'[133] applies only briefly when it comes to Kleist. When he reads to his friends the tragic ending of his debut play *The Family Schroffenstein*—which he began writing in Thun and in which two children imagine their own rebirth beyond the reach of their fathers' repressive worlds, only to ultimately die at their hands—"the audience's laughter, along with the writer's," turns "so fierce and boundless" that it becomes "impossible for him to reach the final murder scene."[134] Together they succeed in ridiculing their despair about the fact that their desire for unfettered self-determination is naïve. Without his friends, however, in the solitude of his room, Kleist becomes once again overcome by melancholia. His sister Ulrike becomes a victim of his permanent mood swings. When her brother writes home "that he is seriously ill" and in need of financial support, she rushes, worried, from Frankfurt an der Oder to Switzerland. She beats her way through the turmoil of the Swiss civil war, taking a carriage "the entire way to Bern passed armed troops," and when she finally meets her brother, he is doing well and jokes about her travel outfit.[135] But soon after, Ulrike's vigor is needed after all. Ludwig Wieland allegedly fooled around with Kleist in front of the Bernese generals' quarters and is being expelled from the country. Consequently, Ulrike commissions a wagoner, orders their luggage to be packed, and "within two hours everything" is "ready to leave for their journey." On October 17, 1802, the two siblings embark on their journey with Ludwig Wieland.

The stay in Switzerland may have been short, but it was significant for Kleist. It was here that he substituted the 'project self-cultivation' with the 'project literature.'[136] For nomads such as Kleist, limiting oneself to one project does not work—not solely the civil servant, the estate owner, or the farmer. He preferred the intermezzo, he preferred to live in liminal spaces and times, like those of literature. Thun was Kleist's second place of birth, so to speak, the place of his rebirth as a writer, which was only made possible by the temporary forgetting of reality—in the heterotopia described by Swiss writer Robert Walser in his short sketch "Kleist in Thun" of 1907. 'How and why did Kleist become a writer?' Walser implicitly asks—and 'how and why me myself?' This form of self-reflexivity is to be expected when a writer portrays a writer. Answers to these questions are hard to find, but the search must be attempted, with the debut play *The Schroffenstein Family* serving as a test piece.

CHAPTER VI

On the Gradual Fabrication of the Writer and His Works

Kleist's Theory of Creativity and His First Literary Experiments

"We laymen have always been intensely curious to know [...] from what sources that strange being, the creative writer, draws his material." With these modest words Sigmund Freud opens his lecture "Creative Writers and Day-dreaming" in Vienna on December 6, 1907, only then to conclude triumphantly and without a doubt: "His Majesty the Ego" is the origin and object of such "egocentric" work, which allows a writer to locate and affirm the self. Creativity, for Freud, is a compensatory activity that serves to satisfy instinctual desires in the imaginary that cannot be fulfilled in the real. Through poetic techniques the writer disguises his fantasies about himself so that they are met with general approval.[1] What is one to make of this? An author's early works are often autobiographical in nature—from Johann Wolfgang Goethe's *Werther* (1774) to Thomas Mann's *Buddenbrooks* (1901) and Günter Grass' *The Tin Drum* (1959). Kleist's debut play *The Schroffenstein Family*, too, demonstrates that life provides the raw material for literature and that literature, in turn, negotiates alternative life plans. Beyond Freud's simple compensation thesis, one can think of creativity as an experiment in which writers test, in their fiction, potential solutions for real crises. But does this help us understand why somebody like Kleist becomes a writer, or how great literature comes into being? Not really. The reciprocal illumination of life and writing has its pitfalls.

The problem is rooted in the fact that every biography necessarily focuses on the facts of an author's life, though the very impetus to know is owed to the author's fictions. The work is fascinating and exceptional, though the person behind it is not necessarily so. He or she may have entirely ordinary traits. How are we, then, to understand the leap into the extraordinary? Is it easier to understand if the author is a 'project-maker' and adventurer like Kleist? That, too, is problematic. The life of a writer is, at best, a sufficient but by no means a necessary condition for the genesis of great works. It would be easy to find biographies similar to those traumatic ones of Kleist or Franz Kafka, for example. There were plenty of dispossessed aristocrats and one-time child soldiers in Prussia at the turn of the 19th century, just as there were plenty of sons in Prague at the turn of the 20th century who had to endure the disciplinary measures of their authoritarian Jewish fathers without giving their suffering such

© WILHELM FINK VERLAG, 2021 | DOI:10.30965/9783846765746_007

grandiose expression in literary works. With regard to the lives of Kleist and Kafka, it is impossible to explain the greatness and singularity of their work in terms of cause and effect.

Writers themselves fall short when attempting to explain the true origins of their creativity. In his *Critique of the Power of Judgment* of 1790, Immanuel Kant wrote that the origin of creativity is unknown to genius; it thus "cannot itself describe or indicate scientifically how it brings its product into being, [...] and hence the author of a product that he owes to his genius does not know himself how the ideas for it come to him, and also does not have it in his power to think up such things at will or according to plan, and to communicate to others precepts that would put them in a position to produce similar products."[2] Analyses of literary and artistic depictions of creativity confirm Kant's notion.[3] From the internal perspective of the author, but even more so from the external perspective of the observer, scientific attempts to explain the origin of creativity fail, as Kant suggests in his *Anthropology from a Pragmatic Point of View* of 1798, in which he had to acknowledge—albeit reluctantly—that the faculty of genius is characterized by the "*invisibility* (of the cause of an effect)."[4] According to Kant, the true origin of creativity is beyond all rational analysis.

Since the origin of creativity is so elusive, the danger of producing legends within the vitae of writers and artists is imminently present, no matter whether biographies or autobiographies. The mystification and auratization of genius by way of the anachronistic topoi of creativity from the biblical story of Genesis or the Classical invocation to the Muse; the pathologizing of genius through the linking of creativity to biographical traumas—each of these reductive formulas means to render the extraordinary understandable to the ordinary reader. German writer Wolfgang Hildesheimer once juxtaposed the many disparate Mozart legends in order to defamiliarize old images of his genius and make it appear entirely anew.[5] In his prose sketch "Kleist in Thun" of 1907, Swiss writer Robert Walser proceeds in a similar fashion. The narrator initially presents Kleist as an extreme character. He is torn between the "old voices" of his "distant northern home" and the intensities of southern nature, "ready for the death leap into the image of that lovely depth" in which he finds the leisure to write. Apollonian clarity and Dionysian frenzy alternate. Inner and outer mobility correspond to each other: Kleist "rushes down the darkening hill" and, "[b]ack in his room he sits down, determined to work till frenzy comes, at his writing table." He appears a restless man who knows no self-care, whose life in Thun is determined by the rhythm of his creative moments, with no healthy variation between tension and release, only mania and melancholic paralysis. Walser's narrator creates a collage made of the topoi of genius informed by the history of the artist novella—by Georg Büchner's "Lenz" (1835), Eduard

Mörike's *Mozart's Journey to Prague* (1855), or Thomas Mann's Schiller-novella "A Weary Hour" (1905). But at the end he makes a sudden leap into the present, introducing himself as a one-time "clerk in a brewery" in Thun and, like a tour guide, presenting incidental facts, such as the Thun trade fair four years prior, among other banal things, thus forcing the reader to question his ability to draw a subtle psychological profile of Kleist:

> [A]nd last of all one can permit oneself the observation that on the front of the villa where Kleist lived hangs a marble plaque which indicates who lived and worked there. Travelers who intend to tour the Alps can read it, the children of Thun read it and spell it out, letter by letter, and then look questioning into each other's eyes. A Jew can read it, a Christian too, if he has the time and if his train is not leaving that very instant, a Turk, a swallow, insofar as she is interested, I also, I can read it again if I like. Thun stands at the entrance of the Bernese Oberland and is visited every year by thousands of foreigners.

This is an absurd list by which Walser's 'tour guide' succeeds to render Kleist's genius foreign and unreadable again.[6]

How does one—as a non-genius—approach a genius appropriately? What can reliably be said from a scholarly perspective concerning literary creativity? Kant suggests considering the question of creativity not in terms of the *origin of production* but in terms of the *produced work*, about whose exceptionality the community of readers has, after all, passed a judgment.[7] Genius thus becomes recognizable only through its product. Kleist himself mentions another method in a nothing less than groundbreaking essay which analyzes the conditions of the *creative process* and which, even today, challenges creativity studies: "On the Gradual Fabrication of Thoughts While Speaking." Kleist presumably wrote it during his time in Königsberg in 1805/06 and dedicated it to Rühle von Lilienstern, his old friend from his time in the Potsdam guard regiment.

Kleist's essay starts out rather innocuously by proposing a "precept" which states that ideas come as we are speaking just like the appetite comes as we are eating. A series of rather heterogeneous case studies is supposed to illustrate this claim. What they all have in common is that, following a precarious beginning or silence, they present the 'gradual' fabrication of thoughts as a 'creativity test' whose distinguishing feature is that the communication between the test subject and its observer has an agonistic structure. Evidently, Kleist considers aggression to be a catalyst for creativity, regardless of whether it is scholarly, artistic, or political in nature. In each case the aggression is directed toward an opponent who embodies—actually or symbolically—social institutions that restrain the individual's self-expression. In the first case, Kleist—while grappling with a mathematical problem—becomes "agitated" and, "like a great general," talks over his, in actuality, peaceful and silent sister as if he were performing an urgent act of self-assertion against a representative of familial demands and expectations. In the second case, Molière asserts himself with his maidservant at home, who—as an imaginary opponent—anticipates the judgment of the literary audience on his developing drama. The third case deals with political acts of liberation, with the onset of the French Revolution, in particular with Mirabeau's speech of June 1789, in which he defies Louis XVI's order to disperse the assembly of the estates. The fourth case recounts Jean de La Fontaine's fable "The Animals Sick with the Plague." The lion, the king of animals, looking for someone to blame for the outbreak of the plague, condemns the fox—the worst offender among the animals—to death. The lion represents the constraining power of the naturally strongest, but the fox manages to save his neck thanks to an artful speech. Kleist's final example describes the ritual of a university examination. The creativity test fails here, as the examiner, unversed in the "art of intellectual midwifery," does not allow for any competition with the examinee, expecting to hear his ideas simply echoed back at him—nothing but reproductions of knowledge—rather than playing on the examinee's mind to sound its "proper tone."[8]

Nothing new can come from mere imitation. Kleist's notion of creativity demonstrates his commitment—in terms of literary history and the history of mentalities—to the artistic debates of the 17th and 18th centuries: to the *Querelle des Anciens et des Modernes* among the members of the Académie Française in 1687—the famous quarrel about the merit of contemporary culture compared with Classical culture—and its continuation in the genius discourse of European Enlightenment. Here, the competition between the generations—the necessary rebellion of the new against the old, the notion of nonconformity as a precondition for originality—becomes a prominent figure of thought which has stayed relevant to the present day. Edward Young's compendium *Conjectures on Original Composition*—first published in London in 1759 and translated into German as early as one year later—serves as a model for the rebellious German authors of the Sturm und Drang movement in that it once again unsettles the three main pillars of the centuries-old theory of poetry—the conviction that the origin and formation of literary works is owed, primarily, to the *trias* of *ingenium* (as divine inspiration), *ars* (as a technical mastery of the rules of art), and *doctrina* (as scholarly knowledge). To claim that original works of art like those of William Shakespeare "were written by angels" would mean "to deny that we are men" with talents that we ought to use because, as Young notes, nature "brings us into the world all *Originals*: No two faces, no two minds, are just alike; but all bear nature's evident mark of separation on them. Born *Originals*, how comes it to pass that we die *Copies*? That meddling ape *Imitation* [...] snatches the pen, and blots out nature's mark of separation, cancels her kind intention, destroys all mental individuality."[9] Thus, to Young the model of genius is the model of individuality, which is to be recognized and expressed—in Kleist's own words—in one's "proper tone." *Individuum est ineffabile* and therefore *ingenium* is too. Despite its significant historical impact, Young's definition of genius is ultimately aporetic insofar as *individuum* and *ingenium* are rendered incomparable. The question of the origin of creativity, of the genealogical authority of the creative subject, cannot be answered in this manner. After the renunciation of the old model of transpersonal creativity, there is no universal theory of causes for the new, personal model anymore. What remains from the debates of the 18th century to this day is a negative foundation of genius: Young's suggestion that a genius should leave the "beaten road" of the many to follow his own "path" and, for the rest, trust in chance or competition with a rival. Originality, to Young, is what "chance often discovers, either by a lucky chosen theme, or a mighty premium, or an absolute necessity of exertion, or a noble stroke of emulation from another's glory."[10]

Kleist's view of creativity as a critical test in which the singularity of the creative subject must assert itself is hardly original. He is, however, more radical than Young, and especially more radical than the aesthetic philosophies of Weimar Classicism. In German Idealism—for instance, in Friedrich Schiller's concept of aesthetic education—the precondition for the autonomy of genius is the division of its sphere, separating the art of invention and self-discovery from day-to-day life in a rebellion against social convention. In Kleist's "Letter from a Young Writer to a Young Painter," the writer also advises—in keeping with Schiller—that, "in spite of [one's] inhuman teachers," one could at least "lock [one's] doors at night for [one's] secret experiments in the mysteries of artistic creation—that calling of the elect."[11] In his essay "On the Gradual Fabrication of Thoughts While Speaking," however, Kleist does not allow for this playful exit strategy. Ultimately, the social institutions are the testing grounds on which one has to prove oneself as a creative mind, to assert creativity by dominating or destroying the powers that restrain self-expression. A second criteria for differentiating Kleist from German Idealism, crucial for situating him historically, is that the self-realization of genius is no longer bound to any moral legitimation, as we see in each of the examples in his essay on creativity. Even the writers of the Sturm und Drang movement had rebelled against authority in the name of heart, reason, and morality. In Kleist's essay, however, there is no prescribed criteria for the contents of the creative person's thoughts, nor does creativity play an essential role in the education of man, as it does in German Idealism. Hence, in Kleist's rendering of La Fontaine's fable, the fox's situation before the lion resembles Scheherazade's test of creativity, spinning tales to have her life spared. Unlike the fox, however, Scheherazade takes on martyrdom in the place of the virgins whose lives are threatened. Her tales entertain and teach the King so that, in the end, he becomes a benevolent and virtuous ruler. In Kleist's adaptation the fox has no intentions of stopping the animal king's plan for sacrifice. His rhetoric does not aim at facilitating the lion's aesthetic education, but at saving his own neck with a destructive stroke of genius, establishing a better candidate for sacrifice among his listeners: the innocent donkey.

Kleist's identification of aggression as a catalyst for creativity may be attributed to his military background. He does not render the *Querelle des Anciens et des Modernes* a merely aesthetic and cognitive quarrel, but reflects quite deliberately on the mental driving forces behind artistic creativity and, in doing so, lays open the relation between construction and destruction. This notion of creativity also explains his writerly competition with Shakespeare, Molière, Schiller, or Goethe, in which world literature itself appears as a drama of struggle with the succeeding generation of writers and their precursors—a struggle that ends in either failure or triumph. As Harold Bloom notes, only the 'strong poet,' driven by the "creative's mind desperate insistence upon priority," survives this conflict and comes to play a role in the merciless history of literature.[12]

Kleist's essay does not reveal much about the talent of the creative subject, the different phases of creative thinking, or the final product—the mathematical, political, or literary idea. From today's perspective it could be said that Kleist works like a psychologist, defining ambition and aggression as catalysts for the creative process, independent of the substance of the thoughts produced. But it could also be said that he works like a media theorist and cognitive scientist.[13] This is captured most clearly in the sensational and, to this day, groundbreaking dimension of Kleist's theory of creativity, whose element of surprise is captured as soon as the essay's title, where thoughts are 'gradually fabricated while speaking,' that is, in and through their medium. Kleist thus reverses the basic assumption of traditional rhetoric according to which thinking precedes speaking, with the speaker expanding on a preconceived thought in controlled and effective speech. For Kleist it is more: No sooner thought than said. Thoughts—gradually fabricated while speaking—owe themselves to the "obstinacy of the medium of language." They are not "transcendent of language," but "contents exclusively pertaining to language."[14]

The creative process thus consists neither of a simple transcription from the inside—from a language of thought, a 'mentalese' of any kind whatsoever—nor does it stem from a simple transcription from the outside—from reproduction or mimesis. Any speaker or writer knows how hard first sentences or the first pages of a manuscript are until the right wording is found for formation into a clear thought. Kleist does not present creativity as the representation of an experience made or planned in advance, but as the modus of experience made within a medium itself—by means of speaking and potentially unsettling, disruptive objections. In this way a *perceptio confusa* turns into a *perceptio distincta*:

> But because I do start with some sort of dark notion remotely related to what I am looking for, my mind, if it has set out boldly enough, and being pressed to complete what it has begun, shapes that muddled idea into a form of new-minted clarity, even while my talking progresses, with the result that my full thought, to my astonishment, is completed with the period. I mumble inarticulately, drawl out my conjunctions, use unnecessary appositions, and avail myself of all other dilatory tricks to gain the time required for fabricating my idea in the workshop of Reason. Nothing on such occasions can have a more salutary effect than a casual gesture from my sister as if to interrupt, for my intellect, already sorely exercised, becomes all the more agitated at this external threat to tear it away from the speech which is guiding it, and like a great general when circumstances marshal against him, I am suddenly a degree more capable of my objective.[15]

Order from noise is the method. The "precept" is: One should abandon oneself to the medium itself—to its figures of control—while trying to speak in a controlled manner without knowing what one's actions will ultimately amount to. The situation is thus paradoxical, the speech act recursive: The speaker gains time by speaking in an, as yet, unstructured manner to differentiate his thoughts, thoughts he himself acquires only by listening to himself speaking, by deploying the formative power of the medium itself. The medium, in this case spoken language—in its resistant nature, in the obstinacy of its possible semantic, syntactic, and pragmatic applications and restrictions—proves to foster creativity. The listener—portrayed by Kleist as agonistic—is also resistant, both disciplining and stimulating the speaker. Because language is—as any medium—a scheme of consensus reliant on interaction, a hybrid cross of subjectivity and intersubjectivity.

For Kleist the medium in which thoughts are expressed is itself the fuel for ideas, the friction that ignites them. There is no consciousness outside of language, as consciousness is, first and foremost, generated and structured in and through language. The medium has priority, consciousness always follows. This helps to explain why Kleist's shift from *origin* to *process* in the question of creativity has remained so productive. Creativity is precisely not—as claimed by the aesthetics of genius of the 18th century and sometimes even today—the independent cognitive competence of the ingenious subject, readily available prior to any action, and actualized within a medium. Rather, it is a knowledge that can only be generated *in actu*, in the act of using a medium. Provocatively, and in contrast to the aesthetics of genius, Kleist insists: "For it is not *we* who 'know'; it is rather a certain condition, in which we happen to be, that 'knows.'"[16] In this respect creativity is in no way, as Kleist's examples illustrate, a predictable process; it is not a transformation of knowledge and intention into practical action, but a mode of experience immanent in one's actions: while speaking, while writing, in the process of painting, sculpting, composing. Art is experience,[17] the experience of distributed agency between artist and medium or material, between artist and the imaginary or real observer.[18] The creative person is him- or herself part of the experimental setup; there is no outside in creative experiments. And according to Kleist, it is primarily those experiments in which something unpredictable happens—an interference disrupting the creative process—that allow for innovation. Creativity always requires an openness to risk, above all, the recognition of an interference's creative potential, and the willingness to be 'overwritten' by the medium or observer, so to speak. Kleist agrees that necessity begets ingenuity—or, as German sociologist Niklas Luhmann put it: Creativity is about "using chance to generate structures."[19] A description that is well suited for Kleist, the 'project-maker.'

Sometimes, too, it is owed to chance that one finds a circle of peers—people who listen to and read one's work in progress, experts who can discipline and stimulate it, as Kleist did in Switzerland with the writers Heinrich Zschokke and Ludwig Wieland as well as the bookseller and publisher Heinrich Geßner. And, so, while it may be hard to tell from where Kleist's exceptional talent originates, this is not the case with regard to the question of why he becomes a writer in Switzerland, particularly if one abides by Kleist's own views on how to foster the literary process of creation in terms of its mental, social, and medial functions. The question 'What is creativity?' is therefore to be substituted with the question *where* and *how* one becomes creative—in which medial context, which work environment, through which intellectual tensions. The beginnings of Kleist's writings are nurtured within a community of friends which serves as shelter and catalyst for his creativity. According to Zschokke, they inspired each other for the "art of beauty, for poetry, literature and literary fame," discussed Goethe, Schiller, Friedrich Schlegel, and Ludwig Tieck, "freely shared their own poetic creations among each other"—Kleist, for example, read from his *The Schroffenstein Family*—and united in a "poetic competition" in response to a copper engraving, entitled *The Judge, or the Broken Jug* (*Le juge, ou la cruche cassée*), which hung in Zschokke's room. Zschokke writes that Kleist's *The Broken Jug* "bore the prize away."[20] Kleist's circle of friends thus acts—wholly in line with his essay "On the Gradual Fabrication of Thoughts While Speaking"—as a creative workshop. Kleist's first biographer Eduard von Bülow relates that Kleist, according to Zschokke, "had written" the fifth act of *The Schroffenstein Family* "in prose only and that the editors Wieland and Geßner allegedly put it into verse. He also maintained the very same Wieland moved Kleist to rewrite his play once more and relocate the plot—first meant to be set in Spain—to Switzerland [Swabia]."[21]

Just as he would later in Dresden, Kleist finds in Switzerland a social context that stimulates his writing. The small group of writers in Bern and Thun seeking intellectual and political freedom in the Helvetic Republic, far away from the Prussian homeland, can hardly be compared in their joint inventiveness with an avant-garde center such as the Zurich Dada a century later. Nor does the group establish a programmatic aesthetic as do contemporary groups of Romantic era writers, who defend the novelty of their generation against the old. What seems to unite this group is their fascination with writing against all opposition, primarily against their families. It is even no use if your father himself is a writer as well-established as Christoph Martin Wieland. In a letter to his son Ludwig of August 1802, he warns him against his own profession:

> Do you know what writing, as a livelihood, in and of itself and especially these days in Germany means? It is the most miserable, uncertain, and despicable craft a person could pursue—the surest way to die in a hospital. [...] I know what you are going to say—novels, plays, journals, paperbacks—and the examples of Goethe, Schiller, Richter [Jean Paul], Kotzebue, La Fontaine.—Indeed, these five are an exception, but what are five against the more than six thousand writers there are at present? [...] The publishing industry is in such a profound decline and is getting so much worse with each book fair, even prestigious booksellers are terrified when offered a manuscript that does not bear an already famous name to guarantee its success. [...] With journals one cannot earn a dime at all anymore; there are indeed several dozen new ones year after year, sprouting like mushrooms from swampy soil, from the boggy big heads of our literary youth; but they wither early, most do not survive their second quarter. [...] I gladly admit that everything I said about the misery of the writing profession, regarded as a *modus acquirendi*, may be somewhat modified were we talking about a young man who decided to become a writer resulting from the urge of an inner calling, with the awareness of great and exceptional mental faculties and talents, hence with an anticipated certainty to create a sensation among our tasteless and weary reading public, which likes best to feed on the excrements of dimwitted minds. I do not know if *you* are that young man, although I have reason to doubt it very much.[22]

The Schroffenstein Family

Kleist was familiar with the doubts family is capable of harboring about one's emergent talents. His family back home in Frankfurt an der Oder expected him to finally take up a bread-and-butter job. Kleist, however, sees himself as a philosophical mind. In October 1801 he writes to his fiancée from Paris: "But *writing* for *money*—O speak not of it! [...] I have [...] been at work giving form to my imaginings, but I cannot understand how a writer can hand over his love child to so coarse a mob as the public."[23] Kleist no longer wants to become a science communicator and write works of popular science—which is what he once declared as the secret money-making objective for his journey to Paris. He wants to become a writer, which is not a bread-and-butter job but a calling. In May 1802 Kleist writes to Ulrike from his writer's retreat in Thun: "Occasionally Geßner or Zschokke or Wieland visit from Bern, listen to some of my writing, and say flattering things—in short, I have no other wish but to die if I might achieve three things: a child, a beautiful piece of writing and a great deed."[24] He starts the "beautiful piece of writing" in Thun, an extraterritorial place, in which he seeks to develop his "proper tone" through writing, to reinvent himself as a writer, far away from the heteronomy of his family in the Prussian homeland. Kleist's first play, *The Schroffenstein Family*, seems to be affected by this: It breaks with all the contemporary models of family life and shows at once how frail the children's fantasies of self-creation are. It is no wonder, then, that Kleist advises his sister and his family not to read the play.

This is Kleist's only commentary on his first work. Unlike the detailed accounts of inspiring apples or wine, nightly agonies at their desk, and writer's block found in Schiller, Goethe, or Kafka, one does not find remarks on the specific circumstances of his literary work in Kleist. In a letter to his sister Ulrike of March 14, 1803, he reacted to a review of his play, published anonymously ten days earlier in the Berlin journal *The Liberal* (*Der Freimüthige*). Kleist believed the critic to be August von Kotzebue, the journal's editor, but in actual fact it was a certain Ludwig Ferdinand Huber who announced, quite generously, the "Emergence of a New Writer."[25] Huber did not know the writer's name, as Geßner published *The Schroffenstein Family* in 1803 in Bern and Zurich anonymously. Kleist was happy about this fact, as he deemed his play a "wretched old book (*Scharteke*)." That, at least, is what he wrote in his letter to Ulrike before crossing the words out. What he did not cross out were his stark words of warning to his family: "Also, would you do me the favor to *not read the book*. I beg you not to. In short, do not do it. Are you listening?"[26]

By *Scharteke* one understands—as we learn from the *German Dictionary* (*Deutsches Wörterbuch*) by the Brothers Grimm—an old book or piece of

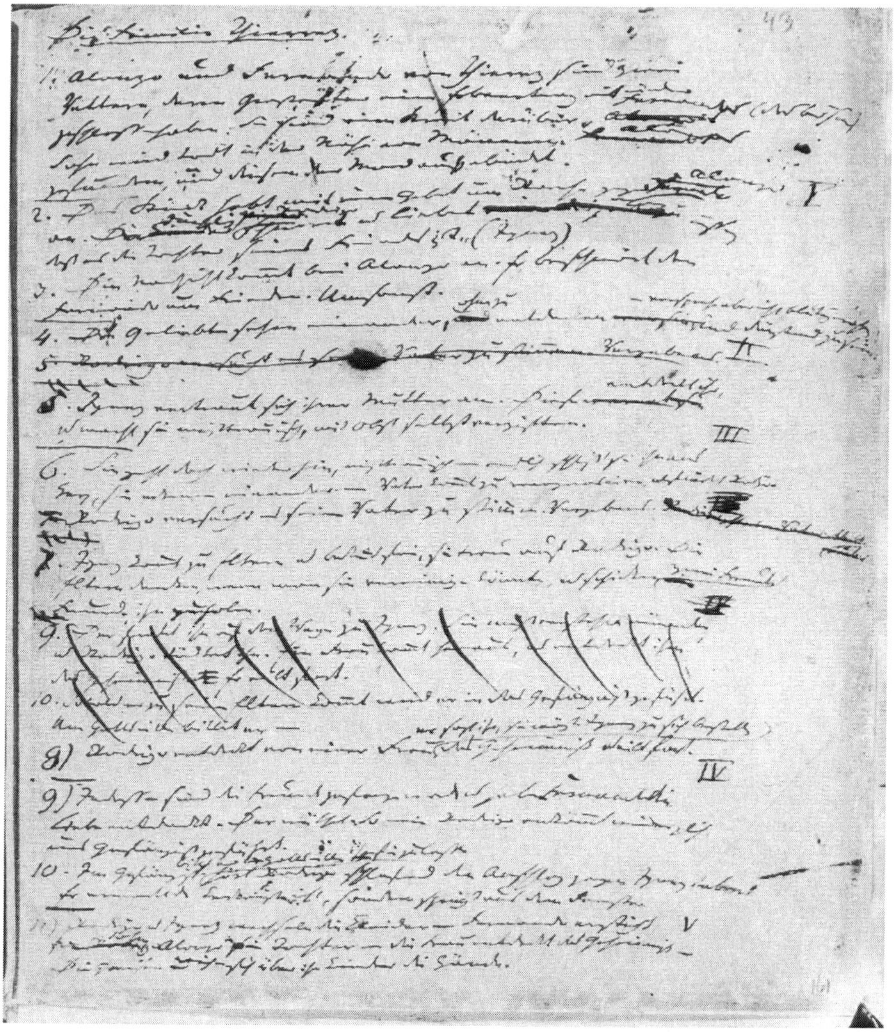

Fig. 30 Draft of Kleist's *The Schroffenstein Family*, here under its original title *The Thierrez Family*

writing that has become worthless as the ideas it expresses have been deemed obsolete.[27] Kleist's first work cannot be considered an old *Scharteke*; at most it could be considered a derivative one, reminiscent of ideas and motifs of the 18th century family tragedies and thus proving their lasting relevance.

Originally, the play was to be set in France; its first draft, of which only a fragment survived, was entitled *The Thierrez Family*. The fully developed second draft, entitled *The Ghonorez Family*, is set in Spain. Ludwig Wieland then advised Kleist to relocate the setting to medieval Swabia. The play's gruesome and somewhat confusing plot may be briefly recounted as follows: The family, with the telling name Schroffenstein, is divided into two rival houses: the House of Rossitz and the House of Warwand. Rupert reigns in Rossitz with his wife Eustache, and in Warwand, Sylvester rules with his wife Gertrude. Rupert has a legitimate son named Ottokar as well as an illegitimate one named Johann, who is mentally unsound. Sylvester has a daughter named Agnes. These, at least, are the children still living at the beginning of the play. The feud between the Schroffensteins of the House Warwand and those of the House Rossitz stems from an inheritance contract stipulating that if the line of descent in one branch of the family is broken, their estate should fall to the other. The feud begins with Rupert's vow of revenge when he mistakenly believes his cousin Sylvester had his youngest son Peter killed by two men who were taken by surprise with bloody knives in their hands next to Peter's dead body—the child's left hand missing its little finger. Hence Rupert's desire to wipe out the House of Warwand without further ado, obliging all family members to assist him in his murderous plot, including his son Ottokar, who—to make matters worse—loves the enemy's daughter, Sylvester's Agnes. After some initial doubts the latter returns Ottokar's love. She drinks some water that Ottokar hands her during an unexpected meeting in the mountains, fully convinced it had to contain poison because of the feud. She then thanks him affectionately for the fact that she was wrong. From then on Ottokar tries to reconcile the two families, as does his uncle Jeronimus, who belongs to a third house of this labyrinthian family, named Wyk. Jeronimus pays for his determination to reconcile the families with his life; Rupert has him killed by one of his vassals. Unfortunately, Rupert also learns that Ottokar and Agnes are in love and that they met in the mountains, in a cave—a fact which has delighted psychoanalytical Kleist scholars. To their further pleasure it is there that Agnes and Ottokar also switch their clothes. This happens upon Ottokar's advice, as he wants to protect Agnes from his father's persecution. As to be expected, it does not help. The fathers each kill their own child thinking it is the other. It is Agnes' blind grandfather, Sylvius, and Ottokar's mad brother, Johann, who realize the mistaken identities. And, at the end, the initial error is solved by the witch Ursula. Rupert learns that Peter was not killed by the House of Warwand after all, but drowned while playing. It was not Sylvester's men but Ursula—the widow of a gravedigger—who cut off the child's finger to cook in a witches' brew with which to fend off the devil. In the end the fathers shake hands with each other over the dead bodies of their children in reconciliation while the mothers embrace each other.

The ending is peculiar and may prevent a reader from taking this "wretched old book" seriously—from understanding it as a piece of contemplative literature concerned with a problem *in abstracto*, grappling with the historico-philosophical, epistemological, and moral concepts of bourgeois Enlightenment Kleist encountered in his adolescence. In this more 'serious' perspective, *The Schroffenstein Family* is three different things: a tragedy of society, a tragedy of knowledge and language, and a family tragedy.

As a societal tragedy the play appears to negotiate the problem of regulating social relations according to Jean-Jacques Rousseau's triadic model of history in *Discourse on the Origin and Foundations of Inequality among Men* of 1753. Rousseau describes a pre-societal ideal state without knowing whether it ever existed, but of which he wants to devise a clear concept to be able to better judge the contemporary condition of man. He assumes that there had once been a golden age of man, which, over time, had fallen victim to decadence—a nomadic age in which man lived peacefully with his own kind in small manageable tribal communities. It was an age which knew of no property ownership, as the land one roamed belonged to nobody, and thus there was no need for laws regulating communal life. It was not until the establishment of property—which started with the occupation and settlement of land as man became sedentary—that inequality was born, with disastrous repercussions. A rampant struggle for property, justice, and power broke loose, Rousseau writes, and the relations between individual interest groups had to thenceforth be regulated by way of contracts. It is Rousseau's utopian hope that, with his use of free reason, man will give up thinking in terms of domination and ownership and thereby restore the original natural community.

In a sense the story of *The Schroffenstein Family* mirrors this Rousseauist history of mankind. Jeronimus, who initially believes he can treat the feud between the Rossitz and Warwand families as a mere rivalry between individuals, is informed by the warden that it was the inheritance contract—according to which, should one line of the family die out, its entire estate should fall to the other—that gave rise to the feud, in the way the apple did to the Fall of Man.[28] Accordingly, the Schroffensteins' inheritance contract—originally a reasonable social contract, a legal practice quite common among noble houses—destroys a once harmonious family community that did not know the difference between 'mine' and 'yours,' causing the 'unnatural' rivalry between the brothers Rupert and Sylvester. Their coveting for the other's property gives rise to mistrust, mistrust gives rise to misunderstandings (which are no more than egocentric constructions of reality), and misunderstandings give rise to hate and murder. Where human relationships are merely regarded in terms of property, human nature becomes corrupted; blood relatives turn into deadly rivals. Only between the children Agnes and Ottokar, who surrendered their egoistic sense of ownership out of free reason, does trust still exist. They dream—faithful to Rousseau—of a future that restores the original ideal state of community.

But the tragedy of the Schroffenstein family is also rooted in a conflict of language and knowledge; the problem of describing and analyzing reality is at issue. Appearance and reality, sign and referent, name and thing rarely correspond in this play. Agnes transforms into Ottokar, Ottokar into Agnes, and—appearing as something other than they are—they fall victim to their own fathers. The tragedy ends the same way it begins: with a misunderstanding. Catastrophe befalls the family because an accident is mistaken for murder. Initially, nobody actually knows the truth; the play offers two possibilities for managing the uncertainty of knowledge that Kleist's Kant crisis brings upon its characters. The first option is to act, the second to analyze. Scenes of action alternate with scenes of interrogation throughout the play.[29] Rupert acts according to a preconceived suspicion that remains unquestioned. By contrast, Jeronimus von Schroffenstein of the House of Wyk, in his attempt to mediate between the Rossitz and Warwand families, examines the evidence like a detective, albeit in vain. Yet his efforts are not without value. His interrogations do not uncover the real circumstances of Peter's death, but they do disclose the terms in which his death is understood—how the unverified suspicion, beginning as a mere rumor, slowly solidifies into reality. For instance, Rupert's assumption that Sylvester is responsible for Peter's death is based entirely on a single word the former extorts from a Warwand by torturing him to death. With his last breath the latter whispers his master's name, which is enough for Rupert to pass his assumption off as a fact, since he dominates the discourse in his house. The dialogue between the characters in Kleist's first play does not represent 'reality'; it merely provides a self-characterization of the respective speaker. Put in terms of the imagery of Kleist's Kant letters: We come to learn that everything depends on the glasses with which one perceives reality. Rupert's perspective is one of self-interest and hate. Ottokar's is one of trust. Accordingly, their versions of reality follow completely contrary rules and come into conflict with each other.

Let us now approach *The Schroffenstein Family* as a family tragedy. The play revolves around the problem of how to justify paternal authority; related to this is the issue of the children reaching majority status. The question of what it means to be a proper father, the question of how to legitimize patriarchal authority of any kind—that of the father of a family, the father of a country, and of God the Father—was a subject typical of Enlightenment literature, which Kleist's play brings back to mind. In the 18th century the authority of the father was justified in two ways: on the one hand, in terms of private law, through the power of the father, the *patria potestas*, and on the other hand, in terms of natural law, through the care of the sympathetically loving father. The private law justification was sufficient in aristocratic families, who did not consider themselves a community based on feelings, but on social station. Family members' interactions were determined by etiquette, children were taken care of by servants and private tutors, and were raised without regard for child-appropriate behavior. Children were supposed to be integrated into the adult world as soon as possible and to act according to their station—Kleist's own example shows this. Things were different in the new bourgeois nuclear family, which was not a public affair but a safe haven—a sanctuary, a private sphere of intimacy. The tendency to separate public and private life can be observed down to the functionalization of living spaces, through which children were separated from the public day-to-day life of the adults. They were to grow up in a sheltered space that provided the freedom necessary for the natural unfolding of their individuality.[30] Thus goes the ideal of the new model of childhood, developed most notably by Rousseau in Kleist's favorite book *Emile* of 1762. Accordingly, it was the duty of the father to reconcile 'power' and 'tenderness.'[31] In real life this rarely worked out, and even in the bourgeois tragedies of the 18th century often only in a precarious way. When a father kills his child—as is the case in Gotthold Ephraim Lessing's *Emilia Galotti*—he exercises his *patria potestas* as an ultimate form of care, as he sees no other way to protect his daughter's virtue—both father and daughter seeming to value virtue more than life.

But the Schroffenstein fathers do not kill out of care, nor does their tragedy result from a conflict between the aristocracy and the bourgeoisie, as in the bourgeois tragedy of the 18th century. Rather, the tragedy unfolds within the family itself, and this family is not a bourgeois one. Rupert and Sylvester are both counts, and the play is set in the Middle Ages. There are two 'houses,' which is historically and terminologically correct, and the family is defined as a community bound by law and property.[32] However, the House of Warwand is, anachronistically, contaminated by ideas of bourgeois Enlightenment. Sylvester embodies the justification of paternal authority through natural law. He is a loving, caring father—a weak one too—who faints when faced with the suspicion that he may have killed Rupert's son. Rupert, by contrast, is the pure embodiment of the *patria potestas*; his authority rests completely on his power to rule. To think in terms of natural law à la Rousseau is foreign to him, as evidenced in his first scene, where he exposes such thinking as powerless fiction:

> Enough of nature.
> 'Tis but a pleasant little fairy tale
> Which poets, mankind's nurses, tell to man.

> We know that faith and innocence and love,
> Fidelity, religion and the fear
> Of Gods are fabulous as beasts that speak.[33]

Kleist does not reconcile the two images of the father—forcefully dominating and tenderly loving—in a single figure, but rather splits them into two and positions them in an irreconcilable opposition. The final reconciliation of the two fathers is indeed a "merry jest,"[34] a matter of 'laughing oneself to death,' as Johann, the madman, puts it—the fool who tells the truth. This ending is a parody of the tableau at the end of the bourgeois melodrama. *The Schroffenstein Family* is a hopelessly pessimistic play. The family will die out due to the death of their last heirs, and none of the problems the play raises is actually solved: the problem of regulating social relationships outside of property ownership, which destroys everybody and everything; the problem of knowledge and communication; and the problem of dealing with the children reaching the status of majority. In the end all we know is that the world is out of joint. "If you have killed each other / It was your own mistake,"[35] comments Ursula, the witch. And Johann adds, with words one finds hard to believe were written by Kleist and not some post-war playwright of the theater of the absurd: "Do not be cross. Papa has done it by / Mistake. He meant no harm. Do not be vexed."[36] That is cold comfort, a naïve faith, nothing more. Daddy will do it again. Everywhere in Kleist one finds broken families.[37] In his later works fathers go on killing their own as well as others' children—for instance, in the novellas "The Earthquake in Chile" and "The Foundling." Or they shoot at their daughters as in *The Marquise of O—* (*Die Marquise von O....*). *The Schroffenstein Family* provided Kleist with a model that he reproduced and modified. The children's deaths are utterly senseless and do not serve to defend moral principles as they did in the bourgeois tragedy. They are effectively never a "mistake" in Kleist, as the witch Ursula suggests, but rather the price the children pay for daring to reach majority.[38]

"*Enlightenment*," notes Kant, "*is the human being's emergence from his self-incurred minority* [*Unmündigkeit*]. *Minority* is the inability to make use of one's own understanding without direction from another."[39] The term majority (*Mündigkeit*)—originally a legal term—marks the end of the relationship of dependence between child and father and the beginning of the child's capacity to function as a legal entity. In Kant's broadening of the term, majority signifies the capacity to hold oneself responsible under any authority. It is the good father, therefore, who helps his child gain that autonomy. This notion is foreign to Rupert von Schroffenstein. His son is expected to live according to the plan established by the House of Rossitz, which involves defending the vested rights and maintaining the family feud with the Warwands. The play's opening scene attests to this. The family gathers around Peter's coffin and swears:

> RUPERT. I swear revenge! Revenge here by the Host,
> Revenge upon thy house, Count Schroffenstein!
> *Receives the sacrament.*
> My son, come forward now and swear!
> OTTOKAR. My heart
> Bears up with wings thy curse to God on high.
> I swear revenge as thou dost.
> RUPERT. Speak the name,
> The name, my son, the name!
> OTTOKAR. Revenge I swear,
> Sylvester Schroffenstein, on thee!
> RUPERT. Make no mistake.
> A curse like ours must reach the ears of God,
> Who arms with lightnings every single word.
> So choose thy words with care and do not say
> Sylvester only—say and his whole house.
> So will it be more sure.
> OTTOKAR. Revenge! Revenge!
> Sylvester, on thy murd'rous house!
> *Receives the sacrament.*[40]

Unemancipated, Ottokar repeats his father's vow for revenge word for word, with blind obedience. By contrast, Johann—Rupert's illegitimate son—eludes the cruel father's power. His madness serves exactly this function, as he freely admits:

> Thee only do I trust, for here
> Within these walls it seems to me that in
> A pagan temple I, a Christian, lie,
> And savages with fearful gestures drag
> Me faint with terror toward their blood-spilt god.[41]

Seduced by his love for Agnes, Ottokar, too, renounces the life plan set by his father. To do this, he must develop a new method of self-formation wherein the assertion of individuality follows the law of contradiction against the paternal tutelage and manifests as a fantasy of rebirth—a sudden change of identity whose aim is liberation from the reality of an overbearing family. The precondition for this change of identity is the changing of a name that carries a cruel family history.[42] Ottokar does not reveal his name when he meets Agnes in the mountains, and he insists on calling her Mary. To her question as to why he addresses her this way, he responds:

I would remind thee with that name of that
Blest day when I did christen thee. I found
Thee sleeping here within this dell, which seemed
To cradle thee. The branches of the trees
Protectingly did weave above thy head
An arbor wreath. A waterfall did sing
A lullaby and gentle breezes fanned thee.
A goddess seemed to guard thee. Then thou didst
Awake and gaze on me as if thou wert
My new-born happiness. I did inquire
Thy name and thou didst say they had as yet
Not christened thee. I reached into the spring
And with a drop of water wet thy brow
And breast and said: "Since thou art image of
The virgin, let Mary be thy name."[43]

With this rebirth fantasy Agnes is to have cast off her Warwand identity and, with it, her involvement in the animosity of the two houses. She is to have been born anew, initiated into a new life just as Ottokar is hoping to be by virtue of his love for her. Her baptism functions as the initiation ritual, and her new name is its token. And while the scene takes place in the mountains, in unspoiled nature, it is there—only seemingly far away from the merciless world of their parents' castles—that both Agnes and Ottokar are killed. There are no uncompromised idylls in Kleist. Unlike Rupert's vow of vengeance, the baptismal ceremony does not rest on the masculine image of the sovereign God from the Old Testament, but on the feminine, loving image of God from the New Testament, as the name Mary represents. Ottokar thus tries and fails to substitute the narrative of the inheritance contract—which established, "[l]ong years ago,"[44] the feud between the two houses and, thus, the trajectory of every family member's life—with a new story of origin that fosters a sense of community and identity. Hence, the dramatic conflict can also be understood as the rivalry between these two narratives, and their respective advocates Rupert and Ottokar.[45] In the end the virtuous man succumbs to the violent one. This scenario is also true for the bourgeois tragedy of the 18th century, though here the sacrifice is meant to have a calculated aesthetic effect. Not so with Kleist: Closing with moral appeals is a move Kleist never makes. He seems to refuse to take the denouement of his play seriously. It is worth asking why Kleist recommended Schiller's *Wallenstein* to Wilhelmine, thus presenting Max and Thekla as role models who stick together against all paternal constraints, preferring to sacrifice themselves over their love, or why Kleist ridicules Ottokar's martyrdom at the end of the play: "When, one day, Kleist read his tragedy *The Schroffenstein Family* to us, the audience's laughter, along with the writer's, became so fierce and boundless during the last act that it was impossible for him to reach the final murder scene."[46] Is Kleist's writing—and his laughter—a mere mechanism of self-defense against the feeling of despair?

This could be one, albeit melodramatic, explanation. "But soon, after his love was over, he began writing about it." Thus German writer Arnold Stadler, winner of the Kleist Prize 2009, describes the painful birth of a writer in his novel *Come on, let's go* (*Komm, gehen wir*).[47] Kleist's love affair with Wilhelmine ended during his time in Switzerland, as did his relationship with Lose and, most significantly, his family. Technically, one becomes a writer in childhood, in the unfulfilled longings one remembers as an adult. In Kleist's first work the children die by the hands of their fathers before they reach the age of remembrance—and before their love for each other has come to an end. In writing one becomes a child again. As Zschokke noted about the hikes he took with Kleist and Wieland in Switzerland: "One can easily imagine how the three young poets wandered around finding new sources of pleasure at every step: discovering bowers of paradise and desert wildernesses, goddesses and monsters, where more prosaic eyes would have found nothing to remark on at all. They were hovering about over the meadows, like butterflies just hatched from their winter pupation, attracted by every flower, and detained by none."[48] But the analogy of the insect metamorphosis can also be conceived the other way around, with the poet having "wings in his adolescence," "which he later, as a caterpillar, sheds to feed on the leaf to which he finds himself bounded," writes Adelbert von Chamisso.[49] Throughout his life Kleist seems to have ignored this possibility.

Kleist dreamed about all kinds of metamorphoses during his time in Switzerland, and one of them may have served as the play's generative core: "As Pfuel recounts, it was indeed written in a most curious, random manner. One day the strange crossdressing scene of the final act—this scene alone—occurred to [Kleist], and because it appealed to him, he wrote it down as one would an incoherent fantasy. It was only then that he came up with a plan for weaving it together with some of the other threads of his fiction—possibly even some randomly found material—and he thus gradually wove the entire tragedy around this one scene."[50] Could Pfuel's account have located the creative nucleus of the play?[51] A boy dresses up in girl's clothes, a girl in boy's clothes: This scenario suggests a reading of the children's deaths as a punitive fantasy, as the penalty they must pay for the confusion stirred by their gender crossing, linking their deaths back to the 'gender trouble' in Kleist's own life.[52] Or, beyond this psychoanalytic reading one could say that the fathers are punishing a different kind of metamorphosis—namely, the children's conversion from enemies to lovers. As said before: Their deaths signify the price for daring to reach majority.

And yet their deaths also seem ridiculous and unnecessary. In my opinion the sexual subtext of the hurried exchange of clothes in the face of the approaching fathers has been overrated. It is a motif of comedies, aesthetically and logically out of place here. In all likelihood Kleist and his friends were merely ridiculing the naïve idealist Ottokar, who—in the alleged freedom the mountains provide—does not waste much thought on the viability of his neat fantasy of self-creation. One should keep in mind the agonistic concept of autonomy in Kleist's "On the Gradual Fabrication of Thoughts While Speaking." For Kleist, the one-time soldier, the martyr is not proven right in the end. The final scene of the play is, in the literal sense of the word, absurd. Not only does it discredit the fathers' hypocritical moral reconciliation over the dead bodies of their children and, thus, the sentimental family cult of the bourgeois melodrama; it also discredits Ottokar's strategic behavior as unreasonable, as a failure in the face of reality. Ottokar's self-sacrifice seems senseless insofar as he had already—before the crossdressing scene and thus before Rupert's arrival—been informed about his brother Peter's fatal accident by Barnabe, Ursula's daughter. He could have apprised his father of this and put a stop to his murderous plans altogether. From this perspective his and Agnes' end is anything but *Fatum*. The play is no mythically founded tragedy; moreover, the absence of moral catharsis calls into question the status of tragedy claimed by its subtitle. Rather than shaking the audience, the ending incites laughter at the naïve young man who believes he can save his lover through an exchange of clothes, or, in the last scene, at the fact that a blind grandfather, a madman, and a witch appear to be the only sensible characters of the play.

It is thus difficult to assess the value of Kleist's first work. It blends figures of thought from his 'magazine of ideas' in both content and form—such as the references to Rousseau and the transformation of the law of electric polarization—into the play's symmetry. In its distribution of positive and negative charge, the play is crafted to perfection; the oppositional forces cannot only be found between the Houses of Warwand and Rossitz but also within the families themselves: Eustache, the wife of the hostile Rupert, is conciliatory by nature. Gertrude, the wife of the, ultimately, conciliatory Sylvester, is hostile by nature. The family discourse the play performs is not simply taken from Kleist's personal experience or from the philosophical debates of the 18th century. The play constructs new knowledge about family conflicts. Kleist is far ahead of his time in that he emphasizes the paradox of an education toward autonomy, the double bind of a call that insists: 'Only with my—your father's—help and plan are you to reach majority.' Later, in his novella "The Foundling," Kleist levels criticism against this paradoxical call in an even more radical manner. Despite its Rousseauist figures of thought, the play is at heart anti-idealist because the children's fantasy of being born anew is thwarted by reality; terror breaks into idyllic nature. And while Kleist's reception of Kant may be full of misunderstandings, in its literary transformation it becomes an anticipation of the Modernist skepticism toward language and communication at the turn of the 20th century.

Kleist's first work thus bears witness to a great literary talent. It is a piece of contemplative literature and, yet, it is also conceived as a youthful jest, which Kleist's own reception confirms. What is unsettling is Kleist's encoding of the play as both highbrow and lowbrow literature. Its lowbrow features can be seen in the monstrosities of Dark Romanticism incorporated into its plot—an obvious break from the tragedy typical of the era—such as the old witch cutting off a dead child's finger to use for her apotropaic magic, and her privilege, in the end, of announcing the family catastrophe as a mere "mistake." The minor character becomes a *dea ex machina*. "'Tis thou didst make the tangle. Thou hast loosed / It too. Go hence!" Rupert replies to Ursula at the end; and thereafter, in the play's last lines, the mad Johann contrives a theory of drama: "Go on, old woman, go! / Thy sleight of hand hath served thee well. Go on! / For with this pretty trick I'm well content."[53] With this kind of meta-language, Kleist indicates just how contingent and contrived we may take the plot to be. In any case, it can no longer be perceived as tragic, given the fact that banal coincidences undermine the significance and tragic effect of the inheritance contract as a fateful power that links misfortune and guilt. Nor can we forget the strategic avoidability of Ottokar's and Agnes' deaths and the reversibility of Rupert's blindness, had a child's finger been thrown on stage earlier. Moreover, one has a hard time identifying with Ottokar as a tragic hero due to his peculiarly limited intellect. His death bestows a just punishment on his vicious father Rupert, yet one waits in vain for any sign of his remorse or moral catharsis, as the conventional ending of a tragedy would have it. Neither family ruminates over whether or not it is guilty or deserves punishment. Instead, they sit over a glass of wine as hosts of a poetological cabaret.

Rather than being shaken by the ending, the audience may be surprised by the fact that the author deliberately breaks the laws of tragedy, thus compromising the integrity of his play. It seems as though Kleist had second thoughts and decided to distance himself from his first literary endeavor, as if the grotesque and comical elements—which he so unexpectedly sets against the tragic—ultimately helped him to cope with his anxiety. Perhaps he had sudden insight into the consequences of taking a literary experiment seriously—the philosophical abyss of the contingent and absurd he might face going down that path. The "sleight of hand" at the play's ending conceals Kleist's "mistake" of having dared to frame his reality in terms of sublime tragedy—though only slightly, as the witch's trick is immediately exposed as such through the 'dramatic theorist' Johann's absurd last lines. Yet it is the sleight of hand that brings the play to an end—something Kleist is unable to achieve with his next drama of the absurd, the experiment *Robert Guiscard, Duke of the Normans*. With the Schroffensteins Kleist is consistently inconsistent insofar as he denies his characters a feasible, happy ending in favor of an ambiguous, undecidable "merry jest," laughing oneself to death. In his later plays and stories, Kleist frequently experimented with such ambiguous closing figures, unsettling his audience and readers. The familiar catharsis—as a mix of fear and pity—refuses to transpire and, ultimately, no morality stands a chance in the face of barbaric violence (not only that of fathers) or the futility of sacrifice (not only that of children).

Robert Guiscard

In Shakespeare's *Romeo and Juliet*, the death of children is necessary for reconciling two feuding families. In Kleist's first work, however, the children's deaths are completely senseless. The Shakespeare reference—which every contemporary reviewer noticed—was, on the one hand, likely intended to conceal the fact that the debutant wanted to be perceived as more radical than his role model. On the other hand, it points to a fantasy of grandeur and competition, which only helps a novice writer suffering from self-doubt if he can live up to the comparison.[54] This is what Kleist wants as early as his second work, the tragedy *Robert Guiscard*, with which he begins to measure himself not only against Shakespeare but the great Attic playwrights—an ambition later confirmed by Christoph Martin Wieland, whose praise for Kleist proved to be fatal. After Kleist had recited some scenes from his fragment to Wieland during his stay in Oßmannstedt in January and February of 1803, the latter was so impressed that he later wrote to Georg Wedekind on April 10, 1804: "I admit I was astonished, and I do not think I am saying too much when I assure you: If the genius of Aeschylus, Sophocles, and Shakespeare joined together to create a tragedy, it would be what Kleist's *Death of Guiscard, the Norman* is, provided the entirety corresponds to what he read to me at the time. From that moment on it was clear to me that Kleist was born to fill the great gap in our contemporary literature, which (in my opinion at least) even Goethe and Schiller have not yet filled; and you can easily imagine how eager I was with him now to get him to complete his work."[55] For Kleist, as he wrote to Wieland in December 1807 in retrospect, it was "the proudest moment of my life."[56]

Wieland's correspondent, Dr. Georg Wedekind, was Kleist's physician, and in Mainz in 1804 he was supposed to cure him of the psychological problems brought on by his failure to complete his *Robert Guiscard*. The expectations Wieland had of Kleist, and those Kleist had for himself, were enormous. At the time of Kleist's *Guiscard* recital in Oßmannstedt, neither of them could have foreseen that Kleist's plays would have no success in his lifetime. Kleist never saw any of them on stage. Whether he ever learned of the premiere of his first work *The Schroffenstein Family* in Graz on January 9, 1804, we do not know. He did suffer—from a distance—from the unsuccessful staging of *The Broken Jug* by Goethe on March 2, 1808, in Weimar. Kleist developed the idea for this comedy, as mentioned earlier, in the course of a writing competition among his friends in Bern. He finished it during his time in Dresden, and it is in this context that the comedy will later be discussed. With regard to Kleist's second work, the tragedy *Robert Guiscard*, we cannot be equally certain about when the surviving fragment was written. In May 1802 Kleist began working on it in Thun with both passion and desperation. If *The Schroffenstein Family* was a testing ground for the literary novice, intended more for the drawer than for publication, with *Robert Guiscard* he wanted more: to make a name for himself and to achieve eternal fame—the "wreath of immortality," as he later writes in a letter to Ulrike on July 3, 1803.[57] The play about the death of the Norman king was supposed to survive the death of the playwright, as Kleist biographer Wilhelm von Schütz writes laconically in his *Biographical Notes* (*Biographische Notizen*): Kleist "[l]ives (in Bern and) at Lake Thun. [...] Wrote *The Schroffenstein Family* there [...]. Afterwards, *Robert Guiscard*, with the remark that he wanted to die when it was done."[58] This comment corresponds with a statement in Kleist's letter to his sister Ulrike of May 1, 1802: "I have a strange fear of dying before I have finished my work."[59] Also surviving is the account of an eyewitness who describes Kleist's desperate struggle to complete his play: "He had rented a small country house on an island in the Aar opposite ours; he was brooding over a tragedy in which the hero dies of the plague on stage. We often saw him for hours in brown vestments on his island, fencing with his arms, running up and down, and reciting."[60] On October 5, 1803, Kleist writes to Ulrike from Geneva that he has "labored five hundred consecutive days, with most of the nights thrown in,"[61] and thus put all his strength into the work, but in vain. On October 26, 1803, he informs his sister from France:

> In Paris I have reread my work, as much of it as I had finished, and have torn it up and burned it and there is an end. Heaven denies me fame, the highest earthly possession. I throw back in its face, like a willful child, everything else I have. [...] I go now to my death. [...] I shall die the beautiful death of the battlefield. I have left the capital city of this country, have traveled to its northern coast, I shall enlist in the French army, a military expedition will soon sail against England, our common doom lies in wait beyond the seas, I exult at the prospect of an eternally glorious grave.[62]

Did Kleist really burn everything or only the imperfect parts, retaining a copy of the perfect parts in his 'magazine of ideas'? The question seems justified, even if scholars cannot answer it due to the current state of source material. Four years later, in December 1807 in Dresden, we learn from letters between Adam Müller and Kleist that he was working on his *Guiscard* again.[63] In June 1808, in the art journal *Phöbus*—which the two of them edited—they printed ten scenes of the play, comprising 524 verses, under the title *Fragment from the Tragedy: Robert Guiscard, Duke of the Normans*. We do not know if this fragment matches the one Kleist so successfully recited to Wieland five years earlier; of that, Kleist scholarship is uncertain. On the one hand, due to the stylistic similarity to Kleist's *Penthesilea*—for instance, the contamination of erotic and military imagery that is frequent in Kleist—it is assumed that the *Phöbus* fragment was written in 1808.[64] On the other hand, it has been shown that the musical quality of the *Phöbus* text follows the theory of recitation of Heinrich August Kerndörffer, with whom Kleist took lessons in Leipzig in March 1803.[65] Furthermore, Wieland recounts Kleist's "madness" during his stay in Oßmannstedt in January and February 1803, "that he often muttered something to himself between his teeth at table. He finally had to confess to me that he was dealing with his *play* in such moments of absence."[66] In Thun he ran around, flailing his arms, reciting; in Oßmannstedt he held quiet monologues: Kleist tried to 'fabricate' his play 'while speaking,' which is not surprising, given his theory of creativity.

In my opinion, with his second play Kleist tries in vain to solve the poetological problems of his first, as will later be shown. For the time being, I argue for reading the surviving *Guiscard* fragment as a result of the crisis years 1802/03. It is not very likely that Kleist, who was so busy in 1808—in addition to the difficulty of editing the *Phöbus* and working on his *Katie of Heilbronn* and *The Battle of Herrmann*—should have had another go at a play he had not succeeded in finishing years earlier, after months of desperate effort. Why, moreover, should he have changed a text that had passed Wieland's judgment so brilliantly? It is more plausible that Kleist wanted to make a name for himself by publishing the verses celebrated by Wieland in *Phöbus*. He most likely did not work on a new version. Were that the case, we might have seen additional fragments published in the subsequent issues of *Phöbus* he so desperately needed to fill.

Just as he is in his later plays *The Battle of Herrmann* and *Prince Frederick of Homburg*, in his early work Kleist is fascinated by great men who make history. Volume 9 of Schiller's literary journal *The Horae* (*Die Horen*), in 1797, featured an essay by Karl Wilhelm Ferdinand von Funck on "Robert Guiscard, Duke of Apulia and Calabria" ("Robert Guiscard Herzog von Apulien und Calabrien"), which probably served Kleist as a source, along with the historical *Memoirs from the Life of the Greek Emperor Alexios Komnenos* (*Denkwürdigkeiten aus dem Leben des griechischen Kaisers Alexius Komnenes*) edited by Schiller in 1790 and written by the Emperor's daughter Anna Komnena. Funck's essay begins rather spectacularly:

> In the tumultuous periods of anarchy and ferment that followed the decline of the first ruling imperial families after the restoration of the Western throne, a bold adventurer could not have lacked the opportunity to immortalize himself in history through brilliant exploits.

The Normans—better known as Vikings—occupied Normandy in 911 and England in 1066 as warlike seafarers, and in the first half of the 11th century, they drove the Arab Saracens out of Sicily and lower Italy. They were led by charismatic military leaders, first by William the Conqueror and then by Tankred and his sons William Iron Arm, Drogo, and Robert Guiscard. Robert was the most brilliant warrior of the sons. His main goal was to conquer Byzantium in order to wrest Emperor Alexios Komnenos from power, but his campaign failed due to the outbreak of the plague. In times of crisis, in the absence of stable orders, "restless minds and great geniuses seek" their opportunity, notes Funck.[67] The analogy to Kleist's own time is obvious, on both a small scale—in the civil wars in Switzerland—and a large scale—in Europe. Guiscard is an ingenious figure in world history similar to Napoleon, who, like Guiscard, failed in a campaign of conquest due to the plague in 1799, when he besieged, in vain, the fortress of Acre on the Eastern Mediterranean coast. Like Guiscard, Napoleon, himself, is said to have taken care of the plague-stricken soldiers in his army.

On the surface Kleist's fragment puts the legitimacy of Guiscard's power to the test. As in *The Battle of Herrmann* and *Prince Frederick of Homburg*, the political and private dimensions of *Guiscard* are linked. The play is simultaneously a war and family drama, and the link is formed by an existential borderline situation par excellence: the scandal of death—of human mortality—which becomes the actual subject of the play. The plot of the dramatic fragment begins with a scene that would challenge any director. The Norman people speak as one powerful chorus, not calmly commenting—as one is familiar with from Classical tragedy—but "*in agitated movement*," "mad with fear," because the Norman duke resists, like a "rock," his warriors' urging to give up his campaign against Alexios. The people incite a "deputation of Normans" to present the request to the Duke:

> Side by side we march with you, good fathers,
> praying fervently, to the Guiscard's tent! A cherub
> leads the way, from God's right hand, when you
> go out to shake the rock around which our
> whole army, mad with fear, boils
> and seethes in vain! Fall on him like a thunderbolt,
> that rock, and open up a way to lead
> us out of the horrors of this nightmare camp!
> Unless he acts at once to save us from the plague
> that Hell inflicts on us so cruelly,
> this point of land will rise up from the sea
> a burial mound for all his people's corpses![68]

Kleist establishes this scene from the perspective of the Norman people to emphasize the underlying hierarchy. The play is set in the camp of the Normans; in the foreground several fires are burning, spreading the scent of frankincense, and in the background dark cypresses as symbols of death are framing a hill, on top of which Guiscard's tent stands, which, in the beginning, hides the ruler from all eyes. Beyond it in the background, the fleet by which the Normans want to escape death and return to their Italian homeland is visible. They are rebellious, but not an amorphous, revolutionary mass. Although the plague threatens to sever all social ties—"friends recoil in fear from friends, / bridegrooms from their brides, mothers from their children"[69]—the army maintains its military order. A deputation of twelve warriors with Armin, an old man, as their leader is to urge Guiscard "like a trumpet / of loud brass" to protect his people—is to "thunder what his duty / is into his ear." Armin, by contrast, forbids the Normans any further sound; he wants mediation: "I'll lend / my voice to meek entreaty, not revolt."[70]

The next scene belongs to Helena, Guiscard's daughter, who is tenderly concerned for her father's peace and asks in vain for the Norman people to leave and come back later. Her father "has battled three whole sweating nights / against the raging pest among us," and the people gathering now disturb his sleep "with waves / that never stop their beating."[71] Armin promises to turn the Normans into a calm ocean, but the peace is disturbed by rumors that the

Duke's personal physician had to come into the tent at night because "suddenly / a pitiful groaning started up within": "a heavy panting like a sick lion gasping / out its soul."[72] After Helena it is her brother Robert's and her husband Abelard's turn to try and keep the army in check. Robert commands Armin to lead the insolent rebels away at once. Meanwhile, his brother-in-law shows understanding for their concerns. Two of Guiscard's potential successors are publicly arguing about how to justify political power: Robert defends dynastic succession, while Abelard recalls that Guiscard, after his father's death, was only granted the power to temporarily rule because of his charisma as a political leader. Robert obviously lacks the charisma that Abelard seems to have because he is able to "hold" the Norman people "here by flattery," as Robert angrily points out, through words like these: "If they were mine, these unawed people / who displease you so, I shouldn't wish / them otherwise than as they are, unawed; / for his freedom's what the Norman's wedded to, / and I would hold in veneration the man / and wife who, in the bed of battle, / beget the fame that I enjoy."[73] Abelard's confessions about the ruler's love for his people reveal how selfish his love really is. Yet Armin acknowledges to Abelard that he—"in shape and speech and manner" resembling his uncle Guiscard—"stand[s] here before us" as the people's "friend." Nevertheless, "Guiscard's son"[74] Robert is to be obeyed. Abelard consequently abandons all political prudence in revealing to the Normans that Guiscard is ill and that his personal physician fears that he has contracted the plague. Abelard consorts with the common people and—"*descending the slope*"—becomes talkative:

> I've told you, it's
> a thing by no means certain yet. The only
> sure sign of the plague is death itself,
> a speedy one, so he denies he has
> it. You know him, he would deny
> it even in his throes. Nonetheless
> his doctor, mother, daughter, his own son,
> as you have seen, are quite convinced of it.[75]

Instead of proving himself to be a prudent strategist in a crisis situation, Abelard drives the Normans from doubt to despair with his flowery speeches. He portrays Guiscard as a man lying weak and withered to death by fever, yet with an eye toward Constantinople from his deathbed, "crouching like a tiger" to issue orders—against the will of his people—"for a main assault"[76] once the enemies of Alexios send him the key to the city. Guiscard had agreed to their condition that he himself should take over the rule of Constantinople rather than his daughter Helena, who, as the widow of the former Emperor, actually deserved the throne. Kleist portrays Abelard as an artful speaker who, like Judge Adam in *The Broken Jug*, regularly incriminates himself with his speeches. Guiscard's death would come just in time for Abelard to reclaim the reign in Apulia and Calabria and to reign in Byzantium as Helena's husband. He would hardly be thinking of bringing his plague-stricken people back to Italy. Guiscard's son Robert angrily calls Abelard a "two-face hypocrite"[77] but seems incapable of a convincing speech in reply.

Abelard can thus only be disproved by the entrance of the Duke himself, which marks the end of Kleist's fragment. Under the cheerful shouting of the Norman people, equipped with his armor and his plumed helmet, he answers Armin's anxious question about his illness "*laughing*":

> The pestilence touched me!
> You must be mad, I think! Do I look like
> a man who's sick with plague? A man who stands
> in front of you possessed of all his life
> and vigor? In full command of all his limbs?
> Whose clear-ringing voice peals freely from his breast
> and fills, like steeple bells, the air around?
> That's a man who's caught the plague? Oh please!
> My state is blooming, do you want to haul
> me off among the rotting corpses in the field?
> What the blazes, no! I'm not about to let
> myself be buried yet in this camp here—
> I'll come to stop in Stambul, not before![78]

Abelard describes the Duke's weakness, while the Duke himself demonstrates that he is "possessed of all his life." The bodily signs are to authenticate their dissembling. Guiscard shows himself not only as a lion in war, but also as a cunning fox, a master of simulation and dissimulation—like the Prince of Cherusci in Kleist's later work *The Battle of Herrmann*. With respect to this character trait, Kleist was able to rely on his main source Funck, who writes that the Normans praised Guiscard's "cunning as much as his bravery, and the sobriquet *Guiscard*—the clever one—that they attributed to him was a name of honor."[79] Guiscard seems to have mastered each of the political arts that Niccolò Machiavelli later, in his treatise *The Prince*, recommends to a new ruler for controlling his public communication and securing his power. In the face of death, however, one can no longer disguise oneself. Guiscard is forced to capitulate before a truth and power that is stronger than his rhetoric. Before Armin has even presented the wishes of the Norman people to Guiscard, he visibly loses his strength. Guiscard's daughter pushes a large drum behind him for support, on which Guiscard "*ease*[*s*] *himself down*"—a truly grotesque throne. Armin, who first "*stares down at the ground*," "*thinking*," attempts to deliver his speech while the Duchess "*sink*[*s*] *on her daughter's breast*" and has to be led back into the tent. The stage directions contradict Armin's hopeful words, with which the fragment closes:

> Well, since
> it's short speech you prefer: Oh, lead us from this vale
> of tears! You savior of the people in their need,
> already you have succored scores, don't
> deny your army the only medicine
> can make us well again, oh don't
> deny us Italy's airy skies,
> but lead us home, home to our own land![80]

In Christian imagery the vale of tears is earthly; language is again revealing. Guiscard is unable to return his army to its earthly homeland. He can, at best, lead his men beyond it into death. And where else could the play go from here? Has not everything already been said in these ten short scenes? Was that Kleist's problem? Or was the play supposed to be a plea for "a greater influence of the people on political decisions," even though the Norman people are hardly portrayed as a protagonist?[81] The dispute over the legitimacy of power and the difference between charisma and dynastic succession is of little significance with regard to the play's dramatic composition, though emphasized by older Kleist scholarship which maintained that Kleist wanted to criticize the weakness of the Prussian king Friedrich Wilhelm III as well as the immorality of the charismatic Napoleon when compared to the Norman war hero. But this struggle could not be the basis for Guiscard's tragedy. In his final appearance the eponymous hero seems to be little affected by the dispute, while the supporting characters Robert and Abelard discuss the legitimacy of political power in public, both proving they are neither worthy of succeeding the Duke nor are they deserving of the love of the Norman people. The very conception of the *Guiscard* fragment does not allow for the creation of a play "geared toward" political history or the historical "moment," as Kleist intended with *The Battle of Herrmann*, whose eponymous hero, incidentally, does with his people as he pleases.[82]

Left open, however, is the potential conflict to follow Guiscard's betrayal of the daughter who loves him. That he risks her love to gain political power over Byzantium implies guilt, and could be as destructive to his relationship with his mother and daughter as the Cheruscan prince Herrmann's unscrupulous use of Thusnelda—in his intrigues against the Roman occupiers—is to his relationship with her. But this conflict could not serve as the basis for developing a full-length play, especially since Kleist's Guiscard—unlike his historical counterpart—does not suddenly die of the plague on the long march to Byzantium, but reaches his destination. Consequently, the betrayal of his daughter has no more potential for development. Guiscard is decided and the family knows. It is for this reason that Abelard is able to share this secret with the army without having to fear a reaction from Guiscard in the final scene.

Moreover, the play does little more than suggest a debate about the two bodies of the king, about the representation of divine, absolutist power and the required concealment of physical frailty. This debate does not seem worthy of tragedy. It is indeed ridiculed with the help of a grotesque stylistic device: the large drum used to support the Duke's rule and to camouflage his infirmity. Nor can the answer to the *Guiscard* riddle be found by comparing it to the Oedipus myth. Faced with the outbreak of the plague among the Theban people, Sophocles' Oedipus learns that he has become innocently guilty of incest with his mother and murder with the death of his father; therein lies the source of his tragedy. The plague in Kleist's *Guiscard* is purely accidental. It is in no way presented as a divine punishment for Guiscard's misconduct—be it his usurpation of political power, the betrayal of his daughter, or his stubborn pursuit of war despite his army's illness. Unlike in Sophocles' *Oedipus Rex*, the plague strikes the ruler and his people alike.[83]

Perhaps the play remains a fragment because—as in *The Schroffenstein Family*—Kleist fails to give the hero's death a tragic form; that is, he fails to frame it from a mythical or religious perspective as misconduct or as punishment for a sin. Rather, he presents death as a scandal that defies human reason, and against which every interpretation fails, including one that would render the play a tragedy. Guiscard's fate is not the result of a struggle between myth and subjective reason as in the Attic tragedy. In contrast to Schiller's tragic theory of the pathetically sublime, while Kleist's hero does provide a "portrayal of the suffering nature," he only seemingly provides a "portrayal of moral independence in the suffering" insofar as he simulates his greatness vis-à-vis the Norman people.[84] Nor does the fragment offer a historical example of the proper conduct one should assume in the face of death, as the Baroque tragic drama does. Even though Guiscard is repeatedly depicted in Baroque imagery—as a "rock around which our / whole army, mad with fear, boils / and seethes in vain!"[85]—he appears neither as a stoic Christian martyr nor as a political ruler foundering on the difference between *Fortuna* and *Fatum*, struggling to recognize that every political art is constrained by divine predestination.[86]

Nowhere does Kleist's fragment suggest that Guiscard's death is to be understood as a boundary separating impermanence from the eternal, this world from the next. There is not a single verse that frames the hero's death *sub specie aeternitatis*—from the perspective of eternity. Nor does the significance of Guiscard's earthly existence reveal itself *sub specie mortis*—from the perspective of death. His death—the result of an infection that makes neither ideological nor dramaturgical sense—would serve the simple function of putting a stop to the campaign of conquest against Constantinople. The senselessness of death is Kleist's radical insight as well as his artistic problem. It is worth recalling the eyewitness account from Thun: "[H]e was brooding over a tragedy in which the hero dies of the plague on stage."[87] The depiction of dying on stage is always difficult, it is generally facilitated by an aesthetic trick: In death a last judgment is passed, so to speak, over a failed or good life. It is hard to imagine that Guiscard's last words, if the play had indeed been completed, would have spoken to the fear or comfort of the afterlife. The contempt he shows toward death in the tenth scene by camouflaging it seems entirely the result of his thirst for glory. Perhaps Kleist would have had Guiscard disillusioned in the end, but even that would not have resulted in a proper conclusion for a tragedy. Guiscard's death is absurd in the way the deaths in Albert Camus' novel *The Plague* (1947) are, though Kleist lacks a philosophy of the absurd—such as the one found in Camus' *The Myth of Sisyphus* (1942) or *The Rebel* (1951)—to complement his literature. To some extent, however, he seems to anticipate Camus' comforting conclusion that suffering from the absurdity of the world is not an individual but a collective experience and thus demands acts of solidarity that wrest the individual from his or her loneliness: in the portrayal of both the daughter Helena's and the Duchess' all-forgiving love for the suffering hero. In any case, Kleist later reiterates this gesture of pity in the touching portrayal of Prothoe's tender friendship with Penthesilea even after the latter's murderous confusion of kissing and biting.

It is more likely though that Kleist, in recognizing the absurdity of existence, was simply at a loss for how to carry on with writing and living. The play remained a fragment, then, because life itself can be fragmented, without amounting to a meaningful totality. Kleist's fragment, however, is not compatible with contemporary aesthetics, neither with Goethe's or Schiller's organological thinking in terms of totality nor with the Romantic philosophy of the fragment. For Friedrich Schlegel, for instance, the fragment is never autonomous, but always part of a whole that is either lost or to be restored—ruinous remnant or futuristic promise. In his *Athenaeum Fragment* 24, he notes: "Many of the works of the ancients have become fragments. Many modern works are fragments as soon as they are written." And in his *Athenaeum Fragment* 22, he calls the former "fragments of the past," the latter "fragments of the future," but both are considered to be representations of perfection and completion.[88]

Kleist's fragment, by contrast, lacks this "think[ing] in terms of totality."[89] It is certainly a "revelatory achievement in the field of art," as Kleist promises his sister Ulrike on July 3, 1803.[90] The problem would then be to combine this new, open epistemology with a new conception of tragedy. This challenge would explain Kleist's futile attempts to finish his play over the course of two years. The assumption that he departs from "think[ing] in terms of totality" is supported by the fact that the fragment's plot lacks teleological framework. It instead remains suspended at a point in which neither a return to the past—to the paradise of the plague-free Italian homeland—nor a departure for a future paradise in Constantinople (or Jerusalem) is conceivable.

In Modernist art and literature, the fragment is conceived as self-sufficient; it requires neither completion nor reference to a totality.[91] Kleist, however, regarded the fragment as a deficient form. His will to create was not directed toward a one-act play. Yet this would have been the solution for his *Guiscard* project, which is a radical thought experiment, a lyrico-musical feat of language, but in its stationary character not conducive to a dramatic plot. It is no wonder, then, that the production history of the fragment does not start before the 20th century—with a premiere on April 6, 1901, in the Berlin Theatre under the direction of Paul Lindau.[92] It is also no wonder that a theorist of the fragment such as Rainer Maria Rilke was enthusiastic about Kleist's *Robert Guiscard*[93] and—with the final line of his sonnet "Archaic Torso of Apollo"—may have provided the key to the connection between Kleist's work and his life in the crisis years 1802 and 1803, during which he was working on his play about the Duke of the Normans. Rilke's call at the end of his hymn to the fragmentary form reads: "You must change your life." Kleist's play remains a fragment because he can no longer give meaning to a chance death, can no longer integrate a fragmentary life into an aesthetic whole. Rilke's sonnet, by contrast, instructs the viewer of Apollo's torso to no longer see it as a fragment, but as a striking presence—not as damaged, but as something radiating epiphanically in its fragmentary form. As such, the viewer is encouraged to abandon the distinction between part and whole as the distinction between non-art and art, which is to say life and art. In judging Apollo's torso, one also passes judgment on one's own life. In the bold turn of Rilke's final tercet, the perspective is reversed from Apollo's torso to the viewer and his or her life: "and not burst forth from all its contours / like a star: for there is no place / that does not see you. You must change your life."[94]

Kleist's fragment may have given rise to a similarly challenging look at the author's life, and vice versa. These are no empty musings, for in *Guiscard* Kleist takes his experience of contingency from the carriage accident in Butzbach and heightens it, questioning the possibility of a meaningful human existence in the face of chance death. From Butzbach he concluded that learning to die must mean learning to live, "to seize the moment"[95]—to lead the right life in the present rather than looking to the future or the past for happiness. In the *Guiscard* fragment the question becomes even more pressing in the face of an imminent death that threatens everyone equally. It is no longer an apologia of the present, an abstract call to live truly in the here and now. It is about the concrete: *Guiscard* is concerned with *how* I should act on what could be my last day so that my action has meaning in itself and is not contingent on the before or after. This is the hidden question asked of all the characters in the play, and it is what gives rise to the fragment's fundamental tension. The question does not revolve around the difference between charisma and dynastic succession, but between pity and fame. Helena and Cecilia—Guiscard's daughter and his wife—think solely of the present power of pity and love, while Guiscard, Abelard, and Robert seek future fame and thus ignore the present suffering of the Norman people. Kleist's fragment unmasks the Duke and his potential successors, showing that the only thing hidden beneath the vanity of their masks is death. And yet the fragment does not take a Christian stance, in the sense of a Baroque Everyman play, according to which everyone is equal before death and God, be it ruler or people, and according to which earthly goods are of no value in the hereafter. Kleist argues strictly for the immanence of this life, in the sense of the disillusionment that comes from the unmasking of the seemingly real through the awareness of life's finiteness. Having his daughter push a drum behind Guiscard for support after his powerful speech is a brilliant move: It separates truth from untruth in this life—the Empress' love from the Duke's lies—and, at the same time, turns the tragedy into a satire. Once again, as in *The Schroffenstein Family*, there is a solution in sight for Kleist: a way out from his early failed tragedies to the success of his later comedies *The Broken Jug* and *Amphitryon*, which, with their ambiguous figures, are tragedies as well.

One may thus speculate as to what a final—still-to-be-written—scene of the fragment might have looked like. Perhaps it would have transpired like the main scene from the historical tragedy *Leopold of Austria* (*Leopold von Österreich*), on which Kleist had allegedly been working during his time in Thun. In this respect Adolf Wilbrandt's Kleist biography from 1863 is of interest because it contains a recollection of Ernst von Pfuel. And even if this recollection is misleading—because Pfuel may have actually read the scene he attributes to Kleist in Jakob Hottinger's play *Arnold von Winkelried*, which was published together with Kleist's *The Broken Jug* in 1812 as part of the first volume of the anthology *German Theater* (*Deutsche Schaubühne*)—the comparison of this scene with Kleist's *Guiscard* is worthwhile. According to Pfuel, before the Battle of Sempach, Kleist had Leopold's knights

> roll the dice to see who would get away with their lives and who would not. The proud gentlemen sit together, carousing, and they begin to throw the dice as if in a boisterous game. The dice have three black sides and three white ones; the black sides represent death. The first of the throwers throw black; everyone laughs and jokes about it; the game continues, the next few throwers also throw black, and more and more do the same—gradually the cocky cheering subsides, and a pensive seriousness comes over the party;—in the end *everyone* has thrown black. According to Pfuel's recollections, Kleist described with overwhelming force how this macabre incident slowly creates the most eerie and ultimately most terrifying mood in the proud circle.—One can only assume that Kleist had already written this first act on his island in the Aar; indeed he only completed this one act (as Pfuel asserts).[96]

Imagine the "proud" Guiscard, Abelard, and Robert before the Battle of Byzantium at a table rolling the dice, slowly realizing the certainty of their deaths and the unworthiness of their claim to power and fame. Kleist—the proud author—would sit at the table with them. He wants to achieve fame with a play that serves as an apologia for pity and love and declares the desire for fame itself to be absurd. In this sense Kleist's burning of the *Guiscard* fragment destroyed a work and life project that was full of paradoxes and that reflected, with great veracity, the precariousness of his own writing and life. The *Guiscard* fragment makes an appeal that refrains from suggesting an aesthetic ideal. The directive is, as expressed by Rilke: "You must change your life." Indeed, it was not that Kleist had poorly conceived his play, with no recourse for how to improve it, but rather that, to him, his life generally appeared poorly conceived. Kleist's plan to board a French warship in Normandy in the fall of 1803, from Calais or Boulogne, to seek the "beautiful death of the battlefield"[97] with Napoleon's troops in England—the old Norman Empire—would seem foolish were it merely understood as a desire to emulate the death of his Norman duke and thus the tragedy of a genius' failure in both his work and his life. Kleist contemplated suicide both before and after his fantasies of grandeur surrounding *Guiscard*. And so his plan to ship off to England might be better understood in light of the words of another one-time soldier, German philosopher Martin Heidegger, as a "running ahead toward death" in order to finally achieve some sense of authenticity in his present existence.[98] To put it more plainly: Perhaps Kleist is merely trying to obscure his failures in love and friendship by fashioning himself, melodramatically, as a writer who failed early on in his career and was thus ready and willing to die. Or even more banal is the possibility that a writer, only happy and content in the flow of his writing, is unbearable—to both himself and others—in the pauses, no longer sure if he is really a writer. It is well known that Kleist fell out of the flow of his writing for the first time in August 1802 while in Switzerland, where he suffered bouts of depression. Neither Dr. Wyttenbach in Bern nor Dr. Wedekind in Mainz two years later could cure Kleist of his tendency toward self-deprecation. Bestowing strength upon a creative person plagued by doubts and feelings of insufficiency requires selfless muses or admirers with a commitment of daily presence. Perhaps Kleist would have completed his *Guiscard* had he stayed with Mädeli in Thun or even become Christoph Martin Wieland's son-in-law, a lost opportunity addressed in the next chapter. In the meantime imagine Kleist seeking advice from the memoirs of Françoise Gilot, the mistress of Pablo Picasso, who had to reassure him, every morning when he seemed most depressed—in bed and during breakfast—what a great painter he was until his expression brightened around noon and he hurried to his studio to work fervently until two o'clock in the morning.[99] Pardon my thought experiment, but it is meant quite seriously. What other brilliant texts would Kleist have written had he received the admiration and encouragement he deserved during his lifetime. Not only necessity, but also respect begets ingenuity—and Wieland's praise for Kleist's *Guiscard* was this exception to the rule. It is strange, then, that it did not help Kleist at all. On the contrary, the failure of Kleist's *Guiscard* project may be of his own making and may itself suggest the reasons why. Kleist's career, however, would probably have taken a different course had it not been Wieland whom he visited in Weimar.

CHAPTER VII

The Lost Years?

Liminal Spaces and Times, 1802–1807: Weimar—Leipzig, Dresden—Thun—Paris, St. Omer—Mainz, Berlin—Königsberg—Fort de Joux, Châlons-sur-Marne

"There is nothing constant in me but inconstancy," Kleist allegedly notes to a member of the von Schlieben family.[1] The phrase hits the mark. At the heart of Kleist's life lies the experience of discontinuity. In Thun, in the summer of 1802, he seemed to have found a sense of direction for his life. He wanted to become a writer, and his first work, *The Schroffenstein Family*, was soon published and performed on stage, receiving positive reviews. The public was only too eager to find out who the anonymous author was. Kleist granted neither himself nor the public this favor. Five years passed before Kleist's arrival in Dresden in August 1807, during which time he published nothing and—after overcoming his *Guiscard* crisis—apparently bowed to his family's will to cease his craft, deciding to finally play the part of the Prussian civil servant they had always wanted him to become. During his training period in Königsberg, he of course did nothing but hatch literary ideas—the comedies *The Broken Jug* and *Amphitryon*, the novella "The Earthquake in Chile," and the beginnings of the tragedy *Penthesilea*. In the eyes of the literary public of his time, however, Kleist's career as a writer lasted only four years, though one can hardly speak of a career at all. From the fall of 1807 until his suicide in November 1811, he was more or less a writer on the side of his full-time job publishing journals in Dresden and Berlin. Considering the posthumous fame gained by his small oeuvre of magnificent works, Kleist's life seems one of missed opportunities for becoming a prominent and influential writer in the eyes of his contemporaries. Kleist, it seems, had no talent for seizing the moment that could have made his literary career.

The first and best chance for seizing such an opportunity presented itself in the fall of 1802 in Weimar, Germany's literary capital. Here and in the nearby university town of Jena—which belonged to the duchy of Weimar—representatives of each generation of contemporary writers came together, fighting for dominance in the literary field at the turn of the 19th century: Christoph Martin Wieland, Johann Gottfried Herder, Johann Wolfgang Goethe, Friedrich Schiller, the brothers August Wilhelm and Friedrich Schlegel, Johann Gottlieb Fichte—veterans of the Enlightenment and Rococo, once celebrated

© WILHELM FINK VERLAG, 2021 | DOI:10.30965/9783846765746_008

figures of the Sturm und Drang movement, and representatives of Weimar Classicism and the more recent Romantic school. Weimar had just six thousand inhabitants. People lived in close quarters and knew each other. The literary scene was quite readily accessible, and the alliances had been settled for some time before Kleist came to the small residential town. The Schlegel brothers and Goethe stood by each other, but no one seemed to stand by Wieland anymore. Goethe and Schiller polemicized against Wieland in their *Xenions* and watched as the Romantics tried to bring down this monument of Enlightenment. In a letter to Caroline and August Wilhelm Schlegel of May 1799, Friedrich Schlegel even speaks of a "systematic destruction of all his [Wieland's] poetry or non-poetry. The time is as ripe for it as ever—and there should be no consideration for his age and life."[2] The Schlegel brothers denigrated Wieland's works as intertextual pastimes and accused him of lacking originality. Wieland's agenda for literature based on combinational wit and worldly esprit was considered outdated by his younger contemporaries, with its privileging of relationality over autonomy and its orientation toward reason, morality, and good taste rather than creative freedom.[3]

Kleist was twenty-five years old when he arrived in Weimar, with Wieland almost seventy. Looking at their ideas, their personalities, and their writing from today's perspective, they appear to have little in common. In Kleist's adolescence Wieland was his "teacher" in virtue, happiness, and love. Thus wrote Kleist to Adolphine von Werdeck from Paris in July 1801 in a melancholic remembrance of his Mainz days in 1794 when he had read Wieland's Platonic *Sympathies* (*Sympathien*) of 1756.[4] Wieland's influence thus concerned a phase in Kleist's life prior to his writing and was purely intellectual in nature.[5] When Wieland and Kleist met at the end of 1802, Wieland—even after becoming more skeptical—still stood for the Enlightenment optimism that Kleist had radically abandoned with his Kant crisis. Comparing their personalities, Wieland was of amiable sociability and liberal judgment, which for decades secured him a distinguished position as a German literary authority. Kleist, by contrast, was an unsociable melancholic, an unnoticed outsider in the literary scene. In 1802 Wieland was working on his novel *Aristippus and Some of His Contemporaries* (*Aristipp und einige seiner Zeitgenossen*), which—in continuation of Enlightenment anthropology—dealt with the reconciliation of man's animal and spiritual natures. Kleist, meanwhile, had just completed *The Schroffenstein Family*, the gruesome tragedy that ridicules such reconciliation. If he had presented Wieland with that play rather than the draft of *Guiscard*, Wieland's verdict would have certainly been far less positive. It is obvious that Wieland and Kleist had completely different genre preferences.

Fig. 31
Christoph Martin Wieland (1733–1813)

Unlike Wieland, Kleist was not able to write a light opera libretto, a proper *Bildungsroman*, or a philosophical novel. He preferred the novella, as a genre of catastrophe, and wrote anti-Classical plays that broke completely with the expectations of the contemporary audience. Yet one of Kleist's contemporaries and comrades from his military days in Potsdam, German writer Friedrich de la Motte-Fouqué—whom Kleist would meet again in Dresden in 1803—claimed that Kleist belonged to "the Wieland School," whereas he himself belonged to "Schlegel's." Discussions on "the art of warfare" help them to overcome this "intellectual distance" in Dresden.[6] Nevertheless, Fouqué's claim seems to make sense only if one relates it to Kleist's youth. One cannot speak seriously of Kleist the writer as a disciple of Wieland in 1803. What, then, brought Wieland—the "proud Swabian bourgeois and Weimar state pensioner lovingly cared for by his family"—together with Kleist, the "pennilessly, restlessly, and hopelessly driven descendant of Prussian nobility,"[7] one-time soldier, and novice writer?

Wieland's letter to Georg Wedekind, Kleist's doctor in Mainz, reveals the reasons why. The acquaintance between Wieland and Kleist was itself "the result of a friendly relationship" between Wieland's eldest son Ludwig and Kleist. Kleist had rendered Ludwig "a very essential service"—by helping him return from Switzerland to his father in Thuringia. According to Wieland's letter, Kleist visited the Wielands several times in November and December 1802 in Oßmannstedt, which was a two hours' walk from Weimar. Finally, when Wieland learned of Kleist's poor quarters in Weimar, he invited him to spend Christmas in Oßmannstedt and to live on his estate for a few weeks in January, even though he had certain reservations about this character who had "something enigmatic and mysterious" about him. Accordingly, Wieland found Kleist's demeanor toward him paradoxical: "He seemed to love and honor me like a son, but he could not be made to behave in an open and confidential manner." For Wieland, Kleist was a misfit but a talented one—unlike his own son Ludwig, of whom he does not think much as a writer. What struck him about Kleist was

> a peculiar kind of distraction when one talked to him, so that, for example, a single word seemed to attract a whole series of ideas in his brain—like a chime of bells—and caused him to hear nothing more of what was said to him, and thus to lag behind with his answer. Another peculiarity and an even more fatal one—as it sometimes seemed to border on madness—was this: that quite often during meals, he murmured something to himself between his teeth and had the air of a person who believes himself alone or is busy with his thoughts as though in a different place and concerned with a completely different subject.

Kleist explained to Wieland that, in such moments, he was working on his *Robert Guiscard*. When Wieland asked Kleist to recite from his play, Wieland reacted enthusiastically: "From that moment on it was clear to me that Kleist was born to fill the great gap in our contemporary literature, which (in my opinion at least) even Goethe and Schiller had not yet filled."[8]

This is how Kleist came to find himself at the center of the German literary scene; not intention but simple chance brought him to a friend's father—the wrong person. The commonplace of Kleist scholarship, that Wieland "was the first to have at least suspected Kleist's significance,"[9] is merely an empty, historically questionable phrase, considering the *Schroffenstein* reviews in *The Liberal*, the *Journal for the Elegant World* (*Zeitung für die elegante Welt*), or the *New General German Library* (*Neue Allgemeine Deutsche Bibliothek*) of 1803, which discussed in detail the pros and cons of Kleist's play.[10] Wieland's praise demonstrates, firstly, a lack of empathy; it put a novice writer, already torn between melancholia and feelings of grandiosity, under enormous pressure. Secondly, his praise seems excessive insofar as it was not based on a careful reading of Kleist's work but on the impression gained from a few scenes freely recited to him by Kleist. Those scenes undoubtedly represent a stroke of genius, but they cannot be seriously compared with the dramatic accomplishments of Schiller and Goethe up to that point—with *The Robbers, Fiesco, Intrigue and Love, Don Carlos, Wallenstein, The Maid of Orleans*, or with *Götz von Berlichingen, Clavigo, Iphigenia in Tauris, Egmont*, and *Torquato Tasso*. Thirdly, Wieland's praise is bad feuilleton style, expressing the sentimental enthusiasm of an art critic rather than a review grounded in facts of the text. Kleist's *Guiscard* struck Wieland as though "the genius of Aeschylus, Sophocles, and Shakespeare joined together to create a tragedy." One ought to add that Wieland assumed that Kleist, unlike Goethe and Schiller, sought or even achieved some sort of reconciliation between Classical and Modern tragedy with the intention of "fill[ing] the great gap in our contemporary literature."[11] Kleist's own assessment was quite different, full of self-doubt and uncertain in the conception of his play. Wieland was aware of this insecurity because Kleist admitted it to him with great candor: "Although he has already written down numerous scenes one by one, he destroys them over and over again as he is unable to write anything that satisfies him."[12] Wieland's subsequent encouragement may have been well intended, but it was ill considered and anything but helpful. The analysis of the *Guiscard* fragment in the previous chapter demonstrates that Kleist had problems crafting his tragedy and would have needed serious advice. But the elder Wieland seems to have evaded such a collaboration; instead, he apparently loved to talk about his own life so that Kleist could write it down. And that is what Kleist did—or so he claims in a letter to Ulrike of January 1803.[13] None of these biographical notes have survived.

According to Eduard von Bülow's biography of 1846, Kleist first went to Jena, "where he was well received by Schiller, and shortly thereafter to Weimar to meet Goethe," who also "was very friendly to him."[14] There is no evidence of these encounters, which any young playwright of the time would have undoubtedly been proud to report—but a thought experiment might be permitted. Imagine if, instead of Wieland, Kleist had spoken about his *Guiscard* with Schiller, whose *Wallenstein* he so admired—that is, with an expert in historical drama who would have fully understood a playwright's difficulties in explaining a hero like Guiscard from his Norman camp and who, during Kleist's stay in Thuringia, was working on *The Bride of Messina*. Schiller could have had delightful discussions with Kleist about the transformation of the Classical chorus in contemporary drama, given the daring opening scene of *Guiscard*, which has the Norman people speak as such a chorus. Or imagine that Kleist had in fact met Goethe in Weimar when he was struggling with *The Natural Daughter*, the play that deals with a French duke's 'natural'—which is to say, illegitimate—daughter, who fails to be legitimized at court due to political and familial intrigues. In the end the Duke's daughter marries a commoner, though swearing sexual and worldly abstinence in her marriage. While her problem of legitimacy is not comparable to that of Guiscard, Kleist and Goethe could have shared, at least occasionally, the despair over the impossibility of ending their respective plays. Goethe did not succeed in finding a proper ending for his tragedy. He completed his play, but it did not result in a stroke of genius. Perhaps Kleist could have taken solace in the fact that even a great writer such as Goethe could fail to realize an idea. One might further imagine that Kleist would have shown the *Schroffenstein* reviews to the Schlegel brothers and, in a joint debate on the *Guiscard*, would have profited from their conviction and certainty that it was the task of a literary critic to help conceptually refine a work of literature.

Why did Wieland—the otherwise so liberal, open-minded, and tolerant author—not recommend Kleist to Schiller and Goethe and, with a hymn of praise, provide him access to the leading literary figures of Weimar and Jena? Wieland's *Guiscard* praise is complicated in that it forced Kleist to be partisan and loyal. Wieland was in need of allies during this time of his life, which is understandable from a human perspective, given his mental and economic problems. His wife had died a year earlier; the estate in Oßmannstedt was financially threatened and had to be sold in 1803; and his literary reputation, which he had built up over decades, was at stake. Strategically speaking, Kleist's deference to Wieland—who, at the end of his life, suffered the relegation from the 'first division' of German literature to the 'second,' so to speak—was fatal. Associated with the "Wieland School," to which he, as a writer, did not at all belong, Kleist was made to share Wieland's artistic loneliness in Oßmannstedt. Fouqué regrets that "seriously monitored school regulations—with Kleist belonging to the Wieland School, Fouqué to Schlegel's—kept the two striving spirits alienated from all immediate poetic exchange."[15] And one can only agree with him in his assessment:

> The young man came—how is unknown to me—into contact with Wieland, who encouraged him to further pursue his literary path, which naturally put Heinrich in a polemical, almost hostile position against everything that belonged to the then so-called New School or was brought about by it. Whatever Heinrich conceived, he conceived with enormous love and force, but also with a certain exclusivity, which often prevented him from noticing the good and beautiful things in the paths of others, or at least from appreciating them properly.[16]

But Kleist's loyalty was not only a question of character. Wieland would have probably ended their friendship immediately had Kleist behaved differently. It was not until years later, in Dresden in 1807, that Kleist opened himself up to the "New School." And it was his connection with the Romantic Adam Müller that became sufficient grounds for Wieland to break off the correspondence with Kleist and deny his request for a contribution to *Phöbus*, which Kleist published together with Müller.

Wieland's praise for *Guiscard* forced Kleist into isolation. It prevented him from taking advantage of the opportunities in Weimar—from establishing contacts with Goethe and Schiller and the writers of his generation who could have furthered his career. Also, to the degree to which Wieland's reputation declined, his praise proved to be without significance for the reception of Kleist's work. By contrast, Goethe's feelings of 'horror and revulsion' toward the hypochondriac Kleist remain in the collective memory. This judgment prevented Kleist's canonization in the 19th century while facilitating it in the 20th century, when Modernist writers—invoking Kleist as a radical breaker of tradition—began creating a tradition of their own.[17]

Kleist was in Weimar and the surrounding area for four months. Only four letters from this time have come down to us, all addressed to Ulrike. Descriptions of the city, the people, the countryside—as in the case of Würzburg, Dresden, or Paris—are missing. Nor is there any mention of the brilliant Weimar Court Theater and its fascinating winter program devised under the direction of Goethe. From November 1802 to February 1803, performances included Schiller's *Wallenstein*, Goethe's *Iphigenia in Tauris* and *Clavigo*, as well as Wolfgang Amadeus Mozart's *Don Giovanni*. Aside from his recurring financial worries, Kleist only hinted at private matters to Ulrike, in his usual enigmatic way: At the beginning of January 1803, he writes that he had spent Christmas in Oßmannstedt and had "(despite Wieland's very pretty daughter) decided" to move there completely. And, presumably at the end of January, he relates the following prophecy: "I have lived here for some time now, and I am glad you are pleased about it. But I have found more love than is right, and sooner or later I will have to leave again; my strange fate!—I would like to at least stay here until spring."[18] Kleist only made it to the end of February before he had to move on to Leipzig. The reason was probably a fling with Luise, Wieland's thirteen-year-old daughter, who fell in love with the "magical Kleist."[19] Although he apparently did not return her love, Kleist got into trouble with Luise's siblings, Amalie and Ludwig. The elder Wieland only learned about these problems after Kleist had decided to leave, and he seemed completely unaffected by it in his further correspondence with Kleist. Even after Kleist's departure from Oßmannstedt to Weimar, Wieland still invited him to a celebration in May 1803, which Kleist avoided, apparently because the date fell on Luise's fourteenth birthday. A year later, in the spring of 1804, Kleist visited the Wielands once more, presumably to explain to his patron the failure of his *Guiscard* project. Luise struggled to keep her composure.[20] As she confessed to her fiancé in 1813, it took her "years before [she] lost the traces of the first grief on [her] face,"[21] having mistakenly believed that Kleist had returned her love. Luise never lost interest in Kleist. She read his works and was somewhat shocked by them, drawing connections between their character and that of their author. Two months prior to Kleist's death, in September 1811, she writes to her sister Charlotte:

> What I first had to assume, I later learned to feel: that I was not loved back the way I loved—but I did not fail to imagine that, if he were to see me again after so many years, his sympathy, often truly expressed to me, could easily turn into love, a love similar to mine in strength and purity!—The reading of some of his works, a more mature intellect and more unbiased mind opened my eyes to this, and I often saw and told myself what kind of human being I was dealing with. What you wrote to me of and about him confirms all this only too well, and I am also convinced that I—if it were not for the great obstacles that stood in the way of his relationship, making it impossible—would not be happy in his possession. In spite of these thoughts, my interest in him has not diminished to such an extent that I would not take a lively interest in his fate, which is not a pleasant one.[22]

In Luise's retrospect the whole affair seems like a bourgeois tragedy about a premature bourgeois daughter who finds herself seduced by a rather immoral nobleman:

> Even though he is not one of the most noble of men, who are an exception anyway, his character is nonetheless *good*, and he would not have made himself guilty of this imprudence against me if he had less noble blood (or rather, that of a commoner) in his veins—[23]

It seems to have been of no avail to Kleist to try and hide his homosexual orientation behind gallantries for the fairer sex. Immature bourgeois girls—even those with prominent fathers—are "too weak" to "doubt" such compliments[24] and instead plunge themselves and their flatterers into misery. Meanwhile, on March 13/14, 1803, Kleist—already in Leipzig—writes to Ulrike again: "I had to leave, and I cannot tell you, why? I left, with tears, the house where I had found more love than the whole world can muster together; except you! —! But I *had to* leave! O Heavens, what a world this is!"[25]

In the same letter Kleist calls himself an "*unspeakable* person." "I wish I could tear my heart from my body, pack it into this letter, and send it to you.—Silly thought."[26] As Kleist scholarship points out, this is a highly vivid description, given Kleist's skepticism toward language.[27] Ulrike would have hardly seen it that way, for Kleist's letter revolves around a theme with variations, expressing the supposedly unspeakable—Kleist's despair—with great eloquence. Most noticeable is what Kleist leaves out: We learn nothing about his visit to the publisher Georg Joachim Göschen in Leipzig, even though Kleist had a letter of recommendation from Wieland in his pocket. And he has but two short sentences to spare for his declamation lessons with Heinrich August Kerndörffer before he makes what he had announced come true by putting all his heart into the letter—namely, into a small scene depicting his dialogue with the mathematician Carl Friedrich Hindenburg in Leipzig. It begins as follows:

> "Well, how's the mathematics in Paris?"—A silly answer from my side, and a sad look to the ground from his.—"So you've been just *traveling around*?" Yes, traveling around.—He shakes his head wistfully. Finally, he hears from me that I am actually working *on something*. "*What* are you working on? Well! Don't I know it? You spent this winter at *Wieland's*; certainly! Certainly."—And then I flung my arms around his neck and hugged and kissed him until he laughingly agreed with me: Man must cultivate *the* talent that he feels is *dominant* in him.
>
> Could I not deal with Wünsch in this way too? And Huth? And Hüllmann? & & & & &[28]

Indeed, if only Kleist could speak with such candor about his vocation to writing in Frankfurt an der Oder, if his old professors at the Viadrina—Wünsch, Huth, and Hüllmann—could respond with as much generosity, understanding, and tolerance as Hindenburg did, Kleist could have been free of a guilty conscience and once again been cheerful and happy. Ulrike, the actual recipient of the letter, is supposed to add five more recipients: For every "&" represents a member of the Kleist family. But perhaps she did not understand such allegorical messages concealed in logograms. At the end of his letter, Kleist lifts the literary veil and confesses his longing for understanding and love from his family straight from his heart:

> And now, in my name, kiss every finger of my forever venerated aunt! And, as they stand, like organ pipes, kiss them all, from the topmost to the last, the little mouse carved from the apple core! One single word from you, and before you know it, I am *rolling* in the parlor with joy. Adieu! Adieu! Adieu! O you my most precious one![29]

It is these very last sentences that Ulrike tore out from the letter and gave away[30]—to no avail in the family, one may assume. Kleist continued moving around, and two years later, when he returned home, he found no understanding for his literary vocation.

In April 1803 Kleist moved on from Leipzig to live with two sisters who had been very fond of him during his first stay in Dresden in 1801 and, like him, were always in need of money. The two young Misses von Schlieben—Karoline and Henriette—were still "poor and friendly and good."[31] But Kleist's visit turns out to be somewhat difficult at first due to his quarrel in Basel with

Karoline's fiancé Friedrich Lose. In a letter to her fiancé of April 1803, Karoline describes both herself and Kleist in a state of "awkward confusion." He blames "himself for the past," but she forgives him—for what, she probably does not know, given her innocuous comment that Kleist "still loves and appreciates" Lose "very much, and should that not make me trust him? To me, too, he is very sympathetic and friendly, and seems to mean well."[32] This is true insofar as Kleist tries to help the two sisters, who are struggling to scrape a living by secretly selling homemade millineries, by—also secretly—writing a letter to his experienced 'financial advisor' Ulrike.[33] And yet it is not true insofar as Kleist supplements an underhanded postscript to Karoline's letter to Lose. On the last page of the letter, he recommends to Lose, who is staying in Milan at the time, to either marry Karoline or to do as Kleist did with Wilhelmine von Zenge:

> It may be that, in a moment of hopelessness, you decided to sever your destiny from the destiny of this poor girl. If this is the case, and if staying away from her is a means to achieve, with freer movement of your forces, at least a more bearable fate for yourself (you understand me), then continue your silence as before and I, while I am here, will do everything possible to alleviate the great pain that this poor girl would then suffer.[34]

Lose did not take to Kleist's assumed familiarity and went on to marry Karoline, much to her chagrin, as can be gathered from the travel diary of Auguste von Pannwitz. In 1835 she and her aunt Ulrike visited "Madame Loose" in Milan, whom Kleist's sister had "last seen in Dresden as a cheerful, blossoming, beautiful girl; today she was deathly pale, terribly thin, and looked more like a corpse." As Auguste continues to relate, during a long illness Lose had "maltreated" his wife and children "so badly that his wife had to take him to the asylum and now had to support not only her five children but also her mad husband from the proceeds of her hands' labor, until, after several years, he finally died in the most lamentable way in the asylum."[35]

When a person lives with one suffering from mental illness, a reciprocal struggle with mental health can ensue, which is why therapists today often recommend therapy for partners in such cases. Karoline was distraught before, during, and after her marriage, but at least, in 1803, she found a doctor in Dresden, according to Bülow's account of 1848: "If this condition lasts much longer," said Karoline, stunned in the face of Lose's cruel silence, "I will go mad."—"You are right, countered Kleist, it would be the best thing to do, and if you ever regain your sanity, I will take a pistol and shoot you and me dead. I can certainly do you that favor. These words made such a deep impression on the girl that she regained her senses soon after and recovered from her melancholia." Although Kleist did not sit behind but next to his 'patient' "on the sofa and was strumming the guitar,"[36] he seems to have known—before Freud's conception of the death instinct—how to satisfy it in a compensatory manner by simulating death. Meanwhile, Kleist's biographer Bülow seems to have been familiar with all the Hollywood movies in which the doctors are the actual madmen. More seriously, Bülow's anecdote confirms that it must not have been easy to be Kleist's friend.

It was not easy for Pfuel either in the next few months; he tried—in a friendly and pragmatic way—to help Kleist, who was despairing over his *Guiscard* project and in financial trouble. In the spring of 1803, Pfuel came to Dresden and convinced Kleist to travel with him to Switzerland in order to disperse his melancholia and be, once again, inspired by the atmosphere of Thun. Pfuel offered to cover the travel expenses for both, but Kleist refused. Instead, he instructed Ulrike—his usual money messenger—to come from Frankfurt to Dresden. She hurried to Kleist, as always, while he in the meantime visited the Dresden art gallery, met Fouqué for nostalgic conversations about their military days in Potsdam, and became acquainted with Johann Daniel Falk—an admirer of Wieland—who was, at the time, adapting the Amphitryon myth into a comedy. This acquaintance had consequences for Kleist's writing, as did the readings he found in the Dresden library. The library's check-out record for June 1803 lists Kleist as the recipient of Aristophanes' *The Clouds* and a volume of Sophocles' tragedies, containing his *Electra*, *Oedipus Rex*, *Philoctetes*, and *Antigone*.[37]

At the end of July 1803, Pfuel and Kleist set off on their journey to Switzerland. Pfuel had time, for he had quit his military service after being refused a study leave in Paris. Kleist could not have wished for a better travel partner: Pfuel was calm, humorous, and quick witted, even when confronted with provocative questions. In Dresden Kleist is said to have asked not only Karoline but also Pfuel whether he wanted to die with him; and—as Pfuel recalls—"he kept coming back to it as if seized by a fixed idea." Pfuel's answer: "It is not time yet, just wait: As soon as it is time, I will let you know." This response made Kleist laugh.[38] He probably wanted nothing more than such a deferral—the hidden purpose of the offer of a shared death. The friend is supposed to reject it, which would protect Kleist from the final consequence. A second refrain in the conversations of the two men was Kleist's ambition "to become the greatest poet of his nation" and to "*tear the laurels from* [*Goethe's*] *brow*."[39] Kleist seems to have rarely been relaxed, but the sportsman Pfuel knew of a remedy. He recommended physical exercise to counter Kleist's mood swings between gloom and pride. Hence, the two often traveled on foot during the following months—in Switzerland, in Italy, and in France. It was cheaper too.

Fig. 32
Ernst Heinrich Adolph von Pfuel
(1779–1866)

Kleist hardly found time to write letters during all his travels. Their journey led them via Gera, Hof, Bayreuth, Nuremberg, Koblenz, and Aarau to Thun, their primary residence in Switzerland. In August, Kleist and Pfuel went on hikes in the mountains around Bern with Adolphine von Werdeck and her husband Christoph Wilhelm—a state councilor—whom they knew from their military days in Potsdam. From Adolphine's travel diary we learn that the two Prussians sometimes behaved a little roughly, like "barbares du Nord." Even in the presence of a young Frenchman dressed in fashionable elegance at a Swiss inn, they "kept speaking German, laughed loudly, and took no notice of the stranger," unlike Adolphine, who was quite flirtatious. The gregarious Adolphine had already considered Kleist egocentric, as opposed to the "amiable Pfuel, who always seemed cheerful, always interesting, never as moody as Heinrich Kleist."[40]

To visit Karoline's fiancé Friedrich Lose, Pfuel and Kleist even hiked across high alpine passes—such as the Gotthard—to northern Italy, where they got as far as Varese and Milan. In between their summer trips, Kleist frequently worked on *Guiscard* in Thun; while Pfuel did what was obviously his favorite sport: swimming in Lake Thun. In 1817 Pfuel wrote a treatise *On Swimming* (*Über das Schwimmen*) because the only way to achieve "enjoyment and pleasure" in swimming, he notes, is to properly master the sport.[41] Kleist admires Pfuel's grace when swimming and gives him the highest score—but not from an athletic point of view. On January 7, 1805, in one of his most passionate letters, Kleist reminds Pfuel of their summer in Thun:

> We felt, or I at least, the sweet enthusiasm of friendship! You restored the age of the Greeks in my heart; I could have slept with you, my dear boy; so entirely did my soul embrace you! I had often, as I watched you stepping into the lake at Thun, contemplated your handsome body with almost *maidenly* feelings. It really could have served an artist as a model for study. I, had I been one, could perhaps have grasped the idea of a god through it. Your small head, with its curly hair, your sturdy neck, broad shoulders, lean body, altogether the very picture of vigor, as though modeled after the most beautiful young steer ever bred in honor of Zeus.[42]

I do not know whether this is the "*most beautiful* love letter from one man to another," as Jens Bisky suggests in his Kleist biography, after discussing the discourse of same-sex love at the turn of the 19th century in a most learned and subtle manner.[43] Yet there can be no doubt that this is a love letter. Maybe the desire was one-sided, which the qualification at the beginning ("I at least") speaks to. Maybe it was not. In any case, Pfuel did not destroy the indecent letter, but kept it in his possession. Kleist's sexual orientation was not fixed. He felt as both man and woman, and he loved both men and women; whether or not he did so physically cannot be decided, as Kleist remained discreet in this regard despite all his indiscretion. As pointed out in Chapter II, what is interesting is not so much the defensive but the productive character of Kleist's 'gender trouble'—the possibility of understanding it as a catalyst for artistic creativity. Thus, this ardent letter to Pfuel, too, oscillates between poetry and truth. The effort at camouflage is substantial. Kleist does express his affection directly, but at the same time, he masks it in paradoxical literary images and allusions, as seen in the mixed erotic-military imagery when speaking admiringly of the strong bull that ultimately falls victim to love. This figure of thought also marks the ending of *Penthesilea*, namely the fatal relationship between the Amazon queen and her lover, the exceedingly strong Achilles.

This imagery implies that the relationship between Pfuel and Kleist could have only been peaceful for the duration of one relaxing summer. They left Switzerland in fall, after Kleist failed to finish his *Guiscard*. His self-confidence collapsed. On October 5, 1803, Kleist writes to Ulrike from Geneva about the torturous and futile work on his tragedy and passes judgment on himself, saying: "It was hell that gave me this half-talent of mine: heaven grants a whole one or none at all. [...] Now, on my way to Paris I am fully determined, devoid of choices as I am, to leap at the first thing that comes along."[44] Kleist had no choice because the hope that Geßner would be able to pay him a honorarium for *The Schroffenstein Family* had also been shattered. In Paris Kleist and Pfuel nevertheless dined in the best restaurants, probably paid for with the help of their company at table, the Werdecks. However, nothing and nobody seemed to help against Kleist's melancholia. No laughter, no mockery from Pfuel. At this point, apparently, Kleist's double suicide proposals were meant to be taken seriously—that is, in the sense of the figure of thought described above: Pfuel is meant to assert his love to Kleist, and Kleist his love to Pfuel—by sacrificing themselves for each other, by dying together. This assumption is no more than that: an assumption about the dramatic events in Paris of fall 1803, about which we, unfortunately, have only indirect information by way of the early Kleist biographies of Eduard von Bülow and Adolf Wilbrandt, who rely on Pfuel's oral account. Accordingly, in Paris Kleist "once again" asks Pfuel

> in vain to die with him. His soul also embittered itself against his friend [...], and as he had one day, with the full arrogance of misery, poured himself out to him and provoked him to violent, rebuking opposition, he hurried away despairingly, burnt his "Guiscard" and all his papers, and fled from Paris.[45]

Thus writes Wilbrandt. Bülow's version reads slightly differently: "A dispute about being and nonbeing brought about the catastrophe. Kleist ran off in anger, stayed away for a long time, and when he finally returned home, he found a note from Pfuel, which indicated that he had moved out in the meantime and left him alone in the apartment."[46] In Ulrike's memory, by contrast, the argument was not about life and death, or being and nonbeing:

> One day, however, Heinrich gets into a quarrel with Pfuhl about a small matter, Heinrich gets so furious that he gets up and leaves. One hour passes after another, one day after another—he does not return. The Werdecks and Pfuhl, in the greatest fear, report it to the police and the embassy, searches are held everywhere, no trace of him. In Paris there is a place where all the casualties who cannot be identified are deposited. They go to this dreadful place every day to look for him among the corpses.[47]

They do not find Kleist in the morgue. He is on his way to northern France to join Napoleon's troops, which are stationed in Boulogne-sur-Mer and are to invade England. He tries to join them twice, walks for days without a passport from Paris the 145 miles to the English Channel, each time in vain. He is lucky to have survived. A Prussian naval lieutenant, unable to identify himself, had just been shot dead in Boulogne as an alleged Russian spy. An unfortunate death, with little honor. Kleist desires a different kind of death—the "beautiful death of the battlefield," as he writes his sister Ulrike from St. Omer on October 26, after the burning of the *Guiscard* draft.[48] But another folly saves him from this fate. He asks the Prussian ambassador extraordinary in Paris, Marquis Girolamo Lucchesini, to put in a good word for him with the French minister of war Alexandre Berthier. Lucchesini writes to Berthier and, at the same time, forwards Kleist's letter of request to his own sovereign, King Friedrich Wilhelm III, informing him of Kleist's intentions. Berthier explains to Lucchesini in mid-December 1803 that the French army had no use for unknown foreign officers. And Friedrich Wilhelm III receives Kleist's letter "very ungraciously," as one can imagine. The whole situation ends with Kleist being summoned back from St. Omer to Paris by Lucchesini and, provided with his passport, sent home to Prussia around Christmas time.[49]

It is an old aristocratic rule of prudence not to give account to anyone who has not asked for it, for to apologize is to accuse oneself.[50] But if everyone at home demanded accountability—the King, the family, the former fiancée, the old professors—how is one to return home at all? Kleist's loss of honor was a public affair, word of his French 'suicide mission' had gotten around. As early as the beginning of December 1803, Pfuel's uncle from the small town of Gielsdorf in the Mark of Brandenburg was asking anxiously whether his nephew in faraway Paris was involved: "For several days now news has been circulating here that your traveling companion Kleist has joined the invasion troops, and it is being alleged that you followed him. Is that true? What about your studies?"[51] Kleist's reticence in letters had so far been a tactic to keep his family and friends at home in the dark about his plans, or lack thereof. Now he remained completely silent, writing no letters for months. This silence was no longer a weapon, but an expression of humiliation and shame. He had wanted to return to Frankfurt in triumph; now it would be in disgrace. Consequently, Kleist interrupted his journey back home from France at a place that he knew from his adolescence, yet where he was unknown and could thus stay: in Mainz, where he "at last collapsed, ill, and for nearly five months kept alternately to [his] bed or [his] room," as Kleist would later write to Henriette von Schlieben.[52] In June 1804 he told the Prussian authorities that he had been "physically ill" but was now restored, in order to dismiss the suspicion of a persistent "mental illness" and not to jeopardize an appointment in a government post.[53] One can choose to believe this or not. Physically, Kleist must have been fit after his long walks in the Swiss Alps and Normandy. As Ulrike wrote in retrospect in 1828, the doctor who treated Kleist in Mainz, taking him into his home, initially "did not know what he should cure [...] and advised him to be active, which in his opinion was all that was lacking."[54]

Fig. 33
Dr. Georg Christian Wedekind (1761–1831)

The friendly doctor was Georg Wedekind, born in 1761, a *homo politicus*, which is rare among German intellectuals. A renowned doctor, the Elector of Mainz appointed him as his personal physician and as a university professor in his city in 1787. In the fall of 1792, the Jacobin Wedekind ensured that Mainz was captured without a fight by revealing to the French that they would have no great resistance to overcome. Wedekind thus played a decisive role in the establishment of the Republic of Mainz. In the spring of 1793, when the Republic came to an end, he had to flee from Mainz with Kleist's regiment besieging the city. The two certainly did not meet each other back then. For a long time Wedekind had difficulties finding an acceptable position, but from November 1803 on he was again in Mainz. And in 1808 he became the personal physician of Grand Duke Ludwig I of Hesse-Darmstadt and remained so until his death in 1831.

As Wedekind's patient and house guest, Kleist could have learned a lot from him—from his reflections on rhetoric, on the promotion of reason through emotion, or from his political views, such as his criticism of Napoleon's revocation of the democratic principles of the French Revolution and of Napoleon's faith in an oligarchy of the nobility, which in Wedekind's case, as in Kleist's remarks in the *Berlin Evening Paper*, was more of an appeal than a criticism based on actual experience.[55] One can only speculate. What is certain is that Wedekind was a good doctor to Kleist—a thorough, careful one who sought advice and knew how to give it. His patient must have told him of Wieland's sympathy toward him; in any case, Wedekind requested from Wieland an informal evaluation of Kleist's character, which turned out to be quite the opposite of Wieland's quick and careless praise of *Guiscard* and proves his brilliant knowledge of human nature. Wieland replied to Wedekind within a week, on April 10, 1804:

> The contents of the letter from the 3rd of the month, which I am honored to have received, moved and saddened me quite a bit. It is now almost a year since I have had any news from Mr. von Kleist, and although I had no particular reason to hope for much better, I could not have imagined that I [...] would receive such sad news of his circumstances from a third party. [...]
>
> If I now combine all these circumstances—his *pride*, based on his self-confidence but violently crushed by his fate, the *eccentricity* of his whole life's path on which he has been moving back and forth ever since he left his military career, his terrible *strain*, his *fruitless striving* for an unattainable delusion of perfection, and his *Guiscard*, which had already become a *idée fixe*—with his shattered, weakened health and the bad relation in which he and his family seem to stand; then I am frightened by the thoughts that come to me and almost feel compelled to believe that it was his good genius that inspired him to work as a carpenter in Coblenz. What is certain (at least in my eyes) is that the project—to give him a post in the office of your friend M* [Charles-François-Philibert Masson, secretary general of the prefecture for the department Rhin-et-Moselle], which your so generously sympathetic affection for this loveable unfortunate man inspired you to do—would be doomed to fail for the simple reason that this *type of employment* and *dependency* would soon become quite unbearable for him.[56]

This sentiment is in keeping with Enlightenment tradition, reasonable and sensitive. After diagnosing Kleist's depression according to the criteria of an anthropological doctor of his time, Wieland suggests a course of treatment: Manual labor, which could have been useful, especially since Kleist was ill suited for bureaucracy, be it French or Prussian. But Kleist did not end up becoming a carpenter in Koblenz. Rather, upon his return to Berlin, he put his suitability for bureaucracy to the test.

We basically know nothing about Kleist's months in Mainz. According to Bülow's biography of 1848, Kleist "made the acquaintance of [Karoline von] Günderode and had a tender relationship with the daughter of a preacher near Wiesbaden during this time."[57] This is an unverifiable yet fortunate reference because it later inspired German writer Christa Wolf's *No Place on Earth*, a double portrait of Karoline von Günderrode and Kleist rendered under the sign of their suicides. Published in 1979, three years after German singer-songwriter Wolf Biermann's expulsion from the German Democratic Republic, the novel presents a conversation between two artists—outsiders, strangers—at a large tea party in Winkel am Rhein in 1804, which also included the siblings Clemens and Bettina Brentano among its guests. This text is, without doubt, one of the densest literary portraits of Kleist, written with pathos, knowing that "there is in fact a pain so terrible that one can die of it," while drawing on the topics one might expect: the German plight—the incessant suffering from the opposition between intellect and power; the question of the distinction between the sexes; and the question of the traumatic origin of artistic creativity. It is a "legend that suits" the two "precursors," as noted at the beginning of the novel: "Descended heavenward, separated in remote graves, resurrected again from the dead, still forgiving those who trespass against us, the sorrowful patience of angels."[58]

The dark months of Kleist's life in 1804 have troubled scholars as well. Their biographical montages are no less speculative than Wolf's novel. Carl Bertuch—an acquaintance of the Werdecks who was infatuated with Adolphine—is to blame for fueling these speculations, with the eleven meetings with "Kleist" or "M. de Kleist" or "Mr. de Kleist" he mentions in his Paris diary between February and May 1804. Does this mean that Kleist left Mainz on several occasions on behalf of Wedekind to analyze Napoleon's sensational policy during these months? Did he report from Paris as a courier or foreign correspondent on the infamous transformation of the French Republic into the French Empire? These questions account for some of the efforts within Kleist scholarship to solve the mystery.[59] Other efforts can be captured in a single question: Is it once again—as in the case of the mysterious Würzburg journey—a Freemason, namely Gustav Count von Schlabrendorf, who drew Kleist to Paris so that he could repeatedly smuggle revised sections of his anonymous book *Napoleon Bonaparte and the French People under His Consulate* (*Napoleon Bonaparte und das französische Volk unter seinem Consulate*) to the printer in Germany, despite the fact that the French were searching fiercely for this polemical work, which accuses Bonaparte of betraying the ideals of the Revolution?[60]

It is hard to believe that the melancholic Kleist, who had just become conspicuous to the Parisian authorities, should have swung himself into such dangerous actions and that Wedekind—thus proving himself a completely irresponsible doctor—should have advised him to do so.[61] Kleist scholar Helmut Sembdner suspected as early as 1991 that Bertuch had not met the writer Kleist but an unknown namesake in Paris.[62] This hypothesis would undermine all speculation about Kleist being an agent in the service of Wedekind or Schlabrendorf. And, indeed, Sembdner seems to have been right if we look to Klaus Müller-Salget's astonishing recent discovery in the Berlin journal *Voss' Newspaper* (*Vossische Zeitung*) of May 5, 1804. Under the heading "Incoming" or "Arrived Strangers," the newspaper reports, on May 3, the arrival of "Mr. v. Kleist, Lieut. ret., from Mainz." Bertuch's Paris diary, in turn, records for May 10, 1804: "A 11 heures a Frascanti peu de monde. Kleist, Walther, Mr. de Prusse, Jagemann, moi." Kleist, who had just come to Berlin from Mainz, is supposed to have been back in Paris in less than a week? Nowadays, such a journey would be no problem. In 1804, however, it would have hardly been possible even with the best horses, not to mention the fact that one would also have to explain why Kleist would have traveled from Mainz via Berlin to Paris. So if it was not Heinrich von Kleist who dined with Bertuch at Frascanti, who did? It must have been another member of the extended Kleist family, probably the same person with whom Bertuch had met several times before in Paris in the spring, for he merely added the name to his list of guests without adding any further description.[63]

According to Müller-Salget, one can imagine the events of the spring of 1804 as unfolding in the following chronology: On April 3 Wedekind writes to Wieland, who answers on April 10. The maximum time a letter would have taken to arrive at its destination at that time was seven days; so Wieland's reply could have arrived in Mainz around April 18. Perhaps Wedekind read Wieland's letter to his patient for therapeutic reasons, with Kleist then roused from his lethargy to make his way to Wieland in Weimar. After a short stay there—which Luise Wieland later related to her sister Charlotte Geßner[64]—Kleist went on to Berlin, where he may have arrived on May 3. This thesis sounds plausible.[65] In the eyes of his contemporaries, Wedekind was a good doctor who always had the relationship between body and soul in mind and knew how to look after his patients both medically and psychologically.[66] How he treated Kleist—whether he used Wieland's letter as a sort of shock therapy—we do not know. What we do know is that his treatment was successful. For the strained writer, first driven by ambition and later so ashamed of himself, so distraught and suicidal, was able to face reality again. He traveled to Wieland, probably to explain the failure of his *Guiscard* project. He traveled home to explain himself to his family and the authorities. He talked openly to everyone about his depression of the last months and his mad plan to invade England with Napoleon's troops. He decided to seek a bread-and-butter job and give up his literary vocation, which, at that moment, seemed impossible to fulfill. His "boy's-morning-blossom-dreams"[67] did not come to maturity. He hid them for two years but did not forget about them. Until 1806 it looked as if Kleist had formed himself in the likeness of his family and the Prussian government.

Kleist's letter to his sister Ulrike of June 24, 1804, reveals how hard this reform must have been and how resilient Wedekind had made his patient. It was the first letter from Kleist after what might have been eight months of silence—after his letter of October 26, 1803, from St. Omer, in which he announced that he wanted to "die the beautiful death of the battlefield." What Kleist describes to

Ulrike in his letter of June 1804 is no less cruel. Upon his return to Berlin, Kleist requested an audience with the King, hoping for the "granting of a request for an appointment to a post." Instead of the King, however, Kleist had to make do with the King's *aide-de-camp* Karl Leopold von Köckeritz, who humiliated him in a manner as banal as it was appalling. *German Men and Women* is the name of Walter Benjamin's collection of letters whose writers show character, in keeping with the volume's threefold motto: "Of honor without fame"; "Of greatness without glory"; "Of dignity without pay."[68] Köckeritz was a man without character, a model of Prussian subservient mentality, who wanted to coerce Kleist into submission too. Kleist defended himself from this position of weakness—without fame, without glory, without pay—by resorting to literary means among others. Unfortunately, Kleist's letter is not included in Benjamin's collection. It would make an important contribution to that superb history of German mentalities:

> My dearest Ully,
> Listen to some news about the success of my journey, a scoundrel gives them better than he can.
>
> I arrived Tuesday morning, had to waste Wednesday and Thursday because the King was away, then on to Charlottenburg on Friday, where at last I found Köckeritz in the palace. He received me with a dark mien, and in response to my question, did I have the honor of being known to him? he answered Yes. I came to him, so I went on, to ask for advice in my difficult position. The Marquis von Lucchesini, to whom I had sent a strange letter from St. Omer, had forwarded it to the King. This letter must contain unmistakable signs of mental illness, and might I make so bold as to hope that His Majesty in his fairness would not cause it to be brought before a political tribunal? Might there be grounds for such a hope? And might I, restored to health as I now feel myself, be allowed to rely on the granting of a request for an appointment to a post, if I dared so petition His Majesty? Whereupon, after a pause, he replied: "Are you really restored to health? I mean," he continued, as I looked somewhat embarrassed at him, "are you completely restored after all the notions and giddiness and brainsickliness?" (He used these words!!) I did not understand him, I answered as calmly as I could manage. I had been physically ill, and now felt quite fully restored to health, except perhaps for a certain weakness that the waters might cure. He removed his handkerchief from his pocket and blew his nose. If he were to be completely truthful with me, he began, now showing a far pleasanter expression, he could not conceal the fact that he did not think too favorably of me. I had left the military, turned my back on civilian service, wandered abroad, thought of settling in Switzerland, wrote 'po'try' (O my dear Ulrike!), wished to join the invasion, etc., etc. Moreover, it is a principle of the King's not particularly to protect people who have left the military for private life. He could do nothing for me. Tears actually came to my eyes. I said I was able to give him a completely different explanation for all these events, one quite different, certainly, from what he supposed. As for the matter of embarking for England, incidentally, it had had no political motive

whatever, and should rather be placed before a doctors' forum than the King's cabinet. Suffering from an *idée fixe*, I experienced a certain kind of headache, which, ever increasing to the point of the unbearable, so pressed me with need for relief that to be free of it at last I would have willingly let the world be turned upside down. It would be cruel indeed if one were to make a sick man responsible for his actions committed under the duress of severe pain. He seemed not entirely unsympathetic. As for that principle of the King's, I went on, it could not *always* have been so. For His Majesty had been gracious enough to release me from service with a promise of reappointment; a promise I could hardly believe him now unwilling to fulfill, if I have not made myself entirely unworthy in his eyes. ... For a moment he really seemed undecided. But then his sudden turnabout showed all too well what had already been decided about me at court. For he all at once reassumed the old grimace and said: "It will not help you. The King has already formed an opinion of you; I doubt that you will relieve him of it again. Try it, and write to him; but do not forget to add immediately your request for permission, in the event of a negative reply, to seek your happiness in another country." What have you to say to this, my dear little sister, Ulrike? I replied that I would beg permission to remain in my Fatherland. I wished to serve *my own King*, not another; if he could not make use of me, my wish would be to continue living in retirement, amongst my own. "Compose your letter as you wish," he broke in, somewhat confused. "It is possible the King might change his mind about you, and if you can win him over to appointing you, I promise I shall not stand in your way." I beseeched him formally for that favor, and we broke off our conversation. But then he asked me, in a wholly sincere way, to forgive him if he had insulted me and cursed his position, which brought upon him the ill feelings of so many to whom he could not be of service. I assured him that I took my leave of him with respect, and I rode back to Berlin. On the way I read Wieland's letter which you sent me and, with a deep sigh, lifted myself up again a little from the humiliation I had just experienced. Now I have written the King; but since my offer of my services will most probably bear no fruit, at least I have couched it in such language as I shall not later regret having used. You yourself have declared it my duty not to humiliate myself, and rather forfeit the favor of the whole world than yours. I now have the choice among a number of sour steps, one of which I shall be capable of doing in the end, because I must. But I throw myself at your feet, my great girl; may the wish I am unable to express still touch your heart.

Berlin, June 24, 1804. Your Heinrich.

P.S. Please answer me soon. I shall expect your letter here. Give my regards to everybody.[69]

The office of a civil servant is no place for tragedies, which is why Kleist—in his dramatic rendering of the sad events at Charlottenburg Palace—takes refuge in the burlesque, having the civil servant interrogating him reach for his handkerchief and then blow his nose. In doing so, Kleist demonstrates his penchant, like Kafka did later, for facial expressions and gestures when rendering catastrophes in his letters and stories—those seemingly small, banal catastrophes of everyday life, which he invariably presents from an external rather than internal narrative perspective. One cannot expect a psychological portrait from Kleist, and this is what links him to Kafka, whose interrogated heroes in *The Trial* or *The Castle* must bear witness, powerlessly, to the institutional violence of subaltern government officials. In fact, it is possible to see Kleist's letter of June 1804, in its rendering of asymmetrical communication, as the generative core for Kafka's novels. It is clear from the outset who is master and who is servant in the audience at Charlottenburg Palace. Unlike Kafka's K.s, however, Kleist does not make the mistake of underestimating his opponent Köckeritz by portraying him as obese and dull.[70] Köckeritz obviously masters the basic rules of any arcane politics. He deliberately withholds his knowledge of the King's thoughts concerning Kleist's request for an appointment to a government post and, at the same time, knows everything about Kleist, having thoroughly studied his file, referencing its key points: "left the military, turned [his] back on civilian service, wandered abroad, thought of settling in Switzerland [Helvetic Republic], wrote 'po'try' [...], wished to join the invasion." Köckeritz even appears to have heard word of the publication of *The Schroffenstein Family* and of Kleist's stay in Mainz with Wedekind, who is unlikely to have cured him of his Republican "notions and giddiness and brainsickliness." The implication is that Kleist is considered politically unreliable—unpredictable in his allegiance.

Kleist counters this charge by turning from political to medical discourse, trying to convince Köckeritz that he suffered from a temporary "mental illness." To have been mentally incompetent for a few months would have seemed more excusable and less dangerous, since refuting Köckeritz's accusation is about more than securing a government post. Kleist's intention to join the French army as a former Prussian officer could have been interpreted as high treason. In this precarious situation Kleist acts with cunning and prudence, as aristocrats have done for centuries in agonistic situations at court. Those who act in "self-defense" are allowed to disguise themselves every once in a while: "Truth against the enemy? Forgive me! I sometimes put / His cravat around my neck to enter his camp." This epigram can be found in Kleist's *Berlin Evening Paper* of October 31, 1810,[71] tucked away in a 'tabloid' devoted to the great battle against Napoleon. It also suits Kleist's minor battle against Köckeritz in June 1804, in which Kleist did not want to end up becoming a martyr. Consequently—and this is what is astonishing—there is no evidence suggesting a guilty conscience in Kleist when confronted with the misconducts Köckeritz names. For Kleist the encounter with Köckeritz does not revolve around the question of guilt, but rather shame or humiliation. Kleist's "sour steps" can best be explained with a

Fig. 34
Karl Leopold von Köckeritz (1762–1821)

sentence from German writer Wilhelm Genazino's acceptance speech for the Kleist Prize 2007: "Kleist's concept of bravery included surviving a catastrophe at all costs, even if it meant crippling himself."[72]

"Who talks of victory? To endure is all."[73] Rainer Maria Rilke's verse perfectly captures Kleist's situation after his meeting with Köckeritz in June—which would not be his last. Three weeks later Kleist had still not received an answer from the King regarding his request for an appointment to a post. He bowed and scraped before the King's cabinet councilors, Jean Guillaume Lombard and Carl Friedrich Beyme, before the minister of foreign affairs, Christian Count von Haugwitz, and before his successor, Karl August Baron von Hardenberg. At the direction of Köckeritz, Kleist wrote a second petition letter to Friedrich Wilhelm III, who—even in such an affair of minor political importance—seemed to do full justice to his reputation as a melancholic on the throne, unable to make decisions. Kleist was hoping for another foreign adventure far from his Prussian homeland, this time with Pierre Gualtieri—Marie von Kleist's elder brother—who was to go to Spain as Prussian ambassador and wanted to take Kleist with him as secretary—or, rather, attaché—to his legation. On August 2, 1804, Kleist was finally able to tell Ulrike "the news that the King has reacted favorably to my plea, even though I have not yet received an official resolution about it."[74] But his time of waiting was not over yet. It was not until the end of 1804 that Kleist found out which government position was intended for him. His dream of going to Spain was crushed. Gualtieri left for Madrid, but without Kleist, as the King did not allow him to accompany

Gualtieri. Since Kleist was paid out of the state coffers, the King wanted him to work directly for him—at least this is what Gualtieri suspects,[75] who would have been anything but a diligent Prussian superior for Kleist.

Gualtieri was considered a *bon vivant*. At court he was supported by his Huguenot friend Lombard, and Queen Luise held him in high esteem. He was sociable, cheerful—apparently not obstinate and unsociable like Kleist, who nevertheless dined "every day with [Gualtieri] at *Stadt Paris*," as Kleist wrote to Ulrike in June 1804, the most expensive hotel in Berlin.[76] The twenty-five Reichsthaler a month with which Ulrike and the Kleist family intended to finance Kleist's professional training for three years would not have allowed for such luxury.[77] Gualtieri must have regularly treated Kleist for meals and would have probably tempted him into further idleness had Kleist been allowed to accompany him to Spain. On his way to Madrid, Gualtieri had already run out of money in Paris. Lucchesini secured him a loan, and Hardenberg provided the initial equipment for the legation. It was not until February 1805 that Gualtieri took up his post, but he apparently continued to dine and drink excessively, eventually dying from inflammation of the chest and brain on May 27, 1805. Johann Georg Rist, Danish ambassador in Madrid, described Gualtieri as a torn man: "half soldier, half *bel esprit*, half courtier, half upright citizen, half German, half French," thus rendering him completely unsuited as a diplomat. Rist "had to give him guidance in the basics of the trade" and "in moments of distress" calm "his despair." According to Rist, the Spanish people hated the "non-Catholic" and even hurled curses and stones at his funeral procession and desecrated his grave.[78] Ultimately, Gualtieri's sociability was merely the flipside of his melancholia—and just like Kleist, he lacked a sense of place. This shared melancholia helps us to better understand Kleist's friendship with Gualtieri as well as the "dear Pierre" obituary he wrote for him, which mirrors Kleist himself—a double portrait that could serve as Kleist's own obituary, outlined in a letter to Marie von Kleist on July 20, 1805:

> The dear, good, peculiar Pierre!—I really loved him, even though he despised me, as he did everyone else. I knew that he despised nothing in me but humanity, nothing that he did not despise in himself. I know you are smiling, but I am smiling too. I had this realization under the conditions in which it really *could* be had; in the familiar solitude of a daily and day-long circling of many moons. One side of him was in love with the other, and the latter despised the former more deeply than he despised the worst among us. To me he had a poignant appearance, this man. One of the many creations that nature crushes because she has too many of them. So much potential for happiness, and so little *capacity* for pleasure! I could have wept many a tear on our walks. Our perpetual conversation was about death, continually leafed through, as in Young's *Night-Thoughts*, where it appears on every page. Well, may he rest in peace. He would have rushed

> to his doom any way he could. His mind had mastered all principles; he walked through life—*and knew it*—without a stick to hold on to, on the narrow ridge of a rugged mountain. Any gust of wind would have toppled him.[79]

This split ego is, at once, aware of its duality, helpless in this knowledge, self-destructive in the struggle between its two sides and hopelessly balancing between hubris and despair. No psychoanalyst today could describe the melancholic disposition more accurately than Kleist does here.

But let us return to the fall of 1804, to Kleist's time in Berlin, which is a time of waiting for him as it is for others. Friedrich Wilhelm III wanted to remain neutral in the conflict between the great European powers so as not to provoke in any way Napoleon's desire to conquer. For the sake of peace, Prussia was in abeyance, lingering in a state of indecision. Compared with England or France, Prussia appeared like a developing country. The political stasis, which blocked the modernization of Prussian society in many areas—such as the military, economic, and financial sectors—enabled the arts to strengthen as a counter-culture. The result was the astonishing cultural flowering of Berlin, which began to compete with Weimar and Jena, attracting the German intelligentsia like a magnet. Jean Paul, Johann Gottlieb Fichte, and August Wilhelm Schlegel moved to Berlin. August Wilhelm Iffland directed the Prussian National Theater at Gendarmenmarkt square, and the heyday of the Jewish literary salons began. Rahel Levin ran a salon on Jägerstraße, and Philippine Cohen ran hers in the family home on Münzstraße, which Kleist frequented then as he had done in 1801. There, he met the Cohens' private tutor—Rahel's future husband Karl August Varnhagen von Ense—as well as Adelbert von Chamisso, the later author of *Peter Schlemihl's Wondrous Story*.[80] Inspired by August Wilhelm Schlegel's lectures "On Belles-lettres and Art," the two of them founded the *North Star League* (*Nordsternbund*), a circle of young Romantic writers, which Kleist apparently did not join. In any case, Kleist did not publish in their house publication, the *Green Almanac* (*Grüner Almanach*). Just as in Weimar, Kleist did not promote himself as a writer in Berlin. His decision to keep his "po'try" private, ostensibly committed to the pursuit of a civil service career, seems to have been less a question of his literary allegiance than the result of the internal and external policing conducted by his family, the royal court, and himself.

Did Kleist back down? Did he turn from poet to philistine? Was he simply masking his enduring reluctance to accept a government post, or was he surrendering, in resignation, to the inevitable? One cannot help but wonder if, hidden behind Kleist's sudden acceptance of reality, there was a new scheme to simply mimic the career of bourgeois intellectuals found everywhere in Berlin.

Fig. 35
Rahel Levin (1771–1831)

One possible answer to the question of what made Berlin—a large city with about 150,000 inhabitants that had no court like Weimar, no university like Göttingen, no publishing houses like Leipzig—attractive to the intelligentsia is the large number of well-paid, highly reputable civil service positions that allowed a writer to pursue his bread-and-butter profession during the day and his literary vocation in the evening. Thus, in 1804, Kleist did not give up writing literature, but rather the ideal of becoming an autonomous writer—a dream he had only been able to entertain in the previous years thanks to Ulrike's patronage. It is conceivable that Kleist's career could have taken a different course from this point on, following a model familiar to us from his contemporaries in the Prussian civil service, the 'poet-lawyers' E.T.A. Hoffmann and Joseph Baron von Eichendorff.

At the end of 1804, things seemed to be moving in this direction; Kleist met a new type of civil servant, one whose disposition and competencies surpassed those of Karl Leopold von Köckeritz. The court of Potsdam no longer seemed to be the center of Enlightenment it had been in the times of Friedrich the Great. Compared with those days, the court of Kleist's time was more of an intellectual vacuum—but there were exceptions, such as the group of dedicated reformers who wanted to give the Prussian state a new, Modern order, headed by Minister of Foreign Affairs Karl August von Hardenberg and Superior Privy Councilor of Finance Karl Sigismund Franz Baron von Stein zum Altenstein, both of whom promoted and respected Kleist and were equally respected by him. Christian von Massenbach, Marie von Kleist's brother-in-law, arranged the contact. Kleist seemed to be more motivated than he had been in a long time and, as Ulrike tells us, was training in Altenstein's office "with great diligence" in finance: "Once he told Altenstein: 'Send me quite a lot.' To which Altenstein replied: 'I will send you so much that you will not be able to finish.'—'We shall see about that.'—And so he worked for eight days and nights straight, so that Altenstein was unable to peruse this much."[81]

Altenstein was a Franconian nobleman, seven years older than Kleist. He studied law in Erlangen and Göttingen and, in 1793, became a trainee in the Chamber of War and Domains in Ansbach—at a time when Hardenberg was commissioned to give the Franconian margraviates, recently annexed by Prussia, a new administrative structure. Hardenberg discovered Altenstein's talent and took him with him to Berlin in 1799. Despite occasional criticism Altenstein supported Hardenberg's reform plans for the next two decades, through political and wartime turmoil. After Prussia's defeat in the twin battles of Jena and Auerstedt in 1806, Altenstein wrote a memorandum in which he called for the abolition of aristocratic privileges, demanded freedom of trade, criticized the restriction of crafts and trades by guilds, and called for the reformation of the military, the elimination of the assembly of the estates, and the introduction of a system of popular representation. After 1815 he reformed the Prussian school and education system as minister of education and cultural affairs. He was responsible for the establishment of the Humanist secondary school, for the development of a multi-track school system, for compulsory schooling throughout Prussia, and an obligatory curriculum for secondary schools.[82]

Altenstein—a friend of Fichte's—was a gentle and educated man well versed in philosophy and the natural sciences. He gave Kleist the chance to prove himself among the elite of the political reform movement. Altenstein initially considered sending Kleist to his homeland of Franconia—the testing ground for bureaucratic innovations, far from Prussia. Kleist was euphoric, saying he had "won the favor of this Altenstein fellow." He no longer doubted that he "shall pass the whole test within every reasonable expectation,"[83] as he assured Pfuel in his notorious letter of January 7, 1805, which Kleist scholar Jens Bisky regards as a kind of "marriage proposal" to Pfuel.[84] Why should Pfuel not have taken Kleist's request to go to Franconia with him literally and seriously, now that Kleist had an income that sufficed for both: "They will appoint me certainly, and soon, and remuneratively. Come to Anspach with me and let us enjoy the sweetness of friendship. [...] You shared your resources with me in Leipzig, or at least would gladly have done so, which is the same thing: accept the same from me! I shall never marry, you will be wife to me, children and grandchildren! Do not continue on the path you have begun."[85] But Pfuel did continue. In April 1805 he was reenlisted in the military, as he had wished, and was dispatched to a battalion in Masuria, far from Berlin. Three years later, in March 1808, he married Karoline von Byern. He had one daughter and five sons with her. The marriage lasted twenty-two years, ending in 1830 when he had an affair with Emilie Wahlert, a married woman. It is hard to believe that his marriage to Karoline was a pretend relationship. Pfuel and Wahlert divorced their partners and married in 1832.

It must have been thanks to Wedekind or Altenstein that Kleist was stable enough to tolerate Pfuel's departure. The friendship between the two continued unbroken, as their correspondence attests. One might have expected a violent reaction on Kleist's part, a temporary collapse, such as the one that followed his separation from Lose in Basel at the end of 1801. However, we have no record of such an event. There is only one hint suggesting the persistence of Kleist's latent melancholia. Bülow, who often relies on Pfuel's account in his biography on Kleist, states that in April 1805 Kleist had "a very peculiar conversation with [Pfuel] about suicide"[86]—for obvious reasons, however: Hartmann von Schlotheim, a former regimental comrade of the two, had just tried in vain to commit suicide, apparently by a pistol shot in the mouth, as his face had been disfigured. Caroline von Briest—Fouqué's future wife—writes that Kleist "stayed with Schlotheim day and night. This company did the poor suffering man a great deal of good; he opened himself up to [Kleist] completely, who felt the same way as him, found his deed necessary, and seemed to approve of it, which of course scandalized the people very much and made poor Marie [von Kleist] very worried, who, frightened by the sad experience, feared for all her friends."[87]

Kleist, however, seemed stable during this time. He did not resent Pfuel for taking a path different from the one he had suggested to him. And he did not resent Altenstein for not keeping him at the royal court in Berlin, wanting to send him first to Königsberg for a proper training and afterward to Franconia. As Kleist asserts to Christian von Massenbach on March 23, 1805:

> You do my good, honest, excellent friend Altenstein a great injustice […]. There can be no talk of wanting me removed from the Hardenberg Department by some artifice; instead, this Altenstein fellow—who has great plans for his fatherland (Franconia)—shows the most lively interest in winning me for his purposes. The intention behind sending me to Königsberg is really no other than to train me to become a competent civil servant, and to transfer the exemplary institution of the Prussian Chambers to the Franconian ones with my assistance once I am employed. […] If working in government business is truly my profession, then I have found in Altenstein the one who will lead me to the height of it; but *whether* it is my vocation is another question, on which my heart for now has no voice.[88]

Kleist distinguishes between profession and vocation, mind and heart, and for now follows reason in going to Königsberg—the trading and residential town in East Prussia, which had about fifty thousand inhabitants at the beginning of the 19th century and was far away enough from the Potsdam court to provide the freedom to test experiments in political reform. When Kant had still been teaching at the Albertina, the university of Königsberg had attracted great names to the city, such as Fichte, Herder, J.M.R. Lenz, Moses Mendelssohn, and Friedrich von Gentz.[89] Kant died in February 1804, and it was not until the winter semester of 1805/06 that his chair was filled with Wilhelm Traugott Krug—the husband of Kleist's former fiancée Wilhelmine. Before Krug's arrival Kleist had begun studying at the Albertina. Following Altenstein's advice, Kleist decided against immediate employment as a mid-level civil servant, which would have earned him a salary of 1,200 Reichsthaler a year. He opted instead for a solid but only half as well-paid training, which would have provided him with the qualifications for top offices and made him eligible for consideration. As part of this training, he had to attend the finance lectures of Christian Jacob Kraus, who introduced the German reformers to the economic theories of Adam Smith, according to whom the wealth of nations was dependent on general education, private property, and free competition no longer hindered by aristocratic privileges, guilds, cartels, or monopolies. It was thanks to Kraus' lectures that the basic ideas of Smith's famous treatise *An Inquiry into the Nature and Causes of the Wealth of Nations* of 1776 found their way into Prussian legislation. In Kleist's personal library in Königsberg, the book was not to go missing for a single day; he refused to lend his "Smith" to Pfuel.[90] Even after his death in 1807, Kraus had a lasting impact, and Napoleon's defeat of Prussia in 1806 seems to have pushed the modernization of the Prussian state. In October 1810 the *Berlin Evening Paper* was still engaged in a debate over Kraus' import, with Kleist on the side of the reformers and Adam Müller on the side of the conservative nobility. On October 12, 1810, Müller's polemical obituary on Kraus was printed, in which he marvels that a "completely unproductive and dependent mind" such as Kraus "was able to attain such local authority" and that through him Adam Smith's teachings "achieved this exaggerated prestige." On October 27, 1810, Müller's obituary was followed by a defense of Kraus, arguing that he was a "wise adviser," a "quick-witted mind capable of new ideas of his own," who, "without idly brooding over the theory of the state, had taught practically and incisively how to help a province, how to help a state"—many "thousands of families in Prussia," which were finally freed from socage and had become landowners, had him to thank.[91]

The "Anti-criticism" was written by an author who was proud that he, unlike Müller, had attended Kraus' lectures in Königsberg. And Kleist, during his studies at the Albertina, had already described Kraus as a man who "gives birth to ideas that really made sense. He spreads thoughts like a rich man money—with his hands full."[92] This portrait of Kraus comes from Kleist's letter to Altenstein of May 13, 1805, to whom Kleist repeatedly reported on the progress of both his studies in finance and political economy as well as his professional training in financial administration at the Chamber of Domains. The Chamber's president, Hans Jakob von Auerswald, was as eager for reform as Altenstein and a mild and understanding superior to Kleist. Kleist himself names the "measures taken to liberate the crafts and trades from guilds"—that is, measures to promote freedom of trade against the restrictions imposed by the guilds—his "favorite subject."[93] However, he did not seem to have become too familiar with administrative matters. A year later, on June 30, 1806, he had to admit to Altenstein that he did not know enough about "the circumstances of bourgeois life" and that his "extraordinary lack of familiarity with it" had led him to "mistakes," which the gracious Auerswald had, however, left "unrebuked."[94] Kleist also seemed to have difficulties with speaking in the Chamber of Domains. In the winter of 1805/06, he wrote his essay "On the Gradual Fabrication of Thoughts While Speaking" in Königsberg, which the previous chapter acknowledged as a basic text for understanding Kleist's concept of creativity. The essay had a quite pragmatic context, as its opening paragraph indicates: "Often, while at my desk working, I search for the best approach to some involved problem."[95] This is Kleist's exact situation, the trainee civil servant in the Königsberg Chamber who had to go from studying files at his business desk to reporting his findings to his colleagues in the Chamber. But this task was difficult for Kleist, as he admits to Altenstein: "All winter long I have felt uncertain whenever my turn came to report: my mind turned blank at the subject matter at hand; it seemed I held an empty page before me. But now how I would tremble to appear before the council. It is a great disorder in my nature, I know; but so it is."[96]

In November 1805 Altenstein had to already endure Kleist's medical report on "eternal plagues in [his] abdomen" as well as his reflections on the "marvelous knotting together of a mind and a convolution of entrails and bowels."[97] In June and July 1806, intimate confessions hailed down on Altenstein, Auerswald, and Hardenberg, in which Kleist vividly reported on his "most severe constipation," interpreting it as the "recurrence" of an illness of the "abdomen" he had experienced before in France, which affected his "temper" and made him unfit for work. He requested to be dispensed from his operations and was granted a six-month vacation. Hardenberg, however, asked Auerswald to point out to Kleist that he should "shorten the leave insofar his health conditions allowed in order to then, within a few months, obtain the qualification necessary for his examination."[98]

It would not have been unreasonable to believe that a melancholic man, such as Kleist, was constipated. Even in the autopsy report after his suicide, the doctors granted this to him and concluded from the "thickened black bile" that he was in a "pathological mental state."[99] Kleist may not have faked his illness, but in the summer of 1806, it was all-too convenient timing. Just as his time at the Viadrina, he only lasted for one year of training in Königsberg. Examinations were imminent, but his illness prevented him from taking them—which would have been, for Kleist, its own kind of torturous situation, as he anticipates in "On the Gradual Fabrication of Thoughts While Speaking":

> Perhaps there is no worse opportunity for showing oneself off to advantage than just such a public examination. Not only is the experience a highly disagreeable one, and in the worst possible taste, and the sheer exasperation of it reason enough to balk at an examiner, who, like a horsedealer with only a book knowledge of horses, buys or rejects us as we satisfy or not on a few prescribed counts; but so delicate is the skill required for playing on the mind of another to sound its proper tone, and so surely will it jangle at the least clumsiness of touch, that even the most practiced connoisseur of human nature, masterfully skilled in what Kant calls the art of intellectual midwifery, might nevertheless, in such a confrontation, not knowing the six-week-old, make very sour music of him indeed.[100]

The student may be vexed and contentious, but such feelings are of no use to him. The institutionalized rules of the university examination do not allow him to behave in a recalcitrant and obstinate manner. Kleist's imagery comes from the language of animal trade and it reveals how the business is done: No "horsedealer" would ever "buy[ ]" a stubborn horse that does not move from its place. It would be different if the examiner were not interested in the thoughts of the student moving in his—the examiner's—direction, that is, if he—as a "connoisseur of human nature"—were at all interested in playing on the student's mind to sound its "proper tone." However, this case is rare, as Kleist suspects. For how could the midwife 'know' the six-week-old whom she nursed? It is only after six weeks that, in accordance with Christian tradition, a child is baptized and given a name unique to it.[101] Kleist compares the final examination to this initiation ritual. The imagery reveals exactly what the conditions of such an exam are. The student has to solve the paradoxical task of passing off the foreign—that which he has learned—as his own, so as to be released into autonomy.

This approach, as one can suspect, is not Kleist's style. He is obstinate, he has no desire for subordination. As Bülow relates: "According to his statements to the ladies, the position in which Kleist was employed at the Chamber displeased him to a great extent, and he found it unbearable to see himself subordinate to men to whom he felt superior."[102] However, his stutter—a "flaw in the organ of speech"[103]—and shyness "whenever [his] turn came to report"[104] prevented Kleist from asserting himself against his superiors in the Chamber as well as at private gatherings, such as at the home of philosophy professor Krug, husband of his former fiancée Wilhelmine, whose malice toward Kleist we saw earlier. But what happens if the weapon of the word cannot be accessed quickly enough? The essay "On the Gradual Fabrication of Thoughts While Speaking" paints the consequences:

> One often sees, in a social gathering, when animated conversation produces continuous cross-pollination of ideas, how some people, who usually remain silent because they do not feel that they are themselves very articulate, will suddenly, with a convulsive movement, flare up, grasp at suitable language, and thereby bring something completely unintelligible into the world. Indeed, having attracted everyone's attention in this way, they seem to be trying to indicate by a kind of embarrassed dumb show that they have absolutely no idea of what they had wanted to say. It is likely that such people have had perfectly cogent and clear thoughts. But the sudden shift in purpose, the transition from thought to expression, curtails that mental agitation which was as necessary to the retention of the thought as to the bringing forth of it. [...] And where we may assume equal clarity of thought, he who can talk faster than his opponent will enjoy a distinct advantage, for, in a manner of speaking, he leads more troops into the field. Just how necessary a certain agitation of the mind is, even to reactive ideas that we have already had, may be seen when receptive and well-instructed young minds are being examined, and, without previous introduction, such questions are put to them as "What is the state?" or "What is property?"[105]

Kleist avoided such questions and examinations. Writers are rarely good public speakers. So Kleist returned to his true calling—writing. On August 31, 1806, he writes to his friend Rühle: "The truth is that I find what I imagine beautiful, not what I accomplish. If I were fit for something else, I would love to do it with all my heart: I simply write because I cannot help it. You know that I left my career again. Altenstein, who does not understand how it all fits together, offered me a leave of absence and I took it; but only to get out of the affair more gently."[106] While Kleist had already secretly given up his career as a civil servant, his literature, nevertheless, benefited from his training in Königsberg, particularly the legal discourse he acquired in the Königsberg Chamber. This influence is immediately evident in a 'courtroom play' like *The Broken Jug*, which he completed in Königsberg. Less noticeable to today's readers is that Kleist's narrative technique follows rhetorical rules that were employed for summarizing civil or criminal cases, which trainees, such as Kleist, had to practice. Such reports—called relations—were supposed to help the members of judicial panels make decisions without having to study the files themselves. Accordingly, these relations needed to contain, in chronological order, all of the important facts necessary for the assessment of a case. Names and places had to be abbreviated or encrypted; the presentation of the facts at the beginning of the relation was to be free of any evaluative statements; all arguments of both the prosecution and the defense had to be presented equally; legally irrelevant matters had to be excluded; and a tight page count had to be kept. Yet Kleist's dense, agitated, breathless, hypotactic, and immensely intricate style was not solely derived from the technique used in the Königsberg Chamber. As will later be shown in an analysis of his stories, he followed the technique partially but parodied it at the same time, revealing its disciplinary character, its merely seeming impartiality, and its inadequacy for establishing truth. For the time being, to provide evidence of Kleist's 'relation model,' it should suffice to quote the beginning of *The Marquise of O—*, which, in its abbreviations and hypotactic sentence structure, is modeled after the *species facti*, the narrative found at the beginning of any relation:

> In M—, an important town in northern Italy, the widowed Marquise of O—, a lady of unblemished reputation and the mother of several well-brought-up children, inserted the following announcement in the newspapers: that she had, without knowledge of the cause, come to find herself in a certain situation; that she would like the father of the child she was expecting to disclose his identity to her; and that she was resolved, out of consideration for her family, to marry him. The lady who, under the constraint of unalterable circumstances, had with such boldness taken so strange a step and thus exposed herself to the derision of society, was the daughter of Colonel G—, the Commandant of the citadel at M—. About three years earlier her husband, the Marquis of O—, to whom she was most deeply and tenderly attached, had lost his life in the course of a journey to Paris on family business. At the request of her excellent mother she had, after his death, left the country estate at V— where she had lived hitherto, and had returned with her two children to the house of her father the Commandant.[107]

Following the chronology of events, Kleist recounts them meticulously, encrypting information for the sake of discretion, playing with the form of *species facti* in a story that involves no legal or criminal case as such.[108] He plays with the form insofar as he deviates from the norm of plainly stated facts, emphasizing the peculiar and as yet unheard-of—in keeping with the tradition of the novella—which is that the Marquise "had with such boldness taken so strange a step and thus exposed herself to the derision of society." It is no coincidence, then, that Kleist—like E.T.A. Hoffmann—was the favorite author of lawyer and novella writer Franz Kafka.

"Outwardly, I fulfil my duties satisfactorily in the office, not my inner duties, however, and every unfulfilled inner duty becomes a misfortune that never leaves," writes Kafka, who for many years had to endure the "back and forth" between his legal work with the Workers' Accident Insurance Institute in Prague and his literary work at home.[109] Kleist was able to escape this conflict. When Hardenberg granted him a leave of absence in mid-August 1806, he went to Pillau, a seaside resort near Königsberg, for a five-week cure. But the summer retreat did not work out as planned; he continued to feel ill, was bedridden, and seemed to become completely absorbed in his inner thoughts. Kleist did not provide portraits of the East Prussian Baltic coast, nor did he—unlike in the case of Würzburg, Dresden, and Paris—provide a portrait of Königsberg, even though he lived there for one and a half years and was there inspired to write literature: the comedy *The Broken Jug*; the novella "Jerónimo and Josefa," later published under the title "The Earthquake in Chile"; the comedy *Amphitryon*; and probably the first drafts for *Penthesilea*. From May 1805 to January 1807, Kleist lived at 81 Löbenichtsche Langgasse in Königsberg, very close to the old Hochmeisterschloss, home of the Chamber of War and Domains. In the winter of 1805/06, Ulrike lived with him, and Kleist often visited Johann George Scheffner's house—the retired war and domains councilor and friend of Christian Jacob Kraus—as well as the homes of the Krugs and his superior Auerswald. At heart, however, Kleist was lonely and introverted even in company. His appearance had "something somber and strange" about it, as Scheffner—who was on friendly terms with him—reports in his memoirs. "Just as a diver ascending from the depths of the sea does not, at least in the first moments, remember everything great and beautiful that he saw in the underwater world and is not able to tell it, so it seemed to be the case with Heinrich von Kleist at times."[110]

The image of the diver is an apt description of Kleist's reticence, but it is more than just a metaphor. There was an actual basis for it from his time in Königsberg. In July 1805 Kleist designed an underwater craft, a hydrostatic submersible. He wanted to leave for Australia with his friends Pfuel und Rühle. Hydrostasy refers to an equilibrium of forces in fluids in which the upward gradient of pressure and the downward force of gravity are balanced at all levels of the fluid layer. This balance of forces is controlled, similar to balloons, by dropping trim weights, but mainly with the help of tanks which are filled with water to increase the weight when diving and with compressed air to push out the water when ascending. The body of the submersible thus seems to hover in the water; it seems to defy gravity, like the puppets in Kleist's essay

Fig. 36
Königsberg, 81 Löbenichtsche Langgasse

"On the Puppet Theater." Nothing ever came of Kleist's plan for a submersible. The first German submarine was built by a Bavarian artillery officer named Wilhelm Bauer. In February 1851 it dove to a depth of 65 feet in the Kieler Förde. Then it was unable to maneuver and the crew waited for an agonizingly long time until the internal pressure was as high as the external so the hatch could be opened and they could swim up through the ice-cold water. Kleist had hoped that his submersible could manage "at least 6–8 nautical miles a day." However, he was not the most reliable mathematician and engineer. His calculations of the pressure conditions at depth were incorrect; his submersible—if it had indeed been built—would have undoubtedly sunk.[111] Pfuel did the math too and must have talked Kleist out of his dreams, given Kleist's angry reaction in his letter to Pfuel in August 1805: "[Y]our sadness because nothing ever came of our plans to go to Australia would touch me deeply if I could convince myself that you really had some feelings in the matter. But of all of us, I am the one who in point of fact commits himself. Why should we three, *te duce* [with you as leader], *not* take a boat on the Baltic?"[112]

The fact that the three friends from the Potsdam military days were planning to leave Prussia and risk their careers to do so needs to be explained. After all, Kleist had just begun his career as a civil servant in Königsberg, and Pfuel and Rühle were officers in the King's army. However, the three were anything

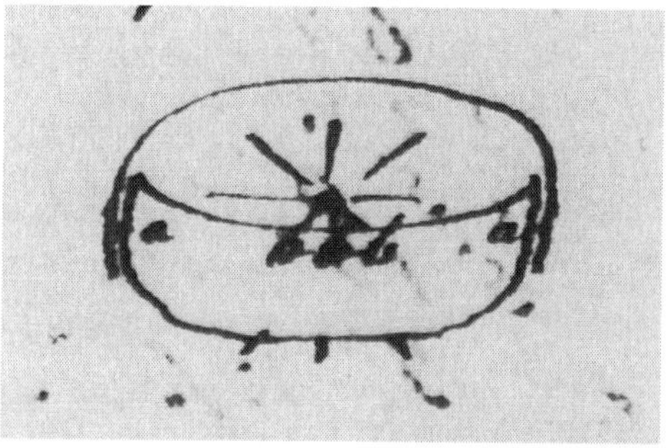

Fig. 37
Kleist's sketch of a submersible

but content with the policy of Friedrich Wilhelm III, and their frustration over it may have been the main reason for their escape fantasies. The Prussian king—even though war against France seemed inevitable—was a melancholic ditherer. His favorite time was the time of respite. And yet France's supremacy over Europe had not been decided, even after Napoleon's coronation as Emperor of France in 1804. England and Russia formed a coalition against France, which Austria joined in 1805. Prussia, however, retained its neutrality and watched passively as the Holy Roman Empire of the German Nation came to an end, and as central states—in between the great powers of Austria and Prussia—with new territorial size and sovereignty consolidated (such as Baden, Württemberg, Bavaria, or Hesse-Darmstadt), which were politically dependent on France. Napoleon experienced a defeat against England at the Battle of Trafalgar, where Nelson destroyed the combined French-Spanish fleet. Consequently, the French emperor concentrated on the continental war and invaded Austria in alliance with the southern German states. He conquered Vienna on November 13, 1805, and defeated Russia and Austria in the Battle of the Three Emperors at Austerlitz on December 2, 1805. In the first half of December 1805, Kleist writes to Rühle full of anger about his indecisive King:

> Are you not convinced as I am that the French will attack *us*, and this very *winter*, if we continue another four weeks to stand by with weapon in hand at the gate of their retreat from Austria? […] Why did the King not instantly, upon the French incursion into Franconia, call all the estates of his realm together, and tell them of his position in a moving speech (the mere painfulness of it would render it moving!)? If he had left it to their sense of honor whether it was their wish to be ruled by a King so ill-used, would not something of a national spirit have bestirred itself? And if this stirring had shown itself, would that not have been the sign to explain to them that it is no ordinary war with which we have to do? It is *To be, or not to be*. And if he could not increase his army by three hundred thousand men, he would have no choice but to die with honor. Do you not think that such a mobilization could have come about? Suppose he had all his gold and

> silver tableware melted down for coin, abolished his chamberlains and horses, had his whole family follow him therein, and he had ascertained, after setting this example, what the nation was willing to do. I do not know how much or how little he enjoys the food he eats off his silver plates; but I am sure the [Austrian] emperor in Ollmütz is not enjoying his meals. [...] The times, it seems, would bring about a new order of things, and we shall live to see nothing of it but the mere overthrow of the old. From the whole of civilized Europe one single huge system of realms will emerge, each throne occupied by new dynasties in thrall to the French. [...] We will soon read in the newspapers: "There is talk of great changes to the constitution of the Holy Roman Empire," and later on: "It is said that a great German (southern) Prince will take over the affairs of the state." In short, within a year, the Bavarian Elector is King of Germany.—Will someone not finally put a bullet through the head of this, the world's evil?[113]

Anger breeds clairvoyance. The Elector of Bavaria did not become King of Germany, but he was made King of Bavaria. Württemberg, too, became a kingdom, while Baden and Hesse-Darmstadt became grand duchies. In the summer of 1806, Napoleon united the southern German states into the Confederation of the Rhine, which had to provide France with troops if necessary. Napoleon was the 'protector' of the Rhenish Confederation; he thus had hegemony in Central Europe. The German central states were sovereign with respect to Prussia and Austria. In August 1806 Franz II abdicated the throne of the Holy Roman Emperor. The overthrow of order was complete, and the almost thousand-year history of the Holy Roman Empire of the German Nation had come to an end. How did Prussia react to this? After the Napoleonic troops had marched through the principality of Ansbach-Bayreuth in the fall of 1805, Friedrich Wilhelm III rattled a little with his weapons, ordering the partial mobilization of his troops, but nothing more. The Prussian king did not join the Austro-Russian coalition prior to the Battle of Austerlitz, even though half of his country demanded war. He sat out every humiliation while Napoleon lost more and more respect for the once so powerful and prestigious Prussia under Friedrich II. Friedrich Wilhelm III's loss of power was evident. He also lacked any political prudence. After Austerlitz, for instance, he allowed himself to be compensated for the loss of Franconia to Bavaria with English Hanover, thus making England his new opponent. Kleist was personally affected by these political developments, as it were. Altenstein's offer to allow him free rein in Franconia—the 'experimental ground' far away from Prussia—after his training in Königsberg was a thing of the past. Friedrich Wilhelm III—accompanied by despondent counselors, such as Köckeritz and Haugwitz—was practically submissive to Napoleon. He only started to act when Napoleon secretly offered Hanover back to the British in August 1806 to conclude a peace treaty with England, and when the anti-French, patriotic opposition in Prussia around

Karl August von Hardenberg and Baron vom Stein—to which Kleist, Rühle, and Pfuel belonged—began to dominate public opinion. The King mobilized the army and demanded the withdrawal of French troops from southern Germany. In response, Napoleon declared war on Prussia on September 9, 1806. At the time Kleist was staying in Pillau for spa treatment. On October 14, 1806, the Prussian troops were crushed in the twin battles of Jena and Auerstedt. Over twenty thousand Prussian and Saxon soldiers lost their lives or were seriously injured. Two weeks later Napoleon captured Berlin. The King and his court fled to East Prussia.

"What terrible times," writes Kleist, still ailing, to his sister from Königsberg on October 24, 1806. Six weeks later, in a letter dated December 6, 1806, again addressed to Ulrike, he placed all his hopes in Queen Luise, who, unlike her husband, was bellicose and had long supported the patriotic opposition in Prussia: "I cannot think of our Queen without emotion. [...] She gathers all the great men around her whom the King neglects, and who yet alone can save us; indeed, she is the one sustaining what has not yet collapsed."[114] In her personal negotiations with the Russian Tsar Alexander I and with Napoleon, Luise repeatedly demonstrated her courage and political skills. But she could not prevent Prussia from losing its position as one of Europe's great powers or from being reduced to half of its pre-war territory in the Treaty of Tilsit in July 1807. The Prussian territories west of the Elbe river were incorporated into the newly founded Kingdom of Westphalia, and Prussia had to relinquish a large part of its territories acquired in the Polish Partitions, which became the French-dominated Duchy of Warsaw. The remaining Prussian state was made to pay an exorbitant war contribution of thirty-two million Reichsthaler, and its army was reduced to one fifth of its original size, to forty-two thousand men. Berlin remained occupied by foreign troops, and it was not until December 1808—at the onset of Napoleon's fight against the Dos de Mayo Uprising of 1808 and the Austrian rearmament efforts, for which Napoleon needed the soldiers he had stationed in Prussia—that Berlin was once again free from French oppression and exploitation. The withdrawal of the French, however, did not give Prussia sovereignty. In November 1808, for example, Napoleon put pressure on Friedrich Wilhelm III to dismiss his chief minister Baron vom Stein, whom Napoleon considered a dissident politician responsible for promoting a popular uprising and a coalition of Prussia and Austria against France. The royal family did not return to Berlin before December 1809. Friedrich Wilhelm III remained dependent on Napoleon's good will while ruling a state that was more or less bankrupt due to the war contributions, plundered by the occupying power, and still in need of reforms in all areas of society.

But let us return to the winter of 1806/07, when the Prussian state was on the verge of dissolution after the defeat of Jena and Auerstedt. For their safety the King and Queen had fled to East Prussia, which the French troops kept away from, given its close proximity to Russia. The Queen, always on Hardenberg's side, supported the reformers. The only hope that Prussia had left was its progressive and learned civil servants and officers, who, in their resistance to Napoleon's world dictatorship, began to express nationalist thoughts, developing ideas for modernizing Prussian society and for transforming the estate-based society into a bourgeois one that would turn the King's subjects into politically responsible citizens committed to their state. In keeping with the idealist concept of self-cultivation, this motivation was about educating the Prussian people toward autonomy as well as political and economic participation in the state beyond all private self-interest. A small elite minority among the educated stratum of aristocrats and bourgeois—especially the younger generation—felt responsible for these changes. The revolution of Prussian society was thus not to come from a mass movement, as in France in 1789, but from above—through a progressive bureaucracy of academically trained civil servants who perceived themselves as the intellectual avant-garde. They gained freedom to act in the power vacuum following the collapse of Prussia in 1806 and in the absence of the royal family.[115] In times of greatest need, people focus on the essentials; measures for 're-education' may thus find a hearing. On December 6, 1806, Kleist notes: "I feel lighter and more pleasant than usual. It seems to me as though the general misfortune were educating people, I find them wiser and warmer, and their view of the world more generous."[116]

So Kleist had hoped. Moreover, considering his castigation of the King for eating from silver plates rather than selling his possessions in support of the war and setting an example for his subjects, Kleist should have—in Prussia's most dire hour—made a temporary sacrifice for the sake of patriotic duty. He should have ended his sick leave and returned to his desk to the reformers in the Chamber. Instead of serving his revered Queen Luise, Hardenberg, or Altenstein in such a manner and remaining in the still unoccupied Königsberg, Kleist, in early 1807, embarked on a daring journey westward, behind the Prussian lines into French territory, only to be arrested in Berlin. How is one to make sense of this recklessness? Did Kleist flee from responsibility in order to continue writing, no matter where, even if it were in the prison of Fort de Joux, where the French took him? On his journey there he reassures his sister in a letter of February 1807 that, in contrast to the other prisoners of war, he "will suffer least from this mishandling; for if [his] situation is at all bearable, [he] can work at [his] writing there as well as anywhere."[117] He likely had "The Earthquake in Chile" under his pen, a novella which—much like the tragedies

The Schroffenstein Family and *Guiscard*—shows that the hope for "a new order of things" after the "overthrow of the old" is misguided. Unlike the works of Schiller or Goethe, Kleist's works never follow the agenda of an aesthetic education. Would it therefore be safe to say that he also wants to revoke his support of political education through reforms in Königsberg? Did he secretly doubt the idealism of the reforms, the Neohumanist notion of self-cultivation that guided them, which focused on refining the intellectual, moral, and aesthetic powers of the individual for the common good? That Kleist was a disappointed idealist—a sceptic—cannot be denied. Nevertheless, from 1808 on he again supported the patriotic and reformist movements, albeit not as a civil servant but in journalistic projects—such as the *Berlin Evening Paper*—or by writing a propaganda play such as *The Battle of Herrmann*, which called for a popular uprising against France, renouncing all selfish interests of station and property.

Kleist did not travel westward from Königsberg alone in January 1807. Pfuel and the officers Carl von Gauvain and Wilhelm von Ehrenberg accompanied him. The four of them first visited Kleist's sister Ulrike in Schorin, near Stolp in Pomerania, where she was staying on the estate of her cousin and brother-in-law Philipp von Stojentin. Then they continued their journey west. Pfuel separated from them shortly before their arrival in Berlin to go to Nennhausen in Havelland, Brandenburg, to see Fouqué. Kleist, Gauvain, and Ehrenberg were arrested in Berlin upon presenting their passports to the French occupation authorities. In April 1807 Henri-Jacques-Guillaume Clarke—at the time governor of Berlin, later French minister of war—informed Kleist's sister of the reason for his arrest after she had beseeched him for help on her brother's behalf: "Your brother exposed himself to the danger of being considered a spy when he went behind the French army lines coming from the enemy headquarters, and I even treated him with leniency by having him brought to France.[118] As a spy Kleist could have easily been executed. Clarke must not have been confident in his suspicions, especially given that Kleist had long been discharged from the Prussian army. Yet Kleist scholarship continues to wonder whether Clarke's suspicions were not justified after all—whether Kleist, Pfuel, Ehrenberg, and Gauvain were on a scouting mission in French territory, or whether they wanted to join a free corps to fight the French.[119] That would have certainly been a foolhardy undertaking with dubious motives—such as Pfuel's desire to compensate for his dishonorable escape from the Battle of Auerstedt. One can also be suspicious of the scant information on the travel routes and dates of the four ex-officers from Königsberg to Berlin, which Kleist and Ulrike outline in their letters. Why did Gauvain and Ehrenberg accompany Kleist on this dangerous journey? Kleist chose his companions carefully on each of his journeys. Gauvain and Ehrenberg, however, were not his friends either before or after the journey. And why did they go with him to Berlin at all, given the fact that the city was so strictly controlled by the French? Why did they not go to their hometowns of Rathenow and Neustadt an der Dosse, adjacent to Pfuel's destination Nennhausen? A stay in these small communities would have been less risky. Gauvain and Ehrenberg would have had to simply part with Kleist when Pfuel did.[120]

The true motivations of the shared journey, if indeed it was carried out together, remain a mystery. Kleist's motive for leaving Königsberg and going to Berlin, however, can be explained in terms of financial problems. At the end of 1806, Kleist was in great financial trouble, as his letters to Ulrike and Marie von Kleist attest. On November 24 he urgently asked Marie to send him his pension, for which he believed he owed gratitude to Queen Luise. As Marie—his actual benefactor and Luise's close confidante—did not answer him, he desperately asked Ulrike again on December 6 and 31: "I must ask you, my dearest Ulrike, to write to Marie immediately. I am sending letters to her without end, and I no longer know if she is alive or dead. She holds thirty Louis d'or of mine—the Queen's pension for the past months April to September." Kleist was worried because "the postal route is disrupted, and I cannot get this money, or even manuscripts I sent to Berlin, nor their value." He was considering whether he could find a publisher for his literary works in Königsberg, but given the "present state" of the Königsberg book trade, this could only be "done with sacrifices." But Kleist could not afford that: "[T]he need is urgent now."[121]

Meanwhile, chaos reigned in Königsberg: The city was overcrowded with refugees, and nobody at the time seemed to know how things would continue for the state and for each individual in the aftermath of the Jena and Auerstedt defeat, following the occupation of Berlin and the flight of the royal court. Even the reformers and patriots did not know what to expect, as Kleist notes on December 6: "General Kalkreuth takes his leave. General Rüchel—who announced to the King that he had recovered and offered his services—has still not received a reply eight days later. Hardenberg, I hear, also wants to resign. Altenstein does not yet know whether he should return to serving a foreign government, or withdraw into private life with a small fortune." It is a time of rumors, an apocalyptic time, but also a time of solidarity. Once again, it seems "as though the general misfortune were educating people," as though they were "wiser and warmer" toward each other.[122] Kleist registered this correlation of misfortune and solidarity. Yet he could not have foreseen that the political crisis would only serve to strengthen the reform movement, and that he—the trainee on leave of absence—would soon again, on Hardenberg's, Stein's, and Altenstein's side, find a place within the reform movement and secure his livelihood. He therefore did not flee from his responsibilities when

Fig. 38 Fort de Joux near Pontarlier

he left Königsberg. On the contrary, he seemed, again, to have a clear life plan. As the postal routes were no longer in service, he had to go to Berlin in person to collect his pension from Marie von Kleist. After that, he planned to go to Dresden, the city where the book trade and publishing industry still seemed to be intact and where he could "peacefully cultivate the literature and arts that he love[d] and to which he ha[d] devoted himself."[123] Kleist wanted to follow his calling as a writer; and this time he did not seem to have a better alternative to secure his existence.

Kleist's arrest in Berlin was probably a mere coincidence, but he bore it with a strange calm, because even as a prisoner he seemed to be taken care of, and he was able to continue writing and hope for peace. In January Kleist, Gauvain, and Ehrenberg were first brought from Berlin to a prison in Wustermark, which—according to Gauvain—was "full of vermin," "underground, damp with unhealthy air without vents." Gauvain protested in vain against "the most indignant treatment," which was completely inappropriate for captured officers.[124] But all petitions and assertions of innocence were of no avail. On March 5 the three men ended up in the prison of Fort de Joux near Pontarlier—a castle from the 11th century in the French Jura, close to the Swiss border—which Kleist describes to Ulrike as follows:

> Nothing can be more desolate than the sight of the castle, lying on a naked bluff, maintained for the sole purpose of securing prisoners. We had to alight and climb on foot; the weather was fearsome, and the storm threatened to blow us from the narrow, icy path into the abyss below. [...] They then began to relieve my companions of their money, and I was the interpreter; from me they could take nothing, since I had nothing. Then they assured us that we should be well treated, and thereupon led us each into a separate vaulted cell, in part hewn from the rock and in part built up of huge ashlars, with neither light nor air. Nothing beats the eloquence of the French. Gauvain came to stay in the cell in which Toussaint Louverture had died; our windows were fitted with triple bars, and how many doors were locked behind us, I do not even know: And yet these enclosures were called decent and tolerable dwellings.[125]

Gauvain thus had the 'honor' of being locked up in the cell in which Toussaint Louverture suffered for months until his death on April 7, 1803. The hero of the Haitian Revolution—which drove the French, English, and Spanish from the island—was captured by Napoleon's troops in June 1802 and deported to France. Kleist's story "The Betrothal in Santo Domingo" recalls the time of that war of independence, "when the blacks were murdering the whites."[126] Gauvain and Ehrenberg—who, according to Kleist, "are sickly by nature"—were afraid they would not be able to hold out for long in the rock prison during winter's cold. Kleist, however, who had been sick and melancholic in Königsberg, now felt "once again at peace and much consoled over [his] lot." He writes to Wieland: "The only change *I* experience as a result of my imprisonment is that I now write in Fort de Joux instead of Dresden or Weimar; and so long as my verses are *good*, what else matters?"[127] One month later the conditions of imprisonment of the three Prussians were eased with a transfer to Châlons-sur-Marne in north-eastern France—in Champagne, the former home of the writer Adelbert von Chamisso, who was born in the Château de Boncourt. In Châlons-sur-Marne the prisoners could move freely "on [their] word of honor," but this was of little use to Kleist because he had no money anyway. His condition was worsening, as he wrote to Ulrike. In the dispute over whether he "should be treated as a state prisoner or a war prisoner," it seems to make "no difference" to the French "whether [he] starve[s] to death in the course of it." Only after two months did "the local commandant" enforce "that [Kleist] receive the usual pay of the prisoner-of-war officers of thirty-seven francs a month."[128] Kleist wrote this letter in June 1807, when he was slowly losing heart. He also wrote a melancholic letter to Marie von Kleist, who—like Ulrike—stood up for him with the French authorities. In the letter Kleist describes to Marie how, sitting on a bench in the yard at dusk, he was addressed by a voice that reminded him of Marie's late brother Pierre von Gualtieri: "It seemed he was once more sitting next to me, as in that summer three years

Fig. 39
Simon Vouet, *Dying Magdalene*, circa 1640

ago, when in every conversation we returned again and again to death as the eternal refrain of life. Ah, it is a wearisome condition, this life. Quite as you once said: a *fatigue*."[129] Kleist's life had always been a struggle and still was—in the agitation of his projects as much as in the endurance of French captivity, where his boredom conceived something as grandiose as his *Penthesilea*, or, as we also find in his letter to Marie, a description of a painting by Simon Vouet that Kleist saw in the Church of Saint-Loup in Châlons-sur-Marne:

> [I]t is the intention, above all, that makes the masterpiece. For the real work of art is not that which is offered to the senses, but which the mind, aroused by the senses, thinks to itself within. A pair of winged angels float downward from the mansions of celestial joy to receive a soul. It is kneeling, as though glazed with the pallor of death, while its mortal part sinks back dying in the angels' arms. How delicately they hold the delicate body, touching with only the tips of their roseate fingers the precious being escaped from the hand of fate. And it casts a final glance at them through dying eyes, as though gazing beyond to fields of infinite blessedness: I have never seen anything more moving or sublime.[130]

Kleist's conversation with the deceased Gualtieri and his feeling of being touched by the view of the portrait of Mary Magdalene—who, in dying, touches the untouchable—is preceded by a sentence that captions and expounds on what follows: "Still, my heart so longs to commune."[131] Kleist's longing to commune—as the two scenes tell us—can only be expressed from the threshold of death, the "refrain of life." In this respect Kleist is a predecessor of Kafka. Kleist's writing always and inevitably separates him from life. It at once expresses the longing for and the impossibility of true communion. This paradox explains why Kleist was able to write just as well in the rock prison of Fort de Joux as Kafka was when he imagined himself writing at a desk in a crypt—surrounded by coffins—in his fragment "Visiting the Dead." These are strange places of inspiration in which we can imagine not only Kleist's *Penthesilea* and *The Marquise of O—* to have been written, but also his *Amphitryon*—though it had already been finished in Königsberg—because they are all "dramas of touching,"[132] illustrating the (im)possibility of every touch in life, between lovers as well as between God and man. In his final days Kleist turned writing on the threshold of death into a game that at least gave him the pleasure of a seemingly successful communication. In an ironic and playful exchange of letters, Kleist and Henriette Vogel mock their love and death before dying together.[133]

For Kleist living and writing are liminal spaces and times, waiting rooms with dark views. We see this even beyond the years 1803 to 1807—although, outwardly, from 1807 on movement had returned to the Mr. von Kleist imprisoned in Châlons-sur-Marne. Following the Treaty of Tilsit, he was released in mid-July and was to go to Berlin to report to General Clarke. Initially, he lacked the travel money, and he wrote begging letters to Ulrike and Rühle until the French granted him the money weeks later. On August 14, 1807, he was in Berlin and at the end of August in Dresden, where Rühle was waiting for him and where the bookseller Christoph Arnold had successfully published Kleist's *Amphitryon* in May. In the fall of 1806, his comedy *The Broken Jug* and the novella "Jerónimo and Josefa"—known under the title of the 1810 book edition as "The Earthquake in Chile"—were also finished. With the yield of his years in Königsberg, Kleist went to Dresden, well prepared and hopeful of finally making a career as a writer.

CHAPTER VIII

Distorting the World to the Point of Recognition

Kleist's Comedies and Novellas I

Court jesters are allowed to tell rulers the truth because they do not have to be taken seriously. The same is true for authors of popular literature. In times of disaster Kleist granted himself small escapes into the genres of comedy and novella—less respected genres than tragedy, which he had failed to fully conceive in *Guiscard*. According to Aristotelian poetics, both tragedy and comedy deal with the violation of a rule—with resistance to a universally accepted norm or to the laws of a society. The tragedy emphasizes the hero's resistance, both justifying and punishing it. The comedy, by contrast, emphasizes not the deviation but the norm, which makes the hero's behavior appear inappropriate and amusing. Etymologically and conceptually speaking, the novella, for its part, is bound to a deviation from the norm: in literature, to a "peculiar and as yet unheard-of event";[1] in jurisprudence, to the amendment of laws. There is no way of telling whether it will be the deviation or the norm that will prevail at the end of a novella. This is true of Kleist's comedies too; one may be unsure whether the heroes are comic or tragic, whether an effort is made to restore the norms or render them completely obsolete, or whether it is the heroes or the norms that one is supposed to deride. Kleist's comedies and novellas are peculiar literary attempts to establish order; in them he does not so much tame the chaos of his time as reflect it, thus distorting his contemporary world to the point of recognition—a world that wants to "bring about a new order of things," yet will result in nothing "but the mere overthrow of the old."[2]

The Broken Jug

One such project is *The Broken Jug*. Kleist began this play in the spring of 1802 in Switzerland, when the old Swiss Confederacy was replaced by the Helvetic Republic and a dispute arose between unitarians and federalists. He finished it in Königsberg in the late summer of 1806, when it became apparent that, for the time, the Prussian reform movement would lose the race against Napoleon's imperialism.[3] The experience of the time was that the institutions of the state no longer provided any support for the individual. In *The Broken Jug* Kleist demonstrates this experience in miniature, using the model of a

© WILHELM FINK VERLAG, 2021 | DOI:10.30965/9783846765746_009

Dutch village court at the end of the 17th century. At the play's conclusion all trust in an authority that pronounces power instead of dispensing justice is shaken. Kleist explains the origins of his play in the preface to the handwritten version:

> The basis of my comedy in all likelihood is an actual case, but more than this I have not been able to discover. I was prompted to write it by a copper engraving which I saw in Switzerland several years ago. One saw depicted in it, first, a judge gravely seated in his chair; standing before him an old woman with a broken jug in her hand, who seemed to be pointing out the injurious treatment it had received; the accused, a young peasant whom the judge thundered at as one whose guilt was already proved, was still defending himself, but feebly; a girl who had probably testified in the case (who knows what the offense was and how it had occurred?) stood between her mother and her fiancé wringing her apron—she couldn't have stood there more shamefacedly if she had given false evidence; and the Clerk (who had probably been staring at the girl a moment before) was now looking sideways at the judge, suspiciously, much as Creon looked at Oedipus in similar circumstances. Below it read: The Broken Jug.—The original, if I am not mistaken, was by a Dutch master.[4]

Kleist was mistaken. The original is by the French painter Philibert-Louis Debucourt. The painting inspired his fellow countryman Jean Jacques André Le Veau to create an engraving entitled *The Judge, or the Broken Jug*, which put the broken jug—a symbol of lost innocence—in a legal context. A print of the engraving hung in the apartment of Kleist's friend Heinrich Zschokke in Bern, and it became the source for a "poetic competition," as Zschokke relates: "In its characters we thought we recognized a sad pair of lovers, a bickering mother with a broken majolica jug, and a big-nosed judge. The challenge was for Wieland to write a satire modeled on it, for Kleist a comedy, and for me a story.—Kleist's *Broken Jug* bore the prize away."[5] In his preface Kleist further expounds on the engraving, disclosing the content of his comedy. Both the engraving and the play deal with a court scene. A young man is accused of having broken a jug—or, according to the play's erotic imagery: of having seduced a girl. The engraving leaves no doubt about this fact. But Kleist reads it differently. He associates the broken jug not with the young couple, but with the judge himself as well as the girl: The court clerk, Kleist notes, looks at the judge suspiciously—like Creon does at Oedipus. This is Kleist's ingenious twist, the generative core of his transformation of the engraving into a play. In Sophocles, as is well known, Oedipus is a judge in his own case. Unbeknownst to him he killed his father, married his mother, and fathered her children. When Thebes is struck by the plague, Oedipus suspects it is the punishment for a crime—a crime he realizes in the end is his own.

Fig. 40 Jean Jacques André Le Veau, *The Judge, or The Broken Jug*, 1782

Unlike Oedipus, Judge Adam is aware of his guilt from the outset. This awareness seems to make the difference between tragedy and comedy—at least in Classical poetics. In Modern literature, however, tragedy and the knowledge of one's own guilt are no longer mutually exclusive. In terms of structure Kleist's *The Broken Jug* does resemble Sophocles' *Oedipus Rex*. They are both analytical dramas. Kleist's comedy, too, gradually brings to light an action that precedes it, while the action on stage, by comparison, appears lacking. The premiere of Kleist's comedy at the Weimar Court Theater on March 2, 1808, failed due to the audience's boredom, not solely because of the director Johann Wolfgang Goethe's mistake of artificially lengthening the play by dividing it into three acts with intermissions, but also because the audience, it seems, did not quite understand that they should have been curious not so much about the *what* but the *how* of the action. Ultimately, it is not the exposing of Judge Adam as the perpetrator that is interesting, but the circumstances of the crime—the psychology of the perpetrator who manages to hide his crime for a long time through artful speech despite the obvious evidence against him. In the deferral of the revelation lies the purpose of Kleist's comedy, but also the problem of staging it successfully. In his acceptance speech at the Kleist Prize 1990 ceremony in Munich, German playwright Heiner Müller noted that Kleist treated "his topics like a sex offender treats a woman,"[6] which caused the festive audience in the Hercules Hall of the Residence to shudder a little. With regard to *The Broken Jug*, one may ask whether Judge Adam is himself a sex offender—who, in abusing the authority of his office by blackmailing Eve, nearly achieves his objective—or a man driven by Eve to his Fall, like his "ne'er-do-well" "ancestor"[7] Adam in Paradise. The court clerk points out this kinship in his first appearance. He is not called Licht (light) for nothing; for him the case is clear from the very beginning—and so, one may assume, it is also clear for the audience. The real question is how Kleist would have expected the audience to perceive the play in its entirety: as a satire of justice and authority, as a tragedy, or as a comedy?[8]

More often than not the audience of *The Broken Jug* is given no choice because the play is mostly staged as a straight-forward comedy—often, even, as a blatant peasant farce. The enduring model for this sort of performance is the 1937 UFA screen adaptation, at the beginning of which Emil Jannings falls out of bed so wretchedly that everyone in the audience knows immediately where his soul lies: below the belt, in the reproductive and digestive tracts. Jannings' Adam is lecherous, brutal, mendacious, dull, and cunning. Anyone who bears in mind Jannings' later association with the Nazis—he became head of the UFA in 1940—will watch his performance with both horror and fascination, and will recognize in it an involuntary portrayal of oppressive, everyday fascism. Kleist's play allows for a crude production when understood simply as a comedy following the dramatic rules that governed the genre until the mid-18th century—that is, as a play in the low style, dealing with the fate of the lower estate unworthy of tragedy. While there is no question that *The Broken Jug* is set in a Dutch village among farmers, the crippled village judge is anything but a bumpkin. Rather, he is an extremely eloquent delinquent whose wit indicates his despair over the fact that he is also a victim. Compared with the simple country folk, his pleasure in language makes him seem like an unloved and misunderstood outsider. Only Licht, the court clerk, can match his intellectual prowess, though he is not a friend, but a competitor for the office of judge. If one were to actually read the beginning of Kleist's play, one would not encounter a clumsy, portly judge falling out of bed. According to the stage directions, Adam is "seated" in the courtroom "bandaging his leg," and then—less abashed than quick witted—begins a verbal duel with Licht, almost as if he were familiar with Kleist's "On the Gradual Fabrication of Thoughts While Speaking":

LICHT. What the devil, Adam, sir! Something's
happened, tell me—oh, you look a sight!
ADAM. A sight, you bet. To stumble, all you need
are feet. On this smooth floor what's there
to stumble over? All the same, I stumbled—
for we've got, each one of us, a nasty stumbling block
inside ourselves.
LICHT. We do! Each one of us—?
ADAM. Inside himself!
LICHT. A curse, damn it!
ADAM. What, what?
LICHT. You've got
an ancestor, a ne'er-do-well he was, who fell
when things began. His fall's notorious.
Your case and his—
ADAM. Well, what? Go on.
LICHT. —are not the same?
ADAM. The same? Get out! I told
you, here, right here, is where I fell.
LICHT. Fell literally?
ADAM. Fell literally.
LICHT. And when did this all happen?
ADAM. Just now, as I was getting out of bed. Lifting
up my voice to welcome in the morning,
I tripped and fell smack into it.
Before the day has started, the Lord God
makes me wrench my foot!
LICHT. And I bet it was
the left one.
ADAM. Left one?
LICHT. This one here, the one
that isn't frolicsome?
ADAM. Yes, that one.
LICHT. God be praised!
The one that found the way of sin too rough
a road?
ADAM. Too rough a road? My foot? Will you explain—
LICHT. Your clumping foot—your clubfoot.
ADAM. Clubfoot! One foot
clumps along just like the other.
LICHT. Pardon me,
but there you do your right foot an injustice.
True, it cannot boast the other's ... gravity,
but then it's not afraid to venture out
on slippery slopes.
ADAM. That's nonsense! Where one dares
to go, the other follows.

LICHT. What's happened to your face,
it's all cut up.
ADAM. My face? Cut up?
LICHT. You mean
to say you don't know it's cut up?
ADAM. I'd be
a liar if—how does it look?
LICHT. How does it look?
ADAM. Yes, old friend.
LICHT. Gruesome!
ADAM. More exactly, please.
LICHT. All scraped and skinned,
not very nice to see. Your cheek has got
a piece gouged out of it. How big a piece?
I'd need a scale to know.
ADAM. The devil!
LICHT (*bringing him a mirror*).
Here,
see for yourself. A sheep the dogs chase through
the briars leaves no more wool behind than you've
left skin somewhere.
ADAM. Dear me, yes, I see! Lord, Lord,
I look a fright. My nose is banged up too.
LICHT. Also an eye.
ADAM. Oh no!
LICHT. Oh yes! A cut
across the brow, so help me God, as if
you had a run-in with a surly peasant.
ADAM. I think
I see the bone. And yet I didn't feel
a thing.
LICHT. Yes, that's what happens in the heat of battle.
ADAM. Battle! If that is what you call it when
you bang your head against that damned goat
on the stove. It's coming back to me. I lost
my balance, and grabbing at the air around me like
a drunkard, I caught hold of my pants which I'd
hung up last night, because they were wet through,
by the belt, above the stove. But poor fool
that I am, the belt it breaks and down we go,
belt and pants and me, head first to the floor,
and on the way I hit my head against
the stove just where the goat has got its nose
stuck out.
LICHT (*laughing*).
Great, great!
ADAM. Damnation!
LICHT. Adam's fall!
Your first time *out* of bed.[9]

The starting point for the dialogue between Adam and Licht is visible bodily evidence: Adam's wounds on his head and leg, which Ruprecht inflicted on the man he caught fleeing from his fiancée's room the previous night without recognizing whom he actually attacked. The judge, who broke the jug during his escape—yet did not rob the girl of her innocence—is marked. Consequently, the play's opening scene revolves around the interpretation of the marks on his body. *The Broken Jug* is a comedy through and through—that is, in the sense of the German *Lustspiel* (comedy), insofar as the play is driven by a delight (*Lust*) in inventing stories, aiming to interpret the physical wounds of the judge as well as the disappearance of his wig, the broken jug, etc. It would be best if the play were, for once, performed on a bare stage so as to bring to the fore its linguistic nuances. Usually the opposite happens. In a typical performance the audience's attention is drawn entirely to the genre picture—to the judge's bedroom, living room, and courtroom, to fluttering chickens, fat sausages, and buxom maids in traditional costumes, who rage, nag, and clamor. If not staged as a peasant farce, Kleist's Adam appears to be a relative of Georg Büchner's language virtuosos Leonce and Valerio from the play *Leonce and Lena* of 1836. Above all, however, in his poetic ingenuity and his abdominal pain, Adam appears—if one bears in mind Kleist's joys and sorrows in Königsberg—as an alter ego of the author himself.

But let us return to the opening scene, to Adam's and Licht's opposing interpretations of Adam's bodily signs. The judge claims to have stumbled over his feet, tripped on "this smooth floor," and slipped. And he insists that this is to be understood "literally." In his first attempt at interpreting his wounds, though, Adam himself suggests a figurative reading: "[W]e've got, each one of us, a nasty stumbling block / inside ourselves." "Stumbling" in the figurative sense—without explicit emphasis on the sensual and vivid quality of the image—can mean: committing a slight "misstep" based "on the weakness of human nature."[10] It is in this moral sense that the word is used in the *Luther Bible*, whose imagery Kleist so frequently draws from. At the beginning of his first response, the judge refers to his ailing body and, at the end, to his ailing soul. His outer injuries reflect his inner ones. He says that he fell over his clubfoot; here, literal and figurative language correspond. What he is implying is that he is a crippled soul who, due to his physical disfigurement, cannot but force a girl like Eve to love him. From the very beginning the imagery of his words presents him more as a victim than a perpetrator. This presentation is reiterated in Licht's words about Adam's battered face: "A sheep the dogs chase through / the briars leaves no more wool behind than you've / left skin somewhere." In the course of the play, we learn that, when Adam fell from Eve's room, he simply got caught in the trellis of Frau Martha's house, losing his wig in the process. In the opening dialogue, however, the 'stigmata' on Adam's face are not attributed to their factual cause, but are instead interpreted through an image that blends the language of the Bible with hunting jargon. Adam is a sheep, not a lamb—he is not a martyr like Christ—and yet he is a chased man, a hunted man, a victim, and the marks of the "briars" are visible on his face. Though this does not make the briars a crown of thorns.

Kleist loves playing with names. In a character's name its very essence is determined, which is why Ottokar in *The Schroffenstein Family* calls his beloved Agnes by the name of Mary. The context of their names—the allusion to the paradisiacal couple—suggests that Adam and Eve could have been destined for each other, that Adam is not a sex offender but rather a man driven by an impossible love. Adam—who, in his interrogation of Eve, is much more considerate toward her than her coarse fiancé is—may have, for a moment, dreamed of a paradisiacal state: He "stared" at her, speechlessly, for "two measured minutes" in her room. This is how Eve later describes her encounter with Adam to District Magistrate Walter, who happens to arrive the very day the trial over the broken jug takes place in order to inspect the Huisum court.[11] Being in love, this encounter must have felt like an eternity to Adam. Ultimately, we do not know what feelings were exchanged between Judge Adam and Eve on the night the jug was broken. The moment of their encounter may have been defined by fear—fear of a love that is socially unacceptable. Kleist himself repeatedly dreamed of this kind of forbidden love; even during his time in Königsberg, he dreamed of Pfuel, and—at least conceivably—of Wilhelmine, who was by then married to Krug.

The crippled Adam has no chance with Eve that night; nor does he stand a chance against his clerk Licht, who outclasses him in the long run. Beginning with their first dialogue, Licht continues to interpret Adam's bodily signs otherwise and, in the course of the trial, strategically asserts his interpretation in order to inherit the judicial office. He has no interest in seeing Adam as a victim—a disappointed and wounded lover. He does not consider Adam's stumble a slight misstep, but a grave sin; and he compares Adam with his "ne'er-do-well" "ancestor," who caused the Fall in Paradise. The judge's foot does not remind him of Oedipus' swollen foot, but of the devil's clubfoot. It is not that Licht actually believes in the devil like the simple village folk—such as aunt Brigitta, who thinks she recognized Satan's footprints in the snow. Licht is merely concerned with accusing the judge of a crime that will lead to his dismissal, in accordance with the principles not of Dutch law but of the *Prussian Civil Code* of 1794 (PCC), which Kleist—a trainee civil servant in Königsberg—knew well. The *Prussian Civil Code* is the first code of law that lists, in great detail, penalties for civil servants, including judicial officers who violate their duties. Adam's Rhine River Inundation Fund is impermissible, according to

District Magistrate Walter, because levies ought only to be collected when the Rhine is inundated. Adam is thus guilty of a "misappropriation of funds," which is punishable under §§418–436 II 20 PCC. Worse still: Adam also violated §477 II 20 PCC by promising to provide a certificate of exemption from military service for the already drafted Ruprecht. He is thus guilty of "active aiding and abetting" for desertion—that is, treason.[12] However, this offense is only dealt with after Adam has already fled the courtroom.

According to the decision of the District Magistrate Walter, Adam's position is to be temporarily filled by Licht, whose name promises to bring light into the darkness of a crime. In truth, however, Licht is anything but a noble adherent of Enlightenment; he is a 'light bearer,' alias 'Lucifer' in Latin—a subdevil working for the government who, for his own benefit, does his utmost to make the judge stumble over his own words. Up until the moment Adam flees, his situation with Licht and the District Magistrate Walter resembles that of the fox in Jean de La Fontaine's fable, which Kleist recounts in his Königsberg essay "On the Gradual Fabrication of Thoughts While Speaking." Adam, who has undoubtedly sinned, must, through artful speech, find another sinner to blame, such as Ruprecht, Lebrecht, etc. If he were to be convicted, he would be a case for the noose, like his corrupt colleague in Holla. 'Lucifer' Licht dramatically details this prospect:

LICHT. I swear to you
Judge Walter showed up yesterday in Holla
unexpectedly, went through all their accounts
and files, then sent the judge and clerk home,
both, suspended. Why? I've no idea—
not officially.
ADAM. The devil! Did the peasant tell
you that?
LICHT. He did, and other things as well.
ADAM. And what were they?
LICHT. You want to know, then, do you?
All right. The judge, placed under house arrest
last night, is looked for in the morning, and found,
guess where: inside his barn, suspended—from the rafter.
ADAM. Oh no!
LICHT. But help arrives, they cut him down,
they chafe his neck and wrists, douse him with cold
water, and bring him back to life, but only
just.
ADAM. They do, do they? Back to life?
LICHT. And now his house is under seal, inventoried,
locked, and bolted—they might have left him hanging,
he's as good as dead. And a new man's
in his place as judge, already.[13]

When District Magistrate Walter arrives, Adam is in a tight spot and begins to lie like La Fontaine's fox. The judge with the devilish clubfoot—not exactly the image of grace—becomes a master of deception, of simulation. But it is of no use to him. He can lie off the cuff, but his repressed desire—the unconscious—becomes manifest in Freudian slips. Walter demands that Adam finally interrogate the parties properly: "Keep up the questioning, I promise you, / and the truth is certain to come out." To this Adam replies: "Gladly. But I'm a villain / if it ever does."[14] The past events, traumatic for both Eve and the disappointed judge, are not confined to the past but burst into Adam's present, into his deceptions, and lead to ambiguity. Adam's words are split like the jug. Even his lies invariably contain the truth. For example, when he blames his missing wig on a cat which he claims used it to birth a litter, this fabrication is the exact description of his split state. The cat used his wig to birth a litter—in other words, the judicial authority that the wig represents has been contaminated, soiled by the physical facts of sexual desire. Adam's world is out of joint and his tall tales cannot restore it. In fact, everything is in shambles, not only the jug, but the world as such—as Martha Rull's lengthy account reveals, with the jug representing the world itself. Broken is Adam's head and soul, Licht's integrity, and the friendship between the two. In an accident the District Magistrate Walter's carriage and his arm are harmed, as is Eve's good reputation. Not only the jug but the wedding has, as Ruprecht puts it, "got a hole in it."[15] Broken is the trust between Eve and Ruprecht as well as the trust in the state authorities. After all, the District Magistrate does not only appoint Licht—who had helped to conceal the offense of the Rhine River Inundation Fund—to replace Judge Adam; he also seriously considers restitution for Adam. Above all, the truth-giving power of language—the congruence between sign and referent, appearance and being—is broken. It is only in dreams that the truth reveals itself directly:

ADAM. I dreamt I was
accused and dragged before the bar, and yet I
was the judge and hounded, skinned, and bullied my
own self and at last condemned myself
to put my neck inside an iron collar.
LICHT. Condemned yourself?
ADAM. I did indeed. And then the two
of us were one and fled into the woods and cowered
there all night.[16]

The judge in Holla is saved, though he almost dies. In Huisum Judge Adam saves his own neck, although, prior to the trial, he dreams that he will soon have to spend the night in "the woods," which does not only refer to his escape, but to a wooden coffin as well. In the end *The Broken Jug* follows a rule that has remained valid since Aristotle's *Poetics*—namely, that the comic "is constituted by a fault and a mark of shame, but lacking in pain or destruction."[17] Adam's premonitions of death are deceptive.

The tragic hero suffers from the clash between his ideal and the norm; the audience suffers along with him. The comic hero may not consider himself comic, but tragic; the audience does not laugh with him, but at him—at a behavior that it finds inappropriate, from which it distances itself through its laughter. *The Broken Jug* is not about the personal ideals of Judge Adam, with which the audience may or may not identify, but about his breaking the rules. In private the judge may be a desperate lover, but he is presented from the outside as a baron of lies. His behavior may be understandable, but it violates the rule of law, which the District Magistrate Walter appears to be restoring in the end, with Adam "lacking in pain or destruction" in body and soul. So, did Kleist write a flawless comedy after all, despite its initial imagery of the Passion? Despite the broken jug's symbolism of the fragility of all earthly things? The complicated thing about *The Broken Jug* is that District Magistrate Walter—as a spectator of Adam's theater of simulation—seems to take pity on the sinful judge at the end; and with his interrogation of Eve, a new play begins, so to speak, which is a tragedy—or at least a satire of authority with a tragic heroine who tries, in vain, to override established norms. Ultimately, Eve is a tragic heroine from the very beginning of the comedy insofar as the audience can identify with her and recognize that her conflict is hopeless from the outset: If she were to tell the truth about the perpetrator, she would not be able to save Ruprecht from being dispatched to the East Indies, because Adam would then no longer forge a certificate of exemption for him. If she were to cover for the judge's lies, she would sacrifice Ruprecht's love for her for the sake of her love for him.

"What use is it to prove I'm innocent? / Unhappy are we both forevermore."[18] Thus Eve begins a chain of lengthy defenses in scene 12, at once anticipating their futility. Her long explanations seem undramatic, even superfluous, for the judge has already been exposed as the guilty party. Eve strains the audience's nerves by belaboring her apologies to the District Magistrate for her aiding and abetting Ruprecht's planned desertion. Apart from a few interruptions, her account continues for 350 verses. Contemporary critics of the comedy's 1808 premiere at the Weimar Court Theater thought this to be a rather poor idea; and so Kleist appended the play's original ending as a variant to the book edition of 1811, thus marking it as dispensable for future productions. And yet today it is mostly included in stagings, and rightly so.

It is only through Eve's testimony that one learns that the judge's case has not only a private but, above all, a political dimension. *The Broken Jug* describes, in every detail, the control mechanisms of an institutionalized power that no longer needs to be exercised in order to be effective. The judge's indication, alone, that Ruprecht would not serve as a soldier in Utrecht to defend his country—which is what Ruprecht had been promised in his conscription letter—but would be sent to the Dutch colonies in the East Indies to fight for his life, is enough to make Eve compliant and put her good name as well as Ruprecht's respect and love for her at risk. "Will he go further than Utrecht?—," Eve anxiously asks Adam, the representative of legal and state authority. According to her account, he replies with distressing words:

> "Will he go further than Utrecht?
> Yes, O righteous God," said he [Adam]. "I don't know
> where he is going. Once he follows the drum,
> the drum follows the Ensign, who follows the Captain;
> the Captain follows the Colonel, who follows
> the General, who then in turn follows the United Provinces,
> and the United Provinces—hang it all—,
> they wander far and wide in thought,
> they sound the drums until the skins are tearing."[19]

The syntax here, at odds with the logic of the sentence, is a stroke of Kleist's genius. Only in the last verse does it become clear what the drum is calling for—that both the drums' and the soldiers' skin will tear. The motif of a soldier's draft dispatch corresponds to the historical reality experienced by destitute families from the German peasantry in the 18th and 19th centuries, when sovereigns pressed into military service every farmer's son they could get their hands on, selling entire regiments to the great European powers, who then used them as cannon-fodder in the colonies. The Dutch Republic, too, used their military conscriptions for colonial purposes. The occupation and exploitation of overseas territories—costing both the native people and the Dutch soldiers their lives—only served the rich merchants of The Hague. Thus notes Eve clear-sightedly, maturing from an innkeeper's daughter to a critic of capitalism in the course of the play, even snapping at District Magistrate Walter:

> EVE. How did he [Adam] continue?
> Sir, he told me what you already know,
> that the militia is to be sent to Batavia
> to rob the local rulers of Bantam,
> of Java, Jakarta—and goodness knows where else?—

of their wealth to fill the coffers of the merchants in the Hague.
[…]
WALTER. I don't know a word about this.
EVE. Your Honor,
I know you are obliged to say exactly that.
WALTER. By my duty!
EVE. That's right, duty compels you.
And your duty is to conceal the truth from us.

Eve does not trust Walter. She knows better from dealing with the deceptive Adam that the state authorities are deceitful themselves:

EVE. "God in heaven," I cried,
"the young men, the bloss'ming, to Batavia!
The isle, the dreadful, where out of
every company disembarking there,
one half ends up burying the other.
That's no fair and honest form
of conscription. That's deception, Your Honor.
The nation is being robbed of its precious youth
to further the trade in pepper and spice."
Ruse against ruse, if he provides me
with a medical certificate for Ruprecht,
I'd give anything in return
that he could righteously demand.[20]

Adam may still hope for the fulfillment of his secret wishes—even during the trial, because his blackmailing scheme had only been interrupted, not cancelled, by Ruprecht's appearance on the night in question. That his scheme is finally revealed owes itself to the coincidence that Adam and Licht each pursue competing interests. District Magistrate Walter is no more a noble representative of the judiciary than the two of them, insofar as his primary concern is not justice, but the restoration of trust in the authorities. He is not actually invested in making Adam's offense public, but rather in the "court's good name," as he "whisper[s]" to Adam.[21] To preserve the honor of the court, he orders Adam to quickly bring the case to an end; and when the villagers try to beat up the real offender, he threatens with the bailiff. Walter protects the abstract authority, not the concrete law. He has little interest in Martha Rull's case regarding the broken jug, thus referring it to the next higher court. And he deceives Eve and Ruprecht in a far more cunning way than Adam did. He gives Eve a purse with twenty guilders—with which she could, if necessary, buy Ruprecht out of his military service—to assure her that his word is true, that the soldiers would not be sent to Asia. But Walter's guilders are as questionable as his words. They show the face of the "King of Spain" and are therefore no longer valid in a time in which the Netherlands has long been independent of Spain, since 1648. Walter notes to Eve: "These are newly minted guilders with the full, prescribed weight. / Behold the face of the King of Spain: / Would the King himself cheat you?"[22] Thus, the evidential value of the coin,[23] with doubtful exchange value, proves that the new order of things is merely the overthrow of the old. At the end of the variant—Kleist's second ending to his play—the comedy itself comes to an end as it gives way to tragedy. It is not the truth that prevails at the end of a tragedy. Rather, the order—which has been revealed as fragile—is restored:

> WALTER. So now do you believe that I was telling you the truth?
> EVE. You wonder if I believe you told the truth?
> Oh these freshly minted coins glinting in the sunlight.
> Oh Lord! May I never see such coins as these again!
> WALTER. Listen, I'm going to give you a kiss now. May I?
> RUPRECHT. And a good one. There. That's good.
> WALTER. So to Utrecht you are going?
> RUPRECHT. Yes, I'll go to Utrecht
> and stand guard on the ramparts for a year,
> and when I'm done, etc. ..... Eve will be mine![24]

When staging the play, one ought to beat the drums—until the skins tear—to poor Ruprecht's words, with his naïve belief that he will marry his Eve after a year's vigil in Utrecht rather than being dispatched to the East Indies. The happy ending of this comedy is but a deception, what else?

Amphitryon

In the end Eve and Ruprecht are not allowed to so much as suspect that they are being deceived, and *The Broken Jug*'s status as a comedy hinges on this fact. Kleist's *Amphitryon*—published by the Dresden bookseller Christoph Arnold in May 1807 while the author was still imprisoned in France—is also titled a comedy. The audience is supposed to laugh about a mistaken identity. Alcmene, the wife of the commander-in-chief of the Thebans, unknowingly sleeps with Jupiter, who has assumed the form of her husband Amphitryon. At least Alcmene is later allowed to learn that she was deceived. Her last word is "Ah!" and this cry of bewilderment—or, better, of horror—at the fact that Amphitryon has reached an agreement with the divine simulator (that, to the consolation of his earthly parents, Alcmene's unborn child will be a demigod) is probably the most famous closing word in the history of German drama. On

October 10, 1927, in a lecture at the Munich Schauspielhaus in celebration of Kleist's 150th birthday, Thomas Mann called Kleist's *Amphitryon* the "wittiest, charmingest, the most intellectual, the profoundest and most beautiful theatre piece in the world."[25] Who could and would contradict him in this? Kleist's wit is charming, gallant, and intellectual, but it is also crude and despairing—so despairing it renders Alcmene speechless.

In *The Broken Jug* the judge's wounds indicate the truth; the bodily signs can be relied upon. The situation is different in *Amphitryon*, in spite of the fact that Alcmene still hopes for this kind of confidence. When a woman 'knows' her husband—the Bible term for intercourse—she trusts in her senses, in the certainty of seeing, hearing, feeling, smelling, and in the certainty of her heart. This is what Alcmene asserts to Charis, her servant, to dispel any doubt about her virtuousness:

> ALCMENE. Oh Charis! As soon mistake myself,
> I would! As soon imagine I'm a Persian
> or a Parthian, in spite of that profoundest feeling,
> sucked in with my mother's milk, which tells
> me I am I, Alcmene. Look, this hand,
> does it belong to me? This bosom? My
> reflection in the mirror? He would have had
> to be stranger to me than my own self!
> Put out my eye, still I would hear him; stop
> my ear and I would feel him; take touch away
> I'd breathe his presence in; take all my senses,
> every one, but only leave my heart,
> that bell—its note is all I need to find
> him out, wherever, in the world.[26]

Alcmene's words, of course, follow a night of passion with Jupiter who, unbeknownst to her, had taken on her husband's form. Alcmene is hurt because Amphitryon denies having made love with her and, in his initial rage, accuses her of cheating on him. Moreover, she is confused as she finds a *J* in place of an *A* on the engraved diadem Amphitryon gave her. Against this confounding lettering she sets the truth of the bodily signs and that of her heart. Amphitryon, by contrast, comes to the conclusion that his wife is not capable of "base deception" and must have therefore fallen for an illusion:

> But to steal a man's own form
> and figure from him and do his office by his wife—
> that is surely one of Satan's tricks!
> In rooms ablaze with candles, no one with his
> five senses still intact ever mistook his friends,
> oh never—till today! Eyes unsocketed

and rolling on a table top—severed limbs,
ears, fingers, stuffed in boxes—these
used to be enough to tell a husband
by. But now—from now on we shall need
to brand the hides of married men, hang
bells around their necks the way we do
with sheep. She is as capable of base
deception as her turtle dove: I'll sooner
trust the honesty of rogues escaped the noose
than think her false. But she has lost her wits;
tomorrow when it dawns, the doctors must
be sent for, I am sure, if only there's
an opportunity for doing so.[27]

In the German original the verb *anknüpfen* in the last verse describes an ambiguous figure, impelling the play to oscillate between tragedy and comedy. It reads: "– Fänd' nur Gelegenheit sich, anzuknüpfen." According to the *German Dictionary* of the Brothers Grimm, *anknüpfen* refers to two things: firstly, "to reattach a torn thread, to attach a new piece of ribbon, to establish a love affair, a relationship, business, negotiation." And indeed, an opportunity for the spouses to reunite presents itself—at least from the point of view of Jupiter and Amphitryon—in the negotiations over Alcmene's baby's status as a demigod. The play thus seems to end as a comedy should end: with no serious damage done. All seems to be well. Unless, of course, one moves the comma in the last verse and discovers an equally possible tragic ending. Read as a reflexive verb (*sich anzuknüpfen*), the last verse could also be read in the following way: "if only there's / an opportunity for me [Amphitryon] to hang myself." This is the second meaning of the verb *anknüpfen* according to the dictionary of the Brothers Grimm.[28]

This second reading seems to be more obvious, given the fact that Amphitryon shows nothing but despair in the preceding verses: He believes his wife to be either insane or to have been seduced by the devil. The latter option is confusing in its anachronism. Satan does not exist in the Roman or Greek pantheon. In Classical mythology the fact that Jupiter (or Zeus) can take on a human form to seduce a woman gives evidence to his omnipotence. In the Christian context, however, such art of simulation is the work of the devil. Satan is a being of shadow, lacking substance. He is reliant on the divine light, which falls on a solid body, to simulate its form in the shape of the shadow. This constitution explains the essential—but also arbitrary—nature of Satan's art of transformation. All evil is parasitic; it depends on the good, existing only insofar as it has some good to live on. In this respect Don Giovanni's theater of seduction in Wolfgang Amadeus Mozart's famous opera, for example, consists merely of the parasitic, vampiric depletion of the life force of his ever-changing lovers—nothing more than the work of the devil. In the end Don Giovanni goes to hell, in accordance with Christian doctrine. To date, however, Kleist scholarship has hardly taken notice of the fact that the precariousness of this play lies not so much in the fact that Jupiter can be identified with the Christian God and his incarnation but rather in the contamination of the images of God and Satan in Jupiter's art of seduction and simulation. It may therefore be comforting for the audience of this comedy to know that the fruit of Alcmene's night of love will not be a hellion, but Hercules, the demigod who is popular even from a Christian perspective, made worthy of ascending to Olympus and gaining immortality through a life of labors and virtuous heroic deeds.

Jupiter thus sugarcoats the pill that Alcmene and Amphitryon—as well as the audience—have to swallow. Nowhere else does Kleist's skepticism toward knowledge seem more radical insofar as even gods, rather than guaranteeing truth, exploit the arbitrary relationship between sign and referent—just as mortals do—and misrepresent themselves for selfish reasons. In its epistemological and metaphysical dimensions, Kleist's *Amphitryon* is anything but the "*Comedy after Molière*" that its title suggests.[29] Molière's play is an earthly comedy of adultery that presents the motif of the erotic contrast between Amphitryon and Jupiter—between husband and divine lover, between love in everyday married life and that in a night of passion—in a way that is as witty as it is immoral. Molière's play remains nothing more than a comedy of mistaken identity, if only because—unlike in Kleist—Alcmene remains unaware of Jupiter's deception. In the end Jupiter and Amphitryon settle the matter themselves, with Jupiter deluding Amphitryon into thinking that he—the god—should in fact be jealous. He reasons as follows:

> To share a love with Jupiter
> Has surely no dishonor in it;
> And surely it must seem a glorious thing
> To be the rival of Olympus' king.
> You have, I think, no shame or wrong to bear,
> And it is I, in this affair,
> Who, god though I am, must utter jealous sighs.
> Alcmene's wholly yours, whatever one does,
> And it should warm your heart to realize
> That the only way for one to please her was
> To assume her cherished husband's guise;
> That Jove, revealed in his immortal splendor,
> Could not have tempted her to be untrue,
> And that her gifts to him of tender
> Love were truly given only to you.

It is evident that Molière's Jupiter, too, tries to sugarcoat the pill for the cuckold but does so in a completely different manner than Kleist's. Molière's play remains entirely in this world: Jupiter serves as an allegory of the 'divine' lover in the figurative sense; he is not a representative of the hereafter. He is a seducer who—like Louis XIV, whose favor Molière enjoyed—is endowed with a quasi-divine sovereign power; he is thus not someone with whom one can argue, which is why Molière's Amphitryon remains silent at the end of the play while his servant Sosias recommends to everyone, including the audience: "But let us cut our speeches short, / And quietly retire now, if you will. / Regarding matters of this sort, / It's wisest always to be still."[30]

While one finds the Amphitryon myth in Homer's *Odyssey* and Hesiod's epic *The Shield of Heracles*, it was Sophocles, Aeschylus, and Euripides who, in the 5th century BCE, transformed the myth into tragedies. In the 2nd century BCE, the Roman playwright Plautus made it into a comedy which had a tremendous, lasting impact, undergoing numerous transformations from Molière to Kleist to Jean Giraudoux and Peter Hacks. The latest adaptation of the myth can be found in the 1997 movie *Face/Off* directed by John Woo, starring John Travolta and Nicolas Cage. The film exploits the dedifferentiating potential of the shapeshifting and cuckoldry motifs, which are capable of destroying identity and even life itself. This potential also serves as the basis for Kleist's playful renditions of the doppelganger motif.

Kleist may have first encountered the myth of Jupiter's night of passion with Alcmene in Molière's classic comedy or in historian August Christian Borheck's 1803 translation of Plautus. Johann Daniel Falk—whom Kleist met in Dresden in 1803, after staying with Wieland near Weimar—certainly could have told him about his work on his *Amphitruon*, which was to be published in 1804.[31] Three years later—after the defeat of Jena and Auerstedt in 1806—when Kleist's comedy was published, it was anything but common for a Prussian writer to adapt a French comedy classic. Thus Adam Müller, who edited Kleist's *Amphitryon* for the bookseller Christoph Arnold, considers in his foreword "the importance of the German and frivolity of Molière's Amphitryon" and emphasizes that Kleist's play "strives for a certain *poetic presence*, in which Antiquity and Modernity [...] will nonetheless relate well."[32] It is true that Kleist often draws on Molière's wit, but he relies on Plautus' *Amphitruo* in that he recognizes the encounter between the divine and the human as a fundamental problem, thus restoring the material to its philosophical and theological dignity. National conservative readers of the play, such as Friedrich Gentz, noticed this immediately. In May 1807 Gentz writes enthusiastically to Müller that Molière's play is "in the end nothing but a farce," while "only an extraordinary genius" like Kleist could solve the task of "keeping the god of gods great and majestic even in such an awkward and suggestive situation as he is presented in here."[33] In his response to Gentz, Müller goes so far as to say that Kleist's *Amphitryon* is "just as much about the immaculate conception of the Holy Virgin as it is about the mystery of love in general." He continues enraptured, every bit the Romantic: "[A]nd so it just sprung up from the great, beautiful time in which, at last, the unity of all faith, of all love and the great, inner community of all religions has opened up—the time to which you and I belong as true contemporaries."[34] The reviewer of the *Tübingen Morning Paper* (*Tübinger Morgenblatt*) is similarly enthusiastic in June 1807: Plautus' adaptation already reveals "a slight trace of contempt for the gods"; Moliere's play is proof of "a genuinely national cuckoldry." Kleist, by contrast, "revives" the myth "with such chastity and sanctity," and interprets it "in such a surprising, superhuman, and noble way." The play comprises "a sentiment which, apart from the Greek, *only* the German is capable of, which had to remain foreign to the Roman, and which the Frenchman will never rise to grasp."[35]

In the prologue the Roman playwright Plautus calls his *Amphitruo* a tragicomedy because—contrary to the so-called estates clause—the play mixes gods, heroes, and servants, giving the Theban commander Amphitryon a doppelganger in Jupiter and one to his servant Sosias in Mercury, so that both of their wives—Alcmene and Charis—are deceived. We will later return to this mirror relation between the characters, which becomes important in Kleist. Like Plautus before him, Kleist is concerned with the possible relation between gods and humans. Apart from the ideological glossing over from the first reviewers, there can be no talk of a "majestic" deity, of "immaculate conception," "chastity," or "sanctity," especially considering the conversation between Jupiter and Alcmene in the famous act 2, scene 5, which, in this particular form, has no equivalent in either Plautus or Molière. The scene unfolds as a play-within-a-play in five acts, so to speak; it is an interrogation play—a test of trust—at the end of which the relationship between man and god is as profoundly shaken as in Goethe's angry hymn "Prometheus."[36]

The dialogue begins with Alcmene's request that Jupiter—who once more approaches her in the guise of Amphitryon—declare her innocence. She wants him to admit that, on the night they made love, he gave her a diadem bearing the initial of a foreign name. If he denies having done so, says Alcmene, "let / my lot be death and night eternal swallow / up my shame." Alcmene initiates a game of death, and her "Ah!" in the play's final verse can thus only be conceived of as a wail, as she is now certain that she has been deceived. But let us return to act 2, scene 5. Jupiter has no intentions to reveal his identity, taking refuge in sophistries: "Even he / who has the luck to be received into your presence, / leaves it pure and blameless still, for nothing

/ not Amphitryon is ever able / to come near you." This distinction between subjective innocence and objective guilt is of little help to Alcmene: "Oh my dear husband, please / do tell me, was it you or not? Speak, it / was you, it was!" Jupiter evades the question: "Yes, it was me. But it's / no matter who it was. I beg you: make / an effort to be calm." For Alcmene this evasion puts an end to their conversation: "Now I / must say good-bye to you forever, my / beloved. Oh, I steeled myself against / this possibility!" Jupiter then tries to console her in the same way he did with Amphitryon in Moliere's comedy, namely by presenting himself—the deceiver—as the deceived, since he had no choice but to borrow Alcmene's husband's guise to be able to deceive her "unerring feeling." Alcmene remains inconsolable, prompting Jupiter to begin act 2 of this interrogation play by revealing: "It was no mortal man / appeared to you but Zeus himself, the Thunder God!" Alcmene's collapsing grammar reflects her fierce revulsion. "[M]adman," "wretch," is how she berates her alleged husband: "You charge, you dare to, the Olympians, / with the crime, blasphemer, that was committed?" Alcmene refuses to believe that the highest god has loose morals. Jupiter, meanwhile, becomes coarse and forbids her to speak, for he is not to be measured by human standards: "Silence, I command / you!" His behavior is so unchivalrous and earthly, it only confirms Alcmene's view: "Oh, lost soul!" she throws at him. And yet Jupiter continues in his machismo, pointing to the many lovers he has pleased and who became famous in bearing him demigods. For Alcmene this turn in conversation is so absurd that she again forgives him, whom she still believes to be Amphitryon, assuming that he, in his "magnanimity," invented the tale of the divine lover only to dispel her "painful thoughts." But now he should go, find another woman, and let her "weep away [her] days." Jupiter, slightly disgruntled, thereupon falls back on the sure proof—the diadem—which bears the initial letter *J* for Jupiter. Alcmene is pleased, but for a different reason than Jupiter had hoped: "I'll / be glad to have suffered all the pain that Jupiter / has caused me, if only everything is nice / again between us." Alcmene speaks of pain rather than fame regarding the night she made love to the god; and she can only tolerate it if it does not further disturb her marital happiness. Jupiter is angry and strikes a more serious note. He begins act 3 of this play-within-a-play by asking: "What—now don't be frightened— / what if you offended him?" Jupiter presents the night of love as a punishment for Alcmene's treatment of her husband Amphitryon like a deity, which betrays Jupiter, the true god. "Who is it that you pray to at His altar? To Him, / perhaps, who sits above the clouds? […] / You grovel in the dust, but always to the man / you love, Amphitryon, am I correct?" Alcmene returns the question: "The involuntary movements of the soul, must they be censured / too? Am I supposed to pray to marble / walls? Well, I need features I can see / if I'm to think of him." Alcmene thus beats Jupiter with his own weapons. He needs to assume Amphitryon's form to love her; she, in turn, needs Amphitryon's shape to love the shapeless god. Where, then, would her guilt lie? Alcmene promises to spend her first waking hour of each day thinking of the god, "[b]ut after that I shall / forget Lord Jupiter." Jupiter—not inclined to be self-reflective—rages on, thus opening act 4 of the play-within-a-play. Alcmene mistakenly believes she senses her husband's concern for his alleged divine rival, and assures the man standing before her in the guise of Amphitryon that she would like to turn back time by one day if she could, to "bolt my closet shut against all gods / and heroes." The plural Alcmene uses, which indiscriminately rejects all gods, tips Jupiter over the edge. He curses the madness of having gotten involved in an affair with Alcmene and brings himself to a sentimental and passionate intercession:

> My good child,
> you have no wish to solace his stupendous being?
> Won't allow his head, that superintends
> the worlds, the pillow of your breast when he seeks to rest
> it there? Olympus too, Alcmene, without love,
> is desolate! What good is it to see
> whole nations bowed down in the dust
> in adoration, to a bosom panting with desire?
> It's love he wants, not all those mad ideas
> they entertain about him.

Alcmene suffocates his pleading and wooing—which she can only understand as hypothetical, since for her it has only ever been Amphitryon standing before her—with an upright theological formula: Her reverence—or *agape*—is for the god, but her love—or *eros*—is for her husband. Understandably, Jupiter is unsatisfied with this distinction. Act 5 of the play-within-a-play begins with the question: "But now suppose / *I* were, for you, the god—?" If Jupiter were to stand before her in the guise of Amphitryon in real time—as is indeed the case—what then? Alcmene feels rather tormented by this next sophistry but soon finds an answer that renders her, in the most fortunate way, unsuitable for embarking on any excursion into the supernatural:

> You were the god embracing
> me, and lo, Amphitryon appeared?—
> I'd be so very sad, oh so dejected,
> and wish that he could be the god and you
> would go on being my Amphitryon
> forever, as you are.

Faced with this unwavering certainty—which is of course deceptive, given Alcmene's confession to Jupiter, whom she believes to be Amphitryon, that his presence means the most to her—Jupiter is finally defeated, but not without turning his defeat into a victory:

> My creature whom
> I worship! In whom I am so blessed—in blessing,
> blessed! So perfectly concordant with
> the great original divine conception,
> in shape and substance, string and sound! Such a one
> as has not issued from my hand in eons![37]

Jupiter successfully transitions from melancholia to mania by celebrating himself, inebriated by the vision of himself as the creator of a being as perfect as Alcmene. He thus insists on maintaining the very distinction between creator and creature he sought to suspend in his union with Alcmene. His original narcissistic desire was to "see himself reflected" in a "living soul,"[38] which is to say Alcmene's. But this longing to recognize oneself in another is less divine than it is human; moreover, it fails. Alcmene does not quietly reflect Jupiter but fiercely opposes him. She cannot help but identify god and husband. Even her last word in her tormented dialogue with Jupiter is "Amphitryon!"[39] She loves her husband as an earthly god—the creator of human life through the entirely earthly act of intercourse. Alcmene is no Virgin Mary willing to accept the blessing of divine visitation—a bold move by Kleist, considering the fact that in the end Jupiter promises Amphitryon in biblical terms: "To you there shall be born / a son, and Hercules his name."[40] It is this promise that first made critics of the play evoke the comparison between Amphitryon and Joseph, Alcmene and Mary, and Hercules and Christ.

As I have sought to demonstrate in this detailed rendering, the arrangement of dialogue in act 2, scene 5 makes it one of the most ingenious pieces of world literature. A play-within-a-play, it is the generative core of Kleist's *Amphitryon*. As in *The Schroffenstein Family*, *Robert Guiscard*, and *The Broken Jug*, it is where the reader is again confronted with a fundamental tension Kleist further unfolds in his subsequent plays. His literature thrives on the conflict between a language of the heart and that of deception. Even after his Kant crisis, the Enlightenment desire for authenticity still informs Kleist's works as a phantasmatic vanishing point. On the one hand, his works expose the ideal of immediacy as a chimera; on the other hand, they bear witness to the fact that only power—not love—can be gained through disguise. "I should like, my angel light, / to have seemed to you a being of a nature all / his own, your conqueror because the gods themselves / instructed him in that fine art"—this is how Jupiter first summarizes, triumphantly, the relationship between the agonistic and theatrical dimensions of his art of simulation, only to finally surrender melancholically: "It's love he wants, not all those mad ideas / they entertain about him." Jupiter pretends to be Amphitryon, and he does it so well that Alcmene turns her affection toward him immediately. But the god is made to bear the consequences of his simulations, for Alcmene's gaze transforms him into someone else. Her heart does not recognize Jupiter's true being; rather, her eyes yield to outward appearances—hence Jupiter, for her, is what he pretends to be: Amphitryon. Jupiter thus falls victim to his own performance insofar as he, in turn, is left having to be what he pretends to be. "His wicked / swindle took *him* in, not you," Jupiter begins to realize. It is always both partners who are deceived and thus both who become victims. For the passive victim of such artful deceptions, like Alcmene, the question arises as to how to distinguish between simulation and truth. The way Kleist sets up this epistemological crisis in *Amphitryon* makes a sound mockery of the ideal of immediate understanding. The linguistic and bodily signs remain equally opaque—and this is what Alcmene despairs of: "A curse on senses that surrendered to so gross / a hoax, a breast that rang so falsely to the touch, / a soul so little worth as not to know / its own true love!"[41]

Is there a way out of this dilemma? Of all people it is Amphitryon who glimpses a way out—the same Amphitryon who finally comes to terms with the disconnect between inner being and outer appearance. Playing along with Jupiter's deception, he seems content with a substitute value, that is, with the glory of being, if not the begetter, at least the father of a demigod. Faced with the mediated nature of perception and the radical deceivability of the senses, Amphitryon comes to see the integrity of Alcmene's love—unwavering and always true to her husband—as an absolute and uncircumventable authority. He voices this insight after Alcmene—at the end of the play, being confronted with Amphitryon's doppelganger Jupiter in the presence of Amphitryon himself and everybody else—once more mistakes his double, Jupiter, for her husband:

> Every word she utters
> is the truth—not gold ten times refined
> is truer. More than oracles—than what
> the lighting writes upon the night, than what
> the thunder says—I trust the strict integrity
> of what her lips have just declared. I'll swear
> upon the altar here and now,
> die ten times over if I'm not
> unshakably persuaded: to her he is
> Amphitryon.[42]

It could be said that Amphitryon's prudence rule provides the answer to Kleist's Kant crisis: If "[w]e can never be certain that what we call Truth is really Truth, or whether it does not merely appear so to us,"[43] then, the substitution of truthfulness for the futile quest for truth could be a solution. While 'true' refers to a judgment in which what is meant actually agrees with the facts, 'truthful' describes the agreement between what is said and the conviction of the person speaking. Truth therefore gives way to the truthfulness of a person or the verisimilitude of judgments, neither of which can be objectified. Amphitryon's insight is that the world, as it relates to the subject, no longer avails of any truth, that it can "only be taken on qua love and not qua knowledge (nor qua knowledge of love)."[44] This insight alone could guarantee the future reconciliation of the two spouses Amphitryon and Alcmene and thus guarantee a happy ending to the comedy, which has yet to be conceived following Alcmene's "Ah!"

For Alcmene, however, this insight is not enough. Feeling cruelly deceived, she is intent on hiding "on a mountain peak" to "keep" her heart "blameless."[45] She believes that only in isolation can the integrity and truth of a person—which inevitably become lost in social interaction—be realized. Kleist expresses a similar sentiment in a letter to his sister Ulrike of February 5, 1801: "Alas," he writes a month before first mentioning his Kant crisis, "there is no way to make oneself completely understood to others, and human nature is such that we must confide only in ourselves. [...] The need to play a role, and an inner repugnance for it, make social gatherings burdensome for me, and I can only be happy in my own company, because there I can be what I really am."[46] For the characters in *Amphitryon*, the real identity behind Jupiter's mask is first revealed at the very end of the play, as Kleist presents a god who literally plays the role of another and decides to finally unmask himself. But what if "no revelation should declare / it to us from on high,"[47] Jupiter asks Alcmene during the interrogation in act 2, scene 5. What if Jupiter were to simply disappear at the end of *Amphitryon* without first playing the helpful lie and simulation detector for the humans who are so prone to deception? What if there were no god behind Jupiter's mask? What if he were only a medium, an allegory for how two lovers, or all human beings, interact? The mask would then be a projection, a vision of oneself, which one holds up to the person opposite. If one takes the image of Jupiter—a god able to create a different mask for every situation—to its radical conclusion, then self-assurance and constancy of being are only possible in social isolation. In social interactions one is meanwhile left to deal with the, in principle, irreducible difference of masks. One's soul cannot be reckoned with, as Achilles' defeat to Penthesilea demonstrates in Kleist's later play.

Kleist was so set on this isolation that even in death he played this masquerade *ad infinitum*—in the so-called "Death Litany" ("Todeslitanei"), his exchange of letters with Henriette Vogel. As unfaltering as Alcmene and as compassionate as Amphitryon may be, a happy ending for the couple is hardly conceivable, considering Kleist's negative anthropology. In his foreword Adam Müller—the editor of Kleist's *Amphitryon*—speculates about the play's ending: "There is one wish the editor cannot suppress, namely that, in the last act, the Theban people might have been reminded of the difference between the divine and earthly Amphitryon, as Alcmene is in act 2. The author did *intend* for the earthly love of the people for their military leader to be defiled just as much as Alcmene's love for her husband is—yet he did not *express* it."[48] Müller's interpretation that Amphitryon became defiled not only as a lover before Alcmene, but "just as much as" a military leader before his people, is hardly substantiated by the text; it rather speaks to the play's relevance for its contemporary context insofar as it no longer reminds the reader of the triad of Amphitryon, Jupiter, and Alcmene, but of a completely different constellation: the weak military leader Friedrich Wilhelm III and his wife Queen Luise, who, as a negotiator, is able to fascinate Napoleon and Tsar Alexander I. This reading would make Jupiter's parting words to Alcmene after their night of love to be misinterpreted in more than one way: "Much better it should stay a secret your / Amphitryon has been in Thebes, these / moments I have offered up on love's / altar have all been stolen from the battlefield. / The world might misinterpret it, my theft."[49] Whether Kleist himself could have really intended such a parallel between Alcmene and Luise is highly doubtful, given his admiration for Luise. Equally audacious are biographical associations within German studies that associate the divine lover with Kleist himself, which is to say, Amphitryon with the philistine marriage theorist Wilhelm Traugott Krug, and Alcmene with Wilhelmine.[50]

The fact that the play is nevertheless intended for the historical moment can be discerned less with regard to the masters than to the servants. On the level of the servants, the problem of authenticity and simulation is not only worked out with words but fought out with blows. Mercury strikes Sosias—whose shape the former has taken on to prepare Jupiter's way to Alcmene—until Sosias ceases to claim his own name, identity, and property in order to save his skin. Without Sosias, the true comical character, the play would not work as a comedy. It is through him that the play is situated in the historical reality of Kleist's time. With Sosias' maltreated body Kleist illustrates the rules of prudence that one should not ignore in times of war—in times of violence and individual powerlessness: that it is sometimes wise not to hold on to one's identity; that it is worthwhile to reflect on the possibility of identity and to explore playful ways of dealing with it, as in the intermingling of fiction and reality, in order to ensure one's survival if nothing else; and that self-assurance and heartfelt immediacy can be possible in isolation but may lead to martyrdom and death in an agonistic society. The latter is attested to in Kleist's novella "The Earthquake in Chile."

"The Earthquake in Chile"

Kleist wrote his novella in Königsberg and first published it under the title "Jerónimo and Josefa. A Scene from the Earthquake in Chile, from 1647" ("Jeronimo und Josephe. Eine Scene aus dem Erdbeben zu Chile, vom Jahr 1647"). It was printed in September 1807 in the most prominent publication of literary entertainment in the first half of the 19th century, Johann Friedrich Cotta's journal *Morning Paper for Educated Classes* (*Morgenblatt für die gebildeten Stände*), which appeared several days a week. Only in the book edition of Kleist's stories, published by Reimer in 1810, does it receive the title commonly used today. In a time of historical disaster—the social destabilization of Prussia caused by the invasion of the French troops—Kleist writes about a natural disaster that temporarily suspends all social order. After an earthquake on May 13, 1647, panic broke out among the people of Santiago de Chile. The apocalyptic event was regarded as God's punishment for the sins of man. A century later, on November 1, 1755, on All Saints' Day, the Lisbon earthquake claimed almost thirty thousand lives, unsettling the Enlightened society of Europe and reigniting the debate over the correlation of moral and natural evils. The ensuing contest between theology, philosophy, and the sciences, vying for authority to interpret the disaster, turned the Lisbon earthquake into a worldwide media event. At issue was theodicy—the problem of how to justify an almighty, omniscient, and benevolent God in the face of evil and suffering and a world so obviously imperfect. The attribution of such a disaster to either God or man was anything but self-evident in an increasingly scientifically oriented age that developed geological theories for explaining the movements beneath the earth and empirical models for calculating and avoiding natural risks, all free from any theological or moral baggage.[51]

Kleist's novella does not play along with this secularization of natural disasters. The historic earthquake in Chile serves as the backdrop for a fictional story that seems to conform to the old theological pattern of sin and divine punishment. The novella has a three-part structure. First the 'fortunate' interruption of two lives by a natural disaster is described. Josefa, a nun of noble birth, falls in love with her former tutor Jerónimo. The result of their union—scandalous in the eyes of the public—is a son named Felipe, whom Josefa delivers on the cathedral steps on the day of Corpus Christi. The nun is put on trial, and she is sentenced to death by decapitation. Meanwhile, Jerónimo is in prison and decides to hang himself at the exact moment of his beloved's execution. The sudden eruption of the earthquake saves the two doomed lovers. The Viceroy's palace, the law court, the cathedral, the convent, the prison—all the public institutions of authority—are reduced to rubble while Jerónimo and Josefa take advantage of the general chaos to escape. Josefa rescues Felipe from the burning convent and finds Jerónimo in the open country, in a valley where all survivors of the disaster have gathered. Here one can see, according to Kleist's narrator, "men and women of every social station […] lying side by side, princes and beggars, ladies and peasant women, government officials and day labourers, friars and nuns: pitying one another, helping one another, gladly sharing anything they had saved to keep themselves alive, as if the general disaster had united all its survivors into a single family."[52] This idyllic scene leads Jerónimo and Josefa to the fateful assumption that their love will now be tolerated by society. They set off to join the others for a mass to show their gratitude in the Dominican church at Santiago. In his sermon, however, the preacher interprets the earthquake as a punishment for Jerónimo and Josefa's sin, turning the congregation—who had been peaceful until that moment—into a murderous mob ready to lynch the two lovers. Josefa and Jerónimo are ultimately slain, as is—inadvertently, instead of their own son Felipe—little Juan, the son of Don Fernando, whose family the unfortunate lovers had just befriended in the valley. The end of the story is at odds with its beginning. The reader is at a loss when it comes to how to interpret the earthquake: as God's punishment for the inhumane treatment of the two lovers, insofar as it saves them but kills their judges, or as the consequence of a forbidden love, insofar as Jerónimo and Josefa are ultimately killed at the preacher's behest? As is typical of Kleist, the closing line of the novella is spectacular, disturbing, and provocative: "Don Fernando and [his wife] Doña Elvira then adopt the little stranger as their own son; and when Don Fernando compared Felipe with Juan and the ways in which he had acquired the two of them, it almost seemed to him as though he must rejoice."[53]

From a psychological perspective this conclusion is completely implausible. In spite of Don Fernando's attempt to protect both children, killing seven attackers in the process, his son Juan, mistaken for Felipe, was killed, smashed against one of the church pillars. Don Fernando's adoption of the orphaned Felipe is a noble deed, but hardly a sufficient cause for joy. The subjunctive mood—"as though"—does not solve the mystery either, but rather contributes to the ending's mysteriousness. Why would Don Fernando rejoice? Whatever the reason, it is worth noting that it would not be a spontaneous expression: It seemed to him as though "he must rejoice." The oxymoron '*must* rejoice' tells us the joy would be contrived. When Don Fernando sees his dead son, "with his brains oozing out," he raises "his eyes to heaven in inexpressible anguish." He is then found at a friend's house with "his bitter tears raining down on the child's face." He initially hides Juan's death from his wife, who ends up learning of it through someone else. She "quietly" weeps "out her maternal grief, and one morning, with the trace of a tear glistening in her eye, [throws] her arms round her husband's neck." She reconciles with him with a kiss and agrees to adopt Felipe. We thus know that the adoption does not take place immediately. But Kleist's narrator keeps the temporal distance between the murderous events and the adoption in the dark, so we never learn exactly what "one morning" means.[54]

Does the story's ending, then, render Kleist's novella a variation on the story of Job? Does Don Fernando—a minor character—suddenly take center stage, coming to the realization that the reconciliation of human suffering and divine will is not a logical problem? After all, God's ways are unpredictable and true faith requires trust in God, even and especially in times of suffering. This is one way of reading the novella—in the context of the theodicy debate. Like Job, Don Fernando would have recognized that the presence or absence of suffering is not an indication of divine punishment or reward—that suffering strikes the righteous and the unrighteous indiscriminately. This experience is distinguished from the revenge fantasies of the false agents of God who slaughter Jerónimo, Josefa, and Juan. Yet, after reading Kleist's *Amphitryon*—which was written at the same time as "The Earthquake in Chile" and which remains entirely immanent in this world—one can hardly suppose that Kleist would have been capable of producing such a serious exercise in Christian faith. The assumption that the novella is a fictional contribution to the theodicy debate is, moreover, inconsistent with the baffling 'rejoice' imperative the traumatized father receives. Nor is the theodicy reading substantiated by the assumption that Kleist, in his Königsberg novella, followed Kant's reflections "On the Miscarriage of All Philosophical Trials in Theodicy" of 1791—that is, the conviction that reason meets its limits with respect to metaphysical questions.[55] On August 31, 1806, Kleist writes to Rühle von Lilienstern from Königsberg: "It cannot be an evil spirit that stands at the world's helm, but merely an uncomprehended one! Do we not laugh when children cry?"[56] In this Kleist follows Kant's view of God as inaccessible to reason. The quote could be placed above the novella as a motto, as a reminder of the failure of all attempts at explaining the senseless suffering the story depicts. One may thus laugh about the childish belief that God could be regarded as an evil or good, just or unjust father.

A second reading of the novella astutely emphasizes the story's gift and exchange economy. Don Fernando's peculiar rejoicing is preceded by a curious comparison: "and when Don Fernando compared Felipe with Juan and the ways in which he had acquired the two of them, it almost seemed to him as though he must rejoice." According to the narrator, Juan is a "poor little creature" and "sickly little boy," his mother has run out of breast milk and the earthquake "injured" her.[57] At Don Fernando's request Josefa helps out and breast-feeds both children, her own and Doña Elvira's. Felipe, however, seems to be more resilient than Juan right from the start; he had, after all, survived the convent fire unscathed. Less viable, however, seems the thesis that Don Fernando's rejoicing can be explained by the fact that the adopted son—being the "child of an ideal mother"—makes him "even forget the dead."[58] Don Fernando "acquired" Juan through natural fatherhood, Felipe through adoption. This constellation is repeated at the beginning of Kleist's novella "The Foundling." The merchant Piachi adopts Nicolo, who is sick with the plague but survives, while Piachi's biological child Paolo, who—first infected with the plague by Nicolo and obviously of weaker constitution than him—dies. I will return to the exchange logic of this novella but would first like to point out one additional feature. Kleist's double adoption fantasy does not suggest an Enlightenment utopia in the sense of Gotthold Ephraim Lessing's *Nathan the Wise* of 1779, according to which stepfathers like Nathan—whose own children and wife were murdered by Christians and who soon thereafter adopted a Christian child—may be the better fathers insofar as they respect and promote their child's individuality, whereas biological fathers dispose of their offspring as if they were their own personal property. To regard Kleist's stepfathers as superior to biological fathers would mean overlooking the fact that Don Fernando "acquired" Felipe and that Piachi merely uses his adoptive son to fill the gap his biological son's death left behind so as to secure the continuation of his family business. How, then, is Don Fernando's economy of comparison and exchange to be understood? Perhaps his adoption of Felipe would make sense in terms of French ethnologist Marcel Mauss' theory of the gift,[59] that is, as a counter-gift through which a gift is reciprocated, which is to say, through which a debt is cancelled. But what would be the gift that Don Fernando reciprocates with the adoption of Felipe? One possible answer lies in the graciousness of Josefa, who gave Juan her breast milk, thus saving him from death. As the first gift a person receives, a mother's milk is the gift par excellence—the model for all gifts to come. Hence, in Christian iconography *Madonna lactans*, the nursing mother, embodies the virtue of charity.[60] This imagery fits into the idyllic middle section of the novella, into the Rousseauist social utopia in the valley, in which the differences between mine and yours, own and foreign, high and low social station are suspended. What is more, Josefa sacrifices her own life at the end of the novella, when she reveals her identity to protect Don Fernando's family: "But as he [Don Fernando] could not overpower the surging mass that pressed in on him, Josefa cried out: 'Farewell, Don Fernando. Here I am, murder me, you bloodthirsty tigers!' and voluntarily threw herself into their midst, to put an end to the fighting. Master Pedrillo struck her dead with his club."[61]

Josefa sacrifices her own life—one cannot give more than that—and she hands her child to Don Fernando at the moment of her certain death. This is a gift of honor inasmuch as the transfer of a family obligation gives the recipient the opportunity to act honorably. This motif is familiar—pardon the comparison—from soap operas and melodramas: A single mother lies on her deathbed and entrusts the care of her soon-to-be-orphaned children to their father, who left the family behind a long time ago to sow his wild oats. He is found in the final seconds of the movie, and bursts into tears at the prospect of taking care of his children because he is given a chance to restore his honor. Similarly, Don Fernando is given an opportunity to prove himself worthy again by caring for Felipe in the future as if he were his own child. He is going to rescind the inferior position he found himself in as a result of the natural disaster: The earthquake forced the nobleman to beg for his son to be fed, while it elevated the disgraced mother Josefa, considered dishonorable in the eyes of the people of Santiago. It is not, then, the poor asking the rich for alms; rather, it is the other way around. Don Fernando does not have much to offer compared with Josefa, whose gift of mother's milk he can only reciprocate with a "small breakfast" in the valley.[62] Later he fails to save his son's life and that of his sister-in-law Doña Constanza. He is unable to keep his word of honor that "he would sooner perish than allow any member of his party to suffer harm."[63] And this hubris is to blame since it is the reason that Don Fernando disregards his sister-in-law Doña Isabel's premonition that going to the mass to show their gratitude would cause harm to everyone.

Don Fernando's standing as a man of honor is of no use to him against the murderous mob; a cobbler like Pedrillo can position himself in front of the aristocrat threateningly and force him to account for his person. In the face of the dissolution of a society divided by social station into an anarchic mob in the aftermath of the natural disaster, neither the symbolic exchange of women, through which the two families—the respected and the outlawed—are mixed, helps (Jerónimo walks with Doña Constanza on his arm, Don Fernando with Josefa), nor does the equating of the two children, in the course of which Juan comes to replace Felipe and thus becomes the mistaken target of a violence intended for Felipe. Don Fernando has failed. Only with the adoption of Felipe does he find recompense equivalent to the gift he received from Josefa: to love a stranger's child as if it were one's own. This may be why Kleist did not opt for an alternative ending—for the survival of Juan. Don Fernando can only prove himself a man of honor by way of the stranger's child—in the elimination of the difference between what is foreign and what is his own—but not by way of his own child. But how much violence is necessary, how high must be the price for Don Fernando's restored image of sublime virtue?

It is understandable that Don Fernando's rejoicing at the story's end is rendered only in the subjunctive. The gift he has to be willing to give has something of the ambivalence implied in the shared etymology of the German words *Gabe* (gift) and *Gift* (poison)—an ambivalence also present in the Greek word *pharmakon*, meaning both remedy and poison. Don Fernando's counter-gift—the adoption of Felipe—may be therapeutic for him, but it is also poisonous because Felipe will forever remind Don Fernando of the one who gave his life for him—of Juan—and therefore of his traumatic failure and guilt. This ambiguity leads to a third reading of the novella, central to an understanding of Kleist's style, which often negotiates opposites in such a way that binaries are suspended into figurations of the third: There is no plus or minus, no either/or in Kleist; opposites form a third, a difference that both divides and unites what is differentiated. Kleist pictures this figure of thought in paradoxes such as his essay "On Thinking Things Over," namely in the image of life as a struggle between two opponents in which the weakness of one becomes the strength of the other and vice versa. We see it, too, in the principle of contrariness and the reversal of polar opposites found in his essay "The Very Last Word in Modern Educational Theory," which was referenced in Chapter III in my discussion of Kleist's productive reception of the sciences, namely Christian Ernst Wünsch's theses on electricity.[64] This figure of thought dominates Kleist's writing insofar as a gesture, a word, a facial expression, a movement can mean, simultaneously, kissing and biting, loving and hating, weakness and strength, submission and dominance, morality and sexuality, compassion and self-love, a sense of justice and an appallingly excessive injustice, etc.

Kleist's novella "The Earthquake in Chile" therefore only appears to follow a distinct three-part plot. In reality, one is confronted with a perpetual interplay of destruction and rescue, happiness and misfortune, undermining any attempt by the reader to establish a fixed meaning.[65] All things initially distinct fall and collapse into one another, thereby holding the story in a state of suspension reminiscent of Kleist's image of the arched gate in Würzburg from his letter of November 16 and 18, 1800: From the initial scene of death—which also becomes a scene of liberation for the two lovers doomed to die by the earthquake—to the mass of the survivors at the end, which turns into a deadly carnage. But it is not only the motifs that describe ambiguous figures.

The meaning they are assigned within the text oscillates. Take, for instance, the reading of the earthquake in the context of the theodicy debate. It bears repeating that, at the beginning of the novella, the earthquake suggests divine punishment for the representatives of Chilean society, whose palaces are destroyed for their merciless behavior toward the lovers Jerónimo and Josefa. At the end of the novella, however, the preacher blames Jerónimo and Josefa for the earthquake. The two are killed, but so are innocent people like Juan and Doña Constanza. Kleist's suspension of the binary in favor of a tertiary order that integrates opposites also manifests in the story's grammar, whose complicated—labyrinthine and nested—syntax, with its artfully displaced subordinate clauses, prevents the reader from clearly attributing and differentiating meaning, inspite or precisely because of the semantic density and concentration, which is to say, the abundance of paradoxical and heterogeneous information. One only has to read closely a few sentences from the final section of the novella to be amazed by Kleist's depiction of the chaos of the masses, the whirlwind of action and counter-action confusing the reader attempting to distinguish between the subjects and objects of these actions. One thus realizes how the aggression of the mob comes to develop its own dynamic, how it de-individualizes its members so entirely that differences in social station as well as all notions of justice, guilt, or innocence become obliterated, rendering anyone capable of becoming victim or perpetrator and all suffering meaningless.

One could consider Kleist a precursor to Modernism, a clairvoyant analyst of the psychology of the masses. What is certain is that his literary world distorts his contemporary world to the point of recognition. It would be erroneous to read into the text a social agenda of freedom, equality, and fraternity. The community of earthquake survivors in the idyllic valley does not last any longer than the social utopia of the French Revolution. Soon thereafter man is a wolf to man once again. The new order established in Europe by the French Revolution and the Napoleonic Wars meant, for Kleist, nothing but the mere overthrow of the old. There is thus nothing unshakable—no more stability, only instability, the destabilization of all coherence in life and thought. In Kleist's style—which often shakes appositions free from their referents and puts into disarray the subjects, objects, and verbs of main and subordinate clauses, kaleidoscopically, in ever-changing twists and turns of punctuation—the historical shock becomes a poetic event. Kleist does not simply claim that time is out of joint. He himself is thrown out of joint in and with his writing, which becomes evident even for today's reader as one loses all sense of direction when reading his story:

> 'Jesus! Holy Mother of God!' screamed Doña Constanza, fleeing to her brother-in-law's side; but: 'Convent whore!' came a cry, and a second blow from another direction struck her down lifeless beside Jerónimo. 'Monsters!' cried an unidentified bystander: 'that was Doña Constanza Xares!' 'Why did they lie to us?' retorted the cobbler. 'Find the right one, and kill her!' Don Fernando, seeing Doña Constanza lying dead beside him, was maddened with rage; drawing and brandishing his sword, he aimed so furious a blow at him that it would have split him in half, the fanatical murderer, who had instigated these horrors, if the man had not dodged aside. But as he could not overpower the surging mass that pressed in on him: 'Farewell, Don Fernando and the children!' Josefa cried out—and: 'Here I am, murder me, you bloodthirsty tigers!' and voluntarily threw herself into the midst, to put an end to the fighting. Master Pedrillo struck her dead with his club.[66]

"The Foundling"

Kleist is a master storyteller, as "The Earthquake in Chile" demonstrates. But where does his fondness for novellas stem from? He had little success with his plays among his contemporaries, but his stories were "devoured." However, according to Pfuel, this reception was "not enough" for Kleist, "having to stoop down from drama to story humiliated him boundlessly." Thus we are told by German writer Clemens Brentano in a letter to his fellow Romantic Achim von Arnim after Kleist's death in 1811.[67] This sentiment is exaggerated and is probably a mere concession to the genre clichés at the turn of the 19th century. Kleist must have felt differently. Why else would he have written eight stories in addition to his eight dramas, stories readers both in Germany and abroad are still enthusiastic about. He had the ambition to excel even in minor literary forms—in the anecdote and novella—to exhaust these popular genres, in both form and content, to such a degree that they would be transformed into great literature. In doing so, Kleist loves to play with tradition, to exceed it, to radicalize its models. He competes with Molière when he writes comedies like *Amphitryon*, and with Giovanni Boccaccio and Miguel de Cervantes when he writes novellas. The revaluation of this genre—its flowering in the German literature of the 19th and 20th centuries—is due to Kleist, alongside E.T.A. Hoffmann, Franz Kafka, and Robert Musil. Both the reading public and scholars agree on this point, though the latter argue about the dates of Kleist's stories. One can only be certain about the dates and locations of the first publication. As mentioned earlier, "The Earthquake in Chile" appeared under a different title in the *Morning Paper for Educated Classes* in 1807. *The Marquise of O—* and *Michael Kohlhaas* were published in full or in excerpts in Kleist's Dresden journal *Phöbus* in 1808. "The Beggarwoman of Locarno" ("Das Bettelweib von Locarno") and "St Cecilia or the Power of Music" ("Die heilige Cäcilie oder die Gewalt der Musik") appeared in Kleist's *Berlin Evening Paper* in 1810 and "The Betrothal in Santo Domingo" in the journal *The Liberal* in 1811. Kleist's collected stories were published in two volumes 1810/11 in Georg Andreas Reimer's Realschulbuchhandlung in Berlin. "The Duel" and "The Foundling" were included in the second volume as first editions.

Whether "The Foundling" is therefore one of Kleist's late rather than early works is still disputed today. Like his first work *The Schroffenstein Family*, "The Foundling" links the main theme of Kleist's pre-literary period—the acquisition of majority and individuality—to the question of its attainability within family discourses, and it concludes with equal skepticism.[68] "The Foundling" is quite rightly regarded as Kleist's darkest novella; his contemporaries warned against reading it. In his foreword to Kleist's *Posthumous Works* (*Hinterlassene Schriften*), Romantic writer Ludwig Tieck called the "situations depicted [...] more distressful than moving,"[69] and German scholar Wilhelm Grimm had no intention of recommending such a "highly sinister, gruesome image of wild passion and diabolic malice" to the readers of the *Journal for the Elegant World* of October 10, 1811.[70] Such appraisals suggest "The Foundling" to be nothing more than a piece of trivial Gothic fiction, meant to entertain crude minds and unsuitable for a sophisticated audience. The numerous intertextual references to Matthew G. Lewis' Gothic novel *The Monk* of 1796, and the incest motif, in particular, speak for this reading. Lewis' hero Ambrosio is a foundling who becomes the murderer of his mother Elvira as well as the rapist and murderer of his sister Antonia. Against this reading, however, I argue that "The Foundling" is a highly elaborate and carefully calculated narrative that demonstrates Kleist's rivalry with the novella tradition particularly well and explains his preference for this genre with regard to both the historical context and the history of the genre's changing function. Kleist's story refers to a period of upheaval and opposes the narrative and conceptual patterns of the *Bildungsroman* in order to expose, mercilessly, the aporias of idealist pedagogy and anthropology.[71] In what follows, I will therefore first discuss "The Foundling," given its uncertain date of origin, before addressing the novellas published in *Phöbus*. This order is also in keeping with the continuity of motifs: "The Foundling" begins the same way "The Earthquake in Chile" ends—with an adoption. And it begins the same way Boccaccio's *The Decameron* does, with a scenario of disaster—the plague.

The novella is a genre without any poetological rules prescribed from Classical Antiquity. Thus, all novellistic writing is measured against the genre's prototype, Boccaccio's collection *The Decameron*, written in the middle of the

14th century.[72] Over the course of ten days, ten young men and women on a country estate near Florence take turns telling each other stories. With only a few exceptions, these stories are remarkably drastic and sexually explicit, such as those about cuckolded husbands and bigoted monks. But the backdrop for this idyllic gathering is a disaster. The storytellers have fled Florence to escape the plague epidemic that hit the city in 1348. Scholarship has argued about how the relationship between apocalypse and blasphemy is to be understood within the frame story—namely, whether the plague should be regarded as divine punishment for the vices of the Florentine people about whom the young people tell stories. The structure of the individual stories, however, mostly following a three-part pattern, speaks against this thesis: A crime is followed by the secular threat of punishment from which the sinner tries to escape using both wit and reason. Corrupt monks rarely succeed in doing so. But ninety percent of the novellas are erotic stories, and sexual transgressions are not always punished. One such example is the seventh story of the second day. A beautiful and noble lady named Filippa is on trial for cheating on her husband. She readily admits to her cheating but objects that the laws according to which she is to be sentenced to death were not made by women. Women, she claims, are much better than men at satisfying multiple lovers; she for one has never denied her husband a single wish. Why, she finally asks, should she not make others, who are in need, happy with her excess love? The audience of the trial applauds the lady, and the judge capitulates before the power of eroticism. They agree to reconcile the positive laws of the state with the laws of nature. The cruel law is amended and its application limited to women who cheat on their husbands for money. The secular court thus dares to annul the divine commandment against adultery. Accordingly, the deadly plague could also be understood in a different way: as the outward sign of the collapse of the medieval Christian world order, against which the protagonists of the novellas had already successfully rebelled. Boccaccio's novella writing thus signals the transition from the Middle Ages to the Early Modern period; it is the expression of a rebellious individuality, of the triumph of an Early Modern rationality over a rigid medieval world order. Kleist's novellas are at once a continuation and transformation of Boccaccio's work in that they present both fantasies of self-creation in situations of crisis and, at the same time, the failure of the rebellious individual within social institutions, resulting in the suppression of individuality.

"The Foundling" is full of intertextual allusions to Boccaccio's *The Decameron*. One immediately recognizes the motif of triangular relationships as well as that of the cuckold, or the criticism of the corrupt, bigoted clergy. The novella begins with a disastrous situation—the plague now rages in Ragusa rather than Florence. A rich property dealer named Antonio Piachi flees the city with his son and on the way picks up an orphaned boy in his carriage, the plague-stricken foundling Nicolo. Nicolo recovers but infects Piachi's son Paolo, who eventually dies. Nicolo takes over his place. At first he follows the education he receives from his stepfather but later opposes it. He is a rebellious hero whose formation of individuality ultimately fails, leading from Ragusa to death.

What unites all of Kleist's novellas formally and conceptually is their opening scenes, the disastrous situations, which stem from Boccaccio. "Something foreign and extraordinary breaks into the lives of ordinary people"—such are the people Kleist consistently deals with, citizens and merchants like Piachi, horse-dealers like Kohlhaas, members of the lower nobility like the Marquise of O—. "Artists, dilettantes, actors, or bourgeois intellectuals and outsiders, that is, the preferred heroes of bourgeois prose" at the turn of the 19th century (such as that of Goethe, Friedrich Hölderlin, and Friedrich Schlegel) do not appear in Kleist's work, writes Gerhard Schulz, with whom one can only agree.[73] What distinguishes Kleist's protagonists is that they do not ruminate in situations of crisis, but simply act. Their desperation is not a philosophical one, but based in reality. A sick boy stops a carriage, and the result is the destruction of a well-off broker's family; a toll-gate is newly erected at a border, and an honorable horse-dealer becomes the most terrible man of his age. Kleist is a crisis specialist, and there are historical reasons that explain why. His stories never mention the disaster of Napoleon; and yet Napoleon determines their structure as a *deus absconditus*, as he does the novellas of E.T.A. Hoffmann, the other great novella writer of the age of Goethe. In the company of his Serapion brethren, Hoffmann's alter ego Theodore compares the time of the German campaign against Napoleon to a "hurricane" that drove the brotherly friends "asunder," leaving no one untouched:

> Of course we none of us *are* the same. [...] But whom of us, all this time, has not the wild whirlpool carried surging on from event to event, and from action to action? The terror, the trouble, the anxiety of that stormy time, could not pass over us without leaving bleeding scars graven on our hearts. The pictures of our early days are pale compared with *that*, and we cannot revive their colours.[74]

According to Theodore, the disaster of Napoleon—similar to a natural disaster like the plague—suddenly disrupted all biographical, historico- and socio-cultural coherence. Thus, for Hoffmann as well as for Kleist before him—who was still in the midst of the turmoil of the Napoleonic Wars when he wrote his stories—the typical situational framework of novellistic storytelling is established, which allows the narrator to focus on exceptional and extraordinary cases, on processes of identity formation that do not proceed successively and linearly, but rather erratically. To repeat: Napoleon is the *deus absconditus* of Kleist's novellas, which are at times historical yet always topical, that is, related to contemporary reality; it is Napoleon who, in the everyday life of Prussia, expels ordinary people "from the 'paradise' of ordinariness,"[75] disrupting the processes of their steady identity formation. Kleist merely uses the abbreviatory novella form to play out his own reality. His novels are experiments on the extent to which an event—in its peculiar and as yet unheard-of nature—can be successfully integrated into an order, on the extent to which the discontinuous can be restored into a continuum. This is the problem of the wartime generation of the German Romantics: searching for fantasies of order that could integrate the contingencies and vicissitudes of life. The most famous contemporary fantasy of order is the coming-of-age novel—the German *Bildungs-* and *Entwicklungsroman*. In his novella "The Foundling," Kleist puts the viability of this fantasy to the test. The plague has profoundly disrupted order in the Piachi family, resulting in Paolo's death. The father reacts to this misfortune by adopting the foundling Nicolo, binding him to the family by contract, and raising him to become a commercially successful and morally educated property dealer.

Yet Nicolo does not become a Wilhelm Meister, as the rest of the plot reveals. He does seem to become a good businessman, but one who—much to Piachi's and his young wife Elvira's chagrin—associates with bigoted clergymen and a lady of dubious reputation named Xaviera Tartini, until he finally marries an attractive young Genoese lady, for which his foster-father rewards him generously. He gives him legal possession of his entire fortune, including his house. But Nicolo's wife soon dies in childbirth, and before she has even been buried, Nicolo already schemes to visit Xaviera. This fact enrages Piachi so much that he, with a forged letter, tricks his disdainful adopted son into coming to the Church of Santa Maria Maddalena for a tryst with Xaviera. In actuality, it is the funeral service for his deceased wife that awaits the love-hungry man there, the date of which was moved up without his knowledge. The thus humiliated man seeks revenge and soon discovers that his adoptive mother Elvira still has a secret passion for a Genoese knight named Colino, who rescued her from a fire in her parents' house when she was still a little girl but later died from the injuries suffered during the rescue. One night Nicolo hides in Elvira's bedroom and waits for her in the guise of the Genoese knight; she falls for the deception and faints at the sight of the man she believes to be dead. Nicolo takes advantage of the opportunity to revive the unconscious woman with burning kisses on her lips and breasts but is taken by surprise by Piachi, who immediately tries to expel the wretched adopted son from his house. But the latter insists on his title to the property, whereupon the old man takes to his heels, leaving Elvira behind, defenseless, in the house with Nicolo. About Elvira we learn that she soon thereafter dies of a sudden fever; and we learn that Piachi returns to his house, "crush[es] out [Nicolo's] brains against the wall"[76] and stuffs the decree confirming Nicolo as the rightful owner of Piachi's property into his mouth. Thus, the foundling is dead, and the adoptive father has become a murderer and is executed—this is certainly not what one would imagine a proper coming-of-age story to look like.

But who is to blame for this disaster: the son or the father? Like so many of Kleist's stories, "The Foundling" stages a trial—the only difference being that its narrator does not follow the narrative technique Kleist adapted from the legal 'relations' in the Königsberg Chamber and thus does not consider the case in terms of pros and cons, but instead brands Nicolo an absolute villain. He calls Nicolo's passion "shameful," his plan "satanic" and "of unutterable vileness." Piachi, by contrast, is described as a "good old man" on two separate occasions and Elvira as an "excellent young wife" and "pure soul."[77] Those who do not question the narrator's authority will either take Nicolo for an inherently bad person ruining good peoples' lives,[78] or excuse his malice as a rebellion against a mercantile society that suppresses love and desire in favor of asceticism and property.[79] Aside from such partisanship it should be noted that the facts of the story contradict the narrator's assessments. The way the narrator depicts Elvira provides a prime example of this discrepancy. As usual, she throws herself in front of the painting of her beloved Colino one night, undressed and in an "attitude of swooning ecstasy." The narrator, however, remains unaffected by this scene despite his earlier comment that Piachi "withdrew with his faithful, virtuous Elvira, whose worldly wishes were few, into retirement."[80] Thus, Kleist thoroughly undermines the authority of the omniscient narrator.

Kleist not only mocks his narrator but with him the principles of bourgeois-idealist storytelling, which is based on two vital links: the ideational or moral nexus and the causal nexus. Since Christian Friedrich von Blanckenburg's *Essay on the Novel* (*Versuch über den Roman*) of 1774, the omniscient narrator of the *Bildungsroman* proves himself as an anthropologist with a precise knowledge of the inner workings of human nature and the ability to describe an individual's development in terms of cause and effect. The representation of cause and effect requires a biographical organizing principle—the telling of life stories in chronological order.[81] The scandal of Kleist's novella, then, is that it abolishes the narrator's one-sided causal psychology. Piachi's feeling of "pity"[82] for the plague-stricken Nicolo, his decision to take him into his carriage, is not—as one would expect—the first link in a chain of good, but instead of evil. The same applies to good deeds such as Nicolo's adoption, his caring upbringing, and the handing over of the family business to him: They invariably lead to bad results. When believing in the virtue of pity is no longer of any avail, it is not only the causal nexus of bourgeois stories of self-cultivation that is affected, but the moral or ideational nexus as well, according to which pity, as Rousseau explains in his *Discourse on the Origin and Foundations of Inequality among Men* of 1753, should be a pillar of reason. In "The Foundling" pity and reason are opposing principles; pity overrides Piachi's reason—with disastrous consequences.[83]

Moreover, in his novella Kleist criticizes the bourgeois-idealist models of family and education that underpin the *Bildungsroman*. In the bourgeois family model, the authority of the father is based on natural law, in his sense of duty to raise his child to majority. In "The Foundling" Kleist shows the deep divide between ideal and reality. Nicolo's upbringing follows a double-bind strategy: 'Only with my—your father's—help are you to reach majority.' In reality, the child can only gain autonomy by leaving the path predetermined by the father. But the old man Piachi does not approve of the fact that the foundling suddenly wants to be independent. Nicolo's murder is the punishment for the attempt to liberate himself, the price he pays for longing for majority, much like the murder of the two Schroffenstein children. One hundred years later in his story "The Sentence" of 1912, Kafka emulates Nicolo's rebellion against his father up to its ultimate consequence: Georg Bendemann's attempt to take over his father's business in his place ends with his father sentencing him to death.

Furthermore, the ideal of the bourgeois family consists in the belief that sensuality and friendship can be united in marriage. How violently and duplicitously this mediation usually transpires in reality is demonstrated by the Piachi family—an artificial construct held together only by substitutions: Elvira replaces Piachi's first wife and yet fulfills neither her role as a mother nor as a lover, Piachi replaces Colino, Nicolo replaces Paolo, and so forth. The attempts to legally protect these substitutions of desire—through adoption, business, and marriage contracts—does not solve the underlying problem, however; the character's suppressed sexuality defies all contracts.

Kleist also gives theoretical reasons for his dismissal of the bourgeois family (as a means of forming and protecting identity) and the idealist conception of education toward majority, namely in his essay "The Very Last Word in Modern Educational Theory," published in the *Berlin Evening Paper* in 1811. Here, Kleist rejects the two most prominent pedagogical concepts of his time. He dismisses both the philanthropic notion of a predictable education toward reason—in which the child is regarded as nothing but a *tabula rasa* on which the educator leaves his stamp, a blank space (whose embodiment the foundling would be)—as well as the Neohumanist notion of the development of a child's individual core through a caring education. According to Kleist, all human socialization is subject to the "universal law of contradiction."[84] Identity formation is thus understood as an act of opposition that depends on a given situation and opponent; it arises from relationships of difference, in which one's self is linked to an other in a struggle defined by mutual dependence. The arbitrariness of the other corresponds to the arbitrariness of one's self. There can be thus no talk of the ideal human's organic development as envisioned in the Neohumanist notions of the *Bildungsroman*, because nothing whole and harmonious could result from ever-changing constellations of influence; there is only the potentiality encountered in the dispositions of one's opponents. The interplay of good and evil in the struggle between Piachi and Nicolo can be understood in the same way as the claim that Kohlhaas "was one of the most honourable as well as one of the most terrible men of his age."[85]

Kleist assumes a general dissociation within the subject, which renders the question of its essence and consistency needless. The idealist notion of individuality inherent in the *Bildungsroman*—with its key elements: originality, authenticity, and singularity—is dismantled by Kleist. For him identity is no longer a question of substance—of the congruence between inner and outer self—but of performance. Nicolo, like his namesake Niccolò Machiavelli—who, in his portrait of "The Life of Castruccio Castracani of Lucca" of 1520, praised the rise of a foundling by means of duplicitous deception—recognizes the art of simulation as a strategy of power.[86] Kleist scholars have always wondered how the evil Nicolo and the good savior Colino could resemble each other—from the perspective of the Swiss physiognomist Johann Kaspar Lavater's physiognomy, for example, this resemblance would be unthinkable. But what gets overlooked here is Nicolo's, like Castruccio's, possession of one particular talent: disguise and acting. He disguises himself as Colino, simulating the latter's image so successfully that Elvira falls for the deception and faints. Her strong reaction is understandable, as from her point of view, she witnesses the uncanny return of her dead savior. Piachi, meanwhile, is first "speechless" then "powerless" in the face of Nicolo's art of simulation.[87] His desperation turns to violence, as his confidence in the foundations of bourgeois-idealist anthropology is radically shaken.

The conflict between Piachi and Nicolo is therefore not merely an Oedipal one, but essentially a conflict between two personality models. In his idealism the bourgeois Piachi trusts that every self-expression is a matter of substance, as Friedrich Schiller demands in *On Grace and Dignity* of 1793, where he conceives of grace as moral grace—as the expression of the beautiful soul as appearance. Nicolo, meanwhile, drawn to the libertinage of the nobility, relies on an anti-idealist, genuinely aristocratic concept of personality, which involves the calculation of images in agonistic times of crisis. Grace, then, derives its meaning from the Latin word *gratia*, which can mean a favor that one enjoys with others, regardless of whether appearances correspond to being.[88] What is at issue here is not the ability to express a beautiful inner being to the outside world, but to control one's public image in order to assert and defend one's interests.[89] As will be shown later, Kleist's essay "On the Puppet Theater" of 1810 also aspires to such calculated self-fashioning—to grace as a means for exerting full control over one's communications, as outlined in the practical guides to proper aristocratic conduct, from Machiavelli's *The Prince* of 1513/31 to Baldassare Castiglione's *The Book of the Courtier* of 1528 and Baltasar Gracián's *The Art of Worldly Wisdom* of 1647.[90]

As an anthropologist Kleist is a moralist rather than a moral philosopher; he is not interested in some ideal behavioral norm, but in the real human condition. Consequently, the agenda of his writing, like that of all skeptical moralists in times of crisis, is one of disappointment. Virtues often disguise vices, as French moralist François de La Rochefoucauld suggests in his *Maxims* of 1664, where he recognizes that self-interest speaks every language and plays every part, even that of altruism. This is also the principle Kleist follows in "The Foundling." Not only is Nicolo self-serving; Piachi is too. His love for his adoptive son is in reality an *amour propre*, a form of self-love. *Proprius* is basically a legal term referring to the authority to dispose of things. *Amour propre*—the combination of love and property—suggests that thinking in terms of property can be applied to areas where notions of ownership are out of place. Piachi disposes of his adopted son as if he were his property. Nicolo's role is to ensure his father's succession to the family business and thereby secure its continuation. When Nicolo tries to assert his own interests against Piachi's, disaster strikes. Idealist thinkers may—as Rousseau's praise of pity attests—regard the virtue of charity, of compassion, as a means of curtailing self-love. In his novella "The Foundling," Kleist, the moralist, proves that even in pity there lies only self-interest. He adheres to empiricism. He agrees with Machiavelli, who in the fifteenth chapter of *The Prince* advises that, in times of crisis, it is "more appropriate to go after the effectual truth of the thing than the imagination of it."[91] It is hence inconceivable for Kleist to produce grand counter-narratives to his current reality. It is impossible for him to write a *Bildungsroman*, but he can write stories like "The Foundling" that undermine the idealist notion of *Bildung* altogether.[92] In doing so, he is radically destructive, incapable of maintaining a joyful distance in the face of affected human behavior and its susceptibility to strong emotions. And the reason for this is simple: Behind Kleist's moralist thinking lies nothing other than disappointed idealism.

The Marquise of O—

Written, presumably, in 1805/06 in Königsberg and published in February 1808 in the Dresden journal *Phöbus*, Kleist's novella *The Marquise of O—* seems to be an exception. At the end of the story, a wedding occurs; two lovers reconcile and start a family—idealism in its purest form, or so one might think. The curious thing is that the bride and groom exchange their vows for a second time after having been married for one year. Apparently, the happy ending is being reassessed, so to speak. And the story begins with a disaster—as is typical of Kleist—thus confirming the gloomy novella definitions of the 19th century, according to which novellas depict exceptional and extraordinary cases that invariably occur "behind the back of bourgeois opinions," writes Romantic critic August Wilhelm Schlegel, or go beyond "the legal measure," presenting "oddities" that are "not immediately in harmony with the moral sense, with appropriateness or custom," writes Ludwig Tieck. German writer Paul Heyse, meanwhile, compares the work of a novella writer with that of a chemist who "has to 'isolate' the effect of certain elements, their struggle for the final result," and thus deals with explosive material, showing which forces drive characters in borderline situations.[93] Kleist's work meets all of these criteria in exemplary fashion with a story that—according to the Dresden painter Dora Stock, whose home Kleist frequented—"no woman could read without blushing."[94] But enough of the preliminary warnings. The novella begins as follows: A respectable Marquise, widowed mother of two children, inserts an announcement in the newspapers looking for the father of her unborn child. She is pregnant and knows neither how she became so nor by whom. Even if one were a virtuous woman, who would not want to read on? Kleist's novella revolves around the difficulty of narrating a matter the characters cannot speak of—namely, that the Marquise was raped in the house of her father, the Commandant of the citadel at M— that was conquered by Russian troops. The leader of the attack, Count F—, first saves the Marquise from being raped by his soldiers, only to then succumb to his own desire when the rescued lady faints, which Kleist's narrator conceals with what is probably the most famous dash in world literature. The Count leaves the fortress without seeing the Marquise again. The latter, awakened from her fainting, continues to gratefully think of the unknown savior, who is now fighting in the distance and is wounded and thought to be dead. After several months, however, Count F— shows up at the Commandant's house again and—to the astonishment of the Marquise and her family—asks for her hand. The lady is unsuspecting, even though the Count gives himself away by revealing that he, in a feverish dream, had mistaken the Marquise for a swan at which he had once thrown excrement. The swan, however, had dived under the surface and re-emerged, washed clean by the water.

The dream of the swan has excited Freudians because it makes the latent—the Count's sexual drives—manifest, which is precisely what psychoanalysts hope for from dream narratives. It has equally delighted German scholars, who in light of the swan, recall Boccaccio's famous falcon novella. The novella tells the story of a poor knight who courts a highly reserved lady and is willing to sacrifice his last possession for her—his valuable falcon. Boccaccio's protagonists are seldom quite as noble and virtuous as this couple, but the falcon—the symbol or leitmotif organizing the conflict of the novella—has remained in the collective memory of German studies thanks to Paul Heyse's theory of the 'falcon.' Generations of German high school and college students have defined stories as novellas by looking for a central motif—a 'falcon'—though they may at times find nothing but what they themselves have projected onto the text. Be that as it may, in the case of *The Marquise of O—* it is easy to identify such a motif. But whether the solution—that the 'falcon' is the swan—will convince any ornithologist is questionable. Similarly, this method of determining the genre of a text is unsuitable if understood in terms of ontology. Genres have no essence; they are merely concepts of practical value and ought to be defined functionally. It would be senseless to use the category of genre to pigeonhole texts and neatly file them away. They should instead be understood as figures of control for the production and reception of texts. Not every novella requires a 'falcon' for the facilitation of readings sensitive to the tensions within the text.[95] Whether or not the Russian Count's dream of the swan proves to be a 'falcon' remains to be shown.

Kleist himself did not refer to his stories as novellas; at the time the term was hardly in use. He had intended to call the anthology—published by Reimer—*Moral Tales* (*Moralische Erzählungen*).[96] About his sources for *The Marquise of O—* one can only speculate.[97] One such source could be Cervantes' story "The Force of Blood," published in *Exemplary Novellas* of 1613, which is—trailing Boccaccio's *The Decameron*—the most influential collection of novellas in the European tradition. Unlike the *Bildungsroman*, the novella is not originally a German invention.

Cervantes' "The Force of Blood" tells the story of a cavalier named Rodolfo, who attacks the beautiful Leocadia, a sixteen-year-old girl, in Toledo. He blindfolds the unconscious woman who has fainted, carries her away to his house, rapes her and then releases her again. Leocadia retains two mementos of this incident—a silver crucifix that she secretly took from her rapist's chamber and a son named Luis, who seven years later is accidentally injured in a horse race and is found and cared for by Rodolfo's father. When Leocadia comes seeking her son, she finds him in the very chamber where she had been raped and presents Rodolfo's outraged parents with the crucifix as proof. They confront their lecherous son with his victim—and the miracle happens: The two fall in love at first sight (after all, Leocadia had not been able to see Rodolfo during the traumatic first encounter years earlier). It is an abstruse story whose happy ending is first brought about by divine providence—epitomized by the crucifix—and by the resemblance between Luis and Rodolfo, but ultimately by Leocadia's awareness of the identity and difference of the lover. Leocadia is capable of 'knowing' her husband in the biblical sense because he has apparently changed from rapist to lover.[98]

Kleist's Marquise has no crucifix to show, but she helps herself through a newspaper announcement, a hidden father puzzle, so to speak, in response to which Count F— comes forward and confesses. The two get married, but not out of love. The husband-to-be is no stranger, but he has proven himself deceptive and is unable to guarantee his conversion. Hence, the Marquise puts her husband to the test for one year. The second wedding is the result of a probationary period in which he had to prove whether the devil had indeed become an angel, the rapist a lover. Looking at it the other way around, one could surmise that the Marquise was just hiding her guilty conscience with the announcement and the probation year, and that she herself was merely misrepresenting herself all along, especially if one takes seriously a distich by Kleist which he published three months after the first print of his novella, in the April/May 1808 issue of *Phöbus*: "This novel is not for you, my daughter. In a faint! / A shameless farce! She merely kept—I know—her eyes closed."[99] What is Kleist's intention with this comment? Is he mocking virtuous readers of the *Phöbus* such as Dora Stock? Or does his distich turn the Marquise into an "inverted Virgin Mary," the "Madonna into a tramp," the "novella of a saint" into a "shameless farce" that relies "on the advertising effect of the pornographic"?[100] It is a mystery. Or perhaps not. Kleist's distich merely shares the Commandant's initial point of view, who does not want to hear anything about his daughter's alleged unknowing conception. He believes her behavior to be a masquerade and chases her out of the family's house with a pistol shot. Her mother takes the opposite stance; she considers her daughter credible and brings the Marquise back home from the country house to which she had retreated. It is back at home where father and daughter are reconciled. This clash of perspectives shows what Kleist is, once again, aiming for in this novella: the undermining of trust in times of crisis. The constellation of war, male violence, sexual aggression, and female innocence is familiar from *Amphitryon*. The Marquise could well be a sister of Alcmene if Kleist's distich did not play so shamelessly with her shamelessness. Kleist's comment fuels doubts about the Marquise, and so does the Count's likening her to a swan, which—according to *Zedler's Universal-Lexicon*—is an ambiguous creature, "a symbol of innocence and piety because, even in the midst of foul waters, it retains its whiteness," but also "of duplicity because it covers its black flesh with white feathers, and is thus different on the outside than inside."[101]

Through the distich and the image of the swan—that is, from both outside and inside the text—the reader is given instructions on how to read the novella: the Marquise might be, much like the Russian Count, an ambiguous figure, united in its difference. The Count is both an angel and a devil; and the Marquise may be an ambiguous figure of both innocence and deceit, like the swan. The respectable family of the Commandant does not come off any better if one looks at the scene of reconciliation between father and daughter at the story's end, which oscillates between tearful sentimentality and incestuous desire. The mother carefully approaches the Marquise's room; "and looking through the keyhole she noticed that her daughter was even sitting on the Commandant's lap, a thing he had never before permitted." The mother is delighted:

> And when finally she opened the door she saw a sight that made her heart leap with joy: her daughter, with her head thrown right back and her eyes tightly shut, was lying quietly in her father's arms, while the latter, with tears glistening in his wide-open eyes, sat in the armchair, pressing long, ardent, avid kisses on to her mouth, just like a lover! His daughter said nothing, he said nothing; he sat with his face bowed over her, as if she were the first girl he had ever loved; he sat there holding her mouth near his and kissing her. Her mother felt quite transported with delight; standing unseen behind his chair, she hesitated to interrupt this blissful scene of reconciliation which had brought such joy back to her house. Finally, she approached her husband, and just as he was again stroking and kissing his daughter's mouth in indescribable ecstasy, she leaned round the side of the chair and looked at him. When the Commandant saw her he at once lowered his eyes again with a cross expression and was about to say something; but she exclaimed: "Oh, what a face to make!" And then she in her turn smoothed it out with kisses, and talked jestingly until the atmosphere of emotion was dispelled. She asked them both to come and have dinner, and as she led the way they walked along like a pair of betrothed lovers; at table the Commandant seemed very happy, though he still sobbed from time to time, ate and spoke little, gazed down at his plate, and caressed his daughter's hand.[102]

The scandal of the novella thus lies in the indistinguishability of good and evil. This indistinguishability is the catalyst for both its action and its interpretation. The story would not advance very much if the Marquise did not idealize her savior into an angelic figure—and if her savior did not idealize the Marquise—and thus purge him of all sexuality before finally recognizing the hybrid nature of all earthly things. The readers of the novella feel the same as its protagonists. Ultimately, Kleist's ambiguous figures undermine any one-sided readings, and at the same time—as the state of indistinguishability is intolerable—set them in motion. Here are some of the more prominent readings Kleist scholars have given of the novella: Firstly, that the novella plays with the analogy of the Marquise and Virgin Mary, with the motif of the Virgin Birth and the Holy Family.[103] Secondly, that Kleist deals with the 18th-century discourse on femininity and that his mockery of the Marquise's reintegration—after she had emancipated herself for a short while by moving to the family's country house—into the bourgeois model of the nuclear family is ultimately unmistakable.[104] Thirdly, that the novella mirrors the territorial and physical rape of the Napoleonic Wars,[105] a claim recently substantiated by a psychoanalytic reading of rape as a means of total war.[106] And fourthly, it is said that the novella glorifies the "absolute feeling," forcing the true out of the false.[107] The scene of banishment is regarded as evidence of this older existentialist reading. After the Commandant learns that his daughter is pregnant and consequently banishes her from the house, sealed by a pistol shot into the ceiling—some Kleist scholars speak of a "leaden ejaculate"[108] due to the incestuous final scene—the Marquise is left to herself and thus gains new self-confidence: "This splendid effort of will gave her back her self-confidence, and as if with her own hands she raised herself right out of the depths into which fate had cast her."[109]

The existentialist reading of the novella is understandable in a generation of German scholars that had just come out of the totalitarianism of World War II, having painfully experienced the indifference of good and evil first hand and, by that point, wishing to put their faith only in skeptical individualism. This reading may come closest to Kleist's experience, who in 1795, after the battles in the Palatinate, wished that "the time that we are now murdering so immorally" could be atoned "with more humane endeavors,"[110] and who, based on his experiences in Paris, concluded about the intermingling of truth and deception: "What does it mean, in terms of results, to do evil? What is *evil*? *Absolute evil*? Myriad, connected and intertwined are the things of this world, every act is the mother of millions of others, and often the worst begets the best.—Tell me, who in this world has ever done something *evil*? Something evil *for Eternity*—?"[111]

CHAPTER IX

The Laurels and the Torch

Kleist in Dresden and Prague, 1807–1809

Phöbus Project (Dresden)

At the end of August 1807, when Kleist arrived in Dresden, which had always been his favorite city, from French-occupied Berlin, he may have felt—as he had before in Switzerland—as though he was entering on a new life. He found peace in 'Florence on the Elbe,' where public life was more or less unrestricted, as Saxony belonged to the Confederation of the Rhine and was therefore not subject to direct control by the French. Dresden was a cultural capital that seemed to favor all of Kleist's expectations for his breakthrough as a writer. He was once again surrounded by friends, old ones like Rühle von Lilienstern and Ernst von Pfuel—both of whom were tutors of Prince Bernhard of Saxony-Weimar after their departure from Prussian military service—and new ones like the conservative Romantic philosopher and state and economic theorist Adam Müller, son of a Prussian tax official. Müller was two years younger than Kleist and, in 1804, published a philosophical work well suited to Kleist's polar thinking, *The Doctrine of Opposites*. "Now I live in Dresden, as the most favorable place in this, for art, highly unfavorable time, to carry out some plans that I have made."[1] Thus Kleist rejoices in a letter to Baron von Stein zum Altenstein. As always his plans are big: He dreams of a "position as a director at the theater in Vienna,"[2] wants to found a publishing house as well as a journal for the arts, and be successful as a playwright. He lived in Dresden for one and a half years until the end of April 1809, first at the Hotel de Russie, then in an apartment in Pirna Suburb, at 123 Rampische Gasse. Rühle got him the apartment; he lived on the same street. Later on Kleist would be joined by another, albeit fictional, neighbor: Michael Kohlhaas takes up quarters in Pirna Suburb. Most likely in March 1809, Kleist moved to Dresden's city center, to "Willsche Gasse, Löwen-Apotheke, four steps up."[3]

In Dresden Kleist lived entirely for his literature; he wrote and wrote and yet never stopped fighting, neither in his works nor in his life. What kept him occupied during his time in Dresden were his war of words with Johann Wolfgang Goethe, the battle of the sexes he envisioned in *Penthesilea*, and the patriotic war he hoped for fueled by Austria's military resistance to Napoleon. With Kleist leisure and the Muse never formed a happy union, not even in

© WILHELM FINK VERLAG, 2021 | DOI:10.30965/9783846765746_010

Fig. 41
Johann Jakob Otto August Rühle von Lilienstern (1780–1847)

peaceful Dresden. On the outside he may have been quiet, but on the inside all the conflicts of his time raged on, and he began to test the political power of his literature. His agonistic nature rendered him tremendously productive. Thomas Mann admired him for his "robustness": "In a single year, 1808, after the ecstatic labors of the *Penthesilea*, he wrote not only the overly sweet *Käthchen von Heilbronn*, but also the entire, savage *Battle of Arminius* and four of his most powerful stories, including the magnificent *Michael Kohlhaas*. Is this not vitality?"[4]

In the beginning everything seemed to be going quite smoothly. Full of optimism and self-confidence, Kleist wrote several letters to Ulrike in September and October 1807. His letters, of course, pertained to her money, which he wanted to invest wisely in a new project he and his friends were pursuing: "I must try to persuade you to invest 500 Reichsthaler at 5 percent in a new corporation for books, maps and works of art, whereof the license patent must be purchased. Adam Müller (a young scholar who gives public lectures here in the winter that are met with great applause), Rühle, and Pfuel (whose brother gives him the money to do so) are the interested parties. To recount the reasons why our enterprise is so opportune and auspicious would not be possible *in writing*." Kleist's withholding of further details from Ulrike served his penchant for mystification—which his sister was used to—when one sentence would have been enough to justify his enterprise: He was looking for a sure landing for the publication of his work and wanted to double his profits, as author and publisher. The opportunity seemed favorable in a city where the book trade was flourishing. It was Kleist's goal to lure his sister to Dresden for the time being, to prove to her how much he was accepted there: "But as I said already—I cannot tell you what is in my heart, you must be present to see our position and judge how truly favorable it is."[5] Ulrike, however, did not move to Dresden as Kleist had hoped. And she did not become a shareholder in the planned publishing house, even though Kleist tried to win her over by mentioning how well connected he was. In his letter he tells her of a Prussian noble family with Polish estates—the von Haza family, which had been residing in Dresden since 1805 and in whose house Kleist's *Amphitryon* had been read at a private gathering. Müller lived in this house, as a private tutor and lover of the lady of the house, Sophie von Haza—a mother of five children, whose husband Peter von Haza grew tired of his wife's affair and, in November 1807, filed for divorce. A year later the divorce was finalized; and in 1809 Sophie von Haza became Sophie Müller. The fact that his former patron von Haza dismissed him—with good reason—in November 1807 only furthered Müller's career. Opportunists like him know how to make a profit even from being disloyal. Thanks to the mediation of Rühle, who knew Müller from the latter's Dresden lectures on dramatic art in the winter of 1806/07, Müller began teaching the young Prince Bernhard in political economy. The Prince's father, Duke Carl August, was so enthusiastic about Müller's teaching that in August 1808 he awarded him the honorary title of privy councilor.

The house of Friedrich Schiller's friend Christian Gottfried Körner was a vibrant place as well, at least for the visitor Kleist, thanks to Körner's foster-daughter Julie Kunze—a possible inspiration for Kleist's Katie of Heilbronn—and his sister-in-law Dora Stock. The latter was a pastel painter, an acquaintance of Goethe, and an easily ruffled critic of Kleist's scandalous texts, such as *The Marquise of O—* and *Penthesilea*. She is said to have successfully disrupted a love affair between Kleist and Julie and to have therefore been caricatured by Kleist as Kunigunde in *Katie of Heilbronn*.[6] Meanwhile, it seems Kleist enjoyed the undivided sympathy of Joseph von Buol, minister of the Austrian legation in Dresden, whose house Kleist also frequented. Von Buol helped place Kleist's plays on Viennese stages and gave him a wonderful gift for his 30th birthday on October 10, 1807. Kleist was "crowned with a laurel wreath" at his table, presumably by Julie—"by the most darling pair of hands in Dresden. I have kept the wreath."[7]

But Kleist's coronation should not be taken too seriously. It was nothing more than a parlor game, as the time of officially crowned writers was long gone. In the 16th and 17th centuries, writers had still been decorated by

Fig. 42
Adam Heinrich Müller (1779–1829)

emperors, princes, or academic institutions with the title of *poeta laureatus*. By the 18th century this practice was already considered obsolete, especially since the honorary title had often been awarded arbitrarily and revealed little about the actual literary talent of the person awarded it. Kleist, however, would have needed and deserved every expression of praise he could have gotten, especially in the fall and winter of 1807, for it was then that he completed his masterpiece *Penthesilea*, whose main character's fate did not leave his friends in Dresden untouched. Kleist notes that, during readings in the literary salons, "tears were shed, in so far as the horror, which is unavoidable, allowed," and that the play "seems less made for women than men." At least Pfuel seems to have liked it: "When I came from my room, pipe in hand, and told him, 'Now she is dead,' two huge tears filled his eyes."[8]

Kleist's play about the Amazon queen would have hardly become a best-seller in the publishing house he was planning. But he had other titles in stock and demanded that Cotta in Tübingen return his "Jerónimo and Josefa," though in vain, as the novella had already been published in the *Morning Paper for Educated Classes*. *The Broken Jug* would have likely sold quite well. Kleist also hoped to serve as the Dresden distribution agent for all French government publications, including the French civil code, *Code Napoléon*, though he warned his sister against "prematurely draw[ing] political inferences from this step."[9] Could Kleist have been opportunistic enough to do business with the enemy? Or would publishing the French civil code have been a clever attempt to disguise the patriotic activities the friends had planned, presenting themselves as pro-French so as to not upset the Saxon government?[10] In any event, the Dresden publishing house did not become a reality, as the clique of established booksellers in Dresden seemed to fear the competition. In January 1808 the already established booksellers—George Friedrich Walther, Christian Gottlob Hilscher, Heinrich Gerlach, August Wagner, and Christoph Arnold—wrote an expert judgment aimed at denying Müller (who took care of the legal formalities for the friends) a publishing license, claiming he lacked "the practical knowledge of the highly comprehensive merchant." The "publishing house of the scholar is always going to be more like a hobby that costs more than it brings in," since it is inspired more by the "fondness" for science and art than "by the mercantile spirit, *without which no action can stand.*" It would be "entirely a mystical publishing house, even if it were composed of scholars from all subjects, and would soon produce in its bodies the disease which in the state is called anarchy."[11] With this argument the five philistine booksellers cunningly blended political and economic biases. Arnold, at least, must have had mixed feelings about the matter. He had, after all, successfully published Kleist's *Amphitryon* following Müller's recommendation in the spring of 1807. Not only did Arnold commission a foreword from Müller, but he also profited from his enthusiasm for Kleist. Müller promoted *Amphitryon* in the Dresden salons, recommended the play to his Prague friend—the political writer and great opposer of Napoleon, Friedrich Gentz—and sent its manuscript to Goethe, as he later did with *The Broken Jug*. Whether Müller's promotion of *Amphitryon* furthered the understanding of the play is doubtful, given his Christian interpretation, having converted to Catholicism in 1805. It is, he notes, "just as much about the immaculate conception of the Holy Virgin as it is about the mystery of love in general."[12] And he assessed Kleist's *The Marquise of O—* in the same way.[13]

On February 22, 1808, Müller's request for a license to open a publishing house was finally rejected. The applicants had waited half a year but made the best use of their time. Kleist completed his *Penthesilea* and eagerly attended Gotthilf Heinrich Schubert's lectures concerning *Views from the Night-side of Natural Science* (*Ansichten von der Nachtseite der Naturwissenschaft*), which shaped his portrayal of both Katie's and Prince of Homburg's somnambulism.[14] At least by mid-December 1807, Kleist—together with Müller and the painter Christian Ferdinand Hartmann, who later became director of the Dresden Academy of Fine Arts—began working on a parallel project to the publishing house: *Phöbus. Journal for the Arts* (*Phöbus. Ein Journal für die Kunst*), the first issue of which appeared on January 23, 1808. The journal's name, Hartmann's cover illustration, Kleist's poetic prologue in the first issue, and Müller's accompanying letters to his friends are prime examples of what literary scholarship

Fig. 43 Frontispiece of Kleist's journal *Phöbus* (copper engraving by Johann Christian Benjamin Gottschick after a drawing by Ferdinand Hartmann)

today calls 'paratexts'—figures of control for steering the readers' expectations in the desired direction.[15]

Phoebus is one of the many epithets of the Greek god Apollo, which identifies him as the god of pure light, the god of sun. At the same time he is regarded as the guarantor of moral order, of measure, as the god of prophecy, of inspiration, of the arts, and as the leader of the Muses. Lyre and bow are the instruments proper to him; he masters both the splendid song and the unerring arrow that avenges and kills. In any case, the etymology of the name Apollo encompasses both prophecy and destruction. Due to his combative strength, Apollo is also suitable as a tutelary god, placed in front of one's house as a gatekeeper. Published by Kleist and Müller in defense of their fatherland and their own contributions to the literature of the Romantic school, *Phöbus* is a rather immodest but by no means bad name for a monthly journal with a hidden political and aesthetic agenda. What is puzzling is the singular 'Art' in the journal's German subtitle—*A Journal for the Art*—given the distinct disciplinary responsibilities of the three editors. Müller writes: "I oversee philosophy and criticism, Kleist poetry, and Hartmann the fine arts." Yet at the same time, they want to make sure to see the one "spirit" they speak of "expressed in quite diverse forms."[16] We can thus see the relationship between the frontispiece and the programmatic prologue of the first issue as the initial test site of this 'unity in difference.'

Designed by Hartmann, the frontispiece features Apollo as a light bearer rising over Dresden, casually directing four horses in a symmetrical motion. He is accompanied by three *Horae* and their winged *genii* in the midst of a zodiac wheel that shows five of the twelve zodiac signs between the rays of the sun. The Libra—Kleist's sign of the zodiac—is in the center and thus occupies the highest position; to the lower left of it is the Virgo—Goethe's sign—and to the lower right of it is the Scorpio—Schiller's sign. This arrangement may or may not have been intentional. At any rate, it is a known fact that Hartmann's drawing was not originally intended for *Phöbus*, but as a sketch for a curtain at the Royal Saxon Court Theater.[17] The initial impulse for *Phöbus* also owed itself to Hartmann,[18] as it was through the interpretation of his image that Kleist and Müller articulated an agenda for *Phöbus*. They did so before the first issue had even appeared, namely in announcements in the Jena *Journal of General Literature* (*Allgemeine Literatur-Zeitung*) of December 26, 1807, and the Berlin *Spener's Newspaper* (*Spenersche Zeitung*) of January 9, 1808, which stated:

> We portray the god whose image and name shields our publication not in a state of calm, amidst the Muses, on Mount Parnassus, but rather as he steers the sun-horses in confident clarity. To represent art through the efforts of a rather large number of like-minded Germans, no matter how different in constitution, is more appropriate to our nation's character than if we were to gather the artists and art critics of our time in uniform symmetry and quiet possession around some summit of beauty no matter how magnificent.—Under the patronage of the god passing by, we commence a race; everyone goes as far as possible and remains unsurpassable, for no one ever reaches the goal completely, but each may ignite new passions for the sublime struggle, forever onward.
>
> We ourselves cannot conceive of a more honorable place for our works than side by side with those of others equally unique and rigorous; opinions and works can very well compete with each other without canceling each other out. But

> since we ourselves are armed, we shall suffer no unarmed or even lightly armed antagonist to confront us in the arena we are hereby opening. Great authors whose fame is long established will be among us; others will follow them, as iron attracts man, once they recognize the spirit of this endeavor in its permanence.[19]

The end of the announcement provides everything else potential subscribers might need to know: The journal is to appear once a month, around the 20th. It will be printed in quarto format, at the cost of ten Reichsthaler, and is to be delivered by mail. Müller and Kleist promise the participation of great authors rather lightly. The language they use to promote the journal is haughty in every respect and strikingly military in nature. There is talk of a "race" between the best armed opponents, of a "sublime struggle" between "artists and art critics," and that "everyone goes as far as possible and remains unsurpassable." Here, Apollo is not a center of calm amidst the Muses; he does not serve a Neoclassical aesthetic that finds its ideal in "uniform symmetry," that gathers the arts "around some summit of beauty no matter how magnificent." These are the terms with which Kleist and Müller interpret Hartmann's drawing upon announcing their journal's first issue. Anyone who looks at the actual frontispiece of the first issue and compares it with the interpretation of the two editors will be surprised by Hartmann's perfectly symmetrical arrangement of Apollo, quadriga, *Hora*, and *genii*. Apollo may be steering the sun-horses dynamically, but the composition of the image fully obeys the integrated Neoclassical ideal of beauty, placing the head of Eirene—the allegory of peace—at its center. Kleist and Müller ignore this harmonious reconciliation of opposites and instead promote a decidedly agonistic, open aesthetics. Consequently, there is not much to the promised unity of the different artistic genres: The illustrations of *Phöbus* by Ferdinand Hartmann, Gerhard von Kügelgen, and other artists follow the ideal of Neoclassical uniformity, while the literary works that Kleist oversees as editor severely violate this artistic ideal. This violation is proven not only by the excerpts from Kleist's *Penthesilea* printed in the journal's first issue, but also by the opening prologue, consisting of a poem by Kleist, which, in its five distichs, offers yet another reading of Hartmann's frontispiece:

> Prologue
>
> Thunder onward, O you, on with your fire-limbed horses,
> Phoebus, bringer of day, onward through infinite space!
> Give yourself to the Hours! Look not beside you, nor back,
> Forward turning your gaze, to where the squadron is stirring!
> Thunder, with no regard, roaring across the fair lands,
> Heedless on whom you arise, whom you will set on at dusk,

Here now steer, and now there, letting your fist be the guide,
'Tis your power, your force, wielded in playful delight.
Strike, and you will not miss, it is the dance round the world,
And from the tower above, watches a scout for the measure.[20]

The hero of Kleist's prologue—a thunderous Jupiter or a dancing Dionysus—has little in common with Hartmann's Phoebus, a calm and measured Apollo. He is characterized by a creative force that, unrestrained by morality, transcends all boundaries, aiming toward the indeterminate, the future, infinity—a creative force that lies beyond good and evil. It is an expression of the arbitrary, of a power "wielded in playful delight" with ever-changing direction, a "dance round the world" not given a measure, but whose measure has to be as yet determined by a "scout" observing the dance below "from the tower above." The aesthetics of production that Kleist envisions in his prologue is not all that sensational. It corresponds perfectly to Kant's definition of genius, which Kant declares in §46 of his *Critique of the Power of Judgment* as "the talent (natural gift) that gives the rule to art," though the genius "does not know himself how the ideas for [his product] come to him, and also does not have it in his power to think up such things at will or according to plan, and to communicate to others precepts that would put them in a position to produce similar products." The rule cannot, Kant notes in §47, "be couched in a formula to serve as a precept, for then the judgment about the beautiful would be determinable in accordance with concepts; rather, the rule must be abstracted from the deed, i.e. from the product."[21] According to Kant, only those who are recognized as a genius by others can be called a genius. This kind of recognition is what Kleist hopes to achieve with the publication of his works in *Phöbus*. The contemporary 'scouts,' however, do not recognize in them the new rule, the "measure," because they are committed to the ideals of harmony and morality of Weimar Classicism. Only the 'scouts' of later generations succeed in recognizing Kleist's genius, as they discover—in his unconventionally open aesthetics and epistemology—the "measure" of Modernist literature.

For Hartmann's visual art, beauty is something that can be objectified; it is founded in regularity and in the unity of the manifold. For Kleist's prologue as for his poetry, however, beauty lies in the unity of opposites and in irregularity—and ultimately, in the eye of the beholder. His aesthetics thus correspond to Müller's "Lectures on Beauty" ("Vorlesungen über das Schöne") held in winter 1807/08, five of which he published in *Phöbus*. In these lectures Müller distinguishes between "*social* beauty" and "*individual* beauty. "*Social* beauty" is that of the beautiful regularity of Classical art or that of Weimar Classicism. According to Müller, "in everyday life" we "often prematurely" call "*individual* beauty ugly." The "true human being" lets himself be "inflamed by that *social* beauty, but only to rekindle all the *individual*, hidden beauty of life, to shine through the dark barks that may cover it and through all the external enchantments of prejudice."[22] There is hence a hidden connection between the inherently contradictory nature of the visual arts and literature featured in *Phöbus*: The copper engravings obey a conception of beauty familiar to contemporary readers; they are the lure intended to seduce the reader into that which is completely different—"into the wide range of individual beauties of life unfolded in the literary texts of the journal," into the "infinite space" of the "individual beauties of life as a whole," in which the reader, "unaffected by the accusations of ugliness," is able to recognize their "measure" after all. Thus notes German scholar Ernst Osterkamp in his brilliant reading of the correspondence between visual arts, literature, and art criticism in *Phöbus*.[23]

As we know, this project did not succeed. The contemporary readers stuck to their prejudices and did not allow themselves to be seduced away from the social beauty of Weimar Classicism to the individual beauty of Kleist's works. Müller and Kleist must have anticipated the failure of their project insofar as they chose not to rely solely on the deceptive allure of the copper engravings, but also tried to oblige the heroes of Weimar Classicism—Goethe and Christoph Martin Wieland—in advance to contribute to their journal. On December 17, 1807, Müller asks Goethe for a "small contribution, or at least permission to write [his] name as a guardian at the beginning" of a journal based on the model of *The Horae*.[24] That same day Kleist writes a letter to Wieland asking whether he could, "in those remaining years that you are still on Earth and not yet in the stars, [...] spare an essay for my *Phöbus*," reminding Wieland of his hymnal response to *Robert Guiscard*.[25] Wieland did not answer him. He was likely uninterested in being associated with Romantics like Müller, whom he later called a "philosophical punchinello" and a "charlatan," a buffoon—more precisely, upon reading Müller's conception of beauty in the March issue of *Phöbus*, which Wieland condemned in its entirety: "I have hardly ever read a droller mishmash of the true and the absurd; only that everything *true* in it is common and has long since been said, whereas everything *new* in it is full of bursting bubbles, will-o'-the-wisps, and wind! wind! wind!"[26] The March issue also contained excerpts of *The Broken Jug*, but Wieland did not comment on these. He had obviously no intention of denouncing Kleist by name. In a letter to German classicist Heinrich Karl Abraham Eichstädt of February 1, 1808, Goethe had already mocked the fact that Müller would "probably exhaust the whole supply of his occupation to feed the sun-horses." And in a letter to Kleist in the same mail, he thanked him for sending the January issue of *Phöbus*, only to confess that he had "as yet been unable to warm" up to Penthesilea, who was "of so singular a race" and inhabited "so alien a region." It just troubled him to see "a young man of talent and spirit awaiting some theater yet to come."[27] In May 1808 he wrote to his friend Karl Ludwig von Knebel: "I broke with the Dresdeners at once. For though I hold Adam Müller in high esteem, and though von Kleist is no common talent, I recognized only too soon that their *Phöbus* would turn into a kind of *phébus* [bombast]; and it is a tried and tested saying, which one simply does not recall often enough: the first ingratitude is better than the last."[28]

Neither Goethe nor Wieland, nor—as also requested and hoped for—Jean Paul, Ludwig Tieck, Friedrich Schlegel, or Friedrich Schleiermacher ever provided Kleist and Müller with contributions for *Phöbus*. The press campaign announcing famous names before the publication of the journal's first issue came to nothing. Even old friends of Kleist were displeased. Karl August Varnhagen scourged Müller's "boastful manner," calling his "insistence on Goethe" simply "disgraceful."[29] The whole thing was essentially a scam—a deception to the subscribers, who were promised authors who had never agreed to contribute. This fact was damaging to *Phöbus* from the very beginning. It did not matter, then, that Kleist and Müller sent a deluxe edition of the January issue to the Austrian emperor and to the King in Westphalia, Napoleon's brother Jérôme. The print run was small and remained small, and the length of the issues was modest, averaging around fifty pages. In a letter to Ulrike of January 5, 1808, Kleist calculated that Schiller's *Horae* sold 3,000 copies and that, "at the time of its release," one could have "hardly" been "more interested in it than in *Phöbus*."[30] This assertion was a complete miscalculation. Kleist was no Schiller: The initial print run of the *Horae* was 2,300 copies in 1795, and it dropped to fewer than 1,000 copies toward the end of 1797. We do not know the initial print run of *Phöbus*, but Karl August Böttiger—also one of those initially courted by the editors as a contributor and certainly no friend of the journal—stated that the number of copies printed from the seventh issue onwards was only 150.[31] Müller and Kleist thus ran into double the trouble. They lacked both funding and contributors, so that they—as Goethe had foreseen—had to supply the journal mainly with their own material, with Müller's art criticism and Kleist's literature. They had intended the journal to publish their own material anyway, but now it was more obvious than originally planned. The contributions by Friedrich de la Motte-Fouqué, Novalis, Gotthilf Heinrich Schubert, and Karl Friedrich Gottlob Wentzel were quantitatively and qualitatively without weight. Issue 1 of *Phöbus* contained a "Prologue" and "Epilogue" from Kleist's pen as well as an excerpt from *Penthesilea* and his poem "The Angel at the Tomb of Our Lord" ("Der Engel am Grabe des Herrn"); issue 2 his novella *The Marquise of O—* and a fable adapted from Jean de La

Fontaine, entitled "The Two Pigeons" ("Die beiden Tauben"). Issue 3 featured excerpts from *The Broken Jug* as well as two fables by Kleist, "The Dogs and the Bird" and "Fable without a Moral"; the double issue 4/5 the *Robert Guiscard* fragment, excerpts from *Katie of Heilbronn*, as well as "Epigrams," in which Kleist mocks his critics. Issue 6, published in mid-November 1808, contained an excerpt from *Michael Kohlhaas* as well as further "Epigrams" and, for reasons of cost, now appeared without Hartmann's frontispiece. From issue 7 onwards the Dresden bookseller Walther took over the publication of *Phöbus*. Prior to that Kleist and Müller had negotiated in vain with Göschen and Cotta to cover their expenses. Issue 8 contained no contribution by Kleist; the double issue 9/10, published in early 1809, featured a second excerpt from *Katie of Heilbronn* as well as the occasional poems "The Higher Peace," "A Young Man's Lament" ("Jünglingsklage"), "Girl's Riddle" ("Mädchenräthsel"), "Catherine of France" ("Katharina von Frankreich"), and "To S.v.H." ("An S.v.H."). The double issue 11/12 was published at the end of February, beginning of March 1809 and contained Kleist's verse idyll "A Fright in the Bath" ("Der Schrecken im Bade").

In view of the financial troubles with *Phöbus*, Kleist imploringly admitted to Rühle, the co-financier, as early as the beginning of May 1808: "We must therefore be willing to make *whatever* sacrifice is necessary. Because the capital that we put into the journal would be lost if it was discontinued [...]. Yes, in order to avoid a scandal, if we were to be granted a credit, we have to be willing to take additional risk."[32] After a little over a year, *Phöbus* was no longer. Müller made major financial concessions in his contract with Walther, without Kleist's knowledge, leading to a quarrel between the two friends, as an angry letter from Kleist of April 5, 1809, attests: If Walther intended to continue publishing *Phöbus*, then he, Kleist, would either resign "from his editorial position" or "look for a co-editor other than Privy Councilor Müller."[33] Apparently, doing so was not an option anyway. That same day Müller wrote to Rühle and Pfuel that he had, "from the very beginning, been responsible for the enterprise of *Phöbus*, the entire business dealings that had occurred in the process, including all the inconveniences," and that, consequently, he had to be the one to save *Phöbus* from debt and sell it. Kleist's thanks for this initiative were "insults of the meanest kind." He had said "things to [his] face" which Müller could "answer only with weapons." In the event that he was "the survivor," he would continue *Phöbus*.[34] Pfuel and Rühle must have prevented the friends' duel, but they were not able to save *Phöbus*. According to Ludwig Tieck's account, who met Kleist and Müller in the summer of 1808 in Dresden, the relationship between the two editors may have been strained for other than purely financial reasons. Tieck found Müller "haughty, catholicizing," and was supposedly "repulsed" by him, whereas he recognized Kleist's literary talent and admired him for his productivity, even though he was so "painstakingly anxious about his works." According to Tieck, Kleist "frequently changed and reworked his writing. He was the hardest to satisfy himself." Tieck's doubt over Kleist's mental stability can be seen in his descriptions of Kleist's obsessions—for instance, "that Kleist seriously tried to push Adam Müller off the Elbe Bridge, as he persuaded himself he was madly in love with the latter's wife and could not live without her." Moreover, it was "hard" on Tieck, the cat lover, that Kleist, who "hated cats," in *The Schroffenstein Family* "had a cat nibble on a jar of preserved pineapple to bring about the catastrophe."[35] It was certainly not easy to be friends with Kleist, even for an opportunist like Müller, who in March 1808, shortly after launching the *Phöbus* project, secretly asked Baron von Müffling for a position as professor in Jena. His involvement in editing *Phöbus*, Müller claims, was "only of secondary importance and subordinate anyway." Dresden was an "element for people like [Karl August] Böttiger, but not for [him]." He finally requested "that [his] intentions, regardless of whether he was offered a position or not, be kept secret for the time being, that is, be withheld particularly from Rühle and [Müller's] local friends, who may consider a betrayal of friendship what a necessary concern for his future and his circumstances forced [him] to do."[36]

What then remains of *Phöbus*? If it were not for the journal, we would have no knowledge of the *Guiscard* or Kleist's poems, no knowledge of the early stages of major works, such as *Penthesilea* or *Michael Kohlhaas*. Moreover, Müller's aesthetic writings and Kleist's literature demonstrate the frontlines of the literary field of the time. The art journal had an agonistic and operative character. Literary and political feuds were fought, overt wars of words against Weimar Classicism and covert ones against the French occupation. In the announcements of December 1807, the editors claimed that *Phöbus* was solely an "art journal," explicitly "excluding the practical arts of government and all criticism of current events"[37]—but this claim was merely camouflage, of course. The poem "The Angel at the Tomb of Our Lord" from the first issue shows particularly well how subtly Kleist disguised political allusions in his poetry. The poem comments on a drawing after a painting by Ferdinand Hartmann; the drawing was included in the journal and bore the title *The Three Marys at the Tomb of Our Lord* (*Die drei Marien am Grabe*):

THE ANGEL AT THE TOMB OF OUR LORD

When calm and cold, with seven fatal wounds,
Our Lord was lying in His tomb; the tomb,
As though it were to bind ten breathing giants,
Into a rocky cleft was hewn with blows;

And with the strength of many men was rolled
A sandstone, deaf to bribes, to shut its door;
Around it had the bailiff's seal been set:
A thought itself could not have slipped away,
Escaped unnoticed from the darkened cave;
And yet, as if it were a thing to fear
That granite block itself was to convert,
A band of guards marched up and down the way,
And gazed upon the image on the seal:
Then, by the early morning's ray, there came,
With everlasting faith, three Marys to the tomb,
To see if Jesus was still lying there:
For He Himself had promised to His friends
That He would rise again the third day's morn.
And now as they approached His woeful grave:
What did the faithful women apprehend?
The guards, who kept their watch upon the place,
Collapsed there lay, their faces in the dust,
Like dead, spread out around the fearful rock;
The stone was rolled far from the entryway;
And on its edge there sat, his pair of wings aquiver,
An angel, swift as lightning he appeared,
His garment was as white as driven snow.
Upon this scene they fell, like dead, themselves,
Onto the ground were struck and felt like dust,
And thought they'd soon be vanishing in glory:
But he, the cherub, said: "Be not afraid!
I know that you seek Jesus, the crucified—
But He's not here, has risen from the dead:
Come here, behold the vacant place inside."
And he, as they beheld the empty tomb,
With hands upraised and at a loss for speech,
Declared to them with mild and noble words:
"Now go and tell the followers He's chosen,
So they go forth and teach to all the nations,
And do as He has done," and disappeared.[38]

Kleist's poem obviously comes across as religious poetry in its dealing with a biblical subject: the resurrection of Christ. Hartmann's painting follows the Gospels of Mark and Luke. The women go to Christ's tomb with anointing vessels in their hands for the body. In Kleist's poem, however, there is no mention of this intention. Instead, the women go to the grave to verify that Christ has risen from the dead, confident that he would keep his promise. For Kleist scholar Klaus Müller-Salget, this deviation from the Gospels is a first indication that the supposedly religious poem should be read as a "disguised political

Fig. 44 *The Three Marys at the Tomb of Our Lord* (copper engraving by Johann Christian Benjamin Gottschick after a painting by Ferdinand Hartmann)

text"—a poem not about faith in the resurrection of Christ, but in the resurrection of Germany. Compared with the Gospels, Kleist exaggerates the protective precautions and thus the fear of the guards at the Lord's tomb. In the Gospels the high priests and Pharisees seal the stone of the tomb; in Kleist's case it is Pontius Pilate himself—who, unlike in the Gospels, is not referred to as "governor" but as "bailiff." With this change Kleist alludes—unmistakably for his contemporaries—to Schiller's *William Tell*, or more precisely, to the bailiff Albrecht Gessler, against whom the freedom fighter rebelled. At the end of the poem, the angel calls upon the three women to proclaim Christ's resurrection to his disciples so that they "do as He has done," that is, follow him in the resurrection (of which there is no biblical mention). According to Müller-Salget, the poem has a political subtext, with parallels easy to draw for the contemporary reader: "Christ, who died and is so carefully guarded, stands for conquered Germany; the bailiff represents Napoleon or his governor; the 'everlasting faith' of the three Marys evokes the unwavering confidence of the Germans; and Kleist's hope and appeal are directed toward a 'resurrection' of Germany, more precisely: of 'Germania and Her Children.'"[39]

Kleist was by no means one of the great German poets. He was neither at home with the genre of poetry nor with the form of self-expression that is constitutive of it. His were not poems of personal experience (*Erlebnislyrik*), but political poetry, occasional poems, and polemical epigrams. The latter dominate the double issue 4/5 and issue 6 of *Phöbus*. They reveal a writer both hurt and hurtful, angry at Goethe, the director of the Weimar Court Theater, for thwarting the production of *The Broken Jug* and for condemning a literature that exceeded his powers of comprehension. It was, of course, no coincidence that Kleist chose the form of the polemical epigram to give expression to his struggle with Goethe. He wanted to defeat Goethe with his own weapons, for the epigrams Goethe co-wrote with Schiller—published in Schiller's *Muses' Almanac of 1797* (*Musenalmanach auf das Jahr 1797*) under the title *Xenions*—too, were attacks aimed against the literary establishment of the time and its representatives, namely Friedrich Nicolai, Christoph Martin Wieland, and the brothers Friedrich Leopold and Christian zu Stolberg-Stolberg. But before paying tribute to Kleist's sharp-tongued epigrams, let us first turn to the facts. What was it that drove Kleist into conflict with Goethe?[40]

In July 1807 Adam Müller sent Goethe *Amphitryon* along with a copy of *The Broken Jug*. Goethe had already read *Amphitryon* thanks to a recommendation from Mr. von Mohrenheim, secretary of the Russian legation in Karlsbad. Goethe was puzzled by the comedy, "the strangest sign of the times," concluding that Plautus aimed "at the discord of the senses," Molière at the "difference between husband and lover," and Kleist at the "confusion of emotions." He found the "situation of Alcmene embarrassing and that of Amphitryon ultimately cruel."[41] In his reply to Müller at the end of August 1807, Goethe subtly rebuked Kleist's *Amphitryon* and criticized *The Broken Jug* as a play belonging to the "invisible theater," with its analytical unfolding of a past event. He recommended that the author "solve a truly dramatic exercise and let an action unfold before our eyes and senses." At the same time, however, he praised "the extraordinary merits" of Kleist's comedy and promised to make the "attempt of a performance" in Weimar, especially since the theater company there had "a perfectly suitable actor" for Judge Adam.[42] This prospect may have encouraged Kleist to see in Goethe an ally willing to contribute to *Phöbus*. On January 24 Kleist sent Goethe the first issue containing excerpts from his *Penthesilea*, hoping for mercy and grace from the Olympian despite the latter's radically different notion of Classical Antiquity. This intention explains Kleist's peculiar devotional formula: "I present it to you 'on the knees of my heart.'"[43] This is a quotation from the penitential prayer of King Manasseh of Judah, an apocryphal text included in the Old Testament of Luther's German translation of the Bible. The English translation in the 1611 King James Version reads as follows:

> Now therefore I bow the knee of mine heart, beseeching thee of grace.
> I have sinned, O Lord, I have sinned, and I acknowledge mine iniquities: wherefore, I humbly beseech thee, forgive me, O Lord, forgive me, and destroy me not with mine iniquities. Be not angry with me for ever, by reserving evil for me; neither condemn me to the lower parts of the earth.
> For thou art the God, even the God of them that repent; and in me thou wilt shew all thy goodness: for thou wilt save me, that am unworthy, according to thy great mercy. Therefore I will praise thee for ever all the days of my life: for all the powers of the heavens do praise thee, and thine is the glory for ever and ever. Amen.[44]

Unlike Manasseh, Kleist was not heard by the Almighty, as Goethe's harsh answer and his rejection of *Penthesilea* in the aforementioned letter to Kleist of February 1, 1807, testifies. Nevertheless, Kleist might not have stopped praising and glorifying Goethe if the Weimar staging of *The Broken Jug* had not failed so thoroughly.

The comedy premiered on March 2, 1808, at the Weimar Court Theater. Goethe divided the play into three acts with intermissions, which merely highlighted the lack of action for which he himself had criticized the play. By the time *The Broken Jug* began, the audience had already sat through a musical prelude: Domenico Della Maria's comic opera *The Prisoner*. At the end of almost four hours of theater, long after Adam's crime had been solved, the actress playing Eve had yet to deliver her lengthy justifications to District Magistrate Walter, straining the nerves of the audience. She did so for the first and last time, as the performance was not repeated. Friedrich Wilhelm Riemer—tutor of Goethe's son August and later Goethe's literary assistant—noted laconically that the audience "liked [the play] at first, then [got] bored, and finally [it was] drummed out by a few, while others clapped at its end."[45] Other eyewitnesses judged with less restraint, reporting of a "genuine pandemonium at the theater," with the audience expressing its displeasure "in a demonstrative manner, by whistling, hissing, etc."[46] The Grand Duke Karl August wrote to Goethe that the "Kleist of the broken jar [sic!]" had "*amused* himself on his own, without having the slightest idea how other people [would] feel about it."[47] The newspapers attacked Kleist; not the director Goethe, not the actors. They relished in describing a theater scandal in which "the thread of patience of an otherwise *very patient* audience finally snapped, and toward the end there was such a noise that nobody was able to understand a single syllable of the endless dialogues."[48] It is no wonder, then, that Kleist—who had not attended the performance in person—was incensed "when he learned that the play had failed so badly. He wanted to challenge Goethe to a duel, etc. He had been made to believe that Goethe had intentionally lengthened the play into three acts and thus caused its failure." Thus goes the memory of the Weimar theologian and publicist Johannes Falk,[49] which is consistent with a statement made by Goethe at the end of 1810, in which he emphasized that the failure of the comedy was due to the lack of "a swiftly performed action." He continued: "But to blame me for the failure of the latter, and even, as he was in the process of doing, to want to send a challenge to Weimar for a duel because of it, points, as Schiller notes, to a serious aberration of nature, which can find the reason for its excuse solely in an excessive irritability of the nerves or in illness."[50]

The duel never took place; Kleist fought Goethe with words, not with weapons. In the third issue of *Phöbus,* he printed excerpts of *The Broken Jug* so the readers could determine for themselves why the comedy had failed on the Weimar stage. And he accompanied it with the fable "The Dogs and the Bird," in which a couple of dogs mistakenly believe that a bird hopping around here and there is easy prey for them until it suddenly flies away: "*Whoever has no grounds / The sage most astounds.*"[51] Thus reads the moral of the fable aimed at the groundling Weimar audience. With his epigrams in the double issue 4/5 of *Phöbus,* the attacks that Kleist leads against hostile literary critics, ignorant readers, and Goethe in particular, seem more direct. The first of a series of distichs in the style of the old master is dedicated to the old master Goethe himself. In Kleist's epigram Goethe—then still a virile and productive fifty-nine-year-old man—is portrayed as an aged epigone of himself:

> *1. Mr. von Goethe*
> See, I call that worthy, for sure, to occupy oneself in old age!
> He now breaks up the ray once thrown by his youth.[52]

Kleist plays the old Goethe against Goethe the young man, or, put differently, the writer of Weimar Classicism against the one of Sturm und Drang. Kleist was able to identify with the young bourgeois genius and his creative force, which we know from the programmatic prologue of *Phöbus.* But he was not able to identify with the elder *von* Goethe who, proud of his noble title, "breaks up the ray once thrown by his youth"—in his defanging of his *Sorrows of Young Werther,* for example—as well as the ray of the younger generation, in his dividing of a strong play like *The Broken Jug* into conventional acts, weakening it. Disappointed love and hate, emulation and rivalry all come together in this epigram. Form and content are congruent. With this distich on Goethe, Kleist wrote an anti-Xenion to Goethe's Xenion "Triumph of the School" ("Triumph der Schule"), with which the latter opposed Newton's theory that white light is composed of prismatic colors—a theory to which Kleist's cherished professor

Christian Ernst Wünsch was also committed. The prefiguration to Kleist's epigram can be found in the *Muses' Almanac of 1797*: "What a sublime idea! We are taught by the immortal master / to split the ray that we always knew as one."[53]

It may be only a legend that Kleist, according to a recollection of his friend Pfuel, had "but one goal: to become the greatest poet of his nation," and that he therefore hated Goethe's "pre-eminence," wanting to *"tear the laurels from his brow."*[54] Apart from the events of 1808, the conflict between Kleist and Goethe was of little importance during Kleist's lifetime. It is significant primarily for Kleist's posthumous reception—for the disdain with which his work was met in the 19th century and its revaluation in the 20th century.[55] But Kleist's epigrams in *Phöbus* are by no means confined to his revenge on Goethe; they are, above all, artful advertising for his own works. With them Kleist mocks himself by appropriating the language of his critics; he exaggerates their polemics, reducing them to their banal, philistine core, hoping for the opposite effect: the dismantling of his critics' ignorance and narrow-mindedness. Below are some examples from the first series of epigrams in the double issue 4/5 that do not require any further explanation—with the exception of "Comedy Playbill," in which Kleist mocks Böttiger's slander in the journal *The Liberal* of February 5/6, 1808. Böttiger was upset by the spectacle of "hordes of Greeks and Amazons, girls and mothers" along with "packs of harnessed dogs and elephants" in Kleist's *Penthesilea*:[56]

> *2. Comedy Playbill*
> Today for the first time, if we may: Penthesilea,
> A dog comedy; actors: heroes and mongrels and women.
>
> *14. Robert Guiscard, Duke of the Normans*
> No, that I call too much! No sooner she gets off stage
> with rabies, he enters with boils of plague.
>
> *19. The Marquise of O—*
> This novel is not for you, my daughter. In a faint!
> A shameless farce! She merely kept—I know—her eyes closed.

Nor does the final example from Kleist's second series of epigrams from issue 6 of *Phöbus* require explanation:

> *10. The Unqualified Critic*
> Why, what an idea you have there! You judge my art of writing
> before you, my dear, have even learned the art of reading.[57]

Kleist's wit pairs self-confidence with despair over the conservative art critics and over the sensitive ladies of Dresden, who find it hard to identify with the female characters of Kleist's stories and plays, neither with the Marquise of O— nor, for certain with Penthesilea—but perhaps with Katie of Heilbronn?

Love in War, Love as War: *Penthesilea*

On August 31, 1806, Kleist wrote to Rühle from Königsberg: "I have a tragedy under my pen."[58] And in the late fall of 1807, he sent a letter to Marie von Kleist from Dresden stating: "I have finished my *Penthesilea*," which supposedly captured his "deepest nature"—"all the filth and radiance of my soul together."[59] Between these two letters lay the defeat of Prussia in the twin battles of Jena and Auerstedt, the escape of the Prussian royal court to Königsberg, and Kleist's captivity as a prisoner of war in France. One of the greatest plays in the history of German literature was written under the most unusual circumstances—in times of war, possibly in a rock prison cell at Fort de Joux. In July 1807 Kleist was released from prison, in his pocket he had drafts for *Penthesilea*; he had used those six months to write. Once he was in Dresden, he completed his play within a few weeks. In 1808 he printed excerpts from the play in *Phöbus* before publishing the completed work with Cotta in Tübingen, with a print run of only 750 copies. It was not until decades later that the play premiered, at the Berlin Court Theater in 1876. But at that time the theater did not have the courage to stage the original—unabridged and unedited—text. This staging did not happen until 1892 at the Munich Court Theater. Kleist had been hopeful that "time alone" would decide whether his play could be performed, knowing that it violated "the public's expectations from the stage," especially women's demands, noting that "the Greek conception of theater could never have developed if women had not been excluded from it."[60] It is, however, also a play that portrays a 'monstrous' woman who—to quote Goethe's verdict once again—was "of so singular a race" and inhabited "so alien a region." Moreover, it troubled Goethe to see that Kleist was "awaiting some theater yet to come."[61] Kleist is thus criticized for the transgression of the limits of both gender and genre.[62] His extreme theater violated not only the expectations of the contemporary audience, but provoked both gender and genre trouble. But unlike *The Broken Jug*, *Penthesilea* never became a popular play. 'No wonder,' Kleist's epigram "Comedy Playbill" mocks. For in this play a woman joins her dogs in devouring her lover, only to then appear before her friends and the audience with all of the signs of madness, full of remorse and willing herself to die with a dagger formed of her own words. What began as a miracle of love between the Amazon queen and the Greek Achilles in the midst of the Trojan War ends in an act of cannibalism. The final scene poses a challenge for any actress playing Penthesilea, and the play is still not performed in cultures whose image of women does not allow for such atrocities. Kleist's peculiar rendering of the Amazon myth is puzzling at first, and thus requires some clarification.

A look at Benjamin Hederich's *Complete Mythological Lexicon* (*Gründliches mythologisches Lexikon*)—first published in 1724 with a revised edition in 1770—is a good place to start. The lexicon was plundered by virtually every writer at the turn of the 19th century when it came to reworking Classical mythology. Under the entry 'Amazons,' Kleist would have been able to read not only the well-known story of the severed breast, but about their peculiar reproductive policy that "[n]one of them was allowed to marry before she had killed an enemy." Regarding Penthesilea in particular, it states:

> Queen of the Amazons, daughter of Mars and the Otrera. [...]. She came with a few thousand of her people to Troy to help Priam, and Hector went to meet her out of sheer honor, whereupon he fell into the hands of Achilles and lost his life [...]; and, since she then ventured to fight the Greeks alone with her people, she and her women fought with great bravery; but finally Achilles approached her, inflicted a fatal wound with his spear, and pulled her off her horse by her hair. [...] According to some [sources other than those previously mentioned by Hederich], Achilles only recognized her beauty and youth after he had killed her. As he now also admired her bravery insofar as she had, more than once, almost subdued him, he wanted to honor her properly. But he was opposed, particularly by Thersites, who not only accused him of performing inappropriate acts with Penthesilea after she died, but also of poking out one of her eyes with his spear. Over this desecration Achilles gave him a blow with his fist so that Thersites dropped to the ground dead, whereupon Diomedes, a relative of Thersites, insisted all the more on Penthesilea's desecration. [...] Other sources, however, relate that she herself killed Achilles, but that he came back to life following the pleading of Thetis, his mother, and in turn put Penthesilea to death. [...] Some also say that Achilles lay with her and fathered Cayster with her.[63]

So much for Kleist's source material. It is evident that he did not draw from the principal sources mentioned by Hederich but rather from the variants given toward the end of the entry, which speak of Achilles' love for Penthesilea and of the possibility that she killed him. Kleist's play is about love as a battle of the sexes and not about the role of the Amazons in the Trojan War, standing in contrast to the principal sources in Hederich. In Kleist, Penthesilea's sole objective is to venture forth with her Amazons onto the battlefield before the gates of Troy in order to conquer men; she is an ally of neither the Trojans nor the Greeks, which rather astonishes the latter—even the smartest among them. Odysseus is beside himself:

> Now begins
> a fight the like of which was never fought
> on earth since Furies were. As far as I
> can see, in Nature there is force and counter-
> force and no third thing. What puts the fire
> out will not make water boil up into
> steam, and vice versa. But now a fierce
> foe of them both appears and when she does,
> Fire's unsure if it shouldn't stream with Wet,
> and Wet if it shouldn't soar with Fire skywards.
> Hard-pressed by Amazons, the Trojan dives
> behind his Greek opponent's shield, the Greek
> protects him from the virgin crowding close
> on his heels, and Greek and Trojan now
> are almost forced, in spite of Helen's rape,
> to stand together side by side against
> the common foe.[64]

For the end of his play—the cruel climax of Achilles' killing—Kleist may have also found a prefiguration in Hederich, one entry further down the alphabet. After the entry 'Penthesilea' comes the entry 'Pentheus.' According to the myth, Pentheus, King of Thebes, banned the orgiastic cult of Dionysus, in which Theban women, including his own mother Agave, participated—a fact Dionysus (or Bacchus) did not tolerate. The myth became popular due to Euripides' tragedy *The Bacchae* of 405 BCE. With respect to Pentheus, Hederich notes:

> When Bacchus came to Boeotia during Pentheus' reign, the latter vigorously opposed his worship, as it was becoming excessive. But, when he went to Mount Cithaeron to witness the Bacchic rites, his own mother and her sisters, in their frenzy, thought him to be a boar. So, with the help of the other women, they struck him down with their thyrsi and tore him, miserably, from limb to limb.[65]

At the end of Euripides' *The Bacchae*, Agave tears her own son to pieces and, with all signs of madness, steps before the chorus bearing Pentheus' bloodied head, unaware of whom she has killed. What appears innovative in Kleist's extreme theater is the result of an adaptation and blending of Classical motifs. Greek mythology and Attic tragedy are rife with cruel scenes. This fact, however, did not correspond to the image of Antiquity that Kleist's contemporaries were used to or wanted to see. In keeping with Johann Joachim Winckelmann's idealization of Classical Antiquity, Schiller and Goethe had explored the ideal of beautiful humanity in the Greeks. Goethe's Iphigenia is the perfect model of the 'noble simplicity and quiet grandeur' that every aristocratic daughter at and after the turn of the 19th century could use as a guide. Penthesilea is her stark counterpart. A first review of the tragedy, published in the *Northern Miscellany* (*Nordische Miszellen*) on December 4, 1808, reads: "According to the aesthetic theory of the Classical philosophers, the tragedy arouses fear and pity; while, here, they are replaced by feelings of horror, revulsion, and disgust. The whole play is supposed to be Classical, we assume; hence, it is not divided into acts. But where is that simplicity of design, that power of genius, that depth of feeling, that high flight of an orderly, chaste imagination? In its place you find here feverish convulsions, stilted unnatural images, rawness, and savagery."[66] By contrast, on September 19, 1885, the poet Detlev von Liliencron passed a completely different judgment in the *Magazine for German and Foreign Literature* (*Magazin für die Literatur des In- und Auslandes*): "It is not incomprehensible that Goethe was cold toward *Penthesilea* [...]. He—will my tongue be torn out now?—did not understand the tragedy; it disgusted him. He only saw a sick Kleist in it. That the good German run-of-the-mill philistine, today and forever, was unable to let this wonderful tragedy into his heart, need not be mentioned. The German philistine, be he a prince or a cigar roller, and—*Penthesilea*!"[67]

Polemics stand here against polemics. Or, to put it more plainly: The shock that Kleist's *Penthesilea* provoked indicates an anti-Neoclassical turn, an aesthetic paradigm shift. Received with dismay at the turn of the 19th century, it was met with approval at the turn of the 20th century. Kleist became an ally of Modernism, as he replaced the hopeful veneration of the Greek Olympus with a chilling gaze into the abyss of the Orcus. He depicts the dark side of the ancient Greeks—repressed by the idealists—in merciless candor, in the affect-driven frenzy of Penthesilea. Kleist thus not only paved the way for the representation of the unconscious in Modernism; his revaluation of the Greek ideal of beauty in German Neoclassicism also produced a more realistic image of Antiquity. With his tragedy Kleist captured the essence—the historical self-conception projected by Greek drama—more precisely than Goethe and Schiller in their adherence to Winckelmann. Kleist was far ahead of his time. Even the Classical philologist Friedrich Nietzsche—who in 1872 published his famous work *The Birth of Tragedy Out of the Spirit of Music*—had difficulties asserting his 'Dionysian' notion of Antiquity against the prevailing one-sided 'Apollonian' notion. In Greek mythology Apollo represents the right measure and harmonious order, while Dionysus stands for ecstasy, madness, and frenzy. According to Nietzsche, Classical tragedy arises from the conflict between these two principles. Kleist's sacrifice of Achilles, fighting plainly and calmly, to the wild Amazon queen—his allowance of the representative of rationality to succumb to the representative of irrationality—is pure heresy in the eyes of the turn-of-the-19th-century admirers of a marble-smooth ideal of Greek beauty. It was Nietzsche's interpretation of Antiquity that first helped the Modernist writers gain a better understanding of *Penthesilea*. In the Amazon queen, fallen away from herself and the world, they found a mirror image of Modern man. The play is not only ahead of Goethe's era, it is also the sign of a new era that no longer expects any redemption, neither from the Classical nor from the humanized gods of the great writers of Weimar Classicism. To put it in the words of Penthesilea's friend Prothoe: "[A]nd what you see around / you here is still the world, the infirm world, / which the gods look down on only from far off." To which Penthesilea responds: "Oh well, But that's good too, that's fine. / It doesn't matter. / […] I'm quite content."[68]

There are, therefore, many images of being torn or torn apart in this play. The end—where Achilles is torn limb from limb because Penthesilea is torn between love and hate—is only the climax. Torn apart is, above all, the relationship between self and world, individual and society. Thus goes the reading of the older scholarship on *Penthesilea*, which emphasizes the conflict between Penthesilea and the Amazon law, interpreting the play as a "tragedy of individuality."[69] What usually goes unmentioned is that even the Greek tragedy was a "tragedy of individuality," as the distinction between epic and dramatic hero in Classical Antiquity demonstrates. The hero of the Homeric epics is a man of action. His deeds are in accordance with the will of the gods, a will that is not concealed from him. His fate represents that of an entire community of people of which he is a part. The epic is intended to create a totality that is visibly predefined, a universal and harmonious world order. He who violates this order cannot be an epic hero. In Homer's *Iliad*, for example, Bellerophontes, the grandson of Sisyphus, stands as the national hero of the Corinthians; his adventures are told in detail, but not his downfall. Bellerophontes conceives the ill-fated idea of storming Mount Olympus on the back of the winged horse Pegasos to discover the secrets behind the rulers of the world. This constitutes a fall from grace comparable to the biblical bite of the apple that also angers a god. Zeus hurls Bellerophontes back to earth, isolates him from all other mortals, and punishes him with madness. We learn of Bellerophontes' offense from a tragedy by Euripides that bears the hero's name in its title, while Homer remains silent about the iniquity. He who demonstrates a lack of concern for the divine order of things is no longer relevant to Homer. Only the hero who acts according to the established set of rules is relevant because in Homer's time no one doubted the mythical order of things. The situation is quite different when it comes to the Attic tragedy, which is founded on different historico-philosophical premises. In the second half of the 5th century BCE, Protagoras,

Gorgias, and Critias dismantled the existing mythical, philosophical, and natural-historical notions of world order into relativism and subjectivism, a phenomenon commonly known as the 'sophistic crisis.' It is from this historical background that the Attic tragedy emerges as a "tragedy of individuality." Sophocles' and Euripides' heroes are characterized, above all, by their obstinacy and subjectivity, which bring them to violate the divine order. The downfall of the hero at the tragedy's end is necessary for the re-establishment of the divine order's validity. The Attic tragedy reflects the sophistic crisis and, at the same time, it is a representation of its temporary overcoming.[70]

The Amazon queen, too, is obstinate insofar as she violates the law of her people. The law of Tanaïs, the founder of the Amazon state, decrees that intercourse is to serve only procreation. Amazons are to conquer any random man in battle, then drag the defeated to the Festival of Roses in Themiscyra and, once the success of their cohabitation is certain—that is, once a child is born—send him back home. Penthesilea is, of course, aware of this tradition, telling Achilles:

> It isn't right for Mars's daughters to go searching
> out opponents of their own. Their duty is
> to take the one the God of Battle puts
> into their way. However—if an ambitious
> spirit shows herself before the princeliest
> foemen, why, well and good![71]

Before the *princeliest* foemen, not a particular one. Penthesilea, however, pursues one person on the battlefield before the gates of Troy in particular, and that is Achilles, son of Peleus—which angers the high priestess of the Amazons, responsible for upholding the law of Tanaïs:

> What business of our nation's is
> Achilles! Is it fitting for a child
> of Mars, a queen, to pay, when she's in battle,
> particular attention to one name?
> [...]
> Whoever heard of anything so mad![72]

Achilles defeats Penthesilea in battle, which he initially conceals in order to enjoy with Penthesilea his bliss as the supposedly defeated foe. His deception is revealed when the Amazons disturb their peace and free Penthesilea, who, troubled by her release, asks if she could follow Achilles to his camp as his prisoner of war. The high priestess thereupon reprimands her Queen in front of all the Amazons:

> Well then, our Queen, with these outrageous words,
> I must confess, you've capped your deeds today
> in proper style. It's not enough you paid
> no heed to custom and went in search of your
> own man to fight; it's not enough, instead
> of making your opponent bite the dust,
> *you* did; it's not enough that his reward
> for that should be your smothering him in roses;
> no, on top of that you fly into
> a passion and abuse your loyal people, those
> who broke your chains, you turn away from us
> and call your conqueror back. All right, you daughter
> of great Tanaïs, I ask your pardon for the rash
> way that we acted, a mistake, no more. I'm sorry
> now for all the blood it cost us, for all
> the prisoners we had to forfeit for your sake,
> with all my heart I wish we had them back.
> In the name of our people, I pronounce you free;
> turn your feet whichever way you please [...].[73]

The opposition established here is clear: the 'one name' that Penthesilea pays particular attention to—that is, Achilles' proper name—stands in contrast to the 'name of her people'; the right to individuality contradicts the right of the collective; the singularity of her love for Achilles goes against the doctrine of impersonal sexual relations. Penthesilea appears self-willed in a double sense: She defies the law of the Amazons and thereby discovers herself in her singularity. The fate of the rebellious Bellerophontes may once again be brought to mind. His offense resulted in two punishments: banishment and madness. The situation is similar with Penthesilea who, should she refuse to submit to the law of Tanaïs, faces banishment from the Amazons by the high priestess. Achilles' offer to fight her a second time saves Penthesilea from having to make the decision. She is thus spared Bellerophontes' first punishment, but not the second: madness. The ending of Kleist's *Penthesilea* could thus be viewed as the ending of an Attic tragedy, with its rebel dead and the mythical order of the Amazons restored. Prothoe's closing words addressed to her dead friend suggest as much:

> She fell because she bloomed too proud and strong!
> The dead oak stands, defying wind and weather,
> the gale pulls down the good wood with a crash,
> for with his fingers he can fasten in its crown.[74]

Kleist quotes a Baroque emblem here, a symbol of the condemnation of human hubris intended to inspire humility before God. While Baroque literature typically employs the image of a small bendable shrub, Kleist's character speaks of a "dead oak" that survives the storm. If one follows the logic of the image further, it is the Amazons, submitting to the law of Tanaïs, who appear to be the dead ones. The mythical order itself thus seems outlived and doomed to death, which is not lost upon the Amazons. Penthesilea speaks quite frankly with Achilles about the tears the women shed having to send away their children's fathers after the celebration of the birth. Before her suicide she explicitly abjures "the law of women" and recommends Prothoe to follow her therein: "And—something I will whisper to you privately, / the others must not hear: the ashes of / Queen Tanaïs, scatter them / to the winds!"[75] The liberation of the Amazon women from the laws of their state seems to be only a question of time. It is therefore questionable to read Kleist's *Penthesilea* as a defense of matriarchy against patriarchy, as Kleist scholars have attempted to do. It would indeed be easier to prove the opposite. After all, Kleist does not justify the law of Tanaïs. Thus, unlike madness in Attic tragedy, Penthesilea's madness is not divine punishment intended to restore mythical order, nor is it the consequence of a *heroic* rebellion. Rather, it is presented as a psychological problem, the manifestation of her liminal position—oscillating between notions of love as a relationship, as unconditional trust in and devotion to the beloved, and love as ownership, the mere physical desire, conquest, and possession of anyone whomever. But what is one to make of the fact that Penthesilea, the huntress, finally pounces on her lover with her dogs and tears him apart? The attempt at individuation through love has obviously failed as well; to speak of a "tragedy of individuality" seems itself questionable when neither the law of Tanaïs nor the departure from it ultimately prevails.

Anyone reading or seeing the play is more or less in the same situation as Odysseus, who—one may recall—is astonished that Penthesilea does not choose between Trojans and Greeks, that she cannot be reduced to a binary logic. And yet the text operates with opposites, especially in distinguishing between Penthesilea and Achilles. One only has to compare their portraits: In her wild reversals of love and aggression that disturb both her friend Prothoe and Achilles, Penthesilea appears like an unpredictable 'affect machine.' She is not portrayed as the subject of her actions, at one with herself, but as an energetic mass, charging and discharging itself—a crosspoint of forces converging in her body.[76] This incongruity becomes particularly evident in the Greeks' vain attempt to create a coherent image of her out of gender stereotypes, such as her "silky curls," "slim hands," and the "silver of her voice."[77] The attempt fails as Penthesilea's extreme fluctuations tear any set image of her apart: "Penthesilea, as a hurricane / the ragged clouds, scatters the Trojan ranks / in front of her." She "rolls all before her like a mountain torrent, / them and us too, Greeks and

Trojans both." She hits them "with a thunder / crack, as if she meant, that crazy girl, / to split the whole Greek tree down to the root."[78] Hurricane, mountain torrent, thunder crack: Compared to the forces of nature, Penthesilea appears both fluid and boundless in her intensity; a clearly defined, integrated image of her self cannot be determined. It is only upon seeing Achilles' form that the troubled gaze finds its way back to a well-ordered perception. Achilles, after having struggled "out of the battle murk," is constructed before our eyes, body part by body part:

> A MYRMIDON (*looking into the distance*).
> Look! Isn't that a head, an armored one,
> appearing just above that ridge, a helmet
> shadowed by its crest? The puissant neck
> that carries it? And now the shoulders and the arms,
> shining in their steel? The mighty frame
> of chest, and see, friends, don't you, strapped
> around his waist the belt of gold?
> [...] Just so the glorious sun car
> climbs the sky on a bright day in spring!
> GREEKS. Hurrah! Achilles! Son of the gods! It's him!
> And whipping on the quadriga himself![79]

It is worth recalling Kleist's journal, whose first issue contained an excerpt from *Penthesilea*; Hartmann's frontispiece; the sun god Phoebus, calmly steering his quadriga (as Achilles does in the verses quoted above); and Kleist's prologue, which presents Phoebus Apollo in a different light—not in harmony, but in wild action, storming and thundering with flaming horses. Perhaps Achilles is not a moderate Apollonian sun god either; there may be a discrepancy between the unambiguous image painted in the passage quoted above and his actions.

It may be tempting to rely on the opposites established in *Penthesilea*, but they cannot be trusted. The play's poetology generates paradoxes throughout the text; all of the relationships in the play are inextricably linked in their differences. As Penthesilea's mother and principal pedagogical authority, Otrera prompts her daughter, on the one hand, to imitate her and, on the other, to go against her. Like her mother, Penthesilea is to become Queen of the Amazons, but unlike her, she is to stake her all on 'one name' at the Festival of Roses, which is Otrera's will. Her last words are: "Dear child, Mars summons you, / now go! You'll catch and crown Pelides, I / am sure."[80] It is also paradoxical that the Amazons adhere to the law of Tanaïs—distinguishing between men and women with respect to their rights—in order to abolish all distinction on the basis of this rigid discrimination, as the choice of the procreation partner must be indiscriminate. The miracle of Achilles and Penthesilea's love *in* the Trojan War lies in love *as* war—a series of physical and psychological duels. Lastly, Achilles playfully reverses his electric charge: He pretends to be weak when he has won and strong when he wants to be defeated; and like a diplomat, he hides his true feelings behind duplicitous speech, as will later be shown.

The law of Tanaïs can also be described heuristically as a rule of prudence, according to which every partner is chosen at random; no love lasts forever, and the partners should be quick to put their guards back up before ultimately fatal traumas ensue. At any rate, the Amazons do not strive to realize an ideal of love, but rather to master the reality of love through a ritual that divides the procreative partnership into three stages: firstly, the physical confrontation in a duel, which symbolizes the overcoming of physical boundaries; secondly, the unification of the sexes in the Festival of Roses, which underlines the possibility of happiness while exposing it as temporary; thirdly, the restoration of physical boundaries through the rule of separation, which is meant to re-establish the lover's inviolability. Remaining trapped in a series of duels, Penthesilea and Achilles never get past the first stage. In the first duel a Trojan warrior interferes, which does not end well for him; the Queen of the Amazons takes the victory. But she loses the next two duels, one due to a deceptive maneuver—a feint by Achilles, who shatters Penthesilea's assault against a rock—and the other due to Achilles' superior physical strength. The wounds the two inflict upon each other are minor, but the duels result in one thing above all: The armor of both opponents comes undone, as the stage directions and second do not tire of mentioning. What had before been a mere mock fight, each opponent sparing the other, now becomes deadly serious.

But Achilles does not seem to understand the seriousness of the situation. In the following duels with Penthesilea, he arms himself purely rhetorically. Although his disdain for Odysseus' eloquence is obvious, as the latter cunningly compelled him to engage in the Trojan War, Achilles is by no means the naïve, upright warrior that the myth portrays. He has apparently inherited from his mother Thetis, a sea nymph, the protean arts—the arts of disguise and deception. What distinguishes him from Odysseus, however, is that he is not a strategist who operates from a distance, but a tactician. He needs close combat, physical contact. He proves in the process to be a seasoned actor in Kleist's play, mastering shifting registers as well as the arts of simulation and dissimulation. Thus, he first faces the Amazons, who put their bows and arrows on him, as a gallant seducer: "Please, please! / Your eyes are better shots, believe me. By / the gods of Mount Olympus, I don't joke, / I feel myself pierced to my innermost / and humbly kneel down at your pretty feet,

/ a disarmed man in every sense."[81] This demeanor, of course, does not prevent him from momentarily switching from the role of the charmer back to that of the soldier who crudely reduces the complexity of the situation by ordering his people to simply kill an Amazon every now and then. He also willingly takes part in deceiving Penthesilea into thinking she defeated him, which Prothoe orchestrates to protect her friend from the shame of being beaten in battle. And he is not sparing with pregnant flattery. The very first words he addresses to Penthesilea are more than just elegant. As he puts it, he is a captive "[i]n every higher sense of that word." He is captive to her beauty as much as he is to his own deception, but by no means is he inhibited when faced with the difficult task of finding the right opening line between two lovers. Penthesilea, by contrast, "*covers her face with her hands*," according to the stage directions.[82] If this gesture were mere acting, it would be the appropriate sign of an *eloquentia corporis* for the expression of an *eloquentia cordis*—a language of the heart. But Penthesilea is not an actress. There is a reason why Odysseus points out that "her face" is "a blank," that "this palm of mine, I swear, / is more expressive than her face." Penthesilea's gestures and facial expressions do not follow any convention, they are not recognizable as renderings of the familiar. There is no puppeteer controlling a marionette, paying attention to the impact of its self-fashioning on the eyes of the beholder, as Kleist's essay "On the Puppet Theater" expects of great actors. Thus, Odysseus' artful attempts at deciphering Penthesilea fail, as does every one of his rhetorical tricks. The master of the art of rhetoric and deception is quite simply astounded that his art finds no audience in Penthesilea: "But in the midst of running on / like this, I notice with astonishment / she doesn't hear a word."[83]

Penthesilea's "soul," as Prothoe warns, "cannot be reckoned with." But that does not prevent Achilles from measuring her by the common yardstick. He wants to love her: "Like men / love women."[84] After all, he has "never played / the coy one with a beauty."[85] As a womanizer he relies on his repertoire and believes—up until the final and fatal duel—that Penthesilea is "a cunning one,"[86] much like himself, and that she will only pretend to fight and defeat him in order to fulfill Tanaïs' terms for celebrating the Festival of Roses with him. Achilles, however, misjudges the situation when he challenges Penthesilea to another duel. In the rose scene Penthesilea had presented him with a misleading idea of providence, according to which her identity and her confidence in her feelings depend solely on seeing herself through him, the son of Peleus, as her mother had predicted:

The nearer I
advanced to the Scamander, the louder all
the valleys we raced through reechoed
with the fighting over Troy, the less pain I
experienced and my soul, expanding wide, embraced
the great world of high-spirited war.
My one thought was: if each most glorious
moment history remembers were reenacted
here before me now, if all the company
of heroes sung in epic song descended
to me from the stars, I'd find no better
one to crown with roses than him my mother
chose—that dear, that savage, charming, dreadful
one by whom brave Hector fell! Pelides!
My one thought waking, one dream sleeping, was
of you! The whole world lay spread out before
me like some piece of woven stuff into
whose every giant square a deed of yours
was worked, and I, I burnt each one into
my heart, so white and pure, like silk, with fire
dyes.[87]

What is overlooked here by Penthesilea—as well as by most of Kleist scholarship—is that Achilles himself is a Proteus. The characters' unstable identity, or merely phantasmatic sense of totality, turns their duels into identity tests and, thus, a perpetual game of misrecognition. It is not only Penthesilea's soul that cannot be reckoned with, but Achilles'. The polarity principle—familiar from Kleist's essay "The Very Last Word in Modern Educational Theory"—serves as the model for their relationship, while in their mutual recognition it is a position of belatedness that ultimately prevails, as it does in all of Kleist's literature. As noted in his essay "On Thinking Things Over: A Paradox": "Reflection, or thinking something over, finds its proper moment *after* rather than *before* an act."[88] Achilles goes into the final duel with his guard down, and only in dying does he realize Penthesilea's true intentions. The same holds true for Penthesilea, who after slaying Achilles, admits that she had mistaken 'biting' for 'kissing' and failed "to have / control over [her] rash mouth."[89]

It is not only Penthesilea's mouth, but Kleist's play that moves at a rash speed, with the action rushing forward in twenty-four scenes, overwhelming the rigid five-act structure of Aristotelian tragedy. At the same time there is little action on stage; characters merely describe actions, which becomes particularly evident in the play's opening and closing scenes. The first few scenes contain lengthy accounts of the battle for Troy conveyed in the traditional forms of the

Greek drama—messenger report and teichoscopy—to represent events that cannot themselves be staged. In Kleist's case, however, the messenger report and teichoscopy serve an additional purpose, one different from the conventional tragedy. They do not simply transfer an event from one place to another, transforming wild action into a tamed narrative—they do not engage in a "distanced and distancing communication."[90] On the contrary, in their impetuous demeanor, their expressive imagery, their hurried rhythm and, above all, in their syntax, whirling everything together, they transport the audience directly into the scene. The audience itself is thus drawn into the action with all its senses. Let me give an example: Diomedes tells the Greeks of Achilles, who, while fighting Penthesilea, gets attacked by the Trojan Deiphobus. Penthesilea surprisingly comes to Achilles' rescue:

> The Queen goes white and down her weapons sink,
> two minutes long; then shaking wrathfully
> her locks around her flaming cheeks, she rears
> up high above her horse's back and brings
> her sword, as if fetched from the sky,
> a thunderstone, straight down on his neck,
> which sends the meddler rolling underneath
> the feet of Thetis' godlike son. He wants,
> the Peleid, by serving her the same,
> to say his thanks. But she, crouched to the neck,
> with streaming mane, of her pied mount that champs
> his golden bit and veers away, eludes
> the murd'rous stroke, gives free rein
> to her horse, looks back, laughs out, and disappears.[91]

This passage presents a terrific choreography—a "body drama," as German scholar Maximilian Nutz calls it.[92] In everyday language the word order would render this passage static, giving it a clear and unified form. Kleist's play, however, shatters the syntax under the excess of kinetic pressure and wild scattering of directional impulses. Three people and a horse collide in frenzied motion. They are not presented as distinct figures, but torn and tangled in their limbs, individual characteristics, circumstances, and motivations. Appositions are torn away from their subjects and wedged between doer and deed. Who does what to whom, how, with what, and to what effect can only be grasped intermittently by the audience or the reader—and initially even with an erroneous reference, which the audience or reader can barely set straight, as the forceful series of sentences will have already rushed on: "But she, crouched to the neck, / with streaming mane, of her pied mount that champs / his golden bit and veers away, eludes / the murd'rous stroke." Whose neck? Not Penthesilea's, but that of her horse. Who eludes the murderous stroke? Not the mount, but Penthesilea. Whose murderous stroke? Not the horse's, but Achilles'. The blurred syntax corresponds to the blurred vision, which can barely distinguish between the back and forth of the action. The iambic rhythm does not create a flowing motion but rapids and maelstroms that draw the audience or reader into the battle, letting them experience the events almost physically, thus creating a more immediate experience than if they had seen the events on stage.

What is being told and said—language itself—replaces the mimetic action. Kleist had after all warned Goethe that *Penthesilea* was "just as little written for the stage" as *The Broken Jug*.[93] The play requires the voice of an actor or the inner voice of the reader; it is a closet drama without external actions—a tragedy of language in performative and formal terms as well as in terms of content, considering its inconceivable final scene. The killing of Achilles, which Penthesilea calls an "error" and a slip of the tongue, is not owed to the disconnect between word and deed, as in Kleist's other plays that are indebted to the Kant crisis. No, Penthesilea "did truly word for word"[94] what others claim only in metaphorical speech—she devoured Achilles for love. To succeed in the reunification of signifier and signified, literal and figurative speech can only be the hope of a mad person, hence engendering acts of madness. The attempt to master reality through language is doomed to fail, as Penthesilea loses control over a language that, in moving from the realm of signification to action, begins to attain autonomy. Once again: "It was a slip— / I swear it, by Diana—of the tongue, no more, / because I am remiss and fail to have / control over my rash mouth the way / I should."[95]

There is no salvation in taking language literally; nor is salvation to be found in a cognizance of the distinction between signifier and signified, in taking refuge in metaphorical speech rather than saying what one actually means. This is what we see in Achilles' figurative language, where metaphors become absolute. When Achilles finally announces to the Greeks that his love for Penthesilea is more important to him than the battle for Troy, Odysseus and Diomedes, believing him mad, want to "[g]rab hold of" the pining lover and "tie him up." A simple remark about his indifference to the yearslong bloody war over the theft of Helen—which seems more absurd to him than a mock fight for the hand of Penthesilea—would have sufficed. Achilles, however, is carried away into mocking comparisons:

> If Dardanusburg, Laertides,
> sank from sight, in its place the waters,
> blue-hued, of a lake; if in the night
> moon-gray fishermen tied their skiffs up
> to the weathercocks of Troy; if a pikefish ruled
> in Priam's palace, rats or otters hugged
> in Helen's bed—I'd care no more than I
> do now.[96]

While he makes these colorful remarks, Penthesilea approaches from afar, ready for their final duel. She is expecting a different Achilles though—the one she had admired, who had dragged Hector mercilessly around Troy and who had defeated her in their last duel. She therefore arms herself with dogs and elephants, which does not frighten Achilles as he is certain of her love. He continues to revel in the imaginary: "I'll have them eating out / of my hand, I'm sure.—Now follow me!—They're all / tame creatures, really, like their Queen!"[97] But what he thinks of as cunning and playful turns into a massacre.

It would be too convenient, however, to consider Penthesilea as capable only of literal speech. Achilles does have reason to believe that Penthesilea understands he had a mock fight in mind when he proposed another duel. After all, the Amazons themselves regard their conquest of men in battle as a mock fight, so to speak. War is, for them, a metaphor for love. In this respect the threat of physical violence is not meant literally but figuratively. It appears that Achilles understood this quite well, based on Penthesilea's detailed explanation of the law of Tanaïs in the rose scene. But what he does not understand is that Penthesilea does not consider him capable of such figurative speech; that she must believe that he is talking like a Greek and a man—and thus according to his culture—for whom war necessarily coincides with violence and death.

Let us recall here the opening scene of *The Broken Jug*. Judge Adam tells his court clerk Licht: "I told / you, here, right here, is where I fell." To which Licht responds: "Fell literally?" And Adam: "Fell literally."[98] The two thus know what to make of each other and of language. Achilles, by contrast, challenges Penthesilea to a duel, despite his love for her, and eventually falls victim to the figurative meaning of his words. Penthesilea, meanwhile, violently reunites figurative and literal speech, twice in a row. She kills Achilles for misspeaking, and then goes on to kill herself with words, with a "killing feeling" that is like "iron ore." Whether understood literally or figuratively, the language games played by Achilles and Penthesilea lack irony and self-reflection. Absolutism leads to catastrophe, which makes for the difference between comedy and tragedy; and yet it also provides an unforgettable pathos formula:

For now I will descend
into myself, as if into a mine,
to dig a killing feeling out as cold
as iron ore. This ore, I will refine it, in the burning
fire of my misery, into hard
steel; then in the hot corrosive poison
of remorse, step it through and through; to hope's
eternal anvil next I'll carry it,
to hone and point it dagger sharp; and to
this dagger now I offer up my breast:
like so! and so! and so! And once
again!—And now all's well.
(*Topples and dies.*)[99]

Beauty and the Beast
Katie of Heilbronn (with an Excursion "On the Puppet Theater")

Penthesilea oscillates between love and hate, devotion and aggression, female and male. She is a hybrid figure, referred to by the names of various hybrid mythological creatures, such as centauress, Sphinx, or raging Megaera. According to Achilles, she is "half Grace, / half Fury," and for Kleist she is—it bears repeating—"all the filth and radiance of [his] soul together."[100] Penthesilea is neither friend nor foe to the Greeks and the Trojans. She is a figure of the third, in-between the two cultures, and she loves Achilles, who is at once master and victim of his simulations. Contemporary parallels could be easily drawn to all the Kleists, Pfuels, or Rühles—to all those Prussian hybrid figures in Saxony oscillating between strength and weakness, male and female gender roles, and between the political systems of their time, with the French Confederation of the Rhine on the one side, and the anti-French Austria on the other. On the outside these figures appear opportunistic, while on the inside, angry. They would like to be whole again. One such figure of wholeness in Kleist is ostensibly Katie of Heilbronn, through whom Kleist construes the wish for wholeness as impossible to fulfill, in spite of his heroine's happy ending. This ending is a long time coming, with Katie having to pass through many ordeals. For the dream of unambiguous love must be asserted against a reality rife with obstacles and contradictions.

Kleist began writing *Katie of Heilbronn* in the fall of 1807, and he finished it in 1808, after completing *Penthesilea*. The play is set in the Middle Ages and begins rather gloomily, in an underground cavern with a tribunal of judges all in disguise. Theobald Friedeborn, a weaponsmith of Heilbronn, sues Friedrich

Wetter, the Count vom Strahl, for allegedly having bewitched and seduced his daughter. What had happened? The Count had come to Friedeborn's workshop to have his armor repaired. At the sight of him, the girl, barely fifteen years old, turned "deathly pale" and flung herself down in front of him without a word, "like she'd been struck by lightning."[101] As soon as the Count left the workshop, she rushed after him and threw herself out the window, still without a sound, breaking both of her thighs in the fall. She was bedridden with a fever for six weeks, never saying a word. And after having barely recovered, she left her parents' house to follow the Count, henceforth, like his shadow. In court Count Wetter vom Strahl breaks the girl's silence by asking her cruel and difficult questions. But the only thing we learn from this interrogation is that he repeatedly pushed Katie away from him in a manner as cruel as his questions, even literally kicking her out of his house. Why the girl is under his spell remains a mystery. The judges acquit the Count, and Katie has to return to her father. At the beginning of the second act, in a long and pompous monologue, the Count confesses that he desires Katie but cannot marry her because of her social station. On a dark stormy night, he then rescues a lady from the hands of her captors in a charcoal burner's hut in the mountains. At first he is unaware that the lady he rescued is Kunigunde of Turneck, who, with the help of her various admirers, has been fighting him for years to gain control of his Staufen properties. The lady reveals her identity to him, but then appears so grateful, beautiful, and polite that the Count generously grants his arch-enemy protection in his castle. There, the housekeeper Brigitte tells Kunigunde about a feverish dream of the Count on New Year's Eve, according to which he would marry a daughter of the Emperor. Kunigunde seems to fulfill this condition; moreover, she pretends to love the Count and tears apart before his eyes the documents that would have conferred on her the title to buy back Staufen. Thereupon the Count, who had just been raving about Katie, changes the object of his desire, assuring his mother: "As sure as I'm a man, she is the wife / For me!" His mother tries to curb his enthusiasm with the words: "Now, now! Keep calm!" such that at least the audience comes to its senses.[102] Her son obviously does not, for in the third act we learn that he wraps into his marriage proposal to Kunigunde a deed of donation for Staufenburg and sends it to Turneck Castle. The castle is in danger. Kunigunde's last admirer, the Rhine-Count vom Stein, wants to take revenge on the deceitful lady who exploited his love to fight the Count vom Strahl. On her way to the convent of the Ursulines, Katie learns by chance—due to the mix-up of two letters—of the Rhine-Count's plan to attack. She hurries to Count vom Strahl, provides him with precise details about the strength and formation of the attackers, and follows the Count to Turneck Castle, which is already ablaze by the time they arrive. Kunigunde manages to escape from the burning castle unharmed but laments that she forgot the Count's portrait and its case. She instructs Katie to retrieve both items from her burning room. The Count wants to rescue Katie, but the house collapses. Katie seems to be dead. It is only then that the Count realize what he has lost: "I'm in despair! / No beauty left on earth! Just leave me! Go!" Kunigunde meanwhile rejoices, as Katie steps out of the ruins carrying a roll of paper. According to the stage directions, she is led by a cherub, which seems visible only to the audience, as the characters in the play do not react to its presence. Katie, however, only retrieved the Count's portrait; she left the case in the castle and is therefore violently berated by Kunigunde. Nobody understands why. How could she possibly have guessed that "the case itself was precious"? For the first time the Count finds sharp words for Kunigunde: "My lady, I am dumbstruck by your kindness!"

The next morning Katie finds the case unharmed in the ashes. Rather than the Count's portrait, it contains the deed of donation that Kunigunde was after. Apprised of this fact, the Count rethinks his relationship for the first time. He even begins to rebuke himself. While he now knows why Kunigunde has pretended to love him, he still does not know why Katie—whom he mistreated and disregarded so disgracefully—"trails along behind [him] through fire and water like a dog [...], wretch that [he is], with nothing to speak for [him] save the coat of arms on [his] shield."[103] The answer can be found in the fourth act. Katie lies under an elder bush in front of Castle Strahl. Knowing only three things about her—that "she sleeps as soundly as a mole," "dreams all the time, like a hunting-hound," and "talks in her sleep"—Count vom Strahl asks her why she loves him. Katie tells him her New Year's Eve dream, which is identical to his. In it a cherub takes the Count by the hand to her room, where he "tenderly [...] hail[s] [her] as [his] bride." A mark on Katie's neck proves the coincidence of dream and reality. Because of her social station, however, the Count continues to waver "on the edge of lunacy's abyss."[104] After all, the cherub had promised him an Emperor's daughter. Meanwhile, Katie is none the wiser. She awakens from her somnambulistic state not remembering the details of her double dream with the Count. The latter sends her to stay at his mother's castle. There, the true bride meets the false one by coincidence: Both ladies want to take a bath in the castle's Gothic grotto. Utterly disturbed by the sight of naked Kunigunde, Katie emerges from the grotto but remains discreet, unlike one of Kunigunde's former lovers, the Burgrave von Freiburg, who still remembers her body very well. According to him, she is a "piece of mosaic, assembled from all three realms of nature. Her teeth belong to a girl from Munich. Her hair was ordered from France. Her cheeks have a healthy glow, thanks to the Hungarian mines, and her figure, which you so much admire, she owes to a corset of Swedish steel, made for her by a blacksmith."[105] Count vom Strahl, of course, must not know anything about Kunigunde's real appearance, which is why Kunigunde tries to poison Katie. But her plan fails.

The fifth and final act is set at the Emperor's palace at Worms. Before the eyes of the Emperor and the Archbishop, Count vom Strahl and Theobald duel to decide whether Theobald or the Emperor is Katie's real father. The unarmed Count is able to push the well-armed Theobald to the ground, as the latter refuses to attack a defenseless man—something that would have meant nothing to Penthesilea. The Emperor attributes the outcome of the duel to divine judgment and reveals, as majestically as apprehensively, that he had lain with Katie's mother Gertrude a long time ago. Upon this revelation Theobald cedes his rights as a father. Katie becomes Kathrina, Princess of Swabia. The Count is meant to apprise her of this fact, but he instead tortures her one last time: He invites her to his wedding with Kunigunde. Katie appears in a fine embroidered dress of silk and satin, as he had requested, just as Kunigunde does. After the entire court has gathered around, the bridegroom announces his decision to marry Katie after all. Kunigunde storms off under curses, and Katie answers the Count's question "My bride! Will you accept me?" with a statement understandable not only from a feminist perspective: "May God and all his saints protect me!" only to then faint briefly.[106] One can only wonder if she will feel any better about her husband than Alcmene does, who, at the end of *Amphitryon*, is left with nothing but the enduring "Ah!"

Yet *Katie of Heilbronn* is Kleist's only play to have achieved success on the stage early on. It was one of the most popular plays of the 19th century, though for many years theatergoers were not given Kleist's original text, but bowdlerized versions of it. At its premiere on March 17, 1810, at the Theater on the Vienna River, the Emperor character's title was replaced with 'Duke of Swabia' for fear of offending the Austrian emperor; the infidelity of an emperor could not be shown on stage. Kleist was not present at the premiere, but he would probably have accepted the change. In May 1811, looking back, he openly admitted to Marie von Kleist that the "judgment of others ha[d] governed me all too often in the past," especially concerning *Katie of Heilbronn*, which "was an altogether fine conception," and "only when I tried to make it more convenient for the stage was I seduced into errors over which I might now weep."[107] Both Marie and we are left to wonder as to what exactly he meant by "fine conception" and what "errors" it is that he lamented.

The first problem is the play's subtitle, which misleadingly identifies the play as a *Great Historical Drama of Knighthood*. The play does not deal with historical material in the way one would expect from a historical drama, such as Schiller's *Wallenstein*. To this day, the search for a historical Katie of Heilbronn has been in vain. Nor does Kleist's play take advantage of a fictional plot for forwarding a particular understanding of medieval times and lives, such as Umberto Eco's *The Name of the Rose* of 1980. Moreover, as a historical drama the play is not very reliable, taking place in four different centuries, as Klaus Müller-Salget has determined: The Burgrave von Freiburg's return from a crusade could only have been, at latest, in the last third of the 13th century, while the institution of the Vehmic Court, by contrast, points to the 14th to 16th centuries. Meanwhile, Katie supposedly wants to join an Ursuline convent, whose order was founded as late as 1535. And then there is the Count's mother, who advises Kunigunde to take the dispute over Staufen to the Imperial Chamber Court at Wetzlar, which was established in 1495 but did not move to Wetzlar until 1693. Kleist was obviously not concerned with a faithful representation of historical facts and details. He mixes historical elements to create dramatic backdrops and costumes—catering to the revival of chivalric tales in the theater of his time—while, at the same time, mocking contemporary public taste.[108]

Thus, *Katie of Heilbronn* can be called 'historical' only insofar as it deals with contemporary problems in historical guise. The codification of intimacy and sexuality at the turn of the 19th century, for example, is projected back onto the Middle Ages to explore it more freely from afar, thus bringing us to a second problem: the representation of women and of the relationship between the sexes, "[f]or whoever loves Kat[i]e cannot find Penthesilea utterly incomprehensible; they belong together as the + and – of algebra, and are one and the same nature, but imagined under opposite circumstances."[109] Kleist suggests this identity in a simple formula, and the general audience gladly falls into this trap. According to this formula, Penthesilea and Katie are identical in the unwavering fixation of their love for one man, the only difference being their behavior. Penthesilea is active and aggressive; she has to and wants to conquer Achilles in battle. Katie is passive, suffering, and submissive. She does not tear her lover to pieces with her dogs like Penthesilea, but obeys Count vom Strahl, following his orders, even against her own will, like a trained dog. Penthesilea clearly contradicts the contemporary image of women at the turn of the 19th century, while Katie conforms to it—an image echoed in the educational experiments Kleist had conducted in his letters to his fiancée Wilhelmine von Zenge, with which he had attempted, albeit in vain, to evoke in writing the asymmetry of the sexes familiar to him from Enlightenment literature, from Jean-Jacques Rousseau to Immanuel Kant and to Theodor Gottlieb Hippel. However, it is only *seemingly* that *Katie of Heilbronn* revives this male fantasy—for two reasons: The Count vom Strahl is anything but a respectable mentor whom one might entrust with the 'civil improvement of women' in the sense of Hippel's 1792 work, and Katie is by no means merely passive and naïve.

It is well known that humans are the only animals for which loving and, in particular, maintaining love, involves talking. What is striking about the conversations between Katie and the Count, however, is that eros plays hardly any role at all. For the Count, at least, their relationship is entirely about power and sex. In court he humiliates Katie to dispel Theobald's suspicion that he got "her to take poison." The judges, Theobald insists, should just "wait nine months" to see "what it was her youthful body absorbed."[110] As soon as he is acquitted and alone, the Count rages with lust: "Katie! But why can I not call you mine? Katie, girl—Katie! Why can I not take you in my arms and carry you off to that fragrant fourposter at home, which my mother installed in my state apartment? Katie! Katie! Katie! You whose young soul was bared before me in the court today, dripping with sensuous beauty, like the bride of a Persian shah, anointed all over with oils, sprinkling the carpets as they lead her to his chamber." The Count does not desire Katie as his wife, given her lower social station; he could easily have had an affair with her. So what exactly is it that he desires? He betrays his reservations when he calls upon the founder of his family, who was still free of any concerns related to social station: "But I would ask you, Winfried—you the leader, first to bear our name, whose godlike brow is that of Zeus—tell me: was the mother of our clan more radiantly virtuous than Katie, in body and soul more spotless, more generously endowed with every lovable charm? ... O greybeard Winfried! I kiss your hand and thank you for my existence ... But had you pressed her to your breast of steel, you would have bred a future race of kings and every ruler on earth would bear the name Wetter vom Strahl!"[111] This biopolitical notion of Katie as the ideal mother of an all-dominating clan is appalling in that it reminds us of the totalitarian power fantasy of Nazi race theory.[112] At the end of the play, the Count has good reason to hope for the fulfillment of his fantasy, knowing that Katie is the Emperor's daughter. There is nothing left standing in the way of their marriage or the begetting of a powerful dynasty. Perhaps this is why he is carried away by his feelings, tearfully assuring Katie of his love:

> First, dear girl, let me assure you now,
> I love you! Love—unspeakable, eternal—
> With all my senses, I devote to you!
> A stag tormented by the noonday heat
> Who with his pointed antlers scrapes the earth,
> Is tempted no less grievously to plunge
> From the rocks and breast the foaming rapids,
> Than I am longing—now that you are mine—
> To steep myself in all your youthful charms.

Katie, "[*b*]*lushing*," responds to this: "My lord! What are you saying? I'm confused!"[113] Her reaction is understandable. What the Count calls love, his imagery reveals as pure violence and possession. In fixating his desire on Katie as the mother of a new strong ruling dynasty, Count vom Strahl is comparable to the Amazon queen Penthesilea, who consciously chooses the strongest of all Greeks as her sexual partner—the very one who dragged Hector around the walls of Troy. In her sexual union with Achilles, the Queen, split into affects, hopes to gain a sense of wholeness and, indeed, the "whole world." It would not matter to her "if all the company / of heroes sung in epic song descended / to [her] from the stars."[114] It has to be that one man. With Penthesilea's concept of providence, Kleist alludes to Plato's notion of love in *Symposium* as the coming together of two separate but originally united parts of the soul. Kleist's first encounter with this idea was likely through Wieland's *Sympathies* of 1755, in which he writes about the love of "sympathetic souls," "who may have already loved each other under a different sky, and now that they see each other, they remember this fact as one remembers a dream of which only a vague but pleasant sensation lingers in the mind! Fate may have separated them as they descended from those blessed shores to embark upon their time of trial in this foreign land. But their friendly angels will reunite them."[115] It thus becomes evident that Wieland's *Sympathies* is also the source for Count vom Strahl and Katie's New Year's Eve double dream, though it could hardly serve as its philosophical reference, for the sympathy between Wieland's two souls is total.[116] Kleist, by contrast, emphasizes the difference between the male and female lover, beginning with the different ways in which they remember the dream. Significantly, Count vom Strahl remembers every detail, but especially well the promise made by the cherub (who had led him into Katie's room) that he would marry a daughter of the Emperor. But what he does not remember is Katie's face or figure. This fact is what presents Kunigunde the opportunity for deception. Katie, in turn, while recognizing Count vom Strahl in her father's workshop, does not remember any details of the dream until the somnambulistic episode under the elderberry bush in which she is questioned by the Count.

Katie is struck by love like lightning when she encounters the Count for the first time in her father's workshop. Love thus appears as absolute, as an end in itself, for which Katie is prepared to sacrifice everything. The Count's desire for a daughter of the Emperor whom he is destined to marry, by contrast, is from the outset nothing but the instrumentalization of his dream. The suddenness and assuredness of Katie's love finds no equivalent in the Count, who remains with the wrong bride for some time before choosing the right one.

Katie of Heilbronn may be attributed to the Romantic era, with its medieval setting and fairy tale motifs, but it only goes so far with the Romantic conception of love. This marks a third problem in the play. The concept of Romantic love as developed in Friedrich Schlegel's *Lucinde* of 1799, for example, is—beyond its common understanding—an art of resolving paradoxes: of saving one's self while surrendering oneself to the other; of discovering and developing one's own individuality through the other in a reciprocal relationship; of ensuring a relationship's stability through the lovers' constant progress. In the Romantic era, love and self-cultivation are one and the same, passion and marriage are not mutually exclusive. The relationship between the two partners should be symmetrical; the man should be able to allow for the female within himself, and the woman should for the male. But how can such unity be forged from duality? How can a difference be construed whose terms are inextricably linked? The prerequisite for lasting Romantic love is, above all, the conjunction of ecstasy and irony, closeness and distance. Love must be understood as a continuously regenerating world apart. One has to be in love with love itself. There are no objective criteria. In the Romantic era the kindling of love is no longer bound to any precondition of property or social station, making chance and the suddenness of falling in love appear as an overwhelming necessity. Nor are there any general laws governing the act of loving. Love itself must serve as a means for communication and, like any art, it requires a degree of talent and originality.

Katie wholly adheres to this paradigm of Romantic love. She stays true to the vision of her lover; and yet it is precisely in her devotion to him that she unfolds the full richness of her individuality. She is not only passive, submissive, and naïve, but, on the contrary, independent and active—namely, in breaking away from her father, stealing the letter like a spy, calculating the troop movements of Kunigunde's opponents in terms of type, extent, and location, handing the Count his sword and shield at Turneck, and bravely entering the burning castle. She is articulate when necessary and silent when unable to answer questions. She fights for her lover but respects his decisions—first for and then against Kunigunde—in spite of the fact that she has been long disillusioned and knows what to expect from her future husband. Count vom Strahl is equally multifaceted—cruel in the initial interrogation of Katie; sappy, sentimental, and narcissistic in his male fantasies; naïve with regard to Kunigunde's deceptions; a master of simulation in his deceptions of both Kunigunde and Katie before it comes to the play's final scene, in which he turns cruel once again. He is a charming, but nevertheless static character, unsuitable as a test subject for Romantic love. In fact, the Count vom Strahl deserves no better than Kunigunde.

Bringing together what does not belong together may or may not be one of the "errors" committed in conforming to public taste, which Kleist complained to his cousin Marie about. After all, the relationship between Katie and Count vom Strahl at first seems anything but conventional. The same cannot be said of the antagonism between Katie and Kunigunde. The failure of an innocent bourgeois girl in her struggle for a man due to a scheming noblewoman is a well-known driving force of the bourgeois tragedy. Kleist turns this conflict into a fairy tale with a happy ending. My guess is that it is precisely this transformation that constitutes the "fine conception" of the play. How does it succeed in saving Beauty from the Beast? What is striking, first of all, is that Kleist's play deals with the perception of beauty not as a philosophical problem, but as a social or political one. From an idealist perspective the beauty of a work of art is, above all, a balm for the soul; as the embodiment of perfection, it provides consolation for the spectator in an imperfect world. By contrast, Kleist, the realist, is concerned with the desire for beauty as power—the power to fascinate and attract. Beauty, in this sense, is geared toward an aesthetic effect, but one whose intentions are ambiguous. Are the 'true' and 'good' concealed behind the 'beautiful,' or is beauty merely the effect of a self-fashioning aimed at winning others over? Katie suggests the former, Kunigunde the latter. Kleist grounds his play in this duality, which is best understood through the notion of grace, whose meaning in aristocratic culture is entirely different from its bourgeois sense.

The best and most influential source of information on the aristocratic conception of grace is Baldassare Castiglione's *The Book of the Courtier* of 1528. Castiglione, like his contemporary Machiavelli, belonged to the generation of the so-called 1494s. In 1494 the French invaded Italy to take control of Naples, thus marking the beginning of a decade-long struggle for supremacy on the Italian peninsula, which forced the city-states of Milan, Venice, Florence, Rome, and Naples to form alternating alliances and stripped them of their former autonomy. The generation of the 1494s was marked by the experience of invasion, of political and military impotence, and of the destabilization of norms. In this respect it resembles Kleist's generation at the turn of the 19th century, which suffered Napoleon's invasion. Castiglione's book is a guidebook on how aristocrats should behave in times of crisis if they want to survive. It is by no means merely a simple manual of decency for noblemen and -women at court. It distinguishes between *grazia* and *affettazione*, between grace and affectation, or pretense. *Grazia* is derived from the Latin word *gratia*. It not only means grace, but also favor, esteem. Whoever wishes to assert himself and win others over in an agonistic court society must master the art of graceful self-fashioning, regardless of whether or not one's outer appearances correspond to an inner substance. *Affettazione*, affectation, or pretense, on the other hand, must be avoided at all costs. To the observer it manifests as a disruption of self-fashioning, exposing it for what it is—artificial and tenuous; while for the self-fashioner affectation manifests as the inability to control one's affects and drives. Castiglione illustrates this phenomenon in the difference between elegant and clumsy dance moves; in the boastfulness of a nobleman who has not understood that one must restrain one's self-praise in order to elicit the applause of others; and in noblewomen's excessive use of makeup, which merely reveals what it is supposed to hide—the transience of all beauty. Affectation and pretense connote a fall from grace because in and through them the animal desire, vanity, and finiteness of man is exposed, as it were. Grace, by contrast—as the effort to conceal effort—cloaks man's earthly animal drives so that he might appear closer to God. It is precisely for this reason that grace became a central tenet of aesthetic education in courtly feudal society.[117]

In the bourgeois culture of the 18th century, the aristocratic art of self-fashioning must have been an uncanny affair, relying solely, as it did, on outer appearances, simulating virtue where vice secretly prevailed. Consequently, the concept of grace was given new meaning. Grace was not to lack substance; it was not to be defined as the mere product of simulation, but as a 'moral grace' in the sense of Shaftesbury or as the correlation of *Grace and Dignity*, as Schiller defined it in his essay of 1793—the manifestation of a beautiful soul, of the congruence of inner and outer beauty. Educated in a bourgeois, Enlightened fashion, this is how Kleist conceives of grace in his early writings, stating in his Happiness essay of 1798 that happiness can only lie "in the gratifying observation of the moral beauty of our own beings."[118] Kleist loses this confidence after his Kant crisis, which culminated in his statement that "[w]e can never be certain that what we call Truth is really Truth, or whether it does not merely appear so to us."[119] Nor did his experience of the French's artful simulations in everyday life in Paris in 1801 help matters. Primarily, however, Kleist's loss of moral grace, so to speak, was a result of the historical upheavals caused by the Napoleonic Wars, which only a person able to defend himself could survive—a person who knows how to control his estimation by both friend and foe. Kleist thus tests the aristocratic concept of grace in his plays of the year 1809—in *Katie of Heilbronn* and *The Battle of Herrmann*—as well as in his most famous article in the *Berlin Evening Paper*, his essay "On the Puppet Theater," published in December 1810.

The essay "On the Puppet Theater" presents a dialogue on the question of who is more graceful in their movement, wooden puppets or human dancers. Mr. C., himself a dancer, favors puppets because, unlike people, they are

Fig. 45
Boy with Thorn (Roman bronze sculpture)

incapable of affectation. This statement at first astonishes his conversational partner, the narrator, who then goes on himself to provide an example confirming the assertion. He tells the story of his encounter with a young man who makes a movement involuntarily reminiscent of a famous model: the Roman sculpture of a boy who sits and removes a thorn from his foot so that he is able to move freely again without pain. Glimpsing himself in the mirror mid-movement, the young man, along with the narrator, notes the resemblance. The narrator, however, refuses to acknowledge the likeness, either, as he states, "to test the self-assurance of the grace with which [the young man] was endowed, or to challenge his vanity in a salutary way." He thus laughs at the young man, prompting him to repeat the gesture, but the young man fails. The narrator's provocation has anything but a "salutary" effect:

> From that day, as though from that very moment, an inconceivable transformation began in that young man. He would stand whole days before the mirror; one charm after the other fell from him. An invisible and incomprehensible force, like an iron net, seemed to spread over the free play of his gestures, and when one year had passed not a trace could be detected of that sweetness which had once so delighted the sight of all who surrounded him.

The vanity of the young man becomes evident because he does not master the effort to conceal his effort. Affectation arises, not grace. According to

Mr. C., the advantage of puppets over humans is that the expression of the puppets' bodies "transpose[s] wholly into the realm of mechanical forces," that "the relation of [the puppeteer's] finger movements to the movements of the puppets attached to them is something quite precise, rather like the relation of numbers to their logarithms or asymptotes to their hyperbola." The grace of the puppets is without inner substance, geared solely toward its aesthetic effect. Puppets are not beautiful souls; rather, they embody the dream of being able to calculate one's expression perfectly, to control one's communication mathematically, to manipulate one's image precisely in order to manipulate others.[120]

Grace proves to be a pure artifact in Kleist's essay, which is the concept of beauty Kunigunde follows in *Katie of Heilbronn*. She is only successful as long as she manages to hide the artificiality of her beauty and simulate love and chivalric magnanimity. But despite her 'mosaic nature'—despite her false teeth and hair, her enhanced cheeks and figure, despite all of her beauty prostheses—she is not a perfect machine, but rather proof that human performance, disrupted by affect, is inferior to puppetry. Kunigunde's display of greed and anger upon learning of her burnt portrait case reveals that she is not a beautiful soul. That her outer beauty is nothing more than a simulation is revealed when she takes a bath in the grotto. Kunigunde passes neither the ordeal by fire nor by water. Kleist scholars have frequently wondered why the play's subtitle reads *Ordeal by Fire* and what kind of ordeal it is, exactly, that Katie undergoes in the burning castle. Kleist adapted the ordeal by fire and water motif from Wolfgang Amadeus Mozart's opera *The Magic Flute*. In act 2, scene 7 of Mozart's opera, the ordeal falls upon the virtuous Tamino and Pamina. In Kleist's case, by contrast, the ordeals are not intended to test Katie's natural innocence but the supposed virtue of Kunigunde. They expose her art of simulation as well as her corrupt nature.

While in the bourgeois tragedy the beautiful soul fails because of the female intriguer, in Kleist's play Beauty triumphs over the Beast. Kleist's "fine conception" consists in catering to the taste of the contemporary audience and, in doing so, exposing the unreality of his literary experiment. *Katie of Heilbronn* is a genre mix of fairy tale, Gothic novel, chivalric drama, and legend. The play blends virtually all of the motifs of the fantastic and miraculous these genres have to offer: the motif of the false and real bride, of the Emperor's secret daughter, of the witch preparing poison, of the ordeal by divine judgment, of the guardian angel. Even Kleist's adaptations from the parapsychological theory of his time—that is, from Gotthilf Heinrich Schubert's remarks on somnambulism in his *Views from the Night-side of Natural Science* of 1808—oscillate between a playful poetics of science and a serious exploration of the unconscious.[121] Kleist exaggerates on purpose; *Katie of Heilbronn* is ironic metapoetry. His play about innocence, beauty, and truth only works because it is set in a time in which the miraculous still found a transcendent legitimation in faith. But Kleist's *Historical Drama of Knighthood* is no more than an artificial rendering of the Middle Ages; it is a purely "literary event," a "phantasm of the Middle Ages."[122] Kleist goes almost too far in his use of fantastic coincidences, historical dates, and disparate genres, and thus provides a happy ending which cannot satisfy the sympathetic reader, given the fact that Katie is misled until the very end. One rather wishes for her the refuge of the convent, and for Count vom Strahl the punishment of life with Kunigunde. Thanks to the cherub as well as the miraculous fire and eerie grotto episodes, Kunigunde's delight in simulation as power has come to an end. At the same time we see the violence necessary for the assertion of the Count and Katie's love, as it appeared so clearly to them in their dream, against all opposition from reality.[123] The absolute and unambiguous thus appear to be untrue.

Dance of Death and Battle Songs (Prague, Aspern)

On October 30, 1807, Kleist writes from Dresden to Adolphine von Werdeck—the friend he made when stationed in Potsdam in his military days, who became his travel companion through Switzerland and Italy in 1803: "What do you think about the world nowadays; that is, the physiognomy of the moment? I find something comical in its contortions. The world is like an old woman who is waltzing and suddenly gives way (she would have been danced to death had she held firm), and you know the effect this has on the partner! I laugh when I think about it. Do you know that I also did a waltz myself, to Fort de Joux, via Châlons-sur-Marne and back again?"[124] *Frau Welt* pauses, as Kleist pauses; but then the dance of death continues. One and a half years later, on April 9, 1809, Austria declared war on France and invaded Bavaria. As part of the Confederation of the Rhine, Saxony sided with France. Being a Prussian patriot, Kleist no longer wanted to stay in Dresden; *Phöbus* and his friendship with Adam Müller had come to an end anyway. So he left again, this time with Friedrich Christoph Dahlmann, who went on to become one of the most famous historians and politicians of the 19th century. Dahlmann was a professor in Kiel, Göttingen, and Bonn, a free and independent mind, fighting for a democratic German nation. He was a member of the Göttingen Seven and co-author of the Constitution of St. Paul's Church. Born in Mecklenburg, Dahlmann was twenty-four years old when he met Kleist, eight years younger than him. He had just come to Dresden intending to publish his translation of

Aristophanes' *The Clouds* in *Phöbus*. Instead, he decided to go to Prague with Kleist, with the intention of "working from Bohemia to the best of his ability to turn the Austrian into a German war," in the hope that Prussia would pull itself together "from its shameful dithering between being and not being while the rest of Germany would follow the united eagles of Austria and Prussia."[125] The passport was supplied by Joseph von Buol, minister of the Austrian legation in Dresden, in whose home Kleist had been crowned with laurels in the fall of 1807. It was issued to "both of them jointly," binding them together like "a married couple." Dahlmann himself spoke jokingly of two "Siamese travelers."[126] In Prague they took up lodgings in two rooms adjacent to each other in a private house near the Charles Bridge. Dahlmann read Kleist from *The Battle of Herrmann*, which was to be staged in Vienna, as it was "entirely calculated for this moment," that is, to incite a war of liberation against the French, as Kleist wrote to Heinrich Josef von Collin.[127] Kleist and Dahlmann continued their journey toward Vienna and on their way met Karl Friedrich von dem Knesebeck in Znojmo, a Prussian colonel, who was on a secret mission to Archduke Karl of Austria to find out whether an alliance between Prussia and Austria could succeed. Six years later, in May 1815—one month before the Battle of Waterloo ended the war against Napoleon—Knesebeck married Adolphine von Werdeck. He was only able to do so because he was lucky enough to have survived an accident in Znojmo in May 1809. Dahlmann had bought two pistols, which Kleist loaded in a crowded inn despite Dahlmann's warning, leaving them lying around in the drawing room. A young officer handled them at breakfast, and a shot was fired, the bullet passing Dahlmann's temple and lodging in Knesebeck's shoulder. One is left to wonder what would have happened had Knesebeck been able to fulfill his mission? But Kleist's recklessness prevented him from doing so.

An accidental death in an inn—not on the battlefield—would be a lamentable end for a Prussian officer. In times of war, killing and being killed ought not be left to chance; military maneuvers ought to obey a choreography practiced with relish on the game board. On their journey Kleist and Dahlmann were obsessed with a war board game passed on to them by Ernst von Pfuel. It was probably an early version of a war game that was quite popular among Prussian officers in the 19th century, developed by Leopold von Reiswitz from a game of chess in 1812 and presented to Friedrich Wilhelm III. Today, the original game can be found in the Prussian Palaces and Gardens Foundation Berlin-Brandenburg.[128] The leap from the fictional to the real battlefield was short in Kleist's time. Dahlmann remembers: "We [Kleist and Dahlmann] were sitting down at our game in Stockerau one early morning when the innkeeper came up to us with the words: 'What, gentlemen, you are sitting down at your game and don't hear that the battle has begun?' It was the Battle of Aspern (on May 21). We, of course, then threw everything together. The day after the battle, we visited the battlefield; the innkeeper gave us horses and a cart and drove us himself. How light-hearted we felt in the midst of this sight of gruesome destruction. I still hold a letter I took out of a dead Frenchman's pocket; it was addressed to his parents." Then things became fraught. The two were mistaken for spies by a farmer collecting bullets: "Hundreds of soldiers came running shouting to each other that two French spies had been captured. It was then that I got truly angry, when Kleist pulled out his poems and handed, namely the one about Franz I, Emperor of Austria, to a few officers. These brave, honest men considered each of his political poems as an unsolicited, insolent interference, and once they fully understood Kleist's name, they practically—with an unbelievable disdain for Prussian military exploits—blamed him for the surrender of Magdeburg by his relative."[129] The relative in question was General Franz Kasimir von Kleist, who—as commander of Magdeburg—had handed over the city to the French without a fight in 1806.

The absurd move that ends Kleist's stroll on the battlefield brings to mind the 'simultaneity of the non-simultaneous.' The war game at the inn was merely a simulation, but it coincided with historical reality insofar as victory or defeat, in Modern warfare, is the result of arithmetic and tactics, and insofar as they depend on the strategic deployment of weapons and troops. On the battlefield of Aspern, however, Kleist came up against soldiers who were still confident in their own bravery and had not yet understood that, to their commander, they were merely pawns in a military game of chess that had long since become reality. Their military virtue owed itself to an inner conviction. It did not require any outside means for instilling in them the courage to die; Kleist's war propaganda is therefore anachronistic. Heroic and passionate verses may drive an anonymous crowd, but with the old swashbucklers such deeds of a desk-bound warrior fail. These soldiers simply distinguish between friend and foe, combatants and non-combatants. What were they to do with a lyrical homage by a Prussian—"To Franz the First, Emperor of Austria" ("An Franz den Ersten, Kaiser von Österreich")—which portrays their sovereign as the Messiah who would save the world from evil, from the "murd'rous spirit" that is Napoleon? It is hard to imagine the soldiers were able to read Kleist's poem in peace and quiet, so let us be satisfied with only the first of three stanzas:

O Sire, you have become our savior,
　By standing up against the murd'rous spirit;
And like the son of this ephem'ral earth,
Who only fell but to grow stronger,
　You strike the murderer anew![130]

Thanks to the intervention of Field Marshal Hiller, Kleist and Dahlmann managed to escape and return to Prague. There, Kleist experimented with political poetry, in spite of his experience in Aspern, which should have taught him that soldiers would only consider it "an unsolicited, insolent interference." After Austria's defeat to Napoleon in Wagram, Kleist's literary commitment seemed to have lost meaning. On July 17, 1809, he writes from Prague:

> Never before have I been so downcast as now. [...] It was the beautiful time after May 21 and 22 [Austria's victory at Aspern], and I found the opportunity, in the house of Count von Kolowrat, to read a few essays that I had once intended for a patriotic weekly. They were struck by the idea of establishing such a weekly. Others, instead of me, took it upon themselves to mobilize a publisher, and nothing was missing but a higher permit, for which they believed we had to officially apply. Never in my life had so many things combined to give me expectations of a happy future; and now the most recent events bring to nothing not only this enterprise but anything whatever that I might have undertaken.[131]

The patriotic weekly Kleist mentions was supposed to be called *Germania*, and was to be distributed in northern Germany, with Kleist as its editor. Franz Anton Count von Kolowrat-Liebsteinsky, the governor at Prague, was one of those meant to help Kleist obtain a permit from the Austrian authorities for such a political journal. The course of history seemed favorable at first, but after the Battle of Wagram the tides turned. Inspired by the initial success of the Spanish war against Napoleon, the hopes of the German patriots for national uprisings in Germany and Italy and for the entry of Prussia and Russia into the war against Napoleon, side-by-side with Austria, had been shattered. Only the Tyroleans under the leadership of Andreas Hofer had succeeded against their Bavarian occupiers. In mid-October 1809 Austria signed the humiliating Treaty of Schönbrunn with Napoleon, according to which they had to cede large territories, pay reparations, reduce their troops, and apply the anti-British Continental Blockade. As a patriot one could no longer count on Austria as an adversary of France, and the experience of recent years had shown that the indecisive Prussian king Friedrich Wilhelm III could not be relied on either. Kleist's profound despair thus seems warranted. There are no surviving letters dating from July to November 1809. As we know from the letters of Achim von Arnim, Clemens Brentano, and Wilhelm Grimm, in Berlin rumor had it that Kleist died in the Monastery of the Brothers of Mercy in Prague.[132] Yet another segment of Kleist's life remains obscure. There is only scant information about time Kleist might have spent in his hometown of Frankfurt an der Oder, Berlin, Frankfurt am Main, or Dresden before eventually moving to Berlin in early February 1810, where he remained until his death.

But let us return to the happier historical moments before and during the War of the Fifth Coalition against France—to Kleist's time in Dresden and Prague from the fall of 1808 to the early summer of 1809. It is the time of Kleist's decisive politicization, in which he conceived or completed patriotic plays—such as *The Battle of Herrmann* and *Prince Frederick of Homburg*—and wrote fomenting texts for his prospective journal *Germania*. He thus joined a propaganda campaign that was conducted entirely officially on Austria's part, but on Prussia's part was the secret affair of a number of conspirators under Baron vom Stein. The propaganda was targeted at the Austrian and German people to incite resistance against the French occupation, to make the war against Napoleon a concern of patriots across the estates. The model for this kind of agitation can be found in the initially successful guerrilla warfare of the Spanish in the Peninsular War against Napoleon, which began in the summer of 1808. Unlike conventional linear tactics, where two armies visibly face each other on the battlefield, guerilla warfare consists of many small wars—hence the diminutive, 'guerrilla.' Guerrilla fighters, or partisans, are able to attack occupational forces anywhere by surprise. This ability, however, presupposes a civilian population who endorses, supports, or even actively participates in the guerrilla war. The Austrian propaganda was intended to fuel the people's willingness to do just that. In Bohemia it was Count von Kolowrat-Liebsteinsky who was involved in this undertaking, along with Franz von Hager zu Allenstein, vice president of the Supreme Police and Censorship Office, and Joseph Count von Wallis, supreme burgrave of Bohemia. Hager advised Wallis on April 23, 1809: "Your Excellency should spread as many individual sheets and pamphlets among the people as possible so that they will be excited and electrified for the good cause."[133] These propaganda campaigns were coordinated with the Imperial Court Chancellery, which was different in Prussia, where government policy had to be oriented toward the pacifism of Friedrich Wilhelm III—at least officially. The patriotic counterbalance around Neidhardt von Gneisenau and the ministers Gerhard von Scharnhorst and Baron vom Stein tried to persuade the Prussian king to change his course with memoranda. They might have even been successful if the French had not intercepted vom Stein's secret courier mail to Prince Wilhelm Wittgenstein. As a consequence, Stein was dismissed. The intercepted letter of August 15, 1808, reads: "The feeling of bitterness increases each day in Germany, and it is advisable to nourish it and have an influence on the people. […] The Spanish affairs leave a very vivid impression, and they prove in a tangible manner what we should have suspected long ago. It will be very useful to cautiously propagate these affairs if possible. For they demonstrate how far cunning and imperiousness can go, and on the other hand, what a nation that possesses strength and courage is capable of achieving."[134]

One can only speculate as to whether Kleist was involved in actual plans of insurrection by Prussian and Austrian patriots, in their negotiations and associations beginning in 1808. There is only one hint at Kleist's immediate involvement: In his memoirs the Prussian patriot H.G.H. von Hüser states that, in the summer of 1808, he rode several times from Berlin, "where the post office was under French control," to Baruth on behalf of a secret group of conspirators "in order to deliver letters to Heinrich von Kleist—known as a poet—who was our like-minded comrade and lived in Dresden."[135] What is certain, however, is that Kleist's political texts of 1808 and 1809 are situated in the context of the propaganda campaigns that were launched in secret on the part of Prussia while being promoted officially on the part of Austria in order to support insurrections against Napoleon through various channels. The style of Kleist's political texts from this period varies quite significantly. In addition to unbearably hateful tirades reminiscent of the darkest times of German history, there are metapolitical texts which lend themselves to being read against the grain insofar as they propagate total war, on the one hand, while critically exposing war's inhumanity, on the other. Nevertheless, the times of the writer peacefully coronated with laurels were over. Kleist became, as Joachim Maass so aptly put it, the 'torch of Prussia.'[136]

As far as the political formations at the turn of the 19th century are concerned, the Napoleonic raids across Europe had one effect above all: the replacement of the Enlightenment culture of cosmopolitanism with an unvarnished nationalism, both among the French and their enemies. Kleist's ode "Germania to Her Children" ("Germania an ihre Kinder") and his introduction to the journal *Germania* already prove this point by way of their titles. Mother Germania calls upon her children—the German tribes—to unite for the common resistance of all the estates against the French. "[M]erchant," "philosopher," "reaper," "knight"—all should unite, as it notes in one variant of Kleist's ode: "Whoever is a German man, / Join this battle if you can!"[137] The oppressed shall liberate themselves and take revenge on the oppressors. What follows is a call for total war:

> Let their whited skeletons
> Cover field and city square.
> Those that fox and vulture spurn,
> Let them be the fishes' share.
> Dam the rivers with their bodies,
> Let their flesh divert the Rhine,
> Send it round the whole Palatinate,
> There to be the borderline.

The chorus provides the slogan: "Shoot him dead and watch him die, / No judge on earth will ask you why."[138] Kleist's ode is a contrafact to Schiller's "Ode to Joy." Without any moral restraint whatsoever, it praises the destruction of the enemy, whose death is still to be killed, whose corpses ought to be desecrated. In his introduction to *Germania*, Kleist expresses the journal's intention in equally explicit terms: "High, on top of the rocks, she shall stand, and her battle song shall thunder down into the valley! You, O Fatherland, she will sing; and your holiness and glory; and what kind of ruin will roll its waves upon you! She will come down when the battle rages, and with red-hot cheeks she will mingle with the combatants and revive their courage, and pour fearlessness and perseverance into their hearts as well as contempt for death." And prior to these lines reads the following declaration: "This journal shall be the first breath of German freedom. It shall proclaim everything that during the last three years, sighed away under the occupation of the French, has had to remain concealed in the bosoms of brave Germans: all concern, all hope, all misery, and all happiness."[139]

This intention is hardly credible. Propaganda texts are never sincere. They only reveal what serves their purposes and conceal whatever does not. What Kleist wrote about French press policy in his satirical "A Primer in French Journalism" ("Lehrbuch der französischen Journalistik") in the spring of 1809 equally applies to German and Austrian journalism: "French journalism is the art of making the people believe what the government considers to be good."[140] The Cheruscan prince in Kleist's *The Battle of Herrmann* takes this political rule of prudence to heart. For Kleist the uprising of the Germans against Napoleon is a question of education; a patriotic elite ought to prepare the German people for battle and indoctrinate them accordingly. Education to majority is not the goal, as his "Catechism of the Germans" ("Katechismus der Deutschen") reveals, which was also written in the spring of 1809. Following a pattern of rhetorical questions and unmistakable answers, love of the fatherland, hatred of Napoleon, and the desire to kill are instilled in a child: "*Question:* Thus—what is the duty of each individual? *Answer:* To immediately, upon the Emperor's command, take up arms, to set an example to others, as the noble-minded Tyroleans did, and to slay the French wherever they may be found."[141]

Kleist's propaganda literature could not be published during his lifetime. Its full impact would only be made later, in the context of national upswing from the founding of the German Empire to the Nazi regime. It was primarily in the jubilant wake of the Battle of Aspern victory that Kleist's political literature turned to the simple and affirmative, as shown above. In times of imminent defeat, skepticism made its way into his pathos; war appeared the destroyer of everything, and so doubts about the significance of his battle songs crept up on the poet. To prove this point, here are some apocalyptic verses from "The

Last Song" ("Das letzte Lied"), written at the time of the French victories in April 1809:

> A race whose dusky hair flows round its head
> Emerges from the night; that bears no name,
> That, like a fantasy of some mythologists,
> Glares from the shattered bones of fallen men,
> A race that was not born, nor was it bred
> By those who rule the German lands of old;
> That can be heard in sound like northern winds,
> When in the reeds on stormy days they moan.
> [...]
> With fiercer hand the bard now strums the chords,
> Lures forth the mighty swell of melody,
> He sings the battle-song of patriots,
> But not an ear to listen to his call,
> And as he sees the banner of the times,
> Come marching on, unfurled from gate to gate,
> He quits his song; and fain with it would end,
> With tearful eyes he lays his lyre down.[142]

But above all, it is his major works of operative, political literature—*The Battle of Herrmann* and *Prince Frederick of Homburg*—that capture just how frail and abysmal Kleist's patriotic fantasies could be.

The Battle of Herrmann, or: The Prince as Performer

The Battle of Herrmann is Kleist's literature of scandal par excellence. It leaves no reader indifferent. What is disturbing is that the infamous, murderous acts the play presents do not happen by mistake or out of an ignorance of truth—as is the case in *The Schroffenstein Family* or *Penthesilea*—but out of political calculation and strategy. Kleist's Herrmann violates every human right. For him the Romans are the enemies of the German people and must be annihilated, no matter whether an individual Roman is good or bad. "The good, indeed! / For they are the very worst!"[143] is Herrmann's motto, meaning the good must be killed first because they could make the enemy appear human and thus weaken the Germans' hatred, their readiness to kill. Herrmann's wife Thusnelda begs him in vain to spare the life of a young Roman centurion who selflessly rescued a German child from a fire. Herrmann's indiscriminate actions, along with the elimination of all ethical values, have provoked Kleist scholars to either critical or apologetic readings of the play. There are those who consider Kleist's *The Battle of Herrmann* to be profoundly inhumane and nationalistic propaganda, with a hero that promotes total war and thus exhibits pre-fascist traits. And, then, there are others who defend Herrmann's infamous actions as *Realpolitik*, as a necessary evil in the struggle of a guerrilla chief against an otherwise overpowering colonial power. Both of these readings are valid, but there is also a third that sees Herrmann's political victory as a moral tragedy.

For his work on *The Battle of Herrmann*, Kleist probably relied on German poet Friedrich Gottlieb Klopstock's Hermann trilogy (1769–87). He did not use the work itself as a model but rather drew from Klopstock's scholarly annotations, in which he listed and translated the historical sources of the Hermann myth, the *Historiae Romanae* by Velleius Paterculus as well as *Germania* and *The Annals* by Tacitus. According to these sources, the historical Hermann was born around 16 BCE. He was a Roman citizen who commanded a Cheruscan auxiliary unit in Roman services and became an opponent of the Romans when Quinctilius Varus, the Roman governor in Germania, sought to introduce Roman law and taxation. The German uprising began as a troop revolt. Unlike in Kleist's play, Marbod, King of the Marcomanni, was not part of the coalition of the German tribes. In the year 9 CE, Hermann defeated the army of Varus in the Teutoburg Forest. After his victory over the Romans, he also defeated Marbod before being killed by his own relatives in 19 CE, who believed he had become too powerful.

The Battle of Herrmann is an operative historical drama insofar as it provides instructions for action in Kleist's contemporary reality. It demonstrates to Kleist's contemporaries how to liberate themselves from French occupation. For this purpose Kleist selects two central motifs from the rather complex Hermann myth: firstly, the motif of the hostility between the German tribes and the Romans and, secondly, the motif of the coalition of the German tribes. While the historical Marbod was not even involved in the Battle of the Teutoburg Forest, Kleist makes him Hermann's ally. He does so for the sake of a contemporary analogy—that two powerful men, the Prussian and the Austrian ruler, are to ally their forces against Napoleon. Equally important is what Kleist omits: That the historical Hermann stood in Roman services; that he never held the title of King of Germania, despite what Kleist claims at the end of his play; and that he was eventually murdered by his own people. Kleist's simplification of the historical source material serves to heroize the Cheruscan prince, affirming the myth of Hermann as the founder of the German nation. Moreover, the historical primal scene of the Teutoburg Forest seems typically German. The elimination of particular—and mutually contradictory—interests seems to have only ever been possible for the Germans through their joint aggression against some external enemy. Otto von Bismarck's foundation of the German Empire and Adolf Hitler's foundation of the Third Reich, respectively, functioned similarly to that of the Cheruscan prince in Kleist's play.

On January 1, 1809, Kleist sent *The Battle of Herrmann* to Collin in Vienna in the vain hope of a stage production. The play was first published in 1821 and premiered in Breslau in October 1860 to mark the anniversary of the Battle of Leipzig in 1813, the decisive battle in the German campaign against Napoleon. On the occasion of the second performance in Dresden in 1861, the critics noted with delight that "the national spirit of the audience expressed itself in thunderous applause." The actor playing Herrmann was repeatedly called back on stage; he was a Polish Jew by the name of Bogumil Dawison. *The Battle of Herrmann* continued to be effective in promoting a frontline against France as well as advancing German unification. After the foundation of the German Empire in 1871, the play's productions on German stages were enthusiastically received. The Berlin theater season of 1914/15 began, almost naturally, with a performance of *The Battle of Herrmann*. In between the acts victories from the French front were reported. In his 1915 work with the obscure title *The Laughing Soldier's Book with a Thinker's Brow* (*Das lachende Soldatenbuch mit der Denkerstirn*), German writer Max Jungnickel recommended Kleist's "wonderful, patriotic frenzies" to the German soldiers with the following justification: "Anyway, we would always win if we could sing this volcanic angel's *The Battle of Herrmann*. What is a regimental march compared with that?"[144]

Kleist's play has served three functions within the chauvinist propaganda of the 20th century: firstly, to strengthen a sense of national identity; secondly, to serve as military instruction; and thirdly, to provide a character study of the Germans. The latter of these functions was ascertained by British cultural philosopher Houston Stewart Chamberlain, who was married to Richard Wagner's daughter Eva, and whose Aryan racial ideology had a strong influence on Nazism: "I would like to know where else the German is portrayed as he is there? […] Kleist [has] simply achieved something miraculous: He has painted the German as he is; in Hermann I do not see anything 'deformed' or ingenious; he is simply a certain, characteristic type of the authentic, unadulterated German, who, through life in nature, through physical strength, and as a result of his fortunate lack of education, appears before us in a more substantial form than his great-grandson, today's secondary school teacher or orchestra conductor."[145] This characterization is not meant ironically, but—as will be illustrated—it looks nothing like Kleist's Herrmann. What is less miraculous is that the character was repeatedly perceived as a quasi-prophetic foreshadowing of the political realist and 'Iron Chancellor' Bismarck or the military strategist Hitler. According to Rainer Schlösser, the Reich drama advisor, *The Battle of Herrmann* became the "cornerstone and foundation of a theatrical repertoire of steel Romanticism" during the Third Reich; the warmongering *furor Teutonicus* was brought on stage as often as possible. In the theater season of 1933/34 alone, the play saw 146 performances.[146]

Even after the end of World War II, Kleist's *The Battle of Herrmann* continued to be used as a propaganda play. The Harz Mountain Theater in Thale in the former German Democratic Republic, in 1957, provides a good example of the play's continued political appropriation. Accompanied by the applause of Walter Ulbricht, chairman of the State Council of the German Democratic Republic, the audience suspected Herrmann's enemies on the other side of the Atlantic: "The motto of the performance was: The Romans are the Americans, and Aristan [the German traitor in Kleist's play] is Adenauer."[147] To recover from the berserk fury of German nationalism—whether it comes from the far-right or far-left side of the aisle—one ought to read Romantic writer Heinrich Heine's mocking caricature of the mythical 'all-purpose weapon' Hermann in *Germany. A Winter's Tale* of 1844. Here, Heine ridicules the initiative of local German patriots to erect the Hermann Monument:

> Behold the wood of Teutoburg,
> Described in Tacitus' pages;
> Behold the classical marsh; wherein
> Stuck Varus, in past ages.
>
> Here vanquish'd him the Cheruscian prince,
> The noble giant, named Hermann;
> 'T was in this mire that triumph'd first
> Our nationality German.
> […]
> Thank heaven! The Romans were driven away,
> A glorious triumph was Hermann's;
> Both Varus and all his legions succumb'd,
> And we remained still Germans!
>
> We Germans remain, and German we speak,
> As we before times have spoken;
> An ass is an ass, not asinus,
> The Swabian line is unbroken.[148]

Propaganda texts characteristically depict reality in simple black and white terms. Kleist's *The Battle of Herrmann* can be regarded as a play à clef at the frontlines of contemporary history, that is, if one is content to settle for analogies—to equate Varus with Napoleon, the gallant Ventidius with the French occupiers, Herrmann with Friedrich Wilhelm III, Marbod with the

Austrian emperor, and the allies of Varus (the German chieftains of the Cimbri, Nervii, and Ubii) with the French-friendly princes of the Confederation of the Rhine. The obvious appeal of this political play is the hope it offers for the end of the foreign occupation of Germany, were Marbod and Herrmann, Austria and Prussia to fight side by side. But things are a little more complicated. Above all, Kleist's *The Battle of Herrmann* demonstrates how to organize national resistance under the watchful eyes of the enemy, which requires the cunning and guile of the partisan. The plans of the Prussian conspirators around Baron vom Stein to import the Spanish guerrilla warfare to Germany never became reality, but they became literature in Kleist's work. Herrmann fights the small war of the partisan, pretending to be the Romans' friend while secretly rejoicing over every single transgression of the Roman army. Every village the Romans set on fire, every German oak tree they cut down, every woman they rape, he exploits to stir up the hatred of his people against the occupiers. And since that does not seem to be enough, he also puts German warriors in Roman uniforms to devastate his own land. In a memorandum of August 11, 1808, Baron vom Stein recommended: "It is therefore necessary to maintain among our people the feeling of unwillingness to accept the pressure from and dependence on a foreign, arrogant people who are growing increasingly vacuous every day—our people must become acquainted with the idea of self-help, of sacrificing one's life and property, which, in any case, will soon become resource and spoils of the ruling nation; certain ideas about the manner of stirring and directing an insurrection must be disseminated and enlivened."[149] Like Baron vom Stein, Herrmann, too, appeals to the willingness of the German people to make sacrifices. They are to wage war against the Romans without regard for property or life:

> In short, as I have already asked you once before,
> If you will just gather together your women and children,
> And bring them to the right bank of the Weser,
> Melt all the gold and silver dishes
> You possess, take your pearls and jewels
> And sell them off or pawn them,
> Lay waste to your lands, slaughter
> Your cattle, set fire to your camps,
> Then I'm your man —:

This strategy of scorched earth baffles the German co-conspirators:

> WOLF. Sorry? What?
> HERRMANN. You don't want —?

THUISKOMAR.
We are to lay waste to our own lands —?
DAGOBERT.
And kill our own herds of cattle —?
SELGAR. And set fire to our camps —?
HERRMANN.
No? No? You won't do it?
THUISKOMAR.
But, you madman, these are the very things
That we are fighting this war to defend!
HERRMANN [*interrupting*].
Forgive me, I thought it was for your freedom.[150]

At the end of the play, Teutoburg lies in ruins. But the scorched earth policy does not make Herrmann the prototype of an anti-capitalist who liberates himself from bourgeois thinking in terms of property, as some more daring Kleist scholars speculated in the spirit of 1968.[151] The play is rather a manual for the Prussian guerrilla fighters. Kleist makes this clear from the outset, through the landscape imagery of the second scene. Herrmann, his wife Thusnelda, and the Roman legate Ventidius are out hunting in the Teutoburg Forest. Herrmann and Thusnelda have Ventidius believe that he saved the German princess from a terrifying animal: the aurochs. Ventidius readily believes this story, but the German people know better. Thusnelda herself was the one who killed the aurochs. The animal would have indeed been a threat on the open field, but not so in the forest. Here, even a feeble German woman, hidden behind trees, can easily defeat an aurochs with bow and arrow. The scene presents the theory of the partisan in a nutshell. Wolf, Prince of the Chatti, grasps the meaning of the example immediately:

If only we could celebrate sometime soon
At dinner victory of a very different kind!
O Herrmann, just as Thusnelda's steady hand
Shot an arrow through that aurochs' throat
We too could flex our brazen war bows,
And drive the dart of battle
Through the neck of the Roman army
That has planted its standard in our German soil.[152]

Like the French, the Romans may be superior in a battle on the open field, but the Germans' familiarity with the native terrain presents an opportunity for them. In *The Battle of Herrmann*, Kleist thus maps out—like a military geographer—the German forests, swamps, mountains, and bushes, in which the Teutons move safely, while the Romans become ensnared. He insists on the significance of the "classical marsh" of the Teutoburg Forest, about which Heine, who had no experience as a soldier, could only mock, given that the victory of the German people depended on it. The Teutoburg Forest becomes a death trap for Varus and his troops, where the Roman general is hunted like a "spotted stag."[153] The enemy is not regarded as a human being but as an animal, and he is hunted down like one accordingly. From its exposition to its cruel conclusion, Kleist's play makes evident that the partisan's asymmetrical warfare necessarily abolishes conventional martial law.[154]

The partisan leader Herrmann is neither a virtuous hero nor the prototype of the "authentic, unadulterated German," who "through physical strength, and as a result of his fortunate lack of education," drives the Roman colonizers out of his land and gives the German people back their freedom, as Houston Stewart Chamberlain believed. Nothing could be less accurate. Kleist's Herrmann is not a noble warrior, but an intellectual whom Kleist portrays as a deskbound warrior. He merely incites other Germans to kill the Romans: Marbod, Fust, and his wife Thusnelda. For him Hamlet's motto—which German intellectuals have always favored—applies: "I will speak daggers [...], but use none."[155] He is the one pulling the levers, taking action only through words. With his sophisticated aesthetics of power, he fulfills the purpose Kleist had in mind for this play: to motivate others to act—namely, the Germans and Austrians in the time of Napoleonic occupation. He is not "authentic" and "unadulterated"; rather, he takes to heart a prudence rule from Niccolò Machiavelli's *The Prince* of 1532, which states that a politician who does not have the strength of a lion must know "how to play the fox," but at the same time, he "must understand well how to disguise the animal's nature," that is, be "a great simulator and dissimulator."[156] The Cheruscan prince perfectly epitomizes what Machiavelli demands of a prince. He is like a stage actor who puts on all kinds of masks and enjoys playing with the Roman clichés of the barbarian. His naïveté toward the Roman occupiers is merely a performance. With utmost control over himself and his emotions, he chooses the mask of the harmless native in order to keep the occupiers in the dark about his actual plans for insurrection. Toward Ventidius he pretends to be the simple-minded husband who could never be a war hero, instead pursuing a "gentler fate," "to be a husband to my wife, / A father to my dear children, / And a good ruler to my people."[157] Ventidius, in turn, does not consider the German people at all capable of simulation; he believes in the image Herrmann paints of himself as a faithful father figure to his children and his people until the bitter end. The same applies to the Roman general Varus, who, recognizing Herrmann's betrayal and looking death in the eye, at least realizes: "O Herrmann, Herrmann! / To have such blonde hair and blue eyes / And yet be as false as a Phoenician."[158]

In *Katie of Heilbronn* Kunigunde's art of simulation fails in the face of Katie's sincerity. *The Battle of Herrmann*, in turn, seems to morally and politically justify the art of simulation as an act of "self-defense"—as the title of a distich in the *Berlin Evening Paper* suggests, which speaks to the underlying tactics: "Truth against the enemy? Forgive me! I sometimes put / His cravat around my neck to enter his camp."[159] Unlike Kunigunde's, Herrmann's play with masks—what Nietzsche calls the "delight in simulation exploding as a power"[160]—serves the good cause of liberating the German people from foreign rule. But does the end really justify the means? When one turns from the political to the private sphere—that is, to the relationship between Herrmann and Thusnelda—one finds reason for doubt. The propaganda play then becomes a moral drama. Unlike Kleist's ode "Germania to Her Children," which preaches total war, *The Battle of Herrmann* has more than political motivations. It ought to be read against the grain, as a defense of the human within the inhumane.

Kleist conceives a counter-figure to Herrmann with Thusnelda, who, for much of the play, serves as an advocate of humanity in this theater of atrocities. She calls Herrmann a "monster" for his intention to execute all Romans indiscriminately, whether good or bad;[161] and she tells her husband she "won't be part of [his] games" with Ventidius, which he does not respect.[162] With Thusnelda Herrmann is calculating; he does not take her seriously, and treats her like a child, addressing her solely in the diminutive (though the German Princess *Thuschen* was too much even for the patriots of the 19th century; in stage productions the diminutive was usually deleted). In order to deceive Ventidius, Herrmann turns Thusnelda into a mistress of simulation. He convinces her that Ventidius' love for her is only pretense—that after defeating the Cherusci, Ventidius would salvage her body, only to, in turn, send her teeth and hair home to adorn Roman women. Ventidius, he argues, treats her like an animal, and so she should treat him as one too. Herrmann's scheming works: Thusnelda invites Ventidius to a rendezvous in a garden and has him torn apart by a bear, since "he has made a bear" of her, and it is the only way to become "worthy of Arminius again."[163]

As always Kleist's imagery hits the mark. As a German saying has it: If one succeeds in deceiving a person, one has tied a bear on his or her back—which can be anything but harmless. Book 15 of Ovid's *Metamorphoses* describes a newborn cub as a shapeless lump that, after the mother bear tenderly licks it, takes on a deceptively human-like, upright shape.[164] It is no wonder that, according to Christian mythology, the bear is considered a hostile, deceitful predator and the embodiment of the devil, whose amorphous protean nature unsettles all honest Christians. We see something similar in Germanic mythology, where a bear's tooth serves as a talisman with which one is able to uncover lies and deceit, as the bear is himself a trickster, a master of simulation.[165] The bear in Kleist's essay "On the Puppet Theater" is no harmless, good-natured teddy bear either; he does not follow his natural instinct nor does he represent a natural state of innocence, as Kleist scholarship generally assumes. The dancer in Kleist's essay recounts a fencing match he had fought and lost against a bear:

> The earnestness of the bear was robbing me of my composure, thrusts and feints followed on one another, I was dripping with sweat: in vain! It was not merely that the bear, like the world's leading fencer, parried every one of my thrusts, but to my feints he reacted not at all (a feat that no fencer anywhere could match). Eye to eye, as though he could read my soul, he stood with his paw poised for the strike, and if my thrusts were not in earnest he simply did not move.[166]

The word *feint* is derived from the Italian word *finta*, the past participle of the verb *fingere*, which means to invent, to imagine, or to feign. It is a term relating to both battles fought with words and swords, referring to material and immaterial aspects of simulation, such as technical tricks. As we know from the famous competition between Zeuxis and Parrhasius, as related by Pliny the Elder, animals typically fall for human feints and fictions.[167] Zeuxis painted grapes in such lively manner that some birds believed them to be real food and began pecking at them. Kleist's bear is obviously smarter than that. The reason he excels in the fencing match cannot be attributed to the fact that he fights 'naturally,' so to speak, without reflecting on his moves—that is, without any recourse to fencing techniques and tactics, tricks and feints.[168] He is not even portrayed as an actively fighting fencer in "On the Puppet Theater." Rather, he excels because he knows how to unmask every one of his opponent's feints, knowing how to "read" his opponent's "soul." He wins a match of encoding and decoding because he himself is a master feinter. His 'natural' style of fencing, too, then, is nothing more than simulation; the opponent must 'bear' with his deceptions, as it were, which may prove fatal, as Ventidius confirms, learning the hard way in *The Battle of Herrmann*. Only in the end does Ventidius realize that Thusnelda's naive infatuation had been merely feinted, that Herrmann has successfully made a bear of his wife.

What allows Herrmann to triumph in advance—"Well then, the first victory has already been won!"[169]—Kleist also presents, with great clarity, as a personal defeat. Ventidius' destruction coincides with Thusnelda's self-destruction and the ruin of the couple's love. As Thusnelda prophesied: "I now no longer want to see this sun! / [...] Go, go, I beg you. Everything, / The whole world is odious to me: Leave me alone!"[170] After her gruesome act of revenge, Kleist shows her speechless, confused, and pale.

Kleist's *The Battle of Herrmann* is thus anything but one-dimensional. Morality gets in the way of politics. There is no end that would justify all means. It is the merit of theater director Claus Peymann and dramaturg Hermann Beil to have brought this aspect to the fore and thus to have 'saved' Kleist's play in their brilliant 1982 production of *The Battle of Herrmann* in Bochum. The Che Guevara beret they put on Herrmann liberated him from German chauvinism while keeping him recognizable as a partisan, positioning him in an international tradition of struggles for liberation with which the German Red Army Faction (RAF) also felt affiliated. The German Autumn of 1977 provided the immediate context for the thoroughly political stage production that made the personal and moral tragedy at the play's end equally palpable. The actors Gert Voss as Herrmann and Kirsten Dene as Thusnelda sit opposite each other on stage with blank looks on their faces as they remove their makeup, abandoning their simulation and their ideals. Peymann owed this idea to his visits with the RAF terrorists at Stammheim Prison, in particular to witnessing Gudrun Ensslin's transformation from Christian or Marxist idealist to nihilist terrorist.

What the German soothsayer tells Varus ultimately applies to Kleist's Herrmann as well. Varus asks, "Where have I come from?" The soothsayer answers, "From nothing, Quintilius Varus!" Varus enquires further: "Tell me, whither am I bound?" And the soothsayer responds: "Into nothing, Quintilius Varus!"[171] Herrmann senses that he is facing the same fate, that he has come from nothing and is bound to return to nothing. After the slaying of Septimus, the noble-minded prisoner of war, Herrmann is incapable of giving the signal for battle: He sinks, as the stage directions note, "[*d*]*eeply moved* [...] *back against the oak trunk again.*"[172]

It is most curious that a propaganda play aimed at encouraging Germans to take *action* toward self-liberation does not present Herrmann as an active agent of war. Herrmann does not defeat the Romans, as Marbod beats him to it. Nor is the battle itself depicted; the slaughter of Ventidius, which Herrmann persuades Thusnelda to perform, stands in its place. Thusnelda, in turn, sends a bear in her stead. After a mock duel Herrmann leaves the killing of Varus to Fust, the Prince of the Cimbri and former traitor to the German cause. Herrmann, as we can see, is not a warrior but an intellectual who drives others to total war. *The Battle of Herrmann* is thus less a propaganda play than a play about the drama of propaganda itself—meta-propaganda—insofar as it reflects the relationship between truth, language, and violence.

What is fatal in Herrmann's verbal sparring is that the "place of truth in this play remains unoccupied." All of Kleist's other characters succumb to their author's Kant crisis; they know language is not an adequate means for finding

Breslauer Theater.

Donnerstag, den 18. October 1860.

Zum ersten Male:

Die Herrmannsschlacht.

Vaterländisches Schauspiel in 5 Acten von Heinrich von Kleist.
Für die Bühne bearbeitet von Feodor Wehl.

Personen:

Herrmann, Fürst der Cherusker	Herr von Ernest.
Thusnelda, seine Gemahlin	Fräul. Schäffer.
Rinold, Adelhard, seine Knaben	Lina Reinhold. Paul Reinhold.
Egbert, ein cheruskischer Anführer	Herr Reinhold.
Gertrud, Vertraute der Thusnelda	[illegible]
Marbod, Fürst der Sueven, Verbündeter des Herrmann	[illegible]
Wolf, Fürst der Katten; Thuiskomar, Fürst der Sicambrier; Dagobert, Fürst der Marsen; Selgar, Fürst der Brukterer — Mißvergnügte	[illegible]
Fust, Fürst der Cimbern; Gueltar, Fürst der Nervier; Aristan, Fürst der Ubier — Verbündete der Römer	[illegible]
Quintilius Varus, römischer Feldherr	[illegible]
Ventidius, Legat von Rom	Herr Vaillant.
Septimius, römischer Anführer	Herr Rohde.
Teuthold, ein cheruskischer Waffenschmied	Herr Meyer.
Hally, seine Tochter	[illegible]
Erster, Zweiter, Dritter cheruskischer Hauptmann	[illegible]
Erster, Zweiter römischer Hauptmann	[illegible]
Ein Mann	[illegible]
Ein Cherusker, Führer des Varus	[illegible]
Komar, ein suevischer Hauptmann	

Deutsche und römische Krieger. Volk.

Kleine Preise.

Das Theater-Bureau ist für den Billet-Verkauf täglich von 10 bis 2 Uhr, an Sonn- und Festtagen von 11 bis 2 Uhr ohne Unterbrechung geöffnet.

Einlaß 6½ Uhr. Anfang 7 Uhr. Ende gegen 10 Uhr.

Morgen (erhöhte Preise): Achtes Gastspiel des Fräulein Victorine Legrain, ersten Tänzerin des Théâtre impérial de l'académie in Paris. Dazu: „Orpheus in der Unterwelt." Burleske Oper in 2 Acten und 4 Bildern mit Tanz von Hector Cremieux. Musik von J. Offenbach.

Fig. 46
Playbill from the premiere of *The Battle of Herrmann* in Wrocław in 1860

truth, which makes them search for it all the more urgently. In Kleist's plays truth acts as a "*deus absconditus*": "It dominates, in the old familiar theological way, through its absence," as Kleist scholar Anthony Stephens notes in his brilliant study of the unique position *The Battle of Herrmann* occupies within Kleist's oeuvre.[173] When it comes to the question of truth, Herrmann is completely unfazed. Talking, lying, and violence are one and the same for him. For the sake of deception, he even toys with sacred texts. For instance, when he has Hally—who was raped by the Romans—cut up into fifteen pieces, he alludes the Book of Judges (19:22–30), in which a Levite divides up his defiled concubine, limb by limb, into twelve pieces and sends them to the twelve tribes of Israel to call for a national fight for justice. In the Book of Judges, this action serves to guarantee truth, while in *The Battle of Herrmann*, it serves to propagate a lie. After all, Herrmann keeps from his people the fact that Hally's rapists had long been punished to death by the Romans themselves. The moral neutralizing of verbal and non-verbal signs in this play is so complete that—as a final result of Herrmann's feats of simulation and dissimulation—all distinctions between German and Roman, friend and foe, good and evil are erased, and all values rendered void. Void, too, is the dream of a liberated and united nation, if one takes this argument to its logical conclusion. In this sense *The Battle of Herrmann* is a propaganda play that cancels itself out. It shows the hopelessness of a world in which falsehood and inhumanity no longer incite resistance on the part of a moral authority.

Portrait of the Author as a Young Hero: *Prince Frederick of Homburg*

> HOMBURG. Except upon command? God, Kottwitz,
> you're content to amble at a pace as slow
> as that? Your heart, man: hasn't it commanded
> you already?[174]

What the Prussian army regulations primarily imposed on the individual was a rhythm of time, of life, of action, and of thinking. Kleist—who quit his military service—fights for the right to his own rhythm in his literature as well as his life. It may be a dream—what else?—that an individual could save his country by following his own rhythm and achieve fame and love in the process. For the demand for one's own rhythm is always directed against a power, almost asking for a counter-reaction. Prince Frederick of Homburg, who follows military orders half awake, half dreaming, wins the Battle of Fehrbellin for his commander-in-chief, the Elector of Brandenburg, precisely because he deviates from the decreed military rhythm—that is, he does so in a rash and impatient assault. He thus embodies a Prussian fantasy wholly different from that of the Cheruscan prince. *The Battle of Herrmann* counts on the figure of the agitator and on the people's support in the struggle for liberation from foreign occupation, whereas *Prince Frederick of Homburg* relies on the self-willed maverick. The play revolves playfully around the question of how to socially and culturally integrate the extraordinary in Prussian society. It does not present the genius of action, but the dreamer and poet who believes that his fictions have become reality. Kleist's Homburg is an ambiguous figure, like an illusion portrait in which one can find the image of the author himself.[175]

> [T]ake a trip up on a Sunday 100 kilometers north of Berlin to the realm of the Great Elector, Fehrbellin, and Frederick's locations: a barren, arid landscape; it's beyond description, little villages, the living image of poverty and deprivation, veritable breeding sites for the causal drive; and you will realize why the

> creator of *Penthesilea* always had to remain an embarrassing and arrogant figure among a people that had been educated by the examples of the farming townsman and chief magistrate to make practical utility the foundation of its colorless emotions.

Thus notes German poet Gottfried Benn in a 1930 radio dialogue entitled "Can Poets Change the World?"[176] Benn is skeptical. Prussia—a cold, barren, flat, a mediocre country—is not suited for elevations, for pinnacles, for geniuses such as Kleist. *Prince Frederick of Homburg* serves as a testing ground for Kleist to explore how Prussian society treats its elite, and how it seeks to drive out the elite's self-will and pride. Kleist translates into reality the insight he ultimately gains from his play's experimental setup. The Prince challenges the system through the symbolic gift of his death,[177] a gift that will also serve as Kleist's final weapon.

The historical petty prince from Hesse—who was born in 1633 during the Thirty Years' War and died in 1708—does not really lend himself to fantasies of grandeur. He was neither a military genius nor a heroic patriot but a war entrepreneur who repeatedly risked his life—and the lives of the soldiers he recruited—for various sovereigns in order to financially secure his small estate in the Taunus region.[178] In 1659 he lost his lower leg in a reckless and, from a military point of view, pointless action as a Swedish mercenary in the battle against the Danish forces and was thereafter forced to wear a prosthesis. In late 1674 the Swedish forces invaded the Mark of Brandenburg and threatened Berlin. Frederick of Homburg had meanwhile become general of the Brandenburg cavalry and, on June 28, 1675, got very lucky. Against the orders of the Great Elector, he and his cavalry troop attacked a Swedish corps, which, apparently unaware of its superior strength, retreated. With him but not through him, the Elector won the battle, thus ushering in the rise of Brandenburg—and hence Prussia—to European power. It is for this reason that the Prince went unpunished—at least according to a historical work by Karl Heinrich Krause, which Kleist borrowed from the Dresden library from January 9 to March 1, 1809:[179]

> Prince Frederick of Hesse-Homburg, aware of his breach of discipline, stood at some distance and did not dare to look up at the strict, just Elector. The Elector beckoned him lovingly to approach. "If I wanted," he addressed him, "to proceed with you according to the severity of martial law, you would deserve to die. But God forbid that I stain my hands with the blood of a man who was such an excellent instrument of my victory." With these words and a fatherly admonition to be more careful in the future, he embraced him and assured him of all his respect and friendship.[180]

Fig. 47 The Great Elector and the Landgrave of Hesse-Homburg after the Battle of Fehrbellin (mezzotint by Johann Joseph Freidhoff after a painting by Carl Kretschmar, circa 1800)

Kleist, then, does not stay true to historical facts in treating his subject: He transforms the mercenary—called "Landgrave with the Silver Leg" due to his prosthesis, who was forty-two years old and married to a niece of the Elector at the time of the Battle of Fehrbellin[181]—into a Romantic young lover. He has him alone proclaimed the victor of Fehrbellin and turns his insubordination into a fatal conflict between Homburg and the Elector. What one finds here is Kleist's typical poetics of extremes and violent reversals, especially regarding the heroization and de-heroization of Homburg. As in many of his other works, the crisis specialist Kleist confronts the exceptional case with the general norm—has the Elector sentence the Prince to death according to "the severity of martial law." Though, as the play's first act shows, the Elector would have had good reasons to spare him, for in Kleist's adaptation the Elector is by no means innocent of Homburg's "breach of discipline."

At the beginning of the play, there stands an interruption, a disruption of the ordinary rhythm. For three whole days the Prince of Homburg has led the cavalry "in a hot chase" of the Swedes, after which he falls asleep "exhausted" at the headquarters in Fehrbellin. He is not supposed to pause there any longer "than three hours' / time to feed his men and mounts" in order to then set off again with his cavalry regiment. Instead, Homburg is introduced as a somnambulist sitting under an oak tree, weaving the glorious "crown of fame" for himself. Count Hohenzollern "[*s*]*hines the torch down on him from the ramp*" on which he is standing along with the Elector, his wife, and his niece Princess Natalie. Playing the part of the audience, these four are situated in the space of reality, while Homburg lingers in a dream state, in the fictional space of his future fame. The spotlight falls on him as it would on an actor at the beginning of a stage production. Thus a play-within-a-play begins in which the audience crosses the boundary between reality and fiction within the fiction. At first the audience does so through comments made by the "kind [...] ladies": "The young man's ill, I'm quite convinced," says the Electress. To which Princess Natalie responds: "He needs a doctor—!" The gentlemen take a somewhat more sober approach to this scene: "Oh, you may take my word / for it, it's nothing more than a fit of mere / distractedness," says Hohenzollern. And the Elector dryly responds: "Well, I must say, I thought / it something you invented! Follow me, / my friends, we will study him a little closer / up."

With these words the four of them join Homburg on stage, they "*descend the ramp*," "*form a circle around him, lit by the Pages' torches*," and thereby present the dream Homburg is acting out in the proper light to Count Hohenzollern: "Oh, what a pity there's / no mirror here! For then he'd run to stand / in front of it and try the wreath on / this way then another, as vain as any / girl with her new bonnet." After having just diagnosed the poor dreamer with mental confusion, Hohenzollern now attributes to him an 'amphibian nature' as well as a narcissistic disorder—the very prejudices that the author Kleist was confronted with throughout his life. The Elector's quick and baseless judgment can be read accordingly. It seems to him that the Prince is falling prey to the sin of pride: "Really—I / must see how far gone the fellow / is!" Consequently, he moves from being a member of the audience to the role of director or fellow actor. According to the stage directions, the Elector "*takes the wreath out of the Prince's hand*," "*winds his neck chain around the wreath and gives it to the Princess*." This action is a decisive manipulation, a disruption and interference that determines not only the course of the dream Homburg is acting out but that of the main play too, insofar as it ultimately leads to Homburg disobeying his orders in the Battle of Fehrbellin, which threatens the Elector's sovereignty. This threat is anticipated in the dream because the Elector and his entourage are made to flee from the "raving" Homburg, who is stammering "Natalie! Dear girl! My bride!" and who is trying to get his wreath back but only manages to capture one of Natalie's gloves instead. The Elector, Natalie, and Hohenzollern hurry to the top of the ramp, where Hohenzollern then drives everyone through the "door" and back into the castle: "In here, my Lord, / at once! So that it's all a blank again / for him!" To which the Elector replies angrily: "Back into nullity and namelessness, / Sir Prince of Homburg, back! It's on the field / of battle, if you please, we'll see each other / next! Such things are never won in dreams!"

The Elector orders that no one is to "breathe a word" to the Prince "about the little joke." After Hohenzollern awakens the "poor mixed-up dreaming fellow," Homburg begins remembering fragments from his nocturnal vision. While he remembers the Elector and Electress as well as some beautiful lady, Natalie's face and name have slipped his mind. His memory of his dream is no better than that of Count vom Strahl. Hohenzollern tries to mislead his friend Homburg, but to no avail: While the orders for the next battle are being issued, the Elector and Natalie inadvertently disclose to whom the glove belongs. This is the reason for Homburg's confusion during the meeting of the war council. He hears that he is not to intervene in the battle until the bridges that could enable the Swedes to escape across the river are blown up, and yet he misses the precise orders because he is focused on Natalie. When he recognizes in her the owner of the glove, he stands—according to the stage directions—"*thunderstruck; then turns and marches triumphantly back among the officers*" and "*pretends to write.*" At the end of the first act, he begins an aria of victory and takes the "pledge" of the glove as a sign of his double fortune in the future—the fortune of victory both in battle and in love, which is the reason why Homburg's aria is also referred to as 'Fortuna monologue': "Already I have felt / your light caress, already, Lady Luck, / as you darted past me, you smiled and shook a pledge / out of your overflowing Horn. Today, / O skittish daughter of the gods, I chase you on / the battlefield, I'll catch you up, dear runaway, / and make you pour out all your blessings at my feet—[...]."[182]

The Prince thus proves himself to be a hero of words, which are to be followed by actions. He is a hero of fiction, both embodying and conceiving fictions that are put to the test in the reality of the play. In his testing of Homburg's dream visions, the Elector performs a role similar to that of the narrator in Kleist's "On the Puppet Theater," who causes the young man, whose posture resembled the Spinario statue, to feel insecure: "but either to test the self-assurance of the grace with which he was endowed, or to challenge his vanity in a salutary way, I laughed and said he was seeing phantoms."[183] The Elector plays a cruel joke on Homburg as he takes his laurels, and an even crueler joke as he sentences him to death. From the outset the relationship between Homburg and the Elector is agonistic; the balance of power in their relationship, however, is different from that in the Spinario episode. This becomes clear in the stage props used to bind dream and reality. After taking Homburg's laurels, which are owed to poets and war heroes alike, the Elector winds his neck chain—the insignia of his power to rule—around the laurel wreath and gives it to Natalie, suggesting his interest in his niece. The somnambulistic Homburg then pursues the two of them. He reaches for the laurels and the chain—for fame and power—but instead captures Natalie's glove, which he later interprets as a sign of love and a promise of her hand. Homburg transgresses the boundary between fiction and reality, beginning with his dream, and thus becomes dangerous to the Elector, who has the door slam shut in Homburg's face, aiming to thrust him into "nullity and namelessness." Or, as Hohenzollern puts it: It is a matter of suspending the connection between fiction and reality, "[s]o that it's all a blank again" for Homburg.[184] However, this attempt to erase the Prince's dream is not successful. When the Elector is said to have fallen in battle, Homburg immediately claims his position. To Natalie's question, "In this awful war, / who'll curb the Swedes now, tell me?" he answers with great matter-of-factness: "Well, then—I'll be the executor of his / last will!"[185] The Elector has survived, but in the end Homburg—the allegedly mentally ill, confused dreamer—is awarded the laurels and chain, as well as Natalie's hand, as indicated by the stage directions of the final act:

> *The Elector hands the wreath, from which the gold chain dangles, to the Princess and leads her by the hand down the ramp, followed by Gentlemen and Ladies. Princess Natalie, surrounded by torchbearers, advances to face the Prince, who rises dumb with wonder; she sets the wreath on his head, hangs the chain around his neck and presses his hand to her heart. The Prince falls in a faint.*[186]

The play's last scene repeats its first: Homburg dreamed of fame and love in advance, and finally fiction has become reality—or is this just a "dream, what else?" as Kottwitz asks at the end.[187] It definitely seems so, given that the ending celebrates a young hero who, like Kleist his author, is and always will be a hero only of fiction. Homburg's initial aria of victory is not followed by any victorious acts. It is only on closer inspection that one sees it is not Homburg who determines the outcome of the battle by way of his spontaneous attack. In Kleist's play the Prince does not intervene until the moment that the infantry under Henning and Truchs has already forced Wrangel's Swedes to retreat. Homburg's cavalrymen all chant together: "Victory! Hurrah! Hurrah! / We've won the victory!" It is only then that the Prince "*run*[*s*] *down the slope*" and orders: "Come, Kottwitz, follow / me!"[188] It is for this reason that any historical parallels to foolhardy soldiers, which are frequently suggested by Kleist scholars, are problematic: parallels, for example, to Prince Louis Ferdinand of Prussia—the impetuous opponent of the hesitant Friedrich Wilhelm III—who fell in 1806 near Saalfeld four days before the Battle of Jena and Auerstedt as the commander of a vanguard mission, or parallels to Ferdinand von Schill, who in 1809 tried to push the Prussian king into fighting the French by single-handedly leaving the Berlin garrison without orders and leading his *Freikorps* into the Battle of Stralsund, where he came to his death. In this regard references to the contemporary discussion about the reform of the Prussian military are equally problematic. Homburg—who "in this past year [...] thanks to his unruliness / and reckless indiscretion, has cost" his Elector "two / great victories"[189]—is not a military genius who could be played against the rigid order of the Prussian army, in a similar way as, for example, military theorist Carl von Clausewitz suggests in his reflections on the modernization of war.[190] A Prussian officer like Homburg—who faints, is characterized as a narcissistic woman, and stands trembling with fear before his own grave—can hardly be considered an exemplary hero. It is no wonder, then, that Kleist's play did not see the success as a patriotic play that he had hoped for with his contemporary audiences. In early 1809 Kleist began researching the material for *Prince Frederick of Homburg* while in Dresden. In March 1810 it was finished and, in June 1811, he offered it to the Berlin publisher Georg Andreas Reimer for publication, but without success. It was first published by Romantic writer Ludwig Tieck in his edition of Kleist's *Posthumous Works* of 1821, and it was in that same year that it premiered at Vienna's Imperial Court Theater. In 1828 it was put on stage in Berlin, where Friedrich Wilhelm III had it removed after just three performances. Even Bismarck said that "this Prince" was "but a weak reed—with his fear of death." And Emperor Wilhelm II recommended that the "fatal scene of cowardice" be deleted, while German novelist Theodor Fontane passed polemical judgment on such "vain, morbid, truly pretentious wimps" as Homburg. At least, however, his judgment that Kleist's Prince is "actually not a hero despite his heroic rhetorics"[191] is accurate.

Homburg is a literary hero imagining himself as a hero because the real heroic, it seems, no longer has a place. It is in this respect that Kleist's play is truly calculated for the historical moment, following his own philosophy of history developed in the *Berlin Evening Paper* on October 9, 1810:

> These civilizations [the Greeks and Romans] began with an epoch of the *heroic*, doubtless the highest to which man can attain; when they could no longer produce heroes in either private or political life, they invented them in *poems*; when they could no longer produce great literature, they discovered the *rules* for it; then, becoming entangled in the rules, they abstracted them into *philosophy*; and once finished with that, they became, simply, *bad*.[192]

The same applies to the Prussians after their defeat at Jena and Auerstedt and the ensuing wild mass retreat of officers from the battlefield: "when they could no longer produce heroes in either private or political life, they invented them in *poems*." Kleist is not an idealist like Schiller, who believes in a progressive development of mankind by means of art. He merely assigns a compensatory function to literature as the site of the heroic in a prosaic society. Kleist is a disappointed idealist, relentlessly honest in his skepticism. As a hero Homburg is as paradoxical and incoherent as Kleist himself; he is a hero of words and an aesthete who—according to Hohenzollern—reflects himself in the mirror 'like a girl,' just as Kleist reflects himself in this play. In the essay "On the Puppet Theater," the young man's narcissistic "glance in[to] a large mirror" and its interruption by the narrator is the beginning of a catastrophe: "He would stand whole days before the mirror; one charm after the other fell from him. An invisible and incomprehensible force, like an iron net, seemed to spread over the free play of his gestures, and when one year had passed not a trace could be detected of that sweetness which had once so delighted the sight of all who surrounded him."[193]

Anthony Stephens has pointed out that the function of the play-within-a-play in Kleist's works is to set in motion this poetics of distortion of an initial vision—that is, the distortion of an ideal, of a protagonist's fantasy of self-creation.[194] This poetics also applies to the Prince of Homburg insofar as his initial dream of fame, power, and love becomes increasingly clouded throughout the course of the play, while he becomes increasingly paradoxical as a hero. Feeling fearful and cowardly after seeing his own grave, he is prepared to sacrifice his love for Natalie in order not to disturb the Elector's marriage policy and to propitiate him: "My every claim to happiness I here / renounce. No longer have I any wish / for Princess Natalie's hand, don't fail to tell / him that—the tenderness I felt for her / is now extinguished, utterly. She / is free [...] to give her hand, her lips to whom / she pleases, as if I never were, and if / it is the King of Sweden, Karl Gustav, / she chooses, why, good luck to her!"[195]

The initial dream is restored in the play's final scene after all, though this restoration is clearly recognizable as a poetic illusion, as fiction-within-a-fiction, due to the symmetrical construction of the play's overall frame; the final return of the stage props—the laurel wreath, the neck chain, and Natalie's glove—to Homburg;[196] and the rhetorical question of the honest Kottwitz: "A dream, what else?" Literature is capable of anything—of conveying both the conflict between dream and reality as well as its reconciliation. It is a distinguishing feature of Kleist's works that they expose their own constructedness in the end. In *Katie of Heilbronn* Count vom Strahl stages his own wedding with Kunigunde and yet marries Katie. *Prince Frederick of Homburg* starts out with a "little joke" and becomes a tragedy for almost four acts, only to finish as a comedy: Homburg, blindfolded, is led to his execution, and then suddenly experiences a reversal of fortune.

Unlike Herrmann or Kunigunde, however, the Prince of Homburg is not someone who deliberately and calculatingly creates an image of himself in order to deceive others. It is not simulation but blindness that he struggles with. He never hides his true feelings, neither in dreaming nor in waking, always displaying himself in all his weakness and his fear of death: "a fearful, / frightened, utterly ignoble figure, / a pitiful, a shameful sight!" as Natalie puts it.[197] The Prince is not a master of simulation who knows how to hide his emotions; he only deceives himself, allowing his desires to get ahead of himself and his reality. This tendency may, indeed, be one of the reasons why Kleist, who was no stranger to such behavior, pardoned the Prince and, at the same time, marked his mercy as ironic. Such a reading, however, would be concerned more with psychology than poetology. Thus, in order to restore the dream of love, power, and, above all, of fame and honor, the play itself needs a motif—a motif that is familiar to Kleist from military and aristocratic culture: the hero's readiness to die.

The fact that Homburg rejects the Elector's offer to pardon him were he to declare his death sentence "unjust" is not the result of an educational process, a moral reformation, or the individual's subordination under a universal law: "I shouldn't want to act / a dishonorable part before a man / who acts so honorably toward me. My offense, / I see it now, is heavy, very heavy; / if the price of his forgiveness is my arguing / it out of him, then I don't want it, no!"[198] What becomes clear in Homburg's words is that he—unlike Natalie in her tender pleading, and unlike his regiment rebelling on his behalf—is not concerned with the difference between an abstract abidance to the law and higher justice, between duty and heart. He acknowledges his guilt and recognizes the martial law. Ultimately, he is looking for a way to restore his honor. The Elector did not pardon him in his letter but challenged him to dispute his sentence, and it is this insult that Homburg wants to rectify, which would not be possible in legal discourse. What Homburg is striving for is the formal symmetry of two men who face each other "honorably," as in the aristocratic ritual of the duel. Accordingly, he accepts the Elector's death sentence. The Prince wants the agonism between the two of them to be carried out in a duel of honor, so to speak, in which the Elector may fire the first shot. In a duel the offender and the offended party face each other "honorably," because the duel is not about guilt and atonement, nor about truth and justice. It is rather about an economy of sacrifice that enables the potential exchange of honor for death. Homburg gives the law and the Elector satisfaction for his offense by proving that he is ready to die. He who does not want to suffer social death must prove that he does not fear natural death, that he is willing to sacrifice his life for the sake of social recognition. Kleist adhered to this aristocratic behavior all the way to his own death in order to deliver himself worthy for posterity. His last play thus shows Kleist a way out through which he seeks not posthumous pity or mercy but recognition.

CHAPTER X

Losing Control

Kleist as a Journalist in Berlin, 1810–1811

Does the city in which one lives reveal something about one's character, about one's wishes and hopes? Cologne, for instance, is considered the northernmost city of Italy, and Berlin has always been a 'colonial city,' set in the sandy soil of the Mark of Brandenburg, inhabited by nomads who regularly change their life plans, who build and tear down, continually making room for the new and unknown. Kleist was one such nomad; he traveled throughout his life until he found, in Berlin, the place to write his last literary and journalistic works. On February 4, 1810, he arrived in the city, where he first lived at the Hotel de Prusse before, presumably at the end of February, renting a room at 53 Mauerstraße in Berlin's city center. The house no longer exists; today, one finds in its place the office of the Federal Government Commissioner for Matters relating to Disabled Persons. It has remained a place dedicated to Kleist, thanks to numerous events commemorating the writer who wrote his essay "On the Puppet Theater" there—an essay that proposes that those who dance with prosthetics after losing a leg in an accident often attain "a lightness, a serenity, and a gracefulness that must amaze every thinking person."[1]

At the end of the French occupation in early December 1808, Berlin was a shadow of its former self. For two years the French troops had been stationed in the city that also served as a staging post, which cost Prussia eight million Reichsthaler, not to mention the costly war contributions that had to continue to be paid. The population of Berlin was divided into those who hated the French occupiers and those who collaborated with them. The civil servants had been forced to swear loyalty to Napoleon; the banks had done business with the French and the states of the Rhenish Confederation; and manufacturers and craftsmen had produced weapons for them. Among those who hated the French were the discharged Prussian soldiers, thousands of whom went begging in the Berlin streets. Everyone was awaiting the return of the Prussian royal couple from Königsberg, which was delayed by Austria's war against France in 1809. On December 23, 1809, the day before Christmas Eve, the dithering King Friedrich Wilhelm III and Queen Luise made a festive entry into the Prussian capital to the cheers of the people. But Friedrich Wilhelm III had little room to act, given the French's stationed troops in Magdeburg, which could have reoccupied Berlin at a moment's notice.[2]

© WILHELM FINK VERLAG, 2021 | DOI:10.30965/9783846765746_011

Fig. 48
Berlin, 53 Mauerstraße (photograph taken between 1890 and 1910)

Fig. 49 Luise, Queen of Prussia (1776–1810)

Fig. 50 Friedrich Wilhelm III, King of Prussia (1770–1840)

Kleist's letters from the spring of 1810 tell us virtually nothing about his everyday life in Berlin. At the time nobody could have guessed that six months later he would become a journalist in the Prussian capital. He frequented the city's literary salons, met with Rahel Robert—née Levin, later Varnhagen—and renewed his friendship with Adam Müller. The Romantic writers Achim von Arnim and Clemens Brentano also lived on Mauerstraße. Each of these neighbors gave very different accounts of Kleist's character. Brentano describes him to German scholar Wilhelm Grimm as "lively and in good health, a frequent guest at our table; a thickset man of thirty-two, with an experienced, round, blunt head; uneven in his moods, good as gold, poor and staunch." Arnim, by contrast, paints a less favorable portrait to Grimm. According to him, Kleist is "a rather strange, slightly unbalanced character," "the most outspoken, almost cynical person I have met for a long time; there is an element of uncertainty in his speech, which comes close to stammering and manifests in the continual deletions and modifications of his works; he lives in a rather curious manner, often spends entire days in bed in order to work undisturbed while smoking his pipe."[3]

In March 1810 Kleist received news of the mixed reception of the premiere of his *Katie of Heilbronn* in Vienna. Romantic writer Friedrich Schlegel castigated the play in the *Austrian Observer* (*Österreichischer Beobachter*) as "a work without inner strength and unity."[4] In Berlin Kleist seemed to have more luck. For Queen Luise's birthday on March 10, he presented her with a sonnet which—as Kleist proudly tells his sister—"moved her to tears before the eyes of the entire court," and he hence trusts that he can "surely [...] count on her favor and good will for something on my behalf."[5] Here is the poem in its third version:

> When I think back, how, in those days of terror,
> The suff'ring sealed within your silent breast,
> How, with such graceful tread, on youthful shoulders,
> With glory you withstood misfortune's test.
>
> How even from the weary chariots of battle,
> The host of men to you came marching on,
> How, despite the wound cut through your heart,
> The banner bore before us you held strong:
>
> O honored Queen, I call those days so blessed!
> We saw the show'ring of your boundless grace,
> We never knew the greatness that you are!
>
> Your head with golden rays seems shimmering;
> You are the star that flickers in full glory,
> As it compels the darkened clouds to part!

It was not only Kleist but all of Berlin that had put its hopes in the popular Queen, whose affinity for the reformers was well known. She did not, however, support Baron von Stein zum Altenstein—whose patronage Kleist had reason to hope for—but instead urged for Karl August von Hardenberg's return to office. The news of her untimely death in July 1810 sent Berlin into deep mourning. The idolizing phenomenon of a 'Queen of Hearts' is anything but new. Luise became a legend because she personified the dream of national rebirth. Numerous memorial services were held in Berlin; and Müller, Ernst von Pfuel, and Kleist were critical of the sermons for being too sober at times. The poets ensured a more worthy posthumous celebration, with Brentano's and Arnim's magnificent cantatas. Six months after her death, Luise was officially interred in a grand mausoleum at the Charlottenburg Palace Gardens.

During his first months in Berlin, Kleist's main concern was to secure his livelihood as a writer. The financial hardship was great, and he could not rely on any other means. His correspondence consisted exclusively of business letters. In April 1810 he received an advance payment of thirty Reichsthaler from the publisher Georg Andreas Reimer for the first volume of his short stories, which were published in the fall in time for the Leipzig Book Fair with a print run of eight hundred copies. The volume included the novellas *Michael Kohlhaas*, *The Marquise of O—*, and "The Earthquake in Chile." Reimer also published Kleist's *Katie of Heilbronn* in time for the Leipzig Book Fair. Kleist had hoped for a production of his play in Berlin and thus inquired with August Wilhelm Iffland, who had served as the director of the Prussian National Theater in Berlin since 1796, and who was also Germany's most famous actor at the time and the author of popular plays. Iffland, however, returned the manuscript in mid-August 1810. Kleist reacted in the way Arnim had described him: cynically. He is hurt, and he hurts Iffland in return: "Through the offices of Councillor Römer you have sent back my play, *Kat[i]e of Heilbronn*, [...] expressing yourself to him as follows: 'I do not like it.' I am sorry, truth to tell, that my Kat[i]e is a girl; had she been a boy, Sir, you would probably have liked her better." That was an underhanded remark, a cheap allusion to Iffland's long-known sexual orientation, especially coming from Kleist, who only a few years prior had offered Pfuel to lead a 'marriage' with him in Franconia. His comment was also anything but politically wise. In Vienna Kleist's play was a success with the public despite mixed reviews. Why, then, did he burn his bridges with the one person who could have secured him success in the Berlin theater? Iffland, who went on to become general director of all representations before royalty in 1811, initially reacted fairly calmly. In a letter to Kleist of August 13, 1810, he points out that he had not told Kleist he did not like his play, but had only expressed his concerns that "the play, whose poetic merit I acknowledge, could not possibly hold the stage without complete reworking." This fact is, continues Iffland, "confirmed by the report of the few performances" of *Katie of Heilbronn* "in Vienna."[6] But Kleist did not let up; he continued to rage against Iffland in the *Berlin Evening Paper*. In the last two years of his life, Kleist was obviously incapable of the artful simulations of his Cheruscan prince, losing, as he did, battle after battle.

On October 1, 1810, Kleist surprised the Berlin public by founding a daily newspaper. For two quarters the *Berlin Evening Paper* appeared daily, with the

Fig. 51
August Wilhelm Iffland (1759–1814)

exception of Sundays, in a convenient octavo format at a price of eight pfennig. It was available at Julius Eduard Hitzig's house in the evening or by subscription, even outside of Berlin. Hitzig was the publisher for the first quarter, but after a sharp decline in circulation he resigned, and August Kuhn, owner of the Berlin Office for Art and Industry and publisher of *The Liberal*, came to Kleist's aid. Among the first subscribers were the Brothers Grimm in Kassel, thanks to whom we have today an almost complete collection of the newspaper as well as a much cited bon mot: In November Wilhelm Grimm called the *Berlin Evening Paper* a "perfect rag."[7] The newspaper provided a diverse mixture of information to suit every taste: police reports alongside polemics against Iffland's theater, military anecdotes, poems, aesthetic essays (such as the famous "On the Puppet Theater"), anti-pedagogical essays (such as "The Very Last Word in Modern Educational Theory"), and political articles, some of which quite bluntly criticized the Prussian government.

Police reports dealing with minor everyday sensations were to ensure that the *Evening Paper* sold well, such as those contained in the October 3 issue: "The writer Seidler, at 56 Friedrichstraße, found a so-called incendiary letter at his address yesterday. According to its contents, Berlin will be set on fire in eight corners within a few days. But, given the vigilance of the chief police authority, the public need not be unduly worried." This sort of news was pretty good publicity for both the police and Kleist's journal, which one had better

Extrablatt
zum 7ten Berliner Abendblatt.

Polizeiliche Tages-Mittheilungen,

Etwas über den Delinquenten Schwarz und die Mordbrenner-Bande.

Die Verhaftung des in den Zeitungen vom 6. d. M. signalisirten Delinquenten Schwarz (derselbe ungenannte Vagabonde, von dem im 1sten Stück dieser Blätter die Rede war) ist einem sehr unbedeutend scheinenden Zufall zu verdanken.

Nachdem er sich bei dem Brande in Schönberg die Taschen mit gestohlnem Gute gefüllt hatte, ging er sorglos, eine Pfeife in der Hand haltend, durch das Potsdamsche Thor in die Stadt hinein. Zufällig war ein Soldat auf der Wache, welcher bei dem Krüger La Val in Steglitz gearbeitet hatte, und die Pfeife des Schwarz als ein Eigenthum des La Val erkannte.

Dieser Umstand gab Veranlassung, den Schwarz anzuhalten, näher zu examiniren, und nach Schönberg zum Verhör zurückzuführen, wo sich denn mehrere, dem ꝛc. La Val und dem Schulzen Willmann in Schönberg gehörige, Sachen bei ihm fanden.

Bei diesem ersten Verhöre in Schönberg standen, wie sich nachher ergeben hat, mehrere seiner Spießgesellen vor dem Fenster, und gaben ihm Winke und verabredete Zeichen, wie er sich zu benehmen habe. Dieses Verhör wurde während des ersten Tumults gehalten, wie der Brand noch nicht einmal völlig gelöscht war, und niemand konnte damals schon ahnden, mit welchem gefährlichen Verbrecher man zu thun habe.

Fig. 52 *Berlin Evening Paper* (October 8, 1810)

buy in the days to follow if one wanted to stay informed about the risk of a fire. After crime followed sex, the report continues: "Last month, due to the vigilance of the police commissioners, eighteen concubinages were turned into legal marriages." Kleist also did not hesitate to fuel the everyday frustrations of the Berlin people, for example on October 5: "Dieme, a hired man in the service of the merchant Grebin, was arrested for going too fast on the road." But gossip alone was not enough. The readers also wanted to be given some food for thought, as was the case on October 6: "The master lace and trimming maker Martin Friedrich Krüger, at 45 Frankfurter Straße, hung himself yesterday, out of melancholia, using his work chair."[8] But Kleist's rendition of the daily news was not always that thrilling. As a result competing newspapers featured parodies of Kleist's *Berlin Evening Paper*, such as the "News of the Day" section of *The Spree Observer* (*Beobachter an der Spree*) on November 19, 1810:

> Last Thursday, due to the negligence of two maidservants, some peas were burnt and were hardly edible.
>
> On the drawbridge on Wednesday morning before the reveille, the gingerbread baker Honigkuchen drowned—two rats caught in one trap and was held responsible for it.
>
> Yesterday evening around seven o'clock, a significant brightness suddenly began spreading in great darkness. On closer inspection it was found that the moon was about to rise ...
>
> With this extensive rendering of the contents of *Krähwinkel's Daily Paper*, we believe that we did [...] fully satisfy its editors [...].[9]

Kleist is obviously being ridiculed as the editor of a local paper that delivered tabloid news to the general public. Why did he peddle the latest news when he had never before attracted attention by making use of the popular? Little is known of the circumstances that led to the founding of the *Evening Paper*. The pleading letters Kleist addressed to publishers and theater directors in the months before the fall of 1810 suggest that he had hoped the journal would put an end to his ongoing financial misery. Moreover, as he had already done with *Phöbus* during his time in Dresden, the newspaper provided him with a forum for making himself known as a writer to the broader public—through the publication of such wonderful anecdotes or stories as "The Beggarwoman of Locarno" and "St Cecilia or the Power of Music." Above all, however, the *Evening Paper* pursued a "patriotic purpose," as Kleist admitted in a letter to Friedrich de la Motte-Fouqué of September 1810.[10] The journal was meant to be a "*popular paper* [...] for people of *every station*," as Kleist announced to writer and historian Eduard Prince von Lichnowsky a month later.[11] In order to open up to as broad an audience as possible for the national cause, Kleist intended to "lure the reader into his snare with all sorts of amusing stories," as Arnim—one of the paper's contributors (along with Müller, Brentano, and Fouqué)—revealed to the Brothers Grimm.[12] But the Prussian government, which had to defer to the French, would not have granted Kleist a license for a patriotic journal. It is for this reason that he asked Berlin's Chief of Police Karl Justus Gruner, who was responsible for censorship, for a license for a popular journal along with the rights to release police reports. The publication of the latter would benefit Gruner insofar as reporting police successes would enhance his reputation. At the same time it would provide Kleist with the necessary cover for his political agenda and would be sure to arouse the curiosity of the readers. Out of sympathy for Kleist's patriotism, Gruner was initially fully supportive of Kleist's project.

The opening article of the first issue of the *Berlin Evening Paper* already engages in political camouflage by presenting Kleist's journalistic agenda in the form of an old Indian prayer card that a traveler allegedly found in the ruins of Palmyra. With the article's title "Prayer of Zarathustra" ("Das Gebet des Zoroaster"), Kleist addresses, it would seem, the learned among his readers, who would know that Zarathustra was the reformer of the ancient Persian religion. Yet the prayer is better understood without such knowledge. The common reader could easily relate it to the shackling of Prussia under French occupation and derive from it the newspaper's agenda:

> God, my Father in Heaven! You have decreed so free, so glorious, so rich a life of Man! Powers of infinite variety, animal and divine, conspire in his breast to make him king of the world. And yet, overwhelmed by invisible spirits, he lies in chains and bondage; what is worthiest he leaves by the wayside, wandering about as though blinded by error, lost amid miseries and trivial things. Indeed he is content in his plight, and if not for the ages long past and the sacred song that remains to tell of them, we should have no glimmer of those heights, O Lord, whence man may look all about him. Still, from time to time, you let it fall as it had been scales from the eyes of your servant, whom you chose as witness to the follies and errors of his race; and whom you arm with the quiver of speech, so that, both fearless and kind, he might go among them and wake them with arrows, now sharper, now gentler, from the strange torpor in which they lie whelmed. I also, the least worthy, O Lord, have been chosen to your purpose, and now set out to answer my calling. Fill me from head to toe with feeling for the afflictions of this fallen age, and insight into the miseries, failings, untruths and hypocrisies from which they spring. Steel me with strength staunchly to bend the just bow, with prudence and discretion, dealing with each as befits him, for your greater glory to fell the malign and incorrigible, to affright the vicious, caution the misguided and twit the foolish with the mere swipe of my sword point above his head. And teach me too to weave the garland, so that I might in my way crown him who pleases you! But above all, Lord, let that love of you awaken, without which nothing, no, not the least consequential thing, can prevail. And thus may your kingdom be ever glorified and magnified in all places and ages, Amen![13]

In "all places and ages"—this may have been too explicit a message in deference to post-hoc censorship. In any case, the prayer was followed by an almost complaisant travel account from Napoleon's Paris—the capital of the dark god Ahriman, so to speak, against whom the historical Zarathustra called for battle. The travel account, in turn, is followed by several fire reports—among others from Steglitz, Schöneberg, Friedrichsfelde, and Lichtenberg—and by the suspicion that the fires were set by a criminal gang.

Zarathustra is thus the mask of the journalist Kleist—an admonisher, equipped with the "quiver of speech," who attacks the "miseries and trivial things," the "failings, untruths and hypocrisies" of his age. These words do not refer to the French occupation alone; rather, they allude to the general decline of morals in the Prussian aristocracy, that is, to its opportunism, egoism, greed, and resistance to reform. It is this sort of decline in morals that the Cheruscan prince in Kleist's *The Battle of Herrmann* aims at when he mockingly asks his brothers-in-arms whether they want to defend their property or their freedom. With the help of the *Evening Paper*, Kleist wanted to awaken his contemporaries from their "strange torpor," from their political passivity. He could no longer bear to sit still in the waiting room of Friedrich Wilhelm III's politics. His newspaper was meant to comment on current affairs and shape public opinion by means of critical articles. Unlike with *The Battle of Herrmann* or "Catechism of the Germans," Kleist no longer saw his journal as an instrument of propaganda, but as a means for independent and free discourse that was to bring movement to the Prussian stagnation through sparking conflict between the various political factions. As editor of the *Evening Paper*, Kleist followed the preamble of his polemical "Primer in French Journalism": "Journalism, in general, is the frank and simple art of informing people what is happening in the world. It is a wholly private affair, and all the ends of the government, whatever they may be, are foreign to it." By contrast, according to Kleist, French journalism deviates from this norm in that it is "the art of making the people believe what the government considers to be good."[14]

Truthfulness, independence, freedom of opinion: Kleist's principles of a free press are both novel and illusionary in the Berlin of the time. As a forum for speaking both in support of and against the government, the *Evening Paper* distinguished itself significantly from Berlin's competing journals, *Spener's* and *Voss' Newspaper*, which commented on government policy in a sympathetic manner and served as an organ for official government announcements. Prussian chancellor Hardenberg tolerated Kleist's newspaper experiment for two whole months. But when the *Evening Paper* published critical articles on Hardenberg's economic and financial reforms, the government retaliated with simple but effective means. Gruner revoked Kleist's rights to print police reports, which had promoted sales. Political articles, in the meantime, fell under censorship. These measures sealed the fate of the *Evening Paper*. After negotiating with the government, Kleist initially still believed that it had an interest in supporting his newspaper with official announcements and financial contributions. This hope, likely fueled by the government itself, turned out to be false. The publisher Kuhn withheld Kleist's salary, demanding compensation for his losses. At the end of March 1811, Kleist had to finally discontinue the journal, which, by that point—mainly reprinting items that had previously appeared in other newspapers—had become unappealing to its readers. In a letter to Reimer of mid-December 1810, Kleist complained that "the indirect destruction" of the *Evening Paper* had been "completely organized."[15]

At the end of February 1811, after a number of diplomatic letters and, by then, in great financial straits, Kleist openly attacks the instigator of the whole affair, Friedrich von Raumer, councilor to Chancellor Hardenberg: "I have the honor to inform Your Right Honorable Sir [Raumer] that I attribute the ruination of the *Evening Paper* entirely to your influence and your sensitivity to the contempt with which I, during our first meeting, refused your offer to accept money to defend the measures of Your Excellency [Hardenberg]."[16] Hardenberg himself rebukes Kleist by pointing out that Kleist had never been offered financial support for a newspaper, "to which he, the Chancellor, by no means wanted to attribute any official status, and indeed appearance proves that it has no such status." And, Hardenberg continues, "it seems imprudent to base a claim for pecuniary compensation on the mere fact that no opportunity had yet presented itself to the authorities to show [you] the favor of providing [you] with government announcements."[17] Kleist does not relent, he repeats his arguments letter for letter and even challenges Raumer to a duel in a letter dated February 22, 1811:

> Since I have now assured His Excellency [Hardenberg], in support of my claim, that Your Right Honorable Sir [Raumer] offered me, at our first meeting, the financial assistance in question for the purpose of running the paper in accord with the interests of the government and as recompense for the paper's popularity that had been sacrificed in doing so: I am asking for an explanation regarding the passage in Your billet I just received, which seems to contradict this fact. Your Right Honorable Sir must realize Yourself that I, in addition to so many offenses against my honor which I have already had to endure, cannot also appear before His Excellency as a liar. And in indicating to You that, in the event of an equivocal or unsatisfactory response, I will demand the satisfaction due to a man of honor under such circumstances, I have the honor to be
> Your Right Honorable Sir's
> most obedient
> H. v. Kleist.[18]

Fig. 53
Friedrich von Raumer (1781–1873)

Hardenberg's tone becomes sharper following this correspondence. He points out that the King had also registered that Kleist, "at the very moment the new finance reform bills were passed," had published articles in the *Evening Paper* "which were basically aimed to attack those very laws." He points out that the *Evening Paper* could have been banned right then and there and that never had anyone tried to "buy" Kleist. "Excerpts from political newspapers that had already been read and a few anecdotes" could not "lay the slightest claim to a subsidy." Hardenberg makes it clear that the decline of the newspaper had to be attributed to its "worthlessness," and that Kleist's "correspondence with Mr. von Raumer" had "displeased him very much."[19] Kleist backs down due to the Chancellor's "displeasure" and agrees—following Hardenberg's suggestion—to attribute the dispute to "misunderstandings," even begging for a job as editor of the "official *Kurmark Gazette* (*Kurmärkisches Amtsblatt*)." Hardenberg replies coldly that he hardly believes that "this necessary yet uninteresting occupation" could "be suited" to Kleist's needs.[20]

Raumer and Hardenberg humiliated Kleist more vigorously than Karl Leopold von Köckeritz had six years earlier when, in 1804, Kleist had applied for a government position at Charlottenburg Palace. Kleist's desperation drove

Fig. 54
Karl August Baron von Hardenberg
(1750–1822)

him to politically imprudent behavior, reaching for last straws. Several weeks later, in late May and mid-June 1811, he wrote to the King's brother, again to Hardenberg, and to the King himself page-long letters intended to restore his honor and substantiate his claim to financial compensation and even an "employment in the King's civil service." He exposed himself without mercy, sometimes even without dignity. He thus claimed to Prince Wilhelm of Prussia that he had founded the *Evening Paper* "to cover the financial deficit" that he had incurred from the loss of Queen Luise's pension after her death. This confession was lacking in dignity and begging for pity. At best it reveals that Kleist had no idea his pension had been coming from his cousin Marie; at worst it made the Prince suspicious, likely believing Kleist's claims to be untrue. More courageous—albeit strangely convoluted—is Kleist's confession that, in a perfect world, he would have sought "to continue the paper, with complete freedom of opinions, as reverence for the existing law allows them, in a liberal order of things, to be expressed."[21] Kleist's confessions and appeals were not heard by the King or his brother. His letters remained unanswered. The failure of his newspaper project was one of many reasons for which Kleist would take his life in November 1811.

The *Evening Paper* represents a brief episode in the struggle for the freedom of the press and for the influence of public opinion on German politics. For a few months it documented the daily and political events in Berlin, most notably the struggle for Prussian reform under Chancellor Hardenberg after the King's return to the capital. In principle Kleist and Hardenberg were in agreement in their analysis of Prussia's situation after the defeats at Jena and Auerstedt, which they saw not only as military defeats but as signs of the bankruptcy of a politically and economically backward state. If Prussia wanted to compete with the modern Enlightenment nation-state of France, it had to reform its education, administration, finance, economy, and military sectors. Moreover, it had to dismantle the immovable structures of the absolutist state so that the Prussian subjects could become involved in matters of the state. The goals of Hardenberg's reform policy were to restore the state's strength and liberate it from foreign occupation; the resulting degree of freedom and equality was at best a means to an end. Hence, from today's perspective the Prussian reforms do not present a coherent image; they are at once progressive and conservative. How is it then that Kleist—who had been well acquainted with the basic ideas of the Prussian reformers at least since his time in Königsberg—came into conflict with Hardenberg in the first place? Did he, at the end of 1810, side with the conservative aristocrats in Berlin, concerned that their privileges would be stripped by Hardenberg?

This explanation seems hardly likely. The thesis, for instance, that the *Evening Paper* was a press organ of the allegedly anti-reform Christian-German Dining Club is utter nonsense.[22] The dining club was created as late as January 1811, at a time when Kleist's journal had already lost all its political influence. Kleist may have attended some meetings; his name appears twice on meeting minutes. Nevertheless, it is doubtful that he could have afforded to be a member of this exclusive dining club, which included names like Iffland, Carl von Clausewitz, Friedrich Carl von Savigny, Friedrich Schleiermacher, Karl Friedrich Schinkel, Johann Friedrich Reichardt, and Johann Gottlieb Fichte, among others. His friends Adam Müller, Achim von Arnim, and Clemens Brentano were opinion leaders in the dining club as well as contributors to the *Evening Paper*, as mentioned earlier. Anti-French patriots dominated the dining club, and one may rightly accuse it of anti-Semitic sentiments. Jews were excluded from membership, as were women and philistines, according to the statutes; and yet the dining club was not a uniform party of anti-reform aristocrats. Its composition was pluralistic, and it valued free discussion. High-ranking civil servants who represented Hardenberg's government policy and could therefore be considered philistines were also among the members, such as Privy Councillor Friedrich August von Staegemann.[23]

Müller's and Arnim's articles in the winter of 1810, which attacked Hardenberg's reforms for different reasons and in varying degrees of severity, were certainly not blameless for the failure of the *Evening Paper*. The editor Kleist printed them regardless. But the mere fact of publication does not reveal anything about his own opinion. Nevertheless, he could have hardly been so naïve as to be unaware of the consequences of his actions. Did Kleist believe he was safe from any repercussions because of his position as a supporter of the reforms? Did he merely want to defend the abstract principle of press freedom against Hardenberg, even at the expense of his livelihood, and even against his own convictions, considering his ties to the reform circles in Königsberg? Do not Kleist's own political articles in the *Evening Paper* speak in support of the government? They do. Most of them, however, date from the time after his conflict with Hardenberg, which means they had to pass the government's approval prior to publication. Was Kleist, then, a progressive or a conservative political thinker? These questions have no simple answers, which is hardly surprising when it comes to Kleist. Perhaps the exemplary analysis of a number of commentaries on one of Hardenberg's many reform measures in the *Evening Paper* can help clarify matters—namely, the Finance Edict of October 27, 1810.

With the help of the Finance Edict, Hardenberg intended to introduce a program to reorganize the state budget. The program proposed a reform of the Prussian economic system in accordance with Adam Smith's liberal principles of economics, combined with a revision of the tax system. Hardenberg hoped that introducing freedom of trade and liberating the peasantry—that is, the abolition of serfdom, of the bond of the peasant to the landed nobility—would increase production and thus prosperity, which in turn would benefit the state through increased tax revenues. In actuality, then, Hardenberg's reform measures were fiscally motivated, though they shook the very foundations of the estate system, providing the basis for both the capitalist private sector of the 19th century and the political emancipation of the peasantry and bourgeoisie. It was foreseeable, though, that he would be met with opposition from the landed nobility, who would pay taxes for the first time.

Hardenberg's Finance Edict was discussed—controversially—in the *Berlin Evening Paper*. Müller was the most outspoken opponent of the economic reforms, which in his opinion contradicted the traditional, feudalistic state order. Müller initially veiled his criticism of Hardenberg in a polemical, even defamatory obituary on the Königsberg economist Jakob Christian Kraus on October 12, 1810. Kraus had made Adam Smith's ideas, on which Hardenberg's reform policy was largely based, popular in Prussia. But because Kleist had benefited from Kraus' lectures in Königsberg, Müller's article did not go unchallenged. On October 22 Kleist sparked a partly serious, partly satirical debate on Kraus in the *Evening Paper*. And on November 16, 1810, Müller went on to openly attack Hardenberg in his article "On National Credit" ("Vom Nationalcredit"). He accuses Hardenberg—to whom he alleges the "artfulness"

Fig. 55
Achim von Arnim (1781–1831)

of an "ingenious administrator"—of acting unilaterally on the legislation and demands its public discussion: "Let us suppose that the legislation of a major state could never be the business of one fine mind alone; but that it could only emerge from the dispute and discussion among those estates most interested in the state's existence; that it could only be maintained and expanded in this way."[24] From today's perspective this presupposition may sound progressive and democratic, but the opposite is true: It is a defense of the privileges of the "most interested estates," meaning the nobility. Müller's overt polemic portrays him as the spokesperson for the aristocratic opposition, and it provoked the King into issuing the cabinet order that would place Kleist's newspaper under strict censorship from that point forward.

Two weeks earlier, in a moderate article published in the *Evening Paper* on October 31, 1810, Achim von Arnim had succeeded in mitigating Müller's polemic against Kraus, if only temporarily. Rather than criticizing Hardenberg's reforms, Arnim took aim at the government's bureaucratic paternalism—its promotion of freedom at the economic level while remaining intolerant of free speech or critical discussions on the reforms. After the King's cabinet order, Kleist published his own political commentaries on Hardenberg's economic and financial policy, primarily opposing the government's critics and the selfish attitude of the aristocratic opposition in particular. In an article on the luxury tax of December 20, 1810, Kleist mocks Müller's defense of the privileges of the nobility, arguing that the tax, which even the aristocrats now had to pay, had not been issued "to finance the courtly conduct of some extravagant prince or his minion's banquets, or the finery and housekeeping for his mistresses, etc." Rather, he reminds readers, the luxury tax had been issued "based on a firm conviction in the nation's generosity and sense of solidarity, that is, as a kind of patriotic contribution in a time of urgent, almost hopeless need."[25] With this statement Kleist takes a clear stance in favor of Hardenberg, delivered in the form of satire. By contrast, Kleist's article "On the Abolition of Peasant Serfdom" ("Über die Aufhebung des laßbäuerlichen Verhältnisses") of December 29, 1810, was far more cunning. Hardenberg had planned for the liberation of the peasantry for purely economic reasons, and along with the abolition of serfdom, the landed nobility's duty to provide social protections to its peasants would also be abolished. The reform had been implemented with hesitation, and in his article Kleist justifies this hesitancy with Hardenberg's supposed considerations of the associated social and humanitarian problems—issues Hardenberg, as everyone in Prussia knew well, had no intention of addressing. But by attributing commendable motives to the government—that is, care for its subjects—Kleist essentially appealed to its responsibility for these problems in the first place. His article emphasizes that the peasants had been dependent for too long and were therefore still acting as if they were reliant. Freedom, he holds, is a learning process: "In short, if a man who was denied the use of particular powers for so long is restored to their free use, he must first learn to make use of this freedom, just as a blind man whose vision is restored through a doctor's charitable hand must gradually learn to see."[26]

Kleist depicts the social problems of his time without haughtiness and with great sensitivity. Yet whether Kleist was pro-nobility and anti-government or anti-nobility and pro-government is still a matter of controversy. But this either/or thinking is futile. It would make more sense to distinguish between reform and government and thus recognize that Kleist was in favor of reforms but not unconditionally supportive of the government. Nor did he criticize the nobility *per se* but rather its thinking in terms of ownership, which posed an obstacle to achieving the common patriotic goals. Kleist's political and humanitarian beliefs were aimed at the future of a national community of free citizens, committed to the state in their freedom. This position is fundamentally different from Hardenberg's thinking in terms of *Real-* and *Machtpolitik*. It also differs fundamentally from the completely amoral considerations of the Cheruscan prince in *The Battle of Herrmann*. Through the *Berlin Evening Paper*, Kleist seems to have been regaining the liberal, Enlightenment, and moral sentiments of his idealist early years, just one year after the at times dreadful propaganda texts of 1809. Kleist's writings from this time are marked, it thus seems, by a 'simultaneity of the non-simultaneous.' Be that as it may, one thing is for certain: The *Evening Paper* comprised controversial political views, and Kleist was willing to risk his livelihood for the sake of fostering freedom of opinion.

Kleist treated theater directors such as Iffland far less sensitively than he did the peasantry. As early as the first week of October, he weaponized his journal to continue his feud with him. On October 4, 1810, he commented on Iffland's performance in a comedy by Julius von Voss, a work now all but forgotten. The title of the comedy—which is actually an adaptation of a one-act play by Bernard-Josephe Saurin—already speaks to its transience. Here is Kleist's review of "Tone of the Day" ("Ton des Tages"):

> Kant says somewhere (I think in his *Critique of Judgment*) that the human Reason and the human hand are two necessarily related and mutually dependent things. The Reason, he believes, when undertaking to effect its ends, requires just such a tool of multifarious and many-sided perfection as the hand; and conversely, the structure of the hand reveals the directing power to be none other than the human Reason. The truth of this at first paradoxical proposition is never clearer than when we see Herr Iffland on the stage. He indeed, in the most dazzling way, expresses with his hand almost every condition and inner motion of his mind. This is not to say that this entire figure does not work effectively in his dramatic characterizations and according to the requirements of his art: for we should then be calling attention to a fault. No actor of our time is likely to compare favorably with him, particularly in the drama of middle-class life. But of all his features, we submit, none as a rule manages the expression of an affection as busily as his hands; it all but distracts attention from his very expressive face. Superb as this mastery in and for itself may be, we believe that a more restrained and less spendthrift display would result in some overall advantage to his artistry, should it on occasion remain in some small measure to be desired.[27]

Kleist's comparison of Immanuel Kant's theory and Iffland's practice of combining hand and mind requires no further explanation; his severe polemic against an institution such as Iffland's theater—which was sponsored by the crown as well as by Hardenberg—displeased the authorities. This was especially true given Kleist's ability to demonstrate, quite cleverly, that the principles of Hardenberg's reform plans—that is, the abolition of an economy based on privileges and the introduction of freedom of trade and thus competition—stood in sharp contrast to Iffland's monopoly in Berlin. He makes this discrepancy particularly clear in an article of October 17, 1810, entitled "Insignificant Remark" ("Unmaßgebliche Bemerkung"). Once again, Kleist substantiates his mockery philosophically, this time taking recourse in Adam Smith rather than Kant:

> For, just as the baker, according to Adam Smith, can tell that his rolls are good without any chemical knowledge of the reason, but simply because they sell well, so the theater director can, without any regard for the critics, conclude that they are staging good plays if the boxes and seats are filled at every performance. But this principle only applies if the trade is free, and unrestricted competition between the stages is made possible. In a city in which several theaters exist side by side, as soon as one of the productions was to degenerate due to a one-sided effort to draw money into the till, certainly the industriousness of another theater director, encouraged by the artistic sensibility of the better part of the nation, will take it upon himself to restore the genre in its original purity.[28]

However, if a theater director held the monopoly, as Iffland did, and was thus free from worry over competition, he was not reliant on "good" plays like *Katie of Heilbronn* or *Prince Frederick of Homburg* to fill his theater. Instead, trite plays—such as August von Kotzebue's *Tenant Farmer Feldkümmel* (*Pachter Feldkümmel*), Theodor Heinrich Friedrich's *Cousin Kuckuck* (*Vetter Kuckuck*), or Matthäus Stegmayer's *Rochus Pumpernickel*—would suffice, as can be gathered from the fictitious joy of an "honest Berliner" in the *Evening Paper* of November 23, 1810. It was not only the political articles, but these commentaries on Iffland's repertoire that contributed to the state-directed ruin of the *Evening Paper*. Iffland complained to the government and threatened with his resignation because Kleist's polemics began to have an effect on the public. The performance of Josef Weigl's *The Swiss Family* (*Die Schweizerfamilie*)—for a long time the most popular German opera next to the *Magic Flute*—was tumultuous, as the *Evening Pape*r reported, not without satisfaction, on November 27, 1810. Two weeks earlier, in the *Evening Paper* of November 13, Kleist had speculated about the casting options for the leading role of Emmeline, suggesting the singers Schmalz, Müller, or Eunicke, without so much as mentioning the singer Herbst, whom Iffland had chosen for the role. In this way Kleist wanted to force Iffland to at least consider his theater criticism. But rather than Iffland, it was the audience who reacted: "A fierce and rather widespread clapping at the entry of Mademoiselle Herbst—which was made rather ambiguous by the fact that *da capo* was called before she had even made a sound—necessitated the lowering of the curtain." The performance could not continue. The review in the *Evening Paper* leaves it open whether the audience was "dissatisfied with Mlle. Herbst, for whom the role of Emmeline did not seem entirely appropriate." In any case, the review notes that the audience seemed "sufficiently compensated" with the performance of Johann Wolfgang Goethe's "Brother and Sister."[29]

Unlike the other major Berlin newspapers, Kleist's journal was anything but an official or semi-official paper. Hardenberg was absolutely right in this regard.

Kleist's political articles and his feud with Iffland prove that the *Berlin Evening Paper* was not just about making money or establishing a name for Kleist as a writer, but that he was beginning to cultivate a powerful public counter-discourse. As with his plays and stories, Kleist conducted a media experiment against contemporary conventions, which, at times, got out of control. One such example is the satirical poem "To Our Iffland upon His Return to Berlin" ("An unseren Iffland bei seiner Zurückkunft in Berlin"), which appeared in the *Evening Paper* of October 3, 1810. The poem disguises itself as an homage to Iffland, but the title already suggests that Iffland, despite his directorship at the National Theater in Berlin, was once again off on one of his numerous guest performances. While the Berlin audience complained about Iffland's recurrent absence, the "patriotic poet" who wrote the poem—that is, Kleist—was less concerned about it: "No way, my friends! and even / If he's gone through the season / That he will wholly shun you / Will never ever come true."[30] The poem offers false consolation, but what makes it scandalous is Kleist's publication, two days later, of a similarly rhymed poem in the *Evening Paper*, titled "Ode upon the King's Return in Winter 1809" ("Ode auf den Wiedereinzug des Königs im Winter 1809"). The close proximity of the two poems' publication had the effect of linking the two 'prides' of the fatherland, both of whom had proven themselves outside of Berlin. Above all, however, it was the order of the poems' appearance in the *Evening Paper* that was offensive. If Kleist had published his homage to the King prior to his ode to Iffland, the tragic fall from grace to persiflage would have been suffered by Iffland alone. The chronological reversal, however, makes the great appear small; the first poem's mockery disrupts the pathos of the second. Kleist's feud with Iffland thus defeats his patriotic intentions with the King, leaving readers confused and in doubt of the editor's sanity.

Kleist's newspaper project was truly adventurous. A closer look at the composition of the *Evening Paper* reveals that Kleist's experiments with and in this medium had been haphazardly conducted, in spite of his claim to have had a plan.[31] With its numerous reports on risky scientific and technological projects, the *Evening Paper* itself resembles an experiment gone out of control, or a fantastical creation inspired by the science fiction of Jules Verne, with its visions of a cannonball postal system, the creation of artificial humans, a canal dug through the center of the earth to Australia, predictions of the occurrence of shooting stars, etc.[32] The *Evening Paper* thus explored the limits of the possible and imaginable while claiming to be based on a rigid plan and to have been thoughtfully constructed. Even before the appearance of its first issue, the editors touted the *Evening Paper* through a notice in *Voss' Newspaper* as a publication that would attempt "to entertain the public in as reasonable a manner as possible," even promising that "[a]t the close of our first year a more complete prospectus will be issued, so that readers may judge to what extent it has been fulfilled."[33] Nothing, of course, ever came of this, as the *Evening Paper* never made it to the end of its first year, being discontinued after just two quarters. And while the final issue of March 30, 1811, reveals no prospectus, it nevertheless vows to make good on its initial end-of-the-year promise: "For reasons that cannot be given here, I have decided to end publication of the *Evening Paper* with this number. The public will be presented elsewhere with a review comparing the actual accomplishment of this enterprise with that which it had believed itself in a position to promise. H.v.K."[34]

The vow to publicly account for the difference between the preconceived plan and the actual accomplishments of his newspaper becomes yet another guarantee that Kleist did not honor. At both the beginning and end of his *Evening Paper*, Kleist thus feigns coherence and forces the reader, in a sort of feedback loop, to search for a hidden plan. And indeed, German scholars have often willingly complied with Kleist, reading, for example, all the contributions retrospectively as camouflage in the struggle against Napoleon. Contemporary readers, by contrast, were presented with a bewildering mix of genres, consisting of police reports, political articles, poems, poetic reflections, anecdotes, theater reviews, etc., with Kleist continually transgressing generic boundaries, deceiving the newspaper reader, against all conventions, by blurring notions of fiction and nonfiction, news and narrative. Kleist claims, for example, that the publication of the fourth part of the article "The Very Last Word in Modern Educational Theory" of November 9 and 10, 1810, was delayed due to the negligence of a messenger. He alleges that a vice-principal by the name of Levanus sent him the short pedagogical treatise in several parts, when, in fact, it was a continuous fictional text written by Kleist himself.

In this sense Kleist's journalistic texts are no less complex, contradictory, self-reflexive, or open to interpretation than his literary works. Through their literary quality they propelled his readers into action, deliberately shifting the instinct for play from a purely aesthetic engagement to real-life action. The texts themselves created the facts on which they allegedly reported from a distance, as can be seen in the tumult surrounding Iffland's production of *The Swiss Family*. Even the police reports were not always able to provide reassurance for the readers in the way Gruner had hoped. On October 9, 1810, the *Evening Paper* reported that, for fear of rabies possibly but not likely introduced by a stray dog, a massacre of farm animals in Charlottenburg had been carried out. This news was followed by the rumor that "the notorious Louise of the gang of incendiaries" had been seen at the post office and was possibly "still in the city at this very moment."[35] Both as writer and editor, a lover of catastrophes and states of exception, Kleist would certainly have appreciated Orson Welles' radio drama *The War of the Worlds*, which in 1938 caused a panic throughout the US when listeners mistook the supposed Martian attack for reality.

The question remains as to whether or not Kleist always overshot the mark deliberately—whether he, as a local news editor, was not apt to fill his paper without close scrutiny of every article in the hustle and bustle of the day, or whether he intentionally reversed the chronology of the homages to Iffland and the King. Did Kleist not choose poorly with the imagery of his opening "Prayer of Zarathustra," enlightening with arrows a people "blinded by error" and struck by a "strange torpor"? Taken literally, these arrows could have put them into a much deeper sleep, just as they would taken figuratively, if one brings to mind Cupid's arrows of love.

The latter may have been an unintentional joke, but such accidental humor is the exception to the rule. In this regard the *Evening Paper* is useful for illuminating Kleist in an entirely different light—that is, not as a melancholic writer but as one who is able to relate the crises and catastrophes of everyday life with a sense of humor; as one who knew how to laugh in the face of the despair brought on by the disruption of the world and individual lives at the turn of the 19th century; as one who proved to be a master of a literary form befitting the situation: the anecdote. The anecdote elaborates on coincidences and extraordinary cases in history but, unlike the novella, does not present itself as fiction from the outset. Rather, the anecdote opens up the narrative toward reality in that it is—or at least seems to be—taken directly from it. The anecdote, therefore, constitutes a liminal genre between narrative and news. And Kleist's are famous for good reason—anecdotes such as "God's Own Chisel" ("Der Griffel Gottes"), "From the Last Prussian War" ("Anekdote aus dem letzten preußischen Kriege"), or the following one, which comes from the *Evening Paper* of October 4, 1810:

> The Perplexed Magistrate
> An Anecdote
>
> A civil militiaman in Hamburg, not very long ago, had left his sentry post without his officer's permission. According to an age-old law, which had once been of strictest importance because of constant marauding among the nobles, the punishment for this crime was death. Although never actually repealed, the law had not been enforced for many hundreds of years; and by a long-standing custom, breakers of the law paid with a small fine instead of their lives, the sum being laid to the city treasury. The aforementioned fellow, however, apparently loath to part with his money, announced before the Magistrate, to the great consternation of the latter, that under the circumstances he would prefer, in accordance

> with the law, to die. The Magistrate, assuming some misunderstanding, sent a deputy to explain the advantages of parting with a few coins rather than face the firing squad. But the man would not budge, saying he was tired of life and would only too gladly take leave of it; with the result that the Magistrate, not wishing to spill blood, had no recourse but to set him free, and was even relieved to hear him concede that under such favorable conditions he might find some relish in living after all.[36]

The anecdote is followed by the critique of the unrestrained interplay of Iffland's mind and hand, quoted above, and the column "News of the Day":

> Just how often the public is worried for no good reason is demonstrated by the testimony—by now already known in the city—of a recently captured military deserter: "He came across a gang of incendiaries who offered that he join them," etc. By all accounts this guy has now confessed that this whole account was a fabrication in order to be granted exemption from punishment.[37]

Thus, on the two inside pages of the *Evening Paper* of October 4, the reader finds two deserters putting on an act, so to speak, as the actor Iffland does in the text in between the anecdote and the news. The deserters, however, do so to escape punishment: one with success, the other presumably without. The "News of the Day" alludes to numerous other reports about a gang of incendiaries in the *Evening Paper*, opening with the words: "Just how often the public is worried for no good reason." A variation on this phrase can be found on the last page of the October 4 issue, in an editorial disclaimer stating that the publication of reports about the gang of incendiaries by no means bears the "intention" of "arousing concern among the public."[38] At the same time the crime reports provide the very material with which readers make up their own stories and rumors, as the second deserter demonstrates. These texts are thus linked together in what can be described as an interactive game between editor and reader. The reader's engagement is determined by what the editor chooses to provide him with. Take, for instance, the anecdote of "The Perplexed Magistrate," where the militiaman transforms the court—which had once been essential and independent—into a stage onto which he can enter as an actor in order to play according to his own rules. His strategy is one of risk; he puts his own life on the line. The anecdote tells a paradoxical tale—the militiaman insists on the law and, by doing so, suspends it in respect to his exceptional case. He has no real control over what will happen to him; and yet he is successful in securing his freedom. The law is not suspended categorically; at least we do not learn anything about such an outcome. All that is reported is that something exceptional happened which, in this particular case, opposed the law. The anecdote thus reflects its own genre laws: The text manifests as an anecdote insofar as its narrative opens up toward both "the reality of the exceptional case and the exceptional case of reality."[39] The whole situation resembles an experiment whose anticipated outcome is disrupted by one more report-worthy. The anecdote thus, in small scale, performs the work of the *Berlin Evening Paper*: a calculation of the incalculable. Typical for Kleist, the 'project maker.'

While Kleist's wit and artful calculations were at their best in 1811, his reality was not looking quite so rosy. Reimer's installments for the second volume of his stories helped Kleist to make ends meet, but his financial straits humiliated him and led to further disgrace after the dispute over the *Evening Paper*. On April 23 Kleist did, however, experience a small success. The actress Henriette Hendel-Schütz performed pantomimes in the concert hall of the Royal National Theater in Berlin, including a pantomime version of *Penthesilea*. Then, at a reception at Hitzig's house, the actress allegedly became too pushy with the shy author, who wanted nothing but to eat his meal. Kleist fled the scene and sought refuge with his friend Christoph Ernst Friedrich Peguilhen.[40] He had always felt lonely in company and yet was dependent on his friends. All in all, Kleist did not have it too bad in Berlin, as his friends all lived within a few blocks from the Gendarmenmarkt square, where the National Theater was located. Kleist, Arnim, and Brentano lived on Mauerstraße; Müller and Hitzig on Charlottenstraße; Rahel Levin, Peguilhen, and Henriette Vogel on Markgrafenstraße. But, at the end of May 1811, Müller and his wife Sophie had to leave the city at Hardenberg's behest. In order to get rid of the troublemaker, Hardenberg sent him on a secret mission to Vienna to see Friedrich Gentz, who had in the meantime allied with Ludwig von der Marwitz, the spokesman for the aristocratic opposition. In late July, early August, Kleist writes to his cousin Marie: "Müller's departure has plunged me into great loneliness." And he continues: "The one with whom I would most like to have a closer relationship now, if I had the choice, is the good Achim Arnim, whom I otherwise neglected only too much. But since he got married, he has not shown his face to me or anyone else. He has practically buried himself alive with his wife in a pavilion in the gardens of the Voss Palace."[41] Arnim—married to Bettina Brentano since March 1811—was apparently unwilling to take over Müller's role of introducing Kleist to Berlin society as Müller had done in Dresden and then again in Berlin.

Müller's departure drove Kleist to his final isolation. In August 1811 he tried to lure his sister Ulrike to Berlin with the promise of securing her a position at the Luisenstift, a girls' school and teachers' seminary. He would probably not have had any success with this undertaking, nor did he have any success convincing Ulrike to apply. Marie von Kleist, meanwhile, was still a source of support for him. In his correspondence with her, he felt like he could pour out his troubles, and his last great letters before his death were addressed to her. Marie presented Princess Marianne with a dedication copy of *Prince Frederick of Homburg* and tried to persuade Prince Wilhelm to grant Kleist a pension. Her efforts were in vain, though, and so was her request that the King grant Kleist's petition to be reinstated in the army as a simple lieutenant. The King did not reject the request categorically, but, unlike Kleist, he had not yet seen the necessity of waging war against Napoleon. Just in case, however, Kleist asked Hardenberg for an allowance so that he could purchase his officer's equipment. But Hardenberg remained silent. Instead, Ulrike provided the money for the equipment, though not to Kleist directly, but to Marie, who was to administer Kleist's finances like a guardian. Kleist considered going to Vienna, although it seemed "desolate" to him "always to be seeking in some other place what I have never yet, because of this strange nature of mine, found anywhere."[42] But to move to Vienna he would have also needed money. Again, it was Ulrike who was to step in. Kleist traveled to Frankfurt an der Oder and, there, was treated by his family like a child, like "a totally useless member of society in their eyes, deserving of no further sympathy," as he writes to his cousin Marie on November 10, 1811.[43] He was deeply hurt, ready to die, and for this purpose he sought and found a new ally, which in turn would hurt Marie: Henriette Vogel, whom he had met in the winter of 1810. Kleist and Henriette served as godparents to Adam and Sophie Müller's daughter Cecilia, who was baptized on November 16, 1810. From November 15 to 17, one of Kleist's last stories appeared in the *Berlin Evening Paper* as a "baptismal gift for Cecilia M ...": "St Cecilia or the Power of Music." One year later the two godparents went together to their death.

CHAPTER XI

On the German Michel and *Stimmung*

Kleist's Novellas II

The first volume of Kleist's stories was published in the Berlin Realschulbuchhandlung at the end of September 1810. It contains *Michael Kohlhaas*, *The Marquise of O—*, and "The Earthquake in Chile," for which Kleist received a honorarium of fifty Reichsthaler. The volume must have sold well, given the fact that Georg Andreas Reimer paid Kleist twice as much for the second volume, which appeared in August 1811, containing "The Betrothal in Santo Domingo," "The Beggarwoman of Locarno," "The Foundling," "St Cecilia or the Power of Music," and "The Duel." "The Foundling" and "The Duel" were first publications, while each of the other stories had been published before, and some as earlier versions, either in Kleist's own journal or in others. It was only through these collected volumes that Kleist, the storyteller, finally gained the recognition from his contemporaries he had so long deserved. On November 24, 1810, the Leipzig *Journal for the Elegant World* featured a review that sang paeans to Kleist's stories, probably written by Wilhelm Grimm. The assertion, the review notes, that "we [Germans] are still very much inferior to our Western neighbors when it comes to the subject of storytelling" is false. Kleist's stories are "by no means French, but indeed German in nature, and only all the more excellent for it." Grimm attributes to them a "thoroughness," a "depth," and a "pure sense of life." They are, he writes, by no means popular fiction for the crowd; rather, everything in them is "exceptional, in terms of disposition, plot, and depicted events."[1]

While the attributes Grimm ascribed to Kleist's stories are accurate, it is inaccurate to render them as German national stereotypes. As Kleist suggested to Reimer, he wanted to publish his collected volumes under the title *Moral Tales*.[2] He thus followed a genuinely French tradition, for which Jean-François Marmontel with his *Moral Tales* (*Contes moraux*) of 1761 provided the genre model. The English translation of Marmontel's title, however, conceals the fact that his stories are anything but moral, that Marmontel understood his 'contes moraux' as 'contes sur les mœurs.' His stories revolve around the analysis of mores, regardless of whether his stories conform to social conventions or not, which is in keeping with the European moralist tradition. In this sense Kleist's novellas can also be regarded as behavioral studies, as illustrated in my readings of "The Earthquake in Chile," "The Foundling," and *The Marquise*

© WILHELM FINK VERLAG, 2021 | DOI:10.30965/9783846765746_012

of O— in Chapter VIII. What makes them comparable to his anecdotes is that they open themselves up to exceptional cases of reality. Kleist can be regarded as a skeptical behaviorist, which is a rather rare type in German literature and thought, with few exceptions from Georg Christoph Lichtenberg to Arthur Schopenhauer and Friedrich Nietzsche to Ernst Jünger. With its directive of self-cultivation, German idealism essentially prevents the reception of the European moralist tradition. Rather than describing how people behave, German idealists prescribe how they *should* behave. Kleist's novellas, by contrast, do not feature characters who are thrown into brooding by their self-cultivation, rapt in melancholic interiority, but rather characters who take action and founder. Kleist is not a moral philosopher, either as a storyteller or as an essayist; rather, he is a moralist. He does not erect systematic intellectual edifices, but assembles individual cases and contradictions. Contrary to what Grimm claims, Kleist does not take a uniquely German path as a storyteller. His novellas are "German in nature" only insofar as they reflect his suffering from German politics. Kleist's most well-known text is a prime example of this kind of suffering and, indeed, this suffering may even be the reason for which it is so well known.

German Virtues, German Vices: *Michael Kohlhaas*

Behind names there are stories. What, then, is the story behind Michael Kohlhaas? According to the *Chronicle of the Margraviate* (*Märkische Chronik*) by Peter Hafftitz—one of the sources for Kleist's novella—the Berlin merchant who led a feud against the noble lawbreaker Junker von Zaschwitz and the state of Saxony was called Hans Kohlhase. He ignited the feud in 1534 due to the mistreatment of his horses and was eventually executed in 1540. A study of the legal and historical background of the feud shows that Kleist was well informed about its dates and facts.[3] The fact that Kleist changed the protagonist's first name is an indication that he wanted to create a personification of the German that could also take on the meaning of two other Mich(a)els: the German Michel—the naïve and foolish German everyman, a national stereotype known since the Early Modern period—as well as the Archangel Michael—the defiant dragon or Satan slayer, patron saint of the Holy Roman Empire and the Germans. And it goes without saying that Kleist changed the name Kohl*hase* into Kohlhaas because the hero of the story proves to be anything but a harmless hare (German: *Hase*). If anything, for Kleist the 'German' animal par excellence would be Thusnelda's bear.

The wealth of readings on *Michael Kohlhaas* could not possibly be reviewed here.[4] Instead, the text shall be read in the context of Kleist's biographical development, that is, as a testimony to the changes in the author's position regarding both the patriotic and anthropological discourses between 1804 and 1810—the time of the novella's creation. Ernst von Pfuel allegedly told Kleist about the historical Kohlhase in Berlin in 1804/05, at least according to Kleist biographer Wilhelm von Schütz.[5] In 1808 Kleist published a fragment of his *Kohlhaas* in the Dresden journal *Phöbus*. The revised, complete version of the story was later published in Berlin, in the first volume of Reimer's collection of 1810. At the beginning of 1804, Baron vom Stein wrote an "Open Letter" to his sovereign, the Prince of Nassau-Usingen, accusing him of having unjustly taken away his imperial knightly estates and of having thus betrayed the very idea of the Holy Roman Empire. While the story of Hans Kohlhase—as recorded in the *Chronicle of the Margraviate*—served as the *historical* source for Kleist's novella, it is conceivable that Stein's letter was its *contemporary* reference, its generative core. Kleist scholarship has thus far overlooked this similarity between the novella and the letter,[6] and so it seems appropriate to present some longer excerpts from Stein's letter:

> Your Serene Highness, by issuing a patent on December 31, 1803, has taken possession of the villages of Frücht and Schweighausen, which have belonged to my family for centuries, with the intention "to secure them against the other estates and to lay claim to territorial sovereignty should the free imperial knighthood be dissolved."
>
> As a commentary to the patent, Your Serene Highness' officials forbade my subjects to pay me my outstanding and currently due rent, and they combined the sanctioned suppression of my independence with what appears to be an unauthorized deprivation of my property. [...]
>
> Germany's independence and autonomy will gain little from the consolidation of the few estates of the free imperial knights with the small territories surrounding them. If these charitable purposes, which are so beneficial to our nation, are to be achieved, these small states must be united with the two great monarchies on whose existence the continuation of the German name depends; and providence may grant that I may experience this happy event.
>
> The blood of the German nobility was spilled in the fierce conflict from which Germany is now recovering. Germany's numerous sovereigns—with the exception of the noble Duke of Brunswick—avoided all participation and sought to preserve their feeble persistence by emigrating, by negotiating with or bribing the French military leaders.
>
> What would Germany's independence gain if its forces were concentrated to an even greater extent in these hands? [...]
>
> Protection is what I expect from the imperial laws on which the personal rights and the sovereignty of the Princes are based, and from the sovereign of

> the Empire, who has made his will clear enough to those Princes guilty of acting on their own authority and perpetuating violence against the weak. [...]
>
> Should the free imperial knighthood be violently shattered, I will renounce my dwelling in a country which surrounds me with objects of bitter memory and where everything reminds me of the loss of my independence and of my new fetters.
>
> It is hard to have to leave an estate that has demonstrably been in the family for seven hundred years; and to have to transplant to distant lands; and to give up the prospect of enjoying the peace and quiet of one's own father's home, with memories of one's youth, after a worksome and—I dare say so—profitable business life and the prospect of expecting the passage to a better life. It is even harder to bring all these sacrifices not for some great noble purpose promoting the common good, but in order to evade the unlawful superiority, in order to—but there is a judging conscience and a punishing God.[7]

After Napoleon declared war on England, the occupation of Hanover in the summer of 1803 marked the beginning of the 'French period' in northern Germany. The dissolution of the Holy Roman Empire was already foreseeable before the defeat at Jena and Auerstedt in 1806. As a precaution the German territorial rulers, such as the Prince of Nassau-Usingen, began declaring their claim to the imperial knightly estates located in their territories. This historical context provides the background to Stein's letter, in which he protests on behalf of the entire free imperial knighthood. What is extraordinary about his letter is the tone that disregards all differences in station. A representative of the lower nobility accuses his sovereign of betraying the very idea of the Empire. The lower nobility sacrificed their lives for this idea, while the high nobility gave it up for the sake of securing their estates. The only hope left is a coalition between the two monarchies of Prussia and Austria. The end of the letter marks its climax, the melodramatically staged farewell—Baron vom Stein's announcement of emigration—for he no longer wants to live in a country that denies him protection, justice, and independence. The Prince's arbitrary actions are ultimately entrusted to divine justice.

Copies of Stein's letter of January 13, 1804, were circulated among the free imperial knights and achieved great publicity.[8] And it was in May 1804 that Kleist came to Berlin. There, he met Jacobin-minded, patriotic people, like Rühle von Lilienstern and Christian von Massenbach, as well as reformist-minded, liberal people, like Ernst von Pfuel. It is conceivable that Stein's letter was the subject of their discussions. In any case, we are invited to consider the parallels between Stein's letter and Kleist's novella. The climax of Stein's letter is characterized by the same sentiment that marks the turning point in Kleist's story. Kohlhaas sets out from Kohlhaasenbrück because, as he points out to his wife Lisbeth, "I do not wish to remain in a country where I and my rights are not defended. If I am to be kicked, I would rather be a dog than a man!"[9] Unlike Stein, he does not find consolation in a "punishing God," but rather usurps the role of the Archangel Michael's emissary, who aims to set the world aright. Like Stein, Kohlhaas criticizes a self-serving, decadent nobility that disdains the people and their rights and that puts its own interests above those of the general public. However, in contrast to Stein, Kohlhaas is himself not a member of the nobility; yet the novella repeatedly emphasizes his righteousness and virtuousness as well as his sense of honor. It is not his aristocratic adversaries but Kohlhaas himself who demonstrates aristocratic behavior.

Perhaps Stein's letter did provide a model for Kleist's novella, but one can only speculate. What is certain is that both the letter and the novella must be considered in the context of the patriotic reform discourse of the time. The rebellion of the horse-dealer corresponds to the discursive position of the aristocratic reformers Stein, Karl August von Hardenberg, Neidhardt von Gneisenau, and Gerhard von Scharnhorst. On the one hand, these reformers wanted to lead the Prussian people before they rose up on their own authority or fell for the allegedly revolutionary promises of the French occupiers. On the other hand, they had to assert themselves against a conservative aristocratic opposition. Kleist sided with the reformers, having nothing to lose, unlike Stein, who was only able to openly voice his criticism of his Hessian sovereign because he was considering selling his family estates and had already purchased property in South Prussia three years earlier. In a rhetorical game Stein's protest letter evokes the dreadful scenario of his fictional displacement. Kohlhaas, meanwhile, shares his name with Kohlhaasenbrück, a place he does not own, and he becomes placeless due to his feud. Likewise, Kleist has always been without a sense of place; he belonged to the dispossessed nobility, whose reputation was no longer self-evident. And it is in this sense that his novella can be regarded as an experimental testing ground for historical and contemporary models of nobility.

The horse-dealer, on his trip from Brandenburg to Saxony, is interrupted by a toll-gate at Tronka Castle, which the new master had built. Kohlhaas remembers the old master nostalgically: "A fine old gentleman, who enjoyed people coming and going and assisted trade and traffic whenever he could. Once he had a road paved because a mare of mine broke her leg out there where the highway leads into the village." To the toll-keeper, carrying out his job with a "sullen face," he adds: "[I]t would have been better for me and for you if the tree for that pole had never been felled."[10] With this scene Kleist alludes to the fundamental transformation of social life in contemporary Prussia. The new master of Tronka Castle, Junker Wenzel, pursues solely his own economic interests. The situation was different under the "fine old gentleman"—a reference that surely would have brought to life the memory of Friedrich the Great, also known as 'The Old Fritz,' in Prussian readers at the turn of the 19th century. Friedrich the Great cared for the well-being of his peasants and was known to especially protect the members of the lower estate from acts of violence by the nobility. His ruling in the Miller Arnold case in 1779 became legendary in Prussia, in which he overturned a supposedly unlawful sentence: The miller Christian Arnold from Pommerzig had been unable to pay rent to his landlord, Count von Schmettau, because someone had partly dammed the watercourse that supplied Arnold's mill to supply his own carp pond with water. As a result of the lawsuit that followed, the sale of the mill was ordered. The miller appealed the ruling and lost, but he found sympathy for his situation with his King. In this case the Old Fritz accused several judicial officers of being too lenient toward the nobility and of therefore having violated their legal obligations. He had them imprisoned and, in addition, Count von Schmettau had to pay damages to the miller.[11] In old Prussia a fairy tale comes true for the miller, which Kohlhaas can only hope for in vain, since Kleist made the setting of Kohlhaas' story a mirror of his own time. The crisis-ridden Prussia at the turn of the 19th century lacked 'fine old gentlemen' like Friedrich the Great, who was "met by fear":

> No one, not the general at the head of a regiment, not the head of one of the *Landescollegii*, nor some official in his business circle, trusted even the least significant person; for the latter had access to the very highest person, the King, just as well as the most respected. The notes the King often attached to submitted reports document the strict attention with which this rare man on the throne monitored his councilors, and with which he warned them just as forcefully as with his cane. [...] This fear produced the most fortunate effects. It made the coward brave, the dawdler diligent, and the deceiver honest. But this fear disappeared along with the spirit of Friedrich the Great and Only.

This nostalgia for a sovereign who allows even the members of the lower estate—the "least significant" ones—be heard and granted justice is taken from Friedrich von Cölln's *Marginalia* to his work *Confidential Letters on the Internal Developments at the Prussian Court* (*Vertraute Briefe über die inneren Verhältnisse am Preußischen Hofe*), published in 1807.[12] Kleist's friend from his time in the Potsdam regiment, Christian von Massenbach, takes a similar stance in his book *Memorabilia on the History of the Decline of the Prussian State since 1794* (*Historische Denkwürdigkeiten zur Geschichte des Verfalls des preußischen Staats seit dem Jahr 1794*), published in Amsterdam in 1809. Such topoi of decadence are common in patriotic discourse. The reformers use them to criticize the contemporary situation, to confront the new generation of self-serving noblemen—who treat their subjects with little fatherly care—with an idealized counter-image of Friedrich the Great. And so does Kleist, to quote his novella once again: "[I]t would have been better for me and for you if the tree for that pole had never been felled." Kohlhaas not only reminds the reader of the "fine old gentleman," he also models his own behavior after him. For example, after being convinced of his groom Herse's innocence with respect to the miserable condition of the horses left at Tronka Castle as collateral, Kohlhaas treats his ailing groom—who was badly abused by Junker Wenzel—with fatherly care, even though, given his age, Kohlhaas could easily be Herse's son: "I am sorry you have not fared better in my service; go, go to bed, Herse, have a bottle of wine brought to you and console yourself with the thought that you will get justice done you!"[13] As with the Old Fritz, Kohlhaas' fatherly care toward his groom induces loyalty and an enthusiasm for fighting. Indeed, Kohlhaas does not have to ask Herse twice for his help in the fight against Wenzel: "Herse had no sooner understood his master than he exultantly cried: 'Sir, this very day!' [...] Kohlhaas then sold his house, and packed his children off in a carriage across the border; at nightfall he gathered together his seven loyal grooms, armed them, gave them mounts, and set off for Tronka Castle."[14]

The Late Medieval material allows Kleist to resurrect the distinction between knightly virtues and vices as both a warning and advice for the contemporary German nobility. Accordingly, the opposition between Kohlhaas and Junker Wenzel turns into a clash between virtues and vices. Wenzel not only acts in an unlawful manner, he also has a penchant for the deadly sins and other sub-sins, such as *superbia, gula, intolerantia*, and *ignavia*. He is proud, immoderate, intolerant, and cowardly. He is portrayed as a drinker and gambler who indulges in joking at Kohlhaas' expense and who would rather hunt harmless hares than fight against Kohlhaas. Kohlhaas, in turn, notwithstanding his name, is anything but a hare, rather invading the enemy territory "like a wolf from the wilderness," as Martin Luther puts it. The cowardly Wenzel does not waste a thought on defending himself and his castle when Kohlhaas, with his "handful of men"—with Herse and his six other grooms—sets fire to the outhouses, descending on the place like "the avenging angel of heaven." "The Junker, amid much laughter, was in the act of reading aloud to a gathering of young friends the edict issued to him by the horse-dealer: but no sooner had he heard the latter's voice in the courtyard than, turning as white as a sheet, he cried out to the company: 'Brothers, save yourselves!' and vanished."[15] Kleist's portrait of Wenzel fits in with the contemporary discourse on nobility, namely with Friedrich von Cölln's criticism in *Confidential Letters* of 1807:

> When I come to think about it: What our nobility once was, and what it is now? Then I do not have the slightest doubt that it will inevitably be destroyed and perish; whether the blow comes from the outside or from within. In France it came from within, for here the nobility had reached its highest level of depravity; its edifice no longer had a foundation, it had to collapse [as does Tronka Castle, by the way]. With us the blow comes from the outside, its effect will be all the more forceful. Our nobility was supposed to defend the fatherland, save the constitution? This task was too difficult for it, who only knows how to enjoy, to reap where others have sown. The opiates that it has been using and consuming to excess through its deposit credit systems are helping to dissolve it completely now that its body is exposed to the hurricane of war. The sleep of death—exhaustion—fatigue now set in, and we will soon see its body being buried, even if peace returns to our country.[16]

According to Cölln, the edifice of the German nobility will collapse from a "blow from the outside"—meaning from Napoleon's troops—since it has already been hollowed out inside. All knightly virtues have disappeared with Friedrich the Great. As Cölln notes: "The royal court led the way in everything that could be called luxury, extravagance, lavishness, licentiousness, and the relegation to last place of all morality."[17] Kleist's Junker Wenzel—with his excessive banquets and his cowardly flight—would be a good, albeit fictional, example of Cölln's argument about the decadence of the German nobility.

"*Reges a regendo vocati*," notes Isidore of Seville and continues: "*Recte igitur faciendo regis nomen tenetur, peccando amittitur*."[18] The Christian world order insists on the correspondence of name and thing. If a king is no longer worthy of his name, he shall lose title and sovereignty. Pope Zachary obeyed this precept of the divine order in 750 when Pippin, the Carolingian Mayor of the Palace, requested that he deny the Merovingian Childeric the title of king and instead bestow it on him, as he had been performing the royal duties in the Frankish kingdom for years. In keeping with New Testament ethics, the Pope decided *in dubio pro re*, that is, for practical truth. Hence, in 751 a change of power from the Merovingians to the Carolingians took place. One thousand years later the German people are far removed from this tradition; and yet every criticism of nobility implicitly recalls it. And in Kleist's case it is the non-noble horse-dealer Michael Kohlhaas who personifies knightly virtues rather than the actual nobleman Junker Wenzel. Kohlhaas exhibits *temperantia, prudentia, iustitia*, and *fortitudo*. He thus acts moderately, prudently, justly, and courageously—at least at the beginning of his legal dispute. Kohlhaas is not a drinker like Wenzel is; he merely consoles his groom Herse with a bottle of wine for the injustice he had suffered, or seals an official legal act with a glass of wine, as was tradition, when selling his estates in Kohlhaasenbrück and Dresden to a Hamburg bank.[19] Nor does he act rashly in assessing his situation when negotiating with the Junker about his horses. He first interrogates Herse in detail to determine whether he might be to blame for the mistreatment of the horses, and he relies on appropriate intermediaries for his case, such as the lawyer, the magistrate, and his wife Lisbeth. Kohlhaas is just insofar as he considers legal action against the Junker only after Herse's innocence has been proven; and he is courageous insofar as he takes up a fight against an all but overpowering opponent.

The conflict between vices and virtues in Kleist's novella has both a medieval foundation and a contemporary reference. Wenzel's vices refer to the decadence of the German nobility, while Kohlhaas' virtues allude to the statutes of the Königsberg *League of Virtue* (*Tugendbund*), a reformist and patriotic society initiated by Baron vom Stein and approved by Friedrich Wilhelm III at the end of June 1808. There were only a few aristocrats among the society's members; it was dominated by members of the bourgeoisie—among them Wilhelm Traugott Krug. Kleist is not recorded as a member. In Paragraph 20 of the statutes of this *Scientific Society for the Exercise of Morality*, one finds a catalog of German virtues:

> The members work in word and letter and by all available means toward the following: love of the fatherland, German selfhood, forthrightness, love of the natural relationships of the family, loyalty to the monarch and the constitution, respect for the law and one's superiors—so that religiosity, love for science, humanity and fraternity, courage and hope, candor and physical strength; so that a hatred of luxury, this poison of faithfulness, genuineness, and sincere simplicity, and this purveyor of falsehood, selfishness, and contrived morals; so that a hatred of flattery, sycophancy, effeminacy, and bashfulness may grow; and so that everyone shall seek out people in all places to lead them to this end.[20]

In a sense Michael Kohlhaas is the perfect embodiment of Paragraph 20. The virtues the paragraph specifies can be interpreted not only in the context of Late Medieval literature, but also in the patriotic reform discourse of Kleist's time. Kohlhaas' "love of the fatherland" can only manifest itself *ex negativo*, namely in his disappointment about a country that is unwilling to protect his rights. His "love for the natural relationships of the family" becomes evident as he "[u]pon his return to Kohlhaasenbrück [...] embraced his devoted wife, Lisbeth, [and] kissed his children, who were jumping for joy round his knees"[21]—but, unfortunately, this happy scene is not the story's ending. What speaks for his "loyalty to the monarch" is his faith that the Elector of Brandenburg is "just." "[I]f only I can succeed," Kohlhass asserts, "in getting past the people who surround him and can reach him in person, I do not doubt I can obtain justice."[22] One may think here of the case of Miller Arnold and

Friedrich the Great. Kohlhaas remains tenaciously faithful to the "constitution" and only breaks away from it when all possibilities to obtain justice seem exhausted. Kohlhaas' respect for the "law and [his] superiors" is as persistent as it is futile; he is religious, humane, fraternal—the epitome of virtue.

There are, however, also French, Russian, and English people who love their country, family, sovereign, constitution, neighbors, and God. What, then, is "German" about these virtues? What justifies the national modifier are, at best and in keeping with contemporary usage of the word, the first two virtues that the *League of Virtue* refers to as German: "German selfhood, forthrightness." To abide by one's German character—one's singularity—and to stay true to oneself coincide here. To "always follow one's own path" and to do so in an "unbendingly sincere or self-confident way of thinking and acting": These are the characteristics that the *German Dictionary* of the Brothers Grimm associates with "forthrightness" (*Geradsinn*). A forthright person is "righteous, sincere, and honest"[23] and thus—according to Johann Christoph Adelung's dictionary of 1774—"German." For under the entry "German" it reads:

> Honest, righteous, in the manner of the old Germans, in which sense the word is still very common in Upper German. Of good German faith. In sincere German trust. [...] Of true German patriotic enthusiasm. A German, genuine, certain promise. A German, genuine, faithful unity. Since the Upper Saxons have strayed quite far from this fine quality of their ancestors by imitating French customs, this meaning is starting to become obsolete for them.[24]

Kohlhaas follows his path unbendingly; he is forthright, one of the "most honourable [...] men of his age."[25] As an honest German Mich(a)el, he would make for an ideal propaganda hero for any patriotic purposes if he did not sometimes appear—in his forthrightness, in his lack of any (Francophile) bad faith—downright simple minded, as a foolish German Michel. To Kohlhaas' naïve question to his wife as to how she intends to make herself heard by the Elector of Brandenburg, his wife Lisbeth replies,

> [l]ooking down in embarrassment, [...] that in the old days, when the castellan of the Electoral palace had held an appointment in Schwerin, he had courted her [...], but that he would not have forgotten her entirely; in short, that he was simply to leave it to her to take advantage of these and certain other circumstances which were too complex to describe.[26]

How far Lisbeth is willing to go is left to the reader's imagination, but not to the guileless Kohlhaas', though, who could not be happier about her suggestion. His forthrightness (*Geradsinn*) is thus reduced to "simplicity" or "naïveté" (*Geradsinnigkeit*).[27] Lisbeth puts, in a manner of speaking, a night cap or pointed cap on her Mich(a)el. The German Michel is an oaf who has no knowledge of Latin or other foreign languages. Such was the stereotype in the Renaissance, which is still present in Adelung's dictionary: "A German Michel [is someone] who understands only his mother tongue, when he should understand other languages as well."[28]

Michael Kohlhaas speaks only the honest language of the heart, not that of deception. Lisbeth, by contrast, puts the enemy's cravat around her neck "to enter his camp" for the sake of "self-defense."[29] While Kohlhaas shows "German" virtue in his honesty, his naïve incomprehension of Lisbeth's suggestive reply proves to be a typically "German" incomprehension, which can—in keeping with Adelung—be defined negatively as a lack of culture. It makes Kohlhaas appear as an enthusiast whose unworldliness is either due to moral rectitude or obsessiveness. Kohlhaas is always forthright; he says what he thinks, even if it puts him in danger, as we see in his open protest at Tronka Castle at the sight of his maltreated horses: "Those are *not* my horses, my lord; those are not the *horses* that were worth thirty gold florins! I want my healthy, well-nourished horses back!"[30] He acts in complete opposition to Kleist's Herrmann. One should therefore be careful not to reduce Kleist's political positions to his literary texts, let alone to any particular one. As exemplified by *Michael Kohlhaas*, his texts are integrated within contemporary discourses; and yet in their indeterminateness they allow for the coupling of contradictory discursive positions: firstly, the nostalgic view on the estate-based society of the Frederician era; secondly, the militant view on the contemporary reform efforts, which were actually dismantling the old estate system by way of economic liberalization; and thirdly, the skeptical moralist view on the true reasons for the behavior of the supposedly noble and virtuous, which does not spare Kohlhaas in the continuation of the fragment originally published in *Phöbus*.

Kleist's ambivalent perspective on the German Mich(a)el Kohlhaas can be explained in part through the history of its publication, that is, through the time that had elapsed between the publication of the *Phöbus* fragment in 1808 and the final version in 1810. The first part of the story—ending with Kohlhaas setting out to storm Tronka Castle—was published at a time when the patriotic reformers, allied with Austria, were pursuing a military confrontation in the conflict between Prussia and France. The image of the horse-dealer's ruined mares can hence be understood as a symbol of Prussia, depleted by war reparations. By contrast, by the time the complete story was published, all patriotic hopes for the liberation of the territories of the former Holy Roman Empire occupied or embattled by Napoleon had been shattered. In view of Napoleon's victories and the defeats of the Prussian reformed nobility against the aristocratic opposition, melancholia took hold of Kleist. In 1808 the *Kohlhaas* fragment could still be read as an immediate call to action; its military enthusiasm would have seemed entirely justified. Indeed, Herse tosses his cap in the air exultantly, and Kohlhaas—after burying his wife, selling his house, and bringing his children to safety—begins his heroic undertaking not without first announcing to the magistrate with pathos: "[T]here could be purposes compared with which his role as father and head of the household was subordinate and unworthy; in short, that he must tell him his mind was set on *higher things*, which might presently be heard of."[31] Against the historical backdrop of 1808, Kohlhaas and his grooms rehearse, so to speak, the national uprising of the German people against Napoleon's exploitative occupation. The uprising is not only rooted in offended honor—of the German patriots or of Kohlhaas, being treated unfairly by Junker Wenzel—but it concerns "higher things," among them the pursuit of fame. Within contemporary military reform discussions, this pursuit was considered a legitimate stimulation of military fervor, as the influential military writer Heinrich Philipp Reinhard von Porbeck notes:

> In the past he [the officer] strove to earn a good reputation; now he fights for admiration, for fame, and—if the limits of his plans extend beyond his grave—for posthumous fame. Thus far he has had a career similar to those of people of other social stations. Now he leaves this career and climbs higher and more perilous steps, which one can only take with a special enthusiasm; steps that still trickle with the blood of his predecessors.[32]

In order to increase combat power, the military reformers paid attention not only to strategic and tactical, but increasingly to anthropological aspects; and they found what they were looking for in Classical Antiquity:

> To confront death, to endure hardships, and to renounce the most beautiful pleasures of life is not a virtue whose seed nature has planted in our heart. The exercise of these virtues therefore requires particular motives. Various legislators of the Ancient times, therefore—in order to arouse these virtues—incited that enrapturing passion to which every mortal sooner or later makes a sacrifice. [...] The means which the Roman legislators used are generally known: The erection of columns of honor that awaken triumphs in the soul of the soldier, a thirst for fame that elevated the forces of nature above itself. Does this art of exalting the minds of the people still shine in its purest light today? Pampering, extravagance, and opulence have poisoned the noble simplicity of German thought and customs and have thus weakened the true love of the fatherland in many. Where are the great, immortal men of our time, willing to sacrifice everything for that love?[33]

The answer is Kleist's literature. Michael Kohlhaas, for example, could be used to demonstrate the functional correlation between all the motives necessary for inciting a new military: virtue, a sense of solidarity, love of the fatherland, honor, fame, heroism, enthusiasm, and the willingness to make sacrifices. Kohlhaas—betrayed in his rights, offended in his honor—develops an appalling enthusiasm for vengeance. He thus initiates a militant attack that takes the form of heroic sacrifice and helps him to achieve an "extremely dangerous military fame."[34]

The novella fragment of 1808, ending with the hero Kohlhaas' departure, suggests only praise for this military enthusiasm regarding the remaining story. In the final version of 1810, however, criticism of this very enthusiasm prevails. This shift is the expression of Kleist's fundamental historical skepticism; the feeling of mania after the victory in the Battle of Aspern is, once again, followed by the feeling of melancholia after the defeat in the Battle of Wagram. For his criticism of Kohlhaas' enthusiasm, Kleist draws on the anthropological and theological discourses of his time. The virtuous, knightly German Mich(a)el—who is at once foolish in his fundamentalism—is portrayed as a religious enthusiast and fanatic who succumbs to the deadly sins of anger and pride.

In *Anthropology from a Pragmatic Point of View* of 1798, Immanuel Kant defines anger as a swift, spontaneous affect and distinguishes it from the passion associated with it as a "*desire for vengeance.*" The latter lasts longer but both anger and vengeance arise from an injustice one has suffered. According to Kant, the "*desire for vengeance*" can express itself as the "*desire for justice*"[35] and, thus, reason. We see this in Kleist's novella insofar as Kohlhaas repeatedly seeks legal justice; and only after he has failed to procure it, does he resort to a militant feud and arson. In so doing, he no longer fights for the "restoration"[36] of his horses maltreated by Junker Wenzel, but for the "establishing [of] a better order of things." He calls himself "an emissary of the Archangel Michael, who has come to punish with fire and sword all those who shall stand on the Junker's side in this quarrel, and to chastise in them the deceitfulness which now engulfs the whole world."[37] Kohlhaas styles himself as an apocalyptic judge and prophet of a new world order, succumbing to the deadly sins *ira et superbia*, anger and pride. The narrator attributes to him a "diseased and deluded fanaticism."[38] He combines "religious enthusiasm" with pathological "fanaticism," as is common in the Enlightenment anthropology and theology of the time.[39] Kohlhaas' evil delusion is interrupted by a proclamation posted by Luther, who accuses the horse-dealer of having taken the law recklessly into his own hands. In the historical source material of the legal case, incidentally,

Luther writes a sympathetic letter to Hans Kohlhase in which he concedes that injustice has been done to him, but then states: "Now, making yourself the judge and taking the law into your own hands is certainly wrong, and God's wrath does not let it go unpunished. What you can achieve justly, you do rightly; if you cannot obtain justice, there is no other counsel but to suffer injustice. [...] And what is the suffering of all of us against the suffering of His son, our Lord Christ's?"[40] In Kleist's story Kohlhaas seeks out Luther, who reacts to him as he does to the devil in the legend according to which Luther put the devil to flight by throwing his inkwell at him: "Leave this place! [...] Your breath is pestilent and your presence perdition!" He calls him an "insane, incomprehensible, terrible man."[41] Luther asks Kohlhaas to forgive Junker Wenzel, and he makes this forgiveness a condition for hearing Kohlhaas' confession and for granting him Communion. On her deathbed Kohlhaas' wife Lisbeth, too, had reminded him in vain of the Christian duty to forgive.

But why is anger considered a deadly sin? In his *Summa Theologica* Thomas Aquinas points out that anger, while considering it a natural passion of man—attributing it to the fluid of the bile—is at the same time an ambivalent passion. The action of the angry man aims to cause suffering in his enemy; it thus constitutes a negative quality, a characteristic of evil. And yet his hope for vengeance also constitutes a positive quality insofar as vengeance is part of a just world order. Aquinas distinguishes between the understandable outburst of anger resulting from the experience of humiliation or injustice and the excessive rage of the angry man, which gets out of hand, with the notion of divine retribution becoming a mere pretext for giving free rein to one's destructive actions. The deadly sin lies in turning against God in anger, not leaving the enforcement of retribution to God or to the rightful worldly institutions that represent God's authority, but taking the law into one's own hands instead. It is then that anger shows itself as the progeny of the worst deadly sin: pride, where man assumes the role of God.[42]

Hence, the contradictory nature of Kohlhaas' actions becomes evident: On the one hand, he severs himself from the divine order of things by proudly declaring himself the judge of his own case and by rejecting the duty to forgive; on the other hand, he believes he is acting in accordance with Christian principles, appealing to just retribution to legitimize his actions. Kohlhaas is caught in the tension between the virtue of *iustitia* and the deadly sins *superbia et ira*, with his anger becoming excessive. Even as his desire for justice ought to be satisfied—as his horses are restored, Tronka Castle is destroyed along with the warden, the steward, and their wives and children—Kohlhaas' anger persists, transforming into a desire for vengeance without regard for justice: a desire for power. Kohlhaas, once a dutiful family man, now assumes the role of a sovereign over life and death and relishes the thrill of violence. He calls upon the entire world to submit to his "Provisional World Government."[43] The only character development that Kohlhaas undergoes stems from his unsettling realization of the evil that lies within him—from realizing that his anger did not serve his desire for justice but his desire for vengeance and power; that the end did not justify the means, with the means becoming the end; that his anger exhausted his humanity. At the end of the story, when Kohlhaas is asked "whether he had anything to say in his defence," he "merely looks at the ground" and replies, "No," and is forthwith sentenced to death.[44] Nevertheless, it is not the insight into his guilt—or at the very least his shame—that ultimately prevails, but Kohlhaas' desire for power. For in the end, instead of saving his own life by handing over the mysterious piece of paper a gypsy-woman had slipped him in Jüterbock, on which the existence of the Elector of Saxony depends, Kohlhaas devours it. Contrary to what Luther suggests to him, Kohlhaas does not want to be a martyr but a hero who usurps upon God's divine justice. And so righteous anger gives way to deadly sin as Kohlhaas becomes "one of the most honourable as well as one of the most terrible men of his age."[45]

According to French moralist Michel de Montaigne, "[t]here is no passion that so shakes the clarity of our judgment as anger."[46] And indeed, anger is a major concern in moralist thought insofar as it suspends reason, if only temporarily. There is no doubt that Kleist is one of the greatest theorists of anger at the turn of the 19th century, not only in his fictional experiments: with the vengeful Kohlhaas, Penthesilea's quick temper, the agitator Herrmann, who himself keeps his cool. In his essay "On the Gradual Fabrication of Thoughts While Speaking," Kleist even explains the outbreak of the French Revolution in terms of Mirabeau's anger, who suddenly attacked the King's Master of Ceremonies with scathing words, as the latter ordered the dismissal of the assembly of the estates. What had agitated him—what, according to Kleist, "precipitated the overthrow of the old order in France"—was, "after all, [...] only the twitch of an upper lip, or the ambiguous fingering of a wrist frill." Mirabeau had charged and then discharged himself "in the manner of a Kleistean Bottle."[47]

The outbreak of the French Revolution is thus attributed to anger over suffered injustice, but its history—the Reign of Terror—demonstrates that anger, initially intertwined with the desire for justice, can turn into a mere desire for vengeance and power, leading to the most gruesome consequences. Germany did not undergo a revolution. All it had, at best, were revolutionary plans and revolutionary works of literature. The German people rather suppressed their anger against the foreign occupiers and the opportunistic nobility; they were not heroic, but turned their anger inward, so to speak, against themselves. The price was stasis and melancholia, the atmosphere of the waiting room of

Friedrich Wilhelm III's government, and, for Kleist, the consequence was suicide. Throughout his life he charged himself with anger over the political situation in Prussia and discharged it as productive energy; with his works Kleist rubbed salt into the wounds Prussia incurred from French occupation and the King's political indifference.

By the time Kleist wrote the second part of *Michael Kohlhaas*, the heroic enthusiasm of the reformers and patriots around Stein, Gneisenau, and Scharnhorst had been significantly dampened. Friedrich Wilhelm III could not be convinced of the urgency of taking military action against Napoleon in 1808/09. The Prussian negotiators in Paris were forced into a corner diplomatically by the notably anti-French actions of the Prussian minister Stein, giving them no option but to ratify an agreement on war contributions that was extremely unfavorable for Prussia. Increasingly, the King considered the reformers' agitation for a popular uprising as a threat to Prussia. In order to prevent a declaration of war by Napoleon, he dismissed Baron vom Stein and dissolved the *League of Virtue*. The failure of the Austrian uprising shattered the last remaining hopes of the patriots. The propagation of military enthusiasm, German virtues, a sense of honor, and heroism now came under suspicion of being out of touch with reality. Besides, the Prussian king had always considered Baron vom Stein to be a dreamer and an eccentric. On the occasion of Stein's first dismissal in 1807, Friedrich Wilhelm III noted:

> It is true that I always considered you to be a thoughtful, talented man, capable of great ideas; but at the same time, I thought you to be eccentric and ingenious—in a word, a man who, since he always considers only his opinion to be true, would not be suited to be a civil servant in a place where there would always be points of contact that sooner or later would have disgruntled him. [...] From all of this I have had to realize with great sorrow that I had unfortunately not been mistaken in my first impression of you. On the contrary, you are to be regarded as an unruly, defiant, obstinate, and disobedient civil servant, who—insisting on his genius and talents, far from having the best interests of the state in mind—acts only by caprice, out of passion, personal hatred, and bitterness.[48]

Against a medieval backdrop the novella *Michael Kohlhaas* traces the transformation of historical awareness at the turn of the 19th century. The first part of the story reflects the expectations of the patriotic reformers up to 1809, the hope for a future renewal of Prussia that would draw its strength from Prussia's Frederician past. The second part shows that the past could no longer provide orientation for the future, that the present sphere of experiences no longer corresponded to the horizon of expectations, that all patriotic hopes were bound to fail. The original story of Hans Kohlhase serves as an example in a chronicle but, unlike in the Late Middle Ages, in Kleist's novella it no longer serves as an example for future behavior—for a teleological coherence between stories in the course of history. On the contrary, Kohlhaas' story was written for Kleist's present time and with it; in its discontinuities it reflects the experience of the unpredictable volatility of the current political developments.[49] The patriotic example of Kohlhaas that Kleist conceived is rendered meaningless by the passing of time. Let me recall once again Kleist's bitter words after the defeat of the Austrians by Napoleon at the Battle of Wagram in July 1809: "Never in my life had so many things combined to give me expectations of a happy future; and now the most recent events bring to nothing not only this enterprise but anything whatever that I might have undertaken."[50] History got ahead of the patriot's hopes and did away with his story. So why still use examples taken from history? What can be salvaged from them? What purpose can they serve? To bear witness to history? But of what history and for whom? To bear witness to indifference, failure, powerlessness? With *Kohlhaas* Kleist had once again reached the endpoint of his writing, so to speak, just as he had done with *Robert Guiscard*. But he works to hide this fact. The story of Kohlhaas ends with the hero's downfall and the anticipated downfall of the corrupt state of Saxony, but it also closes with hope for Kohlhaas' two sons, who are dubbed knights by the Elector of Brandenburg, who also declares that they are to be educated in his school for pages. Despite the experience of incomprehensible times, Kleist reinstalls hope for the future at the story's end by taking recourse to the great past of the Frederician era. This ending is far from consistent, but Kleist never is at the end of his stories. And even this inconsistency is owed to the contemporary reform discourse. In 1807 Friedrich von Cölln writes:

> You, my contemporaries, who, like me, have to live your best years in this state of fermentation—of decay—you I lament as I lament myself. Happy are you old men, who went to your graves along with Friedrich the Great and did not live to see the dissolution of his birth. Happy are you infants, who—conceived and born in such stormy times—as minors do not know the danger that surrounds you. For you the sun will shine again, which thunderclouds, gloomy and frightening, withdrew from our sight. [...] But you men, in whom there is still strength, who are still imbued with Friedrich's spirit, [...] stand united, work together toward the regeneration of the state.[51]

In 1807 the patriotic heroes still view themselves as being called upon; after 1809 they are 'fatally' disappointed—like Kohlhaas—with hope shining only for their children. It may be as comforting as it is illusory to define this grim time as a period of transition. At any rate, Kleist concludes his story with this therapeutic ploy, though it, too, is but a flight of fancy. That such hope for better times was foolish, he could have already known from his time as a child soldier going to war against the French. In October 1793 the *Schleswig Journal* (*Schleswigsche Journal*) featured an article "On Some of the Advantages That Mankind Has Already Received, or Will Receive, as a Result of the Current Political Catastrophe" ("Ueber einige der gewissen Vortheile, welche die gesammte Menschheit durch itzige politische Catastrophe schon erhalten hat, oder noch erhalten möchte"):

> [I]n an age whose affairs are wholly different from the affairs of all previous—where words whose sound previously had an indescribable power have lost all their meaning [...]—only a fool or a dreamer can imagine being able to determine with certainty what might lie hidden in the future; all human knowledge fails, all comparison is impossible because there is no age that could be juxtaposed to the present one.[52]

"The Betrothal in Santo Domingo"

The Romanian writer Marin Sorescu claims that Shakespeare created the world in seven days. On the first day he made the heavens, the mountains, and the chasms of the soul; on the second day he made the rivers, seas, and oceans as well as the other sentiments; on the third day he gathered all the people and taught them tastes—the taste of love, of despair, of jealousy, of glory, and so on until all the tastes were finished. Then some fellows who came late arrived, and the creator patted their heads compassionately. He told them they had nothing left to become but literary critics and argue with his work.[53] Writers do not like critics, unless they are themselves the critics. Literary scholars shy away from making value judgments; they make other mistakes. They know little about the taste of love or despair in Shakespeare. For the sake of scholarship, they concentrate on the cognitive dimension of reading—on the interplay between texts, contexts, and discourses or on cultural and literary theories. Reading, however, has primarily emotional motives. Children are still aware of these motivations. They do not read with the intention of gathering material to serve their education, but for vivid passages that immediately animate their interests, feelings, and activities. Children transcend the one-dimensionality of their experience in the world of fiction—in a 'spiritual regimen.' They take a deep breath from Tom Sawyer, Mowgli, Pippi Longstocking, or Harry Potter when they feel suffocated by their families or at school. Books that make them feel constrained, that narrow their horizon, they put aside. Non-scholarly readers retain this childlike expertise, whereas literary scholars, for the most part, have abandoned it. The latter take a distanced approach to their reading, uninterested in the subjective impact of a text—in its mood or that of its author—and the means by which it was made. Yet it is precisely this *Stimmung*—a German term that references a range of meanings including mood, atmosphere, musical temperament, and sentiment—that I am concerned with in the following notes on the remaining Kleist novellas I have not yet discussed. The intention is not to engender some kind of subjective empathy for a specific 'Kleist sound,' but to read the *Stimmung* resulting from the particular composition of a text, to explore that which fascinates and unsettles.[54]

The starting place for such a reading is "The Betrothal in Santo Domingo," the opening text of Kleist's second volume of stories of 1811. The novella is set on the island of Haiti during the time of the Haitian Revolution. It tells of a "terrible old negro" called Congo Hoango, who puts a bullet in the head of his supposedly kind white master and, thereafter, assembles an armed band of former slaves to ambush and rob white travelers. His concubine Babekan and her fifteen-year-old daughter Toni meanwhile lure passing Europeans into their house and host them there until Congo Hoango returns to kill them. This deception continues until one day, "on a dark and stormy and rainy night," the young Swiss officer Gustav von der Ried—a member of the French colonial troops who is on the run—knocks at the back door of the house, which "stood in an isolated spot by the road," and grasps a hand in the darkness of the night:

> Old Babekan, who was already in bed, got up, merely throwing a skirt round her waist, opened the window and asked who was there. 'By the Blessed Virgin and all the saints,' said the stranger in a low voice, placing himself under the window, 'before I tell you, answer me one question!' And reaching out through the darkness of the night to grasp the old woman's hand, he asked: 'Are you a negress?' Babekan said: 'Well, you must surely be a white man, since you would rather look this pitch-black night in the face than a negress! Come in,' she added, 'there's nothing to fear; I am a mulatto woman, and the only person except myself who lives in this house is my daughter, a mestiza!' and so saying she closed the window, as if intending to come down and open the door to him; but instead, on the pretext that she could not at once lay hands on the key, she snatched some clothes out of the cupboard, crept upstairs to her daughter's bedroom and woke her. 'Toni!' she said, 'Toni!' 'What is it, mother?' 'Quick!' said Babekan. 'Get up at once and dress! Here are clothes, clean white linen and stockings! A white man on the run is at the door and wants to be let in!'[55]

Rainstorm, lonely house, half-dressed women: Thus a 'night piece' begins, creating an uncanny scenario with all the necessary sensual nuance and shivers of excitement. The reader senses the terrible ending and yet hopes that, against all odds, everything will turn out well. He or she feels the way forward like the

Swiss officer in the dark, only to enter a world of hybrid characters—a world in which all distinctions are rendered problematic. The word 'mulatto' probably comes from the Arabic term *muwallad*, while the word 'mestiza' is derived from the Late Latin word *mixticus*. Both words denote people of mixed descent. Mulattoes have European and African ancestry; mestizos have European and Indigenous American ancestry. Their status is precarious because they can be at home in two worlds. They function as intermediaries, figures of cultural exchange, who, in colonial times and from the point of view of indigenous people, can be construed as traitors. The officer, a Swiss member of the French army, trusts that the women's mixed ancestry will have overcome the binary thinking of black and white, friend and foe, but he is mistaken. Babekan's first words suggest sympathy and safety to him as he reaches for her hand in the dark. Later he reaches for her hand again, "presse[s] it to his heart,"[56] then unbuckles his sword, presses her hand again, not realizing that this is the hand that wants to kill him not save him. Toni, who is initially allied with her mother, at first pretends to be a white woman according to her mother's instructions. However, her *eloquentia corporis* becomes an *eloquentia cordis*, the language of deception becomes a language of the heart. After Toni and Gustav make love, the initial two-against-one relation is reversed, as the two are now allied against Babekan. Upon Congo Hoango's return the triangular configuration of their relationship is reshuffled once again, as Toni ties Gustav up for appearance's sake—to save him from what would be a hopeless fight against Congo Hoango and to buy time for Gustav's rescue. And indeed, the rescue succeeds as Toni brings Gustav's family into the house for support. Gustav, however, thinks that Toni has betrayed him; he thus shoots her and, once he realizes his mistake, he shoots himself. The affective and hermeneutic shifts within this triangle keep the narrative in motion and thus the reader too, especially since he or she cannot rely on Kleist's narrator, given the narrative facts frequently contradict the narrator's assessments. All these motions are familiar from the narrative style and familial configurations in "The Foundling" and *The Marquise of O—*.

The novella's game of permutation with hybrid characters makes "The Betrothal in Santo Domingo" a prime subject for feminist and anti- or postcolonial readings. There is no question that these readings have yielded astute reflections on Kleist's position within colonial and race discourses and equally astute insights into gender discourse in Kleist insofar as Toni's name, for example, is ambivalent, simultaneously denoting two genders, woman and man.[57] Such studies inevitably emphasize the cognitive dimension of reading the novella. By contrast, here the question of how to read *Stimmung* in Kleist will be tackled, of how Kleist evokes mood in "The Betrothal in Santo Domingo." One answer to this question lies in the first turning point of the novella: Toni initially simulates a white body for Gustav in order to hide within it her—in the double sense of the word—*black* soul, but shortly thereafter she indeed transforms from Gustav's enemy to his friend. What changed her mind?

It is neither their sexual intercourse nor their secret betrothal—which lends the story its title—that influences Toni's change of heart toward Gustav. For contemporary readers this scene may have been a moment of both excitement and scandal: the older officer's lascivious gaze—described in detail by the narrator—toward the fifteen-year-old girl crouching before him on her knees; toward Toni's "hair, in its abundance of dark curls"; toward "her young breasts"; along with the barely concealed suggestion of their sexual intercourse: "There is no need to report what happened next, for it will be clear to anyone who has followed the narrative thus far."[58] Kleist emphasizes the intensity of the sensual; and yet—at this point of the narration—he places a particular emphasis on a play-within-a-play, on working two anecdotes into the narrative with which Gustav tests and seduces Toni. These anecdotes lead to the reversal of Toni's feelings and sweep both the contemporary and today's reader into an emotional chasm insofar as they open the story toward the real. The first anecdote the officer shares with Toni centers on a sick young girl, a slave who, on the day of the slave revolt, invites her former master, a planter on the run, to stay the night with her. The man receives her invitation as night falls and decides to take his chance: He takes a leap into the dark—the parallel to Gustav is obvious—believing he is going to be safe in the house of his former slave:

> '[…] The wretched man, who knew neither that the girl was sick nor what disease she was suffering from, came to her room full of gratitude, thinking himself saved, and took her in his arms; but he had scarcely been half an hour in her bed caressing her and fondling her when she suddenly sat up with an expression of cold, savage fury and said: "I whom you have been kissing am infected with pestilence and dying of it: go now and give the yellow fever to all your kind!"' And as the old woman [Babekan] loudly proclaimed her abhorrence of such a deed, the officer asked Toni: 'Could *you* ever do a thing like that?' 'No!' said Toni, casting her eyes down in confusion.[59]

We sometimes encounter such anecdotes even today, urban legends, for instance, about men who, after a passionate night of love, find the parting words 'Welcome to the Aids Club' written with lipstick on their bathroom mirror. Nothing is more uncanny than the unpredictability of people, a sudden change in identity that leads to traumatic or even fatal caesurae. This form of the uncanny constitutes a first instance of *Stimmung*, one that Kleist's texts consistently evoke and by means of which they still affect us today, in our very present fears. The caring father, brother, uncle, teacher, priest suddenly proves to be a child molester; the friendly and hard-working fellow student in urban planning at the Hamburg University of Technology turns out to be a terrorist who crashes a plane into the Twin Towers. The continuum of one's lived experience, which had hitherto provided him or her with a sense of trust, is all of a sudden shattered. Kleist's texts are rife with such 'sleeper cells' from which suddenly bursts forth an evil that had long lain dormant behind a guise of goodness.

In Kleist's time, as in ours, evil was thought of as a virus invisibly operating inside a human being. Prothoe's warning to Achilles that Penthesilea's soul cannot be reckoned with reflects a common experience at the turn of the 19th century—an experience Kleist shared with his contemporaries, such as the Romantic writer E.T.A. Hoffmann. While Kleist was writing in the midst of the Napoleonic Wars, Hoffmann did so soon thereafter. They were both acutely aware of the danger posed by the dissolution of fixed identities and social cohesion during this period of upheaval. For the sake of comparison, let us take a look at a passage from Hoffmann's novella *Mademoiselle de Scudery* of 1819. It deals with the clandestine crimes of the seemingly trustworthy goldsmith Cardillac, which further rattle the citizens of Paris, who are already surrounded by "the scene of the most heinous crimes": a series of poisonings that continue even after the murderer is caught. This 'murder virus' triggers an epidemic:

> But it soon became evident that the abominable art of Sainte-Croix had been inherited. Like an invisible, malignant ghost, murder insinuated itself into the most intimate circles of love and friendship and surely and swiftly seized the unfortunate victim. [...] The most sacred bonds were rent by appalling suspicion. The husband trembled before his wife—the father before his son—the sister before her brother. The food and the wine served a friend were left untouched, and where pleasure and gaiety had once prevailed, truculent glances searched for a secret assassin. Fathers of families could be seen anxiously buying provisions in remote districts and preparing the food themselves in some filthy kitchen, afraid of some devilish treachery in their own homes. And yet the greatest precautions were sometimes in vain.[60]

These greatest precautions proved to be taken in vain, since even physiognomy could no longer be trusted—an effect that takes on both a negative and positive sense. Kleist's "The Betrothal in Santo Domingo" also illuminates the absurdity of distrusting a person based solely on his or her outer appearance, as in the case of the color of Toni's skin. In an effort to penetrate a person's inner thoughts, one can develop imaging devices or fantasize about a transparent citizen. Such utopias of surveillance have commonly been devised in both real and fictional responses to historical traumas. If the people of Thomas More's *Utopia* want to marry, for instance, they must first present themselves naked to each other. And Kleist, in a letter to Ulrike from March 13/14, 1803, imagined overcoming the uncertainty of knowledge by tearing his "heart from [his] body, pack[ing] it into this letter, and send[ing] it to" Ulrike.[61]

Evil has no set physiognomy, and nor does the good. The anecdote about the treacherous slave is intended as both a test and warning for Toni. Gustav does not trust her yet. She, in turn, begins to trust him only after hearing another anecdote. While the first one centers on a black slave who brings death to her suitor; the second concerns a noble-minded white woman—Gustav's former bride Marianne Congreve—who sacrificed her life for her lover during the turmoil of the French Revolution in Strasbourg. Toni is meant to, and indeed will, adhere to the anecdote's example; because, as the novella continues, Gustav will soon again find himself in dire straits and in need of a savior. Viewed in this light Toni seems to serve merely as a substitute for Marianne, who died in an attempt to rescue Gustav, with Gustav less a lover than a parasite, so to speak, consuming two lives to save his own.

After making love, Gustav hangs a little golden cross around Toni's neck—originally a gift to him from Marianne, now a "bridal gift" for Toni—allowing the newly betrothed to dream a little of a joint escape to his Swiss homeland: "He described to her the little estate he possessed on the banks of the Aar."[62] The specifics of the location make anyone who knows Kleist's biography stop to wonder what might have inspired Kleist to write this novella, especially when one considers the time in which it is set. Kleist could have easily set his novella in the time of Toussaint Louverture, the Haitian national hero, who was arrested in 1802 and then taken to France, only to die in his cell at Fort de Joux in April 1803. Instead, Kleist's novella is specifically dated 1803.[63] It was, of course, Kleist who fled to the "banks of the Aar" in 1803, gazing lasciviously at Ernst von Pfuel swimming in Lake Thun and dreaming of a betrothal, as he would reveal in his letter two years later. Pfuel, reading Kleist's novella, would have probably understood why a Swiss man finds himself in Haiti, why he gets betrothed to a hybrid character named Toni, and why the story cannot end well. Thus, superimposing the love triangle of Gustav, Toni, and Marianne is that of Kleist, Toni, and Pfuel.

Kleist employs these triangular configurations to give expression to the fact that the human soul cannot be reckoned with. What is uncanny is that these triangle games transcend the fictional space of the story toward the triangle of text, reader, and author, affecting the reality of both reader and author. The monstrous lurking in Kleist's fictional palaces has real-life parallels, unsettling readers at the turn of the 19th century just as much as today.

"The Beggarwoman of Locarno"

The next of Kleist's stories we will read in terms of *Stimmung* is short in content and volume, befitting the format of the *Berlin Evening Paper*. First published in October 1810, "The Beggarwoman of Locarno" is a ghost story—a "chivalric romance[] *with* ghosts," to put it in the mocking terms Kleist had used for the genre in Würzburg in 1800.[64] Ghosts are revenants, of which there are two different kinds: the unredeemed sinners, whose journey into the eternal becomes an eternal journey on earth to atone for unforgivable sins; and then there are the unredeemed victims of crime, who haunt the living until their death is avenged and the guilty party comes to justice. Ghosts are also hybrid beings—lingering between this world and the next—creating an uncanny *Stimmung*. Producing such a mood or atmosphere would require nothing specific of Kleist other than writing in a particular genre. Kleist, however, presents us with a ghost story that is not at all scary. Indeed, what is striking about the story is the absence of any of the Gothic hallmarks; the events are presented in matter-of-fact language, without a trace of sensationalism, much like the police reports in Kleist's *Berlin Evening Paper*.

Out of pity a sick old beggarwoman is given shelter in a castle by the mistress of the house. Upon his return from hunting, her husband, the Marquis, "angrily" orders the old woman to "get up from the corner" of the room in which she was lying down and to "remove herself to behind the stove." On her way there the old woman slips with her crutch and falls, injuring her back so seriously that, once behind the stove, she collapses and dies. Several years later the Marquis finds himself in financial straits and is forced to sell his castle. A Florentine knight is interested in buying the castle but—after spending a night there and hearing a ghostly rustling sound in his room—quickly changes his mind, convinced the place is haunted. Consequently, the Marquis decides to spend the night in the haunted room himself and ends up hearing the same eerie noises. The following night he comes back to further investigate the matter, accompanied by his wife and a loyal servant. The invisible ghost returns, and does so again on the third night as the couple keeps watch with the house dog: "Presently, at exactly midnight, the terrible sounds were to be heard again: someone visible to no human eye, someone on crutches rising and standing up in the corner of the room, the rustling of the straw, the tap, tap, of the advancing steps—and at the very first of these the dog, waking and starting to its feet with ears erect, began growling and barking exactly as if some person were walking towards it, and retreated backwards in the direction of the stove." Thus far the couple had tried "to attribute the occurrence to some trivial and accidental cause which would no doubt come to light," out of fear they would not be able to sell their castle. The dog's reaction causes the Marquise, with "her hair standing on end," to rush out of the room and flee the castle, while the Marquis, "in a frenzy of horror" and "weary of his life," sets fire to the castle. In the vain attempt to rescue him, only "his white bones" are found, which, gathered by the country people, "to this day [...] still lie in that corner of the room in which he had ordered the beggarwoman of Locarno to rise from her bed."[65]

The text unsettles the reader in many different ways. Firstly, there is a disturbing discrepancy between the ghostly event and the 'news style' in which it is presented, which violates the laws of the Gothic genre. Secondly, the laconic narrative style leaves unanswered the question of whether the Marquis kills himself out of guilt or debt. Thirdly, the story deprives the reader of any judgment on the narrated events. The beggarwoman does not incriminate the Marquis, either in life or in death, just as both the Marquise and the narrator refrain from all commentary. Fourthly, the beggarwoman, who, over the course of a mere three pages, walks five times in the same direction across the room, never making more than vague "inexplicable sounds," "moaning and gasping."[66] The story's suspense and entertainment value is rather limited. And since the ghost does not explain itself, the story calls for the reader's interpretative effort. Whether the reader is willing to participate is a different question altogether, as the story's repetition and monotony, lacking a climax (with a dead person at the beginning and one at the end), likely leaves the reader fatigued. Fifthly, there is a disturbing incongruity between the Marquis' cruel ending and his wrongdoing at the beginning. He "angrily" orders the beggarwoman to get up from the corner where he usually places his shotgun to find herself a place behind the stove. He does not kick her out, and it can be assumed that the stove is not the worst place to lie in a cold castle. Moreover, the beggarwoman's death is clearly presented as an accident, the result of a mere slip due to the old woman's weakness. Since the Marquis—on his return from hunting—had just entered the room, he could not have been aware of the old woman's extreme frailty and of the danger his sullen command posed to her. Thus Kleist's ghost story, sixthly, violates the law of justice—both in a legal and a poetic sense. Kleist makes a mountain out of a molehill, so to speak.[67] Lastly, it is odd that the Marquis and his wife never explicitly relate the ghostly noises back to the death of the beggarwoman. They seem to have simply forgotten the incident. This is the scandal of the story—if one may say so—its most astounding gap among many, but one that the inclined reader must first notice.

For literary scholars searching for such gaps is a matter of course. Gaps in the narrative lend themselves perfectly to the production of new readings of a text's cognitive dimensions. The fractures in Kleist's narrative can thus be related to his skepticism of knowledge in a fractured world. One could, for example, accuse the Marquis of a cold heart, of aristocratic haughtiness and greed, and link these traits to Kleist's critique of the nobility. Or one could praise Kleist's open, paradoxical, and gestural narrative style as an anticipation of Modernist—almost Kafkaesque—narration.[68] Such epistemological, moral, political, or narratological approaches produce valuable insights. And yet it would also be appropriate to respect this brief story—which was probably nothing more than a template for the fabrication of a longer story from an anecdote—in its indeterminateness, without burdening it too much with interpretations. Or is a scholarly reader not allowed to do what a non-scholarly reader would take for granted? Would it be unacceptable to refrain from taking this story all too seriously?

When considering the cognitive aspects of Kleist's novella, these questions are not to be understood rhetorically. It is different if one is thinking solely in terms of *Stimmung* and has surrendered to its cracks, gaps, and repetitions. The death of the old woman is forgotten; and yet it is repeated five times in detail. This repetition suggests a traumatic structure to the narrative—trauma understood here as a painful caesura in individual or collective history, which cannot be comprehended immediately but only belatedly through the repetition of "inexplicable sounds." Are, then, the Marquis and Marquise meant to understand the beggarwoman's death as a caesura in *their* lives, but fail to do so? Such a psychoanalytical reading suggests itself but probably constitutes merely another "crutch" with which one can slip on the "polished floor" of the text.[69] The same could be said for a theological reading evoking the dynamics of sin and divine punishment according to Matthew 25:40. What this verse promises on the Day of Judgment is as follows: "Verily I say unto you, Inasmuch as ye have done it unto one of the least of these my brethren, ye have done it unto me." Both of these readings touch on the emotional dimension of Kleist's novella, which is their strength. Their crucial shortcoming, however, is that they insinuate answers that the text, in its composition, manifestly denies. The novella offers no such coherence, instead robbing the reader of any place or stable position, just as it does the beggarwoman and the Marquis.

The beggarwoman crosses the room from one side to the other five times. She slips and falls. Nothing but noises are audible—no last words are uttered that would reveal the meaning of existence or the ways of the world. Any serious effort to engage with *Stimmung* in Kleist's brief story means exposing oneself to and enduring these moments of silence—which is to say, enduring the fact that living and dying are banal and without meaning. Kleist understands how to make the silence of the world audible, which is yet another instance of fascination and disturbance in his writing. The story of the beggarwoman's and Marquis' deaths is presented as just one news item among others in the *Berlin*

Evening Paper. A newspaper is not a place for futuristic utopias; it rather deals with absurd quotidien spectacles, the coming and going of the everyday.

"St Cecilia or the Power of Music"

The story "St Cecilia or the Power of Music" also appeared in the *Berlin Evening Paper*, from November 15 to 17, as a baptismal gift for Adam Müller's daughter Cecilia. Kleist added several passages to the text for publication in his second volume of stories in 1811 and thus altered it decisively. While the earlier version centers on the 'power of music' against the attack of a violent mob of iconoclasts, the later version revolves around the efforts to interpret this attack from different points of view. Consequently, the number of characters in the story is expanded. It centers on a Dutch mother who is desperately searching for her four missing sons but finds them too late to save them. She locates them in the city insane asylum of Aachen: "Wearing long black robes, they were sitting round a table on which a crucifix stood, and this they seemed to be worshipping, with their folded hands silently resting on the table-top." For six years they have been leading "this ghostly existence." They "never utter a word," only get up from their seats once, at midnight, to chant "the *Gloria in excelsis* in voices fit to shatter the windows of the house."[70] What had happened? The reader of the story has already learned that the four Dutch brothers had planned to destroy the convent of St Cecilia during the Feast of Corpus Christi. When they gathered with other rioters as the hour for the celebration approached, the nuns performed an oratorio

> with supreme and splendid brilliance; during the whole performance not a breath stirred from where the congregation stood and sat; especially at the *Salve regina* and even more at the *Gloria in excelsis* it was as if the entire assembly in the church had been struck dead. In short, despite the four accursed brothers and their followers, not even a particle of dust on the floor was blown out of place, and the convent continued to flourish right until the end of the Thirty Years War, when by virtue of an article in the Treaty of Westphalia it was nevertheless secularized.[71]

The orchestra that prevented the outbreak of violence was conducted by Sister Antonia, who had not been expected to take part in the festivities, as she was said to have fallen "violently ill of a nervous fever" and "was lying in a state of complete unconsciousness."[72]

What happens next? The mother sets out to question several witnesses, among them the wardens of the insane asylum, followed by Veit Gotthelf—a former accomplice of the rioters—and finally the Abbess of the convent. The wardens and Gotthelf describe the brothers as suddenly confused, suffering from a religious fanaticism they could not understand. They deem them insane. The Abbess later informs the mother that, throughout the entire orchestra performance, Sister Antonia, the supposed conductor, had actually been lying in her cell, unconscious, dying soon after. The Archbishop of Trier, and subsequently the Pope, had thus attributed the miracle that saved the convent to Saint Cecilia herself, the patron saint of church music. The final words of the story come from the narrator, who labels it a "legend." With this final remark the curtain falls, and the reader is left to wonder whether the events are history or merely legend; nor is the reader able to answer the question raised by the story's title—whether the overpowering of the violent attackers owes itself to Saint Cecilia or to the "Power of Music" alone, to the "dreadful power of the art of sound." In the end the reader is—once more—left with a riddle, a gap in the narrative, which has prompted scholars to bring to mind the pertinent contexts, in particular the Romantic discourses of religion, music, and irony.[73]

My reading, by contrast, strives to engage with the surface of this polyphonic text in order to, once again, detect its *Stimmung*, focusing on its material as well as its making. After all, the question posed by the story's title seems to describe an ambiguous figure that, depending on the reader's interpretation, either elevates the reader from below into the abstract metaphysical sphere of the sacred or lowers him from above into the concrete material of the musical sounds. In the practice of musical composition, such ambiguity is inherent in the principle of 'enharmonic change,' a concept employed since the late 17th century to refer to the sharpening or flattening of a note in the *same* tonal position.[74] A C sharp can thus be understood as a D flat, and an F sharp as a G flat. The pitch is the same, but it can be named and conceptualized differently, modulated according to different keys and modal frameworks. A further fascinating aspect of Kleist's writing is that it links the principle of ambiguity not to the abstract, but to the concrete material of natural or cultural signs. Accordingly, the four brothers sing the *Gloria in excelsis* "in voices that filled us with horror and dread":

> It was a sound something like that of leopards and wolves howling at the sky in icy winter; I assure you, the pillars of the house trembled, and the windows, smitten by the visible breath of their lungs, rattled and seemed about to collapse, as if handfuls of heavy sand were being hurled against the panes.[75]

The *Gloria* derives its pathos from the fact that glory is owed only to God in the highest and from the song's basis in the Gospel of Luke 2:14, which tells of the glorification of God by the angels after the birth of Christ. Kleist's narrator, by contrast, associates the seraphic with the animalistic by comparing the concrete sounds of the heavenly praise of the four brothers—who are either saintly or insane—with the howl of leopards and wolves, devoid of all consciousness. Equally unsettling is the fact that he associates the organic with the inorganic by comparing the voices of living beings to the hurling of heavy sand against window panes. The brothers, who produce noises rather than human or angelic sounds, are not exalted by the 'power of music,' but are stigmatized and banished in their creatureliness. They receive the punishment they deserve. The iconoclasm turns against the iconoclasts themselves.

In its defense of religious iconography, the Roman Catholic Church has traditionally invoked the incarnation of God in the form of Jesus Christ, arguing that the veneration of Christian images serves God and not the images themselves. Kleist's perspective modifies this arrangement in its exchange of the abstract for the concrete, the infinite for the finite. The reader will probably doubt the possibility of undoing this exchange. Accordingly, the incarnation of Saint Cecilia in the body of Sister Antonia, who had fallen ill with a nervous fever, seems just as questionable as the comparison of singing angels with howling animals. Ultimately, the reader is in danger of "collaps[ing]" under the 'attack' of Kleist's visual and sound material—which oscillates between idealization and profanation, between being elevated from below and being lowered from above—like the window panes bombarded with heavy sand. The reader is overpowered by the material of the reading.

With the animal sounds of the four iconoclasts, Kleist quotes himself. On October 13, 1810, one month before the first version of "St Cecilia," Kleist's essay "Feelings before Friedrich's Seascape" ("Empfindungen vor Friedrichs Seelandschaft") appeared in the *Berlin Evening Paper*. In it he interprets Caspar David Friedrich's painting *The Monk by the Sea*, which had just been on display at the Berlin Academy exhibition. In Friedrich's painting a Capuchin monk in a brown habit is standing on a dune gazing into the distance over a dark "boundless watery waste" and a seemingly infinite sky. According to Kleist, however, for the viewer of the picture experiencing the sublime is not possible,

> and that which I should have found within the picture I found instead between the picture and myself; namely, an appeal from my heart to the picture and a rejection by the picture; and so I myself became the Capuchin monk—the picture became the dune, but that across which I should have looked with longing, the sea, was absent completely. Nothing could be sadder or more discomfiting than just this position in the world: the single spark of life in the vast realms of death, the lonely center in the lonely circle. The picture with its two or three mysterious objects lies before one like the Apocalypse, as though it were thinking Young's *Night Thoughts*, and since in its uniformity and boundlessness it has no foreground but the frame, the viewer feels as though his eyelids had been cut off. Nevertheless,

Fig. 56 Caspar David Friedrich, *The Monk by the Sea*, 1808–10

> the painter has doubtless opened an entirely new path in the field of his art, and I am convinced that, through his powers, a square mile of Prussian sand, with a barberry bush and one lonely huddled crow, would have the effect of an Ossian or a Kosegarten. Yes, were such a painting made with its own chalk and water, the foxes and the wolves, I believe, would be set howling by it, which is doubtless the strongest praise one could lavish on this kind of landscape. But my own feelings about this wonderful picture are too confused: therefore, before daring to speak them out more fully, I have tried to learn something by listening to the comments of those who, in pairs, pass before it continually from morning to night.[76]

This time it is not leopards and wolves but foxes and wolves that are howling—they have no consciousness and are without soul. They would, Kleist imagines, fall for the illusion created by the picture if the cliffs were drawn with chalk from the island of Rügen and the Baltic Sea were painted with its own water. Although the human viewer does not mistake art for reality, neither does he succeed in elevating the painting's material by reading it as an expression of the sublime. He is incapable of sharing the monk's experience of sublime nature. He experiences nothing more than the despairing nothingness of his gaze, the confusion of feelings, and he does so not with regard to nature, but rather to the concrete artistic material and the composition of the painting. It is, ultimately, as impossible for the viewer to transcend reality into the ideal as it is for the animal because he himself can no longer frame that which he is seeing; he feels as though "his eyelids had been cut off." In the horizontal strips of dune, sea, and sky, the painting seems to exceed its frame; it is this boundlessness that inundates the perception of the viewer, who is equally unable to contain the picture, conceptually, within himself.

"The Duel"

It is not only the unsettling ambiguity of Kleist's images but, above all, their boundlessness, the dynamics and force of Kleist's language that overpowers the reader. The beginning of "The Duel"—presumably Kleist's last story—can serve as an example for this effect:

> Towards the end of the fourteenth century, just as the night of St Remigius was falling, Duke Wilhelm of Breysach, who, ever since his clandestine marriage to Countess Katharina von Heersbruck, a lady of the family of Alt-Hüningen and regarded as his inferior in rank, had lived in a state of feud with his half-brother Count Jakob Rotbart, was returning home from a meeting with the German Emperor at Worms, whose consent he had won, seeing that all his legitimate children had died, to legitimize his natural son Count Philipp von Hüningen, to whom his wife had given birth before their marriage. Looking forward to the future more hopefully than at any time since his succession to the dukedom, he had already reached the park behind his castle when suddenly, from among the bushes, an arrow sped out of the darkness and transfixed his body just below the breast bone.[77]

Kleist would have loved Formula One racing. He knows how to accelerate from zero to sixty in two sentences. He does not proceed on a straight course, but in curves. Amidst the intense noise of information assailing the reader, he or she is as surprised by the narrated catastrophe as the Duke is by the arrow shooting out of the darkness of the shrubbery. The reader is incapable of keeping a critical distance from the narrated events, as Kleist's language pulls him or her right into the middle of the story. Kleist's novella begins swiftly with a sudden death. Jakob Rotbart is suspected of the Duke's murder, but he has provided an alibi, claiming to have spent the night of the murder with the widowed Littegarde von Auerstein, a beautiful lady who, until his scandalous claims, had been considered virtuous and chaste. Consequently, Littegarde's father is stunned, Littegarde herself faints, and her brothers, once she regains consciousness, chase her from the house and castle. There is only one person who stands by her: Friedrich von Trota, who is intent on marrying her. He challenges the evil Jakob to a duel, the outcome of which is to be taken as a divine judgment by ordeal. If Friedrich wins, God has proven Littegarde's innocence; if Jakob wins, Friedrich and Littegarde must die at the stake. The duel begins with Friedrich lightly slashing Jakob's wrist; Friedrich then takes an unfortunate stumble, which allows Jakob to thrust his sword into his exposed side and twice more into his breast, just under the heart. Littegarde faints again, as the defender of her honor has lost the duel and seems destined to die. She is thrown in jail, but against all odds, Friedrich's seemingly fatal wounds heal, while Jacob's trifling wrist wound grows into a cancerlike ulceration, leaving him to his eventual fate of death while holding on to his claim that he spent the night with Littegarde. Consequently, Littegarde and Friedrich are to be burned at the stake, but, before it comes to that, Littegarde's maid-in-waiting, Rosalie, confesses that she spent the night in question with Jakob pretending to be Littegarde. Faced with his imminent death, Jacob then confesses that he hired an assassin to have his half-brother, the Duke of Breysach, killed in order to secure his inheritance. Now nothing stands in the way of Littegarde and Friedrich's marriage.

A sudden, quick death at the beginning, followed by a slow death at the end: The story builds suspense until the moment of truth, the ritual ordeal by duel, but it then disappoints the reader's expectations as it loses pace. The story supersedes its intermediate resolution with ever-new developments, thus forcing the reader—who is playing the role of the judge—to be patient and continuously revise judgments. It is an exercise in belatedness, to the extent that one cannot rely on a singular moment of divine truth but must remain on a lifelong search until death—or until the artful ending of a story. "Can a fight," thus reasons Friedrich von Trota, "that has not been continued until the death of one of the two opponents be held to have been concluded, if one considers the matter at all rationally?" As long as he is still alive, he has a chance to "win from God with [his] sword a verdict" at any future moment in time.[78] But are one's own actions of any consequence in the establishment of truth? Is not the ultimate revelation of truth merely a matter of chance? Is the maid-in-waiting's confession to be understood as a guarantor of divine providence or as a narrative trick for interrupting—with Rosalie serving as a *dea ex machina*—a process for establishing truth that could, in principle, be further deferred? At the end of the novella, the Emperor gives orders to amend the statutes governing "sacred ordeal by combat" and to insert the words "if it be God's will" wherever it was assumed "that such a trial immediately brings guilt to light."[79]

In the change of pace between its beginning and end, "The Duel" shows how Kleist manages, stylistically, to alternate between accelerating and decelerating the story; to reduce and restore the complexities of perception; to transform his heroes of action into heroes of reflection. Kleist is not only the wild, impetuous storyteller who leaves his characters to act blindly and thus, by extension, the reader in the thicket of compact, meandering sentences. He is also the slow narrator who conveys the insight that the understanding of human actions and failures is, to a certain extent, possible[80]—but only after the fact: "Reflection, or thinking something over, find its proper moment *after* rather than *before* an act."[81] Therein lies the melancholia of moralists like Kleist. Their insights prove hard to generalize and are invariably belated, because every single case is different and a soul cannot be reckoned with (in advance).

Kleist's story finds its logical conclusion in Thomas Mann's *The Magic Mountain* of 1924. The rhetorical duels between the moralist Ludovico Settembrini and the fundamentalist Leo Naphta eventually culminate in a duel with pistols carried out in the snowy landscape of Davos. This duel is, of course, no longer a divine ordeal by combat, but a mere game concerning the truth of the singular and the totality, concerning the conciliation of chance and necessity. Settembrini takes the liberty of taking the ritual that relies on a singular instance of truth-finding for what it is: a theater of honor—a mere comedy, whose players cannot bear the dilemma that all truth is recognized after the fact, if at all. This realization is the reason for which Settembrini shoots his pistol into the air rather than at Naphta, a fundamentalist, who must consider such an action cowardly. Since his opponent refuses to duel, he turns the pistol on himself, shooting himself in the head. He cannot tolerate any deferral.

CHAPTER XII

Economy and Aneconomy of Sacrifice

The Final Scene: Kleist's Suicide at Lake Wannsee

> All these fine and very convincing passages always deal with the fact that someone is dying, that it is hard for him to do, that it seems unjust to him, or at least harsh, and the reader is moved by this, or at least he should be. But for me, who believe that I shall be able to lie contentedly on my deathbed, such scenes are secretly a game; indeed, in the death enacted I rejoice in my own death, hence calculatingly exploit the attention that the reader concentrates on death, have a much clearer understanding of it than he, of whom I suppose that he will loudly lament on his deathbed [...].[1]

It is Franz Kafka, not Kleist, who is writing here. Nonetheless, they are both experts in the depiction of cruel and gruesome dying. Gregor Samsa, for example, the hero of Kafka's "Metamorphosis" of 1912, dies the wretched death of a monstrous bug, swept away by the cleaning woman's broom. Meanwhile, Josef K. in *The Trial* of 1914/15 is stabbed to death with a butcher's knife by his two executioners in a barren quarry outside the city without ever having learned the reason for his guilt. And the officer "In the Penal Colony" of 1914 dies strapped to an execution device that carves the condemned prisoner's sentence on his naked body with needles meant to leave behind 'beautiful' flourishes. In the case of the officer, however, the machine malfunctions, impaling him in the most unaesthetic way. Kleist's deaths are no less horrid and violent. One only needs to bring to mind the death of Nicolo in "The Foundling," whose foster-father "crushed out his brains against the wall";[2] the sight of innocent little Juan in "The Earthquake in Chile," "with his brains oozing out," dashed "against the edge of one of the pillars of the church" by Master Pedrillo;[3] or Penthesilea's cannibalistic tearing apart of Achilles with her dogs. The narrative and dramatic arts of Weimar Classicism generally followed Gotthold Ephraim Lessing's treatise *How the Ancients Represented Death* of 1769, which develops an illusory and serene image of Death as the twin brother of Sleep. This image marks a departure from any real experience of death for the sake of artistic freedom, thereby guaranteeing the autonomy of aesthetic beauty. By contrast, Kleist's images of death refrain from indulging in such escapism; they are anti-idealist and anticipate the literature of Modernism as they pierce through the illusion of beauty that separates art from life, refusing to gloss over reality in all its cruelty and ugliness. And Kafka seems to almost take pleasure in shocking his readers with his death images in order to dispel the

© WILHELM FINK VERLAG, 2021 | DOI:10.30965/9783846765746_013

comforting illusions and deceptions surrounding the repression of death since the early 19th century. For him death is to be in literature what it is in real life: the uncanny, the unfathomable, the unknown—a scandal par excellence.[4] But what if that which is "secretly a game" in literature were to become serious? Is Kafka indeed able to "lie contentedly on [his] deathbed," without lament, as he writes in his diary entry of December 1914? Eight years later, in July 1922, the terminally ill Kafka writes to his friend Max Brod:

> The reason for this fear of death may be divided into two main categories. First he [that is, a writer like Kafka] has a terrible fear of dying because he has not yet lived. [...] The second reason [...] is the belief: "What I have playacted is really going to happen. I have not bought myself off by my writing. I died my whole life long and now I will really die. [...] Of course the writer in me will die right away, since such a figure has no base, no substance, is less than dust. He is only barely possible in the broil of earthly life, is only a construct of sensuality. [...] But I myself cannot go on living because I have not lived, I have remained clay, I have not blown the spark into fire, but only used it to light up my corpse.[5]

Could these also be the words of the melancholic Kleist, who throughout his life played with thoughts of death and who believed that he had squandered his life in writing? Kafka seems helpless in the face of his own death, which gave way to shame and fear that he gave up trying to hide. How did Kleist fare when the real horror of death caught up with the horrific depictions of death in his literature? On the surface the murder-suicide pact of Heinrich von Kleist and Henriette Vogel follows the story of "The Betrothal in Santo Domingo," in which Gustav first puts a bullet through Toni's breast and then one through his own head. Like Kafka, Kleist never "bought [him]self off by [his] writing." What attitude did Kleist and Henriette assume before their deaths? What happens in their case is astonishing.

Baldassare Castiglione's practical guide to aristocratic conduct, *The Book of the Courtier* of 1528, demands grace from aristocrats in all areas of life. More precisely: *sprezzatura*, the effort to conceal effort in order to control one's public image. Kleist killed himself, if I may say so, with grace: on the one hand, light and in high spirits after laughing and joking with Henriette in the bowling alley of Stimming's inn near Lake Wannsee and a picnic on a mild winter's day shortly before the fatal shots; on the other hand, with letters of farewell that can be understood as part of a grandiose staging through which Kleist shaped the history of his own reception. It seems as though Kleist felt the need to take care of his posthumous fame. He had hardly had any success with his writings during his lifetime, but his spectacular and puzzling suicide—as well as the reasons given for it in his suicide letters—caused a sensation among his contemporaries and has continued to shape the image of Kleist's life and work to this day. Put differently, Kleist's suicide gave us the rules by which to understand him as a writer.[6] The farewell letters come to replace, so to speak, a carefully crafted autobiography, characterized by a mixture of 'truth' and 'poetry' otherwise fairly common among writers striving to ensure their remembrance. In a way Kleist's letters are even more effective because the reader does not expect 'poetry' from those doomed to die, only 'truth.' People are always interested in a person's last words as authentic expressions in which the sum of a life is drawn. The tremendous impact of Kleist's suicide letters on readers is based on this 'autobiographical pact'; they are written in and against all despair, following a calculated economy of sacrifice in the way they stage their author's image for posterity. And yet there is one poetic exception to this prosaic rule: the wonderful last epistolary exchange between Kleist and Henriette, the so-called "Death Litany"—the expression of a grandiose aneconomy of sacrifice, of overcoming all calculations in love and in death.

But let us first look at the facts. What happened on Kleist's last days in November 1811? More is known about these days than about any other in Kleist's life. The knowledge comes from Kleist's and Henriette's farewell letters; from the records of Judge Felgentreu, who questioned the eyewitnesses about the last hours before the suicides: the staff of the Stimming's inn on the Kleiner Wannsee, where Kleist and Henriette had spent their last night; and from the autopsy reports of the two surgeons by the names of Sternemann and Greif. According to these accounts, the following transpired: On the morning of November 20, 1811, which fell on a Wednesday, Kleist and Henriette take a cab from Berlin and travel in the direction of Potsdam and, at about two o'clock in the afternoon, draw up at Stimming's inn, located by the bridge separating the Kleiner and Großer Wannsee. They ask for two rooms, drink coffee, and walk to the spot where they will commit suicide the next day. Back from their walk they have dinner at Stimming's, ask for candles and writing materials before retreating to their rooms and asking for coffee twice on Thursday morning to stay awake. At seven o'clock in the morning, Henriette calls for the housemaid to help her dress. In the morning they pay their bills, send letters to Berlin by messenger, joke with each other in the yard of the inn, and Kleist jumps over the boards of the bowling alley and challenges Henriette to do the same, which she refuses. Afterwards they walk to the Kleiner Wannsee, where they dance around a little, constantly being attended to by the staff of the inn, skipping stones over the water, and asking for a table, two chairs, and some coffee on a knoll at the shore of Lake Wannsee. The staff call the idea of dining outdoors on a winter's day "foolish" but perform their duties obligingly and then withdraw discreetly. In the interrogation record of the hired man Riebisch and his wife,

Fig. 57
Henriette Vogel (1780–1811)

the strange mood of the hour of death becomes apparent: "[A]s we were leaving and going home, we saw the two strangers running down the hill toward the lake hand in hand, joking and chasing each other as if they were playing tag. I have never seen such a loving couple as those two on the hill. They kept calling each other 'child' and 'dear child,' and were exceedingly cheerful."[7]

Kleist's and Henriette's farewell letters testify to this cheerfulness as well. The specifics of Henriette's burial wishes, addressed to the Prussian war councilor Christoph Ernst Friedrich Peguilhen, are an example of this spirit:

> My esteemed friend! A great test is in store for the faithful friendship you have always shown me, as the two of us, Kleist, with whom you are acquainted, and I, are here at *Stimming's* on the road to Potsdam, in a very awkward state insofar as we lie here *shot dead*, and we are now counting on the kindness of a sympathetic friend to confide our mortal remains to the secure fortress of the earth. Try, dearest Peguilhen, to arrive here this evening and have everything arranged so that my good Vogel will be as little shocked by this as possible.[8]

We know very little about Henriette Vogel. In 1982 German writer Karin Reschke attempted to retrieve the lost story of Henriette's life in a fictional text, entitled *Persecuted by Happiness. The Diary of Henriette Vogel* (*Verfolgte des Glücks. Findebuch der Henriette Vogel*).[9] Henriette appears here as a thwarted writer whose autobiographical notes Kleist reads on the journey to their shared place of death at Lake Wannsee—a fiction not far from reality. Henriette's letters are elegant and eloquent, as my analysis of the "Death Litany" will make apparent. Peguilhen described Henriette as "ailing" and "irritable," marked by "extravagant religious notions"; she frequently expressed a desire for death as she "placed a high degree of happiness in the continuation of life beyond the grave." He further represented her as a "highly cultivated woman," who liked to surround herself with "cultivated men," such as Kleist, whom Adam Müller had brought to the Vogel family home in 1810. Kleist and Henriette cherished "similar extravagant religious sentiments," played "spiritual chorales" together on the piano and sang, a "sympathy of the souls," a "spiritual love had been born" between them. But there was apparently no more than that between the two because Henriette lived "in a very happy marriage" and had "a ten-year-old daughter that she loved." Thus stated Peguilhen on November 22, 1811, one day after the fatal shots.[10] In 1812 he provided a more detailed portrait, noting with curious meticulousness that Henriette, despite some pockmarks on her face, was a "pride of her sex," "a wonderful, ingenious being," who read William Shakespeare, Homer, Miguel de Cervantes, as well as love stories, such as Johann Wolfgang Goethe's *The Sorrows of Young Werther* or Pierre Choderlos de Laclos' *Dangerous Liaisons*; she "never wrote for publication" but produced some "small highly interesting essays," wished to learn how to fence, and had Kleist teach her "the elements of military tactics and the art of warfare." According to Peguilhen, a doctor had told Henriette about her incurable condition, and Kleist was supposedly unaware of it for some time before granting Henriette her wish for relief. "Without the morbid condition of Madame Vogel, Kleist would probably have left this world alone if his passion had become too powerful to remain within the bounds of virtue and morality."[11]

Friedrich Ludwig (Louis) Vogel was an official paymaster. Müller, who had introduced Kleist to Vogel's house, tried to protect him from rumors. In a newspaper article on Christmas Day 1811, he wrote about the two suicides in a flowery but direct way:

> They both stood above the consolation of a brief passion, so much so that if I am to make myself understood by the world, I must call them cold against each other. There was no communion between them but that of the most glorious dispositions, of the ignorance of their higher, divine destiny, thus of despair and—in the last hours of their lives—of a certain tragic interest in each other.[12]

Adam Müller had every reason to play the noble friend. In the literary estate of Karl August Varnhagen von Ense, Rahel Levin's future husband, there is a record that describes Madame Vogel as a frivolous woman with whom Adam Müller had a "serious love affair." This affair continued until his own friend, Franz Theremin, a Protestant preacher, replaced him because Müller became interested in one Madame Sander, who in turn fell for Theremin, so that Henriette finally had to settle for Kleist.[13] Kleist's cousin Marie von Kleist does not offer a picture of Henriette that is any more favorable. To the King she describes Madame Vogel as a "fame-seeking, vain fool" who "wanted to attain celebrity" at all costs; according to the doctors, Marie claims, she was not even terminally ill.[14] Marie seems jealous and angry. Kleist's farewell letters to her, his comparisons of Marie and Henriette in favor of the latter, left a lasting impression. Kleist biographer Eduard von Bülow, by contrast, tries to remain objective: "There was no passion in their relationship to each other," is his verdict.[15] No passion. That might be true. Be that as it may, Madame Vogel provided finesse rather than tristesse. Her farewell letter to her husband, written at Stimming's inn, is tactful and diplomatic. She assures her husband and her daughter of her love, kisses them both "a thousand times," and anticipates that Louis will soon receive "the highest compensation (which you deserve so much)"—which would have been remarkably clairvoyant if she had meant the widower's remarriage within six months—and she then 'consoles' him that she knows herself to be accompanied in death by a "most fervent love"—which is bold—and wishes "nothing more ardently" than that Kleist "will not be separated from me even in death."[16] In his farewell letter to Peguilhen, Kleist calmly and matter-of-factly asks Peguilhen to pay his barber, his landlord, and the mortician.[17] Peguilhen obeyed their last wishes. On November 22, 1811, after a post-mortem autopsy had been performed, they were buried in two coffins at the very site where they had taken their lives, as recorded in the Stahnsdorf-Machnow church register. On December 2 the Stahnsdorf pastor Johann Gottlob Dreising demanded "church fees for burying the bodies." It can therefore be assumed that they were granted a Christian burial despite their suicides.

In the church register the incident is referred to as a "murder and suicide."[18] The two were found dead by the hired man Riebisch. As the proceedings report by court fiscal Felgentreu states:

> in a small pit, about one foot deep and three feet across, facing each other, sitting feet between feet, their upper bodies, however, slumped backwards, the man wearing a brown cloth coat, a white batiste muslin vest, gray cloth pants, and round-toe high boots; his face slightly stained with blood around his mouth. The woman wearing a dress of white batiste, a fine blue coat, and white kid gloves, with a blood stain the size of a Thaler under her left breast, on the dress, which also appeared to be burned in that spot. Otherwise no outward signs of trauma were discovered on either body.[19]

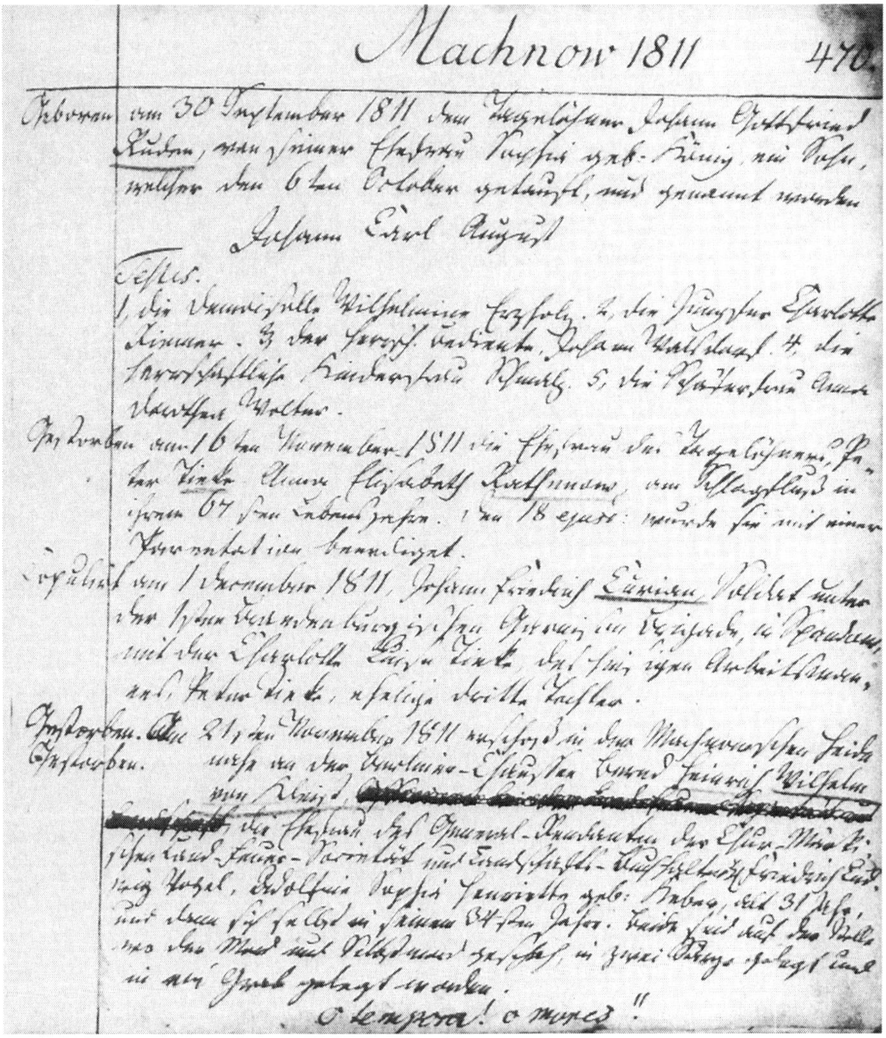

Machnow 1811 470

Testes.

O tempora! o mores!!

Fig. 58 Death entry for Heinrich von Kleist and Henriette Vogel in the church register of Stahnsdorf-Machnow

On November 21, 1811, in the Machnow Heath near the Berlin highway, Bernd *Heinrich Wilhelm von Kleist* shot the wife of the official paymaster of the Kurmark Land-Feuer-Societät insurance company and property accountant Friedrich Ludwig Vogel, Adolfine Sophie Henriette née Keber, thirty-one years old, and then himself in his thirty-fourth year. They were placed in two coffins and buried in one grave at the site where the murder and suicide occurred. *O tempora! O mores!!*

There were three pistols found lying next to the bodies: a larger Italian flintlock pistol by Lazarino Cominazzo and two smaller Terzerol pistols, also called a 'pocket pistol' or 'lady's pistol.'[20] Kleist had shot Henriette in the heart and himself in the mouth, the bullet penetrated his brain, which would have been fatal. However, Kleist did not die from the piece of lead in his brain; as the autopsy revealed, he instead suffocated from the gunpowder. Over the next few weeks, virtually all the newspapers—from Berlin to Leipzig to Vienna and Paris—discuss the circumstances of the double suicide and suspected affair between Kleist and Henriette. Unlike in the case of Goethe's Werther, however, their suicides do not become 'fashionable'—with one exception. In August 1812 the Berlin public mocks a young couple whose attempted suicides in the Tiergarten Park fail because they only shoot gunpowder into their mouths to save the bullets.[21]

Peguilhen is a faithful "executor of the last will of the two deceased," and as such he requested on November 26 and 28 in obituaries in *Voss'* and *Spener's Newspaper* that the "public" not "blindly condemn two beings who were love and purity personified" until he would publish a statement in their defense.[22] But nothing came of it. Friedrich Wilhelm III was not pleased and prohibited the "abuse" of public papers "for the promotion of immorality."[23] In a letter of December 3, 1811, Peguilhen humbly apologized to Prussian chancellor Karl August von Hardenberg for drawing "a parallel to the more glorious death of Ewald von Kleist."[24] The King's condemnation of the double suicide may have also influenced the two doctors who performed the autopsies on Kleist and Henriette. District physician Dr. Sternemann and city surgeon Greif have no difficulty defining a clear motive for Henriette's suicide. Their description of her physique and undergarments is strangely meticulous, and they conclude from their examination of the abdomen what they presumably learned from Peguilhen and Louis Vogel at the scene: that "the deceased Vogel was suffering from an incurable cancer of the womb and chose this easy death for fear of a slow and very hard one." Henriette's desire to die is thus rendered comprehensible; it no longer appears as the result of a tragic love affair. Kleist had provided assisted suicide, so to speak. With Kleist the two doctors have a more difficult time. During the autopsy they carefully search for a physical cause that might have led Kleist to end his life prematurely. And since they cannot find such a cause, they invent one, thus altering their first autopsy report. The first version of November 22, 1811, states: "The liver was very large, however natural, the gall bladder contained a rather large amount of bile; there were, however, no calcareous concretions in the gall bladder. Likewise, the kidneys, spleen, urinary bladder, pancreas, and the entire intestinal tract were in normal condition." In its second version of December 11—written once the King's indignation over

Peguilhen's apologia of the suicide victims was widely known—the report suddenly changes significantly:

> The liver was unnaturally large, its left lobe extended over the stomach, its tissue unnaturally indurated, and it could only be cut open with considerable effort, during which a lot of thick black blood flowed out.
>
> In particular the gall bladder was conspicuously distended and contained a large quantity of thickened gall. [...]
>
> From all these indications we feel justified in concluding, according to the principles of physiology, that the male deceased was of the temperament *sanguino cholericus* in the *first degree*, and must certainly have suffered severe attacks of *hypochondria*, as some colleagues have attested to me, the physician. If a general excess of religious enthusiasm accompanied this eccentric mental condition, a pathological mental state might reasonably be deduced in the case of the male deceased, von Kleist.[25]

This type of 'rewriting' is how to declare a person mad. The two doctors were determined to provide physiological proof that this man, who longed to die and came from a renowned Prussian aristocratic family, could not have been in his right mind. At this point they had already cut open Kleist's head and dissected his brain, layer by layer, but had not discovered anything unusual. Instead, their head saw broke during this procedure, as Kleist had a stubborn head, demonstrating his willfulness even in death. In their desperation the two doctors come up with the idea of declaring the liver unnaturally large, the bile thicker, and of letting a lot of black blood flow. In doing so, they follow the principles of humoral theory, already quite outdated at the time; in other words, they follow the theory of temperaments, which has its roots in Hippocratic medicine and according to which a person's mental and emotional health depends on a balanced mixture of bodily fluids, while a disharmony of these fluids—their disorder—results in illness. Kleist is said to have too much black blood and thickened bile, which would make him a choleric and melancholic hypochondriac. In such a condition depressive and manic states alternate, which could explain the high-spirited amusements, the childish frolicking of the last hours before their deaths. An excess of religious enthusiasm in Kleist though? Considering his letters, this conclusion is out of the question. The autopsy report seems to be inspired by Peguilhen's assessment of Henriette's "extravagant religious notions." There could also have been a medical reason for this wild speculation about the pathological connection of mind and body in Kleist as it was 18th-century medical anthropology that had linked religious enthusiasm—for example, Pietist penitential struggle—to melancholia.[26]

In a letter of November 10, 1811, to his cousin Marie, Kleist anticipated all of this nonsense. He preempts his suicide from being construed as a product

Fig. 59
Marie von Kleist, née von Gualtieri (1761–1831)

of mental illness, and yet he senses that things will turn out differently: "But I swear to you, it is quite impossible for me to go on living; my soul is so sore, if I so much as poke my nose out the window, the light of day, I might almost say, is painful on it. Many will call this sick and exaggerated; but not you, who can see the world from points of view other than your own."[27] Kleist wants to change his cousin's perspective, in hopes that she will join him in justifying his death wish rather than pathologizing it. He starts his letter by rejecting medical explanations for suicide and instead provides social ones, soberly and with utmost clarity: He explicitly talks about feeling excluded by his family, thus implicitly referring to his economic hardship after the failure of the *Berlin Evening Paper*; he speaks of the lack of recognition of his literary and journalistic works—he feels his family regards him as "a totally useless member of society [...], deserving of no further sympathy"—and then speaks of the political misery in Prussia, of the "alliance that the King is now concluding with the French." Kleist thus portrays himself as a nonconformist intellectual who exists outside the familial, aristocratic, aesthetic, and political orders of his time. It is fitting that he concludes his first list of explanations with a *Hamlet* quote. Kleist confesses that he lacks the power to "put these out-of-joint times to rights" and, in the next sentence, goes on to reject the playing of the fool, unlike Hamlet, to reject the desperate wit of the melancholic, whose words do nothing to change the actions of the rulers: "I feel, however, that the will that lives within my heart is very different from that of those who go about repeating this witty allusion [to Hamlet]: and, in short I wish to have nothing more to do with them. If the King concludes such an alliance [with Napoleon], what in the world may we still hope from him?"

Yet it is questionable to understand Kleist's suicide as an appeal to patriotism, especially since he subsequently changes the discourse of his explanations. He tells Marie that his "dejection" is understood by Henriette as of a "higher, more deeply rooted, and incurable, kind." He thus engages in a philosophical discourse, rendering suicide as a heroic sacrifice, as an expression of an almost pre-Existentialist radicalism: the realization that his "one exulting concern can only be to find an abyss deep enough to leap into with [Henriette]."[28] It is worth recalling Kleist's letter to his then-fiancée Wilhelmine von Zenge of July 21, 1801, which expresses Kleist's realization at the time that "there is nothing more disgusting than this fear of death. Life is the one possession that only has value when it is held lightly. It is contemptible if we cannot easily let go of it, and only he who can throw it away lightly and joyfully can use it to great ends. Whoever loves life excessively, he is already morally dead; for his highest vital power, namely his ability to sacrifice it, molders even as he cultivates it."[29] In 1811, as in 1801, Kleist's readiness to die is not a celebration of the hereafter, but of the here and now. When it comes to Kleist, there can be no talk of religious consolation in the face of death; rather, he mocks such consolation, for example, when he writes to Sophie Müller on November 20, 1811, that Henriette and he dream of "heavenly fields and suns, where [they] shall roam in the brightness with long wings on [their] shoulders."[30]

At the end of Kleist's letter to Marie of November 10, 1811, the question regarding his suicide thus shifts away from why he *has to* die—because of his suffering under his unsympathetic family and the weak Prussian state incapable of reform, his lack of success as a writer and his dire financial straits, etc. The question appears banal when the reasons are added up. Instead, what is of interest is why Kleist *was able* to die so calmly, soberly, cheerfully, and without any religious consolation. Kleist's suicide thus becomes comprehensible as an expression of a 'destructive character,' who, throughout his life, suppresses the instinctual drive toward self-preservation and conceives freedom as an act that necessarily violates that same self-preservation. In this sense the destructive act is at once a creative one; for without the sacrifice of every sense of security, innovation is possible neither in life nor in art. The joint journey into death is a "great voyage of discovery," as Henriette puts it in her postscript to Kleist's letter to Sophie Müller of November 20, 1811.[31] It is an enduring nomadism, then, with which Kleist upholds, until the end, the insight he had gained in his life—an insight that he expresses in February 1811 in the *Berlin Evening Paper*: "preservation [is] only possible through destruction, just as life often emerges only from death."[32]

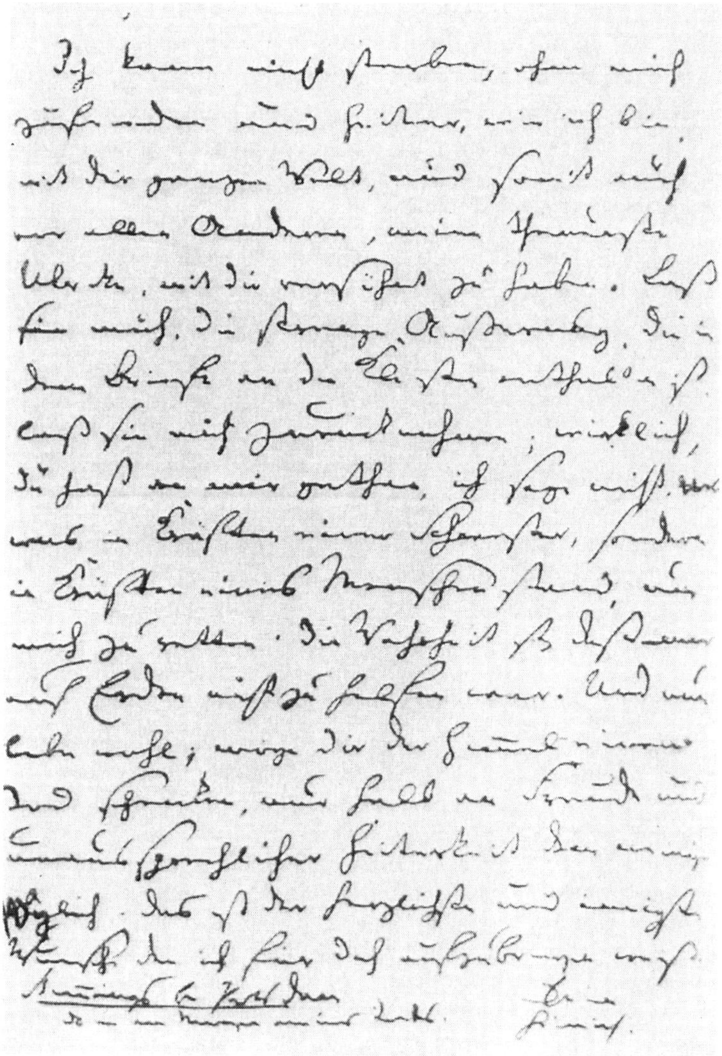

Fig. 60 Kleist's farewell letter to Ulrike of November 21, 1811

I cannot die, serene and happy as I am, without first making peace with the whole world, and so too, and above all others, my dearest Ulrike, with you. Let me call back those strong words in my letter to the family: really, all that was possible, not only for a sister, but for any human being, you in hopes of saving me have done: the truth is, there was no help for me on earth. And now good-bye. If Heaven would grant you a death half as full of joy and inexpressible serenity as my own, it would fulfill my most heartfelt and sincere wishes for you.

Yours,
Heinrich

Stimmings Inn, near Potsdam
On the morning of my death (ADE 205)

Kleist's staging of his suicide follows an economy of sacrifice in two respects. The farewell letters craft an image of their author for posterity. They manifest the suicide as a sacrifice for the sake of art. At the same time they reveal the art of sacrificing oneself for what is right. Not everyone is able to master this art: To suffer "not from a deficit, but from an excess of life."[33] What, then, distinguishes Henriette from Kleist's sister Ulrike? As Kleist writes to his cousin Marie on November 9, 1811, he believes Ulrike has not "comprehended the art of self-sacrifice, of giving oneself entirely for what one loves." And what distinguishes Marie from Henriette? The difference is that Henriette is willing to die with Kleist, as he notes on November 12, 1811, offering little consolation to the disgruntled Marie: "Can it console you to hear that I would never have exchanged you for this woman if she had wanted nothing more than to live with me?"[34]

To be willing to give oneself entirely, beyond any concern for self-preservation, is what Kleist and Henriette have in common; it is this radicality that sets them free and makes them cheerful. A first 'parallel campaign,' preceding their shared death, documents this affinity between the two of them—the 'mirrored letters' of their "Death Litany," which belong to the suicide letters and are unique, indeed unequalled, in the history of letter-writing:

> TO HENRIETTE VOGEL
>
> [presumably Berlin, November 1811]
>
> My *Jettchen*, my dear heart, my beloved, my dove, my life, my dear sweet life, light of my life, my all, my estate and effects, my castles, acres, meadows and vineyards, O sun of my life, sun, moon and stars, heaven and earth, my past and my future, my bride, my girl, my dear friend, my innermost being, my heart's blood, my viscera, apple of my eye, O, dearest, how shall I name you? My golden child, my pearl, my gem, my crown, my queen and empress. Dearly beloved of my heart, my highest and most cherished, my each and all, my wife, my wedding, christening of my children, my tragic drama, my posthumous fame! Ah, you are my other, better self, my virtues, my merits, my hope, the forgiveness of my sins, my future and blessedness, O, dear daughter of Heaven, my child of God, my interceder, my spokesman and pleader, my guardian angel, my Cherubim and Seraph, how I love you![35]
>
> HENRIETTE VOGEL TO KLEIST
>
> [presumably Berlin, November 1811]
>
> My Heinrich, my sweet sounding one, my bed of hyacinths, my ocean of bliss, my dawn and dusk, my Aeolian harp, my dew, my arch of peace, my favorite little child, my dearest heart, my joy in sorrow, my rebirth, my freedom, my fetter, my Sabbath, my golden chalice, my air, my warmth, my thought, my dear sinner, my desired here and beyond, my eyebright, my sweetest woe, my most beautiful youth, my pride, my protector, my conscience, my forest, my splendor, my

> sword and helmet, my magnanimity, my right hand, my Paradise, my teardrop, my Jacob's Ladder, my Saint John, my Tasso, my *knight*, my Count Wetter, my tender page, my arch-poet, my crystal, my life source, my repose, my weeping willow, my protection and safeguard, my hope and perseverance, my dreams, my beloved constellation, my little charmer, my unshakable fortress, my luck, my death, my heart's little fool, my solitude, my ship, my beautiful valley, my reward, my most esteemed![36] my Lethe, my cradle, my incense and myrrh, my voice, my judge, my saint, my sweet dreamer, my longing, my soul, my nerves, my golden mirror, my ruby, my syringa's flute, my crown of thorns, my thousand works of wonder, my teacher and student, I love you above all thoughts of my devising.
>
> My soul belongs to you.
> Henriette.
>
> My shade at noon, my spring in the desert, my beloved mother, my religion, my inner music, my poor sick Heinrich, my tender little white lamb, my Gate of Heaven.
>
> H.[37]

This exchange is beautiful beyond measure, at once tender and mocking; it is a piece of world literature—regrettably largely unknown—a catalog that all the world's lovers could leaf through in search for terms of endearment, only to realize that it is best to refrain from naming the other altogether. Unlike Kleist's, Henriette's letter reveals a lovers' precision, capturing Kleist in all his frailty, inconsistency, and heterogeneity, as well as the 'simultaneity of the non-simultaneous' within him. He comes to be recognizable in the changing allusions of her portrait, whereas she does not in his—far more conventional—portrayal. But both devise motley lists that could, in principle, go on indefinitely. And, indeed, it is the passage into the indefinite that concerns them at that very moment, not long before their shared death at Lake Wannsee on November 21, 1811. And yet we expect truth from last words, not poetry—not gallant masquerades and quotations. But who is to say whether there is true intimacy veiled behind this play? The initial question that sets it in motion is a quotation, modeled after the words of a thoroughly confused man, Count Wetter vom Strahl in Kleist's *Katie of Heilbronn*: "Dearest one, how shall I name you? Katie! But why can I not call you mine [*mein*]? Katie, girl—Katie!" the Count stammers.[38] Kleist's "Death Litany" presents these words in variation: "O, dearest, how shall I name you?" only to then, just like Henriette, use the possessive pronoun "my [*mein*]" suspiciously often.

How do I acknowledge you? What do I call you? What is the right name, your proper name, comprising the incomparable, unique essence of your being?[39] These questions are pertinent to all lovers, but Kleist and Henriette make a mockery of them. What this mockery expresses is that the other cannot be attained; it is precisely through the recognition of this boundary that a different kind of truth emerges, that gallant masquerade and authentic language of the heart coincide, that distance becomes intellectual closeness, maybe even physical proximity. One could imagine that Kleist and Henriette wrote the "Death Litany" on the morning of November 21, 1811, at Stimming's inn. Unfortunately, no original copy of the two letters exists; we only have a handwritten copy by Peguilhen later discovered in his literary estate. Perhaps the two were writing sitting next to each other; in any case, they were on par with each other, seeing eye to eye, unlike Kleist and Wilhelmine, to whom Kleist—in his letters to her—tried constantly to prove himself superior. The "Death Litany" demonstrates a singular symmetry of gift and counter-gift, a mutual recognition derived from the acknowledgment of each other's unattainability; its premise lies in the fact that Kleist and Henriette have already promised each other the ultimate gift: the gift of one's own life. They give themselves up to each other—a deeper devotion would be impossible. In the face of death, Kleist thus not only adheres to an economy but also to an aneconomy of sacrifice.

This aneconomy corresponds to the form of the two letters that mirror each other, published by Kleist scholar Paul Lindau in 1873, accompanied by the comment that their evaluation belonged "less to the domain of the literary critic than to that of the psychiatrist." Rejecting such a pathologization, August Sauer, in his 1907 study, called the epistolary exchange 'Death Litany,' as it emulates the "tone and form" of a litany. Sauer arranged the text into verses and stanzas, thus ignoring the particular epistolary form of Peguilhen's copy.[40] As is well known, a litany is a form of prayer consisting of a series of supplications delivered by the litanist to which the congregation responds in set, monotonous formulas: 'Lord, have mercy on us,' 'Christ, have mercy on us,' etc. Accordingly, Grimm's dictionary defines the word *litany* as a "long, monotonous, repetitive heartfelt effusion or declaration."[41] Kleist and Henriette's last exchange of letters is, however, neither monotonous nor an effusion of the heart in the sense of the imploring invocation of a lover, absolutized as a god in Romantic passion. One is therefore better off settling on the lowest common denominator between Catholic liturgy and "Death Litany" if one wants to retain the name proposed by Sauer: They both offer lists—a poetics of the enumerative, as it were—in the face of the passage into the inestimable.[42]

Such enumerations are familiar from Baroque poems, one of many examples being Georg Rodolf Weckherlin's "On the Early Death etc. of Anna Augusta, Margravine of Baden etc." ("Ueber den frühen tod etc. Fräuleins Anna

Augusta Marggräfin zu Baden etc."). The first stanza reads: "Your life, whose loss so brings us down, / was like a brief and pleasant day, / a star that morning scares away." The poem then continues—as the "etc." in its title anticipates—with many further comparisons until its last stanza summarizes: "Even so your life, so briefly lent, / what was it but a day gone by, / a star, a mist, a dawn, a sigh? / Oh dust, brief anger, dew, snow, scent, / how like to ice, glass, lighting, shower, / sun, rainbow, laughter, echo, flower, / time, dream, flight, shadow, smoke, you went."[43] Weckherlin's pattern of summation is not an echo of the life of a famous Margravine; the poet places no importance on presenting the deceased as a unique individual. In his series of comparisons, he is concerned solely with demonstrating the transience of *all* things earthly. Kleist and Henriette's "Death Litany" lacks a 'memento mori' as well as any Christian purpose; it also offers no verse that would capture a well-rounded image of the two individuals, or the whole of their lives, to be placed as an epitaph. Their invocation of names is dominated by single words; the principle of their series is decontextualization, not contextualization. Nothing in their words seems binding; rather, everything seems interminable and arbitrary in its permutations. The resulting heterogeneous lists are reminiscent of Modernist literary taxonomies in which people become dissociated from their qualities, or classifications become questionable, as in Argentine writer Jorge Luis Borges, who quotes "a certain Chinese encyclopedia" according to which the "animals are divided into (a) those that belong to the Emperor, (b) embalmed ones, (c) those that are trained, (d) suckling pigs, (e) mermaids, (f) fabulous ones, (g) stray dogs, (h) those that are included in this classification, (i) those that tremble as if they were mad, (j) innumerable ones, (k) those drawn with a very fine camel's hair brush, (l) others, (m) those that have just broken a flower vase, (n) those that resemble flies from a distance."[44]

Kleist's staging of his own death marks his final experiment, a feat of calculation on the threshold of the incalculable. The most manifest expression of this experiment is the "Death Litany," which, in its list form, is no less paradoxical in its interweaving of an economy and aneconomy of sacrifice. Let us note that the word *list* does not only refer to an inventory of words but is also etymologically derived from the Old High German *lista*, meaning a "narrow, ribbon-like strip,"[45] a hem, seam, or border. In this sense Kleist's and Henriette's lists are word-strips between this world and the hereafter, delineating and dissolving the borders between two lives. The "Death Litany" illustrates the inadequacy of all attempts at naming, understanding, and ordering (which is instructive for any biographer); and yet it is also the playful attempt to make a name for oneself. There is, in fact, one name that stands out from Kleist's list for the way

Fig. 61 Kleist grave, drawing 1877

that it transcends the temporality of his life: He calls Henriette "my posthumous fame" and thus exposes the futuristic character of his 'death project.' But as a look at the history of Kleist's reception proves, this naming is by no means a self-fulfilling prophecy.

CHAPTER XIII

"Only Whatever Does Not Cease *to Hurt* Stays in the Memory"

Kleist's Posthumous Fame and His Relevance for Today

> HOMBURG. [...] [S]ince I've seen my grave my only thought
> is, Let me live, I don't care how![1]

Let us suppose, for a moment, that Kleist had been forced back to his senses by the shock of killing Henriette. What would have happened? Considering this question, one should bear in mind the verses from German poet Friedrich Gottlieb Klopstock's ode "Clarissa Dead," which Kleist and Henriette had both read shortly before committing their double suicide: "One cruel storm (oh, haste and flee, / Ere it rush down in showers) // Will blast thee in thy brightest gleam: / Yet, even blasted, thou wilt seem / So beautiful, our tears will stream, / Wondering to see the dead."[2] Would Kleist have fled to a place far from Lake Wannsee to write in hiding for some years, to then return to Germany and German literature, under some royal pardon, and die an old man? Would he have finally received his deserved recognition as one of the greats, his early writings—the gruesome *Penthesilea*, the raging *Kohlhaas*—long exonerated as sins of his youth? Did not Johann Wolfgang Goethe and Friedrich Schiller also have their Sturm und Drang period, their *Götz von Berlichingen* and *The Robbers*?

Along with Klopstock's odes, Ernst Friedrich Peguilhen found Ludwig Tieck's translation of Miguel de Cervantes' *Don Quixote* in the possessions of Kleist and Henriette,[3] corresponding to an entry in Franz Kafka's third octavo notebook of October 22, 1917:

> One of the most important quixotic acts, more obtrusive than fighting with windmills, is: suicide. The dead Don Quixote wants to kill the dead Don Quixote; in order to kill, however, he needs a place that is alive, and this he searches for with his sword, both ceaselessly and in vain. Engaged in this occupation the two dead men, inextricably interlocked and positively bouncing with life, go somersaulting away down the ages.[4]

In Cervantes' novel, Don Quixote—after having cursed all chivalric romances and thus his own deluded life, having written his will and received the sacraments—dies a peaceful and faith-filled death. In Kafka's rendition,

© WILHELM FINK VERLAG, 2021 | DOI:10.30965/9783846765746_014

however, the struggle with death becomes yet another fight with windmills; the Christian hope for redemption becomes itself a delusion. Thus, the knight-errant continues to wander the lands in his afterlife, longing to give himself a different end, a death that would truly bring redemption, the end of all reflection on the meaning of death. But he does not succeed in doing so; the thoughts of the dead Don Quixote, revolving around death, are impossible to kill, they seem to have no finite dimension, no "place that is alive" into which he could thrust his sword. In Kafka the dead Don Quixote is therefore condemned to a ceaselessly turning somersault—a salto mortale—with the dead Don Quixote, to perpetually fall and rise again.[5]

If for Kleist "the truth is" that "there was no help for [him] on earth,"[6] if, in the face of death, he was perhaps aware, like Don Quixote, that the journey into the eternal could only become an eternal journey—in other words, a vain quest for the meaning of death—what is he left to do? Would it help to think of posthumous fame, "the immortal brother of mortal honour,"[7] as German philosopher Arthur Schopenhauer calls it? Could there be a fatal correlation between literature that radically defies the expectations of its time and the suicide of its author? Examples of this tragic connection can be found, above all, in the lives and literature of female writers from Virginia Woolf to Sylvia Plath and Anne Sexton. Those who vanish monstrously from history as subjects will eventually return as objects of stories, at long last gaining attention in obituaries, narratives, or oral and written historiography. Such is the paradoxical way of the economy of sacrifice. It imposes a form of remembrance on posterity that is effective precisely because it is anything but harmless; it inscribes a memory into our soul and body so as to keep the memory alive. In *On the Genealogy of Morality* of 1887, Friedrich Nietzsche describes how such a form of remembrance ought to be understood:

> "Something has to be burned in so that it stays in the memory: only whatever does not cease *to hurt* stays in the memory"—that is a main principle from the oldest psychology on earth (unfortunately also the longest). [...] It never got done without blood, torture, sacrifice when humanity considered it necessary to make a memory for itself.[8]

"[O]nly whatever does not cease *to hurt* stays in the memory." This precept applies to all wounds that do not easily heal, be they mental or physical in nature—which is why the Cheruscan prince in Kleist's *The Battle of Herrmann* has the body of Hally, who was raped by the Romans, cut up into pieces and sent to the fifteen German tribes as a memento to keep fresh the hatred against the Roman occupiers. There are many gruesome examples of this principle of the psychology of memory in Kleist's work, but it is his suicide itself that truly puts this principle to the test. Nevertheless, it was not until 1911—in the wake of the centennial celebrations of his death—that Kleist's attempt to shape his image for posterity finally proved successful. In 1811 his suicide caused a sensation among his contemporaries, but it did not bring about the hoped-for understanding of his life and work. His farewell letters remained rather ineffective at first, as it was not until 1848 that they saw partial publication, and not until the early 20th century that a larger number of editions appeared.[9] Before the publication of the letters, it was others who were granted the power to interpret Kleist's suicide. First of all, the doctors Sternemann and Greif, whose autopsy report sought to turn the mystery of the suicides at Wannsee into a solvable riddle—the unfathomable event into something fathomable, the peculiar individual into a pathological melancholic; a dispassionate medical case, stripped of its power to unsettle. The assessment of the two doctors concerning the "eccentric" or "pathological mental state [...] of the male deceased"[10] circulated through various discourses. Most of his contemporaries regarded Kleist as a madman and fool; their condemnation struck the person as much as the playwright and storyteller. In retrospect Kleist's hopeless death helped them comprehend the hopelessness of his works, which seemed to them as mad and excessive as the author himself. Among those who pathologized Kleist were mediocre minds, such as German writer Friedrich Weisser, who wrote a defamatory article calling Kleist a "mad writer" and one of the "most notorious disciples of the notorious Romantic-mystical school," stating in conclusion: "Madness, your name is poetry," a madness that had driven Kleist "to the point of murder." Even the well-known were not exempt from such invectives, including names such as Friedrich Schlegel, whose judgment was just as unsophisticated as Weisser's: Kleist "not only in his works but also in his life took *madness* for genius and confused the two."[11]

In the first half of the 19th century, Kleist's life and work were thus stigmatized as pathological. Those who disregarded Kleist could simply call on a famous example, Goethe, who condemned Romantic writer Ludwig Tieck's "piety" toward Kleist: "This poet, despite my purest intentions to take a sincere interest in him, had always filled me with horror and revulsion, as if a body which nature had intended to be beautiful were afflicted with an incurable disease."[12] Goethe's inability to make sense of Kleist's work results in a medical rather than aesthetic judgment—not at all surprising, given a literature in which lovers are devoured, as Achilles is by Penthesilea, or are torn apart by bears, as Ventidius is, the poor Roman who falls victim to Thusnelda's revenge. The contrast to the formal and moral rigor of Weimar Classicism could hardly have been starker. Only a few in the 19th century defended Kleist's literary experiments, namely E.T.A. Hoffmann, Tieck, Heinrich Heine, and Nietzsche—to no

Fig. 62
Johannes R. Becher (1891–1958)

avail, however. It was only his patriotic plays *The Battle of Herrmann* and *Prince Frederick of Homburg* that found recognition, due to ideological reasons in the course of the unification of Germany after 1860. Yet one cannot seriously speak of a first "Kleist renaissance" in the German Empire, as it was not until the early 20th century that he was rediscovered.[13] The centennial of 1911 was the decisive renaissance moment when Modernist writers began to invoke Kleist. One of them even had the foolish idea of copying Kleist's fatal self-sacrifice.

In April 1910 a Munich high school student, later to become the first minister of culture of the German Democratic Republic (GDR), stages his suicide following a familiar plot. Johannes Robert Becher, then nineteen years old, rents a room with a twenty-six-year-old tobacco dealer named Fanny Fuß, who suffers from a lung disease. She adores him and his juvenile poetic effusions but is unfortunately promised to a jealous engineer. After writing his farewell letters, Becher turns a pistol on his lover and then on himself. In the letters he professes to have lived and died as a poet, but none of this is true—his teachers considered him to be quite childish for his age, and having only dabbled in poetry up to that point, he sought a publisher for his poems in vain. While the poor tobacconist succumbs to her injuries, the high school student survives, as he deviates from the historical model at the critical moment. Kleist had shot himself in the mouth, by sure-fire means, in keeping with soldierly tradition, while Becher shoots himself in the chest and misses his heart. The young man does not seem to have been too serious about dying, as he later reveals in his autobiographical novel *Farewell* (*Abschied*) of 1940. Instead, he was seeking recognition as a poet. The attempted double suicide marked Becher's first initiative in literary policy, so to speak, to further his own interest by using a strategy aimed to influence his reception as a poet. And he was successful with it. The 'poet's madness,' the phrase that Dr. Heinrich Becher, then president of the Munich Higher Regional Court, used in defense of his son made headlines. Becher was committed to a psychiatric hospital in Haar, where he completed his university qualification exams, wrote an elegy for Fanny as well as a Kleist hymn, and soon thereafter gained acceptance as a free spirit in Munich's bohemia.[14] His hymn, entitled "The Struggling" ("Der Ringende"), was published in time for the centennial celebrations of Kleist's death in 1911. There is little mention of the historical Kleist in this poem. Rather, he appears in a dream vision as a revenant from the netherworld. While wandering around on earth, naked, Kleist shows Becher's lyrical alter ego "the fire mark of [his] suffering," while the latter finds comfort in his imaginary brother: "I carry his heart in my heart's throbbing. / O no longer to be lonely, no longer to be broken / in pain and agony??"[15]

Becher's hymn gives a dubious testimony to the veneration Kleist received beginning with the centennial celebrations of 1911. A few years earlier, on November 21, 1900, by contrast, it had been rather quiet at the Kleist grave on the Wannsee, as German dramatist Julius Bab laments:

> No one had come to be here,
> Since many hours, perhaps even for days. — —
> And yet today had been the day he died,
> The day that marked his awful, unforgiven death —
> And not a single flower on his stone.[16]

This situation changes in 1911. The "hearts" now "walk" to the "grave on the Wannsee,"[17] as German writer and critic Julius Hart, touched by the scene, notes in the Berlin newspaper *The Day* (*Der Tag*) on November 21, 1911. Everywhere paeans are sung to Kleist. In Berlin, Munich, and Vienna, special editions of Kleist's works are published to mark the centennial of his death. His *Penthesilea*—long considered impossible to produce on stage—is staged twice in Berlin, by theater directors Paul Lindau and Max Reinhardt, respectively. Modernist writers—such as Richard Dehmel, Arthur Schnitzler, and Hugo von Hofmannsthal—call for the endowment of the Kleist Prize to "prevent struggling literary talents from perishing in the struggle for life by providing them with timely assistance."[18] For the Rhenish playwright Herbert Eulenburg, however, these efforts are not enough. On November 21, 1911, in the *Frankfurt Newspaper* (*Frankfurter Zeitung*), he calls for a national day of remembrance on which all churches are to be "lined in black" in celebration of Kleist, the entire German military is to "fire volleys into the air to the sound of subdued drums and lowered flags in his memory," and all work is to be suspended for one hour.[19] While Eulenburg's call remains unfulfilled, former chancellor of the German Empire, Prince Bernhard von Bülow's voice is heard, loud and clear, in a special supplement to the *Berlin Daily Newspaper* (*Berliner Tageblatt*), indicating the direction in which the reception of Kleist is headed at the advent of World War I. He calls Kleist's fate "tragic" and his gruesome ode "Germania to Her Children," in which Kleist notoriously recommends damming the Rhine with French corpses, the "most beautiful and powerful battle song that ever poured forth from German lips."[20]

There certainly are more respectable testimonies to the fact that, on the occasion of the centennial celebrations of Kleist's death, the image crafted in his suicide letters is finally gaining acceptance, both in public discourse and among Modernist writers. Once again, Hart's commemorative essay gives testimony to Kleist's growing recognition, speaking somewhat flowery of Kleist as a "naked beggar" and "naked Arab."[21] First of all, these words can be understood in a purely material sense. Kleist's poverty, his lack of success with the public, his marginal social position are commonplaces in the commemorative literature of 1911. According to German writers Michael Georg Conrad and Frank Wedekind, Kleist perished due to "death by starvation,"[22] a sentence handed down by public judgment and so familiar to contemporary writers. Kleist, the dispossessed aristocrat living the life of a nomad, thus emerges as the German precursor to French poets Charles Baudelaire or Comte de Lautréamont. But the image of the beggar, so often invoked in the aesthetic discussions at the turn of the 20th century, refers not only to the material—real—poverty of the artist; it also speaks to his ideational poverty, as expressed, for instance, in Rainer Maria Rilke's *The Book of Poverty and Death* of 1903 or in *The Notebooks of Malte Laurids Brigge* published in 1910. The heteronomous misery captured in the notion of ideational poverty is at the same time self-imposed; it signifies the experience of the loss of tradition, which, in the case of the pugnacious Kleist, should of course not be understood merely as the passive form of suffering. This experience of loss is perhaps why Hart supplements the "naked beggar" with a "naked Arab." Kleist's is not, thus reads the full quote, the "mind of a harvester who in possession of all the riches of previous generations is privileged to create perfect works" like Goethe. Nothing is "as understandable as the resistance of a Goethe when the naked Arab Kleist breaks into the world of his Byzantium, rich in treasures and assured of its possessions, when the wild iconoclast shatters and destroys what has been built over thousands of years."[23] This portrait of Kleist is, of course, ultimately a self-portrait of the

Modernist writer, who is unwilling to take on the 'mind of a harvester'—of an epigone or a decadent; he is not interested in perpetuating tradition, but in inhabiting a nomadic and destructive demeanor, the radicality of self-sacrifice. And thus this Modernist self-concept can itself draw from Kleist's self-portrait in his suicide letters. Hart conceives of the rebellion of the Modernist writers at the turn of the 20th century alongside that of Kleist and the writers of the Sturm und Drang movement; and he does so in his Kleist monograph of 1912 as well.[24] Swiss writer Robert Walser also does so in his prose sketch "Kleist in Thun" of 1907, which ingeniously blends the images of the desperate artistic geniuses of Georg Büchner's Lenz, Kleist, and Walser himself.

The fascination with Kleist among Modernist writers is almost typical of their generation. It can be found in authors as diverse as Kafka, Rilke, Wedekind, Gottfried Benn, and Alfred Döblin. It is a paradoxical and yet perfectly understandable phenomenon: Invoking Kleist as a radical breaker of tradition, Modernist writers began creating a tradition of their own. They were looking for role models in the past with which to identify—for great names in order to make a name for themselves; but, in doing so, they found themselves dependent on the bourgeois canon they despised, which retained the names of the heretics, because orthodoxy best defines itself through its opposition to heterodoxy. It was thus Goethe's feelings of "horror and revulsion" toward the hypochondriac Kleist that were responsible for keeping him in the collective memory in the first place. Goethe's judgment prevented Kleist's canonization in the 19th century while facilitating it in the 20th century; exclusion was followed by inclusion. This is the consoling logic of difference to which a historically changing canon adheres. A quote from Döblin attests to this logic: "But how I lit up when I encountered H. v. Kleist's *Penthesilea*; and how my anger turned against the cold-hearted, all too well-tempered Goethe, who rejected this work. Kleist, whom I embraced in my awakening heart, was joined by Hölderlin. Kleist and Hölderlin became the gods of my youth. […] With them I stood up against the calm, the bourgeois, the sated, and the moderate."[25]

It was, of course, not only this anti-idealist attitude of the Modernist writers—who rejected anything remotely Neoclassical, bourgeois, or epigonal—that brought about a new understanding of Kleist, the antipode of Goethe, so that his works were finally read with enthusiasm. It is, above all, Nietzschean figures of thought that inform the Modernist embracing of Kleist, the model for which is the major Kleist biography written by the socialist Wilhelm Herzog. Published in Munich in 1911, Herzog's biography regards Kleist's skepticism as an anticipation of the "thoughts of the Zarathustra poet" Nietzsche.[26] Julius Hart takes a similar stance noting that, after Kleist experienced the "absurdity of the Kantian world of reason," "there could no longer be any talk of God" in his work. Kleist's ideal of art, Hart argues, no longer adheres to "the old ideal of the rational human being as the norm, the harmony, and the measure in all things." On the contrary, Kleist was an "enthusiast, demonically driven by his feeling for nature, his love instinct, ecstatically guided by Promethean artistic drives, a berserker!" The chief witnesses for this Nietzschean reading of Kleist are Penthesilea, Katie, Herrmann, Homburg, and Kohlhaas—all of them driven by a Dionysian force.[27] Even in 1925 German writer Stefan Zweig, in his essay "Kleist, the Dramatist" ("Der Dramatiker Kleist"), puts the author on a par with Nietzsche and emphasizes that the Dionysian in Kleist affects the dramatic form itself; that Kleist never "has complete control over his dramatic language"; that his language is formed "like the breathing of an agitated person, at times seething, swirling and roiling over, at times briefly pausing, a mere panting, or a cry, or a silence."[28]

Zweig's essay conflates arguments by Nietzsche and Sigmund Freud insofar as he doubts that Kleist's creative capacity is sovereign. Accordingly, Kleist does not consciously orchestrate a Dionysian frenzy in order to lend expression to a foreign, chaotic, and alogical unconscious opposing the Apollonian—rational and oppressive—order of reality. Rather, Kleist's specifically Modern character is the product of his inner divisiveness. To Zweig, Kleist appears as a manic-depressive, equally dominated by excessive passions and by fears of failure, ultimately succumbing to his own death plan. His creativity was hence compulsive, not controlled by intellect and reason; not the expression of the individual's sense of wholeness but of isolated pent-up emotions—as manifest in Guiscard's ambition for power, in Penthesilea's sexual lust, and in the hatred of the German people pushed to the point of bestiality in *The Battle of Herrmann*. Unlike Goethe or Schiller, Kleist was not a writer who "mastered his problems, but an obsessive man," "a unique case" in German literary history—if anything, comparable to Fyodor Dostoevsky, whose characters are also "charged" with "all the sick and excessive forces of the nerves."[29] Zweig's portrait of Kleist is an exercise in pathography. Yet, unlike Goethe, Zweig is not trying to condemn Kleist but to understand him. His image of Kleist is shaped by psychoanalysis as well as by the experience of World War I. Kleist becomes, for Zweig, a case study proving that 'the ego is not the master in its own house' and that writing in the Modern age—rather than providing a fixed meaning or serving as a therapeutic exercise—can intensify feelings of helplessness.

Dissociation of the self or renewal of mankind, critique of civilization or Messianism: After 1914 not only the works of German literature but the portraits of Kleist, too, are caught up in this fundamental tension. They thus portray an ambivalent figure. Kleist can be shown, as in Zweig, as a prototype of the dissolution of the self or as a prophet of the renewal of mankind conceived primarily in nationalist terms. These two images of Kleist are mostly thought in either/or terms, but the difference can also be sublated, as in Thomas Mann's *Reflections of a Nonpolitical Man* (1915–18). In a blended portrait of Kleist and himself, Mann notes:

> Chronicler and interpreter of decadence, fancier of the pathological and of death, an esthete with a tendency toward the abyss: how could *I* come to identify myself with Germany, How do *I* come to positive participation in the war, to patriotic enthusiasm? [...] Let me answer this with reference to a great man who was deeply ill from youth on, thoroughly pathological in every selection of artistic themes, hysterical, extreme, romantic, "hypochondriacal," a nuisance to Goethe. And who still, when Germany was in need, found the thunderous phrases of the "community" that could only be destroyed in a bloodbath *that would darken the sun.* [...] [T]his hysterical Junker—logician, propagandist, daredevil and hot-head of irrationality and of regression to subhuman weakness [...] wrote that article, those two pages of powerful and in the most serious sense oratorical prose with the title, "What Is at Stake in This War?" It could have been written word for word two years ago instead of a hundred [...].[30]

The nationalist line in Kleist reception remained dominant during and beyond World War I, while the image of a mentally ill and psychologically dissociated Kleist was mostly forgotten after 1918. Founded in 1920, the Kleist Society played an inglorious role in furthering a nationalist reception of Kleist, as it issued, in 1922, an appeal entitled "To Stand by Kleist Is to Be German!" ("Zu Kleist stehen heißt deutsch sein!"), which was signed by the board members Gerhart Hauptmann, Ricarda Huch, Max Liebermann, and Hans Pfitzner, among others.[31] In 1936 Georg Minde-Pouet, the president of the Kleist Society, was pleased to declare that Kleist had "become a classic of National Socialist Germany."[32] This revaluation was possible because German studies under the Nazis cast Kleist as a propagandist of the German 'people's community,' as a champion of passionate, heroic deeds, and as a model of an enthusiastic willingness to die.[33] In a letter to Reichsführer Heinrich Himmler in 1938, Gerhard Fricke—an authority on Kleist since his 1929 study *Emotion and Fate in Heinrich von Kleist* (*Gefühl und Schicksal bei Heinrich von Kleist*)—looked back with disgust on the Weimar Republic years, during which Kleist's "life and work [...] were to a large extent the hotbed of a subversive, wanton, mostly Jewish psychology and psychoanalysis."[34] He thus polemicized against the Kleist studies of the 1920s—those of Stefan Zweig, Arnold Zweig, or Marieluise Fleißer. The antisemitism of his criticism also targeted the Kleist Foundation—largely financed by the publishing house S. Fischer—and the Kleist Prize it awarded. From Fricke's point of view, the Kleist Prize had invariably gone to the wrong individuals (thanks to the individual entrusted by the Kleist Society to determine the prize recipient)—namely, to Hans Henny Jahnn, Bertolt Brecht, Robert Musil, or Anna Seghers. In fact, Fricke's criticism targeted the entirety of Jewish Kleist reception, which included a fictional representative whose reading of Kleist is among the most touching. I am speaking of the Jewish schoolboy Berthold in Lion Feuchtwanger's 1933 novel *The Oppenheims*, later renamed *The Oppermanns*. Berthold is forced by his Nazi teacher to give a presentation on 'Hermann the German,' in keeping with the spirit of the time. In 1933/34 alone Kleist's *The Battle of Herrmann* was performed 146 times on German stages as an example of what Rainer Schlösser, the Reich drama advisor, called a "steel Romanticism."[35] When Berthold does not deliver on his teacher's demand to praise the Cheruscan prince, he is pilloried in class. Against the nationalist ideologies of the Nazis, he has merely one response, the same that Kohlhaas gives to his wife when she asks him anxiously why he is selling his property. Berthold reads the passage on the eve of his suicide: "I don't wish to remain in a country where my rights are not protected. Better to be a dog, if I am to be trampled on, than a man."[36]

It is clear why exiled German writers quote Kleist—*Michael Kohlhaas*, in particular. In 1935 German playwright Bertolt Brecht drafted a film treatment for the *Kohlhaas* novella, with the intention of restoring the "German classic that the fascists had claimed for themselves to its proper character." "Its subject: the struggle of early capitalist, revolutionary class law (bourgeois law) against feudal privilege."[37] In 1939 Brecht published a sonnet "On Kleist's Play 'The Prince of Homburg'" in the Parisian exile journal *The New World Stage* (*Die neue Weltbühne*), a play he regarded as a lesson on how a hero's backbone can be broken, how he can be turned into a servant, his King's subject. The poem's final stanza reads: "Shattered beside him is his dagger-blade. / Not dead but laid out in the dust he lies, / Struck down like all his country's enemies."[38] The year Brecht's sonnet appeared, Johannes R. Becher was living in exile in Moscow. By then he had developed into an ironclad politician, ideologically armed with communism, in order to separate himself from the youthful bohemian and poet he once was. In a sonnet entitled "Kleist in the Third Reich" ("Kleist im Dritten Reich"), Becher decries the hypocrisy of the fascist reception of Kleist and writes—with good reason—that Kleist, under Nazi rule, would not have needed to kill himself, for: "Suspicious would be deemed what in him glows and burns / He would not have shot himself, you would have done so."[39] Written in exile, Becher's poem is not a fragmented hymn in free verse like his earlier Kleist poem of 1911, which attests to his Expressionist veneration of Kleist. Rather, in its sonnet form it is as neatly closed as his worldview and thus conforms to the conservative demands of the socialist artistic doctrine, to which Kleist would never have complied—a fact Becher, of course, omits. The correspondence between German writer Anna Seghers and Hungarian philosopher Georg Lukács from 1938/39 proves that Kleist's life would have been threatened not only by the Nazis but also by the Communists—had Kleist lived as an exile in Russia, he would have hardly survived the Expressionist debate there.

Lukács is known to have been the chief Marxist theoretician of the exiled writers and intellectuals who fled the Nazi regime and of post-war Socialist Realism in the GDR. For him Kleist—the enemy of the revolutionary Napoleon—represents a "mixture of reaction and decadence" at the turn of the 19th century, which Lukács believes to be the reason Goethe rejected him. The winner of the 1929 Kleist Prize, Seghers—also a Communist, though exiled in Mexico not in Moscow—is committed to Kleist's catastrophic narrative technique in her own novellas and vehemently defends Kleist against Lukács, the socialist Goethe epigone who critiques Kleist for being a Romantic. She sees Kleist as a writer who, like herself, suffered deeply from his fatherland in an era of profound social upheaval, and compares him with other preeminent mad writers and suicide victims of German literature, such as J.M.R. Lenz, Friedrich Hölderlin, and Karoline von Günderrode. In her letters to Lukács, she fiercely points out that Goethe's works of genius—as opposed to those of Kleist—"had been paid for by the writer's close adherence to the established society." Unlike Kleist, Seghers notes, Goethe simply had an aversion to any threat concerning dissolution of the self, a fear of madness and of death.[40] Therefore, one may add, he would have sided with the perpetrators not the victims. Seghers proves courageous in her portrayal of Goethe. What she says about him applies more to some of the German exiles in Moscow—to Becher and Alfred Kurella, for example—who had conformed to the Communist regime in order to reconsolidate their selves, either denying their Expressionist past or publicly denouncing it as an affliction and a sin of their youth while closing their eyes to the Stalinist persecution of former companions who remained loyal to their Expressionist past.[41]

Lukács' negative judgment of Kleist shaped his reception in the GDR. Seghers' objection was of no avail, nor was that of Communist philosopher Ernst Bloch, who, in 1938, had accused Lukács of falsely equating Kleist's "experiment in demolition with a condition of decadence."[42] In the GDR Kleist was either considered a reactionary Romantic and militant Prussian nobleman, or a precursor to Modernist decadence and thus banned from the 'Museum of Socialist Poetry,' to rework a phrase from German poet Hans Magnus Enzensberger. Kleist's literature did not fit the traditionalist agenda of the GDR's official literary policy, which compelled its writers to advance the aesthetic theory and practice of the bourgeois, Humanist tradition represented by

Gotthold Ephraim Lessing, Schiller, and Goethe while forbidding its writers to follow literary movements, past or present, that disrupted this cultural continuum. And yet Kleist did not share the fate of Modernist writers such as Kafka, whose works could not be widely read in the GDR as their print runs were kept small due to censorship. It was only in the course of the temporary liberalization of the GDR's cultural policy after the resignation of Walter Ulbricht, first secretary of the Socialist Unity Party, in 1971 that revisions were made to this traditionalist agenda. Günter Kunert's "Pamphlet for K." ("Pamphlet für K.") of 1975 and Christa Wolf's novel *No Place on Earth* of 1979 were the foremost texts to have reckoned with Kleist's ideological condemnation, in their portrayal of him as a rebel and martyr of his time rather than a pathological reactionary.[43] But it is German playwright Heiner Müller who took up Kleist's experimental poetics most rigorously. His 1977 play *Gundling's Life Frederick of Prussia Lessing's Sleep Dream Scream* features a short scene entitled "Heinrich von Kleist Plays Michael Kohlhaas":

> *Despoiled shore (a lake near Strassburg). Kleist in uniform. A doll of Kleist. A doll of a woman. A doll of a horse. Executioner's block. Kleist touches face breast hands genitals of the Kleist doll. Caresses kisses embraces the woman's doll. Cuts off the head of the horse's doll with his sword. Rips the heart from the woman's doll and eats it. Rips the uniform off his body, wraps the head of the Kleist doll in the tunic, puts on the horse's head, hacks the Kleist doll to pieces with his sword; roses and bowels spill from it. Throws off the horse's head, puts on the wig (hair down to the heels) of the woman's doll, breaks his sword over his knee, approaches the executioner's block. Takes off the wig, spreads the woman's hair over the executioner's block, bites open his artery, sawdust trickles from his arm which he holds over the woman's hair resting on the executioner's block. A white cloth is thrown from the flies onto the scene, a red spot quickly spreads on it.*[44]

The scene unfolds an ingenious mime tracing Kleist's 'destructive character' back to the emotionally charged nature of the Prussian warrior society. One's power to destroy tradition originates itself from tradition; that which is to be destroyed is thus always already one's own, which is why destruction inevitably turns into self-destruction.

It was not only dissident writers in East Germany who discovered Kleist as a rebel against political and cultural regimes. After the failed student movement of 1968, Kleist and his characters provided models for suffering and resisting the state-sponsored violations of the people's rights in West Germany as well: for example, in Peter Stein's 1972 Berlin production of *Prince Frederick of Homburg* and Claus Peymann's Bochum interpretation of Herrmann as a guerrilla. But it is, above all, Kleist's *Michael Kohlhaas* that provided such a model for suffering and resisting. In 1969 Volker Schlöndorff directed the film *Man on*

Horseback, based on Kleist's novella, which also inspired Heinrich Böll's 1974 story *The Lost Honor of Katharina Blum*. In her 1979 historical novel *Kohlhaas*, Elisabeth Plessen attempts to find answers to the disturbing experience of the contemporary terrorism of the Red Army Faction. In his 1985 monograph *Michael Kohlhaas, then and now*, Horst Sendler, then president of the Federal Administrative Court, conducts a historical and legal discourse on the origins of German terrorism. During the 1970s and 1980s, there was a veritable Kleist renaissance in West Germany, thanks to a number of outstanding film and theater productions. This renaissance had more than just political reasons, such as the growing interest in the pathologies of the bourgeois family. Eric Rohmer's 1976 film *The Marquise of O* is a splendid example of this particular interest, as is George Moorse's 1967 film adaptation of "The Foundling." Moreover, an emerging interest in the aesthetics of horror and the sublime characterized these decades, as can be seen in the stage productions of *Penthesilea* by Hans Neuenfels in Berlin in 1981 and Hans-Jürgen Syberberg in Paris in 1987.[45]

One particular Kleist image from the mid-20th century must be called to mind—from Thomas Mann's 1954 Zurich lecture on "Kleist and His Stories," later published as a preface to Martin Greenberg's US edition of translated Kleist stories. Intellectually and stylistically Mann's lecture is a masterpiece that takes to heart Kleist's urging that his self-sacrifice not be simply called "sick" but be considered from different "points of view."[46] His lecture thus seems in many ways indebted to the author image Kleist crafted of himself in his farewell letters. Mann refrains from resolving the many contradictions in Kleist's life and work in his refusal to assume a central point of view. Hence, he paints a truly Modern portrait of Kleist that shows what it must have meant for him to have fallen out of "all known codes and patterns"—out of the social order of his station, out of the moral order of the bourgeoisie, out of the aesthetic order of idealist art. As such, the source of Kleist's unhappiness in life, according to Mann, was also the source of his admirable creative power in literature, understood as a liberation from all literary constraints. Unlike in his *Reflections of a Nonpolitical Man*, Mann thus resists defining Kleist as a sick person, instead defending him against Goethe's notorious judgment. What is more, Mann points out "that the man who had written *Werther* and *Tasso* was hardly in a position to pronounce so haughtily on the subject of morbidity," thus dispensing with the idea of a fundamental opposition between Kleist's two supposed poetic dispositions, which had determined the history of his reception for some one hundred and fifty years. Mann calls Kleist "sullen, melancholy," where melancholia is less an illness than an intellectual attitude, a basic disposition of the Modern genius, whose loss of orientation is not merely a social or psychological problem, but primarily an epistemological and metaphysical one. More strongly than any other portraitist before him, Mann emphasizes Kleist's 'transcendental homelessness': Kleist killed himself "out of a metaphysical longing to cast his fragmented self into the All." His essay "On the Puppet Theater," notes Mann, is a "brilliant piece of aesthetic metaphysics," which however—one should add—no longer offers any real consolation. It is no coincidence, then, that Kleist's essay should be found on Adrian Leverkühn's desk in Mann's *Doctor Faustus*. As melancholic geniuses both Leverkühn and Kleist represent, for Mann, the problem of the Modernist artist: the futile quest to recover a lost sense of totality.[47]

The history of Kleist reception in the 20th century proves that he became an important agent of Modernism in its struggle against anti-Modernism. But when it comes to the question of writers influenced by Kleist or to creative adaptations of his works, things look different, notwithstanding Kleist's minor role in Mann's *Doctor Faustus*. The novel is so complex that one could not unconditionally claim that Kleist's presence as a pre-text is constitutive of Mann's text, nor could one therefore speak of a productive modeling of Kleist in Mann.[48] In his 1922 monograph on Kleist, Friedrich Gundolf already pointed out that Kleist may have many admirers but could not have any real heir, his work being simply the expression of his inimitable character.[49] That Kleist was unique is a commonplace and explains little. I suspect there is another reason to explain the lack of writers modeling their works after Kleist's: It is related to the tendency of Modernist and Postmodernist authors to try to regain their lost sense of purpose and place in the world via the detour of intertextuality. They therefore mostly rely on pre-texts—even if only through parody—through which a sense of totality might be restored, such as Homer's *Odyssey*, Dante Alighieri's *Divine Comedy*, or Goethe's *Wilhelm Meister's Apprenticeship* and *Faust*. Kleist's texts do not lend themselves for such ends, since they do not provide answers, but only pose questions. They stage "paradoxes, dissonances, and disruptions: situations of an indeterminate epistemology,"[50] as one often encounters them today. It is therefore conceivable that the creative adaptation of Kleist's work is just now beginning—in our *Post*modern times. And it is not the Kleist of the Kant crisis, the disappointed idealist—in his lament that his longing for the absolute will inevitably remain unfulfilled—but Kleist the moralist who could serve as a model, as he remains entirely immanent in this world, an observer of human behavior without illusions—albeit not a joyful, calm but an angry and passionate one, always refusing to accept the status quo.

The acceptance speeches of the most recent Kleist Prize winners at the beginning of the 21st century—such as Daniel Kehlmann, Navid Kermani, Marcel Beyer, Monika Rinck, Yoko Tawada, and Christoph Ransmayr—attest to the fact that Kleist has the power to unsettle even in the present day.[51] But the enduring fascination with Kleist goes beyond the German-speaking world. The bicentennial celebrations of Kleist's death in 2011 confirmed that, today, his work clearly belongs within the canon of world literature. On November 21, 2011, the very day of the 200th anniversary of his death, Kleist's works were recited in 148 cities across the globe as part of a Worldwide Reading Day, mostly by young people and streamed on the internet for everyone to follow. Throughout 2011, conferences were organized and theater productions were staged worldwide, and major exhibitions were held in Berlin and Frankfurt an der Oder, the last and first place Kleist lived. In total there were some 2,500 events in honor of Kleist, both in Germany and abroad.[52] As a crisis specialist Kleist may well seem contemporary, for in his life and work, he expressed an experience shared all over the world today, and not just by young people: the experience of the precarious, the uncertain, the unstable, and the non-established. In Kleist's literature the precarious affects the realms of epistemology, ethics, and aesthetics alike. That said, Kleist can hardly serve as a means of identification for the present generation. He remained a stranger to his contemporaries, and the closer we study his life and work, the stranger he becomes. Perhaps we need to discover what is untimely about Kleist and not what is seemingly timely, in order to transcend the boundaries of our time and our selves to revise conventional ways of thinking, to escape the confines and one-dimensionality of the present.

According to Hegel, the owl of Minerva spreads its wings only with the falling of dusk, meaning that wisdom only has a chance to prevail if it looks back to the past, because what one lives through in the present is so difficult to grasp. Shortly before his death Kleist read *Don Quixote*, a novel that reflects on the tradition of chivalric romances when chivalry had long ceased to exist. Perhaps Kleist has something of a Don Quixote figure about him insofar as his Modernity lies in the fact that he embodies a time long gone while also making visible the newness of a time yet to come. In his early biographical and literary adventures, Kleist—the dispossessed aristocrat educated by bourgeois tutors—relentlessly put to the test Enlightenment notions of happiness until an unbridgeable abyss opened up between that which is imaginable and that which is liveable. While bourgeois idealism was rising, he was already showing its downfall. In both real and fictional crises, Kleist continually resorted to aristocratic prudence rules and techniques of communication, thus emerging as a liminal figure transcending boundaries between times and social stations. The oscillation between bourgeois and aristocratic anthropology and aesthetics—reflective of the 'simultaneity of the non-simultaneous' at the turn of the 19th century—seems relevant today, in our times of waiting and transition, in which we hope that appearances will lead to civility and in which happiness primarily means the avoidance of misfortune. The latter, however, is precisely what Kleist rejected. Instead he remained, as the 2007 Kleist Prize winner Wilhelm Genazino puts it, relentless in his "compulsion to happiness"[53]—against all disillusioning experiences. Even in his failures Kleist explored the boundaries of knowledge, pushing toward the new, the unknown. In times of crisis escaping into the next instance of stability would not have helped him, but rather exposing himself to risk. The image of the arched gate, of 'stability in falling,' was merely a feeble consolation in Kleist's life and work, nothing more. Prothoe's closing words addressed to her dead friend Penthesilea are better suited for Kleist. Her words invoke a Baroque emblem that raises the question whether greatness and instability, thoughts concerned for the future and pride go hand-in-hand, and whether we are not 'dead' if, in waiting, we forget our hope for that which awaits us. That would be the untimely question posed by the heroic melancholic Kleist to our post-heroic age, an age that aspires to mediocracy—quite understandably, after the historical catastrophes of the 20th century and more recent ones of this century:

> She fell because she bloomed too proud and strong!
> The dead oak stands, defying wind and weather,
> the gale pulls down the good wood with a crash,
> for with his fingers he can fasten in its crown.[54]

CHAPTER XIV

On Kleist's Fascination with Risk

Encyclopedic Note

The first volume of the paperback series *rowohlt's german encyclopedia* (*rowohlts deutsche enzyklopädie*), published in 1955 and edited by Italian-German philosopher Ernesto Grassi, aimed to map the knowledge of the century. At the end of each volume, one finds an 'encyclopedic note' offering a brief introduction to the volume's general subject. Though positioned at the end, these notes were intended to be read first and were often written by an author different from the volume's main text. In keeping with Grassi's tradition, the final chapter of this biography identifies the central features of Kleist's fascination with risk by turning to the periphery of his work, specifically to his reflections on athletic contests. It does so in the form of five brief theses grounded in an understanding of his 'antiperistatic genius,' the singular creative force of Kleist's life and work. The notion of the antiperistatic genius comes from Arthur Schopenhauer's German translation of Baltasar Gracián's *The Art of Worldly Wisdom*, explained here.[1]

Suppose a lady in polite society invites a rugged man to dance, but he declines, saying, "such trifles were not his business." And when the lady asks him what his business is, he replies, "Fighting!" To which she says:

> I should think it a good thing, now that you are not away at war or engaged in fighting, for you to have yourself greased all over and stowed away in a closet along with all your battle harness, so that you won't grow any rustier than you already are […].

The others present join her in laughter, ridiculing the soldier. This story is found in Baldassare Castiglione's *The Book of the Courtier* of 1528,[2] and the lady must be joking in every respect, for her invitation to dance comes in the midst of wartime, when the Italian city-states were threatened by French, Spanish, and Austrian forces. The choice, therefore, is not to either 'wage war' or 'dance.' The anecdote serves to illustrate that a man must defend his reputation as much on the dance floor as on the battlefield; an aristocrat must know how to fight *and* dance. This convention is not unique to the Italian nobility; it does not apply solely to the Renaissance *gentiluomo*. In the Prussian military academies of Friedrich the Great and his successors, the cadets practiced not only military, but dance maneuvers.

© WILHELM FINK VERLAG, 2021 | DOI:10.30965/9783846765746_015

Warfare and dancing belonged together for Kleist too, the soldier and aristocrat, just as public and private politics did. Politics, as is well known, is the art of gaining and maintaining power over people. Power is won—in public as much as in private life—by those who master communication and other mechanisms of control. Aristocrats knew that dancing was a strategy of self-fashioning to secure power—a form of body politics. They were well aware that their actions and interactions in public spaces were to follow choreographed patterns—that all forms of movement at court, in the military, in politics, or in athletic contests were subject to an artificial, theatrical, or ballet-like performance. The goal of such body politics was to gain full control over one's bodily expressions in order to exert control over one's public image, which would, in turn, work to acquire and secure favor—the Latin *gratia*. Kleist's most famous essay "On the Puppet Theater" deals with this art of self-fashioning, arguing for the marionette's grace and thus advantage over human dancers, given the puppeteer's capacity to "transpose[]" the puppet's movement "wholly into the realm of mechanical forces" and thus fully calculate its expression.[3] The grace of the puppets is without inner substance, geared solely toward its aesthetic effect. Puppets are not beautiful souls whose inner being is reflected in their outer appearance, as Friedrich Schiller's notion of grace demands.[4]

The first thesis is already familiar to us from the introduction: Throughout his life Kleist was fascinated by figures of control in discourses as varied as politics, poetry, pedagogy, and psychotechnics. In his letter to his sister Ulrike of May 1799, he insists on the indispensability of a life plan. His own life developed quite differently from his plan, however, manifesting as a series of experiments whose outcomes could not be predicted. Kleist's difficulties in conceiving of and following a life plan were not unique to him. Rather, they were representative of a generational problem faced by those born after 1770. This generation, raised on Enlightenment values of autonomy and self-determination, was caught up in the turmoil of the Napoleonic Wars, which gave rise to political instability, the need for comprehensive social reform, and the destabilization of the estate system in the German states. The lives of aristocrats, in particular, became dangerously indeterminate, as the sense of stability they derived from the social hierarchy of the estate system weakened and the possibility for social mobility increased. Such a gain in freedom could be experienced as a loss of orientation. "On the Puppet Theater" is one of many examples of the recourse Kleist took in the skeptical-moralist systems of the aristocracy for securing power and favor. It shows that in his literary works he could take up and transform the prudence rules devised by Niccolò Machiavelli, Gracián, and others to control private and public communications in his literary works.

The second thesis argues that Kleist's transformation of moralist thought for his own time made him a precursor to Modernism. While the moralists of the 16th and 17th centuries were primarily concerned with measures for avoiding risk in communication, Kleist, by contrast, was increasingly fascinated by behaviors of risk, by moments of lost control and the figures of control one could discover therein. Kleist's early Happiness essay anticipates this fascination in its very effort to cultivate the Enlightenment notion of an orderly bourgeois 'project identity.' Yet, in its attempt to link virtue and happiness, the essay merely draws kaleidoscopically on heterogeneous thought-images from idealist aesthetics, the imagery of Baroque stoicism, the Christian tradition of *Ecce homo*, Aristotelian ethics, the geography of the Harz Mountains, as well as Greek mythology. In the end Kleist directs the problem away from theory to practical life, admitting:

> We do not know the words of the incantation; time alone conducts them in and of itself, in order to calm and pacify the remarkably disharmonious forms that agitate deep inside and drive us to distraction. And all the young men, whom we see alongside and around us, naturally share this fate with us. All their moves and motions appear to be nothing but the effect of an imperceptible but powerful jolt, which irresistibly drags them along. They appear to me like comets that roam the universe in random ovals until they finally find a law of motion and an orbit.[5]

Accordingly, the "law of motion" must first be discovered; it does not precede motion. Advanced, elaborate calculations for determining a life plan or 'the certain path to happiness' hold no sway over the power of chance. Instead, order and disorder are bound to each other. At the heart of Kleist's Happiness essay lies a contradiction that later served as the generative core of his writing. At the essay's beginning chance is understood as an opponent of virtue, while at the end as virtue's midwife. Later in his life Kleist does not avoid risks but seeks them out, which also becomes evident in his essay "On the Gradual Fabrication of Thoughts While Speaking." The text begins with the inversion of the old moralist precept that one should think before speaking, as Gracián demands in rule no. 48 of *The Art of Worldly Wisdom*: "for the flow of words soon ceases where there is no spring of thoughts."[6] For Kleist, by contrast, the prudence rule reads: "*l'idée vient en parlant*."[7] While moralist prudence culminates in Gracián's dictum: "To appeal to an inner Court of Revision makes things safe,"[8] Kleist proposes, when speaking, to "trust to luck and make a start," and to leave the rest to the imminent "necessity to complete what [the mind] has begun."[9] According to the moralist taxonomy, such imprudent actions fall into the category of the monstrous. In Schopenhauer's 1832 translation Gracián's rule no. 56 reads:

> *Have Presence of Mind.* It springs from a happy promptitude of spirit. Owing to its vivacity and wide-awakeness, there are no dangers or mischances for such a spirit. Many reflect much, and then do everything wrong: others get everything without thinking of it beforehand. There are antiperistatic geniuses who work best in an emergency: they are like monsters who succeed in everything they do on the spur of the moment, but fail in everything they think over: what does not occur to them at once will never occur to them: in their mind there is no court of appeal.[10]

With the terms "antiperistatic genius" and "on the spur of the moment," Schopenhauer links mental and physical movement. He who uses the spurs urging his horse forward, he who makes a decision—speaks, etc.—on the spur of the moment, acts at full speed, so to speak, without stopping to reflect. Gracián's rule thus describes a risky communication strategy in a state of emergency, a strategy he then, however, retracts in the subsequent rule for the sake of safety, in order to avoid risk: "*Thoughtful People Are Safer.*"[11] The situation is different with Kleist. Antiperistasis—the refutation of an opponent's argument on the spur of the moment—becomes the principle catalyst for a rhetoric of 'fabrication,' a rhetoric that indeed takes full effect only in an "emergency." Moreover, the rule of antiperistasis applies not only to rhetorical but also to physical duels.

The third thesis proposes that, for Kleist, athletic contests are a kind of laboratory for observing the laws of motion in unpredictable situations. The starting point for this thesis is Kleist's description of a wrestling match in "On Thinking Things Over: A Paradox":

> Life itself is a contest with fate, and the same is true for ordinary action as for wrestling. The athlete, at that moment when he is holding his opponent in his grip, simply has no recourse but to act spontaneously, on inspiration; and if he begins to calculate which muscles to contract and which limbs to move in order to throw him, he will always draw the short straw and be thrown himself. But afterwards, when he has either won or found himself flat on the floor, *that* would be the proper time and place to think it over, and decide which pressure threw his opponent, or with which foot he ought to have tripped him in order to remain standing himself. Whoever does not hold tightly to life like that wrestler, and, at every turn of contest, in the face of whatever oppositions, pressures, retreats and responses, does not feel and act with every fiber of his being, such a man, try as he might, will never make his mark in a conversation, still less on a field of battle.

"On Thinking Things Over: A Paradox" is presented as a father's speech to his son to be delivered in the future, particularly if the son "decides on a military career."[12] It is hardly questionable that the text alludes to the Prussian army's need for reform; to contemporary discourses and practices of disciplining the body in knightly exercises and according to the gymnastic pedagogy of the philanthropists; as well as to military pamphlets that negotiate the tension between mechanical precision and unrestricted spontaneity, drill and instinct. The text delivers these allusions with changing references, including to the poetics of genius within the Sturm und Drang movement.[13]

But allow me to now read Kleist's texts on questions of reflexivity and spontaneity from a somewhat anachronistic perspective—that is, without considering the contemporary military and pedagogical discourses and practices. Or, put differently, allow me to consider his works as philosophical reflections on sports, as contributions to a philosophy of creative action—of creativity *in actu*—viewed from the perspective of athletic contests. What I offer here, then, is not a historical-systematic foundation for the analysis of laws of motion at the turn of the 19th century, but a heuristic praxeological perspective which helps to illuminate what Kleist's logic of *athletic* practice can teach us about the logic of *creative* practice.

Let us therefore take another look at Kleist's reflections on the behavior of the wrestler while fighting. It is significant that Kleist does not associate wrestling with the intentional movements of the athlete; he understands wrestling not as a preconceived strategy, but as a tactic in the sense of the Latin *tangere*—of sensual touch, requiring close contact, binding together, participation. According to Kleist, what matters is that one experiences, "with every fiber of [one's] being," the sensation of bodily movements and counter-movements, rather than maintain a reflexive distance from one's own body. The aesthetic experience inherent in the martial art of wrestling thus consists in the possibility of perceiving one's body apart from an excentric position of self-reflection. In the anthropological terminology of German philosopher Helmuth Plessner, this experience marks the difference between the lived body *I am* (*Leib sein*) and the material body *I have* (*Körper haben*):[14] Wrestling is about experiencing one's *Leib sein*, sensing the opponent's largely unpredictable and inaccessible condition, such as his vigor or fatigue, his strength or weakness. What is at issue is a non-cognitive, almost seismographic ability to sense different bodily states, both in one's own body and in that of the opponent. The interest here is in embodied intelligence, not in the movement of the body as controlled by the mind. The secret of the antiperistatic geniuses in the world of sports would thus be that they feel and defend their own lived bodies opposite their opponent when competing, though they are by no means in full control of themselves. It is not they who know how a competition will gradually develop, but rather—as Kleist puts it regarding verbal duels in "On the Gradual Fabrication of Thoughts While Speaking"—"a certain condition, in which we happen to be, that 'knows.'"[15] The concern then is a lived experience of identity without self-knowledge, as it were, a knowledge immanent in one's actions that owes itself not to the mind but to the practice of movement. The principle of polarity that Kleist develops in "The Very Last Word in Modern Educational Theory" helps to account for the weight he assigns to the interplay of movements rather than to individual states of consciousness that precede one's actions. The essay raises the question as to what happens when two individuals come into "contact" with each other. The answer Kleist gives reads like a theory of wrestling:

> A man in a condition of total indifference [...] as to some issue or other, does not only instantly cease to be so upon contact with someone firmly opinioned in the matter, but his entire being (if we may so express it) modulates into polar opposition: he assumes the term + when the other is –, and – when the other is +.[16]

Applying this polarity principle to wrestling, it becomes apparent that here, too, the interplay of movements is determined by a polar relation of forces; the weakness of one wrestler becomes the strength of the other and vice versa. A struggle simultaneously separates and unites them. Their unity is temporary and relative—a dynamic equilibrium, a relationship of difference, in which one's self is at once opposed and inextricably linked to an other in a struggle defined by mutual dependence. Reflex precedes reflection in this struggle, as thinking would merely delay action, and knowledge is generated only within action. "Reflection, or thinking something over," writes Kleist in his wrestling match paradox, "finds its proper moment *after* rather than *before* an act."[17]

The fourth thesis posits that the essay "On the Gradual Fabrication of Thoughts While Speaking" is about verbal duels, while "On Thinking Things Over: A Paradox" is about physical duels. The *tertium comparationis* between these two forms of duels is the logic of creativity *in actu*. For Kleist creativity is in no way a predictable process; it is not a transformation of knowledge and intention into practical action, but a mode of experience immanent in one's actions.

In his *Critique of the Power of Judgment*, Immanuel Kant notes that genius gives the rule to art yet does not itself know nor can it describe how it brings its product into being.[18] What belongs to creativity are moments of unpredictability and unattainability; scientific as well as literary attempts to understand creativity founder, time and again, on the idea that creativity is an independent competence, readily available, as it were, prior to any action, or a competence that merely requires translation into practical actions in order to be actualized. In traditional inspiration myths, creativity owes itself to the whisper of the

Muses or God; in myths of genius, to the externalization of an *ingenium* buried within the individual's inner core; and in athletics, to the idea that success is the controlled and controllable implementation of strategies devised in practice or that it is the product of a talented and diligent individual able to choose from a larger repertoire of strategies and moves than others. Not so with Kleist. In his essay "On the Puppet Theater," Mr. C. finds himself astonished that the feints he had rehearsed beforehand fail to fool the bear he is opposing in a fencing match. They fail due to the bear's attentiveness; he parries his opponents thrusts only when they are actually dangerous, thus relying on a form of practical reflexivity that is open to whatever happens suddenly, in the flash of an eye. "Eye to eye," the bear stands facing his opponent; yet in this position he does not read the fencer's "soul," as the latter assumes he does.[19] His practical sense, his multisensory perception, is not directed toward his opponent's inner being, but toward his outer appearance, toward that which is visible.

Kleist thus does not hypostatize an animal instinct, which would again be something invisible like the soul. Rather, he refrains from invisibilizing the question of creativity, turning his attention primarily to the processual moment of a 'forma formans' *in actu*—to the gradual fabrication of thoughts while speaking, of wrestling while wrestling, of fencing while fencing. While the example of the marionettes envisions the mechanization, standardization, and regulation of bodily movements on the basis of preconceived mathematical calculations, the example of the bear relies entirely on a practical knowledge that can only be generated *within* movement and is thus subject to constant change. In this respect creativity is in no way a predictable process; it is not a transformation of knowledge and intention into practical action, but a mode of experience immanent in one's actions. The creative person is him- or herself part of the experimental setup; there is no puppeteer controlling the puppet. He or she engages in the behavior of someone taking part in an experiment, not knowing the outcome; he or she fabricates knowledge in the process of wrestling, speaking, fencing, or writing without knowing what the actions will ultimately amount to. As an antiperistatic genius he or she has to devise figures of control in complex, unpredictable situations, in the flash of an eye, in a state of emergency. These figures can integrate the chance events of life and assess interferences as an opportunity to generate new structures, leading to a choreography *in actu*, without a choreographer.

The argument of the fifth thesis centers on the creative logic of athletic contests, namely that any move is prone to risk deliberately staged by way of the move itself. In athletic contests the loss of control becomes the primal scene of a calculated fascination, so to speak, and the same applies to Kleist's literature.

Kleist's "Boxers" anecdote from the *Berlin Evening Paper* is a testimony to this logic of athletic contests. The anecdote concerns two English boxers—one of them from Portsmouth, the other from Plymouth—who behave politely toward each other in the midst of their fight, giving each other compliments and hence ('aristocratic') satisfaction. The fight ends after the Portsmouther deals the Plymouther a fatal punch and is awarded the victory amid the cheers of the spectators. "[S]ome days later," the anecdote continues in the subjunctive mood, the "Portsmouther too, however, was said to have died [...] of a severe hemorrhage."[20] What is remarkable about Kleist's anecdote is that it deliberately deviates from the historical reality of English boxing matches. Since the mid-18th century, a set of rules introduced by Jack Broughton had been implemented according to which no one was allowed to be seriously injured or killed in a boxing match in England, and it required the immediate intervention of spectators if injuries were imminent. One can also look to the pedagogical discourse in Germany, particularly the practice of physical exercises as described by Johann Christoph Friedrich GutsMuths in his influential coursebook *Gymnastics for Youth* of 1793, where it reads: "We are neither greeks, whose little territory required to be perpetually defended against the attacks of neighbouring greeks [...]; nor romans addicted to the base art of subjugating all nations, far and near. [...] As little are we *athletes*; and our youths need not dash out their teeth, fracture their ribs, dislocate their limbs, or strangle one another."[21]

Kleist is neither interested in the pedagogical measures for training and perfecting the body nor in the preventive measures of Broughton's Rules. He destabilizes the rule-ridden sport of boxing, as it were, restoring it to its roots: the Classical fistfight in all its deadly brutality. Kleist, the unillusioned moralist, understands that it is not control but the loss of control that fascinates the audience, in sports as well as in the arts. It is not only loss of control that is demonstrated in sports but the reversal of order into disorder and back again—a transitory process perceptible to the senses, but not necessarily comprehensible. Sports thus becomes not only an analogue of life but of death. It is not the sports whose laws of motion are based on a calculable economy of 'higher, faster, further,' but rather those based on a rush of adrenaline which are the most appealing to spectators and, therefore, the highest paying—boxing, racing, etc. These are the sports in which athletes 'run ahead toward death,' as it were—and the sentiment expressed in this phrase is not merely intellectual.[22] While the athlete hopes to gain the sensation of a fundamentally volatile condition that is constantly under attack—the experience of his or her own lived body—the spectator viewing graceful movements is still dreaming of the body's integrity.

Fig. 63 Contemporary depiction of boxers, 1797

Two famous English boxers, one of them from Portsmouth, the other from Plymouth, had for many years heard of but had never seen each other, and agreed, when they finally met in London, to stage a public bout to decide once and for all which of them deserved the title of champion. With clenched fists they took their stand opposite each other in a tavern garden, in view of a crowd of people; and when the Plymouther, within a few moments, had struck the Portsmouther such a blow on the breast that he spat blood, the latter, wiping his mouth, called "Bravo." But shortly thereafter, when they had squared off again, the Portsmouther dealt the Plymouther such a right-handed punch to the body that his eyes went blank as he sank to the ground, saying "Not so bad yourself!" Thereupon the crowd, standing around them in a circle, cheered loudly, and while the Plymouther was carried away dead of stomach wounds, they awarded the victory to the Portsmouther. The Portsmouther too, however, was said to have died some days later of a severe hemorrhage. (ADE 269, published in the *Berlin Evening Paper* of November 22, 1810)

From the cathartic experience of sport and the insight that the body is neither an object of discursive disciplining nor an instrument of intentional action, but rather an agent, a medium for actualizing and performing cultural meanings, let us return to the arts and the praxeology of artistic creativity. Kleist emerges as a crisis and catastrophe specialist in his novellas and plays because of the way in which they are produced and because of the effect they have on the reader. In sports as well as in literature, it is true what the German soccer idiom says, that '*after* the game is *before* the game.' But it is also true that '*in* the game, one is *within* the game,' in a perpetual process of becoming, ever-threatened by interferences and chance events. From this perspective one's actions no longer appear as solely teleological, deliberate, or calculated, but as indeterminate and unpredictable as the situations that demanded action in the first place. Decisions are made by way of action itself; no clear-cut distinction between theory and praxis exists. Consequently, a decision—like the action from which it cannot be distinguished—can be modified at any moment (and in this sense cannot truly be called a 'decision'). Indeterminacy, loss of control, the 'evasion of stability':[23] These are catalysts of creativity for Kleist.

Notes

I Dead or Alive?

1 Thus goes Diderot's prudence rule. The argument is quoted in its entirety here for the reader to review:

"Nature does not always give the best advice when you are in danger.

When you are sitting in a carriage and the horses suddenly bolt, and when you see yourself being carried off toward a river or a precipice, nothing will seem more urgent to you than to jump out of your carriage. But in which direction will Nature advise you to jump? In the direction of the front wheel, which moves away from you and from which you have nothing to fear? In the direction of the rear wheel, which moves toward you and threatens you? Nature will advise you to jump toward the front wheel, but it ought to give you precisely the opposite advice for your survival.

You are being moved by two forces: the force of your jump and the force moving your carriage away; but you will follow neither the direction of the one nor the other force and, instead, move on a diagonal.

If the direction of the force of your jump grazes the rear wheel, the diagonal necessarily runs between the two wheels, and you are safe and sound.

If the direction of the force of your jump grazes the front wheel, you will be thrown onto that wheel, thrust down and crushed by the rear wheel.

If you jump into the middle of the interval separating the two wheels, you will be hit by the rear wheel, or be thrown onto the front wheel, or you escape both.

One of those three scenarios will occur depending on the relation between the force of your jump and the force by which the carriage is pulled forward, it is this relation that determines the position of the diagonal.

Thus, the only safe way out is: the direction of the force of the jump must graze the rear wheel; an escape one does not dare to take, even if assured by theory."

This passage can be found in Denis Diderot, "Eléments de physiologie," in *Œuvres complètes de Diderot, revue sur les éditions originales comprenant ce qui été publié à diverses époques et les manuscrits inédits conservés à la Bibliothèque de l'Ermitage. Notices, notes, Table Analytique études sur Diderot et le mouvement philosophe au XVIIIe siècle*, ed. J. Assézat, vol. 9 (Paris: Garnier frères, 1875; repr., Nendeln: Kraus, 1966), 330.—Such artful calculations are analyzed in their historical context in the brilliant study by Bernhard Dotzler, *Papiermaschinen. Versuch über Communication & Control in Literatur und Technik* (Berlin: de Gruyter, 1996), to which I owe the reference to Diderot.

2 Unless otherwise indicated, all English translations of Kleist's letters, essays, and anecdotes are quoted from Heinrich von Kleist, *An Abyss Deep Enough: Letters of Heinrich von Kleist, with a Selection of Essays and Anecdotes*, ed., trans., and introd. Philip B. Miller (New York: Dutton, 1982), with the abbreviation ADE, followed by the page number. In cases where no published English translation exists, Kleist's works and letters are translated from Heinrich von Kleist, *Sämtliche Werke und Briefe*, ed. Ilse-Marie Barth et al., 4 vols. (Frankfurt/M.: Deutscher Klassiker Verlag, 1987–97), and referenced as DKV, followed by the volume and page number. Here: DKV IV, 243.

3 ADE 107.

4 ADE 28.

5 Thomas Mann, "Kleist and His Stories," in *"The Marquise of O—" and Other Stories*, trans. with an introd. Martin Greenberg (New York: Criterion, 1960), 5f.

6 Two of many possible references on the period of transition at the turn of the 19th century: Reinhart Koselleck, *Preußen zwischen Reform und Revolution. Allgemeines Landrecht, Verwaltung und soziale Bewegung von 1791 bis 1848* (Munich: Klett, 1989), and Niklas Luhmann, *Gesellschaftsstruktur und Semantik. Studien zur Wissenssoziologie der modernen Gesellschaft*, 4 vols. (Frankfurt/M.: Suhrkamp, 1980–95), see esp. chap. "Interaktion in Oberschichten," 1:72–161.

7 Walter Benjamin, "The Storyteller. Observations on the Works of Nikolai Leskov," trans. Harry Zohn, in *Selected Writings*, ed. Michael W. Jennings, vol. 3, *1935–1938* (Cambridge, MA: Belknap, 2002), 156.

8 Peter-André Alt rightly criticizes this tendency in the Anglo-American tradition of life-writing in his "Mode ohne Methode? Überlegungen zu einer Theorie der literaturwissenschaftlichen Biographik," in *Grundlagen der Biographik. Theorie und Praxis des biographischen Schreibens*, ed. Christian Klein (Stuttgart: Metzler, 2002), 28.

9 Thus writes Adam Müller in a letter to Friedrich von Gentz of February 6, 1806, to defend Kleist's play *Penthesilea*. Published in: Helmut Sembdner, ed., *Heinrich von Kleists Lebensspuren. Dokumente und Berichte der Zeitgenossen* (Frankfurt/M.: Insel, 1984), no. 226, hereinafter referred to as LS, followed by the entry number.

10 See Heiner Müller's acceptance speech from the Kleist Prize 1990 ceremony in Munich, published as "Deutschland Ortlos. Anmerkungen zu Kleist," *Kleist-Jahrbuch* (1991): 16. The *Kleist-Jahrbuch* is referred to hereinafter as *KJb*.

11 Thus reads the title of Helmut Lethen's study on the German intellectuals' reception of the European moralist tradition at the beginning of the 20th century, published as *Cool Conduct. The Culture of Distance in Weimar Germany*, trans. Don Reneau (Berkeley: U of California P, 2002).

12 Friedrich Nietzsche, *On the Genealogy of Morality*, trans. Adrian Del Caro (Stanford: Stanford UP, 2014), 249.

II Noblesse Oblige

1 The image of the Kleist family coat of arms is a reproduction of the frontispiece of the first written history on the Kleist family: Gustav Kratz, ed., *Geschichte des Geschlechts von Kleist*, 4 vols. (Berlin: Schindler, 1862–87), see esp. vol. 1, *Urkundenbuch*. Source material from this volume is hereinafter referred to as Urkundenbuch, followed by the page and document number.

2 See, for example, Wolf Kittler, *Die Geburt des Partisanen aus dem Geiste der Poesie. Heinrich von Kleist und die Strategie der Befreiungskriege* (Freiburg: Rombach, 1987), 18. Also see Wolf Baumgart, "Die preußische Armee zur Zeit Heinrich von Kleists," *KJb* (1983): 46.

3 Quoted in Sigismund Rahmer, *Das Kleist-Problem* (Berlin: Reimer, 1903), 41.

4 Baltasar Gracián, *The Art of Worldly Wisdom*, trans. Joseph Jacobs (London: Macmillan, 1904), no. 220. See Niccolò Machiavelli, "The Prince," in *The Chief Works and Others*, trans. Allan Gilbert, 3 vols. (Durham: Duke UP, 1965), 1:65.

5 I am indebted to Hans Jürgen Scheuer (Stuttgart) for his advice on the heraldic logic of colors in Kleist's coat of arms.

6 In Lessing's fable, a young wolf is proud of his father who lost his life in battle, killing two hundred enemies. The fox—a master in the art of cunning, experienced in differentiating between appearance and reality—disillusions the wolf by sharing with him the basis of such heroism (with regard to this particular case and in general): Military glory comes from the defeat of the weak, dying in battle from defeat by the strong.

7 Anke Tanzer's study on this minor poet is therefore commendable. See Anke Tanzer, *"Mein theurer zweiter Kleist." Franz Alexander von Kleist (1769–1797) – Leben und Werk* (Oldenburg: Igel, 1998).

8 For these numbers, see Kurd Wolfgang von Schöning, *Die Generale der Chur-Brandenburgischen und Königlich-Preußischen Armee von 1640–1840* (Berlin: Lüderitz, 1840); Bogislav von Kleist, *Die Generale der Königlich-Preußischen Armee von 1840–1890 (1891–1892)*, 2nd ed. (Leipzig: Zuckschwerdt & Möschke, 1895); Baumgart, "Die preußische Armee," 41.

9 See Urkundenbuch, 34f. (U 75).

10 See Urkundenbuch, 53 (U 96), 56 (U 101), 57 (U 102), 58 (U 104), 59 (U 105).

11 See Urkundenbuch, 67f. (U 125).

12 See Martin Wehrmann, *Geschichte von Pommern*, vol. 1 (Gotha: Perthes, 1904), 154.

13 Thus reads the apt formulation in Kittler, *Die Geburt des Partisanen*, 28.

14 See, among others, Volker Press, "Adel im 19. Jahrhundert. Die Führungsschichten Alteuropas im bürgerlich-bürokratischen Zeitalter," in *Der Adel an der Schwelle des bürgerlichen Zeitalters 1780–1860*, ed. Armgard von Reden-Dohna and Ralph Melville (Wiesbaden: Steiner, 1988), 5.

15 See August Sauer, ed., *Ewald von Kleist's Werke*, vol. 1 (Berlin: Hempel, 1880), XVI.

16 Ewald Christian von Kleist, *Sämtliche Werke* (Stuttgart: Reclam, 1971), 98 ("Funeral Song"), 171 ("Birth Song"), 95 ("Ode to the Prussian Army").

17 See Baumgart, "Die preußische Armee," 48, who quotes from *Fragments* (*Bruchstücke*) written by the Royal Prussian Field Marshal Karl Friedrich von dem Knesebeck (printed as manuscript: Magdeburg: self-published at the editor's expense, 1850, 17f.). Baumgart's crucial study makes available numerous sources for assessing the social situation of Prussian officers at the end of the 18th century, sources from which I later quote.

18 Baumgart, "Die preußische Armee," 48.

19 See Rudolf Loch, *Kleist. Eine Biographie* (Göttingen: Wallstein, 2003), 420, who uses a study on Leopold's ideas for reforming the military in his argument. Also see Reinhard Kusch, *Leopold von Braunschweig 1752–1785. Herkommen, Leben und Tod. Portraitskizze eines fürstlichen Philanthropen* (Frankfurt/O.: Kleist-Gedenk- und Forschungsstätte, 1995).

20 Immatriculation on November 18, 1748; see Ernst Friedlaender, ed., Ältere Universitäts-Matrikeln I: Universität Frankfurt a. O., vol. 2, *1649–1811* (Osnabrück: Zeller, 1965), 370.

21 There is a painting of Kleist's birth house from the 1930s, which is on display at the Kleist Museum in Frankfurt an der Oder. See Wolfgang Barthel, Hans Jochen Marquardt, and Barbara Wilk-Mincu, eds., *Heinrich von Kleist (1777–1811). Leben – Werk – Wirkung. Blickpunkte. Katalog der Dauerausstellung des Kleist-Museums* (Frankfurt/O.: Kleist-Gedenk- und Forschungsstätte, 2000), 43 (no. 2/2). Photographs of his birthplace from circa 1920, located in the Prussian Cultural Heritage Image Archive, can also be found in Eberhard Siebert, ed., *Heinrich von Kleist. Leben und Werk im Bild* (Frankfurt/M: Insel, 1980), 26–28.

22 Located in the Secret State Archives Prussian Cultural Heritage Foundation, Berlin, and printed in Siebert, *Heinrich von Kleist*, 14. A facsimile is on display in the permanent exhibition of the Kleist Museum in Frankfurt an der Oder.

23 See DKV IV, 138: "Yes, my birthday is today, and I feel as if I hear the wishes that your heart secretly makes for me today, as if I felt the pressure of your hand expressing to me all these wishes at once."

24 Horst Häker, "10. oder 18. Oktober? Ein Plädoyer für Kleist," *Beiträge zur Kleist-Forschung* 7 (1993), points out the potential faultiness of written records in church registers. Recent Kleist scholarship seems to be finally yielding to his sensible plea. See, for instance, Klaus Müller-Salget, *Heinrich von Kleist* (Stuttgart: Reclam, 2002), 18.

25 See the limited amount of source material in the section on Kleist's childhood in LS 1–12. The English translation of Leopold's poem can be found in Joachim Maass, *Kleist. A Biography*, trans. Ralph Manheim (New York: Farrar, Straus & Giroux, 1983), 8.

26 See LS 9 (songwriting competition), 3 (cheerful early years), 10 (embittered childhood), and 5a (Martini's description of Kleist's temperament).

27 In a letter to Ludwig Tieck of November 26, 1816, Johanna von Haza, daughter of Sophie von Haza, the wife of Adam Müller, purports the existence of such a text. She claims it was written for Kleist's friend Rühle von Lilienstern, kept by her mother, and was later probably lost. See Helmut Sembdner, ed., *Heinrich von Kleists Nachruhm. Eine Wirkungsgeschichte in Dokumenten* (Frankfurt/M.: Insel, 1984), no. 134, hereinafter referred to as NR, followed by the entry number. In his letter to Wilhelmine von Kleist of March 22, 1801, Kleist does use the phrase "story of my soul," common in the 18th century, to explain his concept of education to his fiancée. See DKV VI, 204.

28 On Kleist's skepticism toward the bourgeois ideal of family and education as well as on his novella "The Foundling," see chap. VIII.

29 These portraits can be found in the America Memorial Library/Berlin Central Library in the form of photographs of a lost painting (in the case of Kleist's father) and a lost miniature (in the case of Kleist's mother). The latter is presumably a double portrait of Kleist's mother and her seven-year-old son Heinrich holding a book in his right hand, but this has not been verified.

30 Kleist's letter to his aunt was written in March 1793, for the passages on his mother see DKV IV, 12f., 15f. He only mentions his mother once more, in a letter to Rühle von Lilienstern of December 1808, see DKV IV, 425.

31 Kleist mentions his nanny in a letter to his sister Ulrike of February 25, 1795, see DKV IV, 17. The information on the duration of her employment as a nanny in the Kleist household comes from Nogier herself and is taken from a Frankfurt court record of 1823, a transcript of which can be found in Paul Hoffmann's partial literary estate of Kleist at the German Literature Archive in Marbach.

32 For Martini's remarks see LS 5a, where he also speculates about an "agreement" between Kleist and Pannwitz "to both die by their own choice." For Carl von Pannwitz's suicide, see the memory of Ernst von Schönfeldt in LS 5b.

33 Seminal with respect to Kleist's first stay in Berlin are the essays by Horst Häker, who published and evaluated documents from Georg Minde-Pouet's literary estate. See Horst Häker, "Kleists Beziehungen zu Mitgliedern der französisch reformierten Gemeinde in Berlin," *KJb* (1983); Horst Häker, "Kleists Aufenthalt bei Cartel in Berlin im Jahre 1788," *KJb* (1988/89). Also see the comprehensive monograph by Horst Häker, *Kleists Berliner Aufenthalte. Ein biographischer Beitrag* (Berlin: Haude & Spener, 1989).

34 See the entry "Frankfurt/Oder" in *Berlin und Brandenburg*, ed. Gerd Heinrich (Stuttgart: Kröner, 1973), 177ff.

35 Thus suggests Rudolf Loch, who, taking into consideration the history of Frankfurt before 1800, also speculates whether Kleist may have adopted positions of Enlightenment

philosophy from the Frankfurt regimental commander Prince Leopold von Braunschweig or from the intellectual circle surrounding theology professor Josias Friedrich Christian Löffler. But this seems questionable: Leopold died in 1785 when Kleist was seven years old, and Löffler's intellectual circle existed from 1782 to 1788, from Kleist's fifth to eleventh year of life. See Loch, *Kleist*, 14–18, in particular 14.

36 ADE 16.

37 For these details on the Kleists' financial situation, see the Kleist Museum's volume by Wolfgang Barthel, ed., *Heinrich von Kleist 1777–1811. Chronik seines Lebens und Schaffens auf Grund von Selbstaussagen, Dokumenten und Aussagen Dritter* (Frankfurt/O.: Kleist-Gedenk- und Forschungsstätte, 2001), 9f. Also see LS 11a, 11b (inheritance dispute), as well as Loch, *Kleist*, 425f., n. 38, who details the discrimination the Kleist family suffered from the crown.

38 DKV IV, 17.

39 On the career and education path of 'learned' officers in Prussia in the second half of the 18th century, see Baumgart, "Die preußische Armee." For the term 'learned officers,' see ibid., 54.

40 Thus writes Kleist reflecting on his military service after his resignation in a letter to his sister Ulrike of May 1799, ADE 27.

41 See Carl von Reinhard, *Geschichte des Königlich Preußischen Ersten Garde-Regiments zu Fuß 1740–1857* (Potsdam: Stein, 1858), 539, who reproduces the list of the ranks and quarters of the 2nd and 3rd Guard Battalion for December 1792.

42 For this and subsequent quotes, see DKV IV, 9–16, partially translated in ADE 15–18.

43 See ADE 82.

44 See the documentation by Günther Gieraths, ed., *Die Kampfhandlungen der brandenburgisch-preußischen Armee 1626–1807. Ein Quellenhandbuch* (Berlin: de Gruyter, 1964), 55–57 (Infantry Regiment No. 15: Guard).

45 In his memories, famously published as *The Life Story and Real Adventures of the Poor Man of Toggenburg*, Swiss mercenary Ulrich Bräker (1735–89)—after he had fallen prey to a Prussian recruiter in 1755—describes everyday life in the Prussian army in the 18th century in a particularly impressive and credible manner, as historical research has shown. See Helmut Eckert, "Ulrich Bräckers Soldantenzeit und die preußische Werbung in Schaffhausen," *Schaffhauser Beiträge zur Geschichte* 53 (1976): 151ff.

46 See Baumgart, "Die preußische Armee," 59f. Contrary to what Kleist scholarship likes to assert, the strategy of using the German woodlands advantageously against the Romans, as employed by the Prince of Cherusci in Kleist's *The Battle of Herrmann*, may thus be linked to more than the guerilla warfare in the Spanish War of Independence against Napoleon.

47 See the brilliant study by Michael Sikora, *Disziplin und Desertion. Strukturprobleme militärischer Organisation im 18. Jahrhundert* (Berlin: Duncker & Humblot, 1996).

48 Carl von Clausewitz, *On War*, trans. Michael Howard and Peter Paret (Oxford: Oxford UP, 2007), 61.

49 ADE 19.

50 DKV III, 401.

51 See, among others, Christoph Martin Wieland's *On War and Peace*, published in 1794, and Immanuel Kant's essay "Perpetual Peace," published the following year.

52 According to DKV IV.

53 Quoted in Sikora, *Disziplin und Desertion*, 346. Sikora cites August Wilhelm Leopold von Rahmel's polemical work, *Dienst* (n.p. 1783), and verifies the credibility of its critique through recourse to historical sources.

54 See Curt Jany, *Geschichte der Preußischen Armee vom 15. Jahrhundert bis 1914*, ed. Eberhard Jany, vol. 3, *1763–1807*, 2nd ed. (Osnabrück: Biblio, 1967), 59.

55 See publications critical of the military, for example Jacob de Cognazo as early as 1780. See Johannes Kunisch, "Das 'Puppenwerk' der stehenden Heere. Ein Beitrag zur Neueinschätzung von Soldatenstand und Krieg in der Spätaufklärung," *Zeitschrift für Historische Forschung* 17 (1990).

56 ADE 22.

57 ADE 221f.

58 LS 532d.

59 LS 21, Kleist's first biographer, Eduard von Bülow, in 1846.

60 LS 19, Brentano to Achim von Arnim on 10 December 1811, shortly after Kleist's death.

61 DKV IV, 28, Kleist's letter of March 1799.

62 See Loch, *Kleist*, 432.

63 ADE 159f.

64 See, for instance, Gerhard Neumann during the discussion of his paper: "'… Der Mensch ohne Hülle ist eigentlich der Mensch.' Goethe und Heinrich von Kleist in der Geschichte des physiognomischen Blicks," *KJb* (1988/89): 278.

65 Quoted in Ewald Christian von Kleist, *Ihn foltert Schwermut, weil er lebt. Gedichte, Prosa, Stücke*, ed. Gerhard Wolf (Frankfurt/M.: Fischer, 1983), 303.

66 See the biography by Hans Dieter Zimmermann, *Kleist, die Liebe und der Tod* (Frankfurt/M.: Athenäum, 1989), 47ff.

67 Zimmermann, *Kleist*, 50.

68 Loch, *Kleist*, 424f., who replicates the letter of the father, Karl Wilhelm von Pannwitz (1743–1807). The letter is kept in the Brandenburgian State Main Archive Potsdam, Sign. Pr Br Rep 37 Gulben no. 5, 4.

69 See ADE 146, Kleist's letter of May 1, 1802.

70 Kept in the Berlin State Library – Prussian Cultural Heritage and printed on the cover of virtually every Kleist biography.

71 As Kleist calls it, with reference to Kant, in his "On the Gradual Fabrication of Thoughts While Speaking," ADE 222.

72 See the subtle readings in Heinrich Detering, *Das offene Geheimnis. Zur literarischen Produktivität eines Tabus von Winckelmann bis Thomas Mann* (Göttingen: Wallstein, 1994).

73 Heinrich von Kleist, *The Marquise of O— and Other Stories*, trans. with an introd. David Luke and Nigel Reeves (London: Penguin, 1978), 247, hereinafter referred to as MO, followed by the page number.

74 See László Földényi, "Die Inszenierung des Erotischen. Heinrich von Kleist 'Über das Marionettentheater,'" *KJb* (2001).

75 Aristotle, *Nicomachean Ethics*, ed. and trans. Roger Crisp, rev. ed. (Cambridge: Cambridge UP, 2014), 18.

76 Quoted, without individual references, from Heinrich von Kleist, "Essay: How to find the certain Path to Happiness and—even amid Life's greatest Tribulations—enjoy the Journey undeterred!" trans. Jeffrey L. High, *KJb* (2018).

77 ADE 26, 28.

78 See ADE 23f., Kleist's letter to Martini of March 1799.

79 DKV IV, 35.

80 See Loch, *Kleist*, 433.

81 ADE 23.

82 ADE 23.

83 Ewald von Bülow contradicts himself in his Kleist biography when he remarks that Kleist's plans to study had incurred "the displeasure of his superior, General von Rüchel," only to acknowledge two sentences later that von Rüchel wanted to keep Kleist from leaving the military because "he was flattered by the fact that he had well-educated officers under his command." Tieck refers to the possibility of the King granting Kleist a leave to pursue his studies. See LS 21 (Bülow), 23a (Tieck).

84 DKV IV, 26f.

85 See Thomas Stamm-Kuhlmann, *König in Preußens großer Zeit. Friedrich Wilhelm III. Der Melancholiker auf dem Thron* (Berlin: Siedler, 1992), 165 (Panin's dispatch including source citation).

86 ADE 79f.

87 This often-reiterated thesis is most recently argued in Loch, *Kleist*.

88 On the concept of 'being noble,' see Heinz Reif, *Adel im 19. und 20. Jahrhundert* (Munich: Oldenbourg, 1999), and the collection by Hans-Ulrich Wehler, ed., *Europäischer Adel 1750–1950* (Göttingen: Vandenhoeck & Ruprecht, 1990). On Kleist's appropriation of 'being noble' in his literary works, see Jochen Strobel, "Adel und Autorschaft um 1800. Heinrich von Kleist und sein Schauspiel 'Prinz Friedrich von Homburg,'" in *Deutscher Adel im 19. und 20. Jahrhundert*, ed. Günther Schulz and Markus A. Denzel (St. Katharinen: Scripta-Mercaturiae, 2004).

89 ADE 147, Kleist's letter of May 20, 1802, from Lake Thun.

90 DKV IV, 317; ADE 151, 153, Kleist's letters to Ulrike of July 3, October 5, and October 26, 1803.

91 DKV IV, 474.

92 In this regard I fully agree with Strobel's insightful essay, "Adel und Autorschaft." For a general approach to life-writing in the period of crisis at the turn of the 19th century, see the collection by Jürgen Fohrmann, ed., *Lebensläufe um 1800* (Tübingen: Niemeyer, 1998).

93 ADE 23.

94 The argument that the aristocratic and artistic ways of life converge in their avoidance of the stigma of breadwinning—and also in the sense of a selfless service for the public good, however, demanding the entire person—can also be found in Reif, *Adel*, 25ff.

III Science or Fiction?

1 *Viadrus* is the Latin name for the Oder river.

2 The graduate school at the universities of Potsdam and Frankfurt an der Oder is named *Forms of Life and the Know-How of Living* (*Lebensformen und Lebenswissen*).

3 See Gerd Heinrich, "Die Geisteswissenschaften an der brandenburgischen Landesuniversität Frankfurt/Oder um 1800. Bemerkungen zu Studienangebot und Gelehrtenbestand der Hochschule Heinrich von Kleists vor ihrer Auflösung," *KJb* (1983): 78f.

4 See Friedlaender, *Ältere Universitäts-Matrikeln*, 568ff.

5 See ADE 23: "they pointed out the doubtful prospect for bread on my new-chosen path, the promised security of my old one."

6 All quotes from DKV IV, 46–48, partially translated in ADE 30–32.

7 ADE 24.

8 DKV IV, 48f., partially translated in ADE 32.

9 Kleist describes himself as such in his letter to Wilhelmine von Zenge of August 16, 1800, DKV IV, 73.

10 DKV IV, 49.

11 See Heinrich, "Die Geisteswissenschaften," 75f.

12 ADE 34f.

13 DKV IV, 164.

14 See Carl Renatus Hausen, *Geschichte der Universität und Stadt Frankfurt an der Oder, seit ihrer Stiftung und Erbauung, bis zum Schluß des 18. Jahrhunderts, größtenteils nach Urkunden und Archiv-Nachrichten bearbeitet* (Frankfurt/O.: Apitz, im Verlag bei dem Verfasser, 1800).

15 See Friedlaender, *Ältere Universitäts-Matrikeln*, 568.

16 DKV IV, 31.

17 See DKV IV, 88, 186, 198, 312.

18 See DKV IV, 49, 51, 88, 163, 314.

19 See DKV IV, 44, 88, 314.

20 See ADE 48.

21 See ADE 48.

22 ADE 32.

23 DKV IV, 51. Also see Wilhelmine von Zenge's letter to Wilhelm Traugott Krug of June 16, 1803: "At the time, he [Kleist] studied experimental physics with Dr. Wünsch and took great interest in entertaining us with what he learned after his lectures. We, too, took such an active interest in everything he told us that we, his sisters, and a few other girls from our circle went to Dr. Wünsch to ask him to give lectures to us as well. He did so, and we were a very attentive audience, repeated what we learned with our assistant teacher, Mr. von Kleist, and even wrote essays about it." (LS 36)

24 DKV IV, 163.

25 Alexander von Humboldt, "Ich über mich selbst," in *Aus meinem Leben. Autobiographische Bekenntnisse*, ed. Kurt-R. Biermann (Munich: Beck, 1987), 33; Johann Wolfgang von Goethe, "Zur Farbenlehre," in *Sämtliche Werke, Briefe, Tagebücher und Gespräche*, ed. Manfred Wenzel, vol. 23.1 (Frankfurt/M.: Deutscher Klassiker Verlag, 1991), 488, 992, 1026f. My discussion of Wünsch's reception in Kleist's time and in current scholarship is based on the seminal essay by Christoph Meinel, "'des wunderlichen Wünsch seltsame Reduktion ….' Christian Ernst Wünsch, Kleist unzeitgemäßer Zeitgenosse," *KJb* (1996).

26 Christian Ernst Wünsch, *Esoterika*, vol. 2 (Zerbst: Füchsel, 1817), 192, 194. Quoted in Meinel, *Christian Ernst Wünsch*, 20.

27 In the discussion following Christoph Meinel's paper on Wünsch and Kleist, Klaus Müller-Salget even suggested Kleist might have read Wünsch's *Cosmological Conversations* as early as 1793, during the Rhine campaign. See *KJb* (1996), 33.

28 On the history of the concept of 'project-maker,' see Daniel Defoe, *Essay upon Projects* (1697); Johann Heinrich Zedler, *Universal Lexicon Aller Wissenschafften und Künste* (1741); Friedrich Heinrich Gottlob von Justi, *Gedanken von Projecten und Projectmachern* (1761); or the comedies by Christian Felix Weiße, *Der Projektmacher* (1766) and Josef Richter, *Die lächerlichen Projectanten* (1811). Also see the fascinating essay by Georg Stanitzek, "Der Projektmacher. Projektionen auf eine 'unmögliche' moderne Kategorie," *Ästhetik und Kommunikation* 17, no. 65/66 (1987), whose ideas I am indebted to. Stanitzek does not refer to Kleist but emphasizes that the common practice of philosophical and literary geniuses distancing themselves from 'project-makers' might have served merely as camouflage. This need they felt to distance themselves only goes to show that the distinction may not have been so great after all, which is why "the similarity of [the genius'] work to that of the 'project-maker' had to be kept a trade secret." (ibid., 146)

29 LS 226, Adam Müller's defense of Kleist's *Penthesilea* in a letter to Friedrich Gentz of February 6, 1808.

30 Friedrich Schlegel, *Philosophical Fragments*, trans. Peter Firchow (Minneapolis: U of Minnesota P, 1991), 21.

31 See ADE 161. In his letter to Ernst von Pfuel, written in Königsberg in August 1805, Kleist mentions their plan "to go to Australia."

32 Kleist's sketch and calculations for the submersible can be found in his letter to Ernst von Pfuel of July 2 and 4, 1805, see DKV IV, 342–344. For context and description of the submersible, see chap. VII.

33 See "Project for a Cannonball Postal System," in *Berlin Evening Paper*, October 10, 1810, translated in ADE 245f.: "Therefore, in order [...] that business communications be accelerated and multiplied at least within the boundaries of the civilized world, we propose a *projectile* or *cannonball* express: an institution that, with suitably situated artillery stations spaced within firing range of each other, would discharge, from mortars or howitzer, hollow shells, which have been stuffed full not of powder but letters and packages, and which could very easily be observed in flight, and wherever they might fall, short of some morass, be retrieved; so that these shells, opened at each station, their respective letters for each locality removed and new ones packed in, could then be resealed, loaded into a new mortar, and dispatched to the next station." Compared with the equestrian mail system, Kleist expects a "tenfold gain in time" or a shortening of distances (ADE 246). Kleist's reference to the dangers of "some morass" suggests that he is not entirely committed to this project, even though the *Berlin Evening Paper* frequently relays Kleist's fascination with technological projects to the public: innovations concerning the art of ballooning, cleaning laundry with steam, modifying the arrangement of the keys on keyboard instruments, etc.

34 The essay can be found in the historical-critical Brandenburg edition of Kleist's *Sämtliche Werke*, ed. Roland Reuß and Peter Staengle (Basel: Stroemfeld, 1988–2010), hereinafter referred to as BKA, followed by the section/volume and page number. Here: BKA II/8, 178–181, 185f., 188–190. See Helmut Sembdner, *Die Berliner Abendblätter Heinrich von Kleists, ihre Quellen und ihre Redaktion* (Berlin: Weidmann, 1939), who disputes Kleist's authorship and asserts natural scientist and physician Friedrich Gottlob Wetzel's. Cf. Walter Hinderer, "Ansichten von der Rückseite der Naturwissenschaften. Antinomien in Heinrich von Kleists Welt- und Selbstverständnis," *KJb* (2005): 42f., who—based on Peter Staengle's judgment—thinks it possible that if Kleist was not the author, he at least made editorial changes to it.

35 I thus agree with Hinderer, "Rückseite der Naturwissenschaften," 27, that Wünsch's "role in Kleist's intellectual development was similar to the role Abel performed with Schiller," because he taught Kleist "the scientific and philosophical discourses and insights representative of the time."

36 Johann Christian Polykarp Erxleben, *Anfangsgründe der Naturlehre*, ed. G.C. Lichtenberg, 6th ed. (Göttingen: Dieterich, 1794), 513.

37 See Christian Ernst Wünsch, *Kosmologische Unterhaltungen*, 2 vols., 2nd ed. (Leipzig: Breitkopf, 1791–94), 2:662: "[I]f two bodies—that hang closely enough together and are insulated from each other—are given like charges, they repel each other and, by contrast, attract each other if they have opposite charges or if only one is charged and the other is left neutral."

38 All quotes from ADE 220.

39 ADE 223f.

40 See Friedrich Wilhelm Joseph Schelling, "Von der Weltseele," in *Sämtliche Werke*, ed. Karl F.A. Schelling, 14 vols. (Stuttgart: Cotta, 1856–61), 2:489.

41 See Herminio Schmidt, *Heinrich von Kleist. Naturwissenschaft als Dichtungsprinzip* (Bern: Haupt, 1978), regarding the genealogy of the law of polarity's role within philosophical discourse, and the distinction drawn between Kleist and the harmonizing natural philosophy of the Romantics. Also see Otto Lorenz, "Experimentalphysik und Dichtungspraxis. Das 'Geheime Gesetz des Widerspruchs' im Werk Heinrich von Kleists," in *Die deutsche literarische Romantik und die Wissenschaften*, ed. Nicholas Saul (Munich: Iudicium, 1991); Jürgen Daiber, "'Nichts Drittes ... in der Natur?' Kleists Dichtung im Spiegel romantischer Selbstexperimentation," *KJb* (2005); Roland Borgards, "'Allerneuester Erziehungsplan.' Ein Beitrag Heinrich von Kleists zur Experimentalkultur um 1800 (Literatur, Physik)," in *Literarische Experimentalkulturen. Poetologien des Experiments im 19. Jahrhundert*, ed. Marcus Krause and Nicolas Pethes (Würzburg: Königshausen & Neumann, 2005).

42 ADE 217.

43 Kleist's essay "The Very Last Word in Modern Educational Theory" is allegedly—that is, according to the editor of the *Berlin Evening Paper*—written by a certain vice-principal C.J. Levanus. As his name suggests he is a follower of Jean Paul's pedagogical work *Levana* of 1806 and thus a proponent of the Neohumanist theory of education which argues that every child "bears within itself an independent and intrinsic capability for development and the blueprint for all higher conditions of mind and spirit" (ADE 227). Levanus thus rejects the competing doctrine of philanthropy promoted by Johann Bernhard Basedow or Joachim Heinrich Campe—the notion that indeterminacy and plasticity are characteristic of the human being, resulting in what is assumed to be a virtually unlimited pedagogical power. According to Levanus, the child is by no means "made of wax" (ADE 227), to be molded by the hands of his educator, which the "universal law of contradiction" (ADE 223) ensures. In reality, however, this law overrides both the philanthropic and Neohumanist pedagogy. For a discussion of the pedagogies at play in Kleist's work, see my remarks on *The Schroffenstein Family* and "The Foundling" in chap. VI and VIII.

44 MO 114.

45 ADE 217.

46 ADE 93.

47 ADE 152.

48 See Oliver Hochadel, *Öffentliche Wissenschaft. Elektrizität in der deutschen Aufklärung* (Göttingen: Wallstein, 2003).

49 LS 36, Wilhelmine von Zenge's letter to her future husband Wilhelm Traugott Krug.

50 ADE 92, Kleist's letter to his sister Ulrike of February 5, 1801.

51 ADE 74f.

52 DKV IV, 159.

53 DKV IV, 157f.

54 DKV IV, 159, partially translated in ADE 76.

55 Heinrich von Kleist, *Five Plays*, trans. with an introd. Martin Greenberg (New Haven: Yale UP, 1988), 204, hereinafter referred to as FP, followed by the page number. For select publications, of which there is an abundance, on the trope of the arched gate, see Bianca Theisen, *Bogenschluß. Kleists Formalisierung des Lesens* (Freiburg: Rombach, 1996); Bernhard Greiner, "Sturz als Halt. Kleists dramaturgische Physik," *KJb* (2005); Alexander Honold, "Die Sonne steigt, der Apfel fällt. Bewegte Körper und ihre Bahnen auf Kleists astronomischem Theater," *KJb* (2005).

56 See, among others, Sybille Peters, "Die Experimente der 'Berliner Abendblätter,'" *KJb* (2005); Roland Borgards, "Experimentelle Aeronautik. Chemie, Meteorologie und Kleists

Luftschiffkunst in den 'Berliner Abendblättern,'" *KJb* (2005); Monika Schmitz-Emans, "Wassermänner, Sirenen und andere Monster. Fabelwesen im Spiegel von Kleists 'Berliner Abendblättern,'" *KJb* (2005).

57 DKV IV, 164.

58 See, once again, Heinrich, "Die Geisteswissenschaften," 71–97. Also see Dietmar Willoweit, "Heinrich von Kleist und die Universität Frankfurt an der Oder. Rückblick eines Rechtshistorikers," *KJb* (1997); Loch, *Kleist*, 49ff.

59 See Hans Joachim Kreutzer, *Die dichterische Entwicklung Heinrichs von Kleist. Untersuchungen zu seinen Briefen und zu Chronologie und Aufbau seiner Werke* (Berlin: Schmidt, 1968), 46–49, 57, 68–70, who points out that Kleist employs images and concepts in an unconventional manner, often changing their contexts and meanings.

60 See the introductions in Joseph Vogl, ed., *Poetologien des Wissens um 1800* (Munich: Fink, 1999), and Joseph Vogl, *Kalkül und Leidenschaft. Poetik des ökonomischen Menschen* (Munich: Sequenzia, 2002). Also see Gabriele Brandstetter and Gerhard Neumann, eds., *Romantische Wissenspoetik. Die Künste und die Wissenschaften um 1800* (Würzburg: Königshausen & Neumann, 2004); or Krause and Pethes, eds., *Literarische Experimentalkulturen*, which contains the previously mentioned essay by Roland Borgards, which brilliantly demonstrates Kleist's transformation of scientific experiments into literary experiments.

61 Heinrich von Kleist, *The Feud of the Schroffensteins*, trans. Mary J. Price and Lawrence M. Price, *Poet Lore* 27, no. 5 (1916), 492 (translation modified), hereinafter referred to as FS, followed by the page number.

62 See DKV I, 622. Hinrich C. Seeba is likely responsible for this annotation, see DKV I, 485f.

63 Daiber, "Kleists Dichtung," 53, was the first to call attention to this context without, however, specifying the quote's poetological function within the play. Daiber assumes Kleist knew Alexander von Humboldt's *Experiments on Stimulated Muscular and Nervous Fibers; with Conjectures on the Chemical Process on Animal and Vegetable Life* (*Versuch über die gereizte Muskel- und Nervenfaser nebst Vermuthungen über den chemischen Proceß des Lebens in der Thier- und Pflanzenwelt*), published in 1797, the second part of which contains annotations by Johann Wilhelm Ritter, which is what made him well known. Ritter's *Proof That a Permanent Galvanism Is Combined with the Vital Process in the Animal Kingdom* (*Beweis, daß ein beständiger Galvanismus den Lebensproceß im Thierreich begleite*) was published in 1798. For more on Ritter's impact on his contemporaries, see Walter D. Wetzel, *Johann Wilhelm Ritter. Physik im Wirkungsfeld der deutschen Romantik* (Berlin: de Gruyter, 1973); Jürgen Daiber, "Die Suche nach der Urformel. Zur Verbindung von romantischer Naturforschung und Dichtung," *Aurora* 60 (2000).

64 FS 500.

65 FS 576.

66 Thus remembers Kleist's friend Heinrich Zschokke in his *Autobiography* of 1842, LS 67a. For more on the reception of Kleist's first play, along with my reading of it, see chap. VI.

67 LS 31.

68 LS 32b.

69 ADE 30, Kleist's letter to his sister Ulrike of November 12, 1799.

70 DKV IV, 48.

71 DKV IV, 29, Kleist's letter of March 1799.

72 ADE 222.

73 See Hinderer, "Rückseite der Naturwissenschaften," 36f.

74 ADE 222.

75 See Günter Blamberger, "Agonalität und Theatralität. Kleists Gedankenfigur des Duells im Kontext der europäischen Moralistik," *KJb* (1999). On the role of media in agonistic relationships, see Dominik Paß, "Die Beobachtung der allmähligen Verfassung der Gedanken beim Reden. Eine systemtheoretische Lektüre," *KJb* (2003).

76 LS 33a.

77 LS 33b.

78 LS 32a.

79 DKV IV, 139.

80 See Martin Roussel, "Zerstreuungen. Kleists poetische Meditation 'Über das Marionettentheater,'" *KJb* (2007).

81 LS 534, partially translated in ADE 208. See chap. XII.

82 ADE 24, Kleist's letter to Martini of March 1799.

83 The most brilliant analysis of this oft-interpreted engraving is found in Raymond Klibansky, Erwin Panofsky, and Fritz Saxl, *Saturn and Melancholy. Studies in the History of Natural Philosophy, Religion, and Art* (Montreal: McGill-Queen's UP, 2019).

84 For more on the phenomenon of 'remanence,' see Hubertus Tellenbach, *Melancholy. History of the Problem, Endogeneity, Typology, Pathogenesis, Clinical Considerations*, trans. Erling Eng (Pittsburgh: Duquesne UP, 1980).

85 ADE 94–97.

86 ADE 98.

87 ADE 98f.

88 ADE 107f.

89 This theory of cognition became well known under the name 'radical constructivism.' It is an interdisciplinary discourse that led to significant contributions, for example, from Niklas Luhmann in the social sciences or from Paul Watzlawick in communication studies. For a still-valid analysis of the discourse's genealogy and filiations (including its reception in literary studies), see Siegfried J. Schmidt, *Der Diskurs des Radikalen Konstruktivismus* (Frankfurt/M.: Suhrkamp, 1987).

90 ADE 97f.

91 A literary survey of the Kant crisis is beyond the scope of an endnote; here is a brief overview: Ludwig Muth, *Kleist und Kant. Versuch einer neuen Interpretation* (Cologne: Universitätsverlag, 1954) (argues that Kant's *Critique of the Power of Judgment* of 1790 triggered the crisis); Ulrich Gall, *Philosophie bei Heinrich von Kleist. Untersuchungen zu Herkunft und Bestimmung des philosophischen Gehalts seiner Schriften* (Bonn: Bouvier, 1977) (suspects, among other things, that Kleist had, at best, a secondary knowledge of Kant through his reading of Karl Leonhard Reinhold's *Essay on a New Theory of the Human Capacity for Representation* of 1789); Hanna Hellmann, "Heinrich von Kleist und 'Der Kettenträger,'" *Germanisch-Romanische Monatsschrift* 13 (1925) (names Klinger's novel and Wünsch's *Cosmological Conversations* as possible sources for the thought-image of the "green glasses"); Peter Struck, "Kleists Wahrheitskrise und ihre frühromantische Quelle" (PhD diss., University of Hanover, 1985) (points to a similar thought-image in Tieck's *William Lovell*); Michael Mandelartz, "Von der Tugendlehre zur Lasterschule. Die sogenannte 'Kantkrise' und Fichtes 'Wissenschaftslehre,'" *KJb* (2006) (argues that Kleist took the glasses example from Fichte's "Juridical Defense" of 1799 and that Kleist's phrase "more recent so-called Kantean philosophy" is—in accordance with Ernst Cassirer—simply a "*terminus technicus* for Fichte's science of knowledge"; ibid., 126); Bernhard Greiner, *Kleists Dramen und Erzählungen. Experimente zum 'Fall' der Kunst* (Tübingen: Francke, 2000) (deems Kleist's reception of Kant possible and shows, in a thoughtful

and detailed way, how fruitful such an assumption—even if only heuristic—can be for generating new Kleist readings); Jochen Schmidt, *Heinrich von Kleist. Die Dramen und Erzählungen in ihrer Epoche* (Darmstadt: Wiss. Buchgesellschaft, 2003) (believes the Kant crisis to be merely "staged"; ibid., 15).

92 FS 576.

93 DKV IV, 313.

94 FP 265f.

95 ADE 121f.

96 Friedrich Schiller, *On the Aesthetic Education of Man in a Series of Letters*, ed. and trans. with an introd. Elizabeth M. Wilkinson and L.A. Willoughby (Oxford: Oxford UP, 1967), 33, 35.

97 ADE 99.

98 ADE 96, 98f.

99 DKV IV, 139.

100 Thus goes Werner Frick's incisive formulation, which also illustrates that Kleist's poetics, with its integration of the sciences, abandons the "autonomous status of a self-contained aesthetic domain." See Werner Frick, "Kleists 'Wissenschaft.' Kleiner Versuch über die Gedankenakrobatik eines Un-Disziplinierten," *KJb* (1997): 227f., which presents an astonishing firework of thoughts.

Kleist's literature thus retains and reflects forms of life and the know-how of living; its perception is—even if it lacks disciplinary grounding—no less precise than that of science. We see this in Kleist's analysis of a university exam in his essay "On the Gradual Fabrication of Thoughts While Speaking," according to which the examiner is interested in having his own ideas echoed back at him instead of playing on the student's mind to sound its "proper tone." Thus, from literature science reemerges. Today, a student at the Frankfurt graduate school for life sciences might deduce from Kleist's essay a theory of the paradoxical double bind structures of asymmetrical communication within pedagogical settings, which preempt all autonomy.

101 Frick, "Kleists 'Wissenschaft,'" 233.

102 ADE 93.

103 ADE 212, 216.

104 ADE 160.

105 ADE 253.

106 See the preface to Brandstetter and Neumann, eds., *Romantische Wissenspoetik*, 9f.

107 E.T.A Hoffmann, *The Serapion Brethren*, trans. Alex Ewing, 2 vols. (London: Bell & Sons, 1892), 2:94.

108 Quoted in Madleen Podewski, "Ästhetik und Chemie. Frühromantische Experimente zwischen Kunst und Naturwissenschaft – eine Problemskizze," *Internationales Jahrbuch der Bettina-von-Arnim-Gesellschaft* 15 (2003): 14.

109 Werner Frick, "'Und sehe, daß wir nichts wissen können….' Poetische Wissenschaftsskepsis bei Goethe, Kleist und Büchner," in *'Scientia poetica.' Literatur und Naturwissenschaft*, ed. Norbert Elsner and Werner Frick (Göttingen: Wallstein, 2004), 262f.

110 ADE 122, 95.

111 See Albert Camus, *The Myth of Sisyphus and Other Essays*, trans. Justin O'Brien (New York: Knopf, 1955), 35f.

112 ADE 95.

113 See the passages on Paris in chap. V.

114 ADE 59, Kleist's letter to Wilhelmine von Zenge of September 13, 15, and 18, 1800.

115 Erich Kästner, *Fabian. The Story of a Moralist*, trans. Cyrus Brooks (Evanston, IL: Northwestern UP, 1993).—For further context, see Alexander Košenina, *Der gelehrte Narr. Gelehrtensatire seit der Aufklärung* (Göttingen: Wallstein, 2003).

IV The Misused Love Letters

1 Walter Benjamin, "One-Way Street," trans. Edmund Jephcott, in *Selected Writings*, ed. Michael W. Jennings, vol. 1, *1913–1926* (Cambridge, MA: Belknap, 1999), 460.
2 ADE 54, Kleist's letter to Wilhelmine of September 5, 1801.
3 Monika Maron, "Nach Maßgabe meiner Begreifungskraft," *KJb* (1993): 20.
4 ADE 135.
5 Gottfried Keller, "The Misused Love Letters," trans. Michael Bullock, in *Two Novellas. The Misused Love Letters. Regula Amrain and Her Youngest Son*, trans. Michael Bullock and Anne Fremantle (New York: Ungar, 1974), 26–30.
6 Thus reads the literal translation of the famous 1792 work by Theodor Gottlieb von Hippel, *On Improving the Status of Women*, trans. and ed. with an introd. Timothy F. Sellner (Detroit: Wayne State UP, 1979).
7 This trend in Kleist scholarship has not changed in nearly three decades, namely since the publication of Hans-Jürgen Schrader, "Unsägliche Liebesbriefe. Heinrich von Kleist an Wilhelmine von Zenge," *KJb* (1981/82); Hans-Jürgen Schrader, "'Denke Du wärest in das Schiff meines Glückes gestiegen.' Widerrufene Rollenentwürfe in Kleists Briefen an die Braut," *KJb* (1983).
8 Thus reads Kleist's previously quoted term for complex or confused circumstances, see ADE 17.
9 Wilhelm Traugott Krug, *Krug's Lebensreise in sechs Stazionen von ihm selbst beschrieben. Nebst Frank Volkmad Reinhard's Briefen an den Verfasser*, rev. ed. (Leipzig: Baumgärtner, 1842), 129.
10 LS 36, Wilhelmine to Krug in 1803.
11 Carl Friedrich Pockels, *Versuch einer Charakteristik des weiblichen Geschlechts. Ein Sittengemählde des Menschen, des Zeitalters und des geselligen Lebens*, 5 vols. (Hanover: Ritscher, 1797–1802), 3:277.
12 ADE 31, Kleist's letter to Ulrike of November 12, 1799.
13 LS 36, Wilhelmine to Krug in 1803.
14 ADE 31.
15 In his "On the Gradual Fabrication of Thoughts While Speaking," Kleist reflects on the necessity of speaking swiftly and effortlessly when among nobles at a social gathering, where every duel with words resembles a duel with weapons, ADE 218–222, see esp. 221f.
16 ADE 31.
17 LS 36, Wilhelmine to Krug.
18 LS 38, Wilhelmine to Krug.
19 A watercolor painting on cardboard, currently on display at the Kleist Museum in Frankfurt/O.
20 LS 38, Wilhelmine to Krug.
21 Gerhard Schulz, *Kleist. Eine Biographie* (Munich: Beck, 2007), 105.
22 See Georg Stanitzek, *Blödigkeit. Beschreibung des Individuums im 18. Jahrhundert* (Tübingen: Niemeyer, 1989).

23 DKV IV, 110. In his letter to Wilhelmine of September 5, 1800, Kleist uses this term to describe the shortcomings of the letter medium—namely, the temporal 'phase delay' of letters and the fact that they are read in places other than which they were produced—only to then use these shortcomings to his advantage (see below).

24 Sophie von La Roche, *The History of Lady Sophia Sternheim*, ed. James Lynn, trans. Joseph Collyer (New York: New York UP, 1992), 18.

25 Thomas Mann, *The Magic Mountain*, trans. H.T. Lowe-Porter (New York: Knopf, 1960), 602.

26 LS 38, Wilhelmine to Krug.

27 Thus writes Albrecht Koschorke, *Körperströme und Schriftverkehr. Mediologie des 18. Jahrhunderts* (Munich: Fink, 1999), 97, whose work on the literature of sentimentalism is worth reading with regard to an understanding of Kleist's letters to his fiancée.

28 LS 38, Wilhelmine to Krug.

29 LS 38, Wilhelmine to Krug.

30 DKV IV, 53–57, partially translated in ADE 34.

31 Thus argues—nuanced yet decisive—Müller-Salget, *Heinrich von Kleist*, 38–40, reflecting the consensus among Kleist scholars.

32 See Britta Herrmann, "Auf der Suche nach dem sicheren Geschlecht. Die Briefe Heinrich von Kleists und Männlichkeit um 1800," in *Wann ist der Mann ein Mann? Zur Geschichte der Männlichkeit*, ed. Walter Erhart and Britta Herrmann (Stuttgart: Metzler, 1997).

33 See Schrader, "Widerrufene Rollenentwürfe," 122 (first quote), and Schrader, "Unsägliche Liebesbriefe," 95 (second quote), 88 (third quote).

34 Peter Staengle, *Heinrich von Kleist* (Munich: dtv, 1998), 33f.

35 LS 62a, Wilhelmine to Krug.

36 ADE 38. Kleist's letter of August 16, 1800, from Berlin is just one of many examples.

37 LS 38, Wilhelmine to Krug.

38 See Georg Simmel, "Treue. Ein sozialpsychologischer Versuch," in *Gesamtausgabe*, ed. Otthein Rammstedt, vol. 8.2, *Aufsätze und Abhandlungen 1901–1908* (Frankfurt/M.: Suhrkamp, 1993).

39 NR 167, Wilhelmine Krug's letter, from Leipzig, to Mrs. Henriette Solger, in Dresden, of August 26, 1823.

40 See DKV IV, letters no. 11, 12, and (with some limitations) no. 30, 33.

41 Schrader, "Unsägliche Liebesbriefe," 86, 91f.

42 Christian Fürchtegott Gellert, *Briefe, nebst einer praktischen Abhandlung von dem guten Geschmacke in Briefen* (Leipzig: Wendler, 1751), 56.

43 ADE 34.

44 All quotes from Staengle, *Heinrich von Kleist*, 34f., which reflect the dominant position among Kleist scholars.

45 DKV IV, 58–60, partially translated in ADE 36f.

46 ADE 43 (translation modified), Kleist's letter to Wilhelmine of August 20, 1800, from Pasewalk.

47 Immanuel Kant, "Anthropology from a Pragmatic Point of View," trans. Robert B. Louden, in *Anthropology, History, and Education*, ed. Günter Zöller and Robert B. Louden (Cambridge: Cambridge UP, 2007), 315 (first quote), 404 (second quote), 400 (third quote).

48 Quoted in William H. Hubbard, *Familiengeschichte* (Munich: Beck, 1983), 50.

49 Jean-Jacques Rousseau, "Emile, or, On Education," trans. Christopher Kelly and Allan Bloom, in *The Collected Writings of Rousseau*, ed. Roger D. Masters and Christopher Kelly, vol. 13 (Hanover: UP of New England, 2010), 540.

50 Jean Paul, *Titan. A Romance*, trans. Charles T. Brooks, vol. 1 (Boston: Ticknor & Fields, 1864), 441.

51 See Johann Gottlieb Fichte, *Fichtes Werk*, ed. Immanuel Hermann Fichte, 11 vols. (Berlin: de Gruyter, 1971), 3:310ff. For the Fichte reference of Kleist's example, see Gerhard Neumann, "Hexenküche und Abendmahl. Die Sprache der Liebe im Werk Heinrich von Kleists," *Freiburger Universitätsblätter* 25, no. 91 (1986).

52 ADE 67f., Kleist's letter to Wilhelmine of October 10, 1800, from Würzburg.

53 See Klaus Müller-Salget's annotations in DKV IV, 677.

54 LS 38, Wilhelmine to Krug.

55 Thus reads Varnhagen von Ense's judgment in his letter to Ernst von Bülow—the first Kleist biographer—of February 20, 1847, LS 43. For Kleist's enthusiastic portrayal of Brockes in his letter to Wilhelmine of January 31, 1801, from Berlin, see DKV IV, 186ff.; Hermann F. Weiss, "Heinrich von Kleists Freund Ludwig von Brockes," *Beiträge zur Kleist-Forschung* (1996).

56 Kleist presents Brockes' willingness to join him as a sudden decision made in Pasewalk in August: Brockes put aside "[a]ll that was in his own best interest […] to come with me." (ADE 88, Kleist's letter to Wilhelmine of January 31, 1801)

57 For the pathos formula for his departure, see Kleist's letter to Wilhelmine of August 16, 1800, ADE 39; for the reassuring information on his state of mind in Berlin, see Kleist's letter to Ulrike of August 14, 1800, ADE 37.

58 ADE 37 (translation modified).

59 Johann Gottfried Herder, *Briefwechsel mit Caroline Flachsland*, ed. H. Schauer, 2 vols. (Weimar: Goethe-Gesellschaft, 1926–28), 1:174 (first quote; letter of April 23, 1771), 1:286f. (second quote; letter of August 17, 1771).

60 A reproduction of the tea cup and saucer is on display in the permanent exhibition of the Kleist Museum in Frankfurt/O.

61 DKV IV, 71, Kleist's letter to Wilhelmine of August 16, 1800, from Berlin.

62 ADE 42f., Kleist's letter to Wilhelmine of August 20, 1800, from Pasewalk.

63 DKV IV, 70, Kleist's letter to Wilhelmine of August 16, 1800, from Berlin, partially translated in ADE 39.

64 ADE 50, Kleist's letter to Wilhelmine of September 1, 1800, from Leipzig.

65 ADE 42, Kleist's letter to Wilhelmine of August 20, 1800, from Pasewalk.

66 Jean-Jacques Rousseau, "Julie, or the New Heloise: Letters of Two Lovers Who Live in a Small Town at the Foot of the Alps," trans. Philip Stewart and Jean Vachéin, in *The Collected Writings of Rousseau*, ed. Roger D. Masters and Christopher Kelly, vol. 6 (Hanover: UP of New England, 1997), 197, 200.

67 ADE 64, Kleist's letter to Wilhelmine of September 20, 1800, from Würzburg.

68 Rousseau, "Julie, or, The New Heloise," 9.

69 LS 38, Wilhelmine to Krug.

70 ADE 147, Kleist's letter to Wilhelmine of May 20, 1802, from Thun.

71 Franz Kafka, *Letters to Milena*, trans. and with an introd. Philip Boehm (New York: Schocken, 1990), 223.

72 DKV IV, 81f., Kleist's letter to Wilhelmine of August 21, 1800, from Pasewalk.

73 DKV IV, 95, Kleist's letter to Wilhelmine of September 3, 1800, from Dresden.

74 DKV IV, 130f., Kleist's letter to Wilhelmine of September 19, 1800, from Würzburg.

75 Franz Kafka, *The Trial*, trans. Idris Parry (London: Penguin, 1994), 169.

76 DKV IV, 177, Kleist's letter to Wilhelmine of January 11, 1801, from Berlin, partially translated in ADE 83.

77 DKV IV, 184, Kleist's letter to Wilhelmine of January 21, 1801, from Berlin.

78 ADE 123, Kleist's letter to Wilhelmine of August 15, 1801, from Paris.
79 Thus on love letters in general Roland Barthes, *A Lover's Discourse: Fragments*, trans. Richard Howard (New York: Hill & Wan, 1978), 157.
80 "May you find it resembles me more than I do. There is a touch of mockery in it that I do not like, I wish he had portrayed me more *truthfully*" (DKV IV, 217, Kleist's letter to Wilhelmine of April 9, 1801, from Berlin). Wilhelmine, by contrast, emphasizes that the portrait "closely resembled him"—which is what she tells her fiancée Professor Krug in 1803, LS 62a. For the history of the portrait, currently kept at the Berlin State Library – Prussian Cultural Heritage (with a copy on display at the Kleist Museum Frankfurt/O.), see Eva Rothe, "Die Bildnisse Heinrich von Kleists. Mit neuen Dokumenten zu Kleists Gefangenschaft," *Jahrbuch der Deutschen Schillergesellschaft* 5 (1961): 136–145.
81 ADE 94, Kleist's letter to Wilhelmine of March 22, 1801, from Berlin.
82 Rousseau, "Emile," 638 (first quote), 640 (second quote), 646, 648 (third quote).
83 ADE 40, Kleist's letter to Wilhelmine of August 16, 1800, from Berlin.
84 DKV IV, 168–170, Kleist's letter to his sister Ulrike of November 25, 1800, from Berlin, partially translated in ADE 79f.
85 DKV IV, 172, Kleist's letter to Wilhelmine of November 29, 1800, from Berlin. For the opposition between book learning and practical knowledge, illustrated with the image of the arched gate, see Kleist's letter to Wilhelmine of November 16, 1800, ADE 76.
86 DKV IV, 101f., Kleist's letter to Wilhelmine of September 4, 1800, from Dresden.
87 See Kleist's letters to Wilhelmine of November 13, 1800, ADE 75 (his plan to live in French Switzerland), and of November 22, 1800, ADE 78 (Wilhelmine's rejection of his plan).
88 ADE 132.
89 ADE 134.
90 ADE 138.
91 DKV IV, 154, Kleist's letter to Wilhelmine of November 13, 1800, from Berlin.
92 Rousseau, "Emile," 667.
93 DKV IV, 297, Kleist's letter to Heinrich Zschokke of February 1, 1802, from Thun.
94 DKV IV, 285, Kleist's letter to Wilhelmine of December 2, 1801, from Frankfurt/M., partially translated in ADE 138.
95 See ADE 144, Wilhelmine's letter to Kleist of April 10, 1802.
96 LS 62a.
97 DKV IV, 224, Kleist's letter to Wilhelmine of May 21, 1801, from Leipzig.
98 ADE 113f., Kleist's letter to Wilhelmine of July 21, 1801, from Paris.
99 ADE 142, Kleist's letter to Ulrike of January 12, 1802, from Bern.
100 See Wolfgang Schmidbauer, *Die Rache der Liebenden* (Reinbek: Rowohlt, 2005); Wolfgang Schmidbauer, "Kleists Narzissmus," *KJb* (2008/09).
101 ADE 142, Kleist's letter to Ulrike of January 12, 1802, from Bern.
102 ADE 142, Kleist's letter to Ulrike of January 12, 1802, from Bern.
103 LS 62a, Wilhelmine to Krug.
104 ADE 115, Kleist's letter to Wilhelmine of July 21, 1801, from Paris.
105 ADE 203 (translation modified), 205, Kleist's letter to Marie von Kleist of November 9 and 12, 1811, from Berlin.
106 ADE 147f.
107 Rainer Maria Rilke, "Narcissus," in *Poems 1906 to 1926*, trans. J.B. Leishman (New York: New Directions, 1957), 145.
108 See Rilke's self-reflections on dealing with "doll souls" in his essay "Dolls. On the Wax Dolls of Lotte Pritzel," trans. Idris Parry, in *On Dolls*, ed. with an introd. Kenneth Gross (London: Notting Hill, 2012).

109 For the opposition between "destructive character" and "etui-man," see Walter Benjamin, "The Destructive Character," trans. Edmund Jephcott, in *Selected Writings*, ed. Michael W. Jennings, vol. 2, *1927–1934* (Cambridge, MA: Belknap, 1999), 542.

110 See DKV IV, 286, Kleist's letter to Wilhelmine of December 2, 1801, from Frankfurt/M.: "Give Louise a kiss, and ask her to put in a good word for me with you. Tell her that if I did not marry a *friend from my youth*, I would never have a wife. That will move her—."

111 ADE 147, Kleist's letter to Wilhelmine of May 20, 1802, from Thun.

112 LS 146, quoted from Wilhelm Traugott Krug's autobiography *Krug's Lebensreise* (1842).

113 NR 44, quoted from Wilhelm Traugott Krug's autobiography *Krug's Lebensreise* (1842).

114 LS 288, Wilhelm von Pannwitz in his letter to Philipp von Stojentin of August 13, 1808, from Gulben.

115 Regarding the fate of the miniature, see LS 552ff.

116 DKV IV, 217.

117 The oil painting is kept at the German Literature Archive/Schiller National Museum in Marbach am Neckar.

118 The record was discovered by Hermann F. Weiss, *Funde und Studien zu Heinrich von Kleist* (Tübingen: Niemeyer, 1984), 105.

V "I Felt as Though I Were Entering on a New Life"

1 Benjamin, "One-Way Street," 466.

2 ADE 55, Kleist's letter to Wilhelmine of September 5, 1800.

3 This objection does not apply to the more recent biographies on Kleist. With regard to the Würzburg journey, the works by Müller-Salget, *Heinrich von Kleist*, Schulz, *Kleist*, and Jens Bisky, *Kleist. Eine Biographie* (Berlin: Rowohlt, 2007), strive to differentiate between what is a true secret and what is just a smokescreen—while others avoid making a decision altogether, like Staengle, *Heinrich von Kleist*, or Herbert Kraft, *Kleist. Leben und Werk* (Munich: Aschendorff, 2007). The latter were preceded in their austerity by the literary survey in Diethelm Brüggemann, *Drei Mystifikationen Heinrich von Kleists. Kleists Würzburger Reise. Kleists Lust-Spiel mit Goethe. Aloysius, Marquis von Montferrat* (New York: Peter Lang, 1985), 15–87.

4 For the distinction between *mysterium* and *arcanum*, see Aleida Assmann and Jan Assmann, "Zur Einführung," in *Schleier und Schwelle*, ed. Aleida Assmann and Jan Assmann, vol. 1, *Geheimnis und Öffentlichkeit. Archäologie der literarischen Kommunikation V,1* (Munich: Fink, 1998).

5 Gilles Deleuze and Félix Guattari define this form of "secrecy, speed, and affect" as elements of Kleist's "most uncanny modernity," without, however, referring to the Würzburg journey. Gilles Deleuze and Félix Guattari, *Thousand Plateaus. Capitalism and Schizophrenia*, trans. Brian Massumi (Minneapolis: U of Minnesota P, 2005), 356.

6 ADE 37f. (translation modified).

7 ADE 40, Kleist's letter to Wilhelmine of August 16, 1800.

8 ADE 47, Kleist's letter to Wilhelmine of August 26, 1800. See Adam Soboczynski, *Versuch über Kleist. Die Kunst des Geheimnisses um 1800* (Berlin: Matthes & Seitz, 2007), who gives detailed attention to the strategic calculations of Kleist's art of secrecy in his life and work, with an emphasis on relations to power.

9 Johann Christoph Adelung, *Versuch eines vollständigen grammatisch-kritischen Wörterbuches der Hochdeutschen Mundart, mit beständiger Vergleichung der übrigen Mundarten, besonders aber der oberdeutschen*, vol. 1 (Leipzig: Breitkopf, 1774), 23f.

10 See the lucid and in many ways inspiring article by Linda Simonis, "Poetologie des Abenteuers. Casanova und das Problem der Kontingenz," *Poetica* 34, no. 3/4 (2002): 347.

11 Georg Simmel, "The Adventure," trans. David Kettler, in *Georg Simmel, 1858–1918. A Collection of Essays*, ed. Kurt H. Wolff (Columbus: Ohio State UP, 1959), 244.

12 DKV IV, 81.

13 DKV IV, 80, Kleist's letter to Ulrike of August 21, 1800.

14 ADE 45, Kleist's letter to Wilhelmine of August 21, 1800.

15 ADE 62, Kleist's letter to Wilhelmine of September 15, 1800.

16 DKV IV, 82f., partially translated in ADE 45.

17 For this date, see Kleist's letter to Wilhelmine of August 30, 1800, from Leipzig: "But since I had to see Struensee once again before leaving the following morning" and "I left Berlin for Potsdam with *Brockes* accompanied by *Carl* on 28th at eleven o'clock in the morning" (DKV VI, 89f.).—Kleist relays nothing about the meeting with Struensee itself.

18 DKV IV, 149, Kleist's letter to Struensee of November 1, 1800, from Berlin.

19 This thesis has been consistently promoted since the mid-19th century. For an extensive collection of the source material, see Eberhard Siebert, "War Heinrich von Kleist als Industriespion in Würzburg?" *Jahrbuch Preußischer Kulturbesitz* 22 (1989).

20 LS 40.

21 ADE 80 (translation modified).

22 ADE 45, Kleist's letter to Wilhelmine of August 21, 1800, from Coblentz.

23 ADE 38.

24 See Gall, *Philosophie bei Kleist*.

25 ADE 67.

26 See ADE 24.

27 ADE 73, 75.

28 LS 46, Kunth to Struensee.

29 See Kleist's letters to Wilhelmine of April 9, 1801, and to Kunth of April 12, 1801, particularly DKV IV, 213, 218.

30 See Dirk Grathoff, *Kleists Geheimnisse. Unbekannte Seiten einer Biographie* (Opladen: Westdeutscher Verlag, 1993); Dirk Grathoff, "Heinrich von Kleists Würzburger Reise – eine erweiterte Rekonstruktion," *KJb* (1997).

31 For Brockes as a Freemason, see Peter Struck, "Ein biographisches Detail zu Ludwig von Brockes," *KJb* (1986).

32 See Müller-Salget, *Heinrich von Kleist*, 48, with whom I can only agree.

33 DKV IV, 148, Kleist's letter to Ulrike of October 27, 1800.

34 LS 42, protocol of the Würzburg town council of September 18, 1800.

35 ADE 88, Kleist's letter to Wilhelmine of January 31, 1801, from Berlin.

36 See Schrader, "Widerrufene Rollenentwürfe," 135ff.; Zimmermann, *Kleist*, 105.

37 DKV IV, 140–143, partially translated in ADE 66.

38 ADE 66.

39 Schrader, "Widerrufene Rollenentwürfe," 151, n. 35.

40 See Max Morris, *Heinrich von Kleists Reise nach Würzburg* (Berlin: Skopnik, 1899), 28f.

41 Günter Blöcker, *Heinrich von Kleist oder Das absolute Ich* (Berlin: Argon, 1960), 50.

42 See Uffe Hansen, "Der Schlüssel zum Rätsel der Würzburger Reise Heinrich von Kleists," *Jahrbuch der Deutschen Schillergesellschaft* 41 (1997).
43 See Katharine Weder, *Kleists magnetische Poesie. Experimente des Mesmerismus* (Göttingen: Wallstein, 2008), 109ff., 114, n. 17.
44 Hansen, "Schlüssel zum Rätsel," 199.
45 See DKV IV, 79, 80f., 83, partially translated in ADE 44–46.
46 DKV IV, 164.
47 Goethe's letter to Schiller of December 19, 1798, in Friedrich Schiller and Johann Wolfgang von Goethe, *Correspondence between Schiller and Goethe. From 1794 to 1805*, trans. L. Dora Schmitz, vol. 2 (London: Bell & Sons, 1890), 182 (translation modified).
48 For this particular mode of perception and writing in Kleist, see Gerhard Neumann, "Anekdote und Novelle. Zum Problem literarischer Mimesis im Werk Heinrich von Kleists," in *Heinrich von Kleist und die Aufklärung*, ed. Tim Mehigan (Rochester: Camden, 2000).
49 ADE 46.
50 ADE 42.
51 ADE 51.
52 ADE 40, Kleist's letter to Wilhelmine of August 16, 1800, from Berlin.
53 DKV IV, 79, partially translated in ADE 87.
54 See Horst Häker, "Kleist auf Rügen," *Beiträge zur Kleist-Forschung* (2000).
55 See Weiss, "Kleists Freund."
56 DKV IV, 125.
57 DKV IV, 193f., partially translated in ADE 88f. For more on the critique of ownership at the turn of the 19th century, particularly with regard to the history of literature and mentalities, see Ulrich Fülleborn, *Besitzen als besäße man nicht. Besitzdenken und seine Alternativen in der Literatur* (Frankfurt/M.: Insel, 1995).
58 László Földényi, *Heinrich von Kleist. Im Netz der Wörter* (Munich: Matthes & Seitz, 1999), 71–76.
59 DKV IV, 191.
60 DKV IV, 191.
61 On the difference between Kleist's journeys to Würzburg and Paris, see Gonthier-Louis Fink, "Zwischen Frankfurt an der Oder und Paris. Variationen des Deutschland- und Frankreichbildes des jungen Kleist," *KJb* (1997).
62 ADE 52.
63 DKV IV, 106f., partially translated in ADE 54.
64 ADE 56f.
65 See Friedrich Nicolai, *Beschreibung einer Reise durch Deutschland und die Schweiz im Jahre 1781*, vol. 1 (Berlin: Nicolai, 1783).
66 ADE 57.
67 DKV 115.
68 ADE 105.
69 See Helmut Pfotenhauer, "Kleists Rede über Bilder und in Bildern. Briefe, Bildkommentare, erste literarische Werke," *KJb* (1997): 129ff.
70 ADE 59f.
71 See Brüggemann, *Drei Mystifikationen Kleists*, 63f.
72 See Ralf Konersmann, "Das Versprechen der Wörter. Kleists erste und letzte Dichtung," in *Heinrich von Kleist* (*Text + Kritik, special issue*), ed. Heinz Ludwig Arnold (Munich: edition text + kritik, 1993).

73 See Heinz Politzer, "Auf der Suche nach Identität. Zu Heinrich von Kleists Würzburger Reise," *Euphorion* 61 (1967).

74 In this respect Földényi, *Heinrich von Kleist*, is a both intelligible and ingenious attempt to virtually reconstruct Kleist's "magazine of ideas," including its register and correspondences. Though it is not without precedent. The guiding concepts of Kleist's letters can already be found in a classic of Kleist scholarship, in Kreutzer, *Die dichterische Entwicklung*.

75 For the validity of this image as a figure of thought and its pseudo-scientific derivation in Kleist, see chap. III.

76 ADE 69f.

77 ADE 61.

78 ADE 91f.

79 DKV VI, 213.

80 DKV VI, 212.

81 DKV VI, 214.

82 ADE 119f.

83 For this portrait, see Arthur Eloesser, "Neue Kleist-Miniaturen," *Jahrbuch der Kleist-Gesellschaft* (1923/24).

84 DKV VI, 296. For Kleist's and Ulrike's 'gender trouble,' see Herrmann, "Suche nach dem Geschlecht."

85 DKV VI, 288.

86 Hans Joachim Kreutzer, "Über die Geschicke der Kleist-Handschriften und über Kleists Handschrift," *KJb* (1981/82): 82f.

87 ADE 201: "So I assure you I would suffer death ten times over rather than endure again what I had to endure over the luncheon table with my two sisters in Frankfurt, [...] but let Ulrike tell you about it sometime. [...] [T]o see myself a totally useless member of society in their eyes, deserving of no further sympathy: this is exceedingly painful to me, and truly, it not only robs me of the joys I had hoped for in future but poisons my entire past as well." It does not seem to have helped Ulrike that Kleist, in his last letter to his sister—see ADE 205—calls back on those "strong words" and reassures her: "really, all that was possible, not only for a sister, but for any human being, you in hopes of saving me have done: the truth is, there was no help for me on earth."

88 See the inspiring, short—yet rich in source material—biography on Kleist's sister by Sigrid Weigel, who I am indebted to: Sigrid Weigel, "Ulrike von Kleist 1774–1849. Lebens-Spuren hinter dem Bild der Dichter-Schwester," in *Schwestern berühmter Männer. Zwölf biographische Porträts*, ed. Luise F. Pusch (Frankfurt/M.: Insel, 1985), 281.

89 ADE 105 (translation modified).

90 See Roussel, "Zerstreuungen."

91 ADE 105.

92 ADE 105.

93 DKV IV, 225, partially translated in ADE 106.

94 On Kleist's reception of the visual arts, see Gernot Müller, *"Man müsste auf dem Gemälde selbst stehen." Kleist und die bildende Kunst* (Tübingen: Francke, 1995).

95 See ADE 108, Kleist's letter to Wilhelmine of June 3, 1801.

96 ADE 108f.

97 See chap. II for a short biography of Ewald von Kleist.

98 Johann Wilhelm Ludwig Gleim, "To Death," in *German Poetry from the Beginnings to 1750*, ed. Ingrid Walsøe-Engel (New York: Continuum, 1992), 291: "Death! what good's to you my

sweetheart? / With your lipless teeth you surely / Cannot mean to give him kisses." For Kleist's peculiar rendition of the poem, see DKV IV, 740, as well as Bisky, *Kleist*, 132.

99 ADE 111.

100 This is typical of the melancholic's sense of time. See Ludwig Binswanger, *Melancholie und Manie. Phänomenologische Studien* (Pfullingen: Neske, 1960), 45.

101 ADE 120.

102 DKV IV, 243.

103 Michel de Montaigne, "That to Philosophize Is to Learn to Die," in *The Complete Essays of Montaigne*, trans. Donald M. Frame (Stanford: Stanford UP, 1966), 60–62, 65, 67.

104 ADE 115.

105 ADE 217.

106 See the end of chap. III. Kleist's turn to becoming a moralist has various reasons: philosophical, biographical, and, most of all, historical. The latter becomes obvious in Kleist's life and work after the defeat of Prussia in the twin battles of Jena and Auerstedt in 1806—see chap. VIIff.

107 Rainer Maria Rilke, *The Notebooks of Malte Laurids Brigge*, trans. Stephen Mitchell (New York: Random, 1990), 3.

108 DKV 237f., partially translated in ADE 111.

109 ADE 129.

110 ADE 129.

111 DKV IV, 267.

112 ADE 127.

113 See Ingrid Oesterle, "Werther in Paris? Heinrich von Kleists Briefe über Paris," in *Heinrich von Kleist. Studien zu Werk und Wirkung*, ed. Dirk Grathoff (Opladen: Westdeutscher Verlag, 1988). Oesterle shows which particular sources—from Louis-Sébastien Mercier's *Panorama of Paris* to Tieck's *William Lovell*—Kleist drew from to blend the contemporary discourse on Paris with the sentimental tone prevailing in his private correspondences, all the while considering the similarities and differences between Kleist and those intertexts. For the broader context, also see Karsten Witte, ed., *Paris. Deutsche Republikaner reisen* (Frankfurt/M.: Insel, 1980).

114 ADE 125. Similarly, François de La Rochefoucauld notes in his *Maxims*, trans. Louis Kronenberger (New York: Random, 1959), 1: "What we consider virtues are often merely a group of actions and personal promptings displayed with care or the help of luck; and it is not always through valor and chastity that men are valiant and women chaste."

115 ADE 113.

116 ADE 121.

117 Regarding Kleist's activities in Paris, it is still worth reading the standard work by Paul Hoffmann, *Kleist in Paris* (Berlin: Wegweiser, 1924), as well as Weiss, *Funde und Studien*.

118 DKV IV, 287f.

119 See Klaus H. Kiefer, *Wiedergeburt und Neues Leben. Aspekte des Strukturwandels in Goethes "Italienischer Reise"* (Bonn: Bouvier, 1978).

120 See Günter Blamberger, "'Ein anderer ist nun der wirkliche Anfang.' Die Weltreisenden Peter Schlemihl und Adelbert von Chamisso," in *Hermenautik – Hermeneutik. Literarische und geisteswissenschaftliche Beiträge zu Ehren von Peter Horst Neumann*, ed. Holger Helbig, Bettina Knauer, and Gunar Och (Würzburg: Königshausen & Neumann, 1996).

121 DKV IV, 287.

122 DKV IV, 290.

123 ADE 146 (translation modified).

124 For the speculations that Mädeli might have been Magdalena Furer or Elisabeth Magdalena Stettler and might even have been the mother of a child conceived with Kleist—as well as for Sembdner's critical comment on these speculations—see LS 77b.

125 DKV IV, 301.

126 DKV IV, 300.

127 DKV IV, 301.

128 For Zschokke's recollections, see LS 75a, 75b, and 72.

129 ADE 142.

130 DKV IV, 298.

131 Martin Luther, *D. Martin Luthers Werke. Kritische Gesamtausgabe*, 120 vols. (Weimar: Böhlau, 1883–2009), 19:161. Quoted in Gerd Dicke, "'Mich wundert, das ich so frölich pin.' Ein Spruch im Gebrauch," in *Kleinstformen der Literatur*, ed. Walter Haug and Burghart Wachinger (Tübingen: Niemeyer, 1994), 87. Luther thus rejects the edifying *memento mori* tradition of the saying. See Dicke, who analyzes the transformations and reflections of the saying throughout the centuries.

132 For this figure of thought, see Roussel, "Zerstreuungen."

133 Thus reads the title of Ludwig Völcker's fine work *Muse Melancholie – Therapeutikum Poesie. Studien zum Melancholie-Problem in der deutschen Lyrik von Hölty bis Benn* (Munich: Fink, 1978).

134 Thus Zschokke's recollection in LS 67a.

135 Thus Ulrike's recollections in LS 81a, 81c.

136 See Karl Heinz Bohrer, *Der romantische Brief. Die Entstehung ästhetischer Subjektivität* (Munich: Hanser, 1987), 101, who, however, links the substitution of the one project with the other to the year 1801 and thus to Kleist's time in Paris.

VI On the Gradual Fabrication of the Writer and His Works

1 Sigmund Freud, "Creative Writers and Day-dreaming," in *The Standard Edition of the Complete Psychological Works of Sigmund Freud*, ed. and trans. James Strachey, vol. 9 (London: Hogarth, 1957), 143, 150. The lecture was first published in the Berlin journal *New Revue* (*Neue Revue*) in 1908.

2 Immanuel Kant, *Critique of the Power of Judgment*, ed. Paul Guyer, trans. Paul Guyer and Eric Matthews (Cambridge: Cambridge UP, 2000), 187.

3 See Günter Blamberger, *Das Geheimnis des Schöpferischen, oder: Ingenium est ineffabile? Studien zur Literaturgeschichte der Kreativität zwischen Goethezeit und Moderne* (Stuttgart: Metzler, 1991).

4 Kant, *Anthropology*, 330.

5 See Wolfgang Hildesheimer, *Mozart*, trans. Marion Faber (New York: Farrar, Straus & Giroux, 1982). For a broader context, see Ernst Kris and Otto Kurz, *Legend, Myth, and Magic in the Image of the Artist. A Historical Experiment*, trans. Alastair Laing and Lottie M. Newman (New Haven: Yale UP, 1979), originally published in 1934 and informed by Giorgio Vasari's biographies of artists.

6 Robert Walser, "Kleist in Thun," in *The Walk*, trans. Christopher Middleton and others (London: Serpent's Tail, 2013), 16f., 21, 24. Regarding Walser's various portraits of Kleist, see the studies by Peter Utz, "'Eine Fremdheit bleibt immer.' Robert Walser und der Kleist seiner Zeit," *KJb* (1997); Sabine Eickenrodt, "Kopfstücke. Zur Geschichte und Poetik der literarischen Porträts am Beispiel von Robert Walsers 'Kleist in Thun,'" *KJb* (2004).

7 In the famous §46 of his *Critique of the Power of Judgment*, Kant notes: "*Genius* is the talent (natural gift) that gives the rule to art." And he continues further, in §47: "the rule must be abstracted from the deed, i.e. from the product"—see Kant, *Critique of the Power of Judgment*, 186, 188.

8 All quotes from ADE 218–222.

9 Edward Young, *Conjectures on Original Composition. In a Letter to the Author of Sir Charles Grandison* (London: Millar, 1759), 77, 42f.

10 Young, *Conjectures on Original Composition*, 23, 45f.

11 ADE 238.

12 Harold Bloom, *The Anxiety of Influence. A Theory of Poetry* (New York: Oxford UP, 1973), 13.

13 For this reading, see Paß, "Die Beobachtung der allmähligen Verfassung," which is largely informed by systems theory.

14 See Ludwig Jäger, "Vom Eigensinn des Mediums Sprache," in *Brisante Semantik. Neuere Konzepte und Forschungsergebnisse einer kulturwissenschaftlichen Semantik*, ed. Dietrich Busse, Thomas Niehr, and Martin Wengeler (Tübingen: Niemeyer 2005).

15 ADE 218f.

16 ADE 222.

17 Thus suggests the apt title of John Dewey's study on creativity: John Dewey, *Art as Experience* (New York: Minton, Balch & Company, 1934).

18 On the concept of creativity as a distributed agency between people, media, and devices, see Bruno Latour, "The Berlin Keys or How to Do Words with Things," trans. Lydia Davis, in *Matter, Materiality and Modern Culture*, ed. P.M. Graves-Brown (London: Routledge, 2000); Alfred Gell, *Art and Agency. An Anthropological Theory* (Oxford: Oxford UP, 1998).

19 Niklas Luhmann, "Über 'Kreativität,'" in *Kreativität – ein verbrauchter Begriff?*, ed. Hans Ulrich Gumbrecht (Munich: Fink, 1988), 17.

20 LS 67a.

21 LS 69.

22 LS 80.

23 ADE 131f.

24 ADE 146f.

25 On the contemporary reception of Kleist's first work, see Anett Lütteken, *Heinrich von Kleist – eine Dichterrenaissance* (Tübingen: Niemeyer, 2004), 39ff. (with numerous references to source material).

26 DKV IV, 314. See the concise volume by Helmut Sembdner, ed., *Heinrich von Kleist. Der Dichter über sein Werk*, 2nd ed. (Darmstadt: Wiss. Buchgesellschaft, 1996), 16.

27 See Jacob Grimm and Wilhelm Grimm, *Deutsches Wörterbuch*, 33 vols. (Munich: dtv, 1984), 14:2224–2226.

28 See FS 464.

29 See the still relevant Hinrich C. Seeba, "Der Sündenfall des Verdachts. Identitätskrise und Sprachskepsis in Kleists *Familie Schroffenstein*," *Deutsche Vierteljahrsschrift für Literaturwissenschaft und Geistesgeschichte* 44 (1970).

30 See the standard work by Philippe Ariès, *Centuries of Childhood. A Social History of Family Life*, trans. Robert Baldick (New York: Vintage Books, 1962).

31 Thus reads the apt title of the standard work by Bengt Algot Sørensen, *Herrschaft und Zärtlichkeit. Der Patriarchalismus und das Drama im 18. Jahrhundert* (Munich: Beck, 1984).

32 See Dieter Schwab, "Familie," in *Geschichtliche Grundbegriffe. Historisches Lexikon zur politisch-sozialen Sprache in Deutschland*, ed. Otto Brunner, Werner Conze, and Reinhart Koselleck, vol. 2 (Stuttgart: Klett-Cotta, 1975).

33 FS 459f.

34 FS 576.
35 FS 576.
36 FS 576.
37 See in particular the following two works: Anthony Stephens, "Kleists Familienmodelle," *KJb* (1988/89); Anthony Stephens, *Heinrich von Kleist. The Dramas and Stories* (Oxford: Berg, 1994), to whom I owe many inspirations. Also see the comprehensive study by Joachim Pfeiffer, *Die zerbrochenen Bilder. Gestörte Ordnungen im Werk Heinrich von Kleists* (Würzburg: Königshausen & Neumann, 1989).
38 Thus reads the title of an inspiring study on the family discourse of the Enlightenment, see Peter Horst Neumann, *Der Preis der Mündigkeit. Über Lessings Dramen. Anhang: Über Fanny Hill* (Stuttgart: Klett-Cotta, 1977).
39 Immanuel Kant, "An Answer to the Question: What is Enlightenment?" in *Practical Philosophy*, ed. and trans. Mary J. Gregor (Cambridge: Cambridge UP, 1996), 17.
40 FS 459.
41 FS 471.
42 See Anthony Stephens, "Name und Identitätsproblematik bei Kleist und Kafka," *Jahrbuch des Freien Deutschen Hochstifts* (1985).
43 FS 509f. (translation modified).
44 FS 464.
45 See Anthony Stephens, "'Was hilfts, daß ich jetzt schuldlos mich erzähle?' Zur Bedeutung der Erzählvorgänge in Kleists Dramen," *Jahrbuch der Deutschen Schillergesellschaft* 29 (1985).
46 LS 67a.
47 Arnold Stadler, *Komm, gehen wir* (Frankfurt/M.: Fischer, 2007), 378.
48 LS 75a.
49 Adelbert von Chamisso, "Reise um die Welt mit der Romanzoffischen Entdeckungs-Expedition in den Jahren 1815–18 auf der Brigg Rurik Kapitän Otto v. Kotzebue. Erster Teil: Tagebuch," in *Sämtliche Werke*, ed. Werner Feudel and Christel Laufer, vol. 2 (Munich: Hanser, 1982), 370.
50 LS 70. Pfuel's recollections can be found in Adolf Wilbrandt, *Heinrich von Kleist* (Nördlingen: Beck, 1863).
51 See Kreutzer, *Die dichterische Entwicklung*, 141, who—in a well-founded reference to the play's dramatic structure—already argued against Pfuel that "one can hardly give the actual exchange of clothes any priority with regard to the play's genesis."
52 See Zimmermann, *Kleist*, 51ff.
53 FS 576 (translation modified).
54 On Kleist's productive transformation of Shakespeare, see Bianca Theisen, "Der Bewunderer des Shakespeare. Kleists Skepitizismus," *KJb* (1999); Meta Corssen, *Kleist und Shakespeare* (Hildesheim: Gerstenberg, 1978).
55 LS 89.
56 DKV IV, 399.
57 DKV IV, 317.
58 LS 66.
59 ADE 146.
60 LS 77a.
61 ADE 151.
62 ADE 152f.
63 See Müller's correspondence with Goethe (LS 200b) and Gentz (LS 205) as well as Kleist's letter to Wieland (DKV IV, 399).

64 See Kreutzer, *Die dichterische Entwicklung*, 210f., and in particular Richard Samuel, "Heinrich von Kleists 'Robert Guiskard' und seine Wiederbelebung 1807/08," *KJb* (1981/82).

65 See Michael Kohlhäufl, "Die Rede – ein dunkler Gesang? Kleists 'Robert Guiskard' und die Deklamationstheorie um 1800," *KJb* (1996); Reinhart Meyer-Kalkus, "Heinrich von Kleist und Heinrich August Kerndörffer. Zur Poetik von Vorlesen und Deklamation," *KJb* (2001).

66 LS 89.

67 Quoted in BKA I/2, 39.

68 FP 355.

69 FP 355.

70 FP 356f.

71 FP 357f.

72 FP 360.

73 FP 362f.

74 FP 364f.

75 FP 366.

76 FP 367.

77 FP 368.

78 FP 370.

79 Quoted in BKA I/2, 50.

80 FP 372f. (translation modified).

81 Iris Denneler, "Legitimation und Charisma. Zu 'Robert Guiskard,'" in *Kleists Dramen. Neue Interpretationen*, ed. Walter Hinderer (Stuttgart: Reclam, 1981), 87. Schmidt, *Heinrich von Kleist*, 136, agrees with Denneler when he argues that Kleist proposes that the rule of a prince depends on the "welfare of the people" rather than dynastic principles. Anthony Stephens, "Robert Guiskard, Herzog der Normänner," in *Kleist-Handbuch. Leben – Werk – Wirkung*, ed. Ingo Breuer (Stuttgart: Metzler, 2009), argues against such reading in an inspiring presentation of the state of the research.

82 DKV IV, 432, Kleist's letter to Collin of April 20, 1809.

83 Speculations that Guiscard's death could be a punishment for his hubris—for considering himself invulnerable due to a prophecy that he would die as a crusader in Jerusalem—cannot be substantiated by the play. Cf. Margrit Schoch von Wädenswil, *Kleist und Sophokles* (Zurich: Aschmann & Scheller, 1952), 30, who refers to Anna Komnena's biographical account of Alexios Komnenos, which claims such a prophecy for Guiscard. This may, at best, explain Guiscard's words to Armin that his contact with the plague-stricken people is not "reckless," "nor is it chance" that "explains [his] coming / through unscathed" (FP 371). Nevertheless, this passing remark is not convincing proof of Guiscard's hubristic expectations, neither, incidentally, is Guiscard's anachronistic use of the city name Istanbul (Stambul), which Constantinople first received with the invasion of the Turks in 1453, several centuries after the death of the historical Guiscard.

84 Friedrich Schiller, "On the Sublime," trans. Daniel O. Dahlstrom, in *Essays*, ed. Walter Hinderer and Daniel O. Dahlstrom (New York: Continuum, 1993), 44. On the difference between Schiller's and Kleist's conception of drama with regard to Kleist's *Guiscard*, see Greiner, *Kleists Dramen und Erzählungen*, 124ff.

85 FP 355.

86 On the reception and transformation of the Baroque tragic drama in Kleist's *Guiscard*, see Ulrich Fülleborn, *Die frühen Dramen Heinrich von Kleists* (Munich: Fink, 2007), 56ff.

87 LS 77a.

88 Schlegel, *Philosophical Fragments*, 21.

89 Georg Lukács, *The Theory of the Novel. A Historico-Philosophical Essay on the Forms of Great Epic Literature*, trans. Anna Bostock (London: Merlin, 1971), 56.
90 ADE 150.
91 On the history of the theory of fragment, see Lucien Dällenbach and Christiaan L. Hart Nibbrig, eds., *Fragment und Totalität* (Frankfurt/M.: Suhrkamp, 1984), see esp. the brilliant essay by Peter Horst Neumann, "Rilkes *Archaischer Torso Apollos* in der Geschichte des modernen Fragmentarismus," published therein.
92 See Hinrich C. Seeba's documentation in DKV I, 696–700.
93 See Rilke's recommendation of the fragment to Marie von Thurn und Taxis on December 27, 1913, in NR 424.
94 Rainer Maria Rilke, "Archaic Torso of Apollo," in *New Poems [1908]. The Other Part*, trans. Edward Snow (San Francisco: North Point, 1987), 3.
95 ADE 120.
96 LS 78.
97 ADE 153.
98 Thus read the famous words by Heidegger that sum up his philosophy of death in Martin Heidegger, *Being and Time*, trans. Joan Stambaugh (Albany: SUNY Press, 1996), 246 (translation modified). They are, as is well known, based on Heidegger's biographical experience. As a military weather forecaster, he had to calculate how to fire projectiles from the rear of the front line to the enemy ahead without hitting his own vanguard, which literally ran toward its death.
99 See Françoise Gilot, *Life with Picasso* (New York: McGraw-Hill, 1964).

VII The Lost Years?

1 LS 108. This statement can be found in Eduard von Bülow's biography of 1848, though it is often rather uncritical in its use of oral recollections.
2 Caroline [Schlegel], *Briefe aus der Frühromantik*, ed. Erich Schmidt, vol. 1 (Leipzig: Insel, 1913), 543.
3 For further details on Wieland's reception in Weimar, see Sven-Aage Jørgensen et al., *Christoph Martin Wieland. Epoche – Werk – Wirkung* (Munich: Beck, 1994), 97ff.
4 DKV IV, 250.
5 See Kreutzer, *Die dichterische Entwicklung*, 50.
6 LS 105.
7 Thus reads the apt distinction by Hans-Jürgen Schrader, "Ermutigungen und Reflexe. Über Kleists Verhältnis zu Wieland und einige Motivanregungen, namentlich aus dem 'Hexameron von Rosenheim,'" *KJb* (1988/89): 161. In my analysis of Kleist's references to Wieland, I am equally obliged to Schrader as I am to Lütteken, *Heinrich von Kleist*, 99–110. However, both tend to depict Wieland's partisanship for Kleist more benevolently than critically.
8 LS 89.
9 Thus—representative of the consensus among Kleist scholars—the article by Jan Broch, "Wieland," in *Kleist-Handbuch*, ed. Breuer, 214.
10 See LS 98a, 99, 100a.
11 LS 89.
12 LS 89.
13 See DKV IV, 312: "Wieland tells me his life story; and I write it down."

14 LS 86.
15 LS 105a.
16 LS 106.
17 See chap. XIII as well as Günter Blamberger, "'Nur was nicht aufhört, weh zu thun, bleibt im Gedächtnis.' Zur Typogenese des Kleist-Bildes in der deutschen Literatur der Moderne," *KJb* (1995).
18 DKV IV, 311f.
19 LS 127.
20 See LS 127.
21 LS 93.
22 LS 94b.
23 LS 94a.
24 LS 94a.
25 DKV IV, 313.
26 DKV IV, 313.
27 See the annotations in DKV IV, 527, 812.
28 DKV IV, 313f.
29 DKV IV, 314f.
30 For further details on how the letter and fragment came down to us, see the annotations in DKV IV, 810.
31 ADE 106.
32 LS 109b.
33 See Kleist's request to Ulrike that she make an effort and sell the Schliebens' products "to one of the merchants who come to the market in Gulben." (DKV IV, 319)
34 DKV IV, 315.
35 LS 111.
36 LS 108.
37 LS 103b.
38 LS 112.
39 LS 112.
40 LS 114a.
41 Ernst von Pfuel, *Ueber das Schwimmen* (Berlin: Dümmler, 1817), 3.
42 ADE 159.
43 Bisky, *Kleist*, 233 (emphasis added). Also see ibid, 224–233.
44 ADE 152.
45 LS 117.
46 LS 118.
47 LS 119a.
48 ADE 153.
49 LS 122b. For further details on Kleist's fate in the fall of 1803, see LS 117–123b.
50 See Gracián, *The Art of Worldly Wisdom*, no. 246.
51 LS 132b.
52 ADE 157.
53 ADE 153f.
54 LS 126.
55 For further details on Wedekind, see the highly informative essay by Peter Philipp Riedel, "Jakobiner und Postrevolutionär. Der Arzt Georg Christian Wedekind," *KJb* (1996), which makes use of all available source material.

56 LS 125a.

57 LS 124.

58 Christa Wolf, *No Place on Earth*, trans. Jan van Heurck (New York: Farrar, Straus & Giroux, 1982), 3f., 39.

59 See Hilda M. Brown, "Kleist in Paris. 1804," *Seminar* 13 (1977); Richard H. Samuel and Hilda M. Brown, *Kleist's Lost Year and the Quest for 'Robert Guiscard'* (Leamington Spa: Hall, 1981), which both present these diary entries as supporting evidence.

60 See Grathoff, *Kleists Geheimnisse*, 99ff., see esp. 110.—Schlabrendorf's polemical work is now accessible to readers again thanks to [Hans Magnus Enzensberger], *Gustav von Schlabrendorf. Anti-Napoleon* (Frankfurt/M.: Eichborn, 1991).

61 Thus argues Schulz, *Kleist*, 267, which seems reasonable.

62 See Helmut Sembdner, "Die Doppelgänger des Herrn von Kleist. Funde und Irrtümer der Kleist-Forschung," *Jahrbuch der Deutschen Schillergesellschaft* 35 (1991).

63 See Klaus Müller-Salget, "Kleist im Frühjahr 1804. Eine Aufklärung," *KJb* (2008/09), including all source citations.

64 LS 127.

65 Klaus Müller-Salget informed me of this thesis by email on October 13, 2009, following his discovery in *Voss' Newspaper* that same day, for which I am very grateful.

66 See the medico-historical dissertation by Martin Weber, *Georg Christian Gottlieb Wedekind 1761–1831. Werdegang und Schicksal eines Arztes im Zeitalter der Aufklärung und der französischen Revolution. Mit einem Anhang: Wedekinds Diätetikvorlesung von 1789/90* (Stuttgart: Gustav Fischer, 1988).

67 Johann Wolfgang von Goethe, "Prometheus," in *Werke. Hamburger Ausgabe*, ed. Erich Trunz, vol. 1 (Munich: Beck, 1982), 46.

68 Walter Benjamin, "German Men and Women," trans. Edmund Jephcott, in *Selected Writings*, ed. Michael W. Jennings, vol. 3, *1935–1938* (Cambridge, MA: Belknap, 2006), 167.

69 DKV IV 322–324, partially translated in ADE 153–155.

70 See Friedrich Buchholz, *Gallerie Preussischer Charaktere* (Frankfurt/M.: Zweitausendeins, 1984), 491–494.

71 See Heinrich von Kleist, ed., *Berliner Abendblätter* (1810f.), 4, folio 27, October 31, 1810, hereinafter referred to as BA, followed by the folio and page number.

72 Wilhelm Genazino, "Die Flucht in die Ohnmacht. Dankrede zum Kleist-Preis," *KJb* (2008/09): 18.

73 Rainer Maria Rilke, "Requiem. Für Wolf Graf von Kalckreuth," in *Sämtliche Werke*, ed. Ernst Zinn, vol. 2, (Frankfurt/M.: Insel, 1975), 664.

74 DKV IV, 332, partially translated in ADE 158.

75 See DKV IV, 332f., Kleist's letters to Ulrike of August 2 and 24, 1804.

76 DKV IV, 326.

77 DKV IV, 329.

78 Rist's recollections are quoted in Weiss, *Funde und Studien*, 99f., for whose research efforts any Kleist biographer—not only regarding Gualtieri's case—can only express the greatest gratitude.

79 DKV IV, 345.

80 For Varnhagen's recollections, see LS 132.

81 LS 130.

82 See Paul Goldschmidt, "Stein zum Altenstein, Karl Freiherr von," in *Allgemeine Deutsche Biographie*, ed. Historische Commission bei der Königlichen Akademie der Wissenschaften, vol. 35 (Leipzig: Duncker & Humblot, 1893); Richard Samuel, "Heinrich

von Kleist und Karl Baron von Altenstein. Eine Miszelle zu Kleists Biographie," in *Selected Writings* (Melbourne: University of Melbourne, Department of German Studies, 1965).

83 ADE 160.
84 Bisky, *Kleist*, 233.
85 ADE 160.
86 LS 138a.
87 LS 137b.
88 DKV IV, 337f.
89 For further information on Königsberg, see Jürgen Manthey, *Königsberg. Geschichte einer Weltbürgerrepublik* (Munich: Hanser, 2005).
90 DKV IV, 348.
91 BA 11, October 12, 1810 ("Über Christian Kraus"); BA 24, October 27, 1810 ("Antikritik"). See chap. X.
92 DKV IV, 340.
93 DKV IV, 354.
94 DKV IV, 356.
95 ADE 218.
96 ADE 164.
97 ADE 162.
98 LS 151a.
99 ADE 208.
100 ADE 222 (translation modified).
101 See the article "Sechswöchnerin" in Grimm and Grimm, *Deutsches Wörterbuch*, 15:2794.
102 LS 149.
103 LS 142.
104 ADE 164.
105 ADE 221f.
106 DKV IV, 362.
107 MO 68.
108 See the brilliant in-depth analysis of the story by Hans Kiefner, "Species facti. Geschichtserzählung bei Kleist und in Relationen bei preußischen Kollegialbehörden um 1800," *KJb* (1988/89).
109 Franz Kafka, *The Diaries of Franz Kafka, 1910–13*, ed. Max Brod, trans. Joseph Kresh (Schocken: New York, 1974), 59.
110 LS 142.
111 On Kleist's flawed calculations of the underwater pressure, see Helmut Vogt, "Heinrich von Kleists Hydrostat. Die U-Boot-Idee des preußischen Dichters," *Der Tagesspiegel*, April 18, 1976, 5.
112 ADE 161.
113 DKV IV, 351f., partially translated in ADE 163.
114 DKV IV, 363, 367.
115 For further details on German history at the beginning of the 19th century, see the extensive monograph by Thomas Nipperdey, *Deutsche Geschichte 1800–1866. Bürgerwelt und starker Staat* (Munich: Beck, 1983), which is admirable for its richness in detail, diversity of perspectives, and intellectual density and still indispensable today. Also see, more recently, regarding the global context Jürgen Osterhammel, *Die Verwandlung der Welt. Eine Geschichte des 19. Jahrhunderts* (Munich: Beck, 2009).
116 DKV IV, 106.

117 ADE 168.
118 LS 164b.
119 See Bisky, *Kleist*, 279; Schulz, *Kleist*, 305.
120 See the detailed discussion of these speculations in Stephan Bock, "Croquis. Fußmärsche Routen Ausflüge 1807 – 1801 – 1811," *Heilbronner Kleist-Blätter* 14 (2003): 106ff., who also draws attention to contradictions in Kleist's itinerary, which cannot be discussed in detail here.
121 DKV IV, 368f.
122 DKV IV, 367.
123 Thus writes Ulrike on April 3, 1807, LS 164a; and so does Kleist on multiple occasions, see DKV IV, 379, for instance.
124 LS 119.
125 DKV IV, 373f., partially translated in ADE 169.
126 MO 231.
127 DKV IV, 374f., partially translated in ADE 169; DKV IV, 372.
128 DKV IV, 375, 377.
129 ADE 171.
130 ADE 171.
131 ADE 171.
132 Thus reads the formulation in Martin Roussel, "'Wie zart sie das zarte berühren.' Zur Kunst der Berührung bei Kleist," *KJb* (2008/09): 107, who wonderfully unpacks Kleist's reading of Vouet's painting.
133 See chap. XII.

VIII Distorting the World to the Point of Recognition

1 Thus writes Johann Wolfgang Goethe in his conversation with Johann Peter Eckermann in January 1827, see Johann Wolfgang Goethe and Johann Peter Eckermann, *Conversations of Goethe with Eckermann and Soret*, trans. John Oxenford (London: Bell & Sons, 1875), 209.
2 ADE 163.
3 For further details on the beginning and end of Kleist's writing process, see Heinrich Zschokke's account on the friends' "poetic competition" in response to a French copper engraving, LS 67a. Also see Kleist's letter to Rühle von Lilienstern of August 31, 1806, in which he tells him about having sent his comedy to Marie von Kleist the previous day, ADE 166.
4 FP 87.
5 LS 67a.
6 Müller, "Deutschland Ortlos," 16.
7 FP 89.
8 The consensus among Kleist scholars is that *The Broken Jug* is a comedy, albeit a problematic one. It would be impossible to give a literary survey here; instead I would like to refer the reader to Müller-Salget, *Heinrich von Kleist*, 186ff., who comments on the various interpretative approaches to the comedy.
9 FP 89–91.
10 See the entry on *straucheln* (to stumble) in Grimm and Grimm, *Deutsches Wörterbuch*, 19:984.

11 DKV I, 371.

12 See *Allgemeines Landrecht für die Preußischen Staaten von 1794*, text edition, with an introd. by Hans Hattenhauer and a bibliography by Günther Bernert (Frankfurt/M.: Metzner, 1970). Also see the careful study by Hans-Peter Schneider, "Justizkritik im 'Zerbrochnen Krug,'" *KJb* (1988/89).

13 FP 92f.

14 FP 127.

15 FP 105.

16 FP 99f.

17 Aristotle, *Poetics*, trans. Stephen Halliwell (Chapel Hill: The U of North Carolina P, 1987), 36.

18 DKV I, 362.

19 DKV I, 365.

20 DKV I, 365–367.

21 FP 145.

22 DKV I, 376.

23 There are a number of speculations about the symbolic value of this coin, which is supposed to depict both the King of Spain and the face of God. Müller-Salget, *Heinrich von Kleist*, examines these approaches, coming to the conclusion that an interpretation of "this numismatic impossibility [...] has not yet been achieved satisfactorily" (ibid., 193).

24 DKV I, 376. The ellipsis stands for omitted verses in the printed variant that are preserved in the handwritten manuscript of *The Broken Jug*. In these verses Walter promises Ruprecht a short year of military service all while promising the engaged couple a wedding a year later at Pentecost. See DKV I, 264f.

25 Thomas Mann, "Kleist's *Amphitryon*," in *Essays of Three Decades*, trans. H.T. Lowe-Porter (New York: Knopf, 1947), 202.

26 FP 43.

27 FP 60.

28 Grimm and Grimm, *Deutsches Wörterbuch*, 1:383f.

29 FP 1.

30 Molière, *Amphitryon*, trans. Richard Wilbur (New York: Theatre Communications Group, 2010), 107–109 (act 3, scene 10).

31 Regarding Falk and Kleist, see Fouqué's recollections in LS 107b, 107c.

32 DKV 1, 380.

33 LS 172b.

34 LS 173.

35 LS 175a.

36 Here, the famous 1974 study by Arthur Henkel, "Erwägungen zur Szene II,5 in Kleists 'Amphitryon,'" in *Kleists Aktualität. Neue Aufsätze und Essays 1966–1978*, ed. Walter Müller-Seidel (Darmstadt: Wiss. Buchgesellschaft, 1981), ought to still be followed. Among the fascinating scholarship on Kleist's *Amphitryon*, the following studies should also be noted: Helmut Arntzen, *Die ernste Komödie. Das deutsche Lustspiel von Lessing bis Kleist* (Munich: Nymphenburger, 1968); Peter Szondi, "Fünfmal 'Amphitryon.' Plautus, Molière, Kleist, Giraudoux, Kaiser," in *Lektüren und Lektionen*, ed. Jean Bollack et al. (Frankfurt/M.: Suhrkamp, 1973); Hans Robert Jauß, "Poetik und Problematik von Identität und Rolle in der Geschichte des 'Amphitryon,'" in *Identität*, ed. Odo Marquardt and Karlheinz Stierle (Munich: Fink, 1979); Karlheinz Stierle, "'Amphitryon.' Die Komödie des Absoluten," in *Interpretationen. Kleist Dramen*, ed. Walter Hinderer (Stuttgart: Reclam, 1997); Justus Fetscher, *Verzeichnungen. Kleists "Amphitryon" und seine Umschrift bei Goethe und*

Hofmannsthal (Cologne: Böhlau, 1998); Gabriele Brandstetter, "Duell im Spiegel. Zum Rahmenspiel in Kleists 'Amphitryon,'" *KJb* (1999); Justus Fetscher, "Vorstellungen. Zur Erforschung von Kleists 'Amphitryon' in den Jahren 1978 bis 2001," in *Heinrich von Kleist. Neue Wege der Forschung*, ed. Anton Philipp Knittel and Inka Kording (Darmstadt: Wiss. Buchgesellschaft, 2003).

37 All quotes from act 2, scene 5 can be found in FP 45–56; FP 49 (translation modified).

38 FP 54.

39 FP 56.

40 FP 83.

41 All quotes in this paragraph can be found in FP 19, 54, 47, 80.

42 FP 81.

43 ADE 95.

44 Niklas Luhmann, *Love as Passion. The Codification of Intimacy*, trans. Jeremy Gaines and Doris L. Jones (Cambridge, MA: Harvard UP, 1986), 107.

45 FP 80f.

46 ADE 91f.

47 FP 51.

48 DKV I, 380f.

49 FP 17.

50 See Hanna Hellmann, "Kleists 'Amphitryon,'" *Euphorion* 25 (1924).

51 See Gerhard Lauer and Thorsten Unger, eds., *Das Erdbeben von Lissabon und der Katastrophendiskurs im 18. Jahrhundert* (Göttingen: Wallstein, 2008).

52 MO 60.

53 MO 67 (translation modified).

54 MO 67.

55 See Immanuel Kant, "On the Miscarriage of All Philosophical Trials in Theodicy," trans. George di Giovanni, in *Religion and Rational Theology*, ed. Allen W. Wood and George di Giovanni (Cambridge: Cambridge UP, 1996).

56 ADE 165.

57 MO 58.

58 Thus argues Friedrich Kittler, "Ein Erdbeben in Chili und Preußen," in *Positionen der Literaturwissenschaft. Acht Modellanalysen am Beispiel von Kleists "Das Erdbeben in Chili,"* ed. David Wellbery, 3rd ed. (Munich: Beck, 1993), 33, whose essay is otherwise imaginative and worth reading, just as Wellbery's volume as a whole.

59 Here I follow Pamela Moucha, "Verspätete Gegengabe. Gabenlogik und Katastrophenbewältigung in Kleists 'Erdbeben in Chili,'" *KJb* (2000), who draws from Marcel Mauss, *The Gift. The Form and Reason for Exchange in Archaic Societies*, trans. W.D. Halls (New York: W.W. Norton, 1990).

60 See Jean Starobinski, *Largesse*, trans. Jane Marie Todd (Chicago: U of Chicago P, 1997), 71f.

61 MO 66.

62 MO 58 (translation modified).

63 MO 65f.

64 See chap. III.

65 This ambiguity is why Kleist's style is *also* suited to deconstructivist readings, which ought not to be excluded from Kleist scholarship, so astonishingly diverse in its methodological approaches. This clarification is meant to be directed against both the over-generalizing accusation of a 'deconstructivist turn' in the *Kleist Yearbook* (*Kleist-Jahrbuch*) as well as

the polemics against deconstruction in Schmidt, *Heinrich von Kleist*, who is otherwise highly respected for his Kleist scholarship.

66 MO 66 (translation modified).

67 NR 73a.

68 Among others Kreutzer, *Die dichterische Entwicklung*, 192f., pleads for the late composition of the novella. Cf. Roland Reuß in BKA II/6, 87.

69 Heinrich von Kleist, *Heinrich von Kleists hinterlassene Schriften*, ed. Ludwig Tieck (Berlin: Reimer, 1821), LXII.

70 LS 502.

71 For a more detailed discussion, see Günter Blamberger, "Die Novelle als Anti-Bildungsgeschichte. Anmerkungen zu Kleists 'Der Findling,'" in *Prägnanter Moment. Studien zur deutschen Literatur der Aufklärung und Klassik. Fs. für Hans-Jürgen Schings*, ed. Peter-André Alt et al. (Würzburg: Königshausen & Neumann, 2002).

72 This is what Hannelore Schlaffer, *Poetik der Novelle* (Stuttgart: Metzler, 1993), assumes. The continuation of Boccaccio's writing is not the only inspiration of novellistic writing in 19th century German literature; the functional opposition to the *Bildungs-* and *Entwicklungsroman* plays an equally important role, as I would like to show.—Ingo Breuer, "'Schauplätze jämmerlicher Mordgeschichte.' Tradition der Novelle und Theatralität der Historia bei Heinrich von Kleist," *KJb* (2001), proves as well that studying the poetics of the Early Modern genres of historia and novella can be just as important for understanding German novella writing as referring back to the prototype of the novella, namely Boccaccio's *The Decameron*.

73 Gerhard Schulz, *Die deutsche Literatur zwischen Französischer Revolution und Restauration*, vol. 2, *1806–1830* (Munich: Beck, 1989), 372.

74 Hoffmann, *The Serapion Brethren*, 1:2f.

75 Thus reads the apt formulation in Schulz, *Die deutsche Literatur*, 373.

76 MO 285.

77 MO 270, 272, 277, 283f.

78 See Denis Dyer, *The Stories of Kleist. A Critical Study* (London: Duckworth, 1977).

79 See Jürgen Schröder, "Kleists Novelle 'Der Findling.' Ein Plädoyer für Nicolo," *KJb* (1985).

80 MO 278, 273.

81 See Hans-Jürgen Schings, "Der anthropologische Roman. Seine Entstehung und Krise im Zeitalter der Spätaufklärung," in *Deutschlands kulturelle Entfaltung. Die Neubestimmung des Menschen*, ed. Bernhard Fabian, Wilhelm Schmidt-Biggemann, and Rudolf Vierhaus (Munich: Kraus, 1980).

82 MO 270.

83 See Stephens, "Kleists Familienmodelle," 233.

84 ADE 223. The principle of polarity has already been discussed in the context of Kleist's studies at the Viadrina, see chap. III.

85 MO 114.

86 See Niccolò Machiavelli, "The Life of Castruccio Castracani of Lucca," in *Chief Works and Others*, 2:533–560.

87 MO 284f. (translation modified).

88 See Greiner, *Kleists Dramen und Erzählungen*, 203.

89 See Günter Blamberger, "Agonalität und Theatralität"; Günter Blamberger, "Antiparastatische Genies. Politiken des Privaten in Kleists Essays," in *Politics in Literature. Studies on a Germanic Preoccupation from Kleist to Améry*, ed. Rüdiger Görner (Munich: Iudicium, 2004).

90 For a more detailed discussion, see chap. IX.

91 Machiavelli, *The Prince*, 87.

92 For further readings of the novella, see Ingeborg Harms, "Kleists 'Findling' zwischen Krypta und Handelsgewölbe," in *Gewagte Experimente und kühne Konstellationen. Kleists Werk zwischen Klassizismus und Romantik*, ed. Christine Lubkoll and Günter Oesterle (Würzburg: Königshausen & Neumann, 2001); Günter Oesterle, "'Der Findling.' Redlichkeit versus Verstellung – oder zwei Arten, böse zu werden" in *Interpretationen. Kleists Erzählungen*, ed. Walter Hinderer (Stuttgart: Reclam, 1998); Frank G. Ryder, "Kleists 'Findling': Oedipus manqué?" *Modern Language Notes* 92 (1977); Marianne Schuller, "Ur-Sprung. Kleists Erzählung 'Der Findling,'" in *Moderne. Verluste* (Basel: Stroemfeld, 1997).

93 August Wilhelm Schlegel, *Kritische Schriften und Briefe*, ed. Edgar Lohner (Stuttgart: Kohlhammer, 1965), 218; Ludwig Tieck, *Schriften* (Berlin: Reimer, 1829), XC; Paul Heyse, *Jugenderinnerungen und Bekenntnisse*, 4th ed. (Berlin: Hertz, 1901), 344.

94 LS 261.

95 On the problematics of defining the genre of the novella, see Blamberger, *Das Geheimnis des Schöpferischen*, 81–96.

96 See Kleist's letter to his publisher of Mai 1810, DKV IV, 446.

97 See DKV I, 770ff. The annotations mention, among other sources, an anecdote from Michel de Montaigne's essay on drunkenness of 1588, in which a peasant woman, a widow of the highest regard, falls pregnant as unexpectedly or unknowingly as the Marquise; a farm servant surprised her in her sleep.

98 For a comparison between Cervantes' and Kleist's novella, see Gerhard Neumann, "Skandalon. Geschlechterrolle und soziale Identität in Kleists 'Marquise von O….' und Cervantes' Novelle 'La fuerza de la sangre,'" in *Heinrich von Kleist. Kriegsfall – Rechtsfall – Sündenfall*, ed. Gerhard Neumann, Wolf Kittler, and Manfred Schneider (Freiburg: Rombach, 1994).

99 DKV III, 414.

100 Claudia Liebrand, "*Pater semper incertus est.* Kleists 'Marquise von O….' mit Boccaccio gelesen," *KJb* (2000): 59.

101 Johann Heinrich Zedler, *Grosses vollständiges Universal-Lexicon aller Wissenschafften und Künste, welche bißhero durch menschlichen Verstand und Witz erfunden und verbessert worden*, vol. 35, 2nd complete photomechanical reproduction of the Leipzig edition of 1743 (Graz: Akad. Druck- & Verlagsanstalt, 1996), 1839. I owe the reference to Zedler and to the ambiguity of the swan, including the subsequent reading, to Soboczynski, *Versuch über Kleist*, 170ff.

102 MO 107f. With this scene Kleist scandalizes the reconciliation scene of father and daughter, which he could have found in Rousseau, by turning it incestuous. See Rousseau, "Julie, or, The New Heloise," 144.

103 See, for example, Albrecht Koschorke, *Die Heilige Familie und ihre Folgen. Ein Versuch* (Frankfurt/M.: Fischer, 2000), 188–202.

104 See, for example, Barbara Vinken and Anselm Haverkamp, "Die zurechtgelegte Frau. Gottesbegehren und transzendentale Familie in Kleists 'Marquise von O….,'" in *Heinrich von Kleist*, ed. Neumann, Kittler, and Schneider.

105 See Kittler, *Die Geburt des Partisanen*.

106 See Alison Lewis, "Der Zwang zum Genießen. Männliche Gewalt und der weibliche Körper in drei Prosatexten Kleists," *KJb* (2000), who follows Slavoj Žižek's analyses of the effects of the collapse of the totalitarian regime in former Yugoslavia.

107 See Walter Müller-Seidel, "Die Struktur des Widerspruchs in Kleists 'Marquise von O....,'" *Deutsche Vierteljahrsschrift für Literaturwissenschaft und Geistesgeschichte* 28 (1954): 510ff.

108 See Dirk Grathoff, "Die Zeichen der Marquise. Das Schweigen, die Sprache und die Schriften," in *Heinrich von Kleist*, ed. Grathoff.

109 MO 93.

110 ADE 19.

111 ADE 125.

IX The Laurels and the Torch

1 DKV IV, 403.

2 ADE 172 (translation modified). Thus writes Kleist in a letter to Ulrike von Kleist of September 17, 1807, after a visit to Friedrich Gentz—he did so prematurely, as his expectation was not fulfilled despite his contacts in Vienna.

3 See the address given in a letter to the publisher George Friedrich Walther of April 5, 1809; DKV IV, 430.

4 Mann, "Kleist and His Stories," 13.

5 DKV IV, 388f., partially translated in ADE 172.

6 See LS 269, 270a.

7 ADE 173.

8 ADE 174f.

9 DKV IV, 391.

10 This is what Müller-Salget, *Heinrich von Kleist*, assumes, and perhaps rightly so.

11 LS 204.

12 LS 173.

13 See LS 257, Müller's letter to Gentz of March 10–14, 1808.

14 See Jürgen Barkhoff, *Magnetische Fiktionen. Literarisierung des Mesmerismus in der Romantik* (Stuttgart: Metzler, 1995), 239–267.

15 For further discussion of the term 'paratext,' see Gérard Genette, *Paratexts: Thresholds of Interpretation*, trans. Jane E. Lewin (Cambridge: Cambridge UP, 2001).

16 LS 205. Regarding the confusion caused by the singular and the conflict between the arts in *Phöbus*, see Ernst Osterkamp, "Das Geschäft der Vereinigung. Über den Zusammenhang von bildender Kunst und Poesie im 'Phöbus,'" *KJb* (1990), whom I gladly follow in his inspiring arguments.

17 See LS 222b, Böttiger's description of the frontispiece in the *Dresden Advertiser* (*Dresdner Anzeiger*) of January 28, 1808.

18 See LS 195.

19 LS 206a.

20 Heinrich von Kleist and Adam H. Müller, eds., *Phöbus. Ein Journal für die Kunst*, afterword and annotations by Helmut Sembdner (Darmstadt: Wiss. Buchgesellschaft, 1961), 5, hereinafter referred to as PH.

21 Kant, *Critique of the Power of Judgment*, 186–188. See chap. VI.

22 PH, 104.

23 Osterkamp, "Das Geschäft der Vereinigung," 64.

24 LS 200b.

25 DKV IV, 399.

26 Thus writes Wieland in a letter to Daniel Falk of April 22, 1808, discovered by and published in Weiss, *Funde und Studien*, 147.
27 LS 223b, 224, partially translated in ADE 179.
28 LS 264b.
29 LS 218c, 228a.
30 DKV IV, 405.
31 On Kleist's miscalculation and Böttiger's information on the print run, see DKV IV, 405. Also see the annotations in ibid., 915.
32 DKV IV, 414f.
33 DKV IV, 429.
34 LS 311.
35 All quotes can be found in LS 271, 273a, 275a, 275b. On the cat motif in *The Schroffenstein Family* (act 2, scene 3), see FS 505.
36 LS 258.
37 LS 200a, Adam Müller in a letter to Johannes von Müller of December 17, 1807.
38 DKV III, 407f.
39 Klaus Müller-Salget, "Auferstehung, Apokalypse, Widerstand: Zur Artikulation des Politischen bei Heinrich von Kleist in den Jahren 1808 bis 1811," in *Literatur ist Widerstand. Aufsätze aus drei Jahrzehnten* (Innsbruck: Universität Innsbruck, 2005), 203.
40 On the conflict between Goethe and Kleist, see the standard work by Katharina Mommsen, *Kleists Kampf mit Goethe*, rev. ed. (Frankfurt/M: Suhrkamp, 1979), as well as the multi-faceted synopsis by Bernd Hamacher, "Goethe," in *Kleist-Handbuch*, ed. Breuer. For the epigrams in *Phöbus*, see Justus Fetscher, "'Horen' – 'Athenäum' – 'Phöbus.' Literaturkritische Spitzenzeitschriften," *Beiträge zur Kleist-Forschung* 21 (2007/08).
41 LS 182a.
42 LS 185.
43 ADE 178f.
44 "Prayer of Manasseh," King James Version, King James Bible Online, accessed January 15, 2021, https://www.kingjamesbibleonline.org/Prayer-of-Manasseh-Chapter-1/.
45 LS 239b.
46 LS 243, 244.
47 LS 245.
48 LS 248a, *Journal for the Elegant World* of March 14, 1808.
49 LS 241.
50 LS 252.
51 ADE 229.
52 DKV III, 412.
53 See the annotations in DKV III, 978.
54 LS 112.
55 See chap. XIII.
56 LS 225a.
57 DKV III, 412–414, 416.
58 ADE 166.
59 ADE 174f.
60 ADE 175.
61 ADE 179.
62 For further discussion on these transgressions in *Penthesilea*, see Gabriele Brandstetter, "'Penthesilea.' 'Das Wort des Greuelrätsels.' Die Überschreitung der Tragödie," in

Interpretationen, ed. Hinderer. It goes without saying that a biography will never be able to reflect the wealth of ideas within the existing scholarship, especially when it comes to *Penthesilea*. It can only give recommendations: besides Gabriele Brandstetter's essay especially the recently published collection of brilliant studies on Penthesilea by Rüdiger Campe, ed., *Penthesileas Versprechen. Exemplarische Studien über die literarische Referenz* (Freiburg: Rombach, 2008).

63 Benjamin Hederich, *Gründliches mythologisches Lexikon* (Leipzig: Gleditsch, 1770; repr., Darmstadt: Wiss. Buchgesellschaft, 1996), 206.

64 FP 164.

65 Hederich, *Gründliches mythologisches Lexikon*, 1940.

66 LS 282.

67 NR 611.

68 FP 260.

69 See, for example, Walter Müller-Seidel, "'Penthesilea' im Kontext der deutschen Klassik," in *Interpretationen*, ed. Hinderer, 161.

70 See the still seminal work by Albin Lesky, *Geschichte der griechischen Literatur* (Bern: Francke, 1963). On the epic, also see Lukács, *The Theory of the Novel.*

71 FP 233 (translation modified).

72 FP 193 (translation modified).

73 FP 239f.

74 FP 268.

75 FP 267.

76 See Mathieu Carrière, *Für eine Literatur des Krieges, Kleist* (Basel: Stroemfeld, 1981), a work that is no less stormy than Kleist's play itself; in its intensity it is still worth reading today, even if its readings are not always accurate.

77 FP 166, 168, 177.

78 FP 161, 164.

79 FP 167, 170f.

80 FP 233.

81 FP 208.

82 FP 216.

83 FP 162f.

84 FP 213 (translation modified).

85 FP 179.

86 FP 248.

87 FP 234.

88 ADE 217.

89 FP 265f. (translation modified).

90 Volker Klotz, "Aug um Zunge – Zunge um Aug. Kleists extremes Theater," *KJb* (1985): 139.

91 FP 165 (translation modified).

92 Maximilian Nutz, "Lektüre der Sinne. Kleists Penthesilea als Körperdrama," in *Heinrich von Kleist*, ed. Grathoff, whose congenial reading I follow down to its phrasings.

93 DKV IV, 407.

94 FP 265f. (translation modified).

95 FP 266 (translation modified).

96 FP 247f.

97 FP 248.

98 FP 89.

99 FP 268.
100 FP 245; ADE 174f.
101 Heinrich von Kleist, *Three Plays. Prince Friedrich von Homburg, The Broken Pitcher, Ordeal by Fire*, trans. Noel Clark (London: Oberon, 2000), 167, hereinafter referred to as TP, followed by the page number.
102 TP 206.
103 TP 227f., 233 (translation modified).
104 TP 233, 235, 238.
105 TP 249.
106 TP 259.
107 ADE 196.
108 See Müller-Salget, *Heinrich von Kleist*, 238f.
109 ADE 181f., Kleist's letter to Heinrich Joseph Collin of December 8, 1808, from Dresden.
110 TP 172.
111 TP 184f.
112 See Chris Cullens and Dorothea von Mücke, "'Das Käthchen von Heilbronn.' 'Ein Kind recht nach der Lust Gottes,'" in *Kleists Dramen*, ed. Hinderer, 122ff.
113 TP 256.
114 FP 234.
115 Christoph Martin Wieland, *Werke*, ed. Heinrich Düntzer, 40 vols. (Berlin: Hempel, 1879–82), 39:435.
116 See Gonthier-Louis Fink, "'Das Käthchen von Heilbronn' 'oder das Weib, wie es seyn sollte.' Ein Rittermärchenspiel," in *Käthchen und seine Schwestern: Frauenfiguren im Drama um 1800. Internationales Kolloquium des Kleist-Archivs Sembdner*, ed. Günther Emig and Anton Philipp Knittel (Heilbronn: Stadtbücherei, 2000), 13ff.
117 For the enormous cultural impact of Castiglione, see Peter Burke, *Die Geschicke des "Hofmann." Zur Wirkung eines Renaissance-Breviers über angemessenes Verhalten* (Berlin: Wagenbach, 1996).
118 Kleist, "How to find the certain Path to Happiness," 262. Also see chap. II.
119 ADE 95.
120 ADE 215, 212. Also see Günter Blamberger, "Ars et Mars. Grazie als Schlüsselbegriff der ästhetischen Erziehung von Aristokraten. Anmerkungen zu Castiglione und Kleist," in *Resonanzen*, ed. Sabine Doering, Waltraud Maierhofer, and Peter Philipp Riedl (Würzburg: Königshausen & Neumann, 2000).
121 On Schubert and Kleist, see the meticulous study by Weder, *Kleists magnetische Poesie*.
122 Thus reads the brilliant essay by Jan-Dirk Müller, "Kleists Mittelalter-Phantasma. Zur Erzählung 'Der Zweikampf' (1811)," *KJb* (1998): 11, 13.
123 Yixu Lü is right to emphasize the agonism of dream and reality in Kleist's *Katie of Heilbronn* in *Kleist-Handbuch*, ed. Breuer, 73. Her reading follows Anthony Stephens, *Kleist – Sprache und Gewalt* (Freiburg: Rombach, 1999), 300.
124 DKV IV, 394, partially translated in ADE 174.
125 LS 316.
126 LS 316, 317.
127 DKV IV, 432, Kleist's letter to Collin of April 20, 1809.
128 See Philipp von Hilgers, "Räume taktischer Kriegsspiele," in *Schlachtfelder. Codierung von Gewalt im medialen Wandel*, ed. Steffen Martus, Marina Münkler, and Werner Röcke (Berlin: Akademie, 2003).
129 LS 317.

130 DKV III, 435.
131 DKV IV, 436f., partially translated in ADE 182f.
132 See LS 332a, 332c, 332d.
133 The document can be found in the National Archives in Prague, PG 1807–1810. 16/100. Quoted in Weiss, *Funde und Studien*, 191.
134 Quoted in DKV II, 1072.
135 LS 313.
136 Thus reads the German title of Maass, *Kleist*.
137 DKV III, 429.
138 Maass, *Kleist*, 180.
139 DKV III, 492f.
140 DKV III, 462.
141 DKV III, 488f.
142 DKV III, 438f.
143 Heinrich von Kleist, *The Battle of Herrmann. A Drama*, trans. Rachel Magshamhráin (Würzburg: Königshausen & Neumann, 2008), 78, hereinafter referred to as BH, followed by the page number.
144 NR 429. The outlined reception history follows DKV II, 1087–1100. The quote about the Dresden performance is found in ibid., 1095.
145 NR 375b.
146 Quoted in DKV II, 1099.
147 Quoted in DKV II, 1100.
148 Heinrich Heine, *The Poems of Heinrich Heine. Complete*, trans. Edgar Alfred Bowring (London: Bell & Sons, 1908), 345–347. For further discussion of the Hermann myth, see the recent study by Martina Wagner-Egelhaaf, ed., *Hermanns Schlachten. Zur Literaturgeschichte eines nationalen Mythos* (Bielefeld: Aisthesis, 2008).
149 Quoted in Richard Samuel, "Kleists 'Herrmannsschlacht' und der Freiherr vom Stein," *Jahrbuch der Deutschen Schillergesellschaft* 5 (1961), 72. For the discovery of the transformation of conspiratorial politics into conspiratorial literature, see (in addition to the worthy study by Samuel) above all Kittler *Die Geburt des Partisanen*.
150 BH 18.
151 See Hans Dieter Loose, *Kleists "Herrmannsschlacht": Kein Krieg für Hermann und seine Cherusker: ein paradoxer Feldzug aus dem Geist der Utopie gegen den Geist besitzbürgerlicher und feudaler Herrschaft* (Karlsruhe: von Loeper, 1984).
152 BH 11 (translation modified).
153 BH 115.
154 For further discussion of the historical and systematic context, see Herfried Münkler, *Der Wandel des Krieges. Von der Symmetrie zur Asymmetrie* (Weilerswist: Velbrück, 2006).
155 William Shakespeare, *Hamlet*, ed. Cyrus Hoy, 2nd ed. (New York: Norton, 1992), 57 (act 3, scene 2).
156 Machiavelli, "The Prince," 1:65. On the Machiavelli references in Kleist, see Blamberger, "Agonalität und Theatralität"; Gesa von Essen, "Römer und Germanen im Spiel der Masken. Heinrich von Kleists 'Herrmannsschlacht,'" *KJb* (1999).
157 BH 21.
158 BH 96.
159 BA 27, October 31, 1810. See Martin Dönike, "'... Durch List und den ganzen Inbegriff jener Künste, die die Notwehr dem Schwachen in die Hände gibt.' Zur Gedankenfigur der Notwehr bei Kleist," *KJb* (1999).

160 Friedrich Nietzsche, *The Gay Science*, trans. Walter Kaufmann (New York: Vintage, 1974), 316 ("On the Problem of the Actor").
161 BH 78.
162 BH 24.
163 BH 106.
164 See Ovid, *Metamorphoses*, trans. A.D. Melville (Oxford: Oxford UP, 1998), 363: "A cub to which a bear has just given birth / Is but a lump, hardly alive, until / His mother licks and forms her little bear / To take the big bear's shape she has herself."
165 See the article "Bär," in *Handwörterbuch des deutschen Aberglaubens*, ed. Hanns Bächtold-Stäubli and Eduard Hoffmann-Krayer, vol. 1 (Berlin: de Gruyter, 1987), 902.
166 ADE 216.
167 See Pliny the Elder, *Natural History. A Selection from Philemon Holland's Translation*, ed. J. Newsome (Oxford: Clarendon, 1964), 278f.
168 See the article "Fechtkunst," in *Allgemeine Encyclopädie der Wissenschaften und Künste*, ed. J.G. Ersch and J.G. Gruber, sec. 1, vol. 24 (repr., Graz: Akad. Druck- & Verlagsanstalt, 1971), 190–206.
169 BH 85.
170 BH 83.
171 BH 90.
172 BH 103.
173 Anthony Stephens, "'Gegen die Tyrannei des Wahren.' Die Sprache in Kleists 'Herrmannsschlacht,'" in *Kleist*, 236, 249.
174 FP 294.
175 The idea of the Prince as Kleist's doppelganger is the key idea of Peter Stein's famous 1972 production of the play at the Theatre on Lehniner Square under the title *Kleist's Dream of Prince Homburg* (*Kleists Traum vom Prinzen Homburg*), with Bruno Ganz in the title role.
176 Gottfried Benn, "Can Poets Change the World?" trans. Joel Agee, in *Prose, Essays, Poems*, ed. Volkmar Sander (New York: Continuum, 1987), 100f.
177 For this context, see Jean Baudrillard, *Symbolic Exchange and Death*, trans. Iain Hamilton Grant (Los Angeles: Sage, 2017).
178 For further information on the life of the historical Prince Frederick of Hesse-Homburg, see Holger T. Gräf, *Landgraf Friedrich II.: Der Prinz von Homburg* (Erfurt: Sutton, 2008).
179 LS 307.
180 Karl Heinrich Krause, *Mein Vaterland unter den hohenzollerischen Regenten. Ein Lesebuch für Freunde der Geschichte*, vol. 2 (Halle: Hemmerde & Schwetschke, 1803). Quoted in DKV II, 1168.
181 DKV II, 1162.
182 All quotes can be found in act 1, FP 271–288.
183 ADE 215.
184 FP 274.
185 FP 298f.
186 FP 350.
187 FP 350.
188 FP 293.
189 FP 348.
190 See Clausewitz, *On War*.
191 NR 360 (Bismarck), 584 (Wilhelm II), 575 (Fontane).
192 ADE, 230. See the astute arguments in Susanne Kaul, *Poetik der Gerechtigkeit. Shakespeare – Kleist* (Munich: Fink, 2008), 198ff., from which I benefit here.

193 ADE 215.
194 See Anthony Stephens, "Zur Funktion der 'Schauspiele' in Kleists Erzählungen," *KJb* (2007).
195 FP 317.
196 On the function of the stage props in Kleist's play, see Dagmar Ottmann, "'Das stumme Zeichen.' Zum dramatischen Requisit in Kleists Prinz Friedrich von Homburg," in *Gewagte Experimente*, ed. Lubkoll and Oesterle.
197 FP 322.
198 FP 331.

X Losing Control

1 ADE 213.
2 For an easily accessible overview of Berlin's history during these years, see Frank Bauer, *Napoleon in Berlin. Preußens Hauptstadt unter französischer Besatzung 1806–1808* (Berlin: Berlin Story, 2006).
3 LS 346 (Brentano), 347 (Arnim).
4 LS 353.
5 ADE 184.
6 DKV IV, 448f., partially translated in ADE 185f.
7 LS 422.
8 The quotes can be found in BA 3, 14; BA 5, 22; BA 6, 26.
9 LS 428.
10 DKV IV, 451.
11 DKV IV, 454.
12 LS 396a.
13 ADE 242.
14 DKV III, 462.
15 DKV IV, 461.
16 DKV IV, 471f.
17 DKV IV, 470f.
18 DKV IV, 474.
19 DKV IV, 476f.
20 DKV IV, 476–481, correspondence between Kleist and Hardenberg from February 26 to April 18, 1811.
21 DKV IV, 490, 487.
22 Cf. Reinhold Steig, *Heinrich von Kleist's Berliner Kämpfe* (Berlin: Spemann, 1901).
23 See Stefan Nienhaus, *Geschichte der deutschen Tischgesellschaft* (Tübingen: Niemeyer, 2003).
24 BA 41, 162, 159f.
25 BA 70, 275.
26 BA 76, 301.
27 ADE 243.
28 DKV III, 573.
29 DKV III, 582f.
30 DKV III, 443.

31 See Jochen Marquardt, "Der mündige Zeitungsleser. Anmerkungen zur Kommunikationsstrategie der 'Berliner Abendblätter,'" *Beiträge zur Kleist-Forschung* (1986). Also see Bernhard J. Dotzler, "'Federkrieg.' Kleist und die Autorschaft des Produzenten," *KJb* (1998), the seminal work by Sibylle Peters, *Heinrich von Kleist und der Gebrauch der Zeit. Von der MachArt der Berliner Abendblätter* (Würzburg: Königshausen & Neumann, 2002), and Borgards, "Experimentelle Aeronautik," from whose inspired works I am unfortunately able to incorporate only a few ideas here.

32 For further discussion of Kleist's fantastical science projects, see chap. III.

33 ADE 186.

34 ADE 188 (translation modified).

35 BA 8, 33f.

36 ADE 267. My reading follows the fine essay by Sibylle Peters, "Wie Geschichte geschehen lassen? Theatralität und Anekdotizität in den Berliner Abendblättern," *KJb* (1999).

37 BA 4, 17.

38 BA 4, 18.

39 Peters, "Wie Geschichte geschehen lassen?" 83.

40 LS 490a.

41 DKV IV, 497f.

42 ADE 198, Kleist's letter to Marie von Kleist written in the first half of October 1811.

43 ADE 201.

XI On the German Michel and *Stimmung*

1 LS 370.

2 See Kleist's letter to his publisher of Mai 1810, DKV IV, 446.

3 See Malte Dießelhorst and Arne Duncker, *Hans Kohlhase. Die Geschichte einer Fehde in Sachsen und Brandenburg zur Zeit der Reformation* (Frankfurt/M.: Lang, 1999).

4 For a competent literary survey, see Bernd Hamacher, "Michael Kohlhaas," in *Kleist-Handbuch*, ed. Breuer.

5 See LS 128.

6 To the best of my knowledge, this discovery was made in a master's thesis by Martin Knackstedt, "Heinrich von Kleist and the Military" (master's thesis, University of Kassel, 1996), whose "proper tone" I, as Knackstedt's former thesis advisor, gratefully "sound" here, thus reading Kleist's scolding of university examiners in "On the Gradual Fabrication of Thoughts While Speaking" against the grain.

7 Freiherr vom Stein, *Briefe und amtliche Schriften*, ed. Erich Botzenhart, Walter Hubatsch, and Peter G. Thielen, 10 vols. (Stuttgart: Kohlhammer, 1957–74), 1:721.

8 See Gerhard Ritter, *Stein. Eine politische Biographie* (Stuttgart: Deutsche Verlags-Anstalt, 1958), 88; Max Lehmann, *Freiherr vom Stein* (Leipzig: Hirzel, 1921), 83ff.

9 MO 134.

10 MO 114f.

11 See Malte Dießelhorst, *Die Prozesse des Müllers Arnold und das Eingreifen Friedrichs des Großen* (Göttingen: Schwartz, 1984).

12 Friedrich von Cölln, *Neue Feuerbrände. Marginalien zu der Schrift: Vertraute Briefe über die inneren Verhältnisse am preußischen Hofe*, vol. 2.5 (Amsterdam: Hammer, 1807), 148.

13 MO 115, 126.

14 MO 138.
15 MO 149, 138.
16 Friedrich von Cölln, *Vertraute Briefe über die inneren Verhältnisse am Preußischen Hofe seit dem Tode Friedrichs II*, 5 vols. (Amsterdam: Hammer, 1807), 2:168f.
17 Cölln, *Vertraute Briefe*, 1:113.
18 Isidore of Seville, *Etymologiae*, quoted in Robert Warrand Carlyle and Alexander James Carlyle, *A History of Medieval Political Theory in the West*, vol. 1, 4th ed. (Edinburgh: Blackwood & Sons, 1950), 221, n. 2.
19 See MO 126 (wine to console Herse), 133 (wine to celebrate the conclusion of the deal). On this traditional way of confirming a contract, see Hartmut Boockmann, "Mittelalterliches Recht bei Kleist. Ein Beitrag zum Verständnis des 'Michael Kohlhaas,'" *KJb* (1985): 88.
20 August Lehmann, ed., *Der Tugendbund* (Berlin: Haude & Spener, 1867), 151.
21 MO 121f.
22 MO 134.
23 Grimm and Grimm, *Deutsches Wörterbuch*, 5:3560.
24 Adelung, *Versuch eines vollständigen grammatisch-kritischen Wörterbuches*, 1336f.
25 MO 114.
26 MO 135.
27 Grimm and Grimm, *Deutsches Wörterbuch*, 5:3560.
28 Adelung, *Versuch eines vollständigen grammatisch-kritischen Wörterbuches*, 1336. For a discussion of the positive and negative connotations of the German Michel, see Bernd Grote, *Der deutsche Michel. Ein Beitrag zur publizistischen Bedeutung der Nationalfiguren* (Dortmund: Ruhfus, 1967); Tomasz Szarota, *Der deutsche Michel. Die Geschichte eines nationalen Symbols und Autostereotyps* (Osnabrück: Fibre, 1998).
29 BA 4, 27, 110.
30 MO 121.
31 MO 131 (emphasis added).
32 Heinrich Philipp Reinhard von Porbeck, "Über militärische Ausbildung," *Neue Bellona oder Beiträge zur Kriegskunst und Kriegsgeschichte* 4, no. 3 (1803): 230.
33 Reizenstein, "Ueber den Einfluß des militärischen Geistes, der Disziplin und Subordination auf stehende Heere," in *Denkwürdigkeiten der militärischen Gesellschaft in Berlin*, vol. 2 (Berlin: Wegener, 1802), 346.
34 MO 144 (translation modified).
35 Kant, *Anthropology from a Pragmatic Point of View*, 371.
36 MO 153. The Latin term *restitutio in integrum* allows not only legal but also theological connotations, which can refer to the "return of the world to its prelapsarian state." See Hamacher, "Michael Kohlhaas," 100.
37 MO 148.
38 MO 143.
39 See D. Franz Volkmar Reinhard, *System der christlichen Moral* (Wittenberg: Zimmermann, 1802), 444. For the history of the term *fanaticism*, see Robert Spaemann, "Fanatisch und Fanatismus," *Archiv für Begriffsgeschichte* 9 (1971).
40 Luther, *D. Martin Luthers Werke*, 7:124f. (no. 2151).
41 MO 151–153.
42 For a discussion of anger, see Thomas Aquinas, *Summa Theologiae*, vol. 21, *Fear and Anger*, trans. by John Patrick Reid (Cambridge: Cambridge UP, 2006).
43 MO 148.
44 MO 185.

45 MO 114.
46 Montaigne, "Of Anger," in *The Complete Essays of Montaigne*, 540.
47 ADE 220.
48 Stein, *Briefe und amtliche Schriften*, 2.1:329f.
49 On the specific concepts of time at the turn of the 19th century, see Reinhart Koselleck, Vergangene Zukunft. Zur Semantik geschichtlicher Zeiten (Frankfurt/M.: Suhrkamp, 1989), 300–376.
50 ADE 183.
51 Cölln, *Vertraute Briefe*, 2:170f.
52 Quoted in Koselleck, *Vergangene Zukunft*, 330.
53 The poem "Shakespeare" can be found in Marin Sorescu, *Hands behind My Back. Selected Poems*, trans. Gabriela Dragnea, Stuart Friebert, and Adriana Varga (Oberlin: Oberlin College Press, 1991), 135f.
54 For a historical-systematic as well as exemplary approach to the notion of *Stimmung*, see Hans Ulrich Gumbrecht, *Atmosphere, Mood, Stimmung. On a Hidden Potential of Literature*, trans. Erik Butler (Stanford: Stanford UP, 2012), who has further fueled the debate about this notion, a debate Gumbrecht himself had initiated. For further discussion of the notion of *Stimmung*, see David E. Wellbery, "Stimmung," in *Ästhetische Grundbegriffe. Historisches Wörterbuch in sieben Bänden*, ed. Karlheinz Barck et al., vol. 5 (Stuttgart: Metzler, 2003); Hans Ulrich Gumbrecht, "Erinnerung an Herkünfte. Stimmungen – ein vernachlässigtes Thema der Literatur," *Frankfurter Allgemeine Zeitung*, November 30, 2005. Much would be gained for future literary studies if its original motive and driving force—the pleasure of reading—were to be understood as a legitimate research goal. One strives to remember this pleasure but later forgets it, at best reviving it when writing a speech for an award ceremony or when writing for the literature and arts section of a newspaper. See Günter Blamberger, "'Let's hear, what you can do!' Notizen zur Zukunft der Literaturwissenschaft," *SPIEL* 16, no. 1/2 (1997).
55 MO 231–233.
56 MO 235.
57 See in particular Hans-Jörg Bay, "'Als die Schwarzen die Weißen ermordeten': Nachbeben einer Erschütterung des europäischen Diskurses in Kleists 'Verlobung in St. Domingo,'" *KJb* (1998). Also see Detering, *Das offene Geheimnis*; Sigrid Weigel, "Der Körper am Kreuzpunkt von Liebesgeschichte und Rassendiskurs in Heinrich von Kleists Erzählung 'Die Verlobung in St. Domingo,'" *KJb* (1991); Gerhard Neumann, "'Die Verlobung in St. Domingo.' Zum Problem literarischer Mimesis im Werk Heinrich von Kleists," in *Gewagte Experimente*, ed. Lubkoll and Oesterle.
58 MO 243, 247.
59 MO 242.
60 E.T.A. Hoffmann, *Tales of E.T.A Hoffmann*, ed. and trans. Leonard J. Kent and Elizabeth C. Knight (Chicago: U of Chicago P, 1972), 177, 179f.
61 DKV IV, 313.
62 MO 247.
63 See MO 232.
64 ADE 61.
65 MO 214–216 (translation modified).
66 MO 214f.
67 Kleist just as easily does the opposite. One only needs to think of the Marquise of O—, who ends up marrying her rapist.

68 For a systematic literary survey, see Christian Moser, "Das Bettelweib von Locarno," in *Kleist-Handbuch*, ed. Breuer.

69 MO 214.

70 MO 221.

71 MO 220.

72 MO 218f.

73 MO 227f. For a competent literary survey, see Christine Lubkoll, "Die heilige Cäcilie oder die Gewalt der Musik," in *Kleist-Handbuch*, ed. Breuer. Also see Christine Lubkoll, *Mythos Musik. Poetische Entwürfe des Musikalischen in der Literatur um 1800* (Freiburg: Rombach, 1995).

74 The emphasis lies on the *same* tonal position. The technique of enharmonics has been known in different variations since Classical Antiquity. See Mark Lindley, "Stimmung und Temperatur," in *Geschichte der Musiktheorie*, ed. Frieder Zaminer, vol. 6, *Hören, Messen und Rechnen in der frühen Neuzeit* (Darmstadt: Wiss. Buchgesellschaft, 1987).

75 MO 225 (translation modified).

76 ADE 231f. Kleist's essay is an adaptation of a text by Clemens Brentano and Achim von Arnim. I will not go into the details of the differences here. For a discussion of Kleist's reflections on paintings in general, see Müller, *Kleist und die bildende Kunst.*

77 MO 287 (translation modified).

78 MO 308.

79 MO 320.

80 In a brilliant essay on "The Duel," to which I owe many inspirations, Gerhard Neumann calls this delaying of pace a "narrative of interruption." See Gerhard Neumann, "'Der Zweikampf.' Kleists 'einrückendes' Erzählen," in *Kleists Erzählungen*, ed. Hinderer. Two other equally brilliant essays ought to be recommended for further reading: Müller, "Kleists Mittelalter-Phantasma"; Roland Reuß, "'Mit gebrochenen Worten.' Zu Kleists Erzählung 'Der Zweikampf,'" *Brandenburger Kleist-Blätter* 7 (1994).

81 ADE 217.

XII Economy and Aneconomy of Sacrifice

1 Franz Kafka, *The Diaries of Franz Kafka, 1914–1923*, ed. Max Brod, trans. Martin Greenberg, with the co-operation of Hannah Arendt (New York: Schocken, 1968), 102.

2 MO 285.

3 MO 67.

4 See Günter Blamberger, "Der Tod nach dem Tode Gottes. Über die Lust am Spiel mit der Tradition thanatologischer Phantasmen in der Literatur der Jahrhundertwende," in *Das Imaginäre des Fin de siècle. Ein Symposion für Gerhard Neumann*, ed. Christine Lubkoll (Freiburg: Rombach, 2002).

5 Franz Kafka, *Letters to Friends, Family, and Editors*, trans. Richard and Clara Winston (London: Calder, 1978), 334.

6 For further discussion, see Günter Blamberger, "Ökonomie des Opfers. Kleists Todes-Briefe," in *Adressat: Nachwelt. Briefkultur und Ruhmbildung*, ed. Detlev Schöttker (Munich: Fink, 2008); Günter Blamberger, "Freitod am Wannsee. Heinrich von Kleist und Henriette Vogel 1811," in *Ökonomie des Opfers. Literatur im Zeichen des Suizids*, ed. Günter Blamberger and Sebastian Goth (Munich: Fink, 2013).

7 LS 532.
8 DKV IV, 513f.
9 Karin Reschke, *Verfolgte des Glücks. Das Findebuch der Henriette Vogel* (Berlin: Rotbuch, 1982).
10 LS 522.
11 LS 523a.
12 LS 523b.
13 LS 523c.
14 LS 532d, 532e.
15 LS 524.
16 LS 528.
17 DKV IV, 514f.
18 LS 537.
19 LS 533.
20 LS 535b.
21 NR 40.
22 LS 540.
23 LS 541.
24 LS 542.
25 Georg Minde-Pouet, *Kleists letzte Stunden. Teil I: Das Akten-Material* (Berlin: Weidmann, 1925), 11, 48–50, partially translated in ADE 208.
26 On the concept of melancholia of 18th-century philosophical doctors, see the standard work by Hans-Jürgen Schings, *Melancholie und Aufklärung. Melancholiker und ihre Kritiker in Erfahrungsseelenkunde und Literatur des 18. Jahrhunderts* (Stuttgart: Metzler, 1977).
27 ADE 201.
28 All quotes from Kleist's letter to Marie can be found in ADE 201–203.
29 ADE 115.
30 ADE 204.
31 DKV IV, 512.
32 BKA II/8, 190. On the question of whether Kleist or Friedrich Gottlob Wetzel authored the essay, see chap. III, n. 34
33 Thus reads the apt expression by László F. Földényi in Günter Blamberger et al., "'Kleists letzte Inszenierung.' Podiumsdiskussion in der Akademie der Künste in Berlin, 12.10.2000," *KJb* (2001): 250.
34 ADE 203 (translation modified), 205.
35 ADE 204.
36 The German "m Werthester" could also be understood as referring to the protagonist of Goethe's *The Sorrows of Young Werther*, in the sense of "my most Werther of Werthers"—Trans.
37 DKV IV, 519f.
38 TP 184 (translation modified).
39 For further discussion of these questions, which are also central to Kleist's *Katie of Heilbronn*, see in particular Neumann, "Hexenküche und Abendmahl."
40 Quoted in a lucid study by Holger Helbig that meticulously traces the reception history of the "Death Litany": Holger Helbig, "Herr von Kleist und Frau Vogel beschließen ihren Tod und verwirren die Wissenschaft. Der Briefwechsel zwischen Heinrich von Kleist und Henriette Vogel als philologische Grenzsituation," in *Grenzsituation. Wahrnehmung,*

Bedeutung und Gestaltung in der neueren Literatur, ed. Dorothea Lauterbach, Uwe Spörl, and Uli Wunderlich (Göttingen: Vandenhoeck & Ruprecht, 2002).

41 Grimm and Grimm, *Deutsches Wörterbuch*, 12:1071.

42 On the specifically Modern character of lists, see Sabine Mainberger, *Die Kunst der Aufzählung. Elemente zu einer Poetik des Enumerativen* (Berlin: de Gruyter, 2002).

43 Georg Rodolf Weckherlin, "On the Early Death of Anna Augusta, Margravine of Baden," in *Sing for the Taxman*, trans. Sheenagh Pugh (Bridgend: Seren, 1993), 59f.

44 Jorge Luis Borges, "The Analytical Language of John Wilkins," in *Other Inquisitions. 1937–1952*, trans. Ruth L.C. Simms (Austin: U of Texas P, 1975), 103. As is well known, Michel Foucault's *The Order of Things. An Archaeology of the Human Sciences* (New York: Random, 1970) first arose out of the "wonderment of this taxonomy" (ibid., XV).

45 Grimm and Grimm, *Deutsches Wörterbuch*, 12:1069.

XIII "Only Whatever Does Not Cease *to Hurt* Stays in the Memory"

1 FP 316.

2 Friedrich Klopstock, *Odes of Klopstock. From 1747 to 1780*, trans. William Nind (London: Pickering, 1848), 71.

3 According to Peguilhen, the pages were "particularly opened" to the poems "Clarissa Dead" and "The Graves of Rothschild" (NR 39).

4 Franz Kafka, "The Eight Octavo Notebooks," in *Dearest Father. Stories and Reflections*, trans. Ernst Kaiser and Eithne Wilkins (New York: Schocken, 1954), 69f.

5 My reading follows the brilliant interpretation by Frank Schirrmacher, *Verteidigung der Schrift. Kafkas "Prozeß"* (Frankfurt/M.: Suhrkamp, 1987), 138ff.

6 ADE 205, Kleist's letter to Ulrike of November 21, 1811.

7 Arthur Schopenhauer, *Parerga and Paralipomena. Short Philosophical Essays*, trans. Sabine Roehr and Christopher Janaway, vol. 1 (Cambridge: Cambridge UP, 2014), 342.

8 Nietzsche, *On the Genealogy of Morality*, 249f.

9 For further details on the history of the editions of Kleist's letters, see DKV IV, 1159–1163.

10 ADE 208.

11 NR 24 (Weisser), 33.

12 NR 274. Goethe's judgment is found in the context of his 1833 review of Ludwig Tieck's *Dramaturgical Pages* (*Dramaturgische Blätter*) of 1826.

13 Cf. the thesis about two Kleist renaissances in the otherwise highly regarded study by Lütteken, *Heinrich von Kleist*, 151. For further details on the reception of Kleist in the 19th century, see Walter Müller-Seidel, "Kleists 'Hypochondrie.' Zu seinem Verständnis in klassischer und moderner Ästhetik," in *Texte, Motive und Gestalten der Goethezeit. Festschrift für Hans Reiss*, ed. John L. Hibberd and H.B. Nisbet (Tübingen: Niemeyer, 1989).

14 On Becher's fantasies and acts of self-creation, see the "Jahresbericht des Münchner Wilhelmsgymnasiums 1984/85," in which Rolf Selbmann published the school files from 1910, including Becher's farewell letters. Also see Michael Rohrwasser, *Der Weg nach oben. Johannes R. Becher. Politiken des Schreibens* (Basel: Stroemfeld, 1980).

15 Quoted from Helmut Sembdner, ed., *Kleist in der Dichtung*, 2nd ed. (Frankfurt/M.: Insel, 1985), 47.

16 Quoted from Sembdner, ed., *Kleist in der Dichtung*, 23.

17 Quoted from Peter Goldammer, ed., *Schriftsteller über Kleist* (Berlin: Aufbau, 1976), 120.

18 NR 415. The call appeared in *The Literary Echo* (*Das literarische Echo*) on December 1, 1911, in Berlin.
19 NR 400.
20 NR 399a.
21 Quoted from Goldammer, ed., *Schriftsteller über Kleist*, 117f.
22 Quoted from Goldammer, ed., *Schriftsteller über Kleist*, 116, 148.
23 Quoted from Goldammer, ed., *Schriftsteller über Kleist*, 118.
24 See Julius Hart, *Das Kleist-Buch* (Berlin: Borntraeger, 1912).
25 NR 623b.
26 Wilhelm Herzog, *Heinrich von Kleist. Sein Leben und sein Werk* (Munich: Beck, 1911), 155.
27 Quoted from Goldammer, ed., *Schriftsteller über Kleist*, 122f.
28 Quoted from Goldammer, ed., *Schriftsteller über Kleist*, 216.
29 Quoted from Goldammer, ed., *Schriftsteller über Kleist*, 213, 221, 223.
30 Thomas Mann, *Reflections of a Nonpolitical Man*, trans. Walter D. Morris (New York: Ungar, 1987), 110f.
31 See NR 441.
32 Georg Minde-Pouet, "Die Kleist-Gesellschaft," quoted in Rolf Busch, *Imperialistische und faschistische Kleist-Rezeption 1890–1945. Eine ideologiekritische Untersuchung* (Frankfurt/M.: Akad. Verlagsgesellschaft, 1974), 11. On Minde-Pouet's position, which does not necessarily speak for the Kleist Society as a whole, see Hans Joachim Kreutzer, "'… der erste nationalsozialistische Dichter der Vergangenheit ….' Georg Minde-Pouets Krisenbericht von 1936," *KJb* (1992). On the reception of Kleist during the Third Reich, see Claudia Albert, ed., *Deutsche Klassiker im Nationalsozialismus: Schiller, Kleist, Hölderlin* (Stuttgart: Metzler, 1994). Also see more recently Martin Maurach, *"Betrachtungen über den Weltlauf." Kleist 1933–1945. Ausstellungsbegleitbuch* (Berlin: Theater der Zeit, 2008); Martin Maurach, ed., *Kleist im Nationalsozialismus. Themenband der Beiträge zur Kleist-Forschung 19* (Würzburg: Königshausen & Neumann, 2007).
33 The quotation can be found in an expert opinion on Gunther Haupt's Kleist biography *Der Empörer*. The opinion was written at Heinrich Himmler's request and is reproduced in Joseph Wulf, *Literatur und Dichtung im Dritten Reich. Eine Dokumentation* (Reinbek: Rowohlt, 1966), 397.
34 On the history of the Kleist Prize, see Hans Joachim Kreutzer, "Der Kleist-Preis 1912–1932–1985," *KJb* (1986).
35 NR 484.
36 Lion Feuchtwanger, *The Oppermanns*, trans. James Cleugh (New York: Viking, 1934), 236.
37 NR 687a. Also see Siegfried Mews, "Brechts 'dialektisches Verhältnis zur Tradition.' Die Bearbeitung des 'Michael Kohlhaas,'" *Brecht-Jahrbuch* (1975).
38 Bertolt Brecht, "On Kleist's Play 'The Prince of Homburg,'" trans. Timothy Adès, *Translation and Literature* 15, no. 2 (2006): 237.
39 Quoted from Sembdner, ed., *Kleist in der Dichtung*, 132.
40 Quoted from Goldammer, ed., *Schriftsteller über Kleist*, 290 (Seghers), 293 (Lukács).
41 In 1937 Alfred Kurella, under the pseudonym Bernhard Ziegler, renounced his Expressionist past in the exile journal *The Word* (*Das Wort*). The article is reproduced as "Nun ist dies Erbe zuende," in *Die Expressionismusdebatte. Materialien zu einer marxistischen Realismuskonzeption*, ed. Hans-Jürgen Schmitt (Frankfurt/M.: Suhrkamp, 1973). Johannes R. Becher betrays his own past in his sentimental entry about his Moscow exile of January 29, 1950, see Johannes R. Becher, *Auf andere Art so große Hoffnung. Tagebuch 1950. Mit Eintragungen 1951* (Berlin: Aufbau, 1952).

42 Ernst Bloch, "Discussing Expressionism," in *Aesthetics and Politics. The Key Texts of the Classical Debate within German Marxism*, ed. and trans. Ronald Taylor (London: Verso, 2002), 22.

43 See Theo Honnef, *Heinrich von Kleist in der Literatur der DDR* (New York: Lang, 1988); Bernd Leistner, "Kleist in der neueren DDR-Literatur," in *Heinrich von Kleist*, ed. Grathoff.

44 Heiner Müller, *Hamletmachine and Other Texts for the Stage*, ed. and trans. Carl Weber (New York: Performing Arts Journal Publications, 1982), 76.

45 For further details on stage productions and film adaptations of Kleist after 1968, see Klaus Kanzog, ed., *Erzählstrukturen – Filmstrukturen. Erzählungen Heinrich von Kleists und ihre filmische Realisation* (Berlin: Schmidt, 1981); Klaus Kanzog, "Vom rechten zum linken Mythos. Ein Paradigmenwechsel der Kleist-Rezeption," in *Heinrich von Kleist*, ed. Grathoff. Also see Rolf Bäumer and Peter Seibert, "Kleists Theatertexte als Medienereignis der 80er Jahre. Bühne, Film und Bildschirm oder Paradoxien der Transformation bei Neuenfels, Syberberg u.a.," *Zeitschrift für Literaturwissenschaft und Linguistik* 21 (1991); William C. Reeve, *Kleist on Stage. 1804–1987* (Montreal: McGill-Queen's UP, 1993).

46 ADE 201.

47 Mann, "Kleist and His Stories," 5f. (translation modified), 13.

48 Cf. Gunter Reiss, "Sündenfall-Modell und Romanform. Zur Integration von Kleists Marionettentheater-Thematik im Werk Thomas Manns," *Jahrbuch der Deutschen Schillergesellschaft* 13 (1969): 427, 435, who argues that Kleist's "On the Puppet Theater" is for Mann as well as for post-war authors—such as Heinrich Böll and his novel *The Clown*—an "aesthetic *in nuce*," and that the essay, in its reference to the fall of man, points to "the center of the problem of art" in *Doctor Faustus*: As a contemplative artist, Reiss notes, Adrian Leverkühn finds himself in a state of affectation, so to speak. By contrast, Echo, the boy he loves, appears as a symbol of pure grace. I, by contrast, read Mann's Kleist reference in a different way: as an ironic self-distancing of Mann from his patriotic Kleist reception in *Reflections of a Nonpolitical Man*. Serenus Zeitblom notices the Kleist essay on Leverkühn's desk the very moment he is saying goodbye to him and leaving for the war. During his parting dialogue with Leverkühn, he declares the swift military "break-through to world power" as a way out of the loneliness of the Germans and their boundedness to reflection—as a "break-through to the world," a "thirst for unification." He then seamlessly identifies this "[c]raving to break through" with an aesthetic longing—with the overcoming of the artist's 'includence' in subjectivity, as Leverkühn outlined to him by way of Kleist's essay. Leverkühn initially responds "with a half-laugh," finally giving his friend Zeitblom a look he "carried with [him] to war—perhaps it was that, and not the typhus infection from lice, which brought me home so soon, back to his side." Thomas Mann, *Doctor Faustus. The Life of the German Composer Adrian Leverkühn as Told by a Friend*, trans. H.T. Lowe-Porter (New York: Vintage, 1992), 306–309.

49 See Friedrich Gundolf, *Heinrich von Kleist* (Berlin: Bondi, 1922).

50 See the title of a collection of essays on what has become the intellectual signature of Postmodernism: Hans Ulrich Gumbrecht and K. Ludwig Pfeiffer, eds., *Paradoxien, Dissonanzen, Zusammenbrüche. Situationen offener Epistemologie* (Frankfurt/M.: Suhrkamp, 1991).

51 See the *Kleist-Jahrbuch* of 2007 (Kehlmann), 2013 (Kermani), 2015 (Beyer), 2016 (Rinck), 2017 (Tawada), and 2019 (Ransmayr).

52 The events of the bicentennial celebration of Kleist's death are documented in *KJb* (2011) and *KJb* (2012) as well as in the comprehensive catalog of the 2011 double exhibition in

Berlin and Frankfurt an der Oder. See Günter Blamberger and Stefan Iglhaut, eds., *Kleist. Krise und Experiment* (Bielefeld: Kerber, 2011).

53 Genazino, "Die Flucht in die Ohnmacht," 21.

54 FP 268.

XIV On Kleist's Fascination with Risk

1 It was a student in one of my Kleist courses at the University of Cologne who drew my attention to this phrase: Andreas Rosenfelder, who today is editor of the literature and arts section of the newspaper *The World* (*Die Welt*).

2 Baldesar Castiglione, *The Book of the Courtier*, trans. Charles S. Singleton (New York: Anchor Books, 1959), 33.

3 ADE 212.

4 See Blamberger, "Agonalität und Theatralität."

5 Kleist, "How to find the certain Path to Happiness," 265.

6 Gracián, *The Art of Worldly Wisdom*, no. 48.

7 ADE 218.

8 Gracián, *The Art of Worldly Wisdom*, no. 132.

9 ADE 218f. (translation modified).

10 Baltasar Gracián, *Handorakel und Kunst der Weltklugheit*, ed. Arthur Hübscher, trans. Arthur Schopenhauer (Stuttgart: Reclam, 1992), no. 56.

11 Gracián, *The Art of Worldly Wisdom*, no. 57 (translation modified).

12 ADE 217.

13 See Kittler, *Die Geburt des Partisanen*.

14 Helmuth Plessner, *Die Stufen des Organischen und der Mensch: Einleitung in die philosophische Anthropologie*, 3rd ed. (Berlin: de Gruyter, 1975).

15 ADE 222.

16 ADE 223.

17 ADE 217.

18 Kant, *Critique of the Power of Judgment*, 186f.

19 ADE 216.

20 ADE 269.

21 Johann Christoph Friedrich GutsMuths, *Gymnastics for Youth: Or a Practical Guide to Healthful and Amusing Exercises for the Use of Schools*, trans. C.G. Salzmann (London: Johnston, 1800), 185.

22 See Hans Ulrich Gumbrecht, *In Praise of Athletic Beauty* (Cambridge, MA: Belknap, 2006).

23 See Roussel, "Zerstreuungen," to whom I owe the discovery of this figure of thought in Kleist.

Works Cited

Abbreviations

ADE Kleist, Heinrich von. *An Abyss Deep Enough: Letters of Heinrich von Kleist, with a Selection of Essays and Anecdotes*. Edited, translated, and introduced by Philip B. Miller. New York: Dutton, 1982.

BA Kleist, Heinrich von, ed. *Berliner Abendblätter*. 1810f.

BH Kleist, Heinrich von. *The Battle of Herrmann. A Drama*. Translated by Rachel Magshamhráin. Würzburg: Königshausen & Neumann, 2008.

BKA Kleist, Heinrich von. *Sämtliche Werke. Brandenburger [1988–91: Berliner] Ausgabe*. Edited by Roland Reuß and Peter Staengle. Basel: Stroemfeld, 1988–2010.

DKV Kleist, Heinrich von. *Sämtliche Werke und Briefe*. Edited by Ilse-Marie Barth, Klaus Müller-Salget, Stefan Ormanns, and Hinrich C. Seeba. 4 vols. Frankfurt/M.: Deutscher Klassiker Verlag, 1987–97.

KJB *Kleist-Jahrbuch*. Edited by Andrea Allerkamp, Andrea Bartl, Anne Fleig, Barbara Gribnitz, Hannah Lotte Lund, and Martin Roussel. Stuttgart: Metzler, 1992ff.

LS Sembdner, Helmut, ed. *Heinrich von Kleists Lebensspuren. Dokumente und Berichte der Zeitgenossen*. Frankfurt/M.: Insel, 1984.

MO Kleist, Heinrich von. *The Marquise of O— and Other Stories*. Translated with an introduction by David Luke and Nigel Reeves. London: Penguin, 1978.

NR Sembdner, Helmut, ed. *Heinrich von Kleists Nachruhm. Eine Wirkungsgeschichte in Dokumenten*. Frankfurt/M.: Insel, 1984.

FP Kleist, Heinrich von. *Five Plays*. Translated with an introduction by Martin Greenberg. New Haven: Yale UP, 1988.

FS Kleist, Heinrich von. *The Feud of the Schroffensteins*. Translated by Mary J. Price and Lawrence M. Price. *Poet Lore* 27, no. 5 (1916): 457–576.

PH Kleist, Heinrich von, and Adam H. Müller, eds. *Phöbus. Ein Journal für die Kunst*. Afterword and annotations by Helmut Sembdner. Darmstadt: Wiss. Buchgesellschaft, 1961.

TP Kleist, Heinrich von. *Three Plays. Prince Friedrich von Homburg, The Broken Pitcher, Ordeal by Fire*. Translated by Noel Clark. London: Oberon, 2000.

Kleist's Works and Primary Sources

Kleist, Heinrich von. *An Abyss Deep Enough: Letters of Heinrich von Kleist, with a Selection of Essays and Anecdotes*. Edited, translated, and introduced by Philip B. Miller. New York: Dutton, 1982.

—. *The Battle of Herrmann. A Drama*. Translated by Rachel Magshamhráin. Würzburg: Königshausen & Neumann, 2008.

—, ed. *Berliner Abendblätter*. 1810f.

—. "'Essay: How to find the certain Path to Happiness and—even amid Life's greatest Tribulations—enjoy the Journey undeterred!'" Translated by Jeffrey L. High. *KJb* (2018): 260–269.

—. *The Feud of the Schroffensteins*. Translated by Mary J. Price and Lawrence M. Price. *Poet Lore* 27, no. 5 (1916): 457–576.

—. *Five Plays*. Translated with an introduction by Martin Greenberg. New Haven: Yale UP, 1988.

—. *Heinrich von Kleists hinterlassene Schriften*. Edited by Ludwig Tieck. Berlin: Reimer, 1821.

—. *Sämtliche Werke. Brandenburger [1988–91: Berliner] Ausgabe*. Edited by Roland Reuß and Peter Staengle. Basel: Stroemfeld, 1988–2010.

—. *Sämtliche Werke und Briefe*. Edited by Ilse-Marie Barth, Klaus Müller-Salget, Stefan Ormanns, and Hinrich C. Seeba. 4 vols. Frankfurt/M.: Deutscher Klassiker Verlag 1987–97.

—. *The Marquise of O— and Other Stories*. Translated with an introduction by David Luke and Nigel Reeves. London: Penguin, 1978.

—. *Three Plays. Prince Friedrich von Homburg, The Broken Pitcher, Ordeal by Fire*. Translated by Noel Clark. London: Oberon, 2000.

—, and Adam H. Müller, eds. *Phöbus. Ein Journal für die Kunst*. Afterword and annotations by Helmut Sembdner. Darmstadt: Wiss. Buchgesellschaft, 1961.

Kratz, Gustav, ed. *Geschichte des Geschlechts von Kleist*. 4 vols. Berlin: Schindler, 1862–87.

Sembdner, Helmut, ed. *Heinrich von Kleist. Der Dichter über sein Werk*. 2nd ed. Darmstadt: Wiss. Buchgesellschaft, 1996.

—, ed. *Heinrich von Kleists Lebensspuren. Dokumente und Berichte der Zeitgenossen*. Frankfurt/M.: Insel, 1984.

—, ed. *Heinrich von Kleists Nachruhm. Eine Wirkungsgeschichte in Dokumenten*. Frankfurt/M.: Insel, 1984.

Other Works

Adelung, Johann Christoph. *Versuch eines vollständigen grammatisch-kritischen Wörterbuches der Hochdeutschen Mundart, mit beständiger Vergleichung der übrigen Mundarten, besonders aber der oberdeutschen*. Vol. 1. Leipzig: Breitkopf, 1774.

Albert, Claudia, ed. *Deutsche Klassiker im Nationalsozialismus: Schiller, Kleist, Hölderlin*. Stuttgart: Metzler, 1994.

Allgemeines Landrecht für die Preußischen Staaten von 1794. Text edition, with an introduction by Hans Hattenhauer and a bibliography by Günther Bernert. Frankfurt/M.: Metzner, 1970.

Alt, Peter-André. "Mode ohne Methode? Überlegungen zu einer Theorie der literaturwissenschaftlichen Biographik." In *Grundlagen der Biographik. Theorie und Praxis des biographischen Schreibens*. Edited by Christian Klein, Stuttgart: Metzler, 2002. 22–39.

Aquinas, Thomas. *Summa Theologiae*. Vol. 21, *Fear and Anger*. Translated by John Patrick Reid. Cambridge: Cambridge UP, 2006.

Ariès, Philippe. *Centuries of Childhood. A Social History of Family Life*. Translated by Robert Baldick. New York: Vintage Books, 1962.

Aristotle. *Nicomachean Ethics*. Edited and translated by Roger Crisp. Rev. ed. Cambridge: Cambridge UP, 2014.

—. *Poetics*. Translated by Stephen Halliwell. Chapel Hill: The U of North Carolina P, 1987.

Arntzen, Helmut. *Die ernste Komödie. Das deutsche Lustspiel von Lessing bis Kleist*. Munich: Nymphenburger, 1968.

Assmann, Aleida, and Jan Assmann. "Zur Einführung." In *Schleier und Schwelle*. Edited by Aleida Assmann and Jan Assmann. Vol. 1, *Geheimnis und Öffentlichkeit. Archäologie der literarischen Kommunikation V,1*. Munich: Fink, 1998. 7–16.

Bächtold-Stäubli, Hanns, and Eduard Hoffmann-Krayer, eds. *Handwörterbuch des deutschen Aberglaubens*. Vol. 1. Berlin: de Gruyter, 1987.

Bäumer, Rolf, and Peter Seibert. "Kleists Theatertexte als Medienereignis der 80er Jahre. Bühne, Film und Bildschirm oder Paradoxien der Transformation bei Neuenfels, Syberberg u.a." *Zeitschrift für Literaturwissenschaft und Linguistik* 21 (1991): 89–104.

Barkhoff, Jürgen. *Magnetische Fiktionen. Literarisierung des Mesmerismus in der Romantik*. Stuttgart: Metzler, 1995.

Barthel, Wolfgang, ed. *Heinrich von Kleist 1777–1811. Chronik seines Lebens und Schaffens auf Grund von Selbstaussagen, Dokumenten und Aussagen Dritter*. Frankfurt/O.: Kleist-Gedenk- und Forschungsstätte, 2001.

Barthel, Wolfgang, Hans Jochen Marquardt, and Barbara Wilk-Mincu, eds. *Heinrich von Kleist (1777–1811). Leben – Werk – Wirkung. Blickpunkte. Katalog der Dauerausstellung des Kleist-Museums*. Frankfurt/O.: Kleist-Gedenk- und Forschungsstätte, 2000.

Barthes, Roland. *A Lover's Discourse: Fragments.* Translated by Richard Howard. New York: Hill & Wan, 1978.

Baudrillard, Jean. *Symbolic Exchange and Death.* Translated by Iain Hamilton Grant. Los Angeles: Sage, 2017.

Bauer, Frank. *Napoleon in Berlin. Preußens Hauptstadt unter französischer Besatzung 1806–1808.* Berlin: Berlin Story, 2006.

Baumgart, Wolf. "Die preußische Armee zur Zeit Heinrich von Kleists." *KJb* (1983): 43–70.

Bay, Hans-Jörg. "'Als die Schwarzen die Weißen ermordeten': Nachbeben einer Erschütterung des europäischen Diskurses in Kleists 'Verlobung in St. Domingo.'" *KJb* (1998): 80–108.

Becher, Johannes R. *Auf andere Art so große Hoffnung. Tagebuch 1950. Mit Eintragungen 1951.* Berlin: Aufbau, 1952.

Benjamin, Walter. "The Destructive Character." Translated by Edmund Jephcott. In *Selected Writings.* Edited by Michael W. Jennings. Vol. 2, *1927–1934.* Cambridge, MA: Belknap, 1999. 541f.

—. "German Men and Women." Translated by Edmund Jephcott. In *Selected Writings.* Edited by Michael W. Jennings. Vol. 3, *1935–1938.* Cambridge, MA: Belknap, 2006. 167–235.

—. "One-Way Street." Translated by Edmund Jephcott. In *Selected Writings.* Edited by Michael W. Jennings. Vol. 1, *1913–1926.* Cambridge, MA: Belknap, 1999. 444–488.

—. "The Storyteller. Observations on the Works of Nikolai Leskov." Translated by Harry Zohn. In *Selected Writings.* Edited by Michael W. Jennings. Vol. 3, *1935–1938.* Cambridge, MA: Belknap, 2002. 143–166.

Benn, Gottfried. "Can Poets Change the World?" Translated by Joel Agee. In *Prose, Essays, Poems.* Edited by Volkmar Sander. New York: Continuum, 1987. 99–106.

Binswanger, Ludwig. *Melancholie und Manie. Phänomenologische Studien.* Pfullingen: Neske, 1960.

Bisky, Jens. *Kleist. Eine Biographie.* Berlin: Rowohlt, 2007.

Blamberger, Günter. "Agonalität und Theatralität. Kleists Gedankenfigur des Duells im Kontext der europäischen Moralistik." *KJb* (1999): 25–40.

—. "Antiparastatische Genies. Politiken des Privaten in Kleists Essays." In *Politics in Literature. Studies on a Germanic Preoccupation from Kleist to Améry.* Edited by Rüdiger Görner. Munich: Iudicium, 2004. 25–39.

—. "Ars et Mars. Grazie als Schlüsselbegriff der ästhetischen Erziehung von Aristokraten. Anmerkungen zu Castiglione und Kleist." In *Resonanzen.* Edited by Sabine Doering, Waltraud Maierhofer, and Peter Philipp Riedl. Würzburg: Königshausen & Neumann, 2000. 273–281.

—. *Das Geheimnis des Schöpferischen, oder: Ingenium est ineffabile? Studien zur Literaturgeschichte der Kreativität zwischen Goethezeit und Moderne.* Stuttgart: Metzler, 1991.

—. "Der Tod nach dem Tode Gottes. Über die Lust am Spiel mit der Tradition thanatologischer Phantasmen in der Literatur der Jahrhundertwende." In *Das Imaginäre des Fin de siècle. Ein Symposion für Gerhard Neumann.* Edited by Christine Lubkoll. Freiburg: Rombach, 2002. 299–312.

—. "Die Novelle als Anti-Bildungsgeschichte. Anmerkungen zu Kleists 'Der Findling.'" In *Prägnanter Moment. Studien zur deutschen Literatur der Aufklärung und Klassik. Fs. für Hans-Jürgen Schings.* Edited by Peter-André Alt, Alexander Košenina, Hartmut Reinhardt, and Wolfgang Riedel. Würzburg: Königshausen & Neumann, 2002. 479–494.

—. "'Ein anderer ist nun der wirkliche Anfang.' Die Weltreisenden Peter Schlemihl und Adelbert von Chamisso." In *Hermenautik – Hermeneutik. Literarische und geisteswissenschaftliche Beiträge zu Ehren von Peter Horst Neumann.* Edited by Holger Helbig, Bettina Knauer, and Gunar Och. Würzburg: Königshausen & Neumann, 1996. 109–117.

—. "Freitod am Wannsee. Heinrich von Kleist und Henriette Vogel 1811." In *Ökonomie des Opfers. Literatur im Zeichen des Suizids.* Edited by Günter Blamberger and Sebastian Goth. Munich: Fink, 2013. 219–234.

—. "'Let's hear, what you can do!' Notizen zur Zukunft der Literaturwissenschaft." *SPIEL* 16, no. 1/2 (1997): 53–58.

—. "'Nur was nicht aufhört, weh zu thun, bleibt im Gedächtnis.' Zur Typogenese des Kleist-Bildes in der deutschen Literatur der Moderne." *KJb* (1995): 25–43.

—. "Ökonomie des Opfers. Kleists Todes-Briefe." In *Adressat: Nachwelt. Briefkultur und Ruhmbildung.* Edited by Detlev Schöttker. Munich: Fink, 2008. 145–160.

—, and Stefan Iglhaut, eds. *Kleist. Krise und Experiment.* Bielefeld: Kerber, 2011.

—, László Földényi, Joachim Pfeiffer, Eva S. Poluda, Alexander Weigel, and Gisela Stelly. "'Kleists letzte Inszenierung.' Podiumsdiskussion in der Akademie der Künste in Berlin, 12.10.2000." *KJb* (2001): 245–264.

Bloch, Ernst. "Discussing Expressionism." In *Aesthetics and Politics. The Key Texts of the Classical Debate within German Marxism.* Edited and translated by Ronald Taylor. London: Verso, 2002. 16–27.

Blöcker, Günter. *Heinrich von Kleist oder Das absolute Ich.* Berlin: Argon, 1960.

Bloom, Harold. *The Anxiety of Influence. A Theory of Poetry.* New York: Oxford UP, 1973.

Bock, Stephan. "Croquis. Fußmärsche Routen Ausflüge 1807 – 1801 – 1811." *Heilbronner Kleist-Blätter* 14 (2003): 81–122.

Bohrer, Karl Heinz. *Der romantische Brief. Die Entstehung ästhetischer Subjektivität.* Munich: Hanser, 1987.

Boockmann, Hartmut. "Mittelalterliches Recht bei Kleist. Ein Beitrag zum Verständnis des 'Michael Kohlhaas.'" *KJb* (1985): 84–108.

Borgards, Roland. "'Allerneuester Erziehungsplan.' Ein Beitrag Heinrich von Kleists zur Experimentalkultur um 1800 (Literatur, Physik)." In *Literarische Experimentalkulturen. Poetologien des Experiments im 19. Jahrhundert.* Edited by Marcus Krause and Nicolas Pethes. Würzburg: Königshausen & Neumann, 2005. 75–101.

—. "Experimentelle Aeronautik. Chemie, Meteorologie und Kleists Luftschiffkunst in den 'Berliner Abendblättern.'" *KJb* (2005): 142–161.

Borges, Jorge Luis. "The Analytical Language of John Wilkins." In *Other Inquisitions. 1937–1952.* Translated by Ruth L.C. Simms. Austin: U of Texas P, 1975. 101–105.

Brandstetter, Gabriele. "Duell im Spiegel. Zum Rahmenspiel in Kleists 'Amphitryon.'" *KJb* (1999): 109–127.

—. "'Penthesilea.' 'Das Wort des Greuelrätsels.' Die Überschreitung der Tragödie." In *Interpretationen. Kleists Dramen.* Edited by Walter Hinderer. Stuttgart: Reclam, 1997. 75–115.

—, and Gerhard Neumann, eds. *Romantische Wissenspoetik. Die Künste und die Wissenschaften um 1800.* Würzburg: Königshausen & Neumann, 2004.

Brecht, Bertolt. "On Kleist's Play 'The Prince of Homburg.'" Translated by Timothy Adès. *Translation and Literature* 15, no. 2 (2006): 237.

Breuer, Ingo. "'Schauplätze jämmerlicher Mordgeschichte.' Tradition der Novelle und Theatralität der Historia bei Heinrich von Kleist." *KJb* (2001): 196–225.

Broch, Jan. "Wieland." In *Kleist-Handbuch. Leben – Werk – Wirkung.* Edited by Ingo Breuer. Stuttgart: Metzler, 2009. 208–214.

Brown, Hilda M. "Kleist in Paris. 1804." *Seminar* 13 (1977): 88f.

Brüggemann, Diethelm. *Drei Mystifikationen Heinrich von Kleists. Kleists Würzburger Reise. Kleists Lust-Spiel mit Goethe. Aloysius, Marquis von Montferrat.* New York: Peter Lang, 1985.

Buchholz, Friedrich. *Gallerie Preussischer Charaktere.* Frankfurt/M.: Zweitausendeins, 1984.

Burke, Peter. *Die Geschicke des "Hofmann." Zur Wirkung eines Renaissance-Breviers über angemessenes Verhalten.* Berlin: Wagenbach, 1996.

Busch, Rolf. *Imperialistische und faschistische Kleist-Rezeption 1890–1945. Eine ideologiekritische Untersuchung.* Frankfurt/M.: Akad. Verlagsgesellschaft, 1974.

Campe, Rüdiger, ed. *Penthesileas Versprechen. Exemplarische Studien über die literarische Referenz.* Freiburg: Rombach, 2008.

Camus, Albert. *The Myth of Sisyphus and Other Essays.* Translated by Justin O'Brien. New York: Knopf, 1955.

Carlyle, Robert Warrand, and Alexander James Carlyle. *A History of Medieval Political Theory in the West*. Vol. 1. 4th ed. Edinburgh: Blackwood & Sons, 1950.

Carrière, Mathieu. *Für eine Literatur des Krieges, Kleist*. Basel: Stroemfeld, 1981.

Castiglione, Baldesar. *The Book of the Courtier*. Translated by Charles S. Singleton. New York: Anchor Books, 1959.

Chamisso, Adelbert von. "Reise um die Welt mit der Romanzoffischen Entdeckungs-Expedition in den Jahren 1815–18 auf der Brigg Rurik Kapitän Otto v. Kotzebue. Erster Teil: Tagebuch." In *Sämtliche Werke*. Edited by Werner Feudel and Christel Laufer. Vol. 2. Munich: Hanser, 1982. 81–371.

Clausewitz, Carl von. *On War*. Translated by Michael Howard and Peter Paret. Oxford: Oxford UP, 2007.

Cölln, Friedrich von. *Neue Feuerbrände. Marginalien zu der Schrift: Vertraute Briefe über die inneren Verhältnisse am preußischen Hofe*. Vol. 2.5. Amsterdam: Hammer, 1807.

—. *Vertraute Briefe über die inneren Verhältnisse am Preußischen Hofe seit dem Tode Friedrichs II*. 5 vols. Amsterdam: Hammer, 1807.

Corssen, Meta. *Kleist und Shakespeare*. Hildesheim: Gerstenberg, 1978.

Cullens, Chris, and Dorothea von Mücke. "'Das Käthchen von Heilbronn.' 'Ein Kind recht nach der Lust Gottes.'" In *Kleists Dramen. Neue Interpretationen*. Edited by Walter Hinderer. Stuttgart: Reclam, 1981. 116–143.

Dällenbach, Lucien, and Christiaan L. Hart Nibbrig, eds. *Fragment und Totalität*. Frankfurt/M.: Suhrkamp, 1984.

Daiber, Jürgen. "Die Suche nach der Urformel. Zur Verbindung von romantischer Naturforschung und Dichtung." *Aurora* 60 (2000): 75–103.

—. "'Nichts Drittes ... in der Natur?' Kleists Dichtung im Spiegel romantischer Selbstexperimentation." *KJb* (2005): 45–66.

Deleuze, Gilles, and Félix Guattari. *Thousand Plateaus. Capitalism and Schizophrenia*. Translated by Brian Massumi. Minneapolis: U of Minnesota P, 2005.

Denneler, Iris. "Legitimation und Charisma. Zu 'Robert Guiskard.'" In *Kleists Dramen. Neue Interpretationen*. Edited by Walter Hinderer. Stuttgart: Reclam, 1981. 73–92.

Detering, Heinrich. *Das offene Geheimnis. Zur literarischen Produktivität eines Tabus von Winckelmann bis Thomas Mann*. Göttingen: Wallstein, 1994.

Dewey, John. *Art as Experience*. New York: Minton, Balch & Company, 1934.

Dicke, Gerd. "'Mich wundert, das ich so frölich pin.' Ein Spruch im Gebrauch." In *Kleinstformen der Literatur*. Edited by Walter Haug and Burghart Wachinger. Tübingen: Niemeyer, 1994. 56–90.

Diderot, Denis. "Eléments de physiologie." In *Œuvres complètes de Diderot, revue sur les éditions originales comprenant ce qui été publié à diverses époques et les manuscrits inédits conservés à la Bibliothèque de l'Ermitage. Notices, notes, Table Analytique études sur Diderot et le mouvement philosophe au XVIIIe siècle*. Edited by J. Assézat. Vol. 9. Paris: Garnier frères, 1875. Reprint Nendeln: Kraus, 1966. 235–440.

Dießelhorst, Malte. *Die Prozesse des Müllers Arnold und das Eingreifen Friedrichs des Großen*. Göttingen: Schwartz, 1984.

—, and Arne Duncker. *Hans Kohlhase. Die Geschichte einer Fehde in Sachsen und Brandenburg zur Zeit der Reformation*. Frankfurt/M.: Lang, 1999.

Dönike, Martin. "'… Durch List und den ganzen Inbegriff jener Künste, die die Notwehr dem Schwachen in die Hände gibt.' Zur Gedankenfigur der Notwehr bei Kleist." *KJb* (1999): 53–66.

Dotzler, Bernhard J. "'Federkrieg.' Kleist und die Autorschaft des Produzenten." *KJb* (1998): 37–61.

—. *Papiermaschinen. Versuch über Communication & Control in Literatur und Technik*. Berlin: de Gruyter, 1996.

Dyer, Denis. *The Stories of Kleist. A Critical Study*. London: Duckworth, 1977.

Eckert, Helmut. "Ulrich Bräckers Soldantenzeit und die preußische Werbung in Schaffhausen." *Schaffhauser Beiträge zur Geschichte* 53 (1976): 122–190.

Eickenrodt, Sabine. "Kopfstücke. Zur Geschichte und Poetik der literarischen Porträts am Beispiel von Robert Walsers 'Kleist in Thun.'" *KJb* (2004): 123–144.

Eloesser, Arthur. "Neue Kleist-Miniaturen." *Jahrbuch der Kleist-Gesellschaft* (1923/24): 141–145.

[Enzensberger, Hans Magnus]. *Gustav von Schlabrendorf. Anti-Napoleon*. Frankfurt/M.: Eichborn, 1991.

Ersch, J.G., and J.G. Gruber, eds. *Allgemeine Encyclopädie der Wissenschaften und Künste*. Sec. 1, Vol. 24. Reprint Graz: Akad. Druck- & Verlagsanstalt, 1971.

Erxleben, Johann Christian Polykarp. *Anfangsgründe der Naturlehre*. Edited by G.C. Lichtenberg. 6th ed. Göttingen: Dieterich, 1794.

Essen, Gesa von. "Römer und Germanen im Spiel der Masken. Heinrich von Kleists 'Herrmannsschlacht.'" *KJb* (1999): 41–52.

Fetscher, Justus. "'Horen' – 'Athenäum' – 'Phöbus.' Literaturkritische Spitzenzeitschriften." *Beiträge zur Kleist-Forschung* 21 (2007/08): 175–190.

—. *Verzeichnungen. Kleists "Amphitryon" und seine Umschrift bei Goethe und Hofmannsthal*. Cologne: Böhlau, 1998.

—. "Vorstellungen. Zur Erforschung von Kleists 'Amphitryon' in den Jahren 1978 bis 2001." In *Heinrich von Kleist. Neue Wege der Forschung*. Edited by Anton Philipp Knittel and Inka Kording. Darmstadt: Wiss. Buchgesellschaft, 2003. 203–224.

Feuchtwanger, Lion. *The Oppermanns*. Translated by James Cleugh. New York: Viking, 1934.

Fichte, Johann Gottlieb. *Fichtes Werk*. Edited by Immanuel Hermann Fichte. 11 vols. Berlin: de Gruyter, 1971.

Fink, Gonthier-Louis. "'Das Käthchen von Heilbronn' 'oder das Weib, wie es seyn sollte.' Ein Rittermärchenspiel." In *Käthchen und seine Schwestern: Frauenfiguren im Drama um 1800. Internationales Kolloquium des Kleist-Archivs Sembdner*. Edited by Günther Emig and Anton Philipp Knittel. Heilbronn: Stadtbücherei, 2000. 9–37.

—. "Zwischen Frankfurt an der Oder und Paris. Variationen des Deutschland- und Frankreichbildes des jungen Kleist." *KJb* (1997): 97–125.

Fleig, Anne, Christian Moser, and Helmut J. Schneider, eds. *Schreiben nach Kleist: Literarische, mediale und theoretische Transkriptionen*. Freiburg: Rombach, 2014.

Földényi, László. "Die Inszenierung des Erotischen. Heinrich von Kleist 'Über das Marionettentheater.'" *KJb* (2001): 135–147.

—. *Heinrich von Kleist. Im Netz der Wörter*. Munich: Matthes & Seitz, 1999.

Fohrmann, Jürgen, ed. *Lebensläufe um 1800*. Tübingen: Niemeyer, 1998.

Foucault, Michel. *The Order of Things. An Archaeology of the Human Sciences*. New York: Random, 1970.

Freud, Sigmund. "Creative Writers and Day-dreaming." In *The Standard Edition of the Complete Psychological Works of Sigmund Freud*. Edited and translated by James Strachey. Vol. 9. London: Hogarth, 1957. 142–153.

Frick, Werner. "Kleists 'Wissenschaft.' Kleiner Versuch über die Gedankenakrobatik eines Un-Disziplinierten." *KJb* (1997): 207–240.

—. "'Und sehe, daß wir nichts wissen können....' Poetische Wissenschaftsskepsis bei Goethe, Kleist und Büchner." In *'Scientia poetica.' Literatur und Naturwissenschaft*. Edited by Norbert Elsner and Werner Frick. Göttingen: Wallstein, 2004. 243–271.

Friedlaender, Ernst, ed. *Ältere Universitäts-Matrikeln I: Universität Frankfurt a.O.* Vol. 2, *1649–1811*. Osnabrück: Zeller, 1965.

Fülleborn, Ulrich. *Besitzen als besäße man nicht. Besitzdenken und seine Alternativen in der Literatur*. Frankfurt/M.: Insel, 1995.

—. *Die frühen Dramen Heinrich von Kleists*. Munich: Fink, 2007.

Gall, Ulrich. *Philosophie bei Heinrich von Kleist. Untersuchungen zu Herkunft und Bestimmung des philosophischen Gehalts seiner Schriften*. Bonn: Bouvier, 1977.

Gell, Alfred. *Art and Agency. An Anthropological Theory*. Oxford: Oxford UP, 1998.

Gellert, Christian Fürchtegott. *Briefe, nebst einer praktischen Abhandlung von dem guten Geschmacke in Briefen*. Leipzig: Wendler, 1751.

Genazino, Wilhelm. "Die Flucht in die Ohnmacht. Dankrede zum Kleist-Preis." *KJb* (2008/09): 16–21.

Genette, Gérard. *Paratexts: Thresholds of Interpretation*. Translated by Jane E. Lewin. Cambridge: Cambridge UP, 2001.

Gieraths, Günther, ed. *Die Kampfhandlungen der brandenburgisch-preußischen Armee 1626–1807. Ein Quellenhandbuch*. Berlin: de Gruyter, 1964.

Gilot, Françoise. *Life with Picasso*. New York: McGraw-Hill, 1964.

Gleim, Johann Wilhelm Ludwig. "To Death." In *German Poetry from the Beginnings to 1750*. Edited by Ingrid Walsøe-Engel. New York: Continuum, 1992. 291.

Goethe, Johann Wolfgang von. "Prometheus." In *Werke. Hamburger Ausgabe*. Edited by Erich Trunz. Vol. 1. Munich: Beck, 1982. 44–46.

—. "Zur Farbenlehre." In *Sämtliche Werke, Briefe, Tagebücher und Gespräche*. Edited by Manfred Wenzel. Vol. 23.1. Frankfurt/M.: Deutscher Klassiker Verlag, 1991. 9–1040.

—, and Johann Peter Eckermann. *Conversations of Goethe with Eckermann and Soret*. Translated by John Oxenford. London: Bell & Sons, 1875.

Görner, Rüdiger. *Gewalt und Grazie. Heinrich von Kleists Poetik der Gegensätzlichkeit*. Heidelberg: Winter, 2011.

Goldammer, Peter, ed. *Schriftsteller über Kleist*. Berlin: Aufbau, 1976.

Goldschmidt, Paul. "Stein zum Altenstein, Karl Freiherr von." In *Allgemeine Deutsche Biographie*. Edited by Historische Commission bei der Königlichen Akademie der Wissenschaften. Vol. 35. Leipzig: Duncker & Humblot, 1893. 645–660.

Gracián, Baltasar. *The Art of Worldly Wisdom*. Translated by Joseph Jacobs. London: Macmillan, 1904.

—. *Handorakel und Kunst der Weltklugheit*. Edited by Arthur Hübscher. Translated by Arthur Schopenhauer. Stuttgart: Reclam, 1992.

Gräf, Holger T. *Landgraf Friedrich II.: Der Prinz von Homburg*. Erfurt: Sutton, 2008.

Grathoff, Dirk. "Die Zeichen der Marquise. Das Schweigen, die Sprache und die Schriften." In *Heinrich von Kleist. Studien zu Werk und Wirkung*. Edited by Dirk Grathoff. Opladen: Westdeutscher Verlag, 1988. 198–222.

—. "Heinrich von Kleists Würzburger Reise – eine erweiterte Rekonstruktion." *KJb* (1997): 38–56.

—. *Kleists Geheimnisse. Unbekannte Seiten einer Biographie*. Opladen: Westdeutscher Verlag, 1993.

Greiner, Bernhard. *Kleists Dramen und Erzählungen. Experimente zum 'Fall' der Kunst*. Tübingen: Francke, 2000.

—. "Sturz als Halt. Kleists dramaturgische Physik." *KJb* (2005): 67–78.

Grimm, Jacob, and Wilhelm Grimm. *Deutsches Wörterbuch*. 33 vols. Munich: dtv, 1984.

Grote, Bernd. *Der deutsche Michel. Ein Beitrag zur publizistischen Bedeutung der Nationalfiguren*. Dortmund: Ruhfus, 1967.

Gumbrecht, Hans Ulrich. *Atmosphere, Mood, Stimmung. On a Hidden Potential of Literature*. Translated by Erik Butler. Stanford: Stanford UP, 2012.

—. "Erinnerung an Herkünfte. Stimmungen – ein vernachlässigtes Thema der Literatur." *Frankfurter Allgemeine Zeitung*, November 30, 2005.

—. *In Praise of Athletic Beauty*. Cambridge, MA: Belknap, 2006.

—, and Friederike Knüpling, eds. *Kleist revisited*. Munich: Fink, 2014.

—, and K. Ludwig Pfeiffer, eds. *Paradoxien, Dissonanzen, Zusammenbrüche. Situationen offener Epistemologie*. Frankfurt/M.: Suhrkamp, 1991.

Gundolf, Friedrich. *Heinrich von Kleist*. Berlin: Bondi, 1922.

GutsMuths, Johann Christoph Friedrich. *Gymnastics for Youth: Or a Practical Guide to Healthful and Amusing Exercises for the Use of Schools*. Translated by C.G. Salzmann. London: Johnston, 1800.

Häker, Horst. "10. oder 18. Oktober? Ein Plädoyer für Kleist." *Beiträge zur Kleist-Forschung* 7 (1993): 149–154.

—. "Kleist auf Rügen." *Beiträge zur Kleist-Forschung* (2000): 225–234.

—. "Kleists Aufenthalt bei Cartel in Berlin im Jahre 1788." *KJb* (1988/89): 445–454.

—. *Kleists Berliner Aufenthalte. Ein biographischer Beitrag*. Berlin: Haude & Spener, 1989.

—. "Kleists Beziehungen zu Mitgliedern der französisch reformierten Gemeinde in Berlin." *KJb* (1983): 98–121.

Hamacher, Bernd. "Goethe." In *Kleist-Handbuch. Leben – Werk – Wirkung*. Edited by Ingo Breuer. Stuttgart: Metzler, 2009. 214–219.

—. "Michael Kohlhaas." In *Kleist-Handbuch. Leben – Werk – Wirkung*. Edited by Ingo Breuer. Stuttgart: Metzler, 2009. 97–106.

Hansen, Uffe. "Der Schlüssel zum Rätsel der Würzburger Reise Heinrich von Kleists." *Jahrbuch der Deutschen Schillergesellschaft* 41 (1997): 170–209.

Harms, Ingeborg. "Kleists 'Findling' zwischen Krypta und Handelsgewölbe." In *Gewagte Experimente und kühne Konstellationen. Kleists Werk zwischen Klassizismus und Romantik*. Edited by Christine Lubkoll and Günter Oesterle. Würzburg: Königshausen & Neumann, 2001. 149–167.

Hart, Julius. *Das Kleist-Buch*. Berlin: Borntraeger, 1912.

Hausen, Carl Renatus. *Geschichte der Universität und Stadt Frankfurt an der Oder, seit ihrer Stiftung und Erbauung, bis zum Schluß des 18. Jahrhunderts, größtenteils nach Urkunden und Archiv-Nachrichten bearbeitet*. Frankfurt/O.: Apitz, im Verlag bei dem Verfasser, 1800.

Hederich, Benjamin. *Gründliches mythologisches Lexikon*. Leipzig: Gleditsch, 1770. Reprint Darmstadt: Wiss. Buchgesellschaft, 1996.

Heidegger, Martin. *Being and Time*. Translated by Joan Stambaugh. Albany: SUNY Press, 1996.

Heine, Heinrich. *The Poems of Heinrich Heine. Complete*. Translated by Edgar Alfred Bowring. London: Bell & Sons, 1908.

Heinrich, Gerd, ed. *Berlin und Brandenburg*. Stuttgart: Kröner, 1973.

—. "Die Geisteswissenschaften an der brandenburgischen Landesuniversität Frankfurt/Oder um 1800. Bemerkungen zu Studienangebot und Gelehrtenbestand der Hochschule Heinrich von Kleists vor ihrer Auflösung." *KJb* (1983): 71–97.

Helbig, Holger. "Herr von Kleist und Frau Vogel beschließen ihren Tod und verwirren die Wissenschaft. Der Briefwechsel zwischen Heinrich von Kleist und Henriette Vogel als philologische Grenzsituation." In *Grenzsituation. Wahrnehmung, Bedeutung und Gestaltung in der neueren Literatur*. Edited by Dorothea Lauterbach, Uwe Spörl, and Uli Wunderlich. Göttingen: Vandenhoeck & Ruprecht, 2002. 107–130.

Hellmann, Hanna. "Heinrich von Kleist und 'Der Kettenträger.'" *Germanisch-Romanische Monatsschrift* 13 (1925): 350–363.

—. "Kleists 'Amphitryon.'" *Euphorion* 25 (1924): 241–251.

Henkel, Arthur. "Erwägungen zur Szene II,5 in Kleists 'Amphitryon.'" In *Kleists Aktualität. Neue Aufsätze und Essays 1966–1978*. Edited by Walter Müller-Seidel. Darmstadt: Wiss. Buchgesellschaft, 1981. 200–222.

Herder, Johann Gottfried. *Briefwechsel mit Caroline Flachsland*. Edited by H. Schauer. 2 vols. Weimar: Goethe-Gesellschaft, 1926–28.

Herrmann, Britta. "Auf der Suche nach dem sicheren Geschlecht. Die Briefe Heinrich von Kleists und Männlichkeit um 1800." In *Wann ist der Mann ein Mann? Zur Geschichte der Männlichkeit*. Edited by Walter Erhart and Britta Herrmann. Stuttgart: Metzler, 1997. 212–234.

Herzog, Wilhelm. *Heinrich von Kleist. Sein Leben und sein Werk*. Munich: Beck, 1911.

Heyse, Paul. *Jugenderinnerungen und Bekenntnisse*. 4th ed. Berlin: Hertz, 1901.

Hildesheimer, Wolfgang. *Mozart*. Translated by Marion Faber. New York: Farrar, Straus & Giroux, 1982.

Hilgers, Philipp von. "Räume taktischer Kriegsspiele." In *Schlachtfelder. Codierung von Gewalt im medialen Wandel*. Edited by Steffen Martus, Marina Münkler, and Werner Röcke. Berlin: Akademie, 2003. 249–263.

Hinderer, Walter. "Ansichten von der Rückseite der Naturwissenschaften. Antinomien in Heinrich von Kleists Welt- und Selbstverständnis." *KJb* (2005): 21–44.

Hippel, Theodor Gottlieb von. *On Improving the Status of Women*. Translated and edited with an introduction by Timothy F. Sellner. Detroit: Wayne State UP, 1979.

Hochadel, Oliver. *Öffentliche Wissenschaft. Elektrizität in der deutschen Aufklärung*. Göttingen: Wallstein, 2003.

Hoffmann, E.T.A. *Tales of E.T.A Hoffmann*. Edited and translated by Leonard J. Kent and Elizabeth C. Knight. Chicago: U of Chicago P, 1972.

—. *The Serapion Brethren*. Translated by Alex Ewing. 2 vols. London: Bell & Sons, 1892.

Hoffmann, Paul. *Kleist in Paris*. Berlin: Wegweiser, 1924.

Honnef, Theo. *Heinrich von Kleist in der Literatur der DDR*. New York: Lang, 1988.

Honold, Alexander. "Die Sonne steigt, der Apfel fällt. Bewegte Körper und ihre Bahnen auf Kleists astronomischem Theater." *KJb* (2005): 79–91.

Hubbard, William H. *Familiengeschichte*. Munich: Beck, 1983.

Humboldt, Alexander von. "Ich über mich selbst." In *Aus meinem Leben. Autobiographische Bekenntnisse*. Edited by Kurt-R. Biermann. Munich: Beck, 1987. 31–40

Jäger, Ludwig. "Vom Eigensinn des Mediums Sprache." In *Brisante Semantik. Neuere Konzepte und Forschungsergebnisse einer kulturwissenschaftlichen Semantik*. Edited by Dietrich Busse, Thomas Niehr, and Martin Wengeler. Tübingen: Niemeyer 2005. 45–64.

Jany, Curt. *Geschichte der Preußischen Armee vom 15. Jahrhundert bis 1914*. Edited by Eberhard Jany. Vol. 3, *1763–1807*. 2nd ed. Osnabrück: Biblio, 1967.

Jauß, Hans Robert. "Poetik und Problematik von Identität und Rolle in der Geschichte des 'Amphitryon.'" In *Identität*. Edited by Odo Marquardt and Karlheinz Stierle. Munich: Fink, 1979. 213–254.

Jørgensen, Sven-Aage, Herbert Jaumann, John A. McCarthy, and Horst Thomé. *Christoph Martin Wieland. Epoche – Werk – Wirkung*. Munich: Beck, 1994.

Kästner, Erich. *Fabian. The Story of a Moralist*. Translated by Cyrus Brooks. Evanston, IL: Northwestern UP, 1993.

Kafka, Franz. *The Diaries of Franz Kafka, 1910–13*. Edited by Max Brod. Translated by Joseph Kresh. Schocken: New York, 1974.

—. *The Diaries of Franz Kafka, 1914–1923*. Edited by Max Brod. Translated by Martin Greenberg, with the co-operation of Hannah Arendt. New York: Schocken, 1968.

—. "The Eight Octavo Notebooks." In *Dearest Father. Stories and Reflections*. Translated by Ernst Kaiser and Eithne Wilkins. New York: Schocken, 1954.

—. *Letters to Friends, Family, and Editors*. Translated by Richard and Clara Winston. London: Calder, 1978.

—. *Letters to Milena*. Translated and with an introduction by Philip Boehm. New York: Schocken, 1990.

—. *The Trial*. Translated by Idris Parry. London: Penguin, 1994.

Kant, Immanuel. "An Answer to the Question: What is Enlightenment?" In *Practical Philosophy*. Edited and translated by Mary J. Gregor. Cambridge: Cambridge UP, 1996. 11–22.

—. "Anthropology from a Pragmatic Point of View." Translated by Robert B. Louden. In *Anthropology, History, and Education*. Edited by Günter Zöller and Robert B. Louden. Cambridge: Cambridge UP, 2007. 227–429.

—. *Critique of the Power of Judgment*. Edited by Paul Guyer. Translated by Paul Guyer and Eric Matthews. Cambridge: Cambridge UP, 2000.

—. "On the Miscarriage of All Philosophical Trials in Theodicy." Translated by George di Giovanni. In *Religion and Rational Theology*. Edited by Allen W. Wood and George di Giovanni. Cambridge: Cambridge UP, 1996. 19–37.

Kanzog, Klaus, ed. *Erzählstrukturen – Filmstrukturen. Erzählungen Heinrich von Kleists und ihre filmische Realisation*. Berlin: Schmidt, 1981.

—. "Vom rechten zum linken Mythos. Ein Paradigmenwechsel der Kleist-Rezeption." In *Heinrich von Kleist. Studien zu Werk und Wirkung*. Edited by Dirk Grathoff. Opladen: Westdeutscher Verlag, 1988. 312–328.

Kaul, Susanne. *Poetik der Gerechtigkeit. Shakespeare – Kleist*. Munich: Fink, 2008.

Keller, Gottfried. "The Misused Love Letters." Translated by Michael Bullock. In *Two Novellas. The Misused Love Letters. Regula Amrain and Her Youngest Son*. Translated by Michael Bullock and Anne Fremantle. New York: Ungar, 1974. 13–94.

Kiefer, Klaus H. *Wiedergeburt und Neues Leben. Aspekte des Strukturwandels in Goethes "Italienischer Reise."* Bonn: Bouvier, 1978.

Kiefner, Hans. "Species facti. Geschichtserzählung bei Kleist und in Relationen bei preußischen Kollegialbehörden um 1800." *KJb* (1988/89): 13–39.

Kittler, Friedrich. "Ein Erdbeben in Chili und Preußen." In *Positionen der Literaturwissenschaft. Acht Modellanalysen am Beispiel von Kleists "Das Erdbeben in Chili."* Edited by David Wellbery. 3rd ed. Munich: Beck, 1993. 24–38.

Kittler, Wolf. *Die Geburt des Partisanen aus dem Geiste der Poesie. Heinrich von Kleist und die Strategie der Befreiungskriege.* Freiburg: Rombach, 1987.

Kleist, Bogislav von. *Die Generale der Königlich-Preußischen Armee von 1840–1890 (1891–1892).* 2nd ed. Leipzig: Zuckschwerdt & Möschke, 1895.

Kleist, Ewald Christian von. *Ihn foltert Schwermut, weil er lebt. Gedichte, Prosa, Stücke.* Edited by Gerhard Wolf. Frankfurt/M.: Fischer, 1983.

—. *Sämtliche Werke.* Stuttgart: Reclam, 1971.

Klibansky, Raymond, Erwin Panofsky, and Fritz Saxl. *Saturn and Melancholy. Studies in the History of Natural Philosophy, Religion, and Art.* Montreal: McGill-Queen's UP, 2019.

Klopstock, Friedrich. *Odes of Klopstock. From 1747 to 1780.* Translated by William Nind. London: Pickering, 1848.

Klotz, Volker. "Aug um Zunge – Zunge um Aug. Kleists extremes Theater." *KJb* (1985): 128–142.

Knackstedt, Martin. "Heinrich von Kleist and the Military." Master's thesis, University of Kassel, 1996.

Kohlhäufl, Michael. "Die Rede – ein dunkler Gesang? Kleists 'Robert Guiskard' und die Deklamationstheorie um 1800." *KJb* (1996): 142–168.

Konersmann, Ralf. "Das Versprechen der Wörter. Kleists erste und letzte Dichtung." In *Heinrich von Kleist* (*Text + Kritik, special issue*). Edited by Heinz Ludwig Arnold. Munich: edition text + kritik, 1993. 100–124.

Koschorke, Albrecht. *Die Heilige Familie und ihre Folgen. Ein Versuch.* Frankfurt/M.: Fischer, 2000.

—. *Körperströme und Schriftverkehr. Mediologie des 18. Jahhunderts.* Munich: Fink, 1999.

Koselleck, Reinhart. *Preußen zwischen Reform und Revolution. Allgemeines Landrecht, Verwaltung und soziale Bewegung von 1791 bis 1848.* Munich: Klett, 1989.

—. *Vergangene Zukunft. Zur Semantik geschichtlicher Zeiten.* Frankfurt/M.: Suhrkamp, 1989.

Košenina, Alexander. *Der gelehrte Narr. Gelehrtensatire seit der Aufklärung.* Göttingen: Wallstein, 2003.

Kraft, Herbert. *Kleist. Leben und Werk.* Munich: Aschendorff, 2007.

Krause, Karl Heinrich. *Mein Vaterland unter den hohenzollerischen Regenten. Ein Lesebuch für Freunde der Geschichte.* Vol. 2. Halle: Hemmerde & Schwetschke, 1803.

Kreutzer, Hans Joachim. "'... der erste nationalsozialistische Dichter der Vergangenheit ....' Georg Minde-Pouets Krisenbericht von 1936." *KJb* (1992): 187–192.

—. "Der Kleist-Preis 1912–1932–1985." *KJb* (1986): 11–18.

—. *Die dichterische Entwicklung Heinrichs von Kleist. Untersuchungen zu seinen Briefen und zu Chronologie und Aufbau seiner Werke*. Berlin: Schmidt, 1968.

—. "Über die Geschicke der Kleist-Handschriften und über Kleists Handschrift." *KJb* (1981/82): 66–85.

Kris, Ernst, and Otto Kurz. *Legend, Myth, and Magic in the Image of the Artist. A Historical Experiment*. Translated by Alastair Laing and Lottie M. Newman. New Haven: Yale UP, 1979.

Krug, Wilhelm Traugott. *Krug's Lebensreise in sechs Stazionen von ihm selbst beschrieben. Nebst Frank Volkmad Reinhard's Briefen an den Verfasser*. Rev. ed. Leipzig: Baumgärtner, 1842.

Kunisch, Johannes. "Das 'Puppenwerk' der stehenden Heere. Ein Beitrag zur Neueinschätzung von Soldatenstand und Krieg in der Spätaufklärung." *Zeitschrift für Historische Forschung* 17 (1990): 49–83.

Kusch, Reinhard. *Leopold von Braunschweig 1752–1785. Herkommen, Leben und Tod. Portraitskizze eines fürstlichen Philanthropen*. Frankfurt/O.: Kleist-Gedenk- und Forschungsstätte, 1995.

La Roche, Sophie von. *The History of Lady Sophia Sternheim*. Edited by James Lynn. Translated by Joseph Collyer. New York: New York UP, 1992.

La Rochefoucauld, François de. *The Maxims of La Rochefoucauld*. Translated by Louis Kronenberger. New York: Random, 1959.

Latour, Bruno. "The Berlin Keys or How to Do Words with Things." Translated by Lydia Davis. In *Matter, Materiality and Modern Culture*. Edited by P.M. Graves-Brown. London: Routledge, 2000. 10–21.

Lauer, Gerhard, and Thorsten Unger, eds. *Das Erdbeben von Lissabon und der Katastrophendiskurs im 18. Jahrhundert*. Göttingen: Wallstein, 2008.

Lehmann, August, ed. *Der Tugendbund*. Berlin: Haude & Spener, 1867.

Lehmann, Max. *Freiherr vom Stein*. Leipzig: Hirzel, 1921.

Leistner, Bernd. "Kleist in der neueren DDR-Literatur." In *Heinrich von Kleist. Studien zu Werk und Wirkung*. Edited by Dirk Grathoff. Opladen: Westdeutscher Verlag, 1988. 329–354.

Lesky, Albin. *Geschichte der griechischen Literatur*. Bern: Francke, 1963.

Lethen, Helmut. *Cool Conduct. The Culture of Distance in Weimar Germany*. Translated by Don Reneau. Berkeley: U of California P, 2002.

Lewis, Alison. "Der Zwang zum Genießen. Männliche Gewalt und der weibliche Körper in drei Prosatexten Kleists." *KJb* (2000): 198–222.

Liebrand, Claudia. "*Pater semper incertus est.* Kleists 'Marquise von O....' mit Boccaccio gelesen." *KJb* (2000): 46–60.

Lindley, Mark. "Stimmung und Temperatur." In *Geschichte der Musiktheorie*. Edited by Frieder Zaminer. Vol. 6, *Hören, Messen und Rechnen in der frühen Neuzeit*. Darmstadt: Wiss. Buchgesellschaft, 1987. 109–332.

Loch, Rudolf. *Kleist. Eine Biographie*. Göttingen: Wallstein, 2003.

Loose, Hans Dieter. *Kleists "Herrmannsschlacht": Kein Krieg für Hermann und seine Cherusker: ein paradoxer Feldzug aus dem Geist der Utopie gegen den Geist besitzbürgerlicher und feudaler Herrschaft*. Karlsruhe: von Loeper, 1984.

Lorenz, Otto. "Experimentalphysik und Dichtungspraxis. Das 'Geheime Gesetz des Widerspruchs' im Werk Heinrich von Kleists." In *Die deutsche literarische Romantik und die Wissenschaften*. Edited by Nicholas Saul. Munich: Iudicium, 1991. 72–90.

Lubkoll, Christine. "Die heilige Cäcilie oder die Gewalt der Musik." In *Kleist-Handbuch. Leben – Werk – Wirkung*. Edited by Ingo Breuer. Stuttgart: Metzler, 2009. 137–142.

—. *Mythos Musik. Poetische Entwürfe des Musikalischen in der Literatur um 1800*. Freiburg: Rombach, 1995.

Lü, Yixu. "Das Käthchen von Heilbronn." In *Kleist-Handbuch. Leben – Werk – Wirkung*. Edited by Ingo Breuer. Stuttgart: Metzler, 2009. 67–76.

Lütteken, Anett. *Heinrich von Kleist – eine Dichterrenaissance*. Tübingen: Niemeyer, 2004.

Lützeler, Paul Michael, and David Pan, eds. *Kleists Erzählungen und Dramen. Neue Studien*. Würzburg: Königshausen & Neumann, 2001.

Luhmann, Niklas. *Gesellschaftsstruktur und Semantik. Studien zur Wissenssoziologie der modernen Gesellschaft*. 4 vols. Frankfurt/M.: Suhrkamp, 1980–95.

—. *Love as Passion. The Codification of Intimacy*. Translated by Jeremy Gaines and Doris L. Jones. Cambridge, MA: Harvard UP, 1986.

—. "Über 'Kreativität.'" In *Kreativität – ein verbrauchter Begriff?* Edited by Hans Ulrich Gumbrecht. Munich: Fink, 1988. 13–19.

Lukács, Georg. *The Theory of the Novel. A Historico-Philosophical Essay on the Forms of Great Epic Literature*. Translated by Anna Bostock. London: Merlin, 1971.

Luther, Martin. *D. Martin Luthers Werke. Kritische Gesamtausgabe*. 120 vols. Weimar: Böhlau, 1883–2009.

Maass, Joachim. *Kleist. A Biography*. Translated by Ralph Manheim. New York: Farrar, Straus & Giroux, 1983.

Machiavelli, Niccolò. *The Chief Works and Others*. Translated by Allan Gilbert. 3 vols. Durham: Duke UP, 1965.

Mainberger, Sabine. *Die Kunst der Aufzählung. Elemente zu einer Poetik des Enumerativen*. Berlin: de Gruyter, 2002.

Mandelartz, Michael. "Von der Tugendlehre zur Lasterschule. Die sogenannte 'Kantkrise' und Fichtes 'Wissenschaftslehre.'" *KJb* (2006): 120–136.

Mann, Thomas. *Doctor Faustus. The Life of the German Composer Adrian Leverkühn as Told by a Friend*. Translated by H.T. Lowe-Porter. New York: Vintage, 1993.

—. "Kleist and His Stories." In *"The Marquise of O—" and Other Stories*. Translated, with an introduction by Martin Greenberg. New York: Criterion, 1960. 5–23.

—. "Kleist's Amphitryon." In *Essays of Three Decades*. Translated by H.T. Lowe-Porter New York: Knopf, 1947. 202–240.

—. *The Magic Mountain*. Translated by H.T. Lowe-Porter. New York: Knopf, 1960.

—. *Reflections of a Nonpolitical Man*. Translated by Walter D. Morris. New York: Ungar, 1987.

Manthey, Jürgen. *Königsberg. Geschichte einer Weltbürgerrepublik*. Munich: Hanser, 2005.

Maron, Monika. "Nach Maßgabe meiner Begreifungskraft." *KJb* (1993): 16–20.

Marquardt, Jochen. "Der mündige Zeitungsleser. Anmerkungen zur Kommunikationsstrategie der 'Berliner Abendblätter.'" *Beiträge zur Kleist-Forschung* (1986): 7–36.

Maurach, Martin. *"Betrachtungen über den Weltlauf." Kleist 1933–1945. Ausstellungsbegleitbuch*. Berlin: Theater der Zeit, 2008.

—, ed. *Kleist im Nationalsozialismus. Themenband der Beiträge zur Kleist-Forschung 19*. Würzburg: Königshausen & Neumann, 2007.

Mauss, Marcel. *The Gift. The Form and Reason for Exchange in Archaic Societies*. Translated by W.D. Halls. New York: W.W. Norton, 1990.

Meinel, Christoph. "'des wunderlichen Wünsch seltsame Reduktion ....' Christian Ernst Wünsch, Kleist unzeitgemäßer Zeitgenosse." *KJb* (1996): 1–34.

Mews, Siegfried. "Brechts 'dialektisches Verhältnis zur Tradition.' Die Bearbeitung des 'Michael Kohlhaas.'" *Brecht-Jahrbuch* (1975): 63–78.

Meyer-Kalkus, Reinhart. "Heinrich von Kleist und Heinrich August Kerndörffer. Zur Poetik von Vorlesen und Deklamation." *KJb* (2001): 55–88.

Minde-Pouet, Georg. *Kleists letzte Stunden. Teil I: Das Akten-Material*. Berlin: Weidmann, 1925.

Molière. *Amphitryon*. Translated by Richard Wilbur. New York: Theatre Communications Group, 2010.

Mommsen, Katharina. *Kleists Kampf mit Goethe*. Rev. ed. Frankfurt/M: Suhrkamp, 1979.

Montaigne, Michel de. *The Complete Essays of Montaigne*. Translated by Donald M. Frame. Stanford: Stanford UP, 1966.

Morris, Max. *Heinrich von Kleists Reise nach Würzburg*. Berlin: Skopnik, 1899.

Moser, Christian. "Das Bettelweib von Locarno." In *Kleist-Handbuch. Leben – Werk – Wirkung*. Edited by Ingo Breuer. Stuttgart: Metzler, 2009. 128–133.

Moucha, Pamela. "Verspätete Gegengabe. Gabenlogik und Katastrophenbewältigung in Kleists 'Erdbeben in Chili.'" *KJb* (2000): 61–88.

Müller, Gernot. *"Man müsste auf dem Gemälde selbst stehen." Kleist und die bildende Kunst*. Tübingen: Francke, 1995.

Müller, Heiner. "Deutschland Ortlos. Anmerkungen zu Kleist." *KJb* (1991): 13–16.

—. *Hamletmachine and Other Texts for the Stage*. Edited and translated by Carl Weber. New York: Performing Arts Journal Publications, 1982.

Müller, Jan-Dirk. "Kleists Mittelalter-Phantasma. Zur Erzählung 'Der Zweikampf' (1811)." *KJb* (1998): 3–20.

Müller-Salget, Klaus. "Auferstehung, Apokalypse, Widerstand: Zur Artikulation des Politischen bei Heinrich von Kleist in den Jahren 1808 bis 1811." In *Literatur ist Widerstand. Aufsätze aus drei Jahrzehnten*. Innsbruck: Universität Innsbruck, 2005. 201–213.

—. *Heinrich von Kleist*. Stuttgart: Reclam, 2002.

—. "Kleist im Frühjahr 1804. Eine Aufklärung." *KJb* (2008/09): 251–253.

—. *Kleist und die Folgen*. Stuttgart: Metzler, 2017.

Müller-Seidel, Walter. "Die Struktur des Widerspruchs in Kleists 'Marquise von O.....'" *Deutsche Vierteljahrsschrift für Literaturwissenschaft und Geistesgeschichte* 28 (1954): 467–515.

—. "Kleists 'Hypochondrie.' Zu seinem Verständnis in klassischer und moderner Ästhetik." In *Texte, Motive und Gestalten der Goethezeit. Festschrift für Hans Reiss*. Edited by John L. Hibberd and H.B. Nisbet. Tübingen: Niemeyer, 1989. 225–250.

—. "'Penthesilea' im Kontext der deutschen Klassik." In *Interpretationen. Kleists Dramen*. Edited by Walter Hinderer. Stuttgart: Reclam, 1997. 144–171.

Münkler, Herfried. *Der Wandel des Krieges. Von der Symmetrie zur Asymmetrie*. Weilerswist: Velbrück, 2006.

Muth, Ludwig. *Kleist und Kant. Versuch einer neuen Interpretation*. Cologne: Universitätsverlag, 1954.

Neumann, Gerhard. "Anekdote und Novelle. Zum Problem literarischer Mimesis im Werk Heinrich von Kleists." In *Heinrich von Kleist und die Aufklärung*. Edited by Tim Mehigan. Rochester: Camden, 2000. 129–157.

—. "'... Der Mensch ohne Hülle ist eigentlich der Mensch.' Goethe und Heinrich von Kleist in der Geschichte des physiognomischen Blicks." *KJb* (1988/89): 259–279.

—. "'Der Zweikampf.' Kleists 'einrückendes' Erzählen." In *Interpretationen. Kleists Erzählungen*. Edited by Walter Hinderer. Stuttgart: Reclam, 1998. 216–246.

—. "'Die Verlobung in St. Domingo.' Zum Problem literarischer Mimesis im Werk Heinrich von Kleists." In *Gewagte Experimente und kühne Konstellationen. Kleists Werk zwischen Klassizismus und Romantik*. Edited by Christine Lubkoll and Günter Oesterle. Würzburg: Königshausen & Neumann, 2001. 93–117.

—. "Hexenküche und Abendmahl. Die Sprache der Liebe im Werk Heinrich von Kleists." *Freiburger Universitätsblätter* 25, no. 91 (1986): 9–31.

—. "Skandalon. Geschlechterrolle und soziale Identität in Kleists 'Marquise von O....' und Cervantes' Novelle 'La fuerza de la sangre.'" In *Heinrich von Kleist. Kriegsfall – Rechtsfall – Sündenfall*. Edited by Gerhard Neumann, Wolf Kittler, and Manfred Schneider. Freiburg: Rombach, 1994. 149–192.

Neumann, Peter Horst. *Der Preis der Mündigkeit. Über Lessings Dramen. Anhang: Über Fanny Hill.* Stuttgart: Klett-Cotta, 1977.

—. "Rilkes *Archaischer Torso Apollos* in der Geschichte des modernen Fragmentarismus." In *Fragment und Totalität.* Edited by Lucien Dällenbach and Christiaan L. Hart Nibbrig. Frankfurt/M.: Suhrkamp, 1984. 257–271.

Nicolai, Friedrich. *Beschreibung einer Reise durch Deutschland und die Schweiz im Jahre 1781.* Vol. 1. Berlin: Nicolai, 1783.

Nienhaus, Stefan. *Geschichte der deutschen Tischgesellschaft.* Tübingen: Niemeyer, 2003.

Nietzsche, Friedrich. *The Gay Science.* Translated by Walter Kaufmann. New York: Vintage, 1974.

—. *On the Genealogy of Morality.* Translated by Adrian Del Caro. Stanford: Stanford UP, 2014.

Nipperdey, Thomas. *Deutsche Geschichte 1800–1866. Bürgerwelt und starker Staat.* Munich: Beck, 1983.

Nutz, Maximilian. "Lektüre der Sinne. Kleists Penthesilea als Körperdrama." In *Heinrich von Kleist. Studien zu Werk und Wirkung.* Edited by Dirk Grathoff. Opladen: Westdeutscher Verlag, 1988. 163–185.

Oesterle, Günter. "'Der Findling.' Redlichkeit versus Verstellung – oder zwei Arten, böse zu warden." In *Interpretationen. Kleists Erzählungen.* Edited by Walter Hinderer. Stuttgart: Reclam, 1998. 157–180.

Oesterle, Ingrid. "Werther in Paris? Heinrich von Kleists Briefe über Paris." In *Heinrich von Kleist. Studien zu Werk und Wirkung.* Edited by Dirk Grathoff. Opladen: Westdeutscher Verlag, 1988. 97–116.

Osterhammel, Jürgen. *Die Verwandlung der Welt. Eine Geschichte des 19. Jahrhunderts.* Munich: Beck, 2009.

Osterkamp, Ernst. "Das Geschäft der Vereinigung. Über den Zusammenhang von bildender Kunst und Poesie im 'Phöbus.'" *KJb* (1990): 51–70.

Ottmann, Dagmar. "'Das stumme Zeichen.' Zum dramatischen Requisit in Kleists Prinz Friedrich von Homburg." In *Gewagte Experimente und kühne Konstellationen. Kleists Werk zwischen Klassizismus und Romantik.* Edited by Christine Lubkoll and Günter Oesterle. Würzburg: Königshausen & Neumann, 2001. 249–276.

Ovid. *Metamorphoses.* Translated by A.D. Melville. Oxford: Oxford UP, 1998.

Paß, Dominik. "Die Beobachtung der allmähligen Verfassung der Gedanken beim Reden. Eine systemtheoretische Lektüre." *KJb* (2003): 107–136.

Paul, Jean. *Titan. A Romance.* Translated by Charles T. Brooks. Vol. 1. Boston: Ticknor & Fields, 1864.

Peters, Sybille. "Die Experimente der 'Berliner Abendblätter.'" *KJb* (2005): 128–141.

—. *Heinrich von Kleist und der Gebrauch der Zeit. Von der MachArt der Berliner Abendblätter.* Würzburg: Königshausen & Neumann, 2002.

—. “Wie Geschichte geschehen lassen? Theatralität und Anekdotizität in den Berliner Abendblättern.” *KJb* (1999): 67–86.

Pethes, Nicolas, ed. *Ausnahmezustand der Literatur. Neue Lektüren zu Heinrich von Kleist*. Göttingen: Wallstein, 2011.

Pfeiffer, Joachim. *Die zerbrochenen Bilder. Gestörte Ordnungen im Werk Heinrich von Kleists*. Würzburg: Königshausen & Neumann, 1989.

Pfotenhauer, Helmut. “Kleists Rede über Bilder und in Bildern. Briefe, Bildkommentare, erste literarische Werke.” *KJb* (1997): 126–148.

Pfuel, Ernst von. *Ueber das Schwimmen*. Berlin: Dümmler, 1817.

Pliny the Elder. *Natural History. A Selection from Philemon Holland’s Translation*. Edited by J. Newsome. Oxford: Clarendon, 1964.

Plessner, Helmuth. *Die Stufen des Organischen und der Mensch: Einleitung in die philosophische Anthropologie*. 3rd ed. Berlin: de Gruyter, 1975.

Pockels, Carl Friedrich. *Versuch einer Charakteristik des weiblichen Geschlechts. Ein Sittengemählde des Menschen, des Zeitalters und des geselligen Lebens*. 5 vols. Hanover: Ritscher, 1797–1802.

Podewski, Madleen. “Ästhetik und Chemie. Frühromantische Experimente zwischen Kunst und Naturwissenschaft – eine Problemskizze.” *Internationales Jahrbuch der Bettina-von-Arnim-Gesellschaft* 15 (2003): 13–26.

Politzer, Heinz. “Auf der Suche nach Identität. Zu Heinrich von Kleists Würzburger Reise.” *Euphorion* 61 (1967): 383–399.

Porbeck, Heinrich Philipp Reinhard von. “Über militärische Ausbildung,” *Neue Bellona oder Beiträge zur Kriegskunst und Kriegsgeschichte* 4, no. 3 (1803): 33–95.

“Prayer of Manasseh,” King James Version, King James Bible Online, accessed January 15, 2021, https://www.kingjamesbibleonline.org/Prayer-of-Manasseh-Chapter-1/.

Press, Volker. “Adel im 19. Jahrhundert. Die Führungsschichten Alteuropas im bürgerlich-bürokratischen Zeitalter.” In *Der Adel an der Schwelle des bürgerlichen Zeitalters 1780–1860*. Edited by Armgard von Reden-Dohna and Ralph Melville. Wiesbaden: Steiner, 1988. 1–19.

Rahmer, Sigismund. *Das Kleist-Problem*. Berlin: Reimer, 1903.

Reeve, William C. *Kleist on Stage. 1804–1987*. Montreal: McGill-Queen’s UP, 1993.

Reif, Heinz. *Adel im 19. und 20. Jahrhundert*. Munich: Oldenbourg, 1999.

Reinhard, Carl von. *Geschichte des Königlich Preußischen Ersten Garde-Regiments zu Fuß 1740–1857*. Potsdam: Stein, 1858.

Reinhard, D. Franz Volkmar. *System der christlichen Moral*. Wittenberg: Zimmermann, 1802.

Reiss, Gunter. “Sündenfall-Modell und Romanform. Zur Integration von Kleists Marionettentheater-Thematik im Werk Thomas Manns.” *Jahrbuch der Deutschen Schillergesellschaft* 13 (1969): 426–453.

Reizenstein, "Ueber den Einfluß des militärischen Geistes, der Disziplin und Subordination auf stehende Heere." In *Denkwürdigkeiten der militärischen Gesellschaft in Berlin*. Vol. 2. Berlin: Wegener, 1802.

Reschke, Karin. *Verfolgte des Glücks. Das Findebuch der Henriette Vogel*. Berlin: Rotbuch, 1982.

Reuß, Roland. "'Mit gebrochenen Worten.' Zu Kleists Erzählung 'Der Zweikampf.'" *Brandenburger Kleist-Blätter* 7 (1994): 3–41.

Riedel, Peter Philipp. "Jakobiner und Postrevolutionär. Der Arzt Georg Christian Wedekind." *KJb* (1996): 52–76.

Rilke, Rainer Maria. "Archaic Torso of Apollo." In *New Poems* [*1908*]. *The Other Part*. Translated by Edward Snow. San Francisco: North Point, 1987. 3.

—. "Dolls. On the Wax Dolls of Lotte Pritzel." Translated by Idris Parry. In *On Dolls*. Edited with an introduction by Kenneth Gross. London: Notting Hill, 2012. 51–62.

—. "Narcissus." In *Poems 1906 to 1926*. Translated by J.B. Leishman. New York: New Directions, 1957. 145f.

—. *The Notebooks of Malte Laurids Brigge*. Translated by Stephen Mitchell. New York: Random, 1990.

—. "Requiem. Für Wolf Graf von Kalckreuth." In *Sämtliche Werke*. Edited by Ernst Zinn. Vol. 2. Frankfurt/M.: Insel, 1975. 657–664.

Ritter, Gerhard. *Stein. Eine politische Biographie*. Stuttgart: Deutsche Verlags-Anstalt, 1958.

Rohrwasser, Michael. *Der Weg nach oben. Johannes R. Becher. Politiken des Schreibens*. Basel: Stroemfeld, 1980.

Rothe, Eva. "Die Bildnisse Heinrich von Kleists. Mit neuen Dokumenten zu Kleists Gefangenschaft." *Jahrbuch der Deutschen Schillergesellschaft* 5 (1961): 136–186.

Rousseau, Jean-Jacques. "Emile, or, On Education." Translated by Christopher Kelly and Allan Bloom. In *The Collected Writings of Rousseau*. Edited by Roger D. Masters and Christopher Kelly. Vol. 13. Hanover: UP of New England, 2010.

—. "Julie, or the New Heloise: Letters of Two Lovers Who Live in a Small Town at the Foot of the Alps." Translated by Philip Stewart and Jean Vachéin. In *The Collected Writings of Rousseau*. Edited by Roger D. Masters and Christopher Kelly. Vol. 6. Hanover: UP of New England, 1997.

Roussel, Martin. "'Wie zart sie das zarte berühren.' Zur Kunst der Berührung bei Kleist." *KJb* (2008/09): 82–114.

—. "Zerstreuungen. Kleists poetische Meditation 'Über das Marionettentheater.'" *KJb* (2007): 61–93.

Ryder, Frank G. "Kleists 'Findling': Oedipus manqué?" *Modern Language Notes* 92 (1977): 509–524.

Samuel, Richard. "Heinrich von Kleist und Karl Baron von Altenstein. Eine Miszelle zu Kleists Biographie." In *Selected Writings*. Melbourne: University of Melbourne, Department of German Studies, 1965. 85–92.

—. “Heinrich von Kleists ‘Robert Guiskard’ und seine Wiederbelebung 1807/08.” *KJb* (1981/82): 315–348.

—. “Kleists ‘Herrmannsschlacht’ und der Freiherr vom Stein.” *Jahrbuch der Deutschen Schillergesellschaft* 5 (1961): 64–101.

—, and Hilda M. Brown. *Kleist’s Lost Year and the Quest for ‘Robert Guiscard.’* Leamington Spa: Hall, 1981.

Sauer, August, ed. *Ewald von Kleist’s Werke*. Vol. 1. Berlin: Hempel, 1880.

Schelling, Friedrich Wilhelm Joseph. “Von der Weltseele.” In *Sämtliche Werke*. 14 vols. Edited by Karl F.A. Schelling. Stuttgart: Cotta, 1856–61.

Schiller, Friedrich. *On the Aesthetic Education of Man. In a Series of Letters*. Edited and translated with an introduction by Elizabeth M. Wilkinson and L.A. Willoughby. Oxford: Oxford UP, 1967.

—. “On the Sublime.” Translated by Daniel O. Dahlstrom. In *Essays*. Edited by Walter Hinderer and Daniel O. Dahlstrom. New York: Continuum, 1993. 22–44.

—, and Johann Wolfgang von Goethe. *Correspondence between Schiller and Goethe. From 1794 to 1805*. Translated by L. Dora Schmitz. Vol. 2. London: Bell & Sons, 1890.

Schings, Hans-Jürgen. “Der anthropologische Roman. Seine Entstehung und Krise im Zeitalter der Spätaufklärung.” In *Deutschlands kulturelle Entfaltung. Die Neubestimmung des Menschen*. Edited by Bernhard Fabian, Wilhelm Schmidt-Biggemann, and Rudolf Vierhaus. Munich: Kraus, 1980. 247–275.

—. *Melancholie und Aufklärung. Melancholiker und ihre Kritiker in Erfahrungsseelenkunde und Literatur des 18. Jahrhunderts*. Stuttgart: Metzler, 1977.

Schirrmacher, Frank. *Verteidigung der Schrift. Kafkas “Prozeß.”* Frankfurt/M.: Suhrkamp, 1987.

Schlaffer, Hannelore. *Poetik der Novelle*. Stuttgart: Metzler, 1993.

Schlegel, August Wilhelm. *Kritische Schriften und Briefe*. Edited by Edgar Lohner. Stuttgart: Kohlhammer, 1965.

[Schlegel], Caroline. *Briefe aus der Frühromantik*. Edited by Erich Schmidt. Vol. 1. Leipzig: Insel, 1913.

Schlegel, Friedrich. *Philosophical Fragments*. Translated by Peter Firchow. Minneapolis: U of Minnesota P, 1991.

Schmidbauer, Wolfgang. *Die Rache der Liebenden*. Reinbek: Rowohlt, 2005.

—. “Kleists Narzissmus.” *KJb* (2008/09): 232–247.

Schmidt, Herminio. *Heinrich von Kleist. Naturwissenschaft als Dichtungsprinzip*. Bern: Haupt, 1978.

Schmidt, Jochen. *Heinrich von Kleist. Die Dramen und Erzählungen in ihrer Epoche*. Darmstadt: Wiss. Buchgesellschaft, 2003.

Schmidt, Siegfried J. *Der Diskurs des Radikalen Konstruktivismus*. Frankfurt/M.: Suhrkamp, 1987.

Schmitz-Emans, Monika. “Wassermänner, Sirenen und andere Monster. Fabelwesen im Spiegel von Kleists ‘Berliner Abendblättern.’” *KJb* (2005): 162–182.

Schneider, Hans-Peter. "Justizkritik im 'Zerbrochnen Krug.'" *KJb* (1988/89): 309–326.

Schöning, Kurd Wolfgang von. *Die Generale der Chur-Brandenburgischen und Königlich-Preußischen Armee von 1640–1840*. Berlin: Lüderitz, 1840.

Schopenhauer, Arthur. *Parerga and Paralipomena. Short Philosophical Essays.* Translated by Sabine Roehr and Christopher Janaway. Vol. 1. Cambridge: Cambridge UP, 2014.

Schrader, Hans-Jürgen. "'Denke Du wärest in das Schiff meines Glückes gestiegen.' Widerrufene Rollenentwürfe in Kleists Briefen an die Braut." *KJb* (1983): 122–179.

—. "Ermutigungen und Reflexe. Über Kleists Verhältnis zu Wieland und einige Motivanregungen, namentlich aus dem 'Hexameron von Rosenheim.'" *KJb* (1988/89): 160–194.

—. "Unsägliche Liebesbriefe. Heinrich von Kleist an Wilhelmine von Zenge." *KJb* (1981/82): 86–97.

Schröder, Jürgen. "Kleists Novelle 'Der Findling.' Ein Plädoyer für Nicolo." *KJb* (1985): 109–127.

Schuller, Marianne. "Ur-Sprung. Kleists Erzählung 'Der Findling.'" In *Moderne. Verluste.* Basel: Stroemfeld, 1997. 9–60.

Schulz, Gerhard. *Die deutsche Literatur zwischen Französischer Revolution und Restauration*. Vol. 2, *1806–1830*. Munich: Beck, 1989.

—. *Kleist. Eine Biographie*. Munich: Beck, 2007.

Schwab, Dieter. "Familie." In *Geschichtliche Grundbegriffe. Historisches Lexikon zur politisch-sozialen Sprache in Deutschland.* Edited by Otto Brunner, Werner Conze, and Reinhart Koselleck. Vol. 2. Stuttgart: Klett-Cotta, 1975. 253–301.

Seeba, Hinrich C. "Der Sündenfall des Verdachts. Identitätskrise und Sprachskepsis in Kleists *Familie Schroffenstein*." *Deutsche Vierteljahrsschrift für Literaturwissenschaft und Geistesgeschichte* 44 (1970): 64–100.

Sembdner, Helmut. *Die Berliner Abendblätter Heinrich von Kleists, ihre Quellen und ihre Redaktion*. Berlin: Weidmann, 1939.

—, ed. *Kleist in der Dichtung*. 2nd ed. Frankfurt/M.: Insel, 1985.

—. "Die Doppelgänger des Herrn von Kleist. Funde und Irrtümer der Kleist-Forschung." *Jahrbuch der Deutschen Schillergesellschaft* 35 (1991): 180–195.

Sevin, Dieter, and Christoph Zeller, eds. *Heinrich von Kleist: Style and Concept. Explorations of Literary Dissonance*. Berlin: de Gruyter, 2013.

Shakespeare, William. *Hamlet*. Edited by Cyrus Hoy. 2nd ed. New York: Norton, 1992.

Siebert, Eberhard, ed. *Heinrich von Kleist. Leben und Werk im Bild*. Frankfurt/M: Insel, 1980.

—. "War Heinrich von Kleist als Industriespion in Würzburg?" *Jahrbuch Preußischer Kulturbesitz* 22 (1989): 185–206.

Sikora, Michael. *Disziplin und Desertion. Strukturprobleme militärischer Organsiation im 18. Jahrhundert*. Berlin: Duncker & Humblot, 1996.

Simmel, Georg. "The Adventure." Translated by David Kettler. In *Georg Simmel, 1858–1918. A Collection of Essays*. Edited by Kurt H. Wolff. Columbus: Ohio State UP, 1959. 243–258.

—. "Treue. Ein sozialpsychologischer Versuch." In *Gesamtausgabe*. Edited by Otthein Rammstedt. Vol. 8.2, *Aufsätze und Abhandlungen 1901–1908*. Frankfurt/M.: Suhrkamp, 1993. 398–403.

Simonis, Linda. "Poetologie des Abenteuers. Casanova und das Problem der Kontingenz." *Poetica* 34, no. 3/4 (2002): 345–367.

Soboczynski, Adam. *Versuch über Kleist. Die Kunst des Geheimnisses um 1800*. Berlin: Matthes & Seitz, 2007.

Sørensen, Bengt Algot. *Herrschaft und Zärtlichkeit. Der Patriarchalismus und das Drama im 18. Jahrhundert*. Munich: Beck, 1984.

Sorescu, Marin. *Hands behind My Back. Selected Poems*. Translated by Gabriela Dragnea, Stuart Friebert, and Adriana Varga. Oberlin: Oberlin College Press, 1991.

Spaemann, Robert. "Fanatisch und Fanatismus." *Archiv für Begriffsgeschichte* 9 (1971): 256–267.

Stadler, Arnold. *Komm, gehen wir*. Frankfurt/M.: Fischer, 2007.

Staengle, Peter. *Heinrich von Kleist*. Munich: dtv, 1998.

Stamm-Kuhlmann, Thomas. *König in Preußens großer Zeit. Friedrich Wilhelm III. Der Melancholiker auf dem Thron*. Berlin: Siedler, 1992.

Stanitzek, Georg. *Blödigkeit. Beschreibung des Individuums im 18. Jahrhundert*. Tübingen: Niemeyer, 1989.

—. "Der Projektmacher. Projektionen auf eine 'unmögliche' moderne Kategorie." *Ästhetik und Kommunikation* 17, no. 65/66 (1987): 135–146.

Starobinski, Jean. *Largesse*. Translated by Jane Marie Todd. Chicago: U of Chicago P, 1997.

Steig, Reinhold. *Heinrich von Kleist's Berliner Kämpfe*. Berlin: Spemann, 1901.

Stein, Freiherr vom. *Briefe und amtliche Schriften*. Edited by Erich Botzenhart, Walter Hubatsch, and Peter G. Thielen. 10 vols. Stuttgart: Kohlhammer, 1957–74.

Stephens, Anthony. "'Gegen die Tyrannei des Wahren.' Die Sprache in Kleists 'Herrmannsschlacht.'" In *Kleist – Sprache und Gewalt*. Freiburg: Rombach, 1999. 229–252.

—. *Heinrich von Kleist. The Dramas and Stories*. Oxford: Berg, 1994.

—. "Kleists Familienmodelle." *KJb* (1988/89): 222–237.

—. *Kleist – Sprache und Gewalt*. Freiburg: Rombach, 1999.

—. "Name und Identitätsproblematik bei Kleist und Kafka." *Jahrbuch des Freien Deutschen Hochstifts* (1985): 222–259.

—. "Robert Guiskard, Herzog der Normänner." In *Kleist-Handbuch. Leben – Werk – Wirkung*. Edited by Ingo Breuer. Stuttgart: Metzler, 2009. 62–67.

—. "'Was hilfts, daß ich jetzt schuldlos mich erzähle?' Zur Bedeutung der Erzählvorgänge in Kleists Dramen." *Jahrbuch der Deutschen Schillergesellschaft* 29 (1985): 301–323.

—. "Zur Funktion der 'Schauspiele' in Kleists Erzählungen." *KJb* (2007): 102–119.

Stierle, Karlheinz. "'Amphitryon.' Die Komödie des Absoluten." In *Interpretationen. Kleists Dramen*. Edited by Walter Hinderer. Stuttgart: Reclam, 1997. 33–74.

Strobel, Jochen. "Adel und Autorschaft um 1800. Heinrich von Kleist und sein Schauspiel 'Prinz Friedrich von Homburg.'" In *Deutscher Adel im 19. und 20. Jahrhundert*. Edited by Günther Schulz and Markus A. Denzel. St. Katharinen: Scripta-Mercaturiae, 2004. 95–138.

Struck, Peter. "Ein biographisches Detail zu Ludwig von Brockes." *KJb* (1986): 176–178.

—. "Kleists Wahrheitskrise und ihre frühromantische Quelle." PhD diss., University of Hanover, 1985.

Szarota, Tomasz. *Der deutsche Michel. Die Geschichte eines nationalen Symbols und Autostereotyps*. Osnabrück: Fibre, 1998.

Szondi, Peter. "Fünfmal 'Amphitryon.' Plautus, Molière, Kleist, Giraudoux, Kaiser." In *Lektüren und Lektionen*. Edited by Jean Bollack, Gert Mattenklott, Hans-Hagen Hildebrandt, Helen Stierlin, Henriette Beese, Senta Metz, and Wolfgang Fietkau. Frankfurt/M.: Suhrkamp, 1973. 153–184.

Tanzer, Anke. *"Mein theurer zweiter Kleist." Franz Alexander von Kleist (1769–1797) – Leben und Werk*. Oldenburg: Igel, 1998.

Tellenbach, Hubertus. *Melancholy. History of the Problem, Endogeneity, Typology, Pathogenesis, Clinical Considerations*. Translated by Erling Eng. Pittsburgh: Duquesne UP, 1980.

Theisen, Bianca. *Bogenschluß. Kleists Formalisierung des Lesens*. Freiburg: Rombach, 1996.

—. "Der Bewunderer des Shakespeare. Kleists Skepitizismus." *KJb* (1999): 87–108.

Tieck, Ludwig. *Schriften*. Berlin: Reimer, 1829.

Utz, Peter. "'Eine Fremdheit bleibt immer.' Robert Walser und der Kleist seiner Zeit." *KJb* (1997): 164–181.

Vinken, Barbara. *Bestien. Kleist und die Deutschen*. Berlin: Merve, 2011.

—, and Anselm Haverkamp. "Die zurechtgelegte Frau. Gottesbegehren und transzendentale Familie in Kleists 'Marquise von O....'" In *Heinrich von Kleist. Kriegsfall – Rechtsfall – Sündenfall*. Edited by Gerhard Neumann, Wolf Kittler, and Manfred Schneider. Freiburg: Rombach, 1994. 127–147.

Vogl, Joseph. *Kalkül und Leidenschaft. Poetik des ökonomischen Menschen*. Munich: Sequenzia, 2002.

—, ed. *Poetologien des Wissens um 1800*. Munich: Fink, 1999.

Vogt, Helmut. "Heinrich von Kleists Hydrostat. Die U-Boot-Idee des preußischen Dichters." *Der Tagesspiegel*. April 18, 1976.

Völcker, Ludwig. *Muse Melancholie – Therapeutikum Poesie. Studien zum Melancholie-Problem in der deutschen Lyrik von Hölty bis Benn*. Munich: Fink, 1978.

Wädenswil, Margrit Schoch von. *Kleist und Sophokles*. Zurich: Aschmann & Scheller, 1952.

Wagner-Egelhaaf, Martina, ed. *Hermanns Schlachten. Zur Literaturgeschichte eines nationalen Mythos*. Bielefeld: Aisthesis, 2008.

Walser, Robert. "Kleist in Thun." In *The Walk*. Translated by Christopher Middleton and others. London: Serpent's Tail, 2013. 15–24.

Weber, Martin. *Georg Christian Gottlieb Wedekind 1761–1831. Werdegang und Schicksal eines Arztes im Zeitalter der Aufklärung und der französischen Revolution. Mit einem Anhang: Wedekinds Diätetikvorlesung von 1789/90*. Stuttgart: Gustav Fischer, 1988.

Weckherlin, Georg Rodolf. "On the Early Death of Anna Augusta, Margravine of Baden." In *Sing for the Taxman*. Translated by Sheenagh Pugh. Bridgend: Seren, 1993. 59f.

Weder, Katharine. *Kleists magnetische Poesie. Experimente des Mesmerismus*. Göttingen: Wallstein, 2008.

Wehler, Hans-Ulrich, ed. *Europäischer Adel 1750–1950*. Göttingen: Vandenhoeck & Ruprecht, 1990.

Wehrmann, Martin. *Geschichte von Pommern*. Vol. 1. Gotha: Perthes, 1904.

Weigel, Sigrid. "Der Körper am Kreuzpunkt von Liebesgeschichte und Rassendiskurs in Heinrich von Kleists Erzählung 'Die Verlobung in St. Domingo.'" *KJb* (1991): 202–217.

—. "Ulrike von Kleist 1774–1849. Lebens-Spuren hinter dem Bild der Dichter-Schwester." In *Schwestern berühmter Männer. Zwölf biographische Porträts*. Edited by Luise F. Pusch. Frankfurt/M.: Insel, 1985. 235–287.

Weiss, Hermann F. *Funde und Studien zu Heinrich von Kleist*. Tübingen: Niemeyer, 1984.

—. "Heinrich von Kleists Freund Ludwig von Brockes." *Beiträge zur Kleist-Forschung* (1996): 102–132.

Wellbery, David E. "Stimmung." In *Ästhetische Grundbegriffe. Historisches Wörterbuch in sieben Bänden*. Edited by Karlheinz Barck, Martin Fontius, Dieter Schlenstedt, Burkhart Steinwachs, and Friedrich Wolfzettel. Vol. 5. Stuttgart: Metzler, 2003. 703–733.

Wetzel, Walter D. *Johann Wilhelm Ritter. Physik im Wirkungsfeld der deutschen Romantik*. Berlin: de Gruyter, 1973.

Wieland, Christoph Martin. *Werke*. Edited by Heinrich Düntzer. 40 vols. Berlin: Hempel, 1879–82.

Wilbrandt, Adolf. *Heinrich von Kleist*. Nördlingen: Beck, 1863.

Willoweit, Dietmar. "Heinrich von Kleist und die Universität Frankfurt an der Oder. Rückblick eines Rechtshistorikers." *KJb* (1997): 57–71.

Witte, Karsten, ed. *Paris. Deutsche Republikaner reisen*. Frankfurt/M.: Insel, 1980.

Wolf, Christa. *No Place on Earth*. Translated by Jan van Heurck. New York: Farrar, Straus & Giroux, 1982.

Wünsch, Christian Ernst. *Esoterika*. Vol. 2. Zerbst: Füchsel, 1817.

—. *Kosmologische Unterhaltungen*. 2 vols. 2nd ed. Leipzig: Breitkopf, 1791–94.

Wulf, Joseph. *Literatur und Dichtung im Dritten Reich. Eine Dokumentation*. Reinbek: Rowohlt, 1966.

Young, Edward. *Conjectures on Original Composition. In a Letter to the Author of Sir Charles Grandison*. London: Millar, 1759.

Zedler, Johann Heinrich. *Grosses vollständiges Universal-Lexicon aller Wissenschafften und Künste, welche bißhero durch menschlichen Verstand und Witz erfunden und verbessert worden*. Vol. 35. 2nd complete photomechanical reproduction of the Leipzig edition of 1743. Graz: Akad. Druck- & Verlagsanstalt, 1996.

Ziegler, Bernhard. "Nun ist dies Erbe zuende." In *Die Expressionismusdebatte. Materialien zu einer marxistischen Realismuskonzeption*. Edited by Hans-Jürgen Schmitt. Frankfurt/M.: Suhrkamp, 1973. 50–60.

Zimmermann, Hans Dieter. *Kleist, die Liebe und der Tod*. Frankfurt/M.: Athenäum, 1989.

Index of Names

Photograph and Image Credits

I would like to express my gratitude for the great pictorial reference books by Eberhard Siebert, *Heinrich von Kleist. Leben und Werk im Bild* (Frankfurt/M.: Insel, 1980) and *Heinrich von Kleist. Eine Bildbiographie* (Heilbronn: Kleist-Archiv Sembdner, 2009), both of which are a treasure trove for every Kleist biographer looking to tap into source material.

p. 8	Colored lithograph by L. Clericus, Kleist Archive Sembdner in Heilbronn, in Eberhard Siebert, *Heinrich von Kleist. Eine Bildbiographie* (Heilbronn: Kleist-Archiv Sembdner, 2009).
p. 10	Engraving by Christian Fritsch, 1760, Berlin State Library – Prussian Cultural Heritage.
p. 12	Photograph of lost painting, Kleist Museum, Frankfurt (Oder).
p. 13	Photograph, Berlin Central and Regional Library.
p. 13	Photograph of watercolor miniature in soft pastel on ivory by Franz Ludwig Close, 1784, original lost, authenticity uncertain, Kleist Museum, Frankfurt (Oder).
p. 15	*Left*: Photograph of lost miniature, Kleist Museum, Frankfurt (Oder).
p. 15	*Right*: Pastel, Friedrich von Kleist, private collection of Friedrich Leopold von Kleist, Ratingen.
p. 18	Colored aquatint etching by J. Hausheer, before 1826, Berlin State Library – Prussian Cultural Heritage, Maps Collection.
p. 23	Prussian army uniforms under the reign of Friedrich Wilhelm II, King of Prussia, 1789, Berlin State Library – Prussian Cultural Heritage, Historical Prints Collection.
p. 38	Lithograph by R. Geißler, circa 1870, Berlin State Library – Prussian Cultural Heritage, Historical Prints Collection, 50 MA 41352: R.
p. 43	Göttingen State and University Library.
p. 46	Drawing, in Daniel Gralath, *Versuche und Abhandlungen der naturforschenden Gesellschaft zu Dantzig* (Danzig: Schreiberische Buchdruckerei, 1747), Universitätsbibliothek Marburg.
p. 51	Drawing, in DKV IV, 165.
p. 57	Print, Städel Museum Frankfurt/Main.
p. 60	Frontispiece, in Immanuel Kant, *Schriften zur Philosophie im Allgemeinen und zur Logik*, vol. 1 (Leipzig: Modes & Baumann, 1838), Berlin State Library – Prussian Cultural Heritage.
p. 71	Photograph of miniature, circa 1800, Kleist Museum, Frankfurt (Oder).
p. 77	State and University Library Hamburg, Campe Collection, CS: Kleist: 1.

p. 81 Kleist Museum, Frankfurt (Oder).

p. 86 Frontispiece, copper engraving by Georg Michael Weißenhahn, in Jean-Jacques Rousseau, *Einsame Spaziergänge* (Munich: Strobl, 1783), Berlin State Library – Prussian Cultural Heritage.

p. 93 Silverpoint drawing by Friedrich August Junge, between 1805 and 1810, Berlin State Library – Prussian Cultural Heritage.

p. 94 Miniature by Peter Friedel, Pastel on ivory, 1801, Berlin State Library – Prussian Cultural Heritage, Manuscripts Collection, Nachlass Heinrich von Kleist 1.

p. 95 Oil on laid paper, 1807, German Literature Archive/Schiller National Museum in Marbach am Neckar.

p. 97 In Robert Gernhardt, *Besternte Ernte* (Frankfurt/M.: Zweitausendeins, 1976).

p. 112 Photograph of lost painting, Kleist Museum, Frankfurt (Oder), on loan from Berlin Central and Regional Library.

p. 117 Museum for Franconia, Würzburg.

p. 119 Miniature, authenticity uncertain, Prussian Cultural Heritage Image Archive.

p. 121 Dresden State Art Collections, Old Masters Picture Gallery.

p. 123 Stipple engraving, Prussian Cultural Heritage Image Archive.

p. 131 In *Kleist-Jahrbuch* (1984).

p. 145 Berlin State Library – Prussian Cultural Heritage, Manuscripts Collection, Ms. germ. quart. 822, 161.

p. 172 Copper engraving by Moritz Steinla after a painting by Ferdinand Jagemann, in Jörn Göres, ed., *Deutsche Schriftsteller im Porträt*, vol. 2 (Munich: Beck, 1980).

p. 181 akg-images, Berlin.

p. 185 Photograph of stipple engraving by G. Reußing, 1799, Kleist Museum, Frankfurt (Oder).

p. 192 Photograph of pastel painting by Wilhelm Ternite, 1811, Kleist Museum, Frankfurt (Oder).

p. 195 Stipple engraving, frontispiece, in Rahel Varnhagen, *Rahel – Ein Buch des Andenkens für ihre Freunde* (Berlin: Duncker & Humblot, 1834), Berlin State Library – Prussian Cultural Heritage.

p. 204 Photograph, early 20th century, Kleist Museum, Frankfurt (Oder).

p. 205 Drawing, in DKV IV, 343.

p. 211 Lithograph, 1828, Prussian Cultural Heritage Image Archive.

p. 213 The French title reads *La Madeleine soutenue par deux anges*. The painting can be found at the Museum of Fine Arts and Archeology of Besançon.

p. 217 Photograph of copper engraving of 1782 after a painting by Louis-Philibert Debucourt, Kleist Museum, Frankfurt (Oder).

p. 262 Photograph of painting, original lost.

p. 264 Painting by Gerhard von Kügelgen, circa 1808, in Horst Häker, *Kleists Berliner Aufenthalte* (Berlin: Haude & Spener, 1989).

p. 266 Berlin State Library – Prussian Cultural Heritage.

p. 275 Berlin State Library – Prussian Cultural Heritage.

p. 305 Prussian Cultural Heritage Image Archive.

p. 324 Playbill of Breslau Theater, 1860, in Eberhard Siebert, *Heinrich von Kleist. Eine Bildbiographie* (Heilbronn: Kleist-Archiv Sembdner, 2009).

p. 327 Photograph, Kleist Museum, Frankfurt (Oder).

p. 336 *Top left*: Photograph, in Horst Häker, *Kleists Berliner Aufenthalte* (Berlin: Haude & Spener, 1989).

p. 336 *Bottom left*: Pastel painting by Wilhelm Ternite, property of the House of Hohenzollern, SKH Georg Friedrich Prince of Prussia.

p. 336 *Bottom right*: Lithograph by P. Jentzen after a painting by E. Gebauer, 1831, Prussian Cultural Heritage Image Archive.

p. 339 Lithograph, 1858, Prussian Cultural Heritage Image Archive.

p. 340 State Archive Berlin.

p. 345 Steel engraving, 1849, in Klaus Rek, *Das Dichterleben des Ludwig Tieck* (Berlin: Unabhängige Verlags-Buchhandl., 1991).

p. 346 Stipple engraving, 1836, Prussian Cultural Heritage Image Archive.

p. 349 Pencil, silverpoint, and pastel colors, circa 1800, in Eberhard Siebert, *Heinrich von Kleist. Eine Bildbiographie* (Heilbronn: Kleist-Archiv Sembdner, 2009).

p. 388 Old National Gallery, Berlin.

p. 395 Photograph of miniature on ivory, artist unknown, circa 1802, Kleist Museum, Frankfurt (Oder).

p. 398 Photograph, Prussian Union of Churches, Church Chancery (Archive/Kirchenbuchstelle), Berlin.

p. 401 Photograph of drawing, 1831, original lost, Kleist Museum, Frankfurt (Oder).

p. 403 Photograph of lost original, Prussian Cultural Heritage Image Archive.

p. 408 Reproduction of a drawing by A. Meinhard, in *Illustrirte Zeitung* (Leipzig) on May 5, 1877, Berlin State Library – Prussian Cultural Heritage.

p. 412 Photograph, 1955, © picture-alliance/dpa.

p. 433 Drawing, in Johann Krünitz, *Die Oeconomische Encyclopädie*, vol. 72 (Berlin: Pauli, 1797).

Acknowledgements

As president of the International Heinrich-von-Kleist-Society since 1996, I have been fortunate to work with Kleist experts from around the world who approach his work as admirers, not polemicists. Many have become personal friends. I hope the reader will notice that my biography develops from this relational sense and thus unites the voices of many scholars, all of whom I strived to recognize in the bibliography. Should I have failed to mention anyone, it was not done intentionally.

I want to express my gratitude to the jury of the German Publishers and Booksellers Association that chose this Kleist biography as the top 2011 non-fiction title in the humanities and thus made it possible to finance its English translation. I would also like to thank the publishing house S. Fischer for granting the publication rights, and Brill Germany for publishing the translation—especially Alexander Roesler and Andreas Knop, for their composure and patience. I would like to express my sincere thanks to the Morphomata International Center for Advanced Studies in the Humanities at the University of Cologne, which provided funding for the printing costs of the English publication through support from the German Federal Ministry of Education and Research. Morphomata research associate Karena Weduwen proofread the English edition with the utmost care, and with her wise comments often threw the translators and me into—always productive—doubt. Björn Moll, also a Morphomata research associate, managed to obtain the standard English translations for countless quotations from German, French, and Italian sources, despite the fact that libraries were closed for much of 2020. Last but not least, thanks are due to Sebastian Goth and Kelly Kawar, who not only translated the biography so meticulously and elegantly over months of pandemic lockdown with two young children at home, but also clarified whatever might have been given to misunderstanding in the original German version. I learned a lot from them. I will conclude this list of acknowledgements with the three people to whom I dedicate this book: my daughters Clara and Charlotte Blamberger and my wife Bettina Woernle.

Cologne, Berlin
January 2021